SHĀSHĪ'S PRINCIPLES OF ḤANAFĪ FIQH

أسرار الإيمان

Foreword by: Faḍīlat ush-Shaykh Moḥammed Ḥabīb ur-Raḥmān Maḥbūbī
Compiled and presented by: Mohammad Asrar ul-Haq

SH̲ĀS̲HĪ'S PRINCIPLES OF ḤANAFI FIQH

Asrar Al-Eman Publications

Care of:	Al-Jamia Suffa Tul Islam, Bradford Grand Mosque, Horton Park Avenue, Bradford, England BD5 0LD
Email contact:	asrar.aleman@gmail.com
Published by:	Asrar Al-Eman Publications, Bradford, UK
Design:	Mohammad Asrar ul-Haq
Cover Design:	Mawlana Mohammad Zahoor Bilali [depicting Barak-Khan Madrasah (Uzbekistan), Masjid of Imam Abū Ḥanīfa رحمة الله عليه (Iraq), Citadel of Muhammad Ali (Egypt)]
Guest Editor:	Shaykh Mohammad Anwar ul-Haq Qadri
Epigraph (Urdu):	Fāḍil of Braeli, Imam Aḥmad Raza رحمة الله عليه

10 9 8 7 6 5 4 3 2 1
First Edition
Printed in Turkey

ISBN 978-0-9555943-1-1

Foreword

Allah, the Most High and Most Wise, has shown the path of contentment in both this world and the Hereafter to His ﷻ chosen people. To enable them to tread that path and to achieve divine intent, He ﷻ blessed them with the knowledge of the directives found in His Final Word, the Quran, and in the Tradition of His Final Prophet ﷺ; a tradition transmitted to succeeding generations by the Companions رضي الله عنهم and preserved as the Sunnah. The primary sources of the Quran and the Sunnah merge into a rich, deep fountain of directives from which the laws of the Shariah are drawn. These directives, acknowledged as the base elements of lived and practiced law, are the subject of the discipline of jurisprudence and its principles, *uṣūl ul-fiqh*.

So, what exactly is *uṣūl ul-fiqh* and why is there a need for it? To begin to unravel this question it is necessary to first come to terms with the true quiddity of both sound judgment, *al-ijtihād*, and inference, *al-istinbāṭ*.

First, let us examine *al-Istinbāṭ*. Lexically, it is the drawing of water from a spring. Technically, it is the deducing of a piece of knowledge from the legislative texts of the Quran and the Sunnah, by means of mental exertion and intellectual ability. In other words, it is the use of sound reasoning alongside credible interpretation of the foundational sources, the Book of Allah ﷻ and the Tradition of the Messenger ﷺ, in the production of case judgements and rulings.

A verse of the blessed Quran warned and guided the Muslim community after some individuals fanned the flames of unfounded rumours:

...وَلَوْ رَدُّوهُ إِلَى الرَّسُولِ وَإِلَى أُوْلِي الأَمْرِ مِنْهُمْ لَعَلِمَهُ الَّذِينَ يَسْتَنبِطُونَهُ مِنْهُمْ ...﴿٨٣﴾

"...had they referred it to the Messenger and to such of them as are in authority, those among them who are able to think out the matter would have known..."

[an-Nisā - 4:83]

Those of authority among them to whom the verse refers to are the erudite intellectuals with the ability to infer and think matters through.

Take note too of verse 59, also of Sūrat un-Nisā:

...فَإِن تَنَازَعْتُمْ فِي شَيْءٍ فَرُدُّوهُ إِلَى اللهِ وَالرَّسُولِ إِن كُنتُمْ تُؤْمِنُونَ بِاللهِ وَالْيَوْمِ الآخِرِ ذَلِكَ خَيْرٌ وَأَحْسَنُ تَأْوِيلاً ﴿٥٩﴾

"...if you have a dispute concerning any matter, refer it to Allah and the Messenger if you are believers in Allah and the Last Day. That is better and more seemly in the end."

[an-Nisā - 4:59]

No doubt, a dispute in any matter will arise when an explicit instruction of the Book or the Tradition is not found. Thus, the disputed matter in which no explicit text is found is to be connected to the text through a common cause or root. The ability to arrive at that cause is reserved for those scholars and intellectuals who have the gift of inference and independent judgement.

al-Ijtihād on the other hand is, lexically, to expend potential strength. Technically, it is the jurist deploying knowledge, inference and judgement. In other words, utilising all reasoning powers at one's disposal to achieve an outcome.

Allah ﷻ has said:

وَالَّذِينَ جَاهَدُوا فِينَا لَنَهْدِيَنَّهُمْ سُبُلَنَا... ﴿٦٩﴾

"As for those who strive in Us, We surely guide them to Our paths..."

[al-'Ankabūt - 29:69]

This verse, with its generic and unrestricted composition, signifies a multitude of understandings. One such understanding is that it is the authoritative scholar, *mujtahid,* who endeavours to derive rulings of the Shariah and infer applicable solutions. They ponder over the texts of the Quran and the Sunnah, and so Allah ﷻ blesses them with the ability to arrive at a sound independent judgement. He ﷻ it is that expands their hearts and minds to put a matter to rest with a deep and unique insight.

It is reported that the blessed Messenger of Allah ﷺ wished to send his noble Companion Muʿādh bin Jabal ؓ to the Yemen. On appointing him, the blessed Messenger ﷺ asked: "When you have to decide a matter, how will you do it?" He replied: "I will base it on the Book of Allah ﷻ." He ﷺ continued: "And if you do not find direction in the Book of Allah ﷻ?"
"Then from the Sunnah of the Messenger ﷺ."
"And if you do not find it in the Sunnah of the Messenger ﷺ?" pressed the Prophet ﷺ.
"I will use my independent judgement and will strive for that."

Muʿādh ؓ says that the Messenger of Allah ﷺ then approvingly patted his chest and exclaimed: "Praise be to Allah ﷻ Who divinely sanctioned for the emissary of the Messenger of Allah ﷺ that which pleases him."

Every mujtahid is deserving of divine reward. No doubt, when armed with sincere efforts a mujtahid deploys God-given comprehension to delve right to the core of a scrutinised case and accumulates an abundance of anointed accolades. Nothing resonates more truly than مَنْ كانَ للهِ كانَ اللهُ لَهُ "the one who is for the Almighty ﷻ, the Almighty is for him." It is worth bearing in mind that entitlement to an abundance of reward and the divine gift, is for the act of *al-ijtihād* itself. Otherwise, in the particulars of a case perhaps one may achieve divine intent in some matters yet be incorrect in others. In the case of correctness a twofold reward is appropriated and with an incorrect outcome there is still a reward, albeit solitary. Moreover, such an honest error in legal judgement is not blameworthy nor the proposer a target of ridicule. As the Persian adage goes: خطائے بزرگاں گرفتن خطاست, fixating on the oversight of elders, is in itself an oversight.

The six canonic Hadith compilations support the aforementioned point by including the following tradition:

عن عمرو بن العاص أنّه سمِعَ النَّبيَّ ﷺ يقول: إذا حَكَمَ الحاكِمُ فاجْتَهَدَ ثُمَّ أصاب فَلَهُ أجْرانِ، وإذا حَكَمَ فاجْتَهَدَ ثُمَّ أخْطأَ فَلَهُ أجْرٌ.

"The noble Companion ʿAmr bin al-ʿĀṣ reports that he heard the Prophet ﷺ saying: "When a judge rules by independent judgement and is correct, he has a double reward. And when he rules by independent judgement and is incorrect, he has a singular reward."
[al-Bukhārī: 7352]

After the passing of the authoritative and stable period of the noble Companions ؓ elements of religious doctrine as well as legislation gradually became the subject of disagreement. It was then that the intellectuals of this Ummah applied themselves vigorously to the task of not only preserving the sacred texts of the Quran and its sciences, and the Sunnah and its related sciences, but also its spirit and observance. As yet jurisprudence was not systematically taught nor was there a need felt for a separate science with its own distinct language and literature. A change soon took place. In the year 80 after *al-Hijra* a man to be given the agnomen Abū Ḥanīfa and honoured with the epithet *al-Imam al-Aʿẓam*, the Greatest Imam, Nuʿmān bin Thābit was born.

Who was this great Imam, and what of his principles in the pursuit for independent judgement and inference? *al-Imam al-Aʿẓam* was and remains the most celebrated of the founders of the schools of jurisprudence, *al-madhāhib*.

Allah ﷻ says in the blessed Quran:

هُوَ الَّذِي بَعَثَ فِي الْأُمِّيِّينَ رَسُولًا مِّنْهُمْ يَتْلُو عَلَيْهِمْ آيَاتِهِ وَيُزَكِّيهِمْ وَيُعَلِّمُهُمُ الْكِتَابَ وَالْحِكْمَةَ وَإِن كَانُوا
مِن قَبْلُ لَفِي ضَلَالٍ مُّبِينٍ ﴿٢﴾ وَآخَرِينَ مِنْهُمْ لَمَّا يَلْحَقُوا بِهِمْ وَهُوَ الْعَزِيزُ الْحَكِيمُ ﴿٣﴾

"He it is Who has sent among the unlettered ones a Messenger of their own, to recite to them His revelations and to make them grow, and to teach them the Scripture and wisdom, though before now they were indeed in manifest error. Along with others of them who have not yet joined them. He is the Mighty, Wise."

[Sūrat ul-Jumu'ah- 62:2-3]

Many of the biographers of *al-Imam al-Aʿẓam* have included a telling tradition in the explanation of this blessed verse. Recorded by both al-Bukhārī [4897] and Muslim [2546], it is reported that the noble Companion Abū Ḥurayra ﵁ said that a group were in the company of the blessed Prophet ﷺ when the aforementioned verses were revealed. A man amongst them asked: "Who are those others, O Messenger of Allah?" The Messenger of Allah ﷺ did not respond until he had repeated the question, perhaps several times. Close by sat the noble Companion Salmān the Persian ﵁. The Prophet ﷺ placed his hand on him and informed: "If faith is by the Pleiades a man of Persia will retrieve it." A great number of scholars have singled out Abū Ḥanīfa Nuʿmān bin Thābit as the manifestation of this prophecy.

The paternal grandfather of *al-Imam al-Aʿẓam*, Zūṭa bin Marzubān, had migrated to the flourishing city of Kūfa from Persia, in the era of our master and fourth Rightly-guided Caliph ʿAlī bin Abī Ṭālib ﵁, Allah ﷻ honour him. Zūṭa took his young son Thābit, the father of *al-Imam al-Aʿẓam*, to the court of our master ʿAlī ﵁, Allah ﷻ honour him, who supplicated for Thābit and his future progeny. Thābit grew, married and was blessed with a child named Nuʿmān, who then later became *al-Imam al-Aʿẓam*, the Greatest Imam.

The enduring influence of culture and one's place of upbringing on behaviours and characteristics have long been known. The town of Kūfa, situated in modern day Iraq, was founded by the noble Companion and second Rightly-Guided Caliph of Islam, ʿUmar bin al-Khattāb ﷺ. It too had an input in the legacy of *al-Imam al-Aʿẓam*.The entire garrison town was designed, its boundaries demarcated and its future planned, under the Caliph's watchful eye and by his instruction. For its spiritual and educational prosperity the Caliph ﷺ appointed the erudite Companion ʿAbdullah Ibn Masʿūd ﷺ. Whilst signifying the importance of this appointment the noble Caliph told the people of Kūfa, that though he needed ʿAbdullah in Madinah, he was favouring them and their city above all else. It is in this city that *al-Imam al-Aʿẓam* was nurtured and came to maturity.

Masrūq bin al-Ajdaʿ, the respected Successor, says that tracing the knowledge of the noble Companions of the Messenger of Allah ﷺ culminated with six individuals: ʿUmar bin al-Khattāb, ʿAbdullah Ibn Masʿūd and Zayd bin Thābit. These three were similar and often referred to each other. And, ʿAlī bin Abī Ṭālib, Abū Mūsā al-ʾAshʿarī and Ubayy bin Kaʿb. These three were similar and often referred to each other. From each group of three, one Companion was dominant and so the knowledge of these six is concentrated in just two: ʿAlī bin Abī Ṭālib and ʿAbdullah Ibn Masʿūd. Incidently, both of these giant personalities shaped the Islamic discourse in and around the city of Kūfa.

The knowledge and intellectual dexterity of ʿAlī bin Abī Ṭalib ﷺ is well known. The Messenger of Allah ﷺ said of him: "I am the city of knowledge and ʿAlī is its entrance," and as at-Tirmidhī states in his Book of Virtues, "I am the abode of wisdom and ʿAlī is its gate." As for Ibn Masʿūd ﷺ, the noble Caliph ʿUmar ﷺ had expressed his need for him yet he sacrificed him for the prosperity of Kūfa. Moreover, when the noble Caliph ʿAlī ﷺ, Allah ﷻ honour him, was greeted by a swarm of scholars on his first arrival in Kūfa, he enquired as to who the men were. He was informed that they are the disciples of Ibn Masʿūd ﷺ. The noble Caliph ﷺ exclaimed, "Ibn Masʿūd has filled this land with knowledge," and in another version he said, "Ibn Masʿūd's students are like beacons for the Muslim nation."

The privileged chain of tutelage of *al-Imam al-Aʿẓam* is vast and noteworthy. Having benefited from teachers numbering four thousand in some estimates, this chain is at the very least influenced by if not directly connected to the two aforementioned leading noble Companions ﷺ. His views and opinions were formed on the foundation of the legal rulings and edicts of these two masters. His acceptance amongst his contemporaries and generations that followed is summed up by the great jurist and founder of the ash-Shāfiʿīy school.

Imam Muḥammad bin Idrīs ash-Shāfiʿīy is famed to have venerated *al-Imam al-Aʿẓam* by stating, "People are posterity to Abū Ḥanīfa in jurisprudence."

The methodology of *al-Imam al-Aʿẓam* for legal judgements and inference is both robust and rational. It is conservative yet allows for normative customs and public interest. Its loyalty to tradition as well as versatility has allowed the Ḥanafī school to become the most widely practiced school of jurisprudence the world over. Some of the more notable principles of this school are its adherence to the Book of Allah ﷻ, conformity to the Prophetic Sunnah and the pursuance of the practice of the noble Companions رضي الله عنهم. *al-Imam al-Aʿẓam* himself states: "I take from the Book of Allah ﷻ. What I do not find, I turn to the Sunnah of the Messenger of Allah ﷺ. If I do not find it in the Book of Allah ﷻ nor in the practice of Allah's Messenger ﷺ, I take from the dictums of his Companions رضي الله عنهم. I take from any of their sayings, and do not reach beyond them to any other."

In short, the aforementioned words are an attempt at furnishing some meaningful insight into matters concerning uṣūl ul-fiqh. Withal, Uṣūl ush-Shāshī is a didactically credible, succinct and unmatched work. I thought it fitting to also include within this foreword a brief account and introduction to the personality of Imam Abū Ḥanīfa رضي الله عنه. Perhaps it will enable the reader to discerningly acknowledge that indeed Imam Abū Ḥanīfa was in fact *al-Imām al-Aʿẓam*, the greatest amongst the Imams. Moreover, the mujtahid pioneers of all other schools of jurisprudence not only held him in esteem but asserted openly and without hesitation "people are posterity to Abū Ḥanīfa in jurisprudence."

With these words I have tried, to the best of my ability, to present a balanced, impartial account of actuality. If I succeeded, هَذا مِنْ فَضْلِ رَبِّي, it is from the grace of my Lord. If not,

نَحْنُ نَتوبُ إلى اللهِ تَعالَى أن يَغْفِرَ لَنا وَيَسْتُرَنا إنَّهُ هُوَ التَّوّابُ الرَّحيمُ وَإنَّهُ هُوَ السَّتّارُ الكَريمُ

we offer perfect contrition to Allah, the Lord, Most-High, that He ﷻ forgives us and conceals our faults, for He is the Coverer, the Most-Generous. I pray Allah, Exalted is His Power, enables all believers to perpetually search for and seek out the truth. That He ﷻ guides them at every step. He ﷻ is the Granter of true prosperity and success.

- Humble seeker of the Truth ﷻ, server to His ﷻ creation, ***Mohammad Habib ur-Rahman****, may the Benefactor ﷻ excuse him.*

طالب الحق
خادم الخلق
محمد حبيب الرحمن عفا عنه

Faḍīlat ush-Shaykh Muḥammad Ḥabīb ur-Raḥmān Maḥbūbī

[Translated: Monday 26 October 2020, 9 Rabīʿ ul-Awwal 1442]

Contents

Foreword v

Preface xv

Introduction 1

PART ONE: al-Kitāb 7

1.0 Introduction to al-kitāb 7

1.1 Word Coinage 11

1.1.1 al-Khāṣṣ and al-'Āmm 12

1.1.2 al-Muṭlaq and al-Muqayyad 36

1.1.3 al-Mushtarak and al-Muawwal 52

1.2 Word Usage 64

1.2.1 al-Ḥaqīqa and al-Majāz 64

1.2.2 Methods of al-Isti'āra 82

1.2.3 aṣ-Ṣarīḥ and al-Kināya 93

1.3 Word Clarity 103

1.3.1 al-Mutaqābilāt - Clarity 104

1.3.2 al-Mutaqābilāt - Ambiguity 118

1.4 Abandoning al-Ḥaqīqa 127

1.5 Text Locations 143

1.5.1 'Ibārat un-naṣṣ and 'Ishārat un-naṣṣ 144

1.5.2 Dalālat un-naṣṣ and Iqtiḍā un-naṣṣ 151

1.6 Introduction to al-Amr 163

1.6.1 al-Amr al-Muṭlaq 167

1.6.2 Functions of al-Amr 170

1.6.3 The types of al-Mamūr Bihī 177

1.6.4 The excellence in al-Mamūr Bihī 191

1.6.5 al-Adā 197

1.6.6 al-Qaḍā 210

1.7 an-Nahī 217

1.8 Techniques to understand a text 231

1.8.1 Some Weak Extractions 239

1.9 Ḥurūf ul-Ma'ānī 247

1.9.1 al-Wāw 247

1.9.2 al-Fā 253

1.9.3 Thumma 262

1.9.4 Bal 265

1.9.5 Lākin 268
1.9.6 Aw 273
1.9.7 Ḥattā 279
1.9.8 Ilā 285
1.9.9 'Alā 288
1.9.10 Fī 290
1.9.11 al-Bā 296
1.10 Types of al-Bayān 301
1.10.1 Bayān ut-Taqrīr and Bayān ut-Tafsīr 301
1.10.2 Bayān ut-Taghyīr 303
1.10.3 Bayān uḍ-Ḍarūra 314
1.10.4 Bayān ul-Ḥāl 316
1.10.5 Bayān ul-'Aṭf 318
1.10.6 Bayān ut-Tabdīl 320

PART TWO: as-Sunna 325

2.0 Introduction to as-Sunna 325
2.1 Types of al-Khabar 326
2.1.1 Types of Reporters 331
2.1.2 Criteria for Accepting Khabar ul-Wāḥid 336
2.1.3 Contrasting Khabar ul-Wāḥid with other Sources 339
2.2 Admitting Khabar ul-Wāḥid 344

PART THREE: al-Ijmā' 347

3.0 Introduction to al-Ijmā' 347

3.0.1 Types of al-Ijmā' as-Sanadī 349

3.0.2 Types of al-Ijmā' al-Madhhabī 351

3.1 'Adam ul-Qāili bil Faṣl 357

PART FOUR: al-Qiyās 363

4.0 Duty of the Mujtahid 363

4.1 Validity of al-Qiyās 371

4.2 Conditions for Authentic al-Qiyās 376

4.3 Authentic al-Qiyās 389

4.3.1 Types of Authentic al-Qiyās 394

4.4 Countering al-Qiyās 404

PART FIVE: al-Aḥkām 419

5.0 Rulings 419

5.1 as-Sabab, al-'Illa and ash-Sharṭ 420

5.2 Causes of Legal Rulings 428

5.3 al-Mawāni' 438

5.4 Types of Rulings in Worship 443

5.5 al-'Azīma and ar-Rukhṣa 447

5.6 Rulings without Evidence 451

About the Author 458

Preface

Allah's name I invoke, Who is most-Merciful and most-Compassionate. Salutations be upon His Beloved, our Beloved, Messenger Muhammad al-Muṣṭafā, the one chosen for blessings, peace and salutations.

The book Uṣūl ush-Shāshī is a significant and vitally important introductory text on the topic of Ḥanafi Uṣūl ul-Fiqh, or Islamic Jurisprudence as understood by adherents of the Ḥanafi madhhab. Being a primary text means that often it is the first text a student of *Darse Niẓāmī* and traditional Islamic studies encounters on the subject, whilst the subject itself has for centuries been an indispensable part of curricula all over the Islamic world.

This Rendering

This English translation and explanation of the text of Uṣūl ush-Shāshī, named Shāshī's Principles of Ḥanafī Fiqh, is intended for the use of second or third year students of the traditional *Darse Niẓāmī* course. It primarily contains the Arabic text with its English translation, an overview and explanation of the topic at hand, and a summary to conclude chapters. The material is introduced at a level that typical second and early third year students can follow comfortably. It is an attempt to speak directly to the students and not beyond them. For a student with a basic grasp of Arabic grammar and familiarity with Islamic texts, the book should be almost self-explanatory; the aim of which is to allow an instructor to use direct-contact time more productively with the student.

QUICK REFERENCE

درس نظامي: *Darse Niẓāmī*

The Islamic studies syllabus implemented by Mulla Niẓām ud-Dīn of Sihālī (d. 1747) in the eighteenth century. It has since been adapted for a modern age throughout generations. It has widespread approval the world over and is a widely accepted benchmark in traditional Islamic Studies.

The layout and order of Shāshī's Principles of Ḥanafī Fiqh is consistent with the original text and follows its systematic course. It is glossed with figures, diagrams, references and terminology legends, amongst other helpful tools. The basic principle is introduced and cases are cited which apply the given rule. Additional examples, as well as presentation of counter-arguments and opinions, allow the principles to be repeatedly used and understood through a multitude of scenarios.

The Approach

After teaching this text for a number of years I have endeavoured to keep the direct approach of talking to the student in a simple, yet precise manner. This is to encourage their thinking and enable development of a deeper understanding and appreciation of the subject matter. The aim is to stimulate them enough to progress and to gift them a firm foundation that ultimately helps them to become competent practitioners in the field. The goal in this undertaking is to offer: i) a supplement to the main lessons; ii) a work that is absorbed by the student in private study with attention and keenness before attending a structured class; iii) an enrichment with a solid foundation in the subject; and iv) a preparation to complete learning by rigorously questioning the teacher and gaining a completed understanding. I pray that this book does *not* find its way into the classroom as a main text used by practitioners to deliver their lesson. This work is intended for the student's personal preparation and to accompany the paragon hours spent with a teacher in the flesh.

The Subject

Uṣūl ul-Fiqh is perceived as a difficult subject, which leaves the majority of students anxious about the whole experience. However, teachers and practitioners point to the fact that its rules are based upon everyday events and occurrences, so a trained mind should have no difficulty in seeing its application and appreciating its relevance.

Before commencing the study of any subject it is imperative to know five features of it to fully gauge maximum benefit: its definition – *at-ta'rīf*; its purpose and outcome – *al-gharaḍ* and *al-ghāya*; its scope – *al-mawḍū'*; its origin and compilation – *at-tadwīn*; and the significance of the text in hand.

QUICK ARABIC

التعريف: *at-ta'rīf*

Definition: A statement that presents the meaning of a word or phrase.

الغرض: *al-gharaḍ*

Purpose: The reason why something is done.

الغاية: *al-ghāya*

Outcome: The end result and consequence of a process.

الموضوع: *al-mawḍū'*

Scope: The extent and range to which something will apply.

التدوين: *at-tadwīn*

Compilation: How something came together.

The Definition

The *at-ta'rīf*, definition, should be known so as to prevent one from seeking a completely anonymous subject. So as far as Uṣūl ul-Fiqh is concerned, the word *uṣūl* is the plural of *aṣl* which means foundation or principle. The word *Fiqh* means subsidiary rulings of the Shariah that are derived from the detailed sources. Subsidiary, *al-far'ī*, are those rulings concerned with practice, as opposed to the main, *al-aṣlī*, that concern belief. So collectively the *at-ta'rīf* and definition of Uṣūl ul-Fiqh is: the science of knowing the principles of deriving canonical subsidiary Islamic rulings.

The Purpose And Outcome

The *al-gharaḍ* and *al-ghāya*, purpose and outcome, should be known to avoid the acquisition of a pointless subject. So, for Uṣūl ul-Fiqh, that is to know the details of the sources of Islamic rulings and to know the principles of deriving solutions to cases from those very sources.

The Scope

The *al-mawḍū'*, scope of a subject, should be known to be able to distinguish the particulars of the subject from that of another subject. For Uṣūl ul-Fiqh both *ad-dalāil,* evidences, and *al-aḥkām*, rulings, are within its range. Both have to be acquired and understood before commencing in this science.

Origin And Compilation

The process of *at-tadwīn*, compilation, of the subject should be known in order to be aware of the historical significance of the subject and its roots. All jurists have had a method of deriving rulings. It is virtually impossible to derive valid rulings without a system of principles in place. As the noble Imam Abū Ḥanīfa Nu'mān bin Thābit رحمه الله was the first compiler of Fiqh, by default he must also be the first to have applied a set of uṣūl and principles to meet that end. However, no such collection of principles has survived him. So, the primary text on the subject is ar-Risāla by Imam ash-Shāfi'ī رحمه الله which also happens to be the introduction to his book Kitāb ul-Umm. After this, many brief and lengthy treatises on the subject have been written by a whole host of scholars.

The Author

In order to appreciate the significance of the text in hand, one must

QUICK TERMS

الأصول: *al-uṣūl*

Principles: The accepted fundamental rules of deriving matters of fiqh.

الفرعي: *al-far'ī*

Subsidiary. The branches of fiqh concerning religious ceremonial and civil practices.

الأصلي: *al-aṣlī*

Main: The root.

الدلائل: *ad-dalāil*

Evidences: That which forms the basis to prove or disprove something in the Shariah.

الأحكام: *al-aḥkām*

Rulings: The decision of the Shariah based on valid evidences.

QUICK DICTIONARY

Fiqh: *fik*

The legal framework of Islamic religious, political and civil life.

know a little about the author and their life; the more significant the author the more valuable the text. The author of Uṣūl ush-Shāshī is from those noble, humble and honourable early scholars who shunned limelight and fame. It is for this reason he has not mentioned his name within the text of his book. The multiple commentaries on the original text even fail to mention his name.

In later commentaries the name of the author is given as Abū Ya'qūb, Isḥāq bin Ibrahīm ash-Shāshī al-Samarqandī who passed away in 325 AH, in Egypt. The book has also been referred to as Kitāb ul-Khamsīn*, the Book of Fifty*, as the author of the book was fifty years of age at the time of writing it or that he completed writing it in just fifty days. Some have contended that the name of the author is Niẓām ud-Dīn however there is no mention of an author of this name in accounts of history. ash-Shāsh is said to be a city in Transoxiana which is most likely close to modern day Tashkent [Figure P-01]. This is where the author is said to have hailed from and so his book is associated with that place.

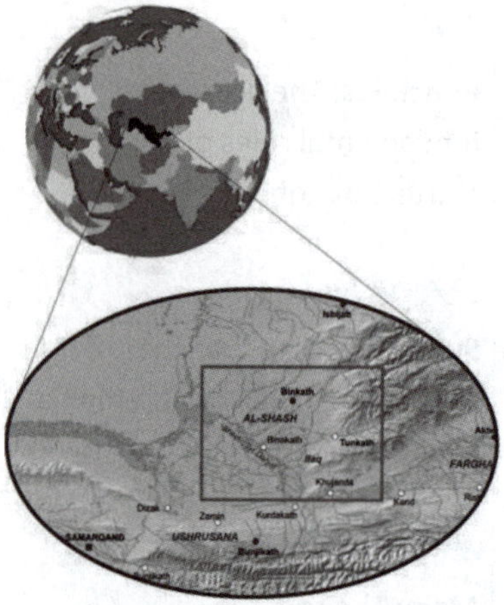

FIGURE P-01:
The world map showing Uzbekistan in black. The magnified map shows the approximate location of the area of ash-Shāsh. It is located to the South-West of the city of Tashkent, and North-East of the city of Samarqand.

As for the author's lifestyle, it is difficult to know exactly what it was as there is uncertainty surrounding his true identity. However, reading the text gives the impression that the author was very scholarly, methodical and an expert in Ḥanafī jurisprudence. He was precise and accurate in presenting the principles, and mindful enough to present several examples of each where necessary. Within the text he has provided the reader with an insight into the application of the principles without lengthening the body of work. His mastery is clear from the text, even if his true circumstances remain obscure.

Personal Attempts

This compilation is an effort that spans more than seven years. What began as partial translations on scraps of paper for the benefit of students, over the years grew into lengthier explanations and soon acquired summaries. I finally decided to collate all the notes, bits and pieces, and present them in the form you have in your hands today. The Urdu books *Ajmal ul-Ḥawāshī* and *Talkhīṣ Uṣūl ush-Shāshī Ma'a Qawāid Fiqhīya*, were greatly helpful in producing a comprehensive final piece. I even took it on myself to attempt to locate the resting place of anyone with either the name Abū Ya'qūb Isḥāq bin Ibrahīm ash-Shāshī al-Samarqandī or Niẓām ud-Dīn ash-Shāshī. The painstaking search of area of The City of the Dead of the Cairo Necropolis, *Qarafa*, over several years from 2009, yielded no results. It was not until April 2017 before the anticipated completion of this book that I finally gave up. In my discussions with various

QUICK REFERENCE

ما وراء النهر: *mā warā an-nahr*

Transoxiana. Beyond the Oxus river. It is an old and obsolete name for the region between Amu Darya and Syr Darya rivers.

scholars, the most fitting explanation of why the grave is unlocatable was that it is likely that as the Fatamid Caliphate [909 CE – 1171 CE] moved to rule over Egypt, the local Sunni population hid and obscured the locations and resting places of notable Sunni scholars. This was an effort to protect them from desecration at the hands of the Ismaili Shia rulers. The only shrines left prominent were of the Ahl ul-Bayt عليهم السلام, as they are revered by all. This theory seems consistent with the current landscape.

Furthermore, I had some notable discussions about the text of Uṣūl ush-Shāshī. Worthy of note is the idea that the text may actually be a combination of a number of pieces of work authored by different people on various occasions. It could be for this reason that the name of the author was removed as it did not represent the work of one person. This explanation also holds some merit given that some of the chapters and sections may seem misplaced to a novice. It could be that several entries have been placed side by side.

Some Remarks

It is worth noting that Uṣūl ush-Shāshī is not a book on comparative Fiqh. It aims to present the Ḥanafī principles in a simple manner, whilst contrasting them with other views on a case by case basis. This helps to reinforce the Ḥanafī principle in the mind of the student and in no way is it an attempt to present the strongest evidence of a given case from both sides. I have spoken to students who in later studies wrongly view the book as unreliable, or worse still, regard some very remarkable scholars as less than ordinary. I feel this is a direct result of not realising that Uṣūl ush-Shāshī is not presenting the others' case, rather just the Ḥanafī case, and for the ease of the student does not necessarily give the strongest evidence of other *madhhabs*.

Acknowledgements

Acknowledgment is not possible without thanking my Lord, first and last, and with every word in between. The truth is as the scholarly mystic Junayd رحمه الله said: حقيقة الشكر العجز عن الشكر – "Real gratitude is (realising) incapability to thank"; I am incapable of thanking Him جل جلاله. Repeating the words of His Khalīl Ibrāhīm عليه الصلاة والسلام. I profess:

"Lo! They are all hostile to me, except the Lord of the Worlds. Who created me, and He does guide me. And Who feeds me and quenches my thirst. And when I

بسم الله الرحمن الرحيم

فَإِنَّهُمْ عَدُوٌّ لِّي إِلَّا رَبَّ الْعَالَمِينَ ۝ الَّذِي
خَلَقَنِي فَهُوَ يَهْدِينِ ۝ وَالَّذِي هُوَ يُطْعِمُنِي
وَيَسْقِينِ ۝ وَإِذَا مَرِضْتُ فَهُوَ يَشْفِينِ ۝
وَالَّذِي يُمِيتُنِي ثُمَّ يُحْيِينِ ۝ وَالَّذِي أَطْمَعُ أَن
يَغْفِرَ لِي خَطِيئَتِي يَوْمَ الدِّينِ ۝ رَبِّ هَبْ لِي
حُكْمًا وَأَلْحِقْنِي بِالصَّالِحِينَ ۝ وَاجْعَل لِّي
لِسَانَ صِدْقٍ فِي الْآخِرِينَ ۝ وَاجْعَلْنِي مِن
وَرَثَةِ جَنَّةِ النَّعِيمِ ۝

صدق الله العظيم

سورة الشعراء 77–85

fall ill, He heals me. And Who causes me to die, then will resurrect me. And Who, I ardently hope, will forgive me my mistakes on the Day of Judgement. My Lord! Bestow me with wisdom and unite me with the righteous. And grant me sincere praise in generations to come. And place me among the inheritors of the Gardens of Delight."

[Blessed Quran – 26:77-85]

Furthermore, the *Ḥabīb's* love cannot be bypassed, ﷺ; Allah Almighty's choicest blessings, peace and salutations be upon him, his family and companions. As the illustrious Ḥassān رضي الله عنه put it:

ما إن مدحت محمدًا بمقالتي ولكن مدحت مقالتي بمحمد – I haven't praised Muhammad ﷺ with my utterance, rather my utterance is elevated due to Muhammad ﷺ.

Thrice do I show gratitude to my mother and to my father. My mother in whose service lies the betterment of my *ad-dunyā* and under whose feet, I pray, my *al-Janna*. My father, teacher and shaykh whose threefold relationship with me is special at every level and whose presence reminds of the Almighty جل جلاله and whose practice instils the love of the sunna of the Beloved ﷺ. His guidance in all matters is so cherished. I personally could not have wished for a more perfect role model and know of no other human being, who has shaped my life quite like he has. May Allah ﷻ preserve him, āmīn.

Special thanks are due to my colleagues, students and the scholars of al-Jamia Suffa-Tul-Islam, who made valuable suggestions throughout. In particular, ash-Shaykh Mohammad Anwar ul-Haq Qadri sahib, my elder brother and inspiration, for reviewing the work with a critical eye and his timely encouragement. I am grateful to many others for their expert advice, input and suggestions too, including Mawlana Mohammad Zahoor Bilali, Mufti Zahid Hussain sahib, Mawlana Masroor-ul-Haq Hussaini sahib, Mawlana Lukman Tahir sahib, Dr Hafiz Ather Hussain sahib and Shaykha H Batool. I am hopeful that I will receive enthusiastic comments and positive criticisms for this book from readers and look forward to making future editions more appealing, *inshaAllah*.

Finally, I reserve a special appreciation for my wife, daughters and son for their continued patience, understanding, encouragement, and support throughout this endeavour. May Allah Almighty keep them forever happy.

Mohammad Asrar ul-Haq
[Monday 11 June 2018, 27 Ramadan 1439]

حديث

عن أبي هريرة رضي الله عنه قال جاء رجل إلى رسول الله ﷺ فقال يا رسول الله من أحق الناس بحسن صحابتي قال أمك قال ثم من قال ثم أمك قال ثم من قال ثم أمك قال ثم من قال ثم أبوك

عليه الصلاة والسلام

صحيح البخاري: كتاب الأدب 5626
صحيح مسلم: كتاب البر والصلة والآداب 2548

QUICK ARABIC

الدنيا: *ad-dunyā*

World. The life of this world.

الجنة: *al-janna*

Paradise. The life of the Hereafter.

Introduction

Introduction

Uṣūl u<u>sh</u>-<u>Sh</u>ā<u>sh</u>ī begins with the formal formula of Allah's Name and Attributes, *al-basmala*, followed by the praise of Allah ﷻ in the exact order set out by the blessed Quran. It also follows the tradition of the blessed Prophet ﷺ in which he has said: "Any important matter begun without invoking the Name of Allah ﷻ is defective". Whilst another narration states: "Any important matter begun without the praise of Allah ﷻ is disjointed and incoherent." Furthermore, it is the custom of the scholarly predecessors to follow this order.

The praise of the Almighty ﷻ is followed by salutations upon the blessed Messenger of Allah, Muhammad ﷺ, his Companions رضي الله عنهم, the founder of the Hanafi juristic school al-Imam ul-A'ẓam Abū Ḥanīfa رحمه الله and those practitioners who worked with and applied his methodology.

After the formal introduction one must know that the sources of Islamic rulings are four; 1) the Book of Allah ﷻ, al-kitāb; 2) the tradition and practice of His Messenger ﷺ, as-sunna 3) the consensus of the Muslim Ummah, al-ijmā'; and 4) analogy, al-qiyās. Based on the fact that rulings as well as these four sources, all make up the contents of the text, this book is divided into five parts.

حديث

عن أبي هريرة رضي الله عنه عن رسول الله أنه قال: "كُلُّ أمْر ذِي بالٍ لا يُبْدأُ فِيهِ بالحَمْدِ لِلَّهِ أقْطَعُ" وفي رواية "بَحَمْدِ اللَّهِ" وفي رواية: "بالحَمْدِ فَهُوَ أقْطَعُ" وفي رواية "كُل كَلامٍ لايُبْدأُ فِيهِ بالحَمْد لِلَّهِ فَهُوَ أجْذَمُ" وفي رواية: "كُلُّ أمْرٍ ذِي بالٍ لا يُبْدأُ فِيهِ بِبِسْمِ اللَّهِ الرَّحْمَنِ الرَّحِيمِ فَهوَ أقْطَعُ"

عليه الصلوة والسلام

روي في سنن أبي داود وابن ماجه، ومسند أبي عوانة الإسفراييني المخرَّج على صحيح مسلم

One part each for the discussion of the four sources and a fifth part discussing rulings.

Text and Translation

بِسْمِ اللَّهِ الرَّحْمَٰنِ الرَّحِيمِ

الحمد لله الذي اعلى منزلة المؤمنين بكريم خطابه ورفع درجة العالمين بمعاني كتابه وخص المستنبطين منهم بمزيد الإصابة وثوابه والصلاة على النبي وأصحابه والسلام على ابى حنيفة وأحبابه

Allah's name I begin with; the Most Merciful, the Most Compassionate.

All praise is for Allah Who elevated the status of the believers with His generous speech; Who raised the rank of the scholars with the understanding of His book; and Who distinguished the extractors (of law) amongst them with increased accuracy and His reward. Blessings be upon the Prophet and his Companions, and peace be on Abū Ḥanīfa and his associates.

❖ ❖ ❖

FIGURE I-02: The Correlation Between Praise and Gratitude

الحمد

هو الثناء باللسان على الجميل الاختياري من نعمة أو غيرها بجهة التعظيم

al-Ḥamd is to **praise** good intentional acts using words, in response to a benefit or otherwise.

الشكر

هو تصرف جميع ما انعم الله به على عبده الى ما خلق لاجله

ash-Shukr and **gratitude** is to use Allah's ﷻ favour upon His creation, in a manner befitting that blessing.

FIGURE I-01: The usage of the particle *al* ال

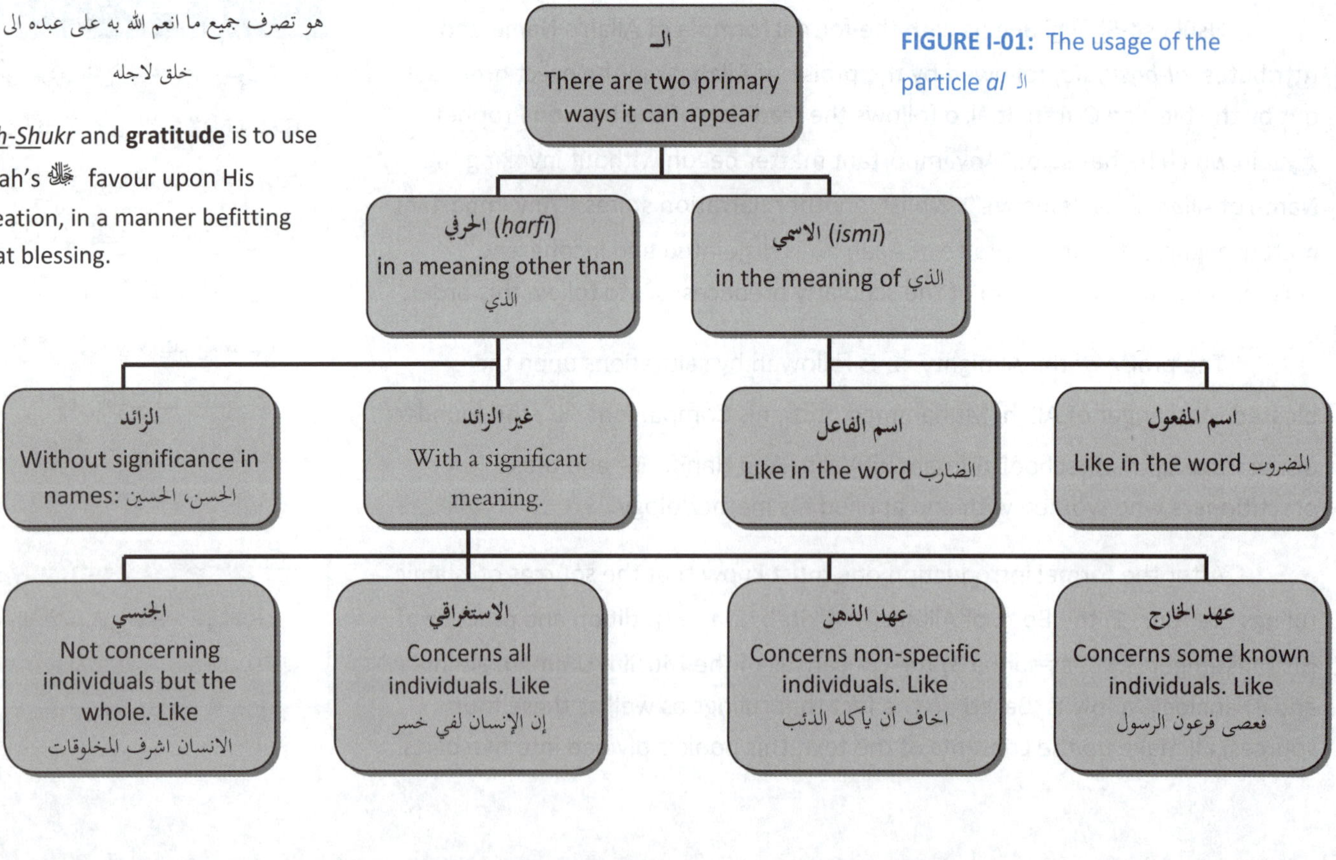

ب In the *basmala* the particle *al-bā* is for assistance or for blessing. The meaning will be either "With the help of Allah's name" or "With the blessing of Allah's name".

لله Allah ﷻ is the name of that Being, Who has all praised qualities and is eternal and everlasting.

الحمد The ال is for *al-jins* or *al-istighrāq* [Figure I-01]. In the case of *al-jins* it will mean the genus of praise and its essence is for Allah ﷻ. In the case of *al-istighrāq* it would mean all individual expressions of praise are for Allah ﷻ, as He is the One Who has granted all ability. Verse 53 of Sūrat un-Naḥl states: "Any blessing you have, is from Allah." Figure I-02 shows the difference between praise, *al-ḥamd*, and gratitude, *ash-shukr*.

المؤمنين This refers to those believers who are truly sincere in their belief.

العالمين This is the plural of *'ālim*. It refers not to all scholars but scholars who are well versed in Quranic sciences and understand its meanings. These scholars have a deep understanding of the blessed Quran, as well as an in-depth knowledge of Hadith and Fiqh as both of these sciences are integral to explaining the blessed Quran.

المستنبطين These are jurists who make sincere and disciplined attempts to deduce legal rulings from the sources.

الصلاة It literally means to supplicate. Its metaphorical meaning has come to mean a set of specified movements of worship. The metaphorical meaning is relevant to the literal as supplication is a significant part of worship. If *aṣ-ṣalah* is from Allah ﷻ it signifies His bestowal of absolute mercy. If it emanates from the angels it is seeking of forgiveness. And should it be from the believers, it is seeking absolute mercy from Allah ﷻ or supplication; and when it is from birds and the like it means praising.

بسم الله الرحمن الرحيم

وَمَا بِكُم مِّن نِّعْمَةٍ فَمِنَ اللَّهِ ثُمَّ إِذَا مَسَّكُمُ
الضُّرُّ فَإِلَيْهِ تَجْأَرُونَ ۝

صدق الله العظيم

سورة النحل 53

FIGURE I-03: Comparing 'prophet' and 'messenger'

	Messenger	Prophet
Similarities	Receives revelation.	Receives revelation.
	Used in the meaning of prophet.	Used in the meaning of messenger.
Differences	*A lawgiver with his own Shariah	*Follows the law of a Messenger
	*Recipient of divine scripture	*Does not receive a separate scripture
	*Revelation received through the angel Jibraīl	*Revelation received in the form of true dreams or from beind a veil.

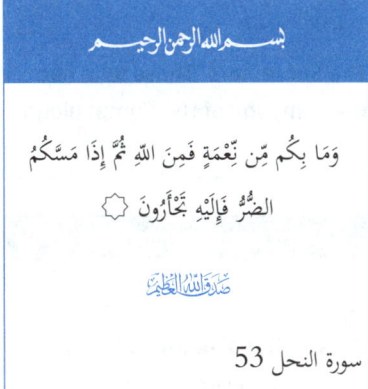

QUICK ARABIC

التابعون: *at-tābi'ūn*

The Successors. Those who had the company of the Companions رضي الله عنهم.

QUICK DICTIONARY

Agnomen: *ag-noh-muh n*

An additional name. It has an allusion to a circumstance.

FIGURE I-04: Usage of قبل (before) and بعد (after)

Both words can denote time or place. Grammatically they appear in three states:

1. Their *muḍāf ilayhi* or genitive noun is explicitly mentioned [Figure I-05];
2. Their *muḍāf ilayhi* is forgotten and thus omitted; or
3. Their *muḍāf ilayih* is figuratively omitted.

In the first two cases both words will be declinable (*al-mu'rab*) and change their endings according to the regent, *al-'āmil*. In the last case they both will be indeclinable (*al-mabnī*) upon the vowel *u*.

النبي The word means 'prophet' and according to some it is synonymous with the word 'messenger'. Others have stated differences between the two [Figure I-03].

أصحاب This is the plural of *ṣāḥib*, the plural of *ṣaḥbun*, the plural of *ṣaḥibun*, or the plural of *ṣaḥībun*. It means a companion of the beloved Prophet صلى الله عليه وسلم. A companion is someone who, in the state of complete faith, has been present in the company of the blessed Prophet صلى الله عليه وسلم, and then passed away with this status.

السلام The usage of this word independently with a non-prophet is disputed. The author of Uṣūl ush-Shāshī feels it can be used with non-prophets without the need to mention a prophet first. The majority however hold that phrases with words الصلاة and السلام should only be used with prophets or angels. If the words are to be applied to non-prophets, the names of the individuals should be subordinate to the prophets.

ابى حنيفة This is the agnomen of the grand master and Imam of the Ḥanafī school of jurisprudence. His name is Nu'mān bin Thābit. He is from the generation of the *at-Tabi'ūn*, the Successors, as it is evidenced that he reported from the noble Companion Anas bin Mālik رضي الله عنه.

أحبابه This refers to the teachers, contemporaries and students of the great Imam Abū Ḥanīfa رحمه الله

❖ ❖ ❖

Text and Translation

وبعد فإن أصول الفقه أربعة كتاب الله تعالى وسنة رسوله وإجماع الأمة والقياس فلابد من البحث في كل واحد من هذه الأقسام ليعلم بذلك طريق تخريج الأحكام

So: the principles of Islamic jurisprudence are four; the Book of Allah Almighty, the Traditions of His Messenger, the Consensus of the Muslim Nation and Analogy. Each of these areas must be discussed to know the method of deriving rulings.

وبعد The particle *al-waw* is for conjunction, *al-'aṭf*. Here, there is a figurative conjunction between two verbal sentences [Figure I-04]. The expanded text would read **احمد الله وأصلي وأسلم** وأقول بعد الحمد والصلاة والسلام أن أصول الفقه أربعة. The first verbal sentence is in bold, and the second verbal sentence is underlined. The particle *al-waw* is the conjunction.

فإن The particle *al-fā* indicates a final clause in a conditional sentence, *al-jazā*. There are then two possibilities: either it is the final clause for the omitted *al-maḥdhūf* word أما or its conditional clause is *al-muqaddar* and understood. If it is the former then the expanded text would read: اما بعد فإن أصول الفقه ; and if the case is the latter, the expanded text would read: إذا فرغت من الحمد والصلاة والسلام فأقول إن أصول الفقه أربعة.

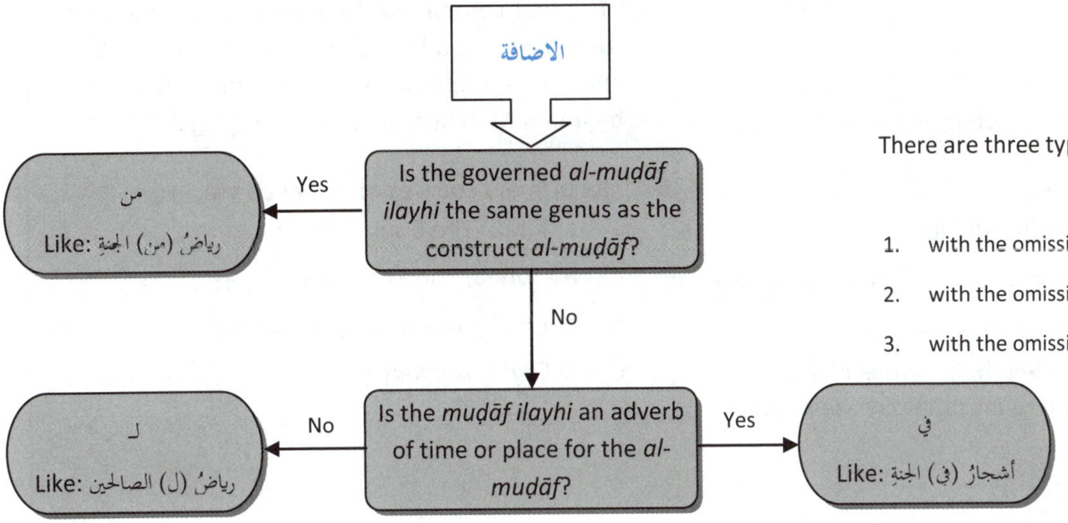

FIGURE I-05: Types of اضافة (genitive construction)

There are three types of *al-iḍāfa* in the Arabic language:

1. with the omission of ل ;
2. with the omission of في ; or
3. with the omission of من.

❖ ❖ ❖

Summary Of The Introduction

1. Before commencing the study of a text on any branch of knowledge it is vital to know the following five features of it: definition (التعريف), subject matter(الموضوع) , aim and purpose (الغرض والغاية), compilation (التدوين) and background to the text you are intending to study (خلفية الكتاب).

2. The definition (التعريف) of Uṣūl ul-Fiqh is:

   أصول الفقه: علم بقواعد يتوصل بها المجتهد إلى استنباط الأحكام من أدلتها التفصيلية

   "Uṣūl ul-Fiqh: is a science of principles that allows a jurist to derive rulings from their exact sources."

3. The scope (الموضوع) of Uṣūl ul-Fiqh:

   موضوع أصول الفقه: الأدلة من حيث انها مثبتة للأحكام والأحكام من حيث أنها مثبتة من الأدلة

   "The scope of Uṣūl ul-Fiqh: is both evidence that supports rulings, and rulings that are supported by evidence."

4. Aim and purpose (الغرض والغاية) of Uṣūl ul-Fiqh:

   غرض أصول الفقه وغايتها: تحصيل القدرة على استنباط الأحكام من أدلتها التفصيلية

   "The aim and purpose of Uṣūl ul-Fiqh is to achieve competence in deriving rulings from their exact sources."

5. Compilation (التدوين) of Uṣūl ul-Fiqh:

   المدون الأول لأصول الفقه: الإمام الأعظم أبو حنيفة نعمان بن ثابت

   والكتاب الأول في أصول الفقه: كان لمحمد بن ادريس الشافعي رضي الله عنه

   "The first compiler of Uṣūl ul-Fiqh was the Grand Jurist Imam Abū Ḥanīfa Nu'mān bin Thābit رحمه الله and the first treatise on Uṣūl ul-Fiqh was written by Imam Muḥammad bin Idrīs ash-Shāfi'ī رحمه الله."

6. The primary sources of evidence are:

   a) al-Kitāb, The Book (الكتاب);

   b) as-Sunna, The Practice (السنة);

   c) al-Ijmā', Consensus (الإجماع); and

   d) al-Qiyās, Analogy (القياس).

al-Kitāb

PART 1

1.0 Introduction to al-Kitāb

The first discussion is on al-kitāb, the blessed Quran and final Word of Allah ﷻ, from the four sources; the other sources being as-sunna - the Practice, al-ijmā' - Consensus, and al-qiyās - Analogy. This is because al-kitāb is the most important of the four and the basis of the rulings of the Shariah.

The author of Uṣūl ush-Shāshī did not define al-kitāb, rather he advanced to the next stage of discussing it. The reason for this is that al-kitāb is well known, and its every word, letter and vowel is undisputedly accounted for. Therefore, he felt it unnecessary to state the obvious. However, many scholars have provided a definition for al-kitāb, which can be summarised as:

القرآن: الكتاب المنزل على الرسول المكتوب في المصاحف المنقول إلينا نقلا متواترا بلا شبهة

"The Quran is the book revealed upon the Messenger ﷺ recorded as scripture, and transmitted to us continuously and unbroken, without any doubt". [al-Manār]

The breakdown of the definition is as follows:

QUICK TERMS

الكتاب: *al-kitāb*

The Book. The inspired final Word of Allah ﷻ. The Quran.

السنة: *as-sunna*

The Practice. The sayings, doings and approval of the blessed Prophet ﷺ.

الإجماع: *al-ijmā'*

Consensus. The unanimous consent of the mujtahids.

القياس: *al-qiyās*

Analogy. The reasoning of the learned.

بِسْمِ اللهِ الرَّحْمٰنِ الرَّحِيْمِ

إِنَّا أَنزَلْنَاهُ قُرْآنًا عَرَبِيًّا لَّعَلَّكُمْ تَعْقِلُونَ ۝

صَدَقَ اللهُ الْعَظِيْمُ

سورة يوسف 2

بِسْمِ اللهِ الرَّحْمٰنِ الرَّحِيْمِ

وَإِنَّهُ لَفِي زُبُرِ الْأَوَّلِينَ ۝

صَدَقَ اللهُ الْعَظِيْمُ

سورة الشعراء 196

QUICK ARABIC

الآيات : *al-āyāt*

Verses. Small sentence-like portions of the Quran.

القراءات : *al-qirāāt*

Readings. Different methods of reciting the Quran.

QUICK DICTIONARY

Genus: jee-nuh s
A class or group. A group of similar closely related things.

Semantics: si-man-tiks
Meanings. Related to the study of words in relation to their meanings.

القرآن	This is *al-jins* or genus in the definition. It is inclusive of both the defined item as well as the non-defined. As the Quran is something that is recited, it is possible that the word *al-qurān* is an *al-maṣdar* from *qaraā yaqrau* (to read) in the meaning of the *al-ism ul-mafʿūl* (the recited). Alternatively, the Arabic word Quran is *al-maṣdar* of *qarana yaqrinu* (to combine) in the meaning of *al-ism ul-mafʿūl* to mean the combined, as the Quran is a combined passage of *al-āyāt*. Either way, both meanings of 'the recited' and 'the combined' would hold true for the Quran and also for other texts, thus this word is a genus.
الكتاب المنزل	This is the first differentiae. It eliminates all non-divine scriptures, whilst true divinely inspired scriptures would remain.
على الرسول	This is the second differentiae. It distinguishes the blessed Quran from other heavenly scriptures as it refers to the beloved Messenger Muhammad ﷺ.
المكتوب	This is the third differentiae. It eliminates those verses that are abrogated and are classified as *al-mansūkh*.
المنقول	This is the fourth differentiae. It eliminates those words that have reached us through *al-āḥād* or singular narrations of *al-qirāat* and recital manners.
بلا شبهة	This is the an explanation, which does not eliminate anything, rather it supports and strengthens the previous differentiae.

It is also worth noting that the word Quran is used for both the written word, as defined above, as well as the semantical relations of those words. In verse 2 of Sūra Yūsuf: "We have sent it down as an Arabic Quran..." the written word being the Quran is signified, and in verse 196 of Sūrat ush-Shuʿarā: "It is without doubt in the Books of former people.", the semantical being Quran is indicated.

Furthermore, not every verse of the blessed Quran is considered a source for rulings. Rather, some five hundred verses concern rulings whilst the remaining are life stories, of the prophets and nations of the past, glad tidings to those who heed the word of Allah ﷻ and warnings to those who are heedless.

The only way we as Muslims can know of the commandments of Allah ﷻ is through these verses that concern rulings. It is thus vital for our ultimate guidance that we understand the Arabic words of the blessed Quran in their written form so by their means we can arrive at what the Almighty ﷻ wishes for us. Now, Arabic words, and indeed words of other languages, differ with each other in their coinage, clarity, usage and sentence positioning. Some words give singular meanings, whilst others have multiple meanings. The understanding we have of some words is clearer than the implications of others. How someone chooses to express themselves can give rise to usage of words with sarcasm or metaphors and so on; similarly, where a word is located or positioned in a sentence changes our understanding and we deduce meanings from that anchoring. Bearing this in mind the author of Uṣūl ush-Shāshī has devoted subsequent chapters to a detailed analysis of the impact on rulings resulting from Arabic words of al-kitāb with respect to meaning, clarity, usage and their positioning as Figure 1.0-01 highlights.

❖ ❖ ❖

QUICK TERMS

المنسوخ: *al-mansūkh*

Abrogated. Verses that are recited but no longer applied.

الآحاد: *al-āḥād*

Singular traditions. Traditions related by single-narrator chains.

الكتاب: *al-kitāb*

The Book. The inspired final word of Allah ﷻ. The Quran.

QUICK GRAMMAR

المصدر: *al-maṣdar*

The infinitive. Root and origin of an Arabic word group.

الاسم المفعول: *al-ism ul-maf'ūl*

Passive Participle. A thing that underwent the act of the verb.

FIGURE 1.0-01

A division of the words of the Quran in terms of impact on rulings.

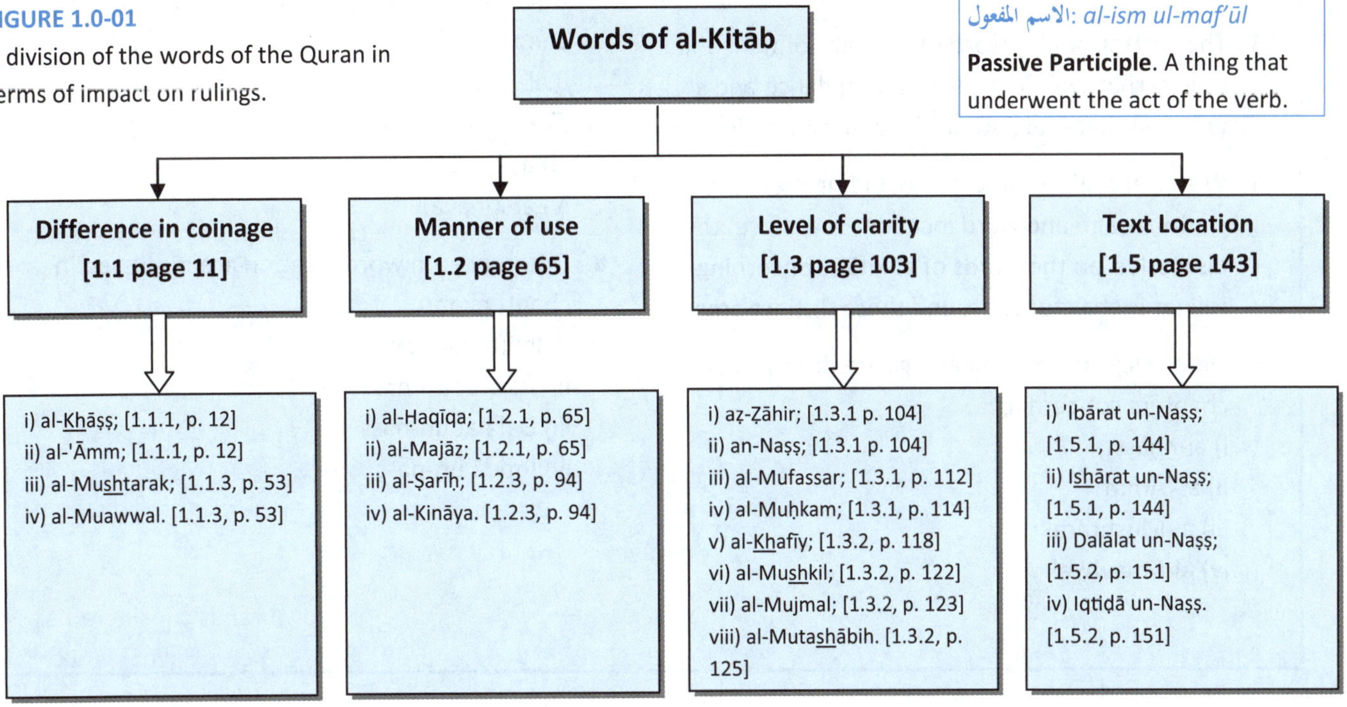

البحث الأول: في كتاب الله

The First Discussion: on the Book of Allah

❖❖❖

Summary Of Introduction To al-Kitāb

1. The primary source of the rulings of the Shariah is the blessed Quran, al-kitāb. It is defined as:
   الكتاب المنزل على الرسول المكتوب في المصاحف المنقول إلينا نقلا متواترا بلا شبهة
   "The book revealed upon the Messenger ﷺ recorded in scripture, and transmitted to us continuously without any doubt."
2. There are some 500 verses concerning rulings, the remaining are life events from the prophets and nations of the past, glad tidings and warnings.
3. The written Arabic word of al-kitāb contains the rulings that we must derive for guidance and so we must first understand the written words.
4. Words are different to each other in meaning, clarity, usage and word location. Therefore, the discussion on the words of al-kitāb concerning rulings is structured around these distinct areas.
5. Differences in word meanings are discussed in chapters concerning:
   i) al-Khāṣṣ
   ii) al-'Āmm
   iii) al-Mushtarak
   iv) al-Muawwal.
6. Differences in word clarity are discussed in chapters concerning:
   i) aẓ-Ẓāhir
   ii) an-Naṣṣ
   iii) al-Mufassar
   iv) al-Muḥkam
   v) al-Khafīy
   vi) al-Mushkil
   vii) al-Mujmal
   viii) al-Mutashābih.
7. Differences in usage are discussed in chapters concerning:
   i) al-Ḥaqīqa
   ii) al-Majāz
   iii) aṣ-Ṣarīḥ
   iv) al-Kināya.
8. Differences in word location are discussed in chapters on:
   i) 'Ibārat un-naṣṣ
   ii) 'Ishārat un-naṣṣ
   iii) Dalālat un-naṣṣ
   iv) Iqtiḍā un-naṣṣ.

1.1 Word Coinage

The previous chapter concluded by showing us how Quranic words are divided for the purpose of extracting rulings of the Shariah. In this chapter, we start looking at the division of the words in terms of their designated and coined meanings. There are four types in all: al-khāṣṣ (the specific), al-'āmm (the general), al-mushtarak (the homograph) and al-muawwal (the precedent). The first two are discussed first in section [1.1.1] whereas the latter two are discussed in section [1.1.3]. This division of coined words is summarised in Figure 1.1-01:

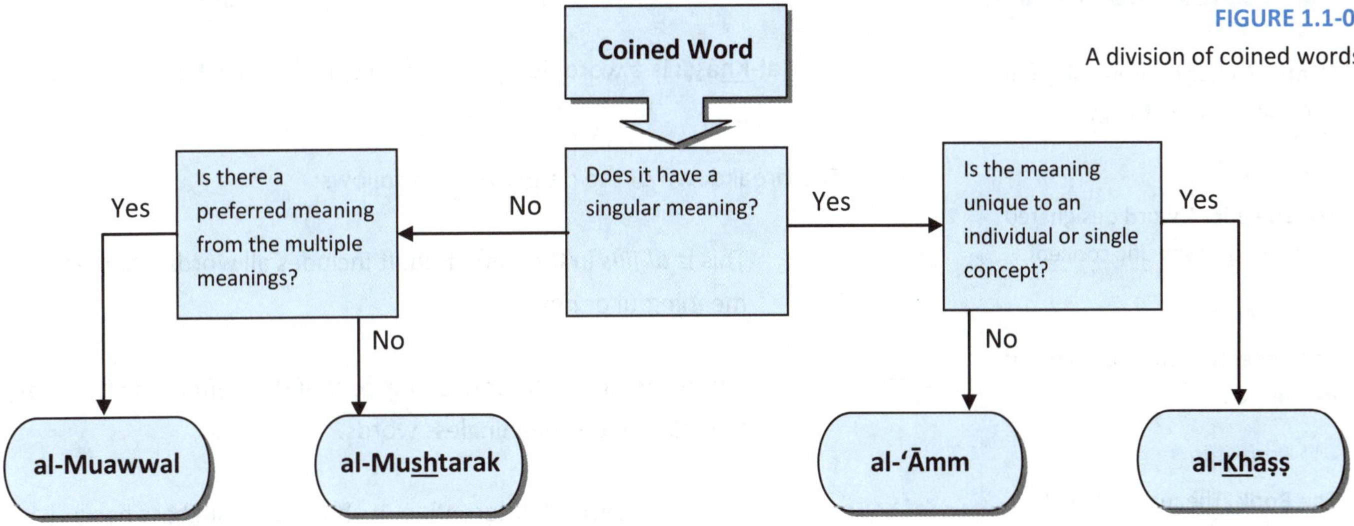

FIGURE 1.1-01
A division of coined words.

The next section [1.1.1] deals with al-khāṣṣ and al-'āmm together as they share the characteristic of having a singular designated meaning. The difference between the two however, is that al-khāṣṣ has a meaning irrespective of personnel and al-'āmm consists of a group of individuals. Furthermore, both of these types give a definitive ruling when compared to al-muawwal and al-mushtarak. al-Khāṣṣ is then discussed before al-'āmm because it is simple in that it is seen as a single unit whereas al-'āmm is seen more like a plurality; the simple comes before the complex.

The text of Uṣūl ash-Shāshī first presents the definition of al-khāṣṣ and its types, before giving the definition of al-'āmm. The ruling of al-khāṣṣ follows this and then three examples in which the ruling is applied are presented. al-'Āmm is then introduced as two types. The ruling on the first type is followed by some examples of its application. This progresses to stating the definitive nature of this type of al-'āmm according to Ḥanafī principles. The definition, ruling and an example of the second type of al-'āmm is then presented. Lastly, the section concludes by providing an easy to understand reason why a substantially weaker piece of evidence is valid in influencing the second type of al-'āmm, in spite of al-'āmm being from al-kitāb.

1.1.1 al-Khāṣṣ and al-'Āmm

The definition of al-khāṣṣ is:

الخاص: لفظ وضع لمعنى معلوم أو لمسمى معلوم على الانفراد

"**al-Khāṣṣ:** is a word designated for a singular specific concept or individual".

The breakdown of the definition is as follows:

لفظ — This is *al-jins* in the definition. It includes all words whether meaningful or not.

وضع لمعنى — This is the first differentiae. It is part of the definition of al-khāṣṣ that eliminates meaningless words.

معلوم — This is the second differentiae. It shows that al-khāṣṣ has a specific meaning. Thus, it will eliminate al-mushtarak from the definition, as al-mushtarak does not have a specified meaning, rather it has numerous possibilities.

على الانفراد — This is the third differentiae. It will eliminate al-'āmm from the definition. This is required as al-khāṣṣ is for an individual in its coinage; al-'Āmm, however, is for a group of individuals.

There are three types of al-khāṣṣ; khāṣṣ ul-fard, the specific and named individual; khāṣṣ un-naw', the specific type; and khāṣṣ ul-jins, the specific genus. The examples of each are *Zayd*, *man* and *human*, respectively. So Zayd is khāṣṣ ul-fard because the word is for a named individual. With one coinage it can only indicate one individual, although different coinages of the same word will allow for numerous individuals to be named Zayd. Man is khāṣṣ un-naw' because in

QUICK TERMS

الجنس: *al-jins*

Genus. A class or group. A group of closely related things.

الخاص: *al-khāṣṣ*

The specific. A word designated for a singular specific concept.

العام: *al-'āmm*

The general. A word designated for a group.

الكتاب: *al-kitāb*

The Book. The inspired final word of Allah ﷻ. The Quran.

خاص الفرد: *khāṣṣ ul-fard*

Specific individual. The named individual.

خاص النوع: *khāṣṣ un-naw'*

Specific type. The word that implies any one individual of a similarly functioning group.

خاص الجنس: *khāṣṣ ul-jins*

Specific genus. The word that implies any one individual of a group that have differing functions.

terms of word coinage it has one meaning but it can be used for various individuals whose Islamic roles are the same. The Islamic role of a man is to be an Imam, to attend Jumu'a and Eid and so on. Human is khāṣṣ ul-jins because though its coinage is for one meaning it could be true of various individuals whose Islamic roles are different. The word human would be appropriate for both a male and a female, whose Islamic roles are not the same. A male's role was described previously, and this is significantly different to a female's role who traditionally is to be a homemaker, raiser of children and so and so forth.

The definition of al-khāṣṣ contains two parameters: *musammā ma'lūm* and *ma'nā ma'lūm*. This is because *ma'nā ma'lūm*, a known concept, would only allow the inclusion of khāṣṣ un-naw' and khāṣṣ ul-jins, and would not include khāṣṣ ul-fard. Khāṣṣ ul-fard is not coined for a concept but for an individual. So, it was necessary to include the words *musammā ma'lūm* in the definition for inclusivity.

Text and Translation

فصل في الخاص والعام فالخاص لفظ وضع لمعنى معلوم أو لمسمى معلوم على الانفراد كقولنا في تخصيص الفرد زيد وفى تخصيص النوع رجل وفى تخصيص الجنس انسان

Chapter on al-khāṣṣ and al-'āmm: al-Khāṣṣ is a word designated for a singular specific concept or individual. Like we say for a single specific individual *Zayd*, for a single specific class *man*, and for a single specific genus *human*.

❖ ❖ ❖

After the definition, types and examples of al-khāṣṣ, we are now presented with the definition of al-'āmm. Its definition is as follows:

العام: كل لفظ ينتظم جمعا من الأفراد

"**al-'Āmm:** is every word containing a group of individuals".

The breakdown of the definition is as follows:

كل لفظ — This is *al-jins* in the definition. It includes all meaningful words, as it is a definition within word coinage. It also indicates that *al-*

QUICK TERMS

الجنس: *al-jins*

Genus. A class or group of closely related things.

QUICK ARABIC

العموم: *al-'umūm*

Generality. An unspecific and indefinite statement.

ʻ*umūm* or generality is a feature of words and not of their meanings.

ينتظم

This is the first differentiae and it has the meaning of *yashtamilu*, to constitute, contain or be made up of something. It eliminates both al-mushtarak and al-khāṣṣ from the definition of al-ʻāmm. al-Khāṣṣ is eliminated because it is not 'made up' of many, and al-mushtarak is eliminated because though it has numerous designations, they can only be used one by one. So, at any one time al-mushtarak does not constitute a group.

جمعا من الأفراد

This is the second differentiae, which is useful in eliminating dual word forms and whole numbers. al-ʻĀmm is for a group of individuals and not a group of parts. Whole numbers are made up of units which collate to make the whole. Parts and individuals are different, so this part of the definition helps eliminate whole numbers from al-ʻāmm.

So, al-ʻāmm is any meaningful word that, due to its spelling or through its meaning, is coined for a group of things or individuals. An example of al-ʻāmm being for a group by its spelling is the word *muslimūn*, as the word form tells us it is a group of adherents of Islam. An example of al-ʻāmm being for a group by its meaning is the word *mā* which tells us whomsoever.

Text and Translation

والعام كل لفظ ينتظم جمعاً من الأفراد إما لفظاً كقولنا مسلمون ومشركون وإما معنى كقولنا من وما

al-ʻĀmm is every word determined for a group of individuals either through the word-form itself like we say *muslimūn* or *mushrikūn*, or through the meaning, like we say *who* or *what*.

❖❖❖

After the definition of al-khāṣṣ, its types, and the definition of al-ʻāmm, we are now given the ruling of al-khāṣṣ as a principle of Fiqh. So, the ruling of al-khāṣṣ is:

وحكم الخاص: وجوب العمل به لا محالة

QUICK TERMS

المشترك: *al-mushtarak*

The concurrent. A word coined for two or more inherently different meanings.

الخاص: *al-khāṣṣ*

The specific. A word designated for a singular specific concept.

العام: *al-ʻāmm*

The general. A word designated for a group.

"**The ruling of al-khāṣṣ** is the necessity to enact it by all means."

This means that the word identified as being al-khāṣṣ is so definite in giving its meaning that it cannot mean anything else, whilst it is so definite no other meaning can be taken into consideration. The underlining reason for this is that if a word did not mean its own meaning, there would be no point of designated meanings for any word. One could practically say anything and then retract by saying "I didn't mean that", there would be no rule or order to follow. As for a metaphorical meaning for that word, it cannot be established without an external sign or indicator that suggests the alternative meaning. So, the coined meaning is definitive, and its definitiveness is not eroded with merely a possibility of a metaphor. So, al-khāṣṣ from al-kitāb is definitive in giving its meaning and must be enforced in all circumstances.

The definitiveness of al-khāṣṣ leads us to conclude that if a weaker piece of evidence like a khabar ul-wāḥid or al-qiyās contradicts it, we will first look to reconcile between them by applying both but without altering the meaning of the al-khāṣṣ word or ignoring it. This is because all evidences are essentially there to be acted upon and not neglected. However, if the weaker evidence and al-khāṣṣ are contradictory, then one of them must be abandoned. As the al-khāṣṣ is definitive in its meaning it cannot be altered or ignored; alteration would render it undefined and abandoning for a weaker piece of evidence would be illogical.

Khabar ul-wāḥid is weaker than al-khāṣṣ of al-kitāb because it is not definitive. Its uncertainty comes from the fact it may or may not have an unbroken chain of transmission to the blessed Prophet ﷺ. al-Qiyās is weaker than al-khāṣṣ of al-kitāb because it is also not definitive and is based upon opinion. The possibility of inaccuracy in an opinion is greater than in something which is definitive. The conclusion is that both khabar ul-wāḥid and al-qiyās will be ignored when they contradict al-khāṣṣ.

Text and Translation

وحكم الخاص من الكتاب وجوب العمل به لا محالة فإن قابله خبر الواحد او القياس فإن أمكن الجمع
بينهما بدون تغيير في حكم الخاص يعمل بهما والا يعمل بالكتاب ويترك ما يقابله

QUICK TERMS

الكتاب: *al-kitāb*

The book. The inspired final Word of Allah جل جلاله. The Quran.

خبر الواحد: *khabar ul-wāḥid*

Singular tradition. Traditions related by single-narrator chains.

القياس: *al-qiyās*

Analogy. The reasoning of the learned.

بِسْمِ اللهِ الرَّحْمٰنِ الرَّحِيْمِ

وَالْمُطَلَّقَاتُ يَتَرَبَّصْنَ بِأَنْفُسِهِنَّ ثَلَاثَةَ قُرُوْءٍ (الآية)

صَدَقَ اللهُ الْعَظِيْم

سورة البقرة 228

QUICK TERMS

الكتاب : al-kitāb

The book. The inspired final Word of Allah ﷻ. The Quran.

الخاص : al-khāṣṣ

The Specific. A word designated for a singular specific concept.

The ruling for al-khāṣṣ of the Quran is the necessity to enact it by all means. If a khabar ul-wāḥid or al-qiyās counters it, and it is possible to reconcile between them both without altering the ruling of al-khāṣṣ then enact them both, otherwise act on al-kitāb and leave its contender.

❖ ❖ ❖

Following the ruling of al-khāṣṣ three examples in which the ruling is applied are presented. The first example is from Sūrat ul-Baqara, verse 228. The al-khāṣṣ word under scrutiny is *thalātha* meaning the number three. To understand the full application of the al-khāṣṣ word *thalātha*, we must first acknowledge that there is a period of waiting, *al-'idda*, for a woman who is given a verbal divorce by her husband. This is the instruction in verse 228 of Sūrat ul-Baqara. However, the duration of this waiting period is disputed regarding a divorced, non-pregnant and menstruating woman, whose marriage was consummated. The Aḥnāf say *al-'idda* should be the duration of three *al-ḥayḍ*, blood discharge phases, whereas the Shawāfi' say it should be the length of three *aṭ-ṭuhr*, pre-discharge phases. Both disputing parties present the same verse because the Quranic word *qurū* has the possibility of both meanings, *al-ḥayḍ* and *aṭ-ṭuhr*. The scenario is summarised in Figure 1.1.1-01:

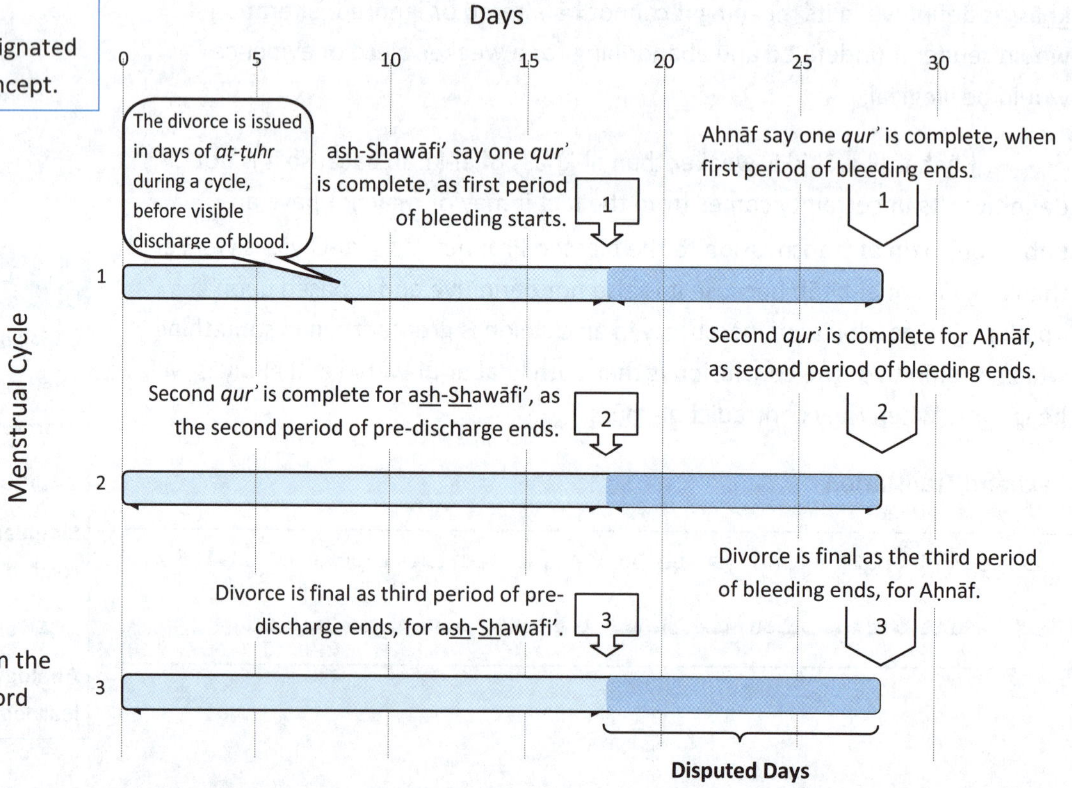

FIGURE 1.1.1-01
Diagram showing dispute in the meaning of the al-khāṣṣ word *qurū'*.

Figure 1.1.1-01 shows how Imam ash-Shāfi'ī ﷺ uses the Quranic words to mean three periods of *aṭ-ṭuhr* and also how Imam Abū Ḥanīfa ﷺ uses it to mean three periods of *al-ḥayḍ*.

One of the pieces of evidence to support the Shafi'ī position is that the verse uses the feminine form of the word for three, *thalātha*. In Arabic the rule regarding usage of numbers 3 through 9 is that if the quantified item, *at-tamyīz*, is masculine the number will be feminine, and if the quantified item is feminine the whole number will be masculine. From the two possible outcomes of the word *qur'*, *aṭ-ṭuhr* is masculine and *al-ḥayḍ* is feminine. So, to be grammatically correct in Arabic the feminine *thalātha* can only couple with the masculine *aṭ-ṭuhr.* In the verse, if the word for three was masculine, *thalāth*, only then would the word *qur'* have the possibility to mean *al-ḥayḍ*.

The Aḥnāf counter this narrative by pointing out that in the words of the blessed Quran the feminine, *thalātha*, is already followed by the masculine *qur*. There is no disagreement in this grammatically. However, when considering the semantics of the word *qur* there is a difficulty in considering the meaning *aṭ-ṭuhr*. The difficulty, according to the Aḥnāf, is that if we consider *al-'idda* period to be *aṭ-ṭuhr*, it will mean that the exact waiting period will be two whole terms and a few days of *aṭ-ṭuhr* in which the divorce was issued [figure 1.1.1-01]. This is not a complete three *aṭ-ṭuhr*, whereas the blessed Quran is explicit in saying the women should be waiting for the duration of "three periods (*qur*)". By stating that *qur* means *aṭ-ṭuhr* you would only be acting upon two and a few days and not three complete periods. The Aḥnāf continue by proposing the meaning of *al-ḥayḍ* for the word *qur*, as we would be able to ensure three whole periods of *qur*, which presents a more befitting solution to the meaning of *qur*. It is befitting as the al-khāṣṣ word, *thalātha*, will be applied wholly as an equal three periods and not as two and a small amount [figure 1.1.1-01]. This is important as al-khāṣṣ gives a definitive meaning that is applicable in all circumstances. If *qur* means *aṭ-ṭuhr* the al-khāṣṣ understanding from *thalātha* is lost, which is not acceptable. So, the only possibility is to apply the meaning of *al-ḥayḍ* to *qur*, this allows for al-khāṣṣ to be applied correctly.

Text and Translation

مثاله في قوله تعالى يتربصن بأنفسهن ثلاثة قروء فإن لفظة الثلاثة خاص في تعريف عدد معلوم فيجب
العمل به ولو حمل الأقراء على الاطهار كما ذهب اليه الشافعي باعتبار ان الطهر مذكر دون الحيض

QUICK ARABIC

العدة: *al-'idda*

The term. The three-month period after a divorce.

الحيض: *al-ḥayḍ*

The menses. A woman's periodic blood flow from the uterus.

الطهر: *aṭ-ṭuhr*

The purity days. The period of no blood flow during a complete menstruation cycle.

القروء: *al-qurū*

The period. A disputed part of the menstruation cycle. It can either mean *al-ḥayḍ* or *aṭ-ṭuhr*.

QUICK GRAMMAR

التمييز: *at-tamyīz*

The qualified. A noun mentioned to clarify what is meant by a previous unclear noun.

QUICK DICTIONARY

Semantics: *si-man-tiks*

Meanings. Related to the study of words in relation to their meanings.

وقد ورد الكتاب في الجمع بلفظ التأنيث دل على انه جمع المذكر وهو الطهر لزم ترك العمل بهذا الخاص
لأن من حمله على الطهر لا يوجب ثلاثة أطهار بل طهرين وبعض الثالث وهو الذي وقع فيه الطلاق

An example of it is the command of Allah Almighty: "women shall wait concerning themselves for three monthly periods". The word thalātha is al-khāṣṣ to determine a known whole number. So it must be enacted. If the word *al-aqrā* is construed to mean *days of purity* like Imam ash-Shāfa'ī has determined based on the word *aṭ-ṭuhr* being masculine and not the word *al-ḥayḍ*, whilst the Quran has a feminine word as the plural. It shows the word is a masculine plural which is *aṭ-ṭuhr*. It necessitates rejecting the enforcing of al-khāṣṣ as those who consider it to mean *aṭ-ṭuhr* cannot obey the ruling of three whole periods of purity but rather two periods of purity and some days of the third period in which the divorce was issued.

❖❖❖

The dispute between the Aḥnāf and the Shawāfi' in the previous text gives rise to a multitude of differences between the two schools in individual cases. These cases and verdicts are matters of Fiqh and do not really enhance on the principles of Fiqh, but do go to highlight how and where differences in application may arise. The differences revolve around whether the three periods, *qurū*, mentioned in the blessed Quran come to an end after the third *aṭ-ṭuhr* ends (Imam ash-Shāfa'īy's position), or if they come to an end after the third *al-ḥayḍ* ends (Imam Abū Ḥanīfa's position). The "disputed days" are marked in Figure 1.1.1-01.

At the onset of the "disputed days" the Shawāfi' consider the divorce final and the marriage over, whereas the Aḥnāf consider the marriage ongoing till the end of the third *al-ḥayḍ*. So, all cases affected by a couple being in wedlock or out of wedlock, will be disputed from this moment to the end of the third *al-ḥayḍ*. To highlight the point the text of ash-Shāshī provides seven cases.

The first dispute is that if a man had voiced an *ar-raj'ī*, revocable divorce, by the onset of the third *al-ḥayḍ* he would still have the right to revoke the divorce and continue the marriage, as according to the Aḥnāf the *al-'idda* doesn't conclude until after the third *al-ḥayḍ*. The Shawāfi' however would contend that as *al-'idda* came to an end after the third *aṭ-ṭuhr* the marriage is already over, so there is no right remaining for the man to revoke the divorce.

QUICK ARABIC

الرجعي: *ar-raj'ī*

The revocable. A divorce issued after which the husband has permission to return to the marriage.

العدة: *al-'idda*

The term. The three-month period after a divorce.

الحيض: *al-ḥayḍ*

The menses. A woman's periodic blood flow from the uterus.

الطهر: *aṭ-ṭuhr*

The purity days. The period of no blood flow during a complete menstruation cycle.

The second affected case mentioned is if the woman enters into a marriage with another man within the disputed days, the Shawāfi' would allow it as her previous marriage is already over after the third *aṭ-ṭuhr*. The Aḥnāf would not allow it as she is still in the previous marriage until the end of the third *al-ḥayḍ*, which is yet to elapse.

The third disputed case mentioned is that the Aḥnāf would maintain that the woman would have to reside in the house of her husband during these disputed days, as she is still in the marriage and it is necessary for her to remain at her husband's residency during *al-'idda*. The Shawāfi' will rule that she is to leave as the marriage is over once the third *aṭ-ṭuhr* has come to an end.

The fourth disputed case is that provision of residency and maintenance are necessary upon the husband throughout a marriage. So, during the disputed days of the third *al-ḥayḍ* according to the Aḥnāf it continues to be necessary. the Shawāfi' do not stipulate this, as the marriage is over after the end of the third *aṭ-ṭuhr*, in their view.

The fifth disputed case is if the husband has previously given one or two revocable divorces to his wife, and currently she is in the disputed days of the third *al-ḥayḍ*, the husband may engage in *al-khul'* or issue a third divorce according to the Aḥnāf. This is because *al-khul'* or a third divorce can only be initiated if the marriage is still valid, which according to the Aḥnāf still remains, therefore both are possible. The Shawāfi' have said that the marriage concluded at the end of the third *aṭ-ṭuhr* so both *al-khul'* and a third divorce are meaningless.

The sixth disputed case is that in the third *al-ḥayḍ* the husband is not permitted to marry his wife's sister, nor four wives other than her. This is because having two sisters in wedlock at the same time is *al-ḥarām*, so as he is still married to his wife, marrying her sister is not permitted. Furthermore, if he was to marry four others, that do not include this woman who is in her *al-'idda*, he would be married to five women, which is also *al-ḥarām*. This is according to the Aḥnāf. As the Shawāfi' consider the marriage over once the third *aṭ-ṭuhr* has come to an end, the man would be permitted to marry the sister of his ex-wife, and to enter marriage agreements with four other women.

The seventh disputed case is that if the husband was to pass away during the last *al-ḥayḍ*, according to the Aḥnāf the divorcee will be entitled to

QUICK ARABIC

الخلع: *al-khul'*

Divorce. An agreement to divorce after compensation is paid by the wife.

الحرام: *al-ḥarām*

The prohibited. That which is unlawful, as opposed to *al-ḥalāl*, lawful.

بسم الله الرحمن الرحيم

قَدْ عَلِمْنَا مَا فَرَضْنَا عَلَيْهِمْ فِي أَزْوَاجِهِمْ

(الآية)

صدق الله العظيم

سورة الأحزاب 50

QUICK TERMS

الخاص: *al-khāṣṣ*

The specific. A word designated for a singular specific concept.

المجمل: *al-mujmal*

The unexplained. Wording that requires explanatory statements.

الكتاب: *al-khāṣṣ*

The book. The inspired final word of Allah ﷻ. The Quran.

QUICK ARABIC

الحيض: *al-ḥayḍ*

The menses. A woman's periodic blood flow from the uterus.

QUICK DICTIONARY

Bequeath: *bih-kweeth*

To dispose. To leave personal property in a last will.

her share of the inheritance and for the husband to bequeath anything to her would be void. The inheritance is given because she still remains his wife in this *al-ḥayḍ* and the bequest is void as one is not permitted to bequest a part of the estate to a relative who automatically inherits. The wife automatically inherits, so cannot be party to a bequest. The Shawāfi' consider the marriage to be over, so an automatic right to inheritance will no longer apply, and the bequest would be permitted due to the woman not being a default inheritor.

Text and Translation

ويخرج على هذا حكم الرجعة في الحيضة الثالثة وزواله وتصحيح نكاح الغير وإبطاله وحكم الحبس والاطلاق والمسكن والإنفاق والخلع والطلاق وتزوج الزوج بأختها وأربع سواها واحكام الميراث مع كثرة تعدادها

Extrapolated, based on this, is the ruling regarding the right to revoke the divorce in the third period of discharge or not; the validity of (the woman) marrying another or its invalidity; the ruling on continual residance, leaving, right of abode and maintenance; possibility of *al-khul'* or (another) divorce; the husband marrying her sister or four others apart from her; and the many rulings on inheritance.

❖❖❖

After highlighting where differences may arise when applying principles, Uṣūl ush-Shāshī returns to giving examples of the ruling of al-khāṣṣ applied to the blessed Quran. So, the second example presented is from Sūrat ul-Aḥzāb, verse 50.

In this verse the al-khāṣṣ word is *faraḍnā*, We have enjoined. The word is clearly definitive in giving its meaning and so enacting it is necessary in accordance with the ruling of al-khāṣṣ. Allah ﷻ sets the mandatory condition of a bridal gift whilst people have no influence in this stipulation. The details of the matter are that Imam ash-Shāfi'ī رحمه الله regards the stipulation of a bridal gift in the marriage contract a right of the parties to the contract. They can set the amount as the Shariah has given no indication of the amount necessary. The reasoning behind this is that Imam ash-Shāfi'ī رحمه الله categorises the marriage contract as any other financial contract, so like other financial contracts the price is set by the two parties, as the Shariah does not stipulate any amount. The two parties have the discretion to specify what they mutually agree to be the acceptable amount.

The Aḥnāf say it is true that the Shariah has not stipulated the higher threshold for bridal gift but it has provided a minimum threshold of ten Dirhams (approximately thirty grams of silver). Any amount less than this set as bridal gift is not acceptable in the Shariah. To state their claim the Aḥnāf have used verse 50 of Sūrat ul-Aḥzāb: "...indeed We know what We have enjoined upon them about their wives." The deduction is that the word *faraḍnā* is al-khāṣṣ to mean Allah جل جلاله has allocated a set amount upon the husbands. Now Allah جل جلاله sets this amount but the exact amount is al-mujmal, unquantified. An al-mujmal amount requires an explanation to clarify what it means, so the sunna has stated: "There is no bridal gift less than ten Dirhams." So, the amount of the bridal gift is set by the Shariah at more than ten Dirhams and it is left at the discretion of the parties to determine an amount equal to or in excess of that.

Building upon this, the text states that as Imam ash-Shāfi'ī رحمه الله considers marriage to be like any other financial agreement and not an act of sunna and not a form of worship. So just as the case is with other financial matters it is better to engage in voluntary prayers than marriage and its consequential affairs. This is when there isn't an unhealthy imbalance of carnal desires in the individual, and the individual needs to make a choice between marriage and freeing up time for worship; otherwise it would be necessary for the person to marry. Contrary to this opinion, the Aḥnāf say that engaging in marriage and upholding conjugal rights, is better than engaging in voluntary prayers. One piece of evidence that supports the Aḥnāf is the Hadith of the blessed Prophet صلى الله عليه وسلم: النكاح من سنتي فمن رغب عن سنتي فليس مني "Marriage is from my tradition, so whomsoever forsakes my tradition is not mine." There is more evidence from al-kitāb, as-sunna, al-ijmā' and al-qiyas to support both points of view but discussing them here is beyond the scope of this book.

Another case Imam ash-Shāfi'ī رحمه الله brings forth is the issue of termination. Just as financial contracts are terminated in various ways without prejudice, the marriage agreement may be terminated in numerous ways without any blame on the husband. This includes terminating the marriage by issuing one, two or three divorces and by granting all three divorces in one cycle

حديث

عن جابر وعبد الله ابن عمر رضي الله عنهما قال صلى الله عليه وسلم:

"لا مهر أقل من عشرة دراهم"

عليه الصلاة والسلام

مصنّف ابن أبي شيبة

حديث

عَنْ عَائِشَةَ قَالَتْ قَالَ رَسُولُ اللَّهِ صلى الله عليه وسلم:

النِّكَاحُ مِنْ سُنَّتِي، فَمَنْ لَمْ يَعْمَلْ بِسُنَّتِي فَلَيْسَ مِنِّي "

عليه الصلاة والسلام

رواه ابن ماجه (1846)

QUICK TERMS

السنة: *as-sunna*

The practice. The sayings, doings and approval of the blessed Prophet صلى الله عليه وسلم.

الإجماع: *al-ijmā'*

Consensus. The unanimous consent of the mujtahids.

القياس: *al-qiyās*

Analogy. The reasoning of the learned.

of *aṭ-ṭuhr* or in different cycles; and even if issuing all three divorces in one sentence. There is no action of termination that is seen as disliked, just as you have in a financial contract. The Aḥnāf however, consider giving two divorces in one cycle a practice of *al-bid'a* and an innovation whose perpetrator is a sinner. The reason for this is that he has acted contrary to the established sunna in a matter as important as marriage. By treating it this way he makes it a trivial matter. He is acting excessively if he issues two or three divorces at once, when he could have easily issued just the one to the same effect. This is why it is disliked.

The third issue is that according to Imam ash-Shāfi'ī ﷺ *al-khul'* is the termination of a marriage, whereas the Aḥnāf consider it to be the equivalent of *aṭ-ṭalāq al-bāin*, an irrevocable divorce. The difference becomes apparent if we consider a man who marries a woman, the woman then enters *al-khul'* arrangement with him, but before she marries another man, she remarries this same individual. The Aḥnāf say the woman has entered this marriage with the right of only two further divorces, so the man can only give her two divorces during the course of this marriage, as he has already issued one divorce to her by way of *al-khul'*. Imam ash-Shāfi'ī ﷺ does not consider *al-khul'* to be a divorce but a termination, so the right of three divorces remain for the duration of the second marriage.

QUICK ARABIC

الطهر: *aṭ-ṭuhr*

The purity days. The period of no blood flow during a complete menstruation cycle.

البدعة: *al-bid'a*

Innovation. An act in the religion that contradicts the sunna.

الخلع: *al-khul'*

Divorce. An agreement to divorce after compensation is paid by the wife.

الطلاق البائن: *aṭ-ṭalāq ul-bāin*

The irrevocable divorce. A divorce after which the husband is not permitted to unilaterally return to the marriage.

Text and Translation

وكذلك قوله تعالى "قد علمنا ما فرضنا عليهم في أزواجهم"خاص في التقدير الشرعي فلا يترك العمل به باعتبار انه عقد مالي فيعتبر بالعقود المالية فيكون تقدير المال فيه موكلاً الى رأى الزوجين كما ذكره الشافعي وفرع على هذا ان التخلي لنفل العبادة أفضل من الاشتغال بالنكاح واباح ابطاله بالطلاق كيف ما شاء الزوج من جمع وتفريق واباح إرسال الثلث جملة واحدة وجعل عقد النكاح قابلاً للفسخ بالخلع

Similarly, the Almighty's word: "...Indeed We know what We have enjoined upon them about their wives", is al-khāṣṣ for a Shariah-allocated quantity. So its enacting cannot be ignored by arguing that it is a financial contract and should be treated like a financial contract. So allocating money in it will be at the discretion of the couple, as Imam ash-Shāfa'īy mentioned. He has deduced, based on this, that abstinence to pursue voluntary salah is better than engaging in marriage. He has made indifferent, terminating it with divorce, howsoever the husband wishes; through collective or seperated divorce. He made indifferent the imparting of all three at once, and he made the marriage contract voidable by way of *al-khul'*.

❖ ❖ ❖

The third example of al-khāṣṣ being applied to the blessed Quran is given from Sūrat ul-Baqara, verse 230. In the verse the word *tankiḥa*, "She marries", is al-khāṣṣ as it gives a definitive meaning and so it must be enacted. The details of this case are that if a mature, sane woman was to enter into her own marriage without the consent of her guardian, the Aḥnāf permit the marriage whereas the Shawāfi' do not. Imam ash-Shāfi'ī رحمه الله takes into account the narration reported by Sayyida Aisha رضي الله عنها which states that any woman entering into marriage without the consent of her guardian is invalid. The verdict is repeated thrice indicating the importance of it. Imam Abū Ḥanīfa رحمه الله says that the word from the blessed Quran, *tankiḥa*, is al-khāṣṣ giving the specific meaning of 'she marries'. The woman establishes the act of marriage and there is no mention of a guardian's consent. So, the al-khāṣṣ of al-kitāb will take preference over the singular al-aḥād narration as combining them is not possible without altering al-khāṣṣ. The Hadith said *any* woman marrying without consent will render the marriage invalid, whereas the Quran tells of a woman who marries on her own accord. The two cannot be validly reconciled.

As the Aḥnāf permit the marriage of a sane, mature woman on her own accord, whilst the Shawāfi' don't, it results in different verdicts if such a marriage takes place. The lawfulness of intercourse between the couple is contested by the Shawāfi', as well as establishing no liability with respect to paying a bridal gift, maintenance costs or providing a place of residence. If the man who is party to this agreement was to issue a divorce, no divorce would occur as there was no marriage from the onset. The Aḥnāf would give different verdicts as the marriage is valid. Intercourse would be lawful, the bridal gift, maintenance and residence would be the responsibility of the husband and any divorce issued would be valid. Furthermore, if three divorces were issued the Shawāfi' would render them all invalid and allow a marriage to take place with the consent of the guardian to the same man. The Aḥnāf would validate all three divorces, so the woman would have to marry another man before she is permitted to marry the ex-husband for a second time. The stated position of the Shawāfi' was held by their earlier scholars and their latter scholars are in agreement with the Aḥnāf in these matters.

بسم الله الرحمن الرحيم

حَتَّىٰ تَنكِحَ زَوْجًا غَيْرَهُ

(الآية)

صدق الله العظيم

سورة البقرة: 230

حديث

عن عائشة رضي الله عنها قالت: قال رسول الله صلى الله عليه وسلم:

"أيما امرأة نَكَحت بغير إذن مواليها فنكاحها باطل ثلاث مرات"

عليه الصلاة والسلام

اخرجه ابو داوود (2083)

QUICK TERMS

الخاص: *al-khāṣṣ*

The specific. A word designated for a singular specific concept.

الكتاب: *al-kitāb*

The book. The inspired final Word of Allah جل جلاله. The Quran.

الآحاد: *al-āḥād*

Singular traditions. Traditions related by single-narrator chains.

Text and Translation

وكذلك قوله تعالى "حتى تنكح زوجاً غيره" خاص في وجود النكاح من المرأة فلا يترك العمل به بما روى عن النبي عليه السلام "ايما امرأة نكحت نفسها بغير اذن وليها فنكاحها باطل باطل باطل "ويتفرع منه الخلاف في حل الوطيء ولزوم المهر والنفقة والسكنى ووقوع الطلاق والنكاح بعد الطلقات الثلث على ما ذهب اليه قدماء اصحابه بخلاف ما اختاره المتأخرون منهم

Similarly The Almighty's saying, "...until she marries another husband..", is al-khāṣṣ for procurement of marriage by the woman. So enforcing it will not be ignored in favour of the narration of the Prophet, peace and blessings be upon him: "The marriage of any woman who enters into it on her own accord without her guardian's consent, is invalid, it is invalid, it is invalid." Differences ensue from this regarding the permissibility of intercourse, the obligation of bridal gift, sustenance and maintenance, the occurrence of divorce and also marriage after three instances of divorce, according to his traditional adherents as opposed to the preference of the latter amongst them.

❖❖❖

Ḥanafī Principles (1)

MEMORISE

	Term	Definition	Ruling	An Example
1	الخاص	لفظ وضع لمعنى معلوم أو لمسمى معلوم على الانفراد	وجوب العمل به لا محالة	يتربص بأنفسهن ثلاثة قروء (البقرة: 228)

❖❖❖

Previously, the definition of al-'āmm was presented with the definition of al-khāṣṣ. The text then went on to cover the ruling and some examples of al-khāṣṣ. To remind ourselves the definition of al-'āmm was given on page 13 as:

العام: كل لفظ ينتظم جمعا من الأفراد

"**al-'Āmm:** is every word containing a group of individuals".

QUICK TERMS

الخاص: *al-khāṣṣ*

The specific. A word designated for a singular specific concept.

العام: *al-kitāb*

The general. A word designated for a group.

Now, we are told of the two types of al-ʻāmm and the ruling on the first type. The ruling on the second type will come later. The two types are:

1. 'Āmmun lam yakhuṣṣa 'anhu shayun: the unrestricted al-ʻāmm, which would imply that there are no exemptions by way of attributes nor exceptions, from the group.

2. . ʻĀmmun khuṣṣa 'anhu ul-ba'ḍ: the restricted al-ʻāmm, which is a word spoken on a group of individuals but some are exempt through attributes or exceptions.

The ruling of the unrestricted al-ʻāmm according to the Aḥnāf is that it gives a definitive understanding, and enacting it is as important as enacting al-khāṣṣ. So, the ruling of ʻāmmun lam yakhuṣṣa ʻanhu shayun is:

وحكم عام لم يخص عنه شيء: وجوب العمل به لا محالة

"The ruling of ʻāmmun lam yakhuṣṣa ʻanhu shayun is the necessity to enact it by all means."

Text and Translation

وأما العام فنوعان عام خص عنه البعض وعام لم يخص عنه شيء فالعام الذي لم يخص عنه شيء فهو بمنزلة الخاص في حق لزوم العمل به لا محالة

As for al-'āmm it is of two kinds: 'āmmun khuṣṣa 'anhu ul-ba'ḍ (restricted al-ʻāmm) and 'āmmun lam yakhuṣṣa 'anhu shayun (unrestricted al-'āmm). The unrestricted al-'āmm is like al-khāṣṣ in terms of the obligation to enact it at all costs.

❖ ❖ ❖

Following the ruling on an unrestricted al-ʻāmm there are some examples of its application. The first example shows al-ʻāmm enacted and the alternative is rejected as there is no conformity. It is a case where a thief is in possession of stolen goods and the goods perish whilst in his possession. A court of law finds him guilty of the crime and his hand is severed as punishment for the theft. The Aḥnāf say there is no additional requirement that the thief must compensate for the damaged goods too. The Shawāfi' on the other hand

QUICK TERMS

عام لم يخص عنه شيء: *ʻāmmun lam yakhuṣṣa ʻanhu shayun*
The general without exemptions. A word designated for a group without exemptions.

عام خص عنه البعض: *ʻāmmun khuṣṣa ʻanhu ul-baʻḍ*
The general with exception. A word designated for a group with possible exemptions.

demand that he must also compensate for the perished goods. The reasoning of the Shawāfi' is based on an agreed upon case that if one was to usurp another's property, and the property was to perish, the usurper would have to compensate for the loss. So similar to the usurper the thief would also have to compensate. The Aḥnāf disagree by citing verse 38 of the Sūrat ul-Māida:

فاقطعوا أيديهما جزاء بما كسبا (المائدة: 38)

"...cut off his or her hands: a punishment for what*(mā)* they committed..."

The Arabic word *mā* is used in the verse and it is an al-'āmm word. Its generality would imply that the thief's punishment is for *all* the crime he or she committed. This means that the punishment of severing is for both the theft and the perishing of the goods. If we were to say that the perished goods are to be compensated for separately this would mean the severing of the hand was for the theft whilst the added compensation is for the perishing of goods. The thief's sentencing would become complex and the generality of the *mā* of al-kitāb would be compromised as now the severing will be for *only* the theft and an additional punishment for the perished goods. To ensure that the *mā* retains its generality it must include *all* of what the thief did. This is vitally important because *mā* is an unrestricted al-'āmm and to enact it is necessary in all circumstances. By adopting the view of the Shawāfi' of likening it to a usurper, al-qiyās is competing with al-'āmm of al-kitāb. In such cases al-qiyās is rejected in favour of al-kitāb.

The evidence supporting the fact that the Arabic word *mā* is al-'āmm is from a fatwa of Imam Muḥammad ﷺ who along with being an exceptional jurist is also a celebrated linguist. He says that if one was to promise his pregnant slave freedom by saying: "If what(*mā*) is in your stomach is a boy, you're free", and she gave birth to a set of twins, one boy and one girl, she will not be free. The reason for this is that the use of the word *mā* means *all* of what is in her stomach must be masculine in gender for her emancipation. However, as she gave birth to a baby girl too, the condition is not met, because a part of what was in her womb is feminine, so she is not free.

Text and Translation

وعلى هذا قلنا إذا قطع يد السارق بعد ما هلك المسروق عنده لا يجب عليه الضمان لأن القطع جزاء جميع ما اكتسبه السارق فإن كلمة ما عامة يتناول جميع ما وجد من السارق وبتقدير ايجاب الضمان

QUICK TERMS

العام: *al-'āmm*

The general. A word designated for a group.

الكتاب: *al-kitāb*

The book. The inspired final Word of Allah ﷻ. The Quran.

القياس: *al-qiyās*

Analogy. The reasoning of the learned.

يكون الجزاء هو المجموع ولا يترك العمل به بالقياس على الغصب والدليل على ان كلمة ما عامة ما ذكره محمد إذا قال المولى لجاريته ان كان ما في بطنك غلاماً فأنت حرة فولدت غلاما وجارية لا تعتق.

Based on this we say if the hand of the thief is severed after the stolen goods perish in his custody there is no liability on him because the act of severing is the compensation for all what the thief has committed. The word *mā* is al-'āmm which entails all what is committed by the thief. By imposing a further penalty it will become a complex punishment. We will not abandon enforcing it based on al-qiyās upon usurpation. The evidence for the word *mā* being al-'āmm is as Imam Muḥammad mentions that if a master says to his slave girl, "If what (*mā*) is in your womb is a boy, you are free", and she gave birth to a boy and a girl, she will not be free.

❖ ❖ ❖

Just as in the previous example the word *mā* is al-'āmm, in this second example the same is true. However, the second example shows that both al-'āmm and the alternative are compatible. Allah ﷻ says in verse 20 of Sūrat ul-Muzzammil:

فاقرءوا ما تيسر من القرآن [المزمل:20]

"...so, you recite of the Quran what is easy for you..."

The word *mā* is al-'āmm and includes all verses that are easily recitable which includes Sūrat ul-Fātiḥa and other verses. As the verse concerns salah it would mean that when a worshiper is to recite from the blessed Quran, he or she can choose to recite any verse to fulfil the requirement. One is not compelled, as an unmissable condition of salah, to recite al-Fātiḥa. However, there is a Hadith that states: "There is no salah without al-Fātiḥa." This would imply that recitation of Sūrat ul-Fātiḥa is essential to the prayer, and without it the salah would be invalid. The *mā* of al-kitāb on the other hand is stating that you may recite from anywhere due to it being al-'āmm.

Despite the apparent contradiction it is possible to apply both sources without affecting the word of the Quran. This is achieved by interpreting the Hadith to mean 'There is no *perfection* in salah without al-Fātiḥa'. Thus, by the instruction of the Quran one must recite from any verse to fulfil the minimum

حديث

عن عبادة بن الصامت رضي الله عنه أن رسول الله ﷺ قال: "لا صلاة لمن لم يقرأ بفاتحة الكتاب"

عليه الصلاة والسلام

صحيح البخاري (723) صحيح مسلم (394)

QUICK TERMS

الكتاب: *al-kitāb*

The book. The inspired final Word of Allah ﷻ. The Quran.

العام: *al-'āmm*

The general. A word designated for a group.

حديث

قال ﷺ: "المسلم يذبح على اسم الله تعالى سمى أو لم يسم"

عليه الصلوة والسلام

سنن ابن ماجه

QUICK TERMS

الواجب: *al-wājib*

The necessary. The non-observance of which is sinful, but denial does not lead to disbelief.

الفرض: *al-farḍ*

The obligatory. The observance of which is necessary and denial leads to disbelief.

الخبر: *al-khabar*

Singular tradition. Traditions related by single-narrator chains.

عام لم يخص عنه شيئ: *'āmmun lam yakhuṣṣa 'anhu ul-ba'ḍ*

The general without exemption. A word designated for a group without exemptions.

QUICK ARABIC

سجدة السهو: *sajdat us-sahw*

Prostration of forgetfulness. Two prostrations made if any *al-wājib* is missed during the salah.

criteria as al-farḍ of salah, and by the instruction of the Hadith include al-Fātiḥa as al-wājib to perfect the prayer and not require a make-up *sajdat us-sahw*.

Text and Translation

وبمثله نقول في قوله تعالى "فاقرءوا ما تيسر من القرآن" فإنه عام في جميع ما تيسر من القرآن ومن ضرورته عدم توقف الجواز على قرآة الفاتحة وجاء في الخبر انه قال لا صلاة إلا بفاتحة الكتاب فعملنا بهما على وجه لا يتغير به حكم الكتاب بأن نحمل الخبر على نفى الكمال حتى يكون مطلق القراءة فرضاً بحكم الكتاب وقراءة الفاتحة واجبة بحكم الخبر

Similar to that is what we say in the Word of the Almighty, "...so, you recite of the Quran what is easy for you..." It is al-'āmm for all easily recitable verses of the Quran. Inevitably this means not limiting permisibility to al-Fātiḥa. It has been reported in a Hadith that he, peace and blessings be upon him, said: "There is no salah without al-Fātiḥa of the Quran." So we enforce both in a manner that does not alter the commandment of the Quran such that we construe the Hadith to mean imperfection. So recitation in general is al-farḍ by the ruling of al-kitāb and the recitation of al-Fātiḥa is al-wājib by the ruling of al-khabar.

❖ ❖ ❖

The third example of enacting *mā* as 'āmmun lam yakhuṣṣa 'anhu shayun concerns the case where someone deliberately fails to mention the name of Allah ﷻ when slaughtering an animal. Imam Abū Ḥanīfa رحمه الله is of the opinion that if it is deliberately omitted the meat would be unlawful. Imam ash-Shāfi'ī رحمه الله says it is permitted in both cases , when purposefully omitted or forgetfully. Imam ash-Shāfi'ī رحمه الله takes his position by presenting a Hadith in which the blessed Prophet ﷺ was questioned about the meat of a slaughtered animal where the name of Allah ﷻ was not invoked. He ﷺ replied: "Eat it, for the name of Allah is in the heart of every believer." Imam Abū Ḥanīfa رحمه الله says that Allah ﷻ has decreed in verse 121 of Sūrat ul-An'ām:

ولا تأكلوا مما لم يذكر اسم الله عليه [الأنعام:121]

"Eat not of that on which Allah's name has not been invoked..."

The word *mā* is al-'āmm and would imply that failure to mention the name of Allah ﷻ before slaughtering is unlawful. When compared to the Hadith presented by Imam ash-Shāfi'ī رحمه الله we can see a direct contradiction. The al-'āmm of al-kitāb says it is unlawful to purposefully omit the name of Allah ﷻ when slaughtering, whilst the Hadith implies the name of Allah ﷻ is already in the heart of the believer who purposefully omits it. It is not possible to reconciliate between them without abrogating the definitive, *al-qat'ī*, verse of the blessed Quran, which is not permitted with the presumptive, *aẓ-ẓannī,* evidence of the al-khabar. The improper abrogation would occur because if for the sake of the Hadith we accept that purposefully omitting the name of Allah ﷻ is permitted, then forgetfully omitting it would most certainly be excused, as forgetfulness is more acceptable than purposeful neglect. So then, as both forgetfully and purposefully omitting are permitted the meaning of the verse, "Eat not of that..." would be redundant. This is not acceptable, as the verse is *al-qat'ī* and cannot be abrogated by an aẓ-*ẓannī* piece of evidence. The only way is to enact the verse and relegate the Hadith.

Text and Translation

وقلنا كذلك في قوله تعالى "ولا تأكلوا مما لم يذكر اسم الله عليه" إنه يوجب حرمة متروك التسمية عامداً وجاء في الخبر انه عليه السلام سئل عن متروك التسمية عامداً فقال كلوه فإن تسمية الله تعالى في قلب كل امرإ مسلم فلا يمكن التوفيق بينهما لأنه لو ثبت الحل بتركها عامداً لثبت الحل بتركها ناسياً فحينئذٍ يرتفع حكم الكتاب فيترك الخبر

Similarly we say about the word of the Almighty, "Eat not of that on which Allah's name has not been pronounced...", that it entails the prohibition of purposefully not pronouncing His name whilst it is mentioned in a Hadith that he, peace and blessings be upon him, was questioned about purposefully not pronouncing, to which he replied: "Eat of it, for the name of Allah is in the heart of every believer." Reconciliation between them both is impossible as permission to purposefully abandon it would in effect permit abandoning it unintentionally too. So at this point the ruling of al-kitāb would be abrogated, and so consequently al-khabar is abandoned.

❖ ❖ ❖

QUICK TERMS

القطعي: *al-qaṭ'ī*

The definitive. Most reliable and certain .

الظني: *aẓ-ẓannī*

The speculative. Reached after careful consideration.

In the final example we are told that khabar ul-wāḥid is to be discarded if it is not possible to enact both it and the 'āmmun lam yakhuṣṣa 'anhu shayun. Allah ﷻ, in verse 23 of Sūrat un-Nisā, whilst listing the women who are forbidden in marriage says:

وأمهاتكم التي أرضعنكم [النساء:23]

"...your foster mothers who gave you suck..."

The generality of the words of the verse indicate that the marriage of the suckling mother is in all cases forbidden to the suckling infant for all his life. There is no indication of a quantity. Merely suckling is sufficient to establish the impermissibility. This is the position taken by the Aḥnāf.

There is, however, a Hadith narrated by Lady 'Āisha رضي الله عنها, which states that suckling on one or two occasions doesn't establish this impermissibility. So, if the infant has sucked on the breast of a woman once or twice, or she has offered her breast milk once or twice by placing it in the infant's mouth, the marriage of the two in future would be possible. This is a position held by Imam ash-Shāfi'ī رحمه الله who says that this suckling can occur up to five times before impermissibility of marriage occurs.

The verse states in absolute terms the impermissibility of marriage to a foster mother through unrestricted al-'āmm words, whereas the Hadith stipulates an amount which is excused. The two cannot be reconciled such that both could be adhered to without altering the generality and openness of the unrestricted al-'āmm. So, al-khabar is relegated to establish the ruling of 'āmmun lam yakhuṣṣa 'anhu shayun, which is to enact it in all circumstances.

Text and Translation

وكذلك قوله تعالى وأمهاتكم التي أرضعنكم يقتضي بعموم حرمة نكاح المرضعة وقد جاء في الخبر لا تحرم المصة ولا المصتان ولا الإملاجة ولا الاملاجتان فلم يمكن التوفيق بينهما فيترك الخبر.

Similarly, The Almighty's says: "...your foster mothers who gave you suck..." implies the generality of marriage to foster mothers being unlawful. It was stated in a Hadith that a child's suckling once or twice does not render it forbidden, nor does the offering of the breast once or twice. As it is not possible to satisfy the two, so the Hadith is yielded.

حديث

عن عائشة رضي الله عنها قالت قال رسول الله صلى الله عليه وسلم:

"لا تحرم المصة والمصتان، وفي رواية أخرى لا تحرم الإملاجة والإملاجتان"

عليه الصلاة والسلام

صحيح مسلم (1450)، (1451)

QUICK TERMS

الكتاب: *al-kitāb*

The book. The inspired final Word of Allah ﷻ. The Quran.

الخبر (الواحد): *al-khabar (ul-wāḥid)*

Singular tradition. Traditions related by single-narrator chains.

عام لم يخص عنه شيء: *'āmmun lam yakhuṣṣa 'anhu shayun*

The general without exemption. A word designated for a group without exemptions.

العام: *al-'āmm*

The general. A word designated for a group.

المصة — The act of sucking; it would be the act of the infant who is feeding.

الإملاجة — This is to offer for sucking. This would be the act of the woman offering the feed.

❖ ❖ ❖

After the ruling and examples of the first type of al-ʻāmm, we are now presented with the definition and ruling of the second type of al-ʻāmm. This is the restricted al-ʻāmm called, ʻāmmun khuṣṣa ʻanhu ul-baʻḍ.

It is important to understand what we mean by *at-takhṣīṣ*, specification. This involves exempting an individual or individuals from a group contained in a word which is al-ʻāmm, using an attached yet independent part of a sentence. This would result in some of the individuals of the group remaining within the limits of the operative part of the sentence, and the rest of the group would not be influenced by it. An independent part of a sentence is one that gives its own complete understanding, and an attached part of a sentence is one that is communicated in one instance and not on separate occasions. If the two parts are separated, the first would be abrogated by the second and it would not constitute *at takhṣīṣ*.

al-ʻĀmm that has undergone *at-takhṣīṣ* and restriction no longer remains definitive and *al-qaṭʻī*. It becomes *aẓ-ẓannī* and speculative. Those individuals that remain within the scope of al-ʻāmm must be enacted whether the excluded individuals are known or not, *al-maʻlūm* or *al-majhūl*. The remainder of those individuals within al-ʻāmm are however still subject to further exclusions.

Once al-ʻāmm has become khuṣṣa ʻanhu al-baʻḍ using a definitive piece of evidence found alongside it, it becomes speculative, so now it is possible to find further exclusions using al-khabar and even al-qiyās, both of which are *aẓ-ẓannī*. This is because they are now of equal weight in strength. However, the extent to which these further exemptions occur are limited to the condition that at least three individuals must remain in the original command. This is because the al-ʻāmm of al-kitāb must make up a group of individuals by its very

QUICK TERMS

عام خص عنه البعض: *ʻāmmun khuṣṣa ʻanhu ul-baʻḍ*

The general with exemptions. A word designated for a group with possible exemptions.

التخصيص: *at-takhṣīṣ*

Specification. Exempting using an attached yet independent clause.

القطعي: *al-qaṭʻī*

The definitive. Most reliable and certain.

الظني: *aẓ-ẓannī*

The speculative. Reached after careful consideration.

QUICK ARABIC

المعلوم: *al-maʻlūm*

The known. The established and attained matter.

المجهول: *al-majhūl*

The unknown. Not in one's knowledge, experience or understanding.

definition. If through exemptions the number of cases drops below a group it would be like altering al-kitāb in order to accommodate lesser sources. This is tantamount to abrogation, which is not permitted with weaker sources.

Text and Translation

وأما العام الذي خص عنه البعض فحكمه أنه يجب العمل به في الباقي مع الاحتمال فإذا قام الدليل على تخصيص الباقي يجوز تخصيصه بخبر الواحد أو القياس إلى أن يبقى الثلاث وبعد ذلك لا يجوز فيجب العمل به.

As for al-'āmm khuṣṣa 'anhu ul-ba'ḍ, its ruling is that it must be enacted in the remaining with (further) possibilities. When a proof is established to exempt from the remainder it is permitted; be it with khabar ul-wāḥid or al-qiyās; until there remains three. After that it is not permitted and it must be enacted.

❖❖❖

The previous discussion about continuing further exemptions using weaker sources once al-kitāb itself has opened up the possibility through an independent attached part of a sentence, requires a bit more clarity. This is so it is not confused with the position that texts that oppose and contradict al-kitāb itself must be rejected and not accommodated. So, to conclude the section we are provided with an easy-to-understand reason why a substantially weaker piece of evidence is valid in influencing the second type of al-'āmm in spite of the al-'āmm being from al-kitāb.

When a definitive *al-qaṭ'ī* piece of evidence has restricted al-'āmm with exemptions and as a consequence some of the individuals previously within the functioning of the al-'āmm word are now not within it, the al-'āmm is no longer *al-qaṭ'ī* and definitive. There is no difference if the exempt individuals are known or not. Now, as the al-'āmm is not *al-qaṭ'ī* any longer, it becomes *aẓ-ẓannī* and speculative. This means that its authority is similar to that of khabar ul-wāḥid and al-qiyās, which are both *aẓ-ẓannī* too. The *at-takhṣīṣ* and restrictions placed on a *aẓ-ẓannī* piece of evidence using another piece of *aẓ-ẓannī* evidence is permitted.

This point is further elaborated in the text of Uṣūl ush-Shāshī. The primary restrictor of al-'āmm will be attached to it in the sentence so the first

QUICK TERMS

عام خص عنه البعض: *'āmmun khuṣṣa 'anhu ul-ba'ḍ*

The general with exemptions. A word designated for a group with possible exemptions.

الخبر (الواحد): *al-khabar (ul-wāḥid)*

Singular tradition. Traditions related by single-narrator chains.

القياس: *al-qiyās*

Analogy. The reasoning of the learned.

الظني: *aẓ-ẓannī*

The speculative. Reached after careful consideration.

الكتاب: *al-kitāb*

The book. The inspired final Word of Allah ﷻ. The Quran.

القطعي: *al-qaṭ'ī*

The definitive. Most reliable and certain.

العام: *al-'āmm*

The general. A word designated for a group.

restriction is from al-kitāb, and thus *al-qaṭ'ī*. The individuals covered by the restriction were either known, *al-ma'lūm*, or they were left unknown, *al-majhūl*. An everyday example of *al-ma'lūm* individuals being restricted would be like instructing a class of students, "Everyone stop writing and only Yusuf continue." *Everyone* is a group of students who are given an instruction. In the very same sentence, a part of it restricts carrying out of the instruction for one individual and that individual is known; namely Yusuf. This is an example of *at-takhṣiṣ* of a known individual. An everyday example of *al-majhūl* individuals being restricted from a sentence would be like, "Everyone stop writing and those with prior permission continue." This is a general instruction to include a group of individuals from whom a certain number *may* be restricted. Those that fall into the restricted bracket are not immediately known.

Now, in the case that the *al-qaṭ'ī* piece of evidence restricted *al-majhūl* members, every individual in the group has an equal possibility of remaining in the group or being in the restriction. All individuals have this 50-50 possibility. The *al-qaṭ'ī* source has done this. All we require now is to individually look at each member of the group and find reason to tip the 50-50 balance in favour of the restriction. This tipping of the balance can be achieved with another *al-qaṭ'ī* piece of evidence or even a *aẓ-ẓannī* piece of evidence, as the possibility is already established through the original *al-qaṭ'ī* source. This would mean, in the case of al-ʻāmm of al-kitāb, that restrictions are possible using *aẓ-ẓannī* pieces of evidence such as al-khabar and al-qiyās.

In the case that the *al-qaṭ'ī* piece of evidence restricted *al-ma'lūm* members, there will be an underlying reason for the restriction of the known individual from the group. That underlying reason has a possibility of being present in any of the other members of the group too. So, if another *al-qaṭ'ī* or *aẓ-ẓannī* piece of evidence is able to show the very same underlying reason in another member, that member will also be restricted from the group. So, this possibility remains in all the remaining members.

To conclude, the passage and with it the chapter, the text says that all members that remain in the directive of the al-ʻāmm after all the restrictions must be enacted, but each remaining member also has the possibility of further exemption. So long as there is a piece of evidence to exempt a member, members will be excluded and if no evidence is present the members will remain under the al-ʻāmm.

QUICK TERMS

التخصيص: *at-takhṣīṣ*

Specification. Exempting using an attached yet independent clause.

QUICK ARABIC

المعلوم: *al-ma'lūm*

The known. The established and attained matter.

المجهول: *al-majhūl*

The unknown. Not in one's knowledge, experience or understanding.

Text and Translation

وإنما جاز ذلك لأن المخصص الذي أخرج البعض عن الجملة لو أخرج بعضاً مجهولاً يثبت الاحتمال في كل فرد معين فجاز أن يكون باقيا تحت حكم العام وجاز أن يكون داخلاً تحت دليل الخصوص فاستوى الطرفان في حق المعين، فإذا قام الدليل الشرعي على أنه من جملة ما دخل تحت دليل الخصوص ترجح جانب تخصيصه وإن كان المخصص أخرج بعضاً معلوماً عن الجملة جاز أن يكون معلولا بعلة موجودة في هذا الفرد المعين، فإذا قام الدليل الشرعي على وجود تلك العلة في غير هذا الفرد المعين ترجح جهة تخصيصه فيعمل به مع وجود الاحتمال.

That is permitted because, had the restrictor that exempted some (members) from the whole, restricted an unknown, it establishes a possibility (of exemption) in all members. So it could remain in the ruling of al-'āmm or be governed by the proof of exemption. Both possibilities are equal for the individual in question. So when a legal proof establishes it to be included in the exempt group, its exemption will gain favour. In the case that the restrictor exempts known members from the whole it may be due to a cause found in that specified individual. So if a legal proof establishes that same cause in another member, its exemption will gain favour and so will be enacted despite the possibility.

❖❖❖

QUICK TERMS

الظني: *aẓ-ẓannī*

The speculative. Reached after careful consideration.

العام: *al-ʿāmm*

The general. A word designated for a group.

Ḥanafī Principles (2)

MEMORISE

	Term	Definition	Ruling	An Example
2	عام لم يخص عنه شيء	لفظ ينتظم جمعا من الأفراد	لزوم العمل به لا محالة	فاقرءوا ما تيسر من القرآن [المدثر: 20]
3	عام خص عنه البعض	لفظ ينتظم جمعا من الأفراد مع تخصيص البعض	يجب العمل به في الباقي مع الاحتمال	اقتلوا المشركين ولا تقتلوا أهل الذمة

❖❖❖

Summary Of al-Khāṣṣ And al-'Āmm

1. Definition of al-khāṣṣ:
   الخاص: لفظ وضع لمعنى معلوم أو لمسمى معلوم على الانفراد
   "al-Khāṣṣ is a word coined for a singular meaning or named individual."

2. There are three types of al-khāṣṣ:
   i) A specific individual, like Zayd.
   ii) A specific kind, like male.
   iii) A specific class and genus, like human.

3. The rulings of al-khāṣṣ are:
   i) وجوب العمل به لا محالة
   "It must be enacted in all circumstances."
   ii) في مقابلة خبر الواحد الجمع بينهما بدون تغيير حكم الخاص وإلا يعمل بخاص الكتاب
   "When contending with al-khabar, satisfy both without altering the ruling of al-khāṣṣ. Otherwise, only enact al-khāṣṣ."

4. An example of al-khāṣṣ is in the verse:
   والمطلقات يتربصن بأنفسهن ثلاثة قروء
   Where the word for three (ثلاثة) is al-khāṣṣ and coined for a number between two and four. It must be adhered to in all circumstances. If the word for cycles (قروء) is considered to mean dry periods in the menstrual cycle, al-khāṣṣ will not be adhered to. So, the word for cycles is the period of bleeding in the menstrual cycle, to ensure al-khāṣṣ is enacted.

5. Definition of al-'āmm:
   العام: لفظ ينتظم جمعا من الأفراد
   "al-'Āmm is a word entailing a group of individuals."

6. The group could be mentioned in the word, like in مسلمون (Muslims) or in meaning, like in من (who) or ما (what).

7. There are two types of al-'āmm:
   i) 'Āmmun lam yakhuṣṣa 'anhu shayun; and
   ii) 'Āmmun khuṣṣa 'anhu ul-ba'ḍ.

8. 'Āmmun khuṣṣa 'anhu ul-ba'ḍ is the general statement limited with restrictions, like in the statement:
   اقتلوا المشركين ولا تقتلوا أهل الذمة
   "Fight the idolaters and don't fight the people in *dhimma*."

9. The ruling of 'āmm khuṣṣa 'anhu al-ba'ḍ is:
   يجب العمل به في الباقي مع الاحتمال
   "It must be enacted in the remainder with a possibility (of more exemptions)."

10. The 'āmmun lam yakhuṣṣa 'anhu shayun is the general statement with no exclusions, like in the verse:
    فاقرءوا ما تيسر من القرآن
    "Recite of the Quran what is easy for you."

11. The ruling of 'āmmun lam yakhuṣṣa 'anhu shayun is:
    لزوم العمل به لا محالة
    "It must be enacted in all circumstances."

1.1.2 al-Muṭlaq and al-Muqayyad

Section 1.1 is about word coinage. Figure 1.1-01 showed that word coinage has four key terms associated with it. al-Khāṣṣ and al-'āmm were discussed in section 1.1.1, and al-mushtarak and al-muawwal will be discussed in section 1.1.3. Here in this section two terms are introduced before we proceed with the discussions on word coinage, the terms are al-muṭlaq and al-muqayyad.

The reason for bringing this discussion here is that in the previous section we were introduced to two types of al-'āmm; one was restricted and the other unrestricted. When a term or idea is left unrestricted, without conditions, exceptions, deferrals or the likes, it is called al-muṭlaq. So, the unrestricted 'āmmun lam yakhuṣṣa 'anhu shayun is like al-muṭlaq in that it has no restrictions, and the 'āmmun khuṣṣa 'anhu al-ba'ḍ is like al-muqayyad in that it has restrictions. Therefore, it is a suitable point at which to provide more details about these terms. However, an important thing to note is that al-muṭlaq and al-muqayyad are terms used with al-khāṣṣ words and not words that are al-'āmm.

The Aḥnāf say that whilst it is possible to enact an unrestricted al-muṭlaq of al-kitāb one is not permitted to add to it using khabar ul-wāḥid nor al-qiyās. If this was permitted it would fall into the category of abrogation and al-kitāb, being *al-qat'ī* and definitive, cannot undergo abrogation with an *aẓ-ẓannī* al-khabar or al-qiyās, as abrogation can only occur with evidences of equal authority. This would also be true for all the properties of the al-muṭlaq, none can be abrogated using an *aẓ-ẓannī* piece of evidence.

An example of al- muṭlaq from the Book of Allah ﷻ is:

فاغسلوا وجوهكم [المائدة :6]

"...so wash your faces...".

In the verse the word for washing, *ghasl*, is said to be al-muṭlaq. The details are as follows: the unrestricted washing of face, arms and feet, as well as the unrestricted wiping of the head, are al-farḍ in the ablution. There is neither stipulation of continuous washing, an intention before the washing, a strict order in washing nor the requirement of reciting the *basmala*. Other Imams have stipulated some of these actions as vital to the ablution to a level of al-

QUICK TERMS

المطلق: *al-muṭlaq*

The unrestricted. Indicates the entity irrespective of qualities.

المقيد: *al-muqayyad*

The restricted. Indicates the entity and some of its qualities.

العام: *al-'āmm*

The general. A word designated for a group.

الخاص: *al-khāṣṣ*

The specific. A word designated for a singular specific concept.

عام لم يخص عنه شيئ: *'āmmun lam yakhuṣṣa 'anhu shayun*

The general without exemptions. A word designated for a group without exemptions.

عام خص عنه البعض: *'āmmun khuṣṣa 'anhu ul-ba'ḍ*

The general with exemptions. A word designated for a group with possible exemptions.

الكتاب: *al-kitāb*

The book. The inspired final Word of Allah ﷻ. The Quran.

الخبر (الواحد): *al-khabar (ul-wāḥid)*

Singular tradition. Traditions related by single-narrator chains.

farḍ. For instance, Imam Mālik رحمه الله considers continuously washing, *al-walā*, a condition for ablution, whereas Imam ash-Shāfi'ī رحمه الله considers the order and an intention to perform ablution as vitally important. Each Imam cites narrations to support their position. The Aḥnāf on the other hand say that Allah جل جلاله has asked for two tasks in the words of the blessed verse. Firstly, to wash, *faghsilū,* and secondly to wipe, *wamsaḥū*. Both these instances are al-khāṣṣ to give specific known understandings of *application of water* and *drawing over a surface*, and they are also al-muṭlaq as neither has any additional conditions or restrictions attached to it, such as *intending to wash* or *continuously washing*. This means that the verse requires the unrestricted application of water to the face, arms and feet, and the unrestricted drawing of water over the surface of the head. If we add the conditions of continuity, intention, order or special recitals, we would be restricting the property of al-muṭlaq of a word of al-kitāb with khabar ul-āḥād. This would be equivalent to abrogation of a stronger authority by way of a weaker authority. We will however, not completely discard the narrations, as we are able to apply the narrations without altering the word of Allah جل جلاله. Therefore, we say, the unrestricted act of washing and wiping is indispensable to the ablution as al-farḍ, and continuity, intention, order and recitals are sunna and highly recommended.

Text and Translation

فصل في المطلق والمقيد: ذهب أصحابنا إلى أن المطلق من كتاب الله تعالى إذا أمكن العمل بإطلاقه فالزيادة عليه بخبر الواحد والقياس لا يجوز. مثاله في قوله تعالى: فاغسلوا وجوهكم فالمأمور به هو الغسل على الإطلاق فلا يزاد عليه شرط النية والترتيب والموالاة والتسمية بالخبر، ولكن يعمل بالخبر على وجهٍ لا يتغيّر به حكم الكتاب فيقال الغسل المطلق فرض بحكم الكتاب والنية سنة بحكم الخبر

Chapter on al-muṭlaq and al-muqayyad: Our jurists hold the view that al-muṭlaq from the Book of Allah Almighty is not to be augmented by khabar ul-wāḥid nor al-qiyās when it is possible to apply it unconditionally. An example of it is the verse of The Most High: "so wash your faces". The duty is to wash without a condition. So there is no adding to it with the condition of intention, order, continuity or recitation of *basmala* using al-khabar. Rather al-khabar will be applied in a manner that doesn't alter the command of al-kitāb. So it is resolved that unconditional washing is al-farḍ from the Book and the intention is sunna using al-khabar.

QUICK TERMS

القياس: *al-qiyās*

Analogy. The reasoning of the learned.

القطعي: *al-qaṭ'ī*

The definitive. Most reliable and certain.

الظني: *aẓ-ẓannī*

The speculative. Reached after careful consideration.

الفرض: *al-farḍ*

The obligatory. The observance of which is necessary and denial leads to disbelief.

خبر الآحاد: *khabar ul-āḥād*

Singular traditions. Traditions related by single-narrator chains.

QUICK ARABIC

الولاء: *al-walā*

To follow. The continual washing of parts in wuḍū without break.

As a second example for al-muṭlaq of al-kitāb not accepting any additions using al-khabar or al-qiyās, verse 2 of Sūrat un-Nūr is presented.

الزانيةُ والزاني فاجلدوا كل واحدٍ منهما مائة جلدةٍ [النور:2]

"The (unmarried) adulteress and the (unmarried) adulterer: flog both of them with one hundred lashes."

If an unmarried man or woman is to fornicate, the Aḥnāf say that the mandatory punishment is one hundred lashes as stipulated by the verse. The Shawāfi' on the other hand say that one hundred lashes and one year's banishment from the locality is the mandatory punishment for the fornicator. They make their case by setting the one hundred lashes stated in the blessed Quran and then providing a Hadith of the blessed Prophet ﷺ, which says for the unmarried there are one hundred lashes and a year's banishment.

The Aḥnāf say that the one hundred lashes are stated unrestricted in the blessed Quran and are al-muṭlaq. That is to say that there is no mention of banishment for one year. The punishment stated in the blessed Quran is mandatory for the crime and does not require any additions. So, if we add to this using al-khabar it would abrogate the unrestricted of al-kitāb and thus it is not permitted. It is not permitted as al-khabar is a *aẓ-ẓannī* piece of evidence and al-kitāb is *al-qaṭ'ī*, so the less authoritative evidence cannot override the more authoritative. However, the Hadith will be adopted in a manner that does not alter the unrestricted al-muṭlaq of al-kitāb, which is to allow banishment for one year as a discretionary punishment for expediency and public order, as and when required. It would be at the discretion of the governor or judge to give this punishment when it is deemed necessary. This is not an addition to the mandatory punishment but to safeguard matters that may arise as a consequence of the mandatory punishment. Furthermore, banishment is not exclusive to the punishment of fornication. The judge may use it in other circumstances too. This shows that the banishment is not an addition to al-kitāb but a separate matter that may or may not make part of the verdict of a judge.

Text and Translation

وكذلك قلنا في قوله تعالى :﴿الزانيةُ والزاني فاجلدوا كل واحدٍ منهما مائة جلدةٍ﴾ إنّ الكتاب جعل جلد المائة حداً للزنا فلا يزاد عليه التغريب حدا لقوله عليه السلام: البكر بالبكر جلد مائة وتغريب

QUICK TERMS

الكتاب: *al-kitāb*

The book. The inspired final Word of Allah ﷻ. The Quran.

الخبر: *al-khabar*

Singular traditions. Traditions related by single-narrator chains.

القياس: *al-qiyās*

Analogy. The reasoning of the learned.

المطلق: *al-muṭlaq*

The unrestricted. Indicates an entity irrespective of any quality.

الظني: *aẓ-ẓannī*

The speculative. Reached after careful consideration.

القطعي: *al-qaṭ'ī*

The definitive. Most reliable and certain.

عام بل يعمل بالخبر على وجه لا يتغيّر به حكم الكتاب فيكون الجلد حدا شرعيا بحكم الكتاب والتغريب مشروعا سياسة بحكم الخبر

Likewise we said that in the Almighty's Word: "The adulteress and the adulterer: flog both of them with one hundred lashes." al-Kitāb has made flogging with one hundred lashes a punishment for adultery so it will not be augmented with a banishment due to the saying of the Prophet, peace and blessings be upon him: "For unmarrieds there are one hundred lashes and a year's banishment". al-Khabar will be applied in a manner that does not alter the ruling of al-kitāb such that the lashes are a legal punishment by the ruling of al-kitāb and banishment is for expediency using the ruling of al-khabar.

❖ ❖ ❖

The next example also shows how al-muṭlaq of al-kitāb is not added to, using the rulings of al-khabar. The example concerns verse 29 of Sūrat ul-Ḥajj:

وليطوفوا بالبيتِ العتيقِ [الحج :29]

"...and encircle the Ancient House."

The Aḥnāf maintain that in the rituals of Hajj, the *ṭawāf uz-ziyāra* is al-farḍ, but ablution for it is neither al-farḍ nor a condition. They classify the ablution as al-wājib. This means that if the encircling of the Ka'ba is performed without the necessary ablution it will be valid as a *ṭawāf* but the lack of purity introduces a deficiency in the worship and so will be made up by sacrificing an animal. The Shawāfi' say that the performance of ablution is a condition for this *ṭawāf* and so the *ṭawāf* is invalid without it. As evidence, they present the verse of Sūrat ul-Ḥajj and a tradition of the blessed Prophet ﷺ which states: "Encircling the House is like salah." Therefore, if it is like the prayers it must also have the condition of ablution, as prayer does.

The Aḥnāf say that the word of the blessed Quran *wal-yaṭṭawwafū* is al-khāṣṣ and al-muṭlaq. It carries the specified meaning of "encircling" and has been left unrestricted, so encircling is possible with or without ablution. Adding the ruling of the Hadith to this, as others have suggested, is adding to to al-kitāb and thus not permitted. This would amount to abrogation of an *al-qaṭ'ī* piece of evidence with the aid of *aẓ-ẓannī* piece of evidence, and that is not permitted.

حديث

قال النبي ﷺ: "الطَّوَافُ بِالْبَيْتِ صَلاةٌ إلا أَنَّكُمْ تَتَكَلَّمُونَ فِيهِ."

عليه الصلاة والسلام

رواه الترمذي (960)

QUICK TERMS

الفرض: *al-farḍ*

The obligatory. The observance of which is necessary and denial leads to disbelief.

الواجب: *al-wājib*

The necessary. The non-observance of which is sinful, but denial does not lead to disbelief.

الخاص: *al-khāṣṣ*

The specific. A word designated for a singular specific concept.

QUICK ARABIC

طواف الزيارة: *ṭawāf uz-ziyāra*

Circumambulation of the visit. The encircling of the Ka'ba performed by the pilgrim on the 10th of *Dhul Ḥijja*.

الطواف: *aṭ-ṭawāf*

Circumambulation. The ritual of encircling the Ka'ba seven times.

We can however take the ruling of al-khabar in a manner that does not alter the authoritative source, which is to rule that just the mere encircling of *aṭ-ṭawāf* is *al-farḍ*, whereas the ablution is al-wājib. So, if one was to leave the ablution and perform *aṭ-ṭawāf*, the deficiency would be compensated for by sacrificing an animal because an al-wājib is missing.

Text and Translation

وكذلك قوله تعالى :﴿وليطوفوا بالبيتِ العتيقِ﴾ مطلق في مسمى الطواف بالبيت، فلا يزاد عليه شرط الوضوء بالخبر بل يعمل به على وجهٍ لا يتغيّر به حكم الكتاب بأن يكون مطلق الطواف فرضا بحكم الكتاب والوضوء واجبا بحكم الخبر فيجبر النقصان اللازم بترك الوضوء الواجب بالدم

Similarly the verse of the Most High: "...and encircle the Ancient House", is al-muṭlaq in assigning the encircling of the House. So it will not be augmented with the condition of ablution using al-khabar. Rather it will be adhered to in a manner that doesn't alter the ruling of the Book, such that mere encircling is al-farḍ by the ruling of the Book and ablution is al-wājib by the ruling of al-khabar. So any inherent deficiency caused by not performing the required ablution is compensated with a sacrificial animal.

Textual Assistance

العتيق — *al-'Atīq* means ancient. It is used as a descriptive of the House of Allah ﷻ, the Ka'ba. The Ka'ba marks the location of the first structure to be built by Sayyidunā Ādam عليه السلام, and thus it is the most ancient.

❖ ❖ ❖

Similar to previous examples, the next example also shows how al-muṭlaq of al-Kitāb is not added to, using the rulings of al-Khabar. The example concerns verse 43 of Sūrat ul-Baqara:

واركعوا مع الراكِعِين [البقرة: 43]

"...and bow with those who bow."

The verse is unrestricted in describing that a bow, *ar-rukū'*, must take place. So long as a bow is achieved, the commandment is fulfilled. There is a Hadith which refers to the actions of a Bedouin Companion, Khallād bin Rāfi' رضي الله عنه,

QUICK TERMS

الخبر: *al-khabar*

Singular tradition. Traditions related by single-narrator chains.

الفرض: *al-farḍ*

The obligatory. The observance of which is necessary and denial leads to disbelief.

الواجب: *al-wājib*

The necessary. The non-observance of which is sinful, but denial does not lead to disbelief.

QUICK ARABIC

الطواف: *aṭ-ṭawāf*

Circumambulation. The ritual of encircling the Ka'ba seven times.

الركوع: *ar-rukū'*

Bowing. A posture in salah in which the head is inclined and hands are placed on the knees.

who performed his prayer without *at-ta'dīl*, which is to be settled during the transitions or motions of salah. He hurriedly completed his prayer. The Prophet ﷺ instructed him to repeat his prayer. Khallād bin Rāfi' رضي الله عنه did exactly as before and was instructed to repeat the prayer again. He was sent again to correct his prayer but failed to make any changes. On this occasion, he asked the Prophet ﷺ to teach him how to pray. The greatest Teacher ﷺ then proceeded to instruct him how to pray, and specifically mentioned *at-ta'dīl*, that he needs to be settled in all the motions. The Hadith shows that the idea of *at-ta'dīl* is essential to the prayer and so should be classed as al-farḍ.

This query is answered by stating that *warka'ū* in the verse is al-khāṣṣ in the meaning of bowing. Furthermore, the verse is al-muṭlaq as it hasn't placed any restrictions or conditions on this bowing, so restricting the bowing to *a settled bowing* using al-khabar is not permitted as al-khabar is *aẓ-ẓannī* and al-kitāb is *al-qaṭ'ī*.

To restrict a definitive bit of evidence with weaker evidence is not valid, so it is not possible to do this here. Therefore, we apply the Hadith in a manner that does not alter al-kitāb. The act of bowing itself is al-farḍ in accordance with the command of the Quran and being settled in salah is deemed to be al-wājib.

Text and Translation

وكذلك قوله تعالى: ﴿واركعوا مع الراكِعِين﴾ مطلق في مسمى الركوع، فلا يزاد عليه شرط التعديل بحكم الخبر ولكن يعمل بالخبر على وجهٍ لا يتغيّر به حكم الكتاب فيكون مطلق الركوع فرضاً بحكم الكتاب والتعديل واجبا بحكم الخبر

Likewise the word of the Most High: "...and bow with those who bow.", is al-muṭlaq in assigning the bow. So it will not be augmented with the condition of being settled, upon the ruling of al-khabar. Rather al-khabar will be applied in a manner that does not alter the ruling of the Book. So merely bowing is al-farḍ due to the ruling of the Book and being settled is al-wājib due to al-khabar.

❖ ❖ ❖

Based on the fact that according to the Aḥnāf al-muṭlaq is not added to, by al-khabar or al-qiyās, they have stated that ablution is permitted when performed with water that has some pure substance dissolved in it, such as

QUICK TERMS

الخاص: *al-khāṣṣ*

The specific. A word designated for a singular specific concept.

المطلق: *al-muṭlaq*

The unrestricted. Indicates an entity irrespective of any quality.

الظني: *aẓ-ẓannī*

The speculative. Reached after careful consideration.

الكتاب: *al-kitāb*

The book. The inspired final Word of Allah ﷻ. The Quran.

القطعي: *al-qaṭ'ī*

The definitive. Most reliable and certain.

القياس: *al-qiyās*

Analogy. The reasoning of the learned.

QUICK ARABIC

التعديل: *at-ta'dīl*

Settling. The calm and proper manner in which each part of salah is to be performed.

saffron, so long as not more than one feature of the water is altered. The three features of water are that it is colourless, tasteless and odourless. So, a pure substance has mixed with water but only changed the colour for example, whilst the other two qualities of taste and odour, remain neutral. Such water is sufficient to perform ablution, and as ablution is possible, *at-tayammum* would not be permissible. *at-Tayammum* would be permitted if there was an absence of water.

The position of others is that saffron-water is not permitted for *ablution* as it is no longer water but a dilute. Verse 6 of Sūrat ul-Māida says:

فان لم تجدوا ماء فتيمموا صعيدا طيبا [المائدة: 6]

"...and if you find no water, then wipe yourselves with clean earth."

To be just *water* saffron-water, *mā uz-za'farān*, must have the same qualities as natural precipitation as it descends from the skies; colourless, odourless and tasteless. Therefore, in the case of having access to saffron-water and no other water, one must perform the dry ablution of *at-tayammum*, as there is no water available.

The Aḥnāf reject this opinion as the genitive construction of *al-iḍāfa* does not render *mā uz-za'farān* into a non-water mixture. Rather, the fact that you still call it *saffron-water* affirms the point that it is essentially water. If it is still water, then in its presence a dry ablution would not be permitted. As for the stipulation that the water should be "of the same quality of precipitation" to be classed as water, it is a restriction on the al-muṭlaq unrestricted water mentioned in Sūrat ul-Māida, verse 6. So, the restriction will be rejected, as the unrestricted of al-kitāb cannot be restricted using a weaker source. As long as a liquid is considered to be water, it would fall into the category of water and would be usable for ablution. How we determine if a mixture is still water is through its qualities: if two qualities out of the three have changed, it is no longer water, and if only one quality is altered, it is still water. Saffron-water has a colour, but remains tasteless and odourless. Should the taste or odour of saffron-water also change when more saffron is added, it will no longer remain water and thus would not be permissible for ablution. The reason for this is not that there is a restriction, but that it is no longer water.

The question remains that ablution is necessary with the availability of a liquid classed as water, so in the presence of filthy-water, *al-mā un-najis*, *at-*

QUICK TERMS

الكتاب: *al-kitāb*

The book. The inspired final Word of Allah ﷻ. The Quran.

المطلق: *al-muṭlaq*

The unrestricted. Indicates an entity irrespective of any quality.

QUICK ARABIC

التيمم: *at-tayammum*

Dry ablution. The ritual ablution performed without water.

QUICK GRAMMAR

الإضافة: *al-iḍāfa*

The apposition. A relationship between consecutive expressions, where the second supplements the first.

QUICK DICTIONARY

Precipitation: *pri-sip-i-tey-shuh n*

Falling. In meteorology it is the falling products of condensation in the atmosphere; snow, rain or hail.

tayammum should not be valid. The filthy-water is *still* water, so it should prevent the performance of a dry ablution. This discrepancy is eliminated as verse 6 of Sūrat ul-Māida says:

ولكِن يريد ليطهركم [المائدة :6]

"...He only wishes to cleanse you..."

Cleanliness cannot be achieved with filthy water, so it defeats the object of the ablution. This means that when the verse instructed "...and if you find no water...", it can only mean *clean* water, the filthy water that may be present is not to be considered as it will not result in cleanliness.

Uṣūl ush-Shāshī makes one other side observation unrelated to our overall principle of al-muṭlaq but relevant to the verse, that in the context of the verse Allah ﷻ saying, "He only wishes to cleanse you" shows that for ablution to be necessary *al-ḥadath* or ritual impurity must have occurred. It is as though earlier in the verse it reads:

إذا قمتم إلى الصلوة فاغسلوا [المائدة :6]

"...when you stand for prayer (and you are ritually impure) then wash..."

In other words, when you wish to stand for prayer, and you are ritually impure, then you must perform ablution. The additional understanding of "and you are ritually impure" is necessary because the purpose of ablution is to gain purity. Gaining purity means the removal of impurity, but that can only be achieved if impurity was there in the first instance. The implied impurity found in the limbs is the cause for the necessity of achieving cleanliness through ablution before a prayer. Therefore, the text informs us in a concise manner that it is impossible to achieve purity if there was no impurity to begin with.

Text and Translation

وعلى هذا قلنا :يجوز التوضي بماء الزعفران وبكلّ ماء خالطه شيء طاهر فغير أحد أوصافه؛ لأنّ شرط المصير إلى التيمم عدم مطلق الماء وهذا قد بقي ماء مطلقاً فإنّ قيد الإضافة ما أزال عنه اسم الماء بل قرره فيدخل تحت حكم مطلق الماء وكان شرط بقائه على صفة المنزل من السماء قيدا لهذا المطلق، وبه يخرج حكم ماء الزعفران والصابون والأشنان وأمثاله، وخرج عن هذه القضية الماء النجس

QUICK ARABIC

الحدث: *al-ḥadath*

Unclean. The state of the one who has not performed ablution or bathed.

بقوله تعالى ﴿ولكِن يريد ليطهركم﴾ والنجس لا يفيد الطهارة، وبهذه الإشارة علم أنّ الحدث شرط لوجوب الوضوء فإنّ تحصيل الطهارة بدون وجود الحدث محال

Based on this we say that ablution with saffron-water is permitted as it is with any water that has a pure substance mixed with it and one quality of the water has changed. This is because the condition for substituting with *at-tayammum* is the lack of water and this remains within the category of water. The genitive state has not removed the label of water from it, but rather reaffirmed it, so it will be under the ruling of water. As for the condition of it remaining in the state of precipitation, it is restricting al-muṭlaq. With it is the deriving of the ruling for water mixed with saffron, soap, saltwort or the likes. Impure water is excluded from this ruling by the statement of the Most High: "He only wishes to cleanse you." Because the impure cannot yield cleanliness. With this subtlety it is known that *al-ḥadath* is the condition that necessitates ablution as acquiring cleanliness without a preceding *al-ḥadath* is impossible.

❖ ❖ ❖

In another example of how al-muṭlaq functions unrestricted and that it cannot be restricted with al-khabar or al-qiyās, Imam Abū Ḥanīfa رحمه الله says if one committed aẓ-ẓihār by saying his wife is eternally forbidden unto him, *al-kaffāra* or expiation becomes necessary. The expiation is to offer one of three things in order; namely to free a slave, if this is not possible to fast two consecutive months, and if this is not possible to feed sixty poor people. Verses 3 and 4 of Sūrat ul-Mujādala say:

وَالَّذِينَ يُظَاهِرُونَ مِن نِّسَائِهِمْ ثُمَّ يَعُودُونَ لِمَا قَالُوا فَتَحْرِيرُ رَقَبَةٍ مِّن قَبْلِ أَن يَتَمَاسَّا ذَٰلِكُمْ تُوعَظُونَ بِهِ وَاللَّهُ بِمَا تَعْمَلُونَ خَبِيرٌ. فَمَن لَّمْ يَجِدْ فَصِيَامُ شَهْرَيْنِ مُتَتَابِعَيْنِ مِن قَبْلِ أَن يَتَمَاسَّا فَمَن لَّمْ يَسْتَطِعْ فَإِطْعَامُ سِتِّينَ مِسْكِينًا [المجادلة: 4-3]

"But those who commit *aẓ-ẓihār* with their wives, then wish to go back on the words uttered, should free a slave before they touch one another; thus you are admonished, and Allah is informed of what you do. The one who cannot should fast for two months consecutively before they touch one another. But if any is unable then the feeding of sixty needy ones..."

As it is evident from the above verses, the first two options of "free a slave" and "fast for two months consecutively" are accompanied by the restriction of "before they touch one another", which is a metaphor for sexual intercourse.

QUICK ARABIC

التيمم: *at-tayammum*

Dry ablution. The ritual ablution performed without water.

الحدث: *al-ḥadath*

Unclean. The state of the one who has not performed ablution or bathed.

الظهار: *aẓ-ẓihār*

Likening to a mother. An archaic practice in which separation between husband and wife occurs until expiation is made.

الكفارة: *al-kaffāra*

Expiation. The prescribed atonement for neglected duties.

QUICK DICTIONARY

Saltwort: *sawlt-wurt*

A particular plant. A bushy plant having prickly leaves, found on beaches or marshes.

The latter option of "feeding sixty needy ones" does not have this restriction, and is thus unrestricted. Therefore, if the one who committed *aẓ-ẓihār* has intercourse before freeing a slave, or before completing two months of fasts, he would be sinful and the expiation would be incomplete. However, if during the feeding of the needy he was to have intercourse with his wife, the expiation would be complete according to the Aḥnāf. This is because this was not restricted in the blessed Quran with "before you touch one another."

Scholars of other schools of Fiqh have said that as the third option of feeding the needy is for the same mistake as the earlier two options of freeing a slave and fasting continuously, then al-qiyās dictates that the condition of "before they touch one another" should be applicable to it as well. Therefore, if someone has intercourse before the completion of the feeding of the sixty needy individuals, then al-qiyās is that this person has wronged and the expiation is incomplete and must be repeated.

The Aḥnāf reject the position of the others because al-qiyās cannot be used to restrict al-muṭlaq of al-kitāb. Freeing a slave and fasting continuously have restrictions from al-kitāb of not touching one another, so both these options are bound by it. Feeding the needy is not bound by the same restriction, so it will remain unrestricted. So, if a husband was to have intercourse during the feeding or after it, both would be permitted. So, al-muṭlaq functions unrestricted and al-muqayyad functions with its restrictions.

Text and Translation

قال أبو حنيفة ﷺ: المظاهر إذا جامع امرأته في خلال الإطعام لا يستأنف الإطعام؛ لأنّ الكتاب مطلق في حق الإطعام فلا يزاد عليه شرط عدم المسيس بالقياس على الصوم بل المطلق يجري على إطلاقه والمقيد على تقييده

Imam Abū Ḥanīfa, Allah be pleased with him, said: when an *al-muẓāhir* has intercourse with his wife during the feeding, the feeding process will not be restarted because the Book is unrestricted with regards to the feeding so it can not be augmented with the condition of no-contact using al-qiyās based on the fasting. Rather al-muṭlaq functions unrestricted and al-muqayyad functions with its restriction.

❖ ❖ ❖

QUICK TERMS

المطلق: *al-muṭlaq*

The unrestricted. Indicates an entity irrespective of any quality.

الخبر: *al-khabar*

Singular tradition. Traditions related by single-narrator chains.

القياس: *al-qiyās*

Analogy. The reasoning of the learned.

الكتاب: *al-kitāb*

The book. The inspired final Word of Allah ﷻ. The Quran.

المقيد: *al-muqayyad*

The restricted. Indicates an entity and some of its qualities.

QUICK ARABIC

المظاهر: *al-muẓāhir*

The one who commits *aẓ-ẓihār*. This occurs when one says words such as, "you are to me as my mother's back". Expiation becomes necessary.

Just as in the previous examples generally, and specifically the preceding example, neither the atonement for *aẓ-ẓihār* nor the atonement of broken vows, *al-yamīn*, can be restricted to emancipating believers only, as is the case in the atonement of accidental killing.

In the case of atonement from accidental killing verse 92 of Sūrat ul-Māida says that a believing slave must be freed:

وَمَن قَتَلَ مُؤْمِنًا خَطَئًا فَتَحْرِيرُ رَقَبَةٍ مُّؤْمِنَةٍ [النساء :92]

"...He who killed a believer by mistake must set free a believing slave..."

Here it is clear that a restriction is placed on the slave that is to be freed. The atonement is al-muqayyad and restricted to slaves that are believing Muslims.

To use this as the base of al-qiyās and extend that the slaves that are to be freed as atonement in cases of *aẓ-ẓihār* and *al-yamīn* is problematic. The verse for *aẓ-ẓihār* is:

فَتَحْرِيرُ رَقَبَةٍ مِّن قَبْلِ أَن يَتَمَاسَّا [المجادلة: 3]

"...free a slave before they touch one another..."

And the verse of broken vows, *al-yamīn*, is:

أو تحرير رقبة [المائدة: 89]

"...or free a slave..."

In both cases of *aẓ-ẓihār* and *al-yamīn*, the verses are al-muṭlaq, and do not restrict the emancipation to a believing or non-believing slave.

The Aḥnāf thus rule that the freeing of a slave for atonement of accidental killing is to be the freeing of a believing slave. The verse is al-muqayyad and as such the restriction of being a believer is necessary; al-muqayyad functions with its restriction. The cases of *aẓ-ẓihār* and *al-yamīn*, however, are both al-muṭlaq, so they must function unrestricted. That is to say that making an analogy with freeing a slave after accidental killing is not permitted as it would be restricting the al-muṭlaq using al-qiyās. So, where al-kitāb is restricted with a believing slave it will remain restricted to it. And where al-kitāb is unrestricted it will remain so by permitting the emancipation of either a believing or a non-believing slave.

QUICK ARABIC

الظهار: *aẓ-ẓihār*

Likening to a mother. A practice in which separation between husband and wife occurs until expiation is made.

اليمين: *al-yamīn*

The oath. A statement strengthened by a solemn appeal using the name of Allah ﷻ.

QUICK DICTIONARY

Atonement: *uh-tohn-muh nt*

Making amends. Correcting the relationship between a sinner and Allah ﷻ.

Emancipate: *ih-man-suh-peyt*

To free. To free a slave from bondage and servitude.

وكذلك قلنا: الرقبة في كفارة الظهار واليمين مطلقة فلا يزاد عليه شرط الإيمان بالقياس على كفارة القتل

Similarly we have said that a slave as atonement for aẓ-ẓihār or for a vow is unrestricted so it will not be augmented with the restriction of being a believer using al-qiyās based on the atonement of murder.

❖ ❖ ❖

To conclude the chapter on al-muṭlaq and al-muqayyad, and the fact that both cannot be altered using khabar ul-wāḥid or al-qiyās, two objections are put forth with their respective answers.

The first query is from the verse of ablution concerning the wiping of the head. The relevant part of verse 6 of Sūrat ul-Māida reads:

وامسحوا برءوسكم [المائدة: 6]

"...and wipe your heads..."

Here the particle *al-bā* is for *at-tab'īḍ* or portioning, so the expanded meaning would read "...and wipe a portion of your heads...". This understanding is accepted by both the Aḥnāf and the Shawāfi' and based on how the Arabic verb *masaḥa* is used. If the verb is *al-muta'ddī* and transitive without a preposition it would mean the whole of the area described, and if it is with a preposition such as *al-bā* it means a portion of the area. Imams Mālik رحمه الله and Aḥmad رحمه الله on the other hand take *al-bā* in the verse to be *az-zāid* and extra, so accordingly they consider it necessary to wipe the whole of the head during the ablution. So, the Aḥnāf and the Shawāfi' say a portion of the head must be wiped, whilst the other two Imams say the whole of the head must be wiped.

The difference between the Shawāfi' and the Aḥnāf arises when the former says that any area of the head that can be termed a portion is sufficient for the act to be complete. So, if one was to wipe an area equivalent to a few hairs on the head, a portion of the head has been wiped, so the act of *al-masḥ* is complete. The Aḥnāf say that an area equivalent to one quarter of the head must be wiped over because in a narration of Mughīra bin Shu'ba رضي الله عنه it is stated that the Prophet صلى الله عليه وسلم came to the grounds of a people. There he answered the call of nature and performed his ablution, whilst wiping over his forelocks, *an-*

QUICK TERMS

القياس: *al-qiyās*

Analogy. The reasoning of the learned.

المطلق: *al-muṭlaq*

The unrestricted. Indicates an entity irrespective of any quality.

المقيد: *al-muqayyad*

The restricted. Indicates an entity and some of its qualities.

الكتاب: *al-kitāb*

The book. The inspired final Word of Allah جل جلاله. The Quran.

خبر الواحد: *khabar ul-wāḥid*

Singular tradition. Traditions related by single-narrator chains.

QUICK GRAMMAR

التبعيض: *at-tab'īḍ*

Portioning. To indicate a part of any whole.

المتعدي: *al-muta'ddī*

Transitive. A verb requiring a direct object.

الزائد: *az-zāid*

Extra. Beyond and more than what is usual in word inflections. Used to add strength to the script.

nāṣiya, and over his leather footwear. The question upon the Aḥnāf here is that when al-kitāb has stated that an unrestricted, al-muṭlaq, portion of the head must be wiped, why do you then restrict this amount to *an-nāṣiya* or a quarter of the head using khabar ul-wāḥid?

The answer to this is that the words in question are not al-muṭlaq, but rather they are al-mujmal [see section 1.3.2, page 123]. The difference is that al-muṭlaq is that which requires the command to be enacted on any one element of it. So, if anyone was to take one individual from those that al-muṭlaq has pinpointed and to carry out the command on that individual, the duty would be complete. al-Mujmal on the other hand is that which is known in terms of meaning but the extent of its application is not immediately clear. The verse above has asked for "a portion" of the head to be wiped, which would intrinsically mean an amount less than the whole of the head. If this wiping of the head was al-muṭlaq it would be true to say that you may perform *al-masḥ* on three hairs, a quarter, a third or nine-tenths of the head, as all of these are "portions of the head". So, if this part of the verse was al-muṭlaq, wiping any portion less than the whole head would be necessary be it two hairs or nine-tenths of the head! However, there is not a single opinion of any *madhhab* that reflects this. Rather each school of thought has given a specific explanation to indicate the portion of the head that must be wiped. This clearly shows that the verse is not al-muṭlaq, rather it falls into al-mujmal. The meaning of the verse is clear that "a portion" of the head must be wiped, but the extent and area of the portion is not clear. This shows that the verse is al-mujmal and falls under a different principle of Fiqh. As it happens, al-mujmal can be clarified using khabar ul-wāḥid and so the Aḥnāf are permitted to use the Hadith of Mughīra ﷛ to clarify the extent of *al-masḥ*. Thus, the question of restricting al-muṭlaq of al-kitāb using al-khabar is not substantiated.

The second objection for the Aḥnāf with regards to restricting al-muṭlaq of al-kitāb is based on verse 230 of Sūrat ul-Baqara:

فإن طلقها فلا تحل له من بعد حتى تنكح زوجا غيره [البقرة: 230]

"So if he (irrevocably) divorces her, he cannot remarry her until she has married another husband..."

The verse informs of how *al-ḥurmat ul-ghalīẓa* ends. *al-Ḥurmat ul-ghalīẓa* is that a woman is divorced three times by a husband, be it in one instance or on

حديث

عن ابن المغيرة بن شعبة عن أبيه أن النبي ﷺ توضأ فمسح بناصيته وعلى العمامة وعلى الخفين."

عليه الصلاة والسلام

رواه مسلم (274)

QUICK TERMS

الكتاب: *al-kitāb*

The book. The inspired final Word of Allah ﷻ. The Quran.

المطلق: *al-muṭlaq*

The unrestricted. Indicates an entity irrespective of any quality.

الخبر (الواحد): *al-khabar (ul-wāḥid)*

Singular tradition. Traditions related by single-narrator chains.

المجمل: *al-mujmal*

The unexplained. Wording that requires explanatory statements.

separate occasions, or by an irrevocable *al-bāina* divorce by metaphor. The couple are then uncoupled and cannot marry or live as husband and wife. This state is of *al-ḥurmat ul-ghalīẓa* or literally an inviolable prohibition. The verse says that this status between the couple can only be removed when the wife has entered into another marriage and the new husband then divorces her. This would mean that the state of *al-ḥurmat ul-ghalīẓa* is ended between the woman and the first husband, so she is permitted to remarry him should they wish. The verse is al-muṭlaq in stating how *al-ḥurmat ul-ghalīẓa* ends. The Aḥnāf however say that it is not a case of the woman simply entering into a marriage contract with the new husband but they must also cohabit and have intercourse for the status of *al-ḥurmat ul-ghalīẓa* to lift with respect to the ex-husband. The understanding is based on the tradition of Rifā'a al-Quraẓī ؓ that his wife ؓ approached the blessed Prophet ﷺ asking if she could remarry Rifā'a ؓ after he had divorced her thrice and she had married another Companion, 'Abdurrahmān bin Zubayr ؓ. The blessed Prophet ﷺ told her that she must first experience the intimacy of 'Abdurrahmān ؓ before she would be permitted to return to Rifā'a ؓ.

The Hadith makes the position of the Aḥnāf clear but it leaves a vital question. al-Kitāb is al-muṭlaq in expressing the end to the status of *al-ḥurmat ul-ghalīẓa* by marrying another husband, however, the Aḥnāf have restricted al-muṭlaq using al-khabar that the marriage is to be consummated too. This is a restriction on the non-restricting al-muṭlaq, which is not permitted.

There are two answers to this objection. The first is that the idea of consummating the marriage is not derived from the Hadith but from the verse itself. The verse reads:

حتى تنكح زوجا غيره [البقرة: 230]

"...until she has married another husband..."

Here the words ta*nkiḥa* and *zawjan* are both used. Both carry their own meaning. The word *nakaḥa* has a literal and figurative meaning. The literal meaning is sexual intercourse, whilst the figurative meaning is the contract of marriage. The word *nakaḥa* is figurative for contract because the contract of marriage renders sexual intercourse halal and permitted. It is better to keep the literal meaning of intercourse from *tankiḥa* because the word *zawjan* is also used in the verse, and it provides the other meaning of *nakaḥa*, the marriage

حديث

عَنْ عَائِشَةَ رضي الله عنها قَالَتْ: جَاءَتِ امْرَأَةُ رِفَاعَةَ الْقُرَظِيِّ إِلَى رَسُولِ اللَّهِ ﷺ، فَقَالَتْ: يَا رَسُولَ اللَّهِ إِنِّي نَكَحْتُ عَبْدَ الرَّحْمَنِ بْنَ الزُّبَيْرِ فَوَاللَّهِ مَا مَعَهُ إِلا مِثْلُ هَذِهِ الْهُدْبَةِ، قَالَتْ: فَقَالَ رَسُولُ اللَّهِ ﷺ: "لَعَلَّكِ تُرِيدِينَ أَنْ تَرْجِعِي إِلَى رِفَاعَةَ، لا، حَتَّى يَذُوقَ عُسَيْلَتَكِ وَتَذُوقِي عُسَيْلَتَهُ."

عليه الصلاة والسلام

رواه البخاري ومسلم (4888)، (2598)

QUICK ARABIC

المسح: *al-masḥ*

Wiping. The wiping of at least a fourth part of the head in wuḍū.

الناصية: *an-nāṣīya*

The forelock. The fore part of the head.

المذهب: *al-madhhab*

School of fiqh. A system of practices according to mujtahids.

البائنة: *al-bāina*

Irrevocably divorced. A woman divorced in a manner that the husband cannot unilaterally return to the marriage.

contract. It is not possible for a man to be a *husband* if a contract of marriage has not already taken place. So *tankiḥa* means sexual intercourse, and *zawjan* means a man with whom a marriage contract has been entered into, a husband.

So, the understanding of the case is not dependent upon a Hadith but rather the case is explained entirely by the verse itself. A woman whose status of *al-ḥurmat ul-ghalīẓa* is established by three divorces from her husband loses the status once she has consummated a marriage to a second husband by sexual intercourse. This would now mean that if the current husband would divorce her, she would be permitted to remarry the earlier husband. In this manner the Aḥnāf are not guilty of restricting al-muṭlaq with al-khabar, and thus it is not a restriction on the non-restricting al-muṭlaq.

The second manner of answering the query is that the Hadith in question, the Hadith of Rifā'a al-Quraẓī ﷺ, is not khabar ul-wāḥid but it is al-khabar ul-mashhūr. This is the opinion held by the majority of scholars. Now to restrict al-muṭlaq of al-kitāb with khabar ul-wāḥid is not permitted but with al-mashhūr it is permitted. So, the question is answered that the Aḥnāf have not placed a restriction on the non-restricting al-muṭlaq.

Text and Translation

فإن قيل: إن الكتاب في مسح الرأس يوجب مسح مطلق البعض وقد قيدتموه بمقدار الناصية بالخبر والكتاب مطلق في انتهاء الحرمة الغليظة بالنكاح وقد قيدتموه بالدخول بحديث امرأة رفاعة، قلنا: إن الكتاب ليس بمطلق في باب المسح فإن حكم المطلق أن يكون الآتي بأي فرد كان آتيا بالمأمور به والآتي بأي بعض كان ههنا ليس بآت بالمأمور به فإنه لو مسح على النصف أو على الثلثين لا يكون الكل فرضا، وبه فارق المطلق المجمل وأما قيد الدخول فقد قال البعض: إنّ النكاح في النص حمل على الوطيء؛ إذ العقد مستفاد من لفظ الزوج وبهذا يزول السؤال وقال البعض: قيد الدخول ثبت بالخبر وجعلوه من المشاهير فلا يلزمهم تقييد الكتاب بخبر الواحد

If it is queried that al-kitāb in the chapter of *al-masḥ* necessitates the wiping of an unrestricted portion whilst you have restricted it to a quarter of the head using al-khabar; and al-kitāb is unrestricted with respect to the ending of *al-ḥurmat ul-ghalīẓa* after marriage yet you have conditioned it with consummation using the Hadith of Rifā'a's wife. We respond that al-kitāb is not

QUICK TERMS

المطلق: *al-muṭlaq*

The unrestricted. Indicates an entity irrespective of any quality.

الخبر (الواحد): *al-khabar ul-wāḥid*

Singular tradition. Traditions related by single-narrator chains.

الخبر (المشهور): *al-khabar ul-mashhūr*

Popular tradition. Traditions that started as singular traditions and later gained in popularity.

الكتاب: *al-kitāb*

The book. The inspired final Word of Allah ﷻ. The Quran.

QUICK ARABIC

الحلال: *al-ḥalāl*

Lawful. That which is permitted in the Shariah, as distinguished from the unlawful, *al-ḥarām*.

الحرمة الغليظة: *al-ḥurmat ul-ghalīẓa*

Inviolable prohibition. The state of a woman divorced three times by a husband.

المسح: *al-masḥ*

Wiping. The wiping of at least a fourth part of the head in wuḍū.

al-muṭlaq in the chapter of wiping. The ruling of al-muṭlaq is that fulfillment of any one component is fulfillment of the task, however, here anyone who fulfils a part has not executed the task. Had he wiped half of the head or two-thirds the whole would still not be compulsory to wipe. With this al-muṭlaq is distinguished from al-mujmal. As for the condition of consummation some have answered that the word *an-nikāḥ* in the text means intercourse, as the contract is derived from the word *az-zawj*. Thus the query is repelled. Others have replied that the condition of consummation is proven by way of al-khabar that reaches the level of al-mashhūr so this does not necessitate conditioning al-kitāb with khabar ul-wāḥid.

❖ ❖ ❖

QUICK TERMS

المجمل: *al-mujmal*

The unexplained. Wording that requires explanatory statements.

Ḥanafī Principles (3)

MEMORISE

	Term	Definition	Ruling	An Example
4	المطلق	ما يدل على نفس الذات دون صفاتها	-المطلق يجري على إطلاقه - إذا أمكن العمل بإطلاقه فالزيادة عليه بخبر الواحد والقياس لا يجوز	الزانية والزاني فاجلدوا كل واحد منهما مئة جلدة (النور: 2)
5	المقيد	ما يدل على الذات مع بعض صفاتها	المقيد يجري على قيده	ومن قتل مؤمنا خطأ فتحرير رقبة مؤمنة

Summary Of al-Muṭlaq and al-Muqayyad

1. Definition of al-muṭlaq:
   المطلق: ما يدل على نفس الذات دون صفاتها
   "What indicates the entity itself irrespective of qualities."

2. The rulings of al-muṭlaq are:
   i) المطلق يجري على إطلاقه
   "al-Muṭlaq functions unrestricted".
   ii) إذا أمكن العمل بإطلاقه فالزيادة عليه بخبر الواحد والقياس لا يجوز
   "When it can be enacted unrestricted, increasing it with khabar ul-wāḥid or al-qiyās is not permitted."

3. An example of al-muṭlaq is in the verse:
   الزانية والزاني فاجلدوا كل واحد منهما مئة جلدة (النور: 2)
   "Adulteress and adulterer, strike each of them one hundred lashes". Here there is a set punishment for adultery. To extend this absolute sanction by adding a year's exile will not be permitted.

Summary of al-Muṭlaq and al-Muqayyad (continued)

1. Definition of al-muqayyad:
ما يدل على الذات مع بعض صفاتها
"What indicates the entity and some of its qualities".

2. The ruling of al-muqayyad is:
المقيد يجري على قيده
"The muqayyad functions with its conditions".

3. An example of al-muqayyad is in the verse:
ومن قتل مؤمنا خطأ فتحرير رقبة مؤمنة
"Whomsoever kills a believer accidentally must free a Muslim slave".

The verse decrees that a slave must be freed for expiation however, the condition is that it is not any slave, just a Muslim slave.

❖ ❖ ❖

1.1.3 al-Mu<u>sh</u>tarak and al-Muawwal

Chapter 1.1 is about word coinage. Figure 1.1-01 showed that word coinage has four key terms associated with it. al-<u>kh</u>āṣṣ and al-'āmm were discussed in section 1.1.1, and in the previous section 1.1.2 the two terms of al-muṭlaq and al-muqayyad were introduced to enrich our understanding. Now we proceed with the discussions on word coinage, by discussing the terms of al-mu<u>sh</u>tarak and al-muawwal.

First, we are presented with the definition of al-mu<u>sh</u>tarak and three common examples of it. The ruling on al-mu<u>sh</u>tarak in three cases follows this, each highlighting a different aspect. A contended case then follows and the Ḥanafī solution to it is applied. Following this, al-muawwal is defined, its ruling and examples are presented to show its application. This section and the chapter, overall, concludes with a type of al-mu<u>sh</u>tarak that becomes al-mufassar, and an example is presented to show this.

❖ ❖ ❖

The definition of al-mu<u>sh</u>tarak is given as:

المشترك: ما وضع لمعنيين مختلفين أو لمعان مختلفة الحقائق

"**al-Mu<u>sh</u>tarak:** is that which denotes two or more inherently different meanings".

QUICK TERMS

الخاص: *al-<u>kh</u>āṣṣ*

The specific. A word designated for a singular specific concept.

العام: *al-'āmm*

The general. A word designated for a group.

المطلق: *al-muṭlaq*

The unrestricted. Indicates an entity irrespective of any quality.

المقيد: *al-muqayyad*

The restricted. Indicates an entity and some of its qualities.

المشترك: *al-mu<u>sh</u>tarak*

The concurrent. A word coined for two or more inherently different meanings.

From the definition we see that al-mushtarak as a term will be applicable to a word; a word that was coined and designated to a meaning on two or more separate occasions. Each time it was first used to describe one particular meaning, the other meaning was not considered. The first example of this is the Arabic word '*al-jārīya*'. In one context it means *slave-girl* and in a second context it means a *boat*. When the word was being used for a slave-girl for the first time, there was no consideration for the use of the word for a ship, nor vice versa. So, each thing was called '*al-jārīya*' irrespective of the other. Thus, the two designated meanings are inherently different. Similarly, the two possible meanings of the Arabic word '*al-mushtarī*', the purchaser in a financial transaction and the planet Jupiter, were both referred to with this one word, however, when the word was first designated for one of the meanings the other was not in the mind of the designator. The third example of this is the Arabic word '*bāinun*', which either means the separation of two things or could mean something that is apparent and clear. When the word was coined for one meaning the other meaning was not in the mind of the one coining the word in each case.

Text and Translation

فصل في المشترك والمؤول: المشترك ما وضع لمعنيين مختلفين أو لمعان مختلفة الحقائق، مثاله قولنا: جارية فإنها تتناول الأمة والسفينة والمشتري فإنه يتناول قابل عقد البيع وكوكب السماء وقولنا: بائن فإنه يحتمل البين والبيان

Chapter on al-mushtarak and al-muawwal: al-mushtarak is that which is coined for two or more inherently different meanings. An example of it is our saying 'al-*jāriya*' which can mean *female-salve* or *ship*; or '*al-mushtarī*' which could mean *the purchaser* in a transaction or the *planet Jupiter*; or our saying "*bāinun*" which has the possibility of meaning *separate* or *apparent*.

❖ ❖ ❖

The ruling of al-mushtarak according to the Aḥnāf is:

حكم المشترك: إذا تعين الواحد مرادا به سقط اعتبار إرادة غيره

"**The ruling of al-mushtarak:** when one meaning is determined, consideration for its other meanings cease."

QUICK TERMS

المؤول: *al-muawwal*

The accepted. The dominant and accepted meaning from concurrent meanings.

المفسر: *al-mufassar*

The explained. Wording with a statement of clarity from the issuer.

The word identified as al-mushtarak has many meanings, which are very different to one another. Finding a common denominator between them is not possible, as they are all independent of each other. By necessity, when the al-mushtarak word is used in one instance it cannot in the same instance have the second or third meaning simultaneously. It is therefore necessary for a scholar to pause when al-mushtarak is present in a text and to ascertain which of its meanings is meant in that instance. If after analysing the indicators and contemplating over the evidences, one meaning becomes clear, the other meanings are then irrelevant and void. According to the Aḥnāf there is no attempt made at trying to find a common understanding that unifies both or all meanings, as when they were coined, they were coined independently, so their usage is also independent.

Given that al-mushtarak only holds for one meaning in one instance, and the other meanings become redundant, all the scholars agree that in verse 228 of Sūrat ul-Baqara, the word *al-qurū* is al-mushtarak between the meanings of *al-ḥayḍ* and *aṭ-ṭuhr*. After examining the evidence, the Aḥnāf settled on the meaning of *al-ḥayḍ* and disregarded the other, whilst the scholars of the ash-Shāfa'ī school settled on the meaning of *aṭ-ṭuhr* and disregarded the other. Neither group finds a common meaning.

Text and Translation

وحكم المشترك أنه إذا تعين الواحد مرادا به سقط اعتبار إرادة غيره، ولهذا أجمع العلماء رحمهم الله تعالى على أن لفظ القروء المذكور في كتاب الله تعالى محمول إما على الحيض كما هو مذهبنا أو على الطهر كما هو مذهب الشافعي

The ruling of al-mushtarak is that when one meaning is determined from it the possibility of the other meaning ceases. That is why the scholars, Allah have mercy on them all, have agreed that the word *al-qurū* mentioned in the Book of Allah Almighty either means days of blood flow, as it is in our school, or means days of no-blood flow, as is the school of ash-Shāfa'ī.

❖ ❖ ❖

To further the understanding of al-mushtarak the author presents an example that illustrates that you cannot have a common combined meaning for

بســـم الله الرحمن الرحيـــم

وَالْمُطَلَّقَاتُ يَتَرَبَّصْنَ بِأَنفُسِهِنَّ ثَلَاثَةَ قُرُوءٍ

(الآية)

صدق الله العظيم

سورة البقرة: 228

QUICK TERMS

المشترك: *al-mushtarak*

The concurrent. A word coined for two or more inherently different meanings.

QUICK ARABIC

الحيض: *al-ḥayḍ*

The menses. A woman's periodic blood flow from the uterus.

الطهر: *aṭ-ṭuhr*

The purity days. The period of no blood flow during a complete menstruation cycle.

القروء: *al-qurū*

The period. A disputed part of the menstruation cycle. It can either mean *al-ḥayḍ* or *aṭ-ṭuhr*.

al-mushtarak. Rather it will take one of its meanings, and in the case that no meaning can be determined, al-mushtarak will leave the whole case unresolved.

An example of it is a verdict of Imam Muḥammad ﷺ which deals with the word *al-mawālī*. It has two possible independent meanings; it can be a master, *al-mu'tiq*, who frees a slave, and it can also mean the freed slave, *al-mu'taq*. Therefore, Imam Muḥammad ﷺ says that if one was to bequest some of his estate to *al-mawālī* of so-and-so saying: "After I die give the *al-mawālī* of so-and-so 1000 of my wealth". After saying this, the one bequeathing passes away without a further explanation. There is also no other indicator to give preference to one *al-mawālī* over the other because multiple reasons could be given to argue the cases of both parties; such as the one bequeathing wished to repay the favour of those that freed him, or he wished to further show his kindness to the one he freed. None of the reasonings would be conclusive to determine the meaning by themselves. Imam Muḥammad ﷺ says the *al-waṣīya* and bequest will be void. This is because the two *al-mawālī* are independent of each other and so there is no possibility to find a common meaning that would include both. This voiding of the bequest shows that al-mushtarak cannot have a common meaning but will take one of its meanings in every instance.

A second example of Imam Abū Ḥanīfa ﷺ was used to further engrain the idea that al-mushtarak cannot adopt a meaning common to and inclusive of all its meanings. Rather just one meaning is to be preferred in one instance. Imam Abū Ḥanīfa ﷺ says that if one was to say the following to his wife, "You are for me like my mother", without an intention of *aẓ-ẓihār* it would not constitute it. This is because saying *you are as my mother* could have two connotations and is al-mushtarak between them. Firstly, it could mean like my mother in *honour*, and secondly it could mean *unlawful for me* like my mother. The first would not constitute *aẓ-ẓihār* but the second would. Therefore, until the intention of the one saying the words is unknown, neither meaning can be conclusively preferred. Therefore, without an intention, the statement is void, and in the case of the presence of an intention, the statement will take the appropriate meaning.

Text and Translation

وقال محمّد عليه الرحمة: إذا أوصى لموالي بني فلان ولبني فلان موال من أعلى وموال من أسفل فمات

QUICK ARABIC

الوصية: *al-waṣīya*

The will. An instruction of a person regarding their property and belongings after death.

الظهار: *aẓ-ẓihār*

Likening to a mother. A practice in which separation between husband and wife occurs until expiation is made.

المظاهر: *al-muẓāhir*

The one who commits *aẓ-ẓihār*. This occurs when one says to his wife words such as "you are to me like my mother's back".

QUICK DICTIONARY

Bequeath: *bih-kweeth*
To dispose. To give personal property and wealth by last will.

بطلت الوصية في حق الفريقين لاستحالة الجمع بينهما وعدم الرجحان وقال أبو حنيفة عليه الرحمة: إذا قال لزوجته: أنت على مثل أمي لا يكون مظاهراً؛ لأنّ اللفظ مشترك بين الكرامة والحرمة فلا يترجح جهة الحرمة إلا بالنية

Imam Muḥammad, mercy be upon him, said: if one bequeathed for *al-mawālī* of so-and-so, and so-and-so has a charge from above and a charge below. So he died. The bequest will be void for both parties as it is impossible to combine them both and there is no preference. Imam Abū Ḥanīfa, mercy be upon him, said: if one said to his wife, "you are to me like my mother", he will not be *al-muẓāhir* because the statement is al-mushtarak to mean honourable or forbidden. So the meaning of forbiddance will not be preferred expect with an intention.

❖❖❖

As the multiple meanings of al-mushtarak cannot be combined, the following ruling highlights it by saying that the Aḥnāf have stated that should a pilgrim in the state of *al-iḥrām* kill an animal, he need not compensate for it by an equivalent animal but may simply pay for it. The details of the case are that hunting prey is forbidden for a pilgrim in the state of *al-iḥrām* because verse 95 of Sūrat ul-Māida has stated:

يأيها الذين آمنوا لا تقتلوا الصيد وأنتم حرم [المائدة: 95]

"O believers, kill not game whilst you are a pilgrim..."

Despite this prohibition if the pilgrim was to kill, then compensation must be given as Allah ﷻ says:

ومن قتله منكم متعمدا فجزآء مثل ما قتل من النعم [المائدة: 95]

"...and if any of you does kill it intentionally, the compensation is an animal equivalent to the one he killed..."

This goes to show that if a pilgrim does kill an animal, an equivalent is to be offered as compensation. However, by *equivalent* it could mean one of two things, equivalent in appearance, or an implied equivalence. Equivalence in appearance is in size or weight for example, like a dear would be an equivalent to a goat. This is called *al-mithl aṣ-ṣūrī*. An implied equivalence would be in

QUICK ARABIC

الإحرام: *al-iḥrām*

Pilgrim's garb and state. The dress of the pilgrim and the state in which he or she is held to be.

المثل الصوري: *al-mithl aṣ-ṣūrī*

Equivalent in appearance. When one thing is the same as the other in size or weight.

المثل المعنوي: *al-mithl al-ma'nawī*

Implied equivalence. When one thing is the same as the other in monetary value.

terms of the monetary value of the animal, where the money is said to be an equivalent of the animal. This is called *al-mithl al-ma'nawī*.

It is the opinion of some scholars that when an equivalent can be found for the hunted animal then the compensation upon the pilgrim will be an animal equivalent in appearance. However, if it is not possible to find an equivalent in terms of appearance, like in the case of a pilgrim killing a pigeon, then these scholars opt for compensating with money. Imam Abū Ḥanīfa رحمه الله and Imam Abū Yūsuf رحمه الله have said that whether there is an animal equivalent in appearance or not, only *al-mithl al-ma'nawī* can be given in charity as compensation, which would be the monetary value. It is not an option to offer *al-mithl aṣ-ṣūrī*. This is because al-kitāb has used the word *al-mithl* and it is al-mushtarak between *al-mithl aṣ-ṣūrī* and *al-mithl al-ma'nawī*. The ruling of al-mushtarak is that if one meaning is selected then the other meaning is invalid. All scholars unanimously agree that if the pilgrim kills the likes of a pigeon then the compensation is monetary, so this meaning is selected for the instance in the verse. This meaning, once selected, becomes the preference and all other meanings are ignored thereafter. If we were to sometimes apply *al-mithl al-ma'nawī* and on other occasions *al-mithl aṣ-ṣūrī* it would amount to *'umūm ul-mushtarak* or an understanding inclusive of every denotation of al-mushtarak; this is not permitted as each coinage is independent of the other. When it is not possible to have both meanings, and one meaning of *al-mithl*, *al-mithl al-ma'nawī*, was agreed upon by all, then that is the preferred meaning. The other *al-mithl*, *al-mithl aṣ-ṣūrī*, is thus abandoned.

Text and Translation

وعلى هذا قلنا: لا يجب النظير في جزاء الصيد لقوله تعالى: ﴿فجزاءٌ مثل ما قتل مِن النعمِ﴾؛ لأنّ المثل مشترك بين المثل صورةً وبين المثل معنى وهو القيمة وقد أريد المثل من حيث المعنى بهذا النص في قتل الحمام والعصفور ونحوهما بالاتفاق فلا يزاد المثل من حيث الصورة؛ إذ لا عموم للمشترك أصلاً فيسقط اعتبار الصورة لاستحالة الجمع

Based upon this we said: a match is not necessary in compensation for game because He Most High says: "...the reprisal is a livestock animal equivalent to what he killed..." The word *al-mithl* is al-mushtarak between *a match in form* and *in implication*, which is its monetary value. The word *al-mithl* has

بسم الله الرحمن الرحيم

وَمَن قَتَلَهُ مِنكُم مُّتَعَمِّدًا فَجَزَاءٌ مِّثْلُ مَا قَتَلَ مِنَ النَّعَمِ

(الآية)

صدق الله العظيم

سورة المائدة: 95

QUICK TERMS

المشترك: *al-mushtarak*

The concurrent. A word coined for two or more inherently different meanings.

عموم المشترك: *'umūm ul-mushtarak*

Generality of the concurrent. The understanding that a word indicates many independently coined meanings in one instance.

unanimously been used to mean implied equivalence in this very text for the case of killing a pigeon, sparrow or the likes. Therefore, equivalence in form will not be added to this, as al-mushtarak has no generality at all. So the possibility of form equivalence is passed over due to the implausibility of combining.

❖❖❖

After establishing the definition, rulings and examples of al-mushtarak, the text goes on to say that when signs, indications and evidence single out one of the meanings of al-mushtarak as the prevalent meaning in a context, it is termed al-muawwal. That is to say, al-mushtarak becomes al-muawwal when a preferred opinion is formed. Thus, the definition of al-muawwal will be:

المؤول: المشترك الذي ترجح بعض وجوهه بغالب الرأي

"**al-Muawwal:** is the al-mushtarak which has a prevalent meaning due to dominant opinion".

The ruling of al-muawwal is presented as:

حكم المؤول: وجوب العمل به مع احتمال الخطأ

"**The ruling of al-muawwal:** it must be enacted with the possibility of an error."

This means that it must be enacted whilst the preferred meaning is most befitting. However, be cautious that the interpretation is prone to error. That is to say, that despite strong evidence pointing to a correct outcome there is a remote possibility that the wrong meaning has been preferred. It is the scholar who has found evidence of this preferred meaning, and the scholar may have overlooked evidence or evidence was unknown at the time. Nevertheless, while no evidence suggests an error, it is necessary to act upon what is known.

An example provided for al-muawwal from the rulings of the Shariah is that in a financial transaction if the currency is left unspecified, the assumption that it is the most prevalent currency in the land would be al-muawwal. So, if one said, "I have bought this book for five", it will be assumed the book is for five pounds sterling if the transaction was in the UK. This is our interpretation and *at-taawīl*, thus making the cost of five pounds sterling al-muawwal. However, if the transaction took place in a land where there were multiple currencies in circulation, like an international zone, and the exact currency was

QUICK TERMS

المؤول: *al-muawwal*

The accepted. The dominant and accepted meaning from concurrent meanings.

التأويل: *at-tawīl*

Interpretation. The process of arriving at a preferred meaning from concurrent meanings.

المشترك: *al-mushtarak*

The concurrent. A word coined for two or more inherently different meanings.

الخاص: *al-khāṣṣ*

The specific. A word designated for a singular specific meaning.

الكناية: *al-kināya*

The concealed. A word or phrase that has a concealed and hidden meaning. A metaphor.

QUICK DICTIONARY

Metonymy: *mi-ton-uh-mee*

Figure of speech. To use the name of one thing for another, to which it is related.

not specified this would render the 'five' al-mushtarak. In the case of the cost being al-mushtarak and unspecified, the transaction would be void, as a common understanding of all the coinages of al-mushtarak in one instance is not permitted, and there is not a way to determine one of the currencies in hindsight without complications due to differences in rates. Therefore, no currency is the prevalent one and the transaction is void.

Furthermore, a couple of previously stated examples also serve as examples of al-muawwal. The Aḥnāf give the Arabic word *qurū* from verse 228 of Sūra tul-Baqara, the preferred meaning of *al-ḥayḍ* as discussed previously on page 16. In the chapter of al-khāṣṣ we discussed that the word *al-qurū* is al-mushtarak between *aṭ-ṭuhr* and *al-ḥayḍ*. So, using the implications of the al-khāṣṣ word *ath-thalātha* we preferred the meaning of *al-ḥayḍ*, thus making the word *al-qurū* al-muawwal in that meaning. Similarly, the Arabic verb *tankiḥa* from verse 230 of Sūrat ul-Baqara has the preferred meaning of sexual intercourse, as discussed on page 50. The word *nakaḥa* is al-mushtarak for both the institution of marriage and sexual intercourse. The Aḥnāf preferred conveying the meaning of sexual intercourse with this word because of the presence of the word *zawjan* in the same speech, which implies the meaning of marriage. Rather than repetition, each word holds different meanings.

Furthermore, another example of al-muawwal is in situations where divorce is under consideration. Metonymy or indirect words of intent, *al-kināya*, convey the meaning of divorce. This is by way of al-muawwal too. So, during an intense argument where divorce is being discussed between husband and wife, if the husband was to use the word *bāin*, it is al-mushtarak between 'clear' and 'separated'. As the discussion is about divorce the meaning of separated is most appropriate and preferred. Thus, the word *bāin* becomes al-muawwal in that meaning.

Text and Translation

ثم إذا ترجح بعض وجوه المشترك بغالب الرأي يصير مؤولا، وحكم المؤول وجوب العمل به مع احتمال الخطأ، ومثاله في الحكميات ما قلنا: إذا أطلق الثمن في البيع كان على غالب نقد البلد وذلك بطريق التأويل ولو كانت النقود مختلفة فسد البيع لما ذكرنا، وحمل الأقراء على الحيض وحمل النكاح في الآية على الوطيء وحمل الكنايات حال مذاكرة الطلاق على الطلاق من هذا القبيل

بسم الله الرحمن الرحيم

وَالْمُطَلَّقَاتُ يَتَرَبَّصْنَ بِأَنفُسِهِنَّ ثَلاَثَةَ قُرُوءٍ (الآية)

صدق الله العظيم

سورة البقرة 228

بسم الله الرحمن الرحيم

فَإِن طَلَّقَهَا فَلاَ تَحِلُّ لَهُ مِن بَعْدُ حَتَّىَ تَنكِحَ زَوْجًا غَيْرَهُ (الآية)

صدق الله العظيم

سورة البقرة 230

QUICK ARABIC

القروء (ج: الأقراء): *al-qurū*

The period. A disputed part of the menstruation cycle. It can be either *al-ḥayḍ* or *aṭ-ṭuhur*.

الحيض: *al-ḥayḍ*

The menses. A woman's periodic blood flow from the uterus.

الطهر: *aṭ-ṭuhr*

The purity days. The period of no blood flow during a complete menstruation cycle.

Then, when one of the meanings of al-mushtarak takes precedence through a dominant opinion it will be termed al-muawwal. The ruling for al-muawwal is that it must be enacted with the possibility of an error. An example of it from the rulings is what we have said that if the currency is unspecified in a transaction it will default to the prevalent currency of the land; this will be by way of interpretation. If there are various currencies in use the transaction will be void as we have mentioned. Interpreting the word *al-aqrā* to mean *al-ḥayḍ*, the word *an-nikāḥ* in the verse to mean intercourse, and all allusions in scenarios of divorce to mean divorce, are all of this type.

❖ ❖ ❖

A case illustrating the application of the principle that when supported by an indicator or evidence al-mushtarak only conveys the supported meaning is as follows. The Aḥnāf say that if one was the owner of the minimum quota of two different classes of zakah whilst simultaneously in debt, the debt will be exclusive to the class that is easiest for repayment. This is because debt is a preventive to the obligation of zakah and not tying it to one class of wealth will enable one to be exempt from all classes of zakah. For this reason, the Aḥnāf consider the debt associated with the easiest method of repayment. Once the easiest class of wealth is singled out for repayment, the other classes are debt-free and so subject to zakah. For example, if one had more than the minimum quota of silver dirhams, the minimum quota of gold dinars, stocks and also the quota for small cattle, whilst simultaneously having a debt, the debt will be associated with either the dirhams or the dinars. This is because it is easier to pay debt using these currencies, without having to sell.

Imam Muḥammad عليه رحمة الله has based a case upon this of someone who entered a marriage by allocating one quota, *an-niṣāb*, as the bridal gift, and he was the owner of *an-niṣāb* in both goats and dirhams. The bridal gift will be due from the dirhams and not the goats, as it is easier to pay the debt of the bridal gift in coins. Now, if the said man was to delay the payment of the bridal gift beyond a whole year, and remain in possession of both classes of wealth, Imam Muḥammad عليه رحمة الله says that the zakah will be necessary on the goats only. The bridal gift that he owes his wife will prevent the compulsion of zakah on the dirhams because debts prevent from compulsion of zakah. He will be encouraged to pay his debts from the dirhams, so effectively the wealth does not belong to him, and he will be instructed to pay the zakah from the goats.

QUICK TERMS

المشترك: *al-mushtarak*

The concurrent. A word coined for two or more inherently different meanings.

المؤول: *al-muawwal*

The accepted. The dominant and accepted meaning from concurrent meanings.

QUICK ARABIC

القروء (ج: الأقراء): *al-qurū*

The period. A disputed part of the menstruation cycle. It can be either *al-ḥayḍ* or *aṭ-ṭuhr*.

الحيض: *al-ḥayḍ*

The menses. A woman's periodic blood flow from the uterus.

النكاح: *an-nikāḥ*

Conjunction. In legal terms it is the marriage contract.

النصاب: *an-niṣāb*

The minimum threshold. The minimum property upon which zakah must be paid.

وعلى هذا قلنا: الدين المانع من الزكاة يصرف إلى أيسر المالين قضاء للدين، وفرع محمد عليه الرحمة على هذا فقال: إذا تزوج امرأة على نصاب وله نصاب من الغنم ونصاب من الدراهم يصرف الدين إلى الدراهم حتى لو حال عليهما الحول تجب الزكاة عنده في نصاب الغنم ولا تجب في الدراهم

Based on this we said: debt that waives zakah will be applied to the easier of two amounts, in order to repay the debt. Imam Muḥammad, mercy be upon him, derived from this, by saying: if someone marries a woman in exchange of *an-niṣāb*, whilst he owns the minimum quota of small cattle and a minimum quota of dirham, the debt will be applied to the dirham. So if a year passed on both quotas, zakah will be payable from the small cattle and not on the dirham according to him.

❖ ❖ ❖

Finally, in this chapter we are told that if one of the meanings of al-mushtarak is preferred by the articulator and originator of the word by explicitly communicating that this is the meaning of the word, then al-mushtarak becomes al-mufassar.

al-Mufassar is distinctly different to al-muawwal because in al-muawwal we interpreted a preferred meaning using the assistance of a third-party indicator or evidence. In al-mufassar the very speaker and articulator of the al-mushtarak word is stating and explaining that this is the meaning of my words. So, al-muawwal has the possibility of an error on our part in that we have interpreted the words of the articulator albeit with evidence. There can be very little doubt regarding al-mufassar as the user of the al-mushtarak word is clarifying it to be of one meaning. There will be more about the definition, strength of clarity, ruling and examples of al-mufassar in a later section [1.3.1, page 111].

Here, we understand that the ruling of al-mufassar is that we must enact it with certainty. This is because there is no possibility of opposing the articulator as it is the articulator who used the word. An example of this is if one confessed: "I owe so-and-so ten dirham of Bukhārā". It can only mean the dirham of Bukhārā and not any other currency. If the type of dirham was not

QUICK TERMS

المفسر: *al-mufassar*

The explained. Wording with a statement of clarity from the issuer.

QUICK ARABIC

النصاب: *an-niṣāb*

The minimum threshold. The minimum property upon which zakah must be paid.

stated we would have interpreted it to be the prevalent currency in that vicinity; we could be wrong. However, when the speaker himself explains that it is the dirhams of Bukhārā the currency is now al-mufassar. It goes without saying that al-mufassar is always preferred over al-muawwal, as the former is definitive and *al-qaṭ'ī*, whilst the latter is tentative and *aẓ-ẓannī*.

Text and Translation

ولو ترجح بعض وجوه المشترك ببيان من قبل المتكلم كان مفسراً، وحكمه أنه يجب العمل به يقينا، مثاله إذا قال: لفلان على عشرة دراهم من نقد "بخارا" فقوله: من نقد "بخارا" تفسير له فلولا ذلك لكان منصرفاً إلى غالب نقد البلد بطريق التأويل فيترجح المفسر فلا يجب نقد البلد

If one of the meanings of al-mushtarak takes precedence due to an explanation of the first speaker it will become al-mufassar. Its ruling is that it must be enacted with certainty. An example of it is, if one stated: I owe so and so ten dirham of Bukhārā. So stating the currency of 'Bukhārā' is his explanation. Had he not stated it, it would have defaulted to the prevalent currency of the land by way of interpretation. So al-mufassar takes precedence and the currency of the land is not necessary.

❖ ❖ ❖

Ḥanafī Principles (4)

	Term	Definition	Ruling	An Example
6	المشترك	ما وضع لمعنيين مختلفين او لمعان مختلفة الحقائق	- إذا لم يتعين الواحد مرادا به سقط اعتبار الجميع - إذا تعين الواحد مرادا به سقط اعتبار إرادة الغير - إذا تعين من قبل المتكلم كان مفسرا	مشتري جارية
7	المقيد	ما يدل على الذات مع بعض صفاتها	وجوب العمل به مع احتمال الخطأ	حتى تنكح زوجا غيره (البقرة: 230)

QUICK TERMS

المفسر: *al-mufassar*

The explained. Wording with a statement of clarity from the issuer.

المؤول: *al-muawwal*

The accepted. The dominant and accepted meaning from concurrent meanings.

القطعي: *al-qaṭ'ī*

The definitive. Most reliable and certain.

الظني: *al-ẓannī*

The speculative. Reached after careful consideration.

المشترك: *al-mushtarak*

The concurrent. A word coined for two or more inherently different meanings.

MEMORISE

Summary of al-Mushtarak and al-Muawwal

1. The definition of al-mushtarak:
المشترك: ما وضع لمعنيين مختلفين او لمعان مختلفة الحقائق
"al-Mushtarak is a word coined for two fundamentally different meanings or for many different meanings".

2. Examples of al-mushtarak are words like المشتري which can mean *purchaser* or the planet *Jupiter*, and the word الجارية which means *boat* or *salve-girl*.

3. The rulings of al-mushtarak are:
i) إذا لم يتعين الواحد مرادا به سقط اعتبار الجميع
"When no meaning can be determined all meanings are abandoned".
ii) إذا تعين الواحد مرادا به سقط اعتبار إرادة الغير
"When one meaning is determined, consideration for others is abandoned".
iii) إذا تعين من قبل المتكلم كان مفسرا
"When the spokesman determines the meaning, it becomes al-mufassar."

4. Definition of al-muawwal:
المؤول: الوجه المرجّح من معاني المشترك بغالب الرأي
"The proposed meaning from the various meanings of al-mushtarak based on dominant opinion".

5. An example of al-muawwal is in the verse:
حتى تنكح زوجا غيره
"Until she has intercourse with another spouse."
The word *nakaḥa* could mean either marriage contract or intercourse. Due to the dominant opinions, based on evidence of higher strength than al-qiyās, the Ḥanafīs assign the meaning of intercourse to the word in this instance. The word *nakaḥa* becomes al-muawwal in the meaning of intercourse, so the same word cannot mean the marriage contract here.

6. The ruling of al-muawwal is:
وجوب العمل به مع احتمال الخطأ
"It is necessary to enact it with the possibility of error."

1.2 Word Usage

The previous chapter 1.1 discussed word coinage and what any given word of al-kitāb is assigned to mean. Four principle terms of al-khāṣṣ (the specific), al-'āmm (the general), al-mushtarak (the homograph) and al-muawwal (the precedent) were all introduced. Further discussions on al-muṭlaq (the unrestricted) and al-muqayyad (the restricted), both types of al-khāṣṣ, were also included.

In this chapter the very same words of al-kitāb are discussed but in terms of how they have been used. It is one thing to know the designated meaning of a word but quite another to understand how it is being used. For example, if one was to say "It's okay". We understand that the word 'okay' is an adjective to describe matters to be normal, satisfactory or under control. However, when someone is upset or angry and says the same sentence, "It's okay", where things are clearly not under control or normal, the manner in which the word is used has changed. Rather than things being okay, they are not okay, and the speaker is understood to be saying matters are not okay given the circumstances. So, we have understood from the previous chapter that the words of al-kitāb have particular assigned meanings, however we need to build upon that to see how those words are put to use.

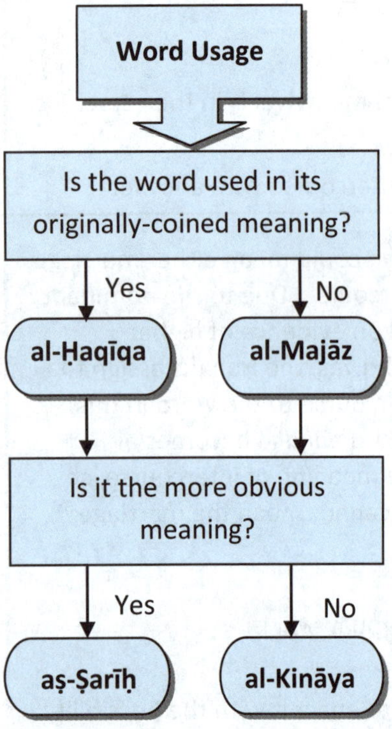

FIGURE 1.2-01
A division of the manner in which words are used.

The four primary terms introduced are al-ḥaqīqa (the literal), al-majāz (the figurative), aṣ-ṣarīḥ (the unequivocal) and al-kināya (the equivocal). Section 1.2.1 discusses the first two whereas the latter two are discussed later in section 1.2.3. This division of word usage is summarised in Figure 1.2-01:

1.2.1 al-Ḥaqīqa and al-Majāz

The chapter begins by defining both al-ḥaqīqa and al-majāz:

الحقيقة: كلّ لفظ وضعه واضع اللغة بإزاء شيء

"**al-Ḥaqīqa:** is every word coined by the lexicographer for an item".

المجاز: كل لفظ مستعمل في غير معناه الحقيقي

"**al-Majāz:** is every word used in other than its literal meaning".

When a word is *coined,* it means that a word is assigned to an item or to an understanding in such a manner that no other indicator is needed to know what

QUICK TERMS

الحقيقة: *al-ḥaqīqa*

The literal. A word coined by the lexicon for an item.

المجاز: *al-majāz*

The figurative. A word used for a meaning other than its coined meaning.

the word in question represents. If a word is used in the assigned meaning it will be literal or al-ḥaqīqa, and if it is used in any other meaning it was not originally coined for, it will be figurative or al-majāz.

Bearing in mind the definition of both al-ḥaqīqa and al-majāz we realise that they cannot merge into one word in one instance according to the Aḥnāf. This means that when a word is used it may appear to be true both literally and figuratively but only one is truly intended in that one instance. ash-Shawāfi' and some others permit the merger of both.

To highlight the Ḥanafī position that it is not possible to merge both al-ḥaqīqa and al-majāz we have a tradition of the blessed Prophet ﷺ. The tradition reads:

لا تبيعوا الدرهم بالدرهمين ولا الصاع بالصاعين

"Do not trade one dirham for two dirham, nor one *aṣ-ṣā'* for two *aṣ-ṣā'*".

The Arabic word *aṣ-ṣā'* has a literal meaning of the actual container used to measure *a cubic measure of around 2.6 Kilograms*, this is al-ḥaqīqa. *aṣ-Ṣā'* also has a figurative meaning of *the contents of such a container*. However, as there is a unanimous agreement that the figurative meaning is the understanding of *aṣ-ṣā'* in the hadith, the possibility of the literal meaning cannot hold true. Therefore, the hadith means you cannot exchange the contents of one *aṣ-ṣā'* for the contents of two measures of *aṣ-ṣā'*; so it is perfectly acceptable to trade one *aṣ-ṣā'* container itself for two containers, as the Hadith cannot mean both al-ḥaqīqa and al-majāz at the same time.

Similarly, in verse 6 of Sūrat ul-Māida the word for *al-mulāmasa*, touching, is al-ḥaqīqa to mean *contact* with the bare skin of the hand and it is al-majāz for sexual intimacy. There is agreement between the Aḥnāf and the Shawāfi' that it is al-majāz in the instance of the verse. So, in the context of the verse if a man is to merely touch a woman it will not necessitate the need for purity, rather purity will be required after sexual intimacy only. This is because both al-ḥaqīqa and al-majāz are not implied by the same word in one instance.

Text and Translation

فصل في الحقيقة والمجاز: كلّ لفظ وضعه واضع اللغة بإزاء شيء فهو حقيقة له ولو استعمل في غيره يكون مجازا لا حقيقة، ثم الحقيقة مع المجاز لا يجتمعان إرادة من لفظ واحد في حالة واحدة، ولهذا قلنا:

بسم الله الرحمن الرحيم

وَإِن كُنتُم مَّرْضَى أَوْ عَلَى سَفَرٍ أَوْ جَاء أَحَدٌ منكُم مِّنَ الْغَائِطِ أَوْ لاَمَسْتُمُ النِّسَاء فَلَمْ تَجِدُواْ مَاء فَتَيَمَّمُواْ صَعِيدًا طَيِّبًا

(الآية)۝

صدق الله العظيم

سورة المائدة: 6

حديث

عَنِ ابْنِ عُمَرَ رَضِيَ اللهُ عَنْهُ قَالَ: قَالَ رَسُولُ اللَّهِ ﷺ: "لَا تَبِيعُوا الدِّينَارَ بِالدِّينَارَيْنِ، وَلَا الدِّرْهَمَ بِالدِّرْهَمَيْنِ، وَلَا الصَّاعَ بِالصَّاعَيْنِ، فَإِنِّي أَخَافُ عَلَيْكُمْ الرَّمَاءَ"، وَالرَّمَاءُ هُوَ الرِّبَا."

عليه الصلاة والسلام

مسند أحمد بن حنبل (5725)

QUICK ARABIC

الصاع: *aṣ-ṣā'*

A cubic measure. An ancient measure which equates to approximately 2.035Kg.

QUICK TERMS

الحقيقة: *al-ḥaqīqa*

The literal. A word coined by the lexicon for an item.

المجاز: *al-majāz*

The figurative. A word used for a meaning other than its coined meaning.

QUICK ARABIC

اهل الحرب: *ahl ul-ḥarb*

Inhabitants of a hostile state. Those dwelling in lands that have not as yet made peace agreements with Muslims.

QUICK REFERENCE

السير الكبير: *as-siyar al-kabīr*

The Major Treatise on Engagement. The first major Islamic treatise on the law between Muslim and non-Muslim nations by Imam Muḥammad رحمه الله.

QUICK DICTIONARY

Bequeath: *bih-kweeth*

To dispose. To give personal property and wealth by last will.

Emancipate: *ih-man-suh-payt*

To free. To free a slave from bondage and servitude.

لما أريد ما يدخل في الصاع بقوله عليه السلام: لا تبيعوا الدرهم بالدرهمين ولا الصاع بالصاعين سقط اعتبار نفس الصاع حتى جاز بيع الواحد منه بالإثنين ولما أريد الوقاع من آية الملامسة سقط اعتبار إرادة المس باليد

Chapter on al-ḥaqīqa and al-majāz: Every word coined by lexicographers for a designated item is al-ḥaqīqa for it. If it is used for other than it, it will be al-majāz and not al-ḥaqīqa. al-Ḥaqīqa and al-majāz are never implied by one word in one instance. For this reason we said: Because the intent is the contents in his saying, peace and blessings be upon him, "Do not trade one dirham for two, nor one *aṣ-ṣā'* for two," the meaning of the measuring container itself is void. So trading one *aṣ-ṣā'* container for two is permitted. And, because intercourse is meant in the verse of *al-mulāmasa* the possibility of mere physical contact is void.

❖❖❖

As merging both al-ḥaqīqa and al-majāz in one word is not possible, Imam Muḥammad رحمه الله has delivered a particular verdict concerning bequests. The case is if one, having never been a slave himself, was to bequest in favour of his slaves who had also freed other slaves saying: I bequest to my *al-mawālī*. The benefactor would only be his directly emancipated slaves and not those emancipated thereafter by the freed-slaves. This is because *al-mawālī* when used for emancipated slaves is al-ḥaqīqa for that meaning and al-majāz for those indirectly emancipated through a freed slave. The al-ḥaqīqa meaning takes precedence in this case and as al-ḥaqīqa cannot merge with al-majāz in one word, it is the only meaning taken. Therefore, the directly emancipated slaves will be lone benefactors.

Similarly, in the book as-Siyar al-Kabīr there is a mention of *ahl ul-ḥarb* combatants who when asking for protection, ask to include their *al-ābā*, fathers. When Muslims grant this protection, it will include the fathers but it will not extend to the grandfathers. This is because *al-ābā* is al-ḥaqīqa for male parents but it is al-majāz for male ancestors. The word is used only in one meaning, which will be male parent, the father. Equally, should the *ahl ul-ḥarb* combatants ask for their protection to include their *ummahāt*, mothers, it will not include the grandmothers. The word *al-umm* is al-ḥaqīqa for a female parent and al-majāz for a female ancestor. The word is used only in one meaning, which will be female parent, the mother.

Furthermore, based on the same rule that al-ḥaqīqa cannot merge with al-majāz in one word, we say that if one was to bequest for virgin-daughters, *al-abkār*, of someone it will not include those who have lost their virginity out of wedlock. For example, if one said words to the effect of: "I bequest a third of my wealth after my death to the virgin-daughters of my friend"; this will not include unmarried non-virgins. The difference arises because according to Imam Abū Ḥanīfa رحمه الله the word *al-abkār* is al-ḥaqīqa for those who are literally unmarried virgins and it is al-majāz for those who have lost their virginity with or without marriage. The bequest is for *al-abkār,* which is either al-ḥaqīqa or al-majāz. As the literal virgins are unanimously included in *al-abkār* in this bequest, the other meaning is abandoned.

Additionally, if one was to bequeath for *al-abnā* of someone and the said person has sons and grandsons, the bequest will be for the sons and not the patrilineal grandsons. This is because the word *al-ibn* is al-ḥaqīqa in the meaning of sons, whilst it is al-majāz for patrilineal grandsons. As al-ḥaqīqa is unanimously agreed upon as the intent of the word, al-majāz is abandoned.

Furthermore, if one was to vow not to make *an-nikāḥ* with a particular woman whilst the woman in question is not his wife at the time, it will mean he will not be party to a marriage contract with that woman. If he was to then go and fornicate with her, the vow is not dishonoured. This is because the word *an-nikāḥ* is al-ḥaqīqa in the meaning of sexual intercourse and al-majāz in the meaning of a marriage contract. As the vow is concerned with the marriage contract and that he will not be party to it, the al-ḥaqīqa meaning is abandoned. Now when he goes to commit the heinous sin of adultery it will not violate his vow, as intercourse is not understood from the vow.

Text and Translation

قال مُحَمَّد عليه الرحمة: إذا أوصى لمواليه وله موال أعتقهم ولمواليه موال أعتقوهم كانت الوصية لمواليه دون موالي مواليه، وفي "السير الكبير": لو استأمن أهل الحرب على آبائهم لا تدخل الأجداد في الآمان ولو استأمنوا على أمهاتهم لا يثبت الأمان في حق الجدات، وعلى هذا قلنا: إذا أوصى لأبكار بني فلان لا تدخل المصابة بالفجور في حكم الوصية ولو أوصى لبني فلان وله بنون وبنو بنيه كانت الوصية لبنيه

QUICK ARABIC

النكاح: *an-nikāḥ*

Conjunction. In legal terms it is the marriage contract.

QUICK DICTIONARY

Patrilineal: *pa-truh-lin-ee-uh l*

Male line. Inheriting or determining through the male line.

دون بني بنيه، قال أصحابنا: لو حلف لا ينكح فلانة وهي أجنبية كان ذلك على العقد حتى لو زنا بها لا يحنث

Imam Muḥammad, Allah have mercy on him, says: when a man bequeaths for his *al-mawālī* and he has slaves which he freed and his freed-slaves have slaves which they freed, the bequest will be for his slaves and not for his slaves' slaves. In as-Siyar ul-Kabīr it is mentioned that if the *ahl ul-ḥarb* seek protection for their fathers, their grandfathers will not be included in the protection. If they sought protection for their mothers, protection would not be inclusive of grandmothers. Based on this we have said: if a bequest is for the virgin-girls of a family, those who are tainted with committing adultery will not be included in the bequest. If a bequest was made for the children of someone and he has children as well as grandchildren, the bequest will be for the children and not the grandchildren. Our scholars have said: if one was to vow not to marry someone who is *al-ajnabīya* it would be construed as a marriage contract such that were he to commit adultery with her, he would not have broken the vow.

❖❖❖

In the following section three objections have been raised to the ruling that al-ḥaqīqa cannot be joined in one word with al-majāz. The objections are then answered in the same order in which they are raised. The objections are as follows:

1) The first objection is if one was to vow not to "set foot in the house of so-and-so", Imam Abū Ḥanīfa ﷺ says the vow is broken if the person enters the house barefooted, in shoes, or even on a ride. This should not be the case because the words "to set foot" are only literally meant when he is barefooted. When he enters with footwear on, or on a ride, this is not literally "to set foot". So why is he said to have broken his vow by entering shod or on a ride? This is merging both al-ḥaqīqa and al-majāz in one instance.
2) The second objection is if one was to vow, "not to reside in the house of so-and-so". This person will be liable if he enters the owned residence of the said person, his rented accommodation or even his borrowed residence. However, "the house of so-and-so" literally means the property owned by the person, whilst rented accommodation and

QUICK ARABIC

اهل الحرب: *ahl ul-ḥarb*

Inhabitants of a hostile state. Those dwelling in lands that have not as yet made peace agreements with Muslims.

الأجنبية: *al-ajnabīya*

Female non-near relative. A woman to whom a man is permitted to marry.

QUICK REFERENCE

السير الكبير: *as-siyar al-kabīr*

The Major Treatise on Engagement. The first major Islamic treatise on the law between Muslim and non-Muslim nations by Imam Muḥammad ﷺ.

QUICK DICTIONARY

Bequeath: *bih-kweeth*

To dispose. To give personal property and wealth by last will.

Shod: *shod*

To fit with a shoe. Past tense and past participle of shoe.

borrowed residence are not his property. By saying that he will have broken his vow in all cases you have merged both al-ḥaqīqa and al-majāz in one instance.

3) The third objection is if one announced that "my slave is free the day so-and-so arrives". This person would be liable if the said person arrives in the daytime or at night. Here, the word "day" is literally daytime and not night-time. In effect, your verdict has merged both al-ḥaqīqa and al-majāz in one instance.

The answers to each of the objections are as follows:

1) In the first case the words, "set foot in the house of so-and-so", are not literal. Therefore, if one were to utter the words of the vow, then proceed to only stand outside the house of the individual, and simply place his foot inside the house, the vow would not be broken. This is because it is understood that "set foot" figuratively means, "to enter"; this will be al-majāz. In effect the person is vowing, "not to *enter* the house of so-and-so." Now, if he enters barefooted, shod or mounted, in all cases the vow will be broken, so long as there is an entrance into the person's house. The vow is not broken because al-ḥaqīqa merges with al-majāz, but it is broken if the al-majāz meaning of *entrance* is found.
2) In the second case, "the house of so-and-so", is al-majāz for the actual residence of so-and-so, whether that individual is the property owner, a tenant or borrowing it in-kind. The vow has obviously come about due to a dispute between the two; hence he has vowed not to remain in the same house as the other. Therefore, wherever the other individual is, this person has vowed to stay away. Now if so-and-so lived in a property that he also owned, and the vowing-individual stayed there too, he would be liable. This is not because it is owned by so-and-so but it is because so-and-so was residing there. Conversely, if the vowing-individual stayed in a property owned by the so-and-so but not his actual residence, the vow would not be broken. Therefore, there is not a merging of al-ḥaqīqa and al-majāz here either. Rather the vow hinges on just the al-majāz, which is "the house that so-and-so is actually resident in".
3) In the third case, "the day so-and-so arrives", means at any time because the word *day*, when attached to a non-prolonged act, means any time. If it were associated with a prolonged act, it would mean

QUICK TERMS

الحقيقة: *al-ḥaqīqa*

The literal. A word coined by the lexicon for an item.

المجاز: *al-majāz*

The figurative. A word used for a meaning other than its coined meaning.

daylight. Examples of a non-prolonged act are to enter, leave or arrive. And examples of prolonged acts are riding, fasting or dining. As the emancipation of the slave was dependent upon the arrival of someone, his arrival is non-prolonged, so anytime the arrival occurs the slave is free. If the arrival is in daylight or during the night the freedom will occur. This is not due to a merger between al-ḥaqīqa and al-majāz rather it is because of the way the words themselves are used.

Text and Translation

ولئن قال: إذا حلف لا يضع قدمه في دار فلان يحنث لو دخلها حافيا أو متنعلا أو راكبا، وكذلك لو حلف لا يسكن دار فلان يحنث لو كانت الدار ملكا لفلان أو كانت بأجرة أو عارية وذلك جمع بين الحقيقة والمجاز، وكذلك لو قال :عبده حر يوم يقدم فلان فقدم فلان ليلا أو نهارا يحنث، قلنا: وضع القدم صار مجازاً ا عن الدخول بحكم العرف، والدخول لا يتفاوت في الفصلين ودار فلان صار مجاز ا عن دار مسكونة له وذلك لا يتفاوت بين أن يكون ملكاً له أو كانت بأجرة له، واليوم في مسئلة القدوم عبارة عن مطلق الوقت؛ لأن اليوم إذا أضيف إلى فعل لا يمتد يكون عبارة عن مطلق الوقت كما عرف فكان الحنث بهذا الطريق لا بطريق الجمع بين الحقيقة والمجاز

If one was to ask: when someone vowed he would not set foot in the house of so-and-so, he would have broken the vow by entering it barefooted, shod or mounted. Similarly, if one were to vow not to reside in so-and-so's house, he would have broken that vow if the house was owned, rented or borrowed by that person. This is merging both al-ḥaqīqa and al-majāz. Similarly, if one said his slave is free the day so-and-so arrives and the person arrives by night or day he will have broken the vow. We answer that setting-foot is al-majāz for entering in everyday usage, and an entrance is present in both (disputed) cases. The house of so-and-so is al-majāz for his place of residence and this is present whether it is owned or rented by him. As for the word 'day' in the case of the arrival, it means any time because when the word *al-yawm* is used in conjunction with a non-prolonged-act it denotes any time as is commonly known. So the breaking of the vow is in this way and not by way of merging both al-ḥaqīqa and al-majāz.

❖ ❖ ❖

QUICK TERMS

الحقيقة: *al-ḥaqīqa*

The literal. A word coined by the lexicon for an item.

المجاز: *al-majāz*

The figurative. A word used for a meaning other than its coined meaning.

QUICK ARABIC

اليوم: *al-yawm*

The day. A day of twenty-four hours.

QUICK DICTIONARY

Emancipate: *ih-man-suh-payt*

To free. To free a slave from bondage and servitude.

Shod: *shod*

To fit with a shoe. Past tense and past participle of shoe.

There are three types of al-ḥaqīqa: namely, al-muta'adhira, al-mahjūra and al-musta'mala.

al-Muta'adhira (impracticable) is, as its name suggests, a literal meaning that is absurd and so unrealistic that it is difficult to realise it. An example of it is if one said, "I will not eat from this tree". Eating or taking a bite from the tree is absurd but achievable though challenging. al-Mahjūra (disused) is, as its name suggests, a literal meaning that is no longer in common use. It is possible to realise the meaning but it is no longer used in that sense. An example of this is if one said, "I will not set-foot in his house". One is very capable of setting just his foot into a house without entering the rest of the body in the building, but this is not what is meant. The actual literal meaning is no longer applicable. al-Musta'mala (in use) is, as its name suggests, not only possible in its literal meaning but is also still in the common vocabulary of people. The ruling of the first two types is given as:

حكم الحقيقة المتعذرة والحقيقة المهجورة: يصار الى المجاز

"Ruling of al-ḥaqīqa al-muta'adhira and al-ḥaqīqa al-mahjūra is to proceed to a meaning of al-majāz."

This means that in both of the circumstances the literal meaning is abandoned and replaced with al-majāz. Therefore, in the case of al-muta'adhira if one vowed, "I will not eat from this tree" or "I will not eat this dish", we will proceed to the figurative understanding of 'the fruit of the tree' and 'the food-content of the dish'. Though it is possible for the individual to take a bite out of the tree or the dish it will not be understood to mean the tree itself or the dish itself, as they would be the impracticable literal meanings. Therefore, if the individual ate the fruit of the tree or the food-content of the dish, he would have broken the vow. Now, with a degree of discomfort if he was to bite into the tree itself or the dish itself, he would not have violated the vow because the literal meaning is not understood from the words.

Similarly, if one were to vow, "not to drink from the well", it would mean to scoop water out of the well using a tool or with his hands. Now, he would have broken the vow if he were to do either of these two things. The literal meaning of actually suspending himself down to the surface of the water in the well, to literally "drink from the well", would be an impracticable meaning. So, if he was to drink from the well directly, with great difficulty, he

QUICK TERMS

المتعذرة: *al-muta'adhira*

The impracticable. The coined meaning is unrealistic in the context.

المهجورة: *al-mahjūra*

The disused. The coined meaning is possible but is abandoned.

المستعملة: *al-musta'mala*

In use. The coined meaning is in common use, alongside a figurative meaning.

QUICK DICTIONARY

Impracticable: *im-prak-ti-kuh-buh l*

Not practical. Incapable of being put into practice with available means.

would not have violated his vow because al-ḥaqīqa is impracticable and the ruling is to proceed to al-majāz, which is to scoop water out.

Text and Translation

ثم الحقيقة أنواع ثلاثة: متعذرة ومهجورة ومستعملة، وفي القسمين الأولين يصار إلى المجاز بالاتفاق، ونظير المتعذرة إذا حلف لا يأكل من هذه الشجرة أو من هذه القِدر فإن أكل الشجرة أو القِدر متعذرة فينصرف ذلك إلى ثمرة الشجرة وإلى ما يحلّ في القِدر حتى لو أكل من عين الشجرة أو من عين القِدر بنوع تكلف لا يحنث، وعلى هذا قلنا: إذا حلف لا يشرب من هذه البير ينصرف ذلك إلى الاغتراف حتى لو فرضنا أنه لو كرع بنوع تكلف لا يحنث بالاتفاق

al-Ḥaqīqa has three types: al-muta'adhira (impracticable), al-mahjūra (disused) and al-musta'mala (in use). The first two cases will lead to al-majāz, unanimously. The example of al-muta'adhira is when one takes a vow not to eat of this tree or this pot, for eating the tree or the pot is impractical. So it will be deflected to be the fruits of the tree or what fills the pot, such that even if he awkwardly ate the tree itself or the pot itself, he would not have broken the vow. Based on this we said: if one vowed not to drink from this well, it would deflect to mean with a ladle such that if we assume that one awkwardly sipped it directly, it is unanimous that he would not have broken the vow.

❖❖❖

The example of al-ḥaqīqa al-mahjūra is vowing, "I will not set-foot in so-and-so's house". This will literally mean that whilst standing outside the person will not enter his foot into the house. This is not how people commonly understand the words 'set-foot'. The literal meaning has been abandoned. What they would understand is that this person does not want to *enter* the house of the other. Therefore, as the literal meaning is abandoned, the ruling is that we proceed to al-majāz, which is that he vows not to enter the person's house. So, the person will have only broken his promise if he enters the person's house and not by literally just placing his foot inside the house.

Similarly, the concept of argumentation is disliked in Islam. However, when a case is to be argued, in the Shariah and by general expectations, both parties are permitted to make an argument. It is as though al-ḥaqīqa is

QUICK TERMS

الحقيقة: *al-ḥaqīqa*

The literal. A word coined by the lexicon for an item.

المجاز: *al-majāz*

The figurative. A word used for a meaning other than its coined meaning.

المتعذرة: *al-muta'adhira*

The impracticable. The coined meaning is unrealistic in the context.

المهجورة: *al-mahjūra*

The disused. The coined meaning is possible but is abandoned.

المستعملة: *al-musta'mala*

In use. The coined meaning is in common use, alongside a figurative meaning.

abandoned in that particular circumstance making it al-ḥaqīqa al-mahjūra. Therefore, if one were to appoint a representative, *al-wakīl,* to argue a case on his or her behalf, it would be permitted because he is not asking for argumentation but for representation. Thus, the representative could respond on behalf of the appointer by affirming or denying because this is the general idea and common understanding of representation in an argument. The representative would not just agree to all the claims to avoid argumentation. Rather, the al-majāz of *responding* is what is required and he has authority to carry out this.

Text and Translation

ونظير المهجورة لو حلف لا يضع قدمه في دار فلان، فإن إرادة وضع القدم مهجورة عادة، وعلى هذا قلنا: التوكيل بنفس الخصومة ينصرف إلى مطلق جواب الخصم حتى يسع للوكيل أن يجيب بنعم كما يسعه أن يجيب بلا؛ لأنّ التوكيل بنفس الخصومة مهجور شرعا وعادة

The example of al-mahjūra is if one vowed not to set-foot in so-and-so's house. Intending *to place the foot* is disused in common usage. Based on this we said that representation in a dispute is construed to mean replying to a dispute such that it is permitted for the representative to reply with a 'yes' as it is permitted for him to reply with a 'no', as representation just for the sake of disputing is disused in Shariah and in practice.

❖ ❖ ❖

The remaining type of al-ḥaqīqa is al-musta'mala. This is a word that is still used in its designated meaning. There are two possibilities; there is a figurative al-majāz meaning which is also prevalently in use alongside the al-ḥaqīqa or there is not. If there is no prevalent al-majāz then it is agreed by all the scholars that the preferred meaning is al-ḥaqīqa. However, if al-ḥaqīqa also has a prevalent al-majāz there is a difference of opinion between Imam Abū Ḥanīfa ﷺ and the Ṣāḥibayn. Imam Abū Ḥanīfa ﷺ says that al-ḥaqīqa will still be preferred whilst the Ṣāḥibayn are of the opinion that *'umūm ul-majāz* will be preferred. *'Umūm ul-majāz* is a meaning which is common and inclusive of both al-ḥaqīqa and al-majāz. Imam Abū Ḥanīfa ﷺ says that al-majāz is just a replacement for al-ḥaqīqa, and when al-ḥaqīqa is in use there is no need to replace it with anything else. The Ṣāḥibayn say that words are used to give

QUICK TERMS

صاحبَين: *ṣāḥibayn*

The Two Colleagues. Imams Abū Yūsuf ﷺ and Muḥammad ﷺ

عموم المجاز: *'umūm ul-majāz*

A general metaphor. A meaning that incorporates both the literal and figurative.

QUICK ARABIC

الوكيل: *al-wakīl*

An agent. A person authorised to act on behalf of another.

meaning, and as both al-ḥaqīqa and al-majāz are in use both their meanings are relevant. Therefore, a meaning, which is inclusive of both, is to be selected; this is *'umūm ul-majāz*.

There are two examples given to highlight the difference of opinion regarding al-ḥaqīqa al-musta'mala when there is a prevalent al-majāz too. The first example is of *al-ḥinṭa*, wheat. The second example is of drinking from a specific river.

If one was to vow, "I will not eat this wheat", according to Imam Abū Ḥanīfa ﷺ it means the grains of the wheat as they are. Therefore, if one were to eat them raw or toasted, his vow would be broken. However, if he were to grind it into flour and eat a chapatti of that wheat the vow would not be broken. This is because normally people eat raw wheat or even prepare it as it is. This would be al-ḥaqīqa of his vow, "I will not eat wheat." People also grind wheat into flour and consume it as bread. This is al-majāz for the word *wheat* because we have given the product a new name. It is now known as bread or chapatti, and not as wheat. Bread and chapatti are recognisable and used. Imam Abū Ḥanīfa ﷺ says that whilst al-ḥaqīqa is in use, the meaning is what is required. The al-majāz is not required. The Ṣāḥibayn say that the vow mentions wheat, which is consumed by way of al-ḥaqīqa and al-majāz. Therefore, it is better to take a meaning, which will include them both. Therefore, the vow means *anything that contains this wheat*. This is *'umūm ul-majāz* of his vow, and as a consequence he will break his vow by eating the wheat raw, cooked, as bread or in any other way.

The second example is that one vows, "I will not drink from the Euphrates." al-Ḥaqīqa of this statement is that I will not step up to the flowing river named the Euphrates and drink from it. This is an understood and used meaning as many people approach the river and kneel over it to drink directly from it. *'Umūm ul-majāz* for the statement would be, "I will not drink from *the water of the Euphrates*", which can be achieved by directly drinking from it or from a cup that contains its water. According to Imam Abū Ḥanīfa ﷺ al-ḥaqīqa is in use, so the vow will only be broken if he drinks directly from the river, but not from the cup that contains its water. The Ṣāḥibayn say that both al-ḥaqīqa and al-majāz are in use, so *'umūm ul-majāz* will be used, and as a consequence he will break the vow by drinking directly from the river, by scooping the water in his hands, in a cup or by any other means.

QUICK TERMS

صاحبَين: *ṣāḥibayn*

The Two Colleagues. Imams Abū Yūsuf ﷺ and Muḥammad ﷺ

عموم المجاز: *'umūm ul-majāz*

A general metaphor. A meaning that incorporates both the literal and figurative.

الحقيقة: *al-ḥaqīqa*

The literal. A word coined by the lexicon for an item.

المجاز: *al-majāz*

The figurative. A word used for a meaning other than its coined meaning.

QUICK ARABIC

الحنطة: *al-ḥinṭa*

Wheat. The plant or grain of a cereal grass.

ولو كانت الحقيقة مستعملة فإن لم يكن لها مجاز متعارف فالحقيقة أولى بلا خلاف، وإن كان لها مجاز متعارف فالحقيقة أولى عند أبي حنيفة عليه الرحمة وعندهما العمل بعموم المجاز أولى، مثاله لو حلف لا يأكل من هذه الحنطة ينصرف ذلك إلى عينها عنده حتى لو أكل من الخبز الحاصل منها لا يحنث عنده، وعندهما ينصرف إلى ما تتضمنه الحنطة بطريق عموم المجاز فيحنث بأكلها وبأكل الخبز الحاصل منها، وكذا لو حلف لا يشرب من الفرات ينصرف إلى الشرب منها كرعا عنده وعندهما إلى عموم المجاز وهو شرب مائها بأي طريق كان

If al-ḥaqīqa is in use and there is no known al-majāz for it then al-ḥaqīqa is preferred without any difference of opinion. If it does have a known al-majāz for it then according to Abū Ḥanīfa, mercy be upon him, al-ḥaqīqa is preferred and according to Ṣāḥibayn *'umūm ul-majāz* is better. An example of it is if one vowed not to eat from this grain of wheat. According to him it will be taken to mean the grain itself, such that were he to eat from bread made of it he would not have broken the vow according to him. According to them two, the meaning will be taken to mean anything containing that wheat by way of *'umūm ul-majāz*. So he will have broken the vow by eating it itself or the bread made from it. Similarly, if one made an oath not to drink from the Euphrates river, it will be construed to mean sipping it directly according to him and according to them both, to the *'umūm ul-majāz* which is to drink its water by any means.

❖ ❖ ❖

The Three Grand Jurists, *al-aimma ath-thalātha*, differ regarding the exact mechanism by which al-majāz is to replace al-ḥaqīqa. They all agree that al-majāz is a replacement for al-ḥaqīqa and that the literal word must be intentional, as well as agreeing that both al-ḥaqīqa and al-majāz are properties of words and not meanings. The only point of contention is how and when the replacement can be carried out.

Imam Abū Ḥanīfa ﷺ holds the opinion that al-majāz replaces the very words that are al-ḥaqīqa. Therefore, when a sentence is grammatically correct, it meets the requirement to be replaced with al-majāz if the need arises. This is true whether al-ḥaqīqa is semantically applicable in reality or not. Now, if a

QUICK TERMS

الأئمة الثلاثة: *al-aimma ath-thalātha*

The Three Grand Jurists. Imams Abū Ḥanīfa ﷺ, Abū Yūsuf ﷺ and Muḥammad ﷺ.

المتعذرة: *al-muta'adhira*

The impracticable. The coined meaning is unrealistic in the context.

المهجورة: *al-mahjūra*

The disused. The coined meaning is possible but is abandoned.

المستعملة: *al-musta'mala*

In use. The coined meaning is in common use, alongside a figurative meaning.

QUICK DICTIONARY

Semantics: *si-man-tiks*

Meanings. Related to the study of words in relation to their meanings.

sentence is grammatically correct but cannot be applied for any reason, Imam Abū Ḥanīfa ﷺ says simply replace the words with its al-majāz counterpart. This will prevent the sentence from being invalid.

The Ṣāḥibayn, Imams Abū Yūsuf ﷺand Muḥammad ﷺ, say that al-majāz is to replace al-ḥaqīqa in application and not in terms of the words. This means we first apply the sentence with al-ḥaqīqa to see if it may hold true. If it could hold true but due to an external factor it is not the required meaning, only then do we move on to al-majāz as a replacement. In this way, al-majāz is not a replacement of the words of al-ḥaqīqa directly, but rather it is the replacement for the *al-ḥukm* and application of al-ḥaqīqa. In the case that al-ḥaqīqa does not hold true when applied, the Ṣāḥibayn simply nullify the statement.

The difference between the two opinions becomes evident through an example. If a young master was to address an elderly slave with "This is my son", Imam Abū Ḥanīfa ﷺ says the slave would be free. The Ṣāḥibayn say the sentence is invalid and therefore without consequence. Imam Abū Ḥanīfa ﷺ explains the emancipation by stating that the sentence, 'this is my son', is grammatically correct. The only issue for al-ḥaqīqa is that it cannot be true for whom it was intended because he is older in age, and so clearly not his son. In this case simply replace the words with al-majāz, as al-majāz replaces al-ḥaqīqa in terms of the words. In the context of slavery al-majāz for 'son' is freedom, because a son once under the ownership of a father would be free. It is as though he has said 'son' to mean freedom, because freedom is a necessary outcome of being a son. Therefore, the words the young master has in fact uttered are, "This is a free-man (son)". Imam Abū Ḥanīfa ﷺ has just replaced al-ḥaqīqa words with the al-majāz equivalent.

The reasoning of the Ṣāḥibayn is that al-majāz is the replacement for the *al-ḥukm* and application of al-ḥaqīqa, so we first apply al-ḥaqīqa of the sentence, 'this is my son'. We find that al-ḥaqīqa cannot be true because the claimer is younger than the one who he is calling son. As al-ḥaqīqa cannot be applied there is no method of replacing it with al-majāz. For al-majāz to be used, al-ḥaqīqa must first be applicable and then due to an external factor substituted with al-majāz. So, the sentence is invalidated due to the impossibility of al-ḥaqīqa and the inability to replace it with al-majāz; thus, the slave will not be free.

QUICK TERMS

صاحبَين: *ṣāḥibayn*

The Two Colleagues. Imams Abū Yūsuf ﷺ and Muḥammad ﷺ

الحقيقة: *al-ḥaqīqa*

The literal. A word coined by the lexicon for an item.

المجاز: *al-majāz*

The figurative. A word used for a meaning other than its coined meaning.

QUICK DICTIONARY

Emancipate: *ih-man-suh-payt*

To free. To free a slave from bondage and servitude.

ثم المجاز عند أبي حنيفة عليه الرحمة خلف عن الحقيقة في حق اللفظ وعندهما خلف عن الحقيقة في حق الحكم، حتى لو كانت الحقيقة ممكنة في نفسها إلا أنه امتنع العمل بها لمانع يصار إلى المجاز وإلا صار الكلام لغوا وعنده يصار إلى المجاز وإن لم تكن الحقيقة ممكنة في نفسها، مثاله إذا قال لعبده وهو أكبر سنا منه: هذا ابني لا يصار إلى المجاز عندهما لاستحالة الحقيقة وعنده يصار إلى المجاز حتى يعتق العبد

Then al-majāz, according to Abū Ḥanīfa, mercy be upon him, replaces al-ḥaqīqa in the word and according to them both it replaces al-ḥaqīqa in application. So if al-ḥaqīqa in itself is possible but not executable due to a preventative, it will become al-majāz, otherwise the statement will become void. According to him, it will become al-majāz even if al-ḥaqīqa itself is not possible. An example of it is if one says to his slave who is elder than him: "This is my son." According to them both it will not become al-majāz as al-ḥaqīqa is not possible. And according to him it becomes al-majāz and the slave will be free.

❖ ❖ ❖

Rulings will differ in some cases based on the previously stated differences between Imam Abū Ḥanīfa رحمه الله and the Ṣāḥibayn. Imam Abū Ḥanīfa رحمه الله said that al-majāz replaces al-ḥaqīqa in the words whilst the Ṣāḥibayn said it replaces it upon application.

The first case is if one confessed, "I or this wall owe him one thousand". Imam Abū Ḥanīfa رحمه الله considers this to imply al-majāz whilst the Ṣāḥibayn consider the statement invalid. The al-ḥaqīqa and literal meaning is that either the individual or the wall owes one thousand. As it is literally impossible for the wall to owe anything the Ṣāḥibayn consider the whole statement invalid and we cannot progress to a meaning of al-majāz. Therefore, this is not a confession to owing one thousand according to them both. Imam Abū Ḥanīfa رحمه الله permits progression to al-majāz by replacing the al-ḥaqīqa words, even though al-ḥaqīqa is not applicable itself. It is as though the person uttered al-majāz, so it will be a confession of owing one thousand. This is because the "or(*aw*)" will be in the al-majāz meaning of "and (*waw*)" and the sentence will be reintroduced as "I and this wall owe him one thousand." The ruling of *al-waw* in a sentence is that it conjoins two elements with no regard for order. Therefore, the confession will stand for the individual as a standalone sentence irrespective of the fact that the wall cannot owe anything.

The second case is if one confessed, "My slave or my donkey is free". As in the previous case, Imam Abū Ḥanīfa رحمه الله considers this to imply al-majāz whilst the Ṣāḥibayn consider the statement invalid. The al-ḥaqīqa and literal meaning is that either the slave or the donkey is free. As it is literally impossible for the donkey to be free, the Ṣāḥibayn consider the whole statement invalid and we cannot progress to a meaning of al-majāz. Therefore, this is not an announcement of emancipation according to them both. Imam Abū Ḥanīfa رحمه الله permits progression to al-majāz by replacing the al-ḥaqīqa words, even though al-ḥaqīqa is not applicable itself. It is as though the person uttered al-majāz, so it will be an announcement of emancipation of the slave. As in the previous case, this is because the "or(*aw*)" will be in the al-majāz meaning of "and (*waw*)" and the sentence will be reintroduced as "My slave and this donkey are free." The ruling of *al-waw* in a sentence is that it conjoins two elements with no regard for order. Therefore, the announcement will stand for the individual as a standalone sentence irrespective of the fact that the donkey is not in need of freedom.

Text and Translation

وعلى هذا يخرج الحكم في قوله: له على ألف أو على هذا الجدار وقوله: عبدي أو حماري حر

Based on this, the ruling will be derived for one's statement: "I or this wall owe him a thousand", and for one's statement: "My slave or my donkey is free."

❖ ❖ ❖

The section on al-ḥaqīqa and al-majāz concludes with an objection on the position held by Imam Abū Ḥanīfa رحمه الله He says that so long as the words are grammatically correct, and it is not possible to act upon al-ḥaqīqa due to an impediment, we must replace it with al-majāz to avoid the words becoming invalid. However, if one says, "This is my daughter", to his wife who has a known lineage to someone other than him, she is still lawful for him. Imam Abū Ḥanīfa رحمه الله does not consider replacing al-ḥaqīqa with al-majāz by stating that this statement equates to a divorce. In fact, Imam Abū Ḥanīfa رحمه الله says that this statement is invalid. It will remain invalid whether the woman in question is

QUICK TERMS

صاحبَين: *ṣāḥibayn*

The Two Colleagues. Imams Abū Yūsuf رحمه الله and Muḥammad رحمه الله

الحقيقة: *al-ḥaqīqa*

The literal. A word coined by the lexicon for an item.

المجاز: *al-majāz*

The figurative. A word used for a meaning other than its coined meaning.

older or younger than the husband. The statement, "This is my daughter", is grammatically correct, so according to the principles set, should we not replace it with al-majāz before stating that it is an invalid statement?

The answer to this objection is that though the statement is correct grammatically, it would void the marriage if true. If it would void the marriage then it would also invalidate a divorce, as divorce is a direct consequence of marriage. You cannot issue a legal divorce to someone you are not married to. As such, if the circumstance in which the sentence is spoken does not allow al-ḥaqīqa to be true, using al-ḥaqīqa as a figurative expression to mean a consequence that would render itself a non-existent is also not possible. Simply, if there is no marriage, then figuratively meaning divorce from the very same words would also be non-existent.

This answer can then be further queried by someone stating the following: 'being a son' invalidates ownership, in that a man cannot be a master to a slave son. This means that being a son is contradictory to an outcome of ownership, which is freedom. You have stated that when two things are contradictory in this manner then figurative expression and al-majāz cannot be formed between them. However, you have accepted this elsewhere. So, when one says, "This is my son", to a slave elder than himself, it should not equate to freedom also. However, Imam Abū Ḥanīfa رحمه الله accepted al-majāz in this case and stated the slave will be free.

The answer to this question is that being a son is not contradictory to ownership. This is to say that a father does become an owner of his slave son in accordance with the hadith that "whomsoever comes to own a close-relative, the relative will become free". A son is a close relative of a father, so if the father buys the slave-son he will become his master. Only after the ownership is established, the freedom will immediately follow. Therefore, if being a son is not contradictory to the father's ownership, then there is a valid relationship between the two. As that is the case, a figurative expression and al-majāz is permitted between the two. That is to say one can say "son" and expressively mean "freedom".

Text and Translation

ولا يلزم على هذا إذا قال لامرأته: هذه ابنتي ولها نسب معروف من غيره حيث لا تحرم عليه ولا يجعل

حديث

عن سمرة بن جندب رضي الله عنه فيما يحسب حماد قال قال رسول الله ﷺ من ملك ذا رحم محرم فهو حر.

عليه الصلاة والسلام

سنن أبي داود (3949)

QUICK TERMS

صاحبين: *ṣāḥibayn*

The Two Colleagues. Imams Abū Yūsuf رحمه الله and Muḥammad رحمه الله

الحقيقة: *al-ḥaqīqa*

The literal. A word coined by the lexicon for an item.

المجاز: *al-majāz*

The figurative. A word used for a meaning other than its coined meaning.

ذلك مجازاً عن الطلاق سواء كانت المرأة صغرى سناً منه أو كبرى؛ لأن هذا اللفظ لو صح معناه لكان منافيا للنكاح فيكون منافيا لحكمه وهو الطلاق، ولا استعارة مع وجود التنافي بخلاف قوله: هذا ابني فإن البنوة لا تنافي ثبوت الملك للأب بل يثبت الملك له ثم يعتق عليه.

This does not contradict with the one who was to say to his wife: "This is my daughter", whilst she has a known lineage other than his, that she becomes unlawful for him. Nor would this be al-majāz for divorce whether the woman is younger in age or older than him. This is because if the statement is correct it would negate the marriage and therefore negate its ruling which is divorce. There can be no figurative expression whilst there is a negation. This is unlike one's statement: "This is my son", as being a son does not negate the father's ownership rather it confirms it and so he becomes free.

❖ ❖ ❖

MEMORISE

Ḥanafī Principles (5)

	Term	Definition	Ruling	An Example
8	الحقيقة	كل لفظ وضعه واضع اللغة بإزاء شيء	- الحقيقة المتعذرة: يصار إلى المجاز بالاتفاق - الحقيقة المهجورة: يصار إلى المجاز بالاتفاق - الحقيقة المستعملة: إن كان لها مجاز متعارف فالحقيقة أولى عنده وعندهما العمل بعموم المجاز أولى. وإن لم يكن لها مجاز متعارف فالحقيقة أولى بلا خلاف.	- الحقيقة المتعذرة: إذا حلف لا يأكل من هذه الشجرة أو من هذه القِدر - الحقيقة المهجورة: لو حلف لا يضع قدمه في دار فلان - الحقيقة المستعملة: لو حلف لا يأكل من هذه الحنطة
9	المجاز	كل لفظ مستعمل في غير معناه الحقيقي	يصار إلى المجاز عند تعذر الحقيقة أو هجرتها	معنى "الدخول" بـ " لا يضع قدمه"

Summary Of al-Ḥaqīqa and al-Majāz

1. Definition of al-ḥaqīqa:

الحقيقة: كل لفظ وضعه واضع اللغة بإزاء شيء

"Every word coined by the lexicographer to represent something".

2. Definition of al-majāz:

المجاز: كل لفظ مستعمل في غير معناه الحقيقي

"Every word used in other than its coined meaning".

3. A word in one instance can be either al-ḥaqīqa or al-majāz; never both.

4. There are three types of al-ḥaqīqa:

i) al-Ḥaqīqat ul-muta'a<u>dh</u>ira: the improbable meaning. This is when the coined meaning is unrealistic in the context it is used. Like if someone said, "I will not drink from this well." The literal meaning is to drink directly from the well unaided. This is unrealistic, as normally you would use a bucket, pump or the cusped palms of the hand. Unaided drinking from the well is unrealistic. So, if one who vowed this statement was to suspend himself directly into the well and drink the water directly, the oath would not be broken as the metaphoric meaning of aided drinking is set.

ii) al-Ḥaqīqat ul-mahjūra: the abandoned meaning. This is that the coined meaning is possible but is not acted upon. Like if someone vowed not to "step into so-and-so's house". It will not mean the literal step. Rather, the metaphorical "I will not enter" will be understood.

iii) al-Ḥaqīqat ul-musta'mala: the meaning in use. This is that the coined meaning is in common use, as is the metaphorical meaning. Like someone says, "I vow not to eat wheat". It could imply the literal eating of raw wheat or the metaphorical flour, paste or bread. Both are possibilities.

5. The ruling of both al-ḥaqīqat ul-muta'a<u>dh</u>ira and al-ḥaqīqat ul-mahjūra:

يصار إلى المجاز بالاتفاق

"Avert to a metaphorical meaning, unanimously".

6. The ruling of al-ḥaqīqat ul-musta'mala:

i) If it has a recognised metaphorical meaning, Imam Abū Ḥanīfa رحمه الله says the literal meaning is preferred. The Two Colleagues say *'umūm ul-majāz* (a general metaphor) will be used.

ii) If there is no recognised metaphorical meaning the literal is preferred, without disagreement.

7. The ruling of *al-majāz*:

يصار إلى المجاز عند تعذر الحقيقة أو هجرها

"The metaphorical will be used when the literal is improbable or abandoned".

1.2.2 Methods of al-Isti'āra

Chapter 1.2 is about word usage. Figure 1.2-01 showed that word usage has four key terms associated with it. The discussion of al-ḥaqīqa and al-majāz was in section 1.2.1, and the details of aṣ-ṣarīḥ and al-kināya are in section 1.2.3, later in the book. Here in this section we are introduced to methods of al-isti'āra before we proceed with further discussions on word usage.

The reason for bringing this discussion here is that the previous section, 1.2.1, introduced us to the idea of al-ḥaqīqa and al-majāz, but more information is required to know the exact connection between the two. When can a word legitimately change from its literal meaning to one that is a figurative expression? Can someone just say a word with a known meaning and then say "no, I actually meant another thing but chose to express it in this way". Clearly, that would be absurd as anyone could say anything and explain it away as a figurative expression. Therefore, there is a mechanism of allowing figurative expressions, al-majāz, once certain criteria are met between it and al-ḥaqīqa. This is called al-isti'āra. We will in the next section 1.2.3 return to the overall discussion of word usage and the remaining two terms of aṣ-ṣarīḥ and al-kināya.

According to jurists al-isti'āra and al-majāz are synonymous, however a rhetor would disagree with the jurist and consider the two to be different. This means that according to the jurist when there is a valid reason to use a word in other than its literal and coined meaning, the used expression can be called al-majāz or al-isti'āra. They are the same.

Uṣūl ush-Shāshī has mentioned two ways in which al-isti'āra is permitted. One is that al-ḥaqīqa and the intended meaning are connected by way of *al-'illa* and its outcome, al-ma'lūl. The other is when the coined al-ḥaqīqa connects to the intended meaning by *as-sabab* and its outcome, al-musabbab.

To understand this let us first look at the definitions of both *al-'illa* and *as-sabab*. *al-'illa* is defined in the Shariah as follows:

العلة: ما يكون واسطة بين السبب والحكم

"*al-'illa* is the means between *as-sabab* and the outcome."

This means that *al-'illa* is the immediate medium and apparatus by which an outcome is achieved. So, by way of example, water is extracted from a well using a bucket. The bucket is directly involved in scooping out the water and

QUICK TERMS

الحقيقة: *al-ḥaqīqa*

The literal. A word coined by the lexicon for an item.

المجاز: *al-majāz*

The figurative. A word used for a meaning other than its coined meaning.

الصريح: *aṣ-ṣarīḥ*

The unequivocal. A word or phrase with a clear and palpable meaning.

الكناية: *al-kināya*

The concealed. A word or phrase that has a concealed and hidden meaning. Such as a metaphor.

الاستعارة: *al-isti'āra*

The figurative. Synonymous with al-majāz.

العلة: *al-'illa*

The means. The method or instrument used to attain an end.

المعلول: *al-ma'lūl*

The effect. The outcome and end with respect to the method and instrument used.

thus is *al-'illa* for how the outcome of extracting water was achieved. The outcome or *al-ḥukm*, when considered in relation to *al-'illa* will be called al-ma'lūl.

as-sabab is defined in the Shariah as follows:

السبب: ما يكون طريقا إلى الحكم بواسطة

"*as-sabab* is the channel to the outcome using a means."

This means that *as-sabab* is the pathway and manner in which the actual means, *al-'illa*, managed to give us the outcome. So, continuing the same example of extracting water from a well using a bucket, we would say that the means by which the bucket was able to scoop up the water is the rope. The rope would be *as-sabab* for the outcome of extracting water from the well. The outcome or *al-ḥukm*, when considered in relation to *as-sabab* is called al-musabbab.

In another example, such as walking to a destination, we would say *as-sabab* is the suitability of the pathway for walking as this is what allows that particular means of travel; *al-'illa* is walking as that is the means that allows the outcome to be realised; and the outcome and *al-ḥukm* is arriving at the destination. So, arrival at the destination is al-musabbab in relation to *as-sabab*, the pathway, whilst also being al-ma'lūl in relation to *al-'illa*, which is walking.

Bearing this in mind, the ruling of al-isti'āra is given as follows:

حكم الاستعارة: يوجب صحة الاستعارة من الطرفين بين العلة والحكم و يوجب صحتها من السبب للحكم

"The ruling of al-isti'āra is that it is permitted both ways between *al-'illa* and its outcome, and it is permitted from *as-sabab* to its outcome."

This means that one can say a word that is *al-'illa* and as al-majāz intend the meaning of al-ma'lūl, and vice versa by uttering al-ma'lūl and figuratively intending *al-'illa*. However, one can also say a word that is *as-sabab* and as al-majāz intend the meaning of al-musabbab, but the reverse is not permitted. So, one cannot utter al-musabbab and figuratively intend *as-sabab*.

The reason for this is that *al-'illa* is inseparable from al-ma'lūl, and vice versa. Therefore, the bucket will directly scoop up the water, and the walking will directly enable arrival at the destination. Due to this immediate and direct

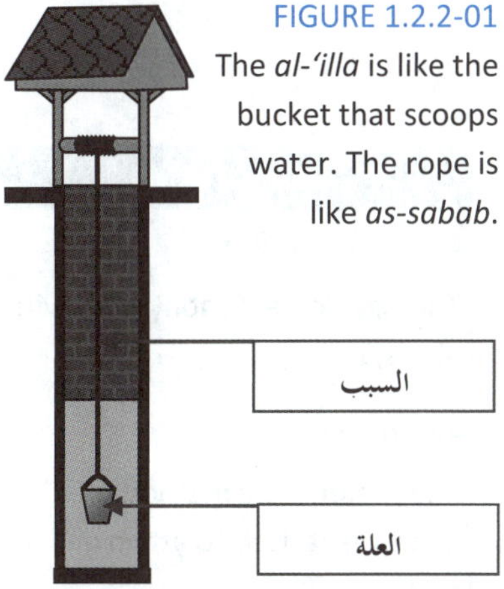

FIGURE 1.2.2-01
The *al-'illa* is like the bucket that scoops water. The rope is like *as-sabab*.

QUICK TERMS

السبب: *as-sabab*

The channel. The route and way in which the means attains the end.

المسبب: *al-musabbab*

The effect. The outcome and end with respect to the route and way it is achieved.

QUICK DICTIONARY

Rhetor: *ret-er*
A master of rhetoric. Rhetoric is the study of effectively using language.

Jurist: *joo r-ist*
Versed in law. An individual experienced as a scholar of the law.

connection, the two are interchangeable. However, the rope will enable the bucket to scoop up the water from the well, and the suitable pathway will allow walking to enable arrival at the destination. Notice that neither the rope nor the pathway, are directly responsible for the outcome in each case. Due to this indirect connection, the source and effective cause can figuratively mean the outcome because *al-'illa* must have been present to reach the outcome. However, when we try to reverse this and connect the outcome to *as-sabab* it is not necessary that *al-'illa* is present. This is because it is possible that the outcome before us was achieved in another way that does not include this *as-sabab*. More details on this will follow in chapter 5.1, page 419.

Text and Translation

فصل في تعريف طريق الاستعارة: اعلم أنّ الاستعارة في أحكام الشرع مطردة بطريقين أحدهما لوجود الاتصال بين العلة والحكم والثاني لوجود الاتصال بين السبب المحض والحكم، فالأول منهما يوجب صحة الاستعارة من الطرفين والثاني يوجب صحتها من أحد الطرفين وهو استعارة الأصل للفرع

Chapter on defining the method of al-isti'āra: Understand that al-isti'āra in the rulings of Shariah are expressed in two ways; one of them is due to a connection between *al-'illa* and its outcome, and the second is due to a connection between *as-sabab al-maḥḍ* and its outcome. The former of the two allows al-isti'āra from both sides and the latter allows it from one side which is to use the source and intend its resultant.

Textual Assistance

السبب المحض — The reason the text includes the word *al-maḥḍ* is to indicate that this is the literal and genuine *as-sabab* and not in the figurative sense. It is very common to use the word *as-sabab* figuratively in the meaning of *al-'illa*. The text wishes to make it clear that this is *as-sabab* in its literal sense.

❖ ❖ ❖

After introducing the two methods of al-isti'āra and their relative rulings, we are now presented with case examples of each of them. Details of al-

QUICK TERMS

الاستعارة: *al-isti'āra*

The figurative. Synonymous with al-majāz.

العلة: *al-'illa*

The means. The method or instrument used to attain an end.

المعلول: *al-ma'lūl*

The effect. The outcome and end with respect to the method and instrument used.

السبب: *as-sabab*

The channel. The route and way in which the means attains the end.

المسبب: *al-musabbab*

The effect. The outcome and end with respect to the route and way it is achieved.

الحقيقة: *al-ḥaqīqa*

The literal. A word coined in the lexicon for an item .

المجاز: *al-majāz*

The figurative. A word used for a meaning other than its coined meaning.

isti'āra between *al-'illa* and al-ma'lūl, and vice versa, is given first, then this is followed by al-isti'āra between *as-sabab* and al-musabbab.

The example concerns two words, the Arabic word for ownership *al-milk*, and the Arabic word for purchasing *a<u>sh</u>-<u>sh</u>irā*. The connection between the two words is of *al-'illa* and al-ma'lūl because purchasing, *a<u>sh</u>-<u>sh</u>irā*, is the direct cause of ownership, *al-milk*. Immediately after purchasing an item one would become the owner of it. Due to this relationship between the two words one can be figuratively used to mean the other, so al-isti'āra is permitted from both sides. The author first presents both words in their literal meaning to show that both words give rise to different rulings. Only then does he state that one can be replaced with the other should one intend it.

In a literal sense if one was to say, "If I own a slave, he is free", only to buy half a slave and then sell that share on. Later, he bought the other half share of the slave, this half share of the slave will not be free; nor will the first half. The reason for this is that normally when people say, "I own something" it does not mean I own a share of it. The norm is that when one uses the word of ownership, it is understood to mean entire ownership. Ownership does not ordinarily increase gradually. So his statement of "If I own a slave, he is free" will not have enabled the emancipation of the first half of the slave because he sold him on and no longer has a right over that half, and similar for the second half as he does not own a whole slave, this half will not be free either.

Contrast the above with one who says in a literal sense, "If I purchase a slave, he is free", only to buy half a slave and then sell that share on. Later, he bought the other half share of the slave; this half share of the slave will be free. The difference is that it is quite normal to purchase something in instalments. Therefore, if one says, "I purchased something" it is commonly acceptable for this to be just an initial instalment with other instalments to follow. Bearing this in mind, his statement "If I purchase a slave, he is free" has occurred in instalments. So, the first half share of the slave will not be free as he sold it on and no longer has a right over it, but the second half share of the slave will become free as he will have purchased a slave, be it in instalments.

The above two cases are presented with both *al-milk* and *a<u>sh</u>-<u>sh</u>irā* used with a meaning of al-ḥaqīqa. It is permitted that the one who said that statement could have used al-majāz in either case by way of al-isti'āra, such that 'ownership' meant 'purchase' and vice versa. Though this is linguistically

QUICK ARABIC

الملك: *al-milk*

Ownership. To have the legal right of possession.

الشراء: *a<u>sh</u>-<u>sh</u>irā*

Purchasing. To acquire by the payment of money or its equivalent.

QUICK DICTIONARY

Emancipate: *ih-man-suh-payt*
To free. To free a slave from bondage and servitude.

permitted, as there is an *al-'illa* and al-ma'lūl connection between the two words, the author highlights that in a court of law the judge will only allow it when it works against the issuer of the statement. So in the case of the statement "If I own a slave, he is free" we stated that both halves of the slave will not be free, but the verdict will be given that the second half is free just like if the statement had been "If I purchase a slave, he is free". This is because the issuer of the statement is set to benefit on the basis of his intention, and thus a man will not be granted freedom should we take the intention into consideration. Therefore, the verdict will be against the issuer of the statement but it will be acknowledged by the court that despite the negative verdict the integrity of the issuer is upheld. The reason why the slave will be free is a matter of integrity and not because al-isti'āra is invalid from both sides.

Text and Translation

مثال الأول فيما إذا قال: إن ملكت عبدا فهو حر فملك نصف العبد فباعه ثم ملك النصف الآخر لم يعتق؛ إذ لم يجتمع في ملكه كل العبد، ولو قال: إن اشتريت عبدا فهو حر فاشترى نصف العبد فباعه ثم اشترى النصف الآخر عتق النصف الثاني ولو عنى بالملك الشراء أو بالشراء الملك صحت نيته بطريق المجاز؛ لأن الشراء علة الملك والملك حكمه فعمت الاستعارة بين العلة والمعلول من الطرفين إلا أنه فيما يكون تخفيفا في حقه لا يصدق في حق القضاء خاصة لمعنى التهمة لا لعدم صحة الاستعارة

The example of the first is when one said: "If I own a slave, he shall be free." So he owned half a slave and then sold it. Then he became an owner of the second half; it will not be free, as he has not owned the whole of the slave. And should he have said: "If I buy a slave, he shall be free." So he bought half a slave and then sold it. Then he bought the second half; the second half will be free. If he intended ownership to mean purchasing or vice versa, the intention will be valid by way of al-majāz. This is because purchasing is *al-'illa* for ownership and ownership is its outcome. So al-isti'āra between *al-'illa* and al-ma'lūl is common to both sides, except that when there is leniency in his favour he will not be believed in jurisdictions due to integrity, not due to the impermissibility of al-isti'āra.

❖❖❖

QUICK TERMS

الاستعارة: *al-isti'āra*

The figurative. Synonymous with al-majāz.

العلة: *al-'illa*

The means. The method or instrument used to attain an end.

المعلول: *al-ma'lūl*

The effect. The outcome and end with respect to the method and instrument used.

السبب: *as-sabab*

The channel. The route and way in which the means attains the end.

المسبب: *al-musabbab*

The effect. The outcome and end with respect to the route and way it is achieved.

المجاز: *al-majāz*

The figurative. A word used for a meaning other than its coined meaning.

The second type of al-isti'āra is between *as-sabab* and its consequence, al-musabbab. This was introduced earlier and we were told that the ruling concerning it is that it is permitted from the cause, *as-sabab*, to the resulting consequence, al-musabbab, and not the other way around. The example of this type is given through two words, *at-taḥrīr* meaning freedom, and *aṭ-ṭalāq* meaning divorce. If one says to his wife, "I have freed you" and intended the meaning of divorce it will be valid. This is because the literal meaning understood from the word 'free' is that one has relinquished authority over the other, and this in turn would mean that there is also no longer a right of gratification with that person. In other words, by saying "you are free" in a literal sense the issuer would no longer have a right of ownership over that person if the person was a slave, and by virtue of this could not now gratify themselves with that person. This means that *at-taḥrīr* is *as-sabab* for diminishing the right of gratification, *zawālu milk il-muta'a*. The word for freedom, *at-taḥrīr*, is not assigned for this meaning nor is it ordinarily connected to this meaning, rather it is leading to this meaning like a pathway or medium. This is the very definition of *as-sabab*; something that is a mere means to an outcome. Therefore, the word 'free' is *as-sabab* and 'divorce' is al-musabbab, and as the ruling stated that al-isti'āra is permitted by stating *as-sabab* and intending al-musabbab, so we ruled that divorce would occur if the husband intended it.

Text and Translation

ومثال الثاني إذا قال لامرأته: حررتك ونوى به الطلاق يصح؛ لأن التحرير بحقيقته يوجب زوال ملك البضع بواسطة زوال ملك الرقبة فكان سببا محضا لزوال ملك المتعة فجاز أن يستعار عن الطلاق الذي هو مزيل لملك المتعة

The example of the second is if one said to his wife: "I have freed you", whilst intending divorce; it will occur, because freedom in reality necessitates the diminishing of ownership of the private parts by way of diminishing ownership of a person. So it is a mere cause for the diminishing of the right of gratification. So to figuratively use it for divorce is permitted which is the same as diminishing the right of gratification.

❖ ❖ ❖

QUICK ARABIC

زوال ملك المتعة: *zawālu milk il-mut'a*

Diminished right of gratification. When one no longer has the right to the benefits of an owner.

التحرير: *at-taḥrīr*

Freedom. The state of not being confined or restrained.

الطلاق: *aṭ-ṭalāq*

Divorce. A release from the marriage tie, it can be revocable or irrevocable.

The previous section gives rise to a tangential question, which does not directly concern our principle. Uṣūl ush-Shāshī looks to dispel the concern before continuing its discussion on al-isti'āra. The question is that we have said that using the word *free* figuratively to mean *divorce* is acceptable because al-isti'āra is permitted from *as-sabab* to al-musabbab. When one word replaces another in this manner of al-majāz, it should also have all the options available that would normally be available. So, should this not then mean that the word *free* takes on the full functions of the word *divorce*, in that there is an option to deliver a revocable *ar-raj'ī* divorce as well as an irrevocable *al-bāin* divorce? This does not seem to be the case because in Ḥanafī Fiqh it states that the divorce issued by the word *free* only results in an irrevocable *al-bāin* divorce.

The Aḥnāf reply to this query by making it clear that the word *free* is not *as-sabab* for all types of divorce, rather it is just *as-sabab* for the divorce that will result in *zawālu milk il-muta'a*; that is the diminishing of the right to benefit. The right to benefit truly diminishes only in the divorce that is *al-bāin* because the husband is not permitted to return to his wife. In a *ar-raj'ī* divorce, however, we do not consider the right to benefit to have diminished entirely. That is why the husband is permitted to return to his wife after it has been issued. So, as the word *at-taḥrīr* is al-majāz for *zawālu milk il-muta'a* by way of al-isti'āra, and as *zawālu milk il-muta'a* is a function of aṭ-ṭalāq *al-bāin* and not *aṭ-ṭalāq ar-raj'ī*, we conclude that the words "I have freed you" will result in an irrevocable *al-bāin* divorce, when intended for divorce.

Text and Translation

ولا يقال: لو جعل مجازا عن الطلاق لوجب أن يكون الطلاق الواقع به رجعيا كصريح الطلاق؛ لأنا نقول لا نجعله مجازا عن الطلاق بل عن المزيل لملك المتعة وذلك في البائن؛ إذ الرجعي لا يزيل ملك المتعة عندنا

It should not be queried that if you have made it al-majāz for *aṭ-ṭalāq* then the divorce that occurs should be revocable like it is in an explicit *aṭ-ṭalāq*, because we will reply: we do not make it al-majāz for *aṭ-ṭalāq*, rather it is for diminishing the right of gratification. This is found only in the irrevocable divorce; because the revocable does not diminish the right of gratification according to us.

❖❖❖

QUICK ARABIC

الطلاق: *aṭ-ṭalāq*

Divorce. A release from the marriage tie, it can be revocable or irrevocable.

الرجعي: *ar-raj'ī*

The revocable. A divorce after which the husband has a right to return to the marriage.

البائن: *al-bāin*

The irrevocable. A divorce after which a husband cannot unilaterally return to the marriage.

التحرير: *at-taḥrīr*

Freedom. The state of not being confined or restrained.

النكاح: *an-nikāḥ*

Conjunction. In legal terms it is the marriage contract.

After dealing with the tangential issue, we return to the discussion of al-isti'āra, and in particular the fact that al-isti'āra between *as-sabab* and al-musabbab is only permitted one way. Therefore, bearing in mind that the word for *freedom, at-taḥrīr*, is *as-sabab* and the word for *an irrevocable divorce, aṭ-ṭalāq ul-bāin*, is al-musabbab, if a master says to his slave-girl, "I divorce you" and intends to free her, it will not suffice. This is because *as-sabab* can be used to mean the resultant but not the other way around.

Moreover, for the same reason we say that we are able to conduct a marriage by using words such as *al-hiba* (to gift), *at-tamlīk* (to own) or *al-bay'* (to sell). Therefore, if a woman was to say to a man, in the presence of two witnesses, "I gift myself to you", and the man accepted, the marriage will be valid. Similarly, the marriage would be valid if she says, "I enter myself into your serfdom" or "I sell myself to you". This is because each of these words is *as-sabab* and *an-nikāḥ* with the right of gratification is al-musabbab. *al-Hiba* grants the recipient of the gift the right of use, whilst in the case of slave-girls this would allow the right of gratification, which is the idea of marriage. Therefore, *al-hiba* can lead to *an-nikāḥ,* but it is not directly linked to it because not everything that is gifted is eligible for marriage. Therefore, as *al-hiba* is *as-sabab* it can be used to mean *an-nikāḥ*, which is its *as-sabab* and thus the marriage will be valid. A similar chain of thought will result in both *al-milk* and *al-bay'*, so both will be valid for the marriage to take place.

The reverse of this is impermissible. Therefore, if one were to try to gift, own or sell something using the word *an-nikāḥ*, it would be unacceptable. This is because it is not permissible to say al-musabbab and mean al-sabab.

Text and Translation

ولو قال لأمته: طلقتك ونوى به التحرير لا يصح؛ لأنّ الأصل جاز أن يثبت به الفرع وأما الفرع فلا يجوز أن يثبت به الأصل؛ وعلى هذا نقول: ينعقد النكاح بلفظ الهبة والتمليك والبيع؛ لأن الهبة بحقيقتها توجب ملك الرقبة وملك الرقبة يوجب ملك المتعة في الأماء فكانت الهبة سببا محضاً لثبوت ملك المتعة فجاز أن يستعار عن النكاح، وكذلك لفظ التمليك والبيع ولا ينعكس حتى لا ينعقد البيع والهبة بلفظ النكاح

QUICK TERMS

الاستعارة: *al-isti'āra*

The figurative. Synonymous with al-majāz.

العلة: *al-'illa*

The means. The method or instrument used to attain an end.

المعلول: *al-ma'lūl*

The effect. The outcome and end with respect to the method and instrument used.

السبب: *as-sabab*

The channel. The route and way in which the means attains the end.

المسبب: *al-musabbab*

The effect. The outcome and end with respect to the route and way it is achieved.

المجاز: *al-majāz*

The figurative. A word used for a meaning other than its coined meaning.

If one said to his slave-girl: "I divorce you", whilst intending freedom, it will not be valid. This is because the cause can be used to establish the resultant but the resultant cannot be used to establish the cause. Based on this we say that marriage is valid with the words of *al-hiba*, *at-tamlīk* or *al-bay`*. As *al-hiba* in its literal meaning grants ownership of the individual. Ownership of the individual grants the right of gratification in slave girls. So *al-hiba* is the mere cause of establishing the right of gratification, therefore it can be used figuratively for marriage; similar are the words *at-tamlīk* and *al-bay`*. The reverse is not valid such that a selling or a gifting are invalid with the word for *an-nikāḥ*.

❖❖❖

The section concludes by stating that when al-majāz is used in a situation, there is no need to consider the intention. There is also a query directed at the Ṣāḥibayn and their answer is provided.

There is no need to consider the intention when al-majāz is used because the intention is to differentiate between two or more possibilities. However, when al-majāz is already taken as the given meaning, there are no other possibilities, so the intention is not required.

The query directed at the Ṣāḥibayn is that previously it was stated that according to them it was necessary for al-ḥaqīqa to be applicable before one can replace it with al-majāz should an impediment obstruct al-ḥaqīqa [see page 77]. However, we see in the examples provided in the previous section that when a free-woman says "I gift or sell myself to you", the Ṣāḥibayn accept that this will be valid as al-majāz for marriage. How can this be when the literal meaning of a free-woman being gifted or sold is not permitted? As al-ḥaqīqa is not possible, the statement should be void according to them, rather than enacting al-majāz because of it.

They reply that it is not impossible for a free-woman to come to be sold or gifted, eventually. They say if a free-woman was to abandon her faith and migrate to the land of non-believers and the Muslims captured her as a prisoner of war. She would come into the ownership of Muslims, and selling or gifting her would be possible. This means that for her to be sold or gifted is not an impossibility, so we are permitted to replace the literal meaning with a figurative one, which is to replace *selling* and *gifting* with *marriage*. This type of *possibility* is the same as if one was to make a vow using words such as "I vow to

QUICK ARABIC

النكاح: *an-nikāḥ*

Conjunction. In legal terms it is the marriage contract.

الهبة: *al-hiba*

To gift. To voluntarily give something without expecting compensation.

التمليك: *at-tamlīk*

To grant ownership. To have the legal right of possession.

البيع: *al-bay'*

To sell. To transfer to another in exchange for money.

الكفارة: *al-kaffāra*

Expiation. The prescribed atonement for neglected duties.

touch the sky"; though this vow is near impossible but expiation would still be necessary. It is normally the case that when someone makes an impossible vow, it is null, but the likes of these are possible through miracles. Therefore, the scholars give the verdict that though these are impossible a miracle could enable them. A miracle would make them possible, and as the one making the vow did not make the miracle happen, *al-kaffāra* and expiation must be paid.

Text and Translation

ثم في كل موضع يكون المحل متعينا لنوع من المجاز لا يحتاج فيه إلى النية، لا يقال: وَ لما كان إمكان الحقيقة شرطاً لصحة المجاز عندهما كيف يصار إلى المجاز في صورة النكاح بلفظ الهبة مع أن تمليك الحرة بالبيع والهبة محال؛ لأنا نقول: ذلك ممكن في الجملة بأن ارتدت ولحقت بدار الحرب ثم سبيت، وصار هذا نظير مس السماء وأخواته

Then on every occasion the place of the appropriate al-majāz is fixed; it doesn't require an intention. It shouldn't be queried: that according to them both the workability of al-ḥaqīqa is a condition for the validity of al-majāz, so how have you figuratively validated marriage with the word for gift when ownership and gifting of a free-woman is invalid? As we will reply: it is possible in principle such that were she to apostate and emigrate to hostile territory and then be captured. This is like 'touching the sky' and the likes.

❖ ❖ ❖

QUICK TERMS

الحقيقة: *al-ḥaqīqa*

The literal. A word coined by the lexicon for an item.

المجاز: *al-majāz*

The figurative. A word used for a meaning other than its coined meaning.

صاحبين: *Ṣaḥibayn*

The Two Colleagues. Imams Abū Yūsuf رحمه الله and Muḥammad رحمه الله

Ḥanafī Principles (6)

MEMORISE

	Term	Definition	Ruling	An Example
10	الاستعارة	استعمال كلمة بدل أخرى لعلاقة التعليل أو السببية	– يجوز من الطرفين بين العلة والحكم – يجوز من السبب للحكم – إذا تعين الاستعارة لا يحتاج فيه إلى النية	– مثال التعليل: العلاقة بين كلمة "التمليك" وكلمة "الشراء" – مثال السببية: العلاقة بين كلمة "التحرير" وكلمة "الطلاق"

Summary Of Methods of al-Isti'āra

1. al-Isti'āra is synonymous with al-majāz.

2. Definition of al-isti'āra is:

   الاستعارة: استعمال كلمة بدل أخرى لعلاقة التعليل أو السببية

   "To use a word in place of another word due to a connection of al-'illa and al-ma'lūl or as-sabab and al-musabbab, between them."

3. Definition of al-'illa is:

   العلة: ما يكون واسطة بين السبب والحكم

   "al-'Illa is the means between al-sabab and the outcome."

4. Definition of as-sabab is:

   السبب: ما يكون طريقا إلى الحكم بواسطة

   "as-Sabab is the channel to the outcome using a means."

5. Ruling of al-isti'āra is:

   حكم الاستعارة: يوجب صحة الاستعارة من الطرفين بين العلة والحكم و يوجب صحتها من السبب للحكم

   "The ruling of al-isti'āra is that it is permitted both ways between al-'illa and its outcome, and it is permitted from as-sabab to its outcome."

6. An example of al-isti'āra using al-'illa and al-ma'lūl is the interchangeable use of the words 'ملكتُ' and 'اشتريتُ'.

7. An example of al-isti'āra using as-sabab and al-musabbab is the use of the word 'التحرير' to mean 'الطلاق'; but not the other way around.

8. When al-isti'āra is determined to have been used, the intention is not taken into consideration because the intention is to select between two or more possibilities.

1.2.3 aṣ-Ṣarīḥ and al-Kināya

Chapter 1.2 is about word usage. Figure 1.2-01 summarised the division of word usage and highlighted the relationship between the four key terms of the chapter. Section 1.2.1 discussed al-ḥaqīqa (the literal) and al-majāz (the figurative), whilst section 1.2.2 was about methods of al-isti'āra. Here, in this section, we will be looking at the remaining two primary terms in this chapter, namely aṣ-ṣarīḥ (the unequivocal) and al-kināya (the equivocal).

The definition of aṣ-ṣarīḥ is:

الصريح: لفظ يكون المراد به ظاهرا

"aṣ-Ṣarīḥ is a word with a clear intent."

This means that the moment one expresses the word, it clearly states its intended purpose and meaning. The examples of this include statements such as "I sold it" and "I bought it". It is clear which act took place and who was responsible for it. The statements are said to be aṣ-ṣarīḥ.

The ruling of aṣ-ṣarīḥ is:

حكم الصريح: يوجب ثبوت معناه بأي طريق كان؛ نوى به ذلك المعنى أو لم ينو

"The ruling of aṣ-ṣarīḥ is that its meaning must be enacted from any form, whether one intended that meaning for it or not."

This means that the understanding expressed by aṣ-ṣarīḥ will be established regardless of how it is delivered. It can form a major part of a sentence or even be an attribute. Furthermore, because it clearly gives its meaning, the intention of the one expressing it becomes redundant. So, this means that divorce will occur irrespective of the intention of the individual in sentences such as, "You are divorced", with the aṣ-ṣarīḥ word of divorce forming part of a exclamatory sentence in the Arabic. This also holds true if one said, "I divorced you", with the aṣ-ṣarīḥ word of divorce used in the Arabic verb form; or if one said, "O divorced one", with the aṣ-ṣarīḥ word of divorce used in the vocative form.

Equally, if one intentionally or accidently said to his slave, "You are free", "I freed you", or "O free one", in all cases the slave will be free. This is because the word for freedom is aṣ-ṣarīḥ, so it must be accounted for with or without an intention.

QUICK TERMS

الصريح: *aṣ-ṣarīḥ*

The unequivocal. A word or phrase with a clear and palpable meaning.

الكناية: *al-kināya*

The concealed. A word or phrase that has a concealed and hidden meaning. A metaphor.

الحقيقة: *al-ḥaqīqa*

The literal. A word coined by the lexicon for an item.

المجاز: *al-majāz*

The figurative. A word used for a meaning other than its coined meaning.

الاستعارة: *al-isti'āra*

The figurative. Synonymous with al-majāz.

QUICK GRAMMAR

جملة إنشائية: *jumla inshāīya*

Exclamatory sentence. A sentence that is not declarative.

النداء: *an-nidā*

Vocative form. Words used for calling or addressing.

الفعل: *al-fi'l*

Verb form. Words that express actions in a tense.

فصل في الصريح والكناية: الصريح لفظ يكون المراد به ظاهرا، كقوله: بعت واشتريت وأمثاله، وحكمه أنه يوجب ثبوت معناه بأي طريق كان من إخبار أو نعت أو نداء، ومن حكمه أنه يستغني عن النية، وعلى هذا قلنا :إذا قال لامرأته: أنت طالق أو طلقتك أو يا طالق يقع الطلاق نوى به الطلاق أو لم ينو، وكذا لو قال لعبده: أنت حر أو حررتك أو يا حر

Chapter on aṣ-ṣarīḥ and al-kināya: aṣ-Ṣarīḥ is a word with a clear intent. Like one saying: I sold, I bought and the likes. Its ruling is that its meaning must be enacted from any form whether it is a predicate of a nominal clause, an attribute or a vocative. Also a ruling of it is that it requires no intention. Based on this we said: if one said to his wife: "You are divorced", "I divorced you" or "O divorced one", the divorce will occur whether he intended it or not. Like this is, if one said to his slave: "You are free", "I have freed you" or "O free one".

❖❖❖

Based on the previously established principle that aṣ-ṣarīḥ is clear and unequivocal in giving its meaning and based on the ruling that no intention is required to establish it, the Aḥnāf say that the ritual of *at-tayammum* grants *aṭ-ṭahāra,* purity. This claim is derived from the verse of the blessed Quran regarding the case when one needs to gain purity but does not have access to water. The relevant part of verse 6 of Sūrat ul-Māida reads, "...and you find no water, then take for yourselves clean sand or earth, and rub therewith your faces and hands, Allah does not wish to place you in difficulty..." The verse then goes on to say:

وَ لكِن يريدِ ليطهركم [المائدة: 6]

".. but He does want to purify you..."

This clearly shows that the function of the dry ablution of *at-tayammum* is to give purity. This verse is aṣ-ṣarīḥ in describing *at-tayammum* as a mechanism of *aṭ-ṭahāra* and purity.

This view is contended. One objection is that if the verse is aṣ-ṣarīḥ in this regard then one of the rulings of aṣ-ṣarīḥ is that there is no requirement of an intention. However, the Aḥnāf have said that an intention is a condition and

بسم الله الرحمن الرحيم

فَلَمْ تَجِدُواْ مَاء فَتَيَمَّمُواْ صَعِيدًا طَيِّبًا

(الآية)

صدق الله العظيم

سورة المائدة: 6

QUICK ARABIC

التيمم: *at-tayammum*

Dry ablution. The ritual ablution performed without water.

الطهارة: *aṭ-ṭahāra*

Purification. To make something pure and free from filth.

thus required for *at-tayammum*. The reply to this is that the intention required for *at-tayammum* is not for it to become a purifying agent, rather it is for it to be used as a replacement for *al-wuḍū*. The verse is aṣ-ṣarīḥ in declaring *at-tayammum* a purifying agent and thus no intention is required for this. The intention is for another purpose, which is to declare the intent of replacing the *al-wuḍū* with *at-tayammum* as an agent of purity in particular circumstances.

Another objection aimed at the aṣ-ṣarīḥ nature of the verse in declaring *at-tayammum* an agent of purity comes from two accounts of Imam ash-Shafi'ī رحمه الله One account is that *at-tayammum* is prescribed only as a necessity, because in its nature soil is contaminated and that which is contaminated is not a purifying agent. It is prescribed by the Sharia as a purifying agent only due to the lack of water and soil being readily available. The other account is that *at-tayammum* acts as a concealing agent, it does not actually purify. Water is the purifier, but as it is not available at the time of need for prayer, the *at-tayammum* conceals the impurity of the worshiper until he comes in possession of usable water or invalidates it in another way.

The Aḥnāf, have the evidence of the aṣ-ṣarīḥ words of verse 6 of Sūrat ul-Māida to say that *at-tayammum* is a purifying agent. As for the reasoning of the Shawāfi' we say aṣ-ṣarīḥ of al-kitāb is more compelling evidence.

Now, depending on which opinion is taken there will be a difference between the Aḥnāf and the Shawāfi' in the verdicts of numerous cases. There are six cases mentioned in the text:

1. The validity of *at-tayammum* before a prayer start time: One would be permitted to perform *at-tayammum* before the onset of a prayer's time according to the Aḥnāf but according to the Shawāfi' it would not be permitted. According to the Aḥnāf *at-tayammum* is an agent of purity just the same as *ablution*, so just as *ablution* is permitted before the time of a prayer has started, *at-tayammum* is also permitted. The Shawāfi' say *at-tayammum* is only purifying due to the necessity of a prayer. The prayer only becomes necessary to perform once the time of the prayer has begun and not before. When necessity arises only then will *at-tayammum* be necessary, therefore it is permitted within the time and not before it.
2. The validity of multiple *al-farḍ* prayers with one *at-tayammum*: According to the Aḥnāf multiple prayers in their own times are

بسم الله الرحمن الرحيم

فَلَمْ تَجِدُواْ مَاء فَتَيَمَّمُواْ صَعِيدًا طَيِّبًا

(الآية) ۝

صدق الله العظيم

سورة المائدة: 6

QUICK TERMS

الصريح: *aṣ-ṣarīḥ*

The unequivocal. A word or phrase with a clear and palpable meaning.

الكتاب: *al-kitāb*

The book. The inspired final word of Allah ﷻ.

الفرض: *al-farḍ*

The obligatory. The observance of which in necessary and denial leads to disbelief.

QUICK ARABIC

التيمم: *at-tayammum*

Dry ablution. The ritual ablution performed without water.

الوضوء: *al-wuḍū*

Ablution. The ritual cleaning to attain purity.

permitted with the same *at-tayammum*. This is to say that *at-tayammum* is not invalidated when the time of one prayer lapses. This is because *at-taymmum* is just like *ablution* and one *ablution* can be performed for multiple prayers, therefore so can *at-tayammum*. The Shawāfi' say one *at-tayammum* cannot suffice for multiple prayers because it is an agent of purity out of necessity. Once the prayer for which *at-tayammum* was first necessary has been performed, the necessity is over. Once the necessity is over, the necessity of purity is no longer and so the *at-tayammum* terminates. When the time for a new prayer begins, there is a new necessity for purity, so in the absence of water another *at-tayammum* is to be performed.

3. The status of the Imam's purity: The Aḥnāf say that if the Imam is leading the prayer having performed *at-tayammum*, he is permitted to do so even if the followers gained their purity by performing *al-wuḍū*. This is because *at-tayammum* is an agent of purity just like *al-wuḍū*. This means that whoever has performed either of the two is pure and their status is equal in purity. It would then follow that it does not make a difference who leads the prayer and who follows. The Shawāfi' on the other hand make a distinction between the two methods of purity. *al-Wuḍū* is the actual agent of purity and therefore grants actual purity. *at-Tayammum* masks the impure status and its purity is due to necessity, thus making it weaker. If the leader of the salah is in a weaker state to those that follow it will invalidate the prayer. It is just like the case of an able-bodied person who is not permitted to follow the one who is unable to perform *as-sajda* or *ar-rukū'* due to the firmer status of the former compared to the latter.
4. Permissibility of *at-tayammum* during illness: The Aḥnāf say when one is ill, they may perform *at-tayammum* whether there is a genuine fear of losing the functionality of a limb or fear of death, and even if there is no such fear. This is because *at-tayammum* is an agent of purity in its own right. However, the Shawāfi' say that if there is no fear of losing a limb or a fear of death arising from *ablution*, no other reason is acceptable to excuse the *al-wuḍū* in favour of *at-tayammum*. This is because the necessity is not established. If one would lose the function of a limb or fear death because of using water, then necessity is established. *at-Tayammum* is an agent of purity only when necessary, so it is valid in these cases only.

QUICK ARABIC

التيمم: *at-tayammum*

Dry ablution. The ritual ablution performed without water.

الوضوء: *al-wuḍū*

Ablution. The ritual cleaning to attain purity.

QUICK DICTIONARY

Imam: *ih-mahm*
Prayer leader. The officiator and leader of the congregational prayer.

5. Permissibility of at-*tayammum* when fearful of missing Eid prayer or the funeral prayer: The Aḥnāf say that if one fears missing the prayers of Eid or a funeral, if they engage in performing *al-wuḍū*, they are permitted to perform *at-tayammum*. This is because there is no replacement or alternative to both of these prayers. So, the worshiper would lose the chance of both these prayers by engaging in *al-wuḍū*, which is replaceable with an independent agent of purity, *at-tayammum*. However, the Shawāfi' have disallowed this because they have opined that there is *al-qaḍā* and an alternative when the Eid or funeral prayers are missed, which is to make them up. If there is an alternative, there is no necessity. If there is no necessity, there is no need for *at-tayammum*, which is only an agent of purity when necessity arises.
6. The intention when performing *at-tayammum*: The Aḥnāf say that the intention for *at-tayammum* is that an agent of purity is being used to gain purity. However, the Shawāfi' do not see *at-tayammum* as an agent of purity and so it will not grant purity. If it does not grant purity then the intention of using it in that manner, is not valid too. Rather, one should intend to perform the necessary prayer with *at-tayammum*, which will only mask the impurity due to the necessity of the *al-farḍ* salah.

QUICK TERMS

القضاء: *al-qaḍā*

To settle. To settle and make up a missed obligatory observance.

الفرض: *al-farḍ*

The obligatory. The observance of which is necessary and denial leads to disbelief.

QUICK ARABIC

التيمم: *at-tayammum*

Dry ablution. The ritual ablution performed without water.

الوضوء: *al-wuḍū*

Ablution. The ritual cleaning to attain purity.

Text and Translation

وعلى هذا قلنا: إن التيمم يفيد الطهارة؛ لأنّ قوله تعالى: ﴿وَ لكِن يرِيدِ ليطهركم﴾ صريح في حصول الطهارة به وللشافعي عليه الرحمة فيه قولان: أحدهما: أنه طهارة ضرورية والآخر: انه ليس بطهارة بل هو ساتر للحدث، وعلى هذا يخرج المسائل على مذهبين من جوازه قبل الوقت وأداء الفرضين بتيمم واحد وإمامة المتيمم للمتوضئين وجوازه بدون خوف تلف النفس أو العضو بالوضوء وجوازه للعيد والجنازة وجوازه بنية الطهارة

Based on this we have said: *at-tayammum* administers purity as He Almighty says: "...but He does want to purify you...". This is unequivocal in stating that purity is obtained from it. Imam ash-Shāfi'ī, mercy be upon him, has two opinions about it: the first is that it is a purifier by necessity; and the second that it is not a purifier but a concealer of impurity. Based on this, rulings of both schools are derived from its permissibility before the entering of the time, the observance of two obligatory prayers with one *at-tayammum*, the performer of *at-tayammum* leading those who performed *ablution*, its permissibility when not in fear of harm to life or limb by performing *ablution*, its permissibility for Eid or funeral prayers and its permissibility with the intention of gaining purity.

❖ ❖ ❖

The definition of al-kināya is:

الكناية: ما استتر معناه

"al-Kināya is that which has a concealed meaning."

This means that any word which is equivocal and unclear in its meaning is termed al-kināya. Words that are figurative, al-majāz, fall into this category due to their obscurity before they become widespread and commonplace. The definition of al-kināya implies that any word, whether used as al-ḥaqīqa or al-majāz, may fall into this category. It is for this reason that Figure 1.2-01 shows the flow diagram with al-ḥaqīqa and al-majāz both potentially categorised as aṣ-ṣarīḥ or as al-kināya; it depends on how clear each of them is in their used meaning.

The ruling of al-kināya is:

حكم الكناية: ثبوت الحكم بها عند وجود النية أو بدلاله الحال

"The ruling of al-kināya is to establish its ruling when there is an intention or the situation supports it."

This means that the meaning of the unclear and equivocal al-kināya will come into force when the originator of the words makes the meaning known by revealing an intention, or there is other evidence that supports a meaning. It is vital that an intention or the circumstance eliminate any ambiguity. The one who hears the words should know of the intention behind the words, or the situation and circumstances in which the words were uttered are known. As an example, during an argument which moves on to the topic of divorce the man uses the figurative expression for divorce, "You are separate". This is an issuance of divorce, even if the husband was to plead that he did not intend it. There must be an intention or other evidence to eliminate the ambiguity, so when either is found, the ambiguity is lifted and the meaning is determined.

QUICK TERMS

الحقيقة: *al-ḥaqīqa*

The literal. A word coined by the lexicon for an item.

المجاز: *al-majāz*

The figurative. A word used for a meaning other than its coined meaning.

الصريح: *aṣ-ṣarīḥ*

The unequivocal. A word or phrase with a clear and palpable meaning.

الكناية: *al-kināya*

The concealed. A word or phrase that has a concealed and hidden meaning. A metaphor.

QUICK ARABIC

التيمم: *at-tayammum*

Dry ablution. The ritual ablution performed without water.

الوضوء: *al-wuḍū*

Ablution. The ritual cleaning to attain purity.

It should be understood that there are multiple meanings for figurative expressions of divorce, such as *al-baynūna* (separate) and *at-taḥrīm* (unlawful), so they require further evidence to eliminate possibilities and establish their meanings. The multiple meanings of "you are separate (*bāin*)" come about because it is not clear what the wife is separate from; separated in marriage i.e. divorced, separate from blame or in viewpoint? Or maybe in another meaning such as you are separate and unique amongst your contemporaries! The multiple meanings of, "You are unlawful (*ḥarām*)", come about because it is not immediately obvious if she is unlawful in marriage to him i.e. divorced, or unlawful to others for marriage due to being his wife! Another meaning of *al-ḥarām* is 'prevented'. So, is she prevented from leaving the house, seeing her friends or from chores?! There are multiple meanings for these figurative expressions of divorce. Therefore, to determine them as meaning divorce it requires the evidence of the circumstances in which the words were said, or the intention of the originator.

There is an objection levelled at these words as expressions of divorce. The objection is that if the words *al-baynūna* and *at-taḥrīm* result in divorce they should function like the word *aṭ-ṭalāq*, which is designated for divorce. Using *aṭ-ṭalāq* the issuer would be delivering a revocable *aṭ-ṭalāq ar-raj'ī* divorce, however, the Aḥnāf state that the divorce issued using al-kināya is an irrevocable *aṭ-ṭalāq al-bāin* divorce.

The answer to this is that these words, *al-baynūna* and *at-taḥrīm,* function in their designated meanings, which are *separated* and *unlawful*, respectively. Both outcomes of *separation* and *unlawfulness* only occur in an irrevocable divorce, so it is this type of divorce that occurs. The question would be valid had we stated that these words *are in the meaning of* the word *aṭ-ṭalāq*, but we have not stated that. We have called them al-kināya because they are unclear and have multiple implications. Once the situation or the intention makes it clear that a divorce was issued, the words function in their own meaning. What follows is that the husband does not have the right to a revocable *aṭ-ṭalāq ar-raj'ī* divorce.

Text and Translation

والكناية هي ما استتر معناه والمجاز قبل أن يصير متعارفا بمنزلة الكناية وحكم الكناية ثبوت الحكم بها
عند وجود النية أو بدلالة الحال؛ إذ لا بد له من دليل يزول به التردد ويترجح به بعض الوجوه، ولهذا

QUICK TERMS

الكناية: *al-kināya*

The concealed. A word or phrase that has a concealed and hidden meaning. A metaphor.

QUICK ARABIC

البينونة: *al-baynūna*

Separation. A word with a metaphorical connotation for divorce .

التحريم: *at-taḥrīm*

Forbiddance. A word with a metaphorical connotation for divorce.

الطلاق الرجعي: *aṭ-ṭalāq ar-raj'ī*

Revocable divorce. A divorce after which the husband has permission to return to the marriage.

الطلاق البائن: *aṭ-ṭalāq al-bāin*

Irrevocable divorce. A divorce after which the husband is not permitted to unilaterally return to the marriage.

المعنى سمي لفظ البينونة والتحريم كناية في باب الطلاق لمعنى التردد واستتار المراد لا أنه يعمل عمل الطلاق، ويتفرع منه حكم الكنايات في حق عدم ولاية الرجعة

al-Kināya is that which has a concealed meaning. al-Majāz, before it is recognisable, serves as al-kināya. The ruling of al-kināya is to establish its ruling when there is an intention or the situation supports it. It is vital for it to have supporting evidence to eradicate doubt and to give preference to an outcome. For this reason the words *al-baynūna* and *at-taḥrīm* are considered as al-kināya in the chapter of divorce due to an element of doubt and ambiguity, not because they function as the word *aṭ-ṭalāq* functions. From this, branch off the rulings of al-kināya with respect to lack of authority in the revocable divorce.

❖❖❖

Due to the unclear and concealed meaning of al-kināya, no legal punishments will result from them. If one was to confess, using words that are al-kināya, to a crime punishable in the Shariah, the punishment cannot be carried out because a clear confession is required. The reason for this is that all punishments must have no element of doubt in them, but al-kināya carries an element of doubt. For example, if one was to confess to adultery with words such as, "Yes, I committed an unlawful act", it is not a clear enough confession as to which unlawful act the person is referring to. Is it the one in question or does it refer to another unlawful act? Simply confessing to an *unlawful act* is not aṣ-ṣarīḥ to mean adultery, so it is not a confession of adultery. Another example of this is if a mute is to use unconventional sign language to communicate an admittance of adultery, it is not admitted as a confession due to the ambiguity. Similarly, in a case of defamation if a person accused another of adultery, and a third person provides evidence by saying "You told the truth". It is inadmissible in this form because he could be testifying to the truth of the individual in the defamation claim or in some other case. Due to the uncertainty and lack of clarity, it will be inadmissible.

QUICK TERMS

الحقيقة: *al-ḥaqīqa*

The literal. A word coined by the lexicon for an item.

المجاز: *al-majāz*

The figurative. A word used for a meaning other than its coined meaning.

Text and Translation

ولوجود معنى التردد في الكناية لا يقام بها العقوبات حتى لو أقر على نفسه في باب الزنا والسرقة لا يقام عليه الحد ما لم يذكر اللفظ الصريح، ولهذا المعنى لا يقام الحد على الأخرس بالإشارة ولو قذف

رجلا بالزنا فقال الآخر: صدقت لا يجب الحد عليه لاحتمال التصديق له في غيره

As there is the element of doubt in al-kināya no punishments can be served by it. Such that if one was to confess in the chapter of adultery or robbery, no punishment will be served till clear wording is used. For this reason no punishment is served on a mute due to gestures. If one accused a man of adultery and the other says: "you're right", no punishment would be administered to him due to the possibility of him confirming something else.

QUICK TERMS

الكناية: *al-kināya*

The concealed. A word or phrase that has a concealed and hidden meaning. A metaphor.

❖ ❖ ❖

Ḥanafī Principles (7)

	Term	Definition	Ruling	An Example
11	الصريح	لفظ يكون المراد به ظاهرا	– يوجب ثبوت معناه بأي طريق كان من إخبار أو نعت أو نداء – يستغني عن النية	وَ لكِن يريدِ ليطهركم [المائدة: 6]
12	الكناية	ما استتر معناه	ثبوت الحكم بها عند وجود النية أو بدلالة الحال	أنت بائن

❖ ❖ ❖

Summary Of aṣ-Ṣarīḥ and al-Kināya

1. Definition of aṣ-ṣarīḥ:
   الصريح: لفظ يكون المراد به ظاهرا
   "A word which has a clear meaning".

2. The ruling of aṣ-ṣarīḥ:
   i) يوجب ثبوت معناه بأي طريق كان من إخبار أو نعت أو نداء
   "Its meaning must be established whether it is an account, an adjective or in the vocative case."
   ii) يستغني عن النية
   "It is independent of the intention."

3. For example, if one said to his wife, "You are divorced." This is clear in its meaning, so it will be applied even if uttered accidentally. This is because it is not dependant on an intention.

4. Definition of al-kināya:
   الكناية: ما استتر معناه
   "The meaning of which is obscure."

5. The ruling of al-kināya:
   ثبوت الحكم بها عند وجود النية أو بدلالة الحال
   "Its meaning is established when there is a known intention or the circumstances indicate it."

6. For example, a man says to his wife, "You are separated." Just saying it will not result in divorce, as we do not know what she is separated from: her wealth, husband or family. That is why for the divorce to be enacted an intention would be necessary, otherwise divorce will not occur.

1.3 Word Clarity

The previous chapters 1.1 and 1.2 discussed word coinage and word usage, respectively. Chapter 1.1 contained the four principle terms of al-khāṣṣ (the specific), al-'āmm (the general), al-mushtarak (the homograph) and al-muawwal (the precedent). Further discussions on al-muṭlaq (the unrestricted) and al-muqayyad (the restricted), both types of al-khāṣṣ, were also a part of this chapter. Chapter 1.2 followed by dividing words in terms of how they may be used. The four primary terms introduced were al-ḥaqīqa (the literal), al-majāz (the figurative), aṣ-ṣarīḥ (the unequivocal) and al-kināya (the equivocal). The section was complimented with a discussion on al-isti'āra, the figurative expression, which is just another name for al-majāz.

In this chapter we discuss the very same words but in terms of how clear they are in their used meanings. We are introduced to a scale of clarity for word use. It ranges from the very clear to the most ambiguous. There are eight terms in total, four for clarity and four for ambiguity.

The four terms of clarity introduced are aẓ-ẓāhir (clear), an-naṣṣ (the clearer), al-mufassar (the explained) and al-muḥkam (the unalterable). Section 1.3.1 discusses these terms. The four terms of ambiguity introduced are al-khafīy (the unclear), al-mushkil (the difficult), al-mujmal (the unexplained) and al-mutashābih (the intricate). These terms are discussed later in section 1.3.2. This scale of word clarity is summarised in Figure 1.3-01:

FIGURE 1.3-01
A scale of clarity for how words may be used.
Each term has an opposite.
Each lower term is contained in the higher term.

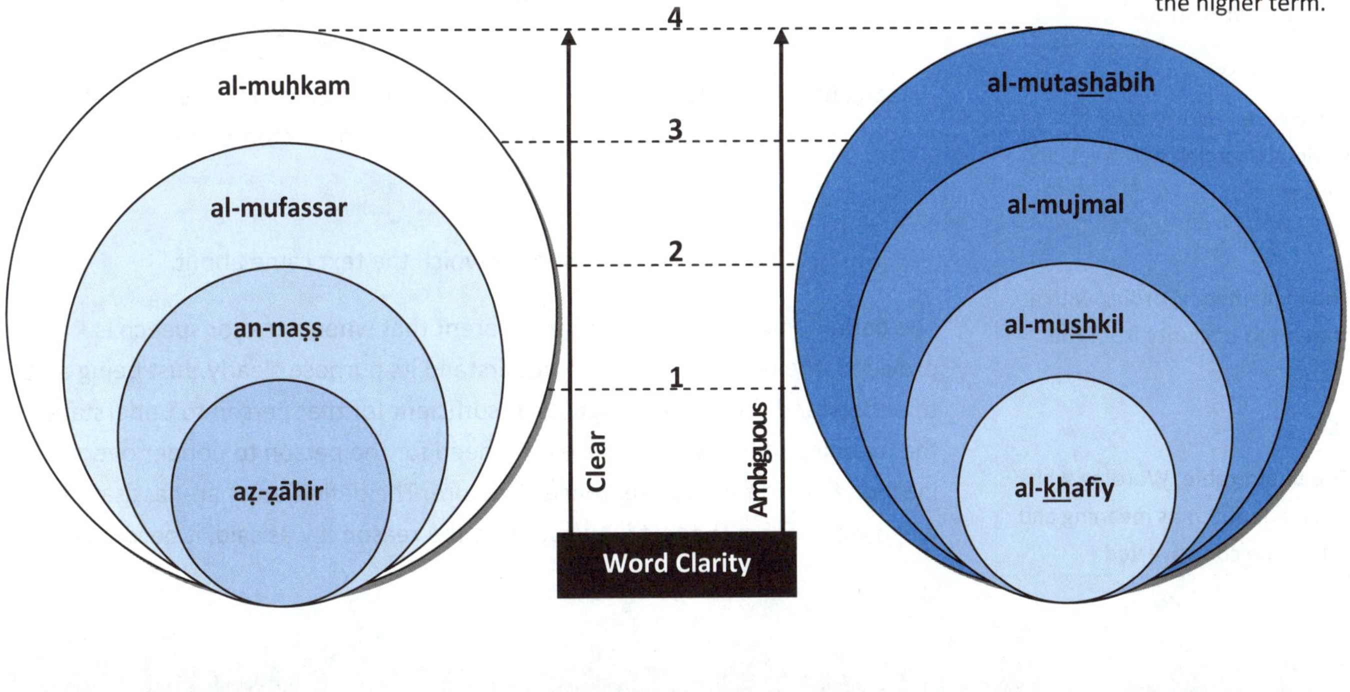

1.3.1 al-Mutaqābilāt – Clarity

In this section the four terms of clarity are presented. The four terms are aẓ-ẓāhir (clear), an-naṣṣ (the clearer), al-mufassar (the explained) and al-muḥkam (the unalterable). The summary of how they relate to each other is shown in Figure 1.3.1-01.

FIGURE 1.3.1-01

A division of terms of clarity.

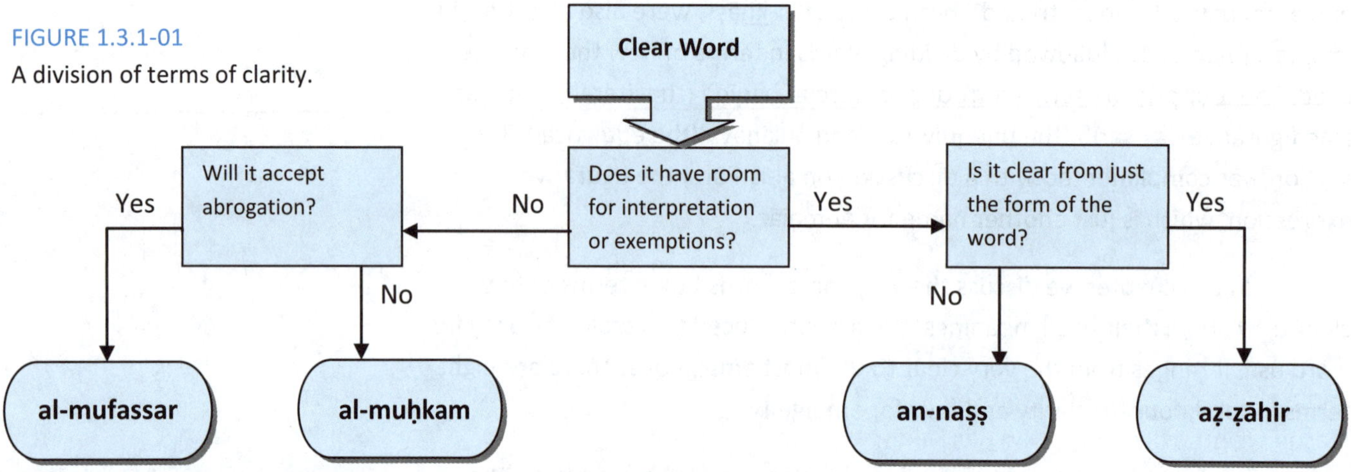

QUICK TERMS

الظاهر: *aẓ-ẓāhir*

The clear. Wording with an obvious meaning without the need for context.

النص: *an-naṣṣ*

The clearer. Wording with obvious meaning which is in its context.

المفسر: *al-mufassar*

The explained. Wording with a statement of clarity from the issuer.

المحكم: *al-muḥkam*

The unalterable. Wording which has no doubt in its meaning and cannot be controverted.

The text of Uṣūl ush-Shāshī mentions the corresponding four terms of ambiguity at this stage, however, they will be discussed later in section 1.3.2.

First, the definitions of aẓ-ẓāhir and an-naṣṣ are given:

الظاهر: كل كلام ظهر المراد به للسامع بنفس السماع من غير تأمل

"aẓ-Ẓāhir is every text that gives a clear understanding to the recipient from merely hearing it and without a need to contemplate."

النص: ما سيق الكلام لأجله

"an-Naṣṣ is the reason for which the text came about."

The definition of aẓ-ẓāhir makes it apparent that when a text or speech is provided, the recipient is able to understand its purpose clearly. Just being able to understand the spoken language is sufficient for that person to understand the meaning of the words. There is no need for the person to ponder over the individual word forms or sentence structure. The definition of an-naṣṣ says that when we connect the text in question to the reason it was said, it becomes known as an-naṣṣ. This implies that a text deemed to be aẓ-ẓāhir, when connected to its reason will be known as an-naṣṣ. This would mean that where we have an-naṣṣ, aẓ-ẓāhir is already present. Moreover, when a clearly understood text connects to its reason and context it becomes clearer. So, on the scale of clarity an-naṣṣ is clearer than aẓ-ẓāhir.

The example for both aẓ-ẓāhir and an-naṣṣ is given from Sūrat ul-Baqara, verse 275. Allah ﷻ says:

وَ أحل الله البيع وحرم الربا [البقرة :275]

"...Allah has permitted trade and He has forbidden usury..."

These words are clear in stating that *al-bay'* is permitted but *ar-ribā* is not. These words are said to be aẓ-ẓāhir in this regard. Anyone who hears the words and understands the meanings of the words will come to this conclusion without the requirement of further thinking or contemplation. The words themselves give this meaning. Now, when we connect these words to the reason why the blessed Quran decreed them, we find the following:

إنما البيع مِثل الربا [البقرة :275]

"...trade is the same as usury..."

This is how the non-believers viewed the two. They said that *al-bay'* is just like *ar-ribā*; the two are the same. In response to this, and to show that the two are actually different, Allah ﷻ said He has forbidden one and permitted the other; therefore, they are very different. So, the statement, "Allah has permitted trade and He has forbidden usury", when viewed by itself is aẓ-ẓāhir in telling us that *al-bay'* is permitted and *ar-ribā* is forbidden; and when viewed with its reason of issuance is an-naṣṣ to differentiate between *al-bay'* and *ar-ribā*. The knowledge of the two being different is clearer than one being *al-ḥalāl* and the other *al-ḥarām*.

QUICK ARABIC

الحرام: *al-ḥarām*

The unlawful. That which is not permitted in the Shariah, as distinguished from the lawful.

البيع: *al-bay'*

To sell. To transfer to another in exchange for money.

الربا: *ar-ribā*

Usury. Excess to the legal standard permitted in a contract of exchange.

الحلال: *al-ḥalāl*

The lawful. That which is permitted in the Shariah, as distinguished from unlawful.

Text and Translation

فصل في المتقابلات: نعني بها الظاهر والنص والمفسر والمحكم مع ما يقابلها من الخفي والمشكل والمجمل والمتشابه، فالظاهر اسم لكل كلام ظهر المراد به للسامع بنفس السماع من غير تأمل، والنص ما سيق الكلام لأجله، ومثاله في قوله تعالى: ﴿وَ أحل الله البيع وحرم الربا﴾ فالآية سيقت لبيان التفرقة بين

البيع والربا ردا لما ادعاه الكفار من التسوية بينهما حيث قالوا: ﴿إنما البيع مِثل الربا﴾ وقد علم حل البيع وحرمة الربا بنفس السماع فصار ذلك نصا في التفرقة ظاهراً في حل البيع وحرمة الربا

Chapter on al-Mutaqābilāt: what we mean by it is aẓ-ẓāhir, an-naṣṣ, al-mufassar and al-muḥkam, along with their opposites, al-khafīy, al-mushkil, al-mujmal and al-mutashābih. aẓ-Ẓāhir is the name given to every text that has a clear denotation for the recipient from merely hearing it and without a need to contemplate. an-Naṣṣ is the reason for which the text came about. An example of it is in the Almighty's word: "...Allah has permitted trade and He has forbidden usury...". The words came about in order to state the difference between trade and usury in response to the claim of the non-believers of their parity when they claimed: "...trade is the same as usury...". The permissibility of trade and prohibition of usury is understood by the same wording, so this becomes an-naṣṣ for the differentiation and aẓ-ẓāhir for the permissibility of trade and prohibition of usury.

❖❖❖

بســم الله الرحمن الرحيـم

قَالُوٓاْ إِنَّمَا ٱلْبَيْعُ مِثْلُ ٱلرِّبَوٰاْ وَأَحَلَّ ٱللَّهُ ٱلْبَيْعَ وَحَرَّمَ ٱلرِّبَوٰاْ (الآية)

صدق الله العظيم

سورة البقرة: 275

QUICK TERMS

الظاهر: *aẓ-ẓāhir*

The clear. Wording with an obvious meaning without the need for context.

النص: *an-naṣṣ*

The clearer. Wording with obvious meaning which is in its context.

المفسر: *al-mufassar*

The explained. Wording with a statement of clarity from the issuer.

المحكم: *al-muḥkam*

The unalterable. Wording which has no doubt in its meaning and cannot be controverted.

The example from Sūrat ul-Baqara verse 275 shows the difference between aẓ-ẓāhir and an-naṣṣ based on their respective definitions. Three more examples highlight the same difference. Two are from the blessed Quran and one is a Hadith.

1. Allah ﷻ has said in the blessed Quran:

فانكِحوا ما طابَ لكم من النساء مثنى وُ ثلاَ ثَ ورباع [النساء :3]

"...then marry other permissible women, two, three or four..."

Upon hearing the words *fankiḥū* (then marry) one would understand that getting married is permitted. There is no need to ponder over the words to arrive at this meaning. This means that the verse is aẓ-ẓāhir in allowing marriage. The reason for the revelation of this verse is to limit the number of women permitted for marriage at one time. So, the words of this verse are an-naṣṣ for the number of marriages.

2. Allah ﷻ has said in the blessed Quran:

لا جناح عليكم إن طلقتم النساء ما لم تمسوهن أو تفرضوا لهن فريضة [البقرة:236]

"You will not be blamed if you divorce women when you have not yet consummated the marriage or fixed a bridal gift for them...".

Upon hearing the words of the verse, we learn that the issuing of a divorce is at the discretion of the man. To arrive at this meaning does not require any pondering. The verse is therefore aẓ-ẓāhir in stating the discretion of the husband in matters of divorce. The reason for revelation of this verse is to state that a husband is permitted to divorce his bride, who has neither had her marriage consummated nor her bridal gift mentioned during the marriage ceremony. The words are an-naṣṣ in this regard. There is also al-ishāra [Chapter 1.5.1, page 144] or an indication in the verse towards the lawfulness of a marriage ceremony without a mention of the amount of bridal gift. This is indicated in the verse because the verse says that when a bridal gift is not mentioned one may divorce them and one can only divorce the one whom one has married. If the marriage became void due to the absence of the mention of a bridal gift, issuing a divorce would not be valid either. The divorce is permitted in the verse, so the marriage must be valid even though the bridal gift was not stipulated.

3. The blessed Prophet ﷺ said:

من ملك ذا رحم محرم منه عتق عليه

"Whoever owns *al-maḥram* relative will oblige freedom".

Upon hearing the words of the narration, one understands that a purchaser becomes the owner of the merchandise immediately after the transaction. This is because one has no authority to use, or in this case free, if there is no ownership established. Another Hadith states:

لا عتق فيما لا يملكه ابن آدم (ابن ماجه)

"There is no emancipation in what a man does not own."

As ownership is understood from the Hadith without need for further pondering, it is said to be aẓ-ẓāhir in establishing ownership for the

حديث

عن عبد الله بن عمر قال قال رسول الله ﷺ من ملك ذا رحم محرم عتق عليه.

عليه الصلوة والسلام

(النسائي)

QUICK TERMS

الإشارة: *al-ishāra*

Hint. A sign or hint given by the order in which words appear in a text.

QUICK ARABIC

المحرم: *al-maḥram*

Unlawful. A near relative with whom it is unlawful to marry.

purchaser. The reason for the statement in the Hadith is to announce the freedom of a close relative if they come into ownership of a relative. Therefore, the words of the Hadith are an-naṣṣ in this regard.

Text and Translation

وكذلك قوله تعالى: ﴿فانكِحوا ما طابَ لكم من النساء مثنى وُ ثلاَ ثَ ورباع﴾ سيق الكلام لبيان العدد وقد علم الإطلاق والإجازة بنفس السماع فصار ذلك ظاهرا في حق الإطلاق نصا في بيان العدد، وكذلك قوله تعالى: ﴿لا جناح عليكم إن طلقتم النساء ما لم تمسوهن أو تفرضوا لهن فريضة﴾ نص في حكم من لم يسم لها المهر وظاهر في استبداد الزوج بالطلاق وإشارة إلى أن النكاح بدون ذكر المهر يصح، وكذلك قوله عليه السلام :من ملك ذا رحم محرم منه عتق عليه، نص في استحقاق العتق القريب وظاهر في ثبوت الملك له

Similarly, the word of He Almighty: "...then marry other permissible women, two, three or four...", has come about to state the number; the allowance and permissibility is understood in the same hearing. So it is aẓ-ẓāhir in respect to allowance and an-naṣṣ in expressing the number. Likewise, the word of He, the Almighty: "You will not be blamed if you divorce women when you have not yet consummated the marriage or fixed a bridal gift for them...". It is ruled as an-naṣṣ for the one whose bridal gift is not mentioned, aẓ-ẓāhir for the husband's discretion in divorce and al-ishāra in stipulating that marriage without mention of a bridal gift is valid. Similarly, his saying, peace and blessings be upon him: "Whoever owns a *al-maḥram* relative will oblige freedom", is an-naṣṣ in the right of freedom for the relative and aẓ-ẓāhir in confirming his ownership.

❖ ❖ ❖

The ruling of both aẓ-ẓāhir and an-naṣṣ is the same. It is given as:

حكم الظاهر والنص: وجوب العمل بهما

"The ruling of aẓ-ẓāhir and an-naṣṣ is the necessity of enacting both."

It is necessary to enforce both of them whether they are al-'āmm or al-khāṣṣ in their original designated meaning [Chapter 1.1.1, page 12]. However, one should bear in mind that there is an element of possibility that another meaning is possible. This is because just as the clear al-khāṣṣ word may have been used

QUICK TERMS

النص: *an-naṣṣ*

The clearer. Wording with obvious meaning which is in its context.

الظاهر: *aẓ-ẓāhir*

The clear. Wording with an obvious meaning without the need for context.

الإشارة: *al-ishāra*

Hint. A sign or hint given by the order in which words appear in a text.

العام: *al-'āmm*

The general. A word designated for a group.

الخاص: *al-khāṣṣ*

The specific. A word designated for a singular specific concept.

QUICK ARABIC

المحرم: *al-maḥram*

Unlawful. A near relative with whom it is unlawful to marry.

figuratively [Chapter 1.2 .1, page 64], aẓ-ẓāhir and an-naṣṣ may be figurative, or there may be limitations or interpretations to be considered.

With the above ruling in mind our scholars have said that when someone buys their close-relative as a slave, the relative is emancipated immediately. Furthermore, the purchaser retains the rights of an emancipator. The right of the emancipator is that provided other inheritors do not take all the inheritance left by the deceased, the emancipator will have a share.

Text and Translation

وحكم الظاهر والنص وجوب العمل بهما عامين كانا أو خاصين مع احتمال إرادة الغير وذلك بمنزلة المجاز مع الحقيقة، وعلى هذا قلنا: إذا اشترى قريبه حتى عتق عليه يكون هو معتقا ويكون الولاء له

The ruling of aẓ-ẓāhir and an-naṣṣ is the necessity of enacting both, whether they are al-'āmm or al-khāṣ, with the possibility of another meaning. This is like al-majāz alongside al-ḥaqīqa. Based on this we have said: if someone bought his close-relative such that he is freed, he will be an emancipator and curatorship will be his.

❖ ❖ ❖

The ruling of both aẓ-ẓāhir and an-naṣṣ is the same; they must be enacted. Differentiating between the two is possible when we look at the strength of each. We have learnt previously that an-naṣṣ is clearer than aẓ-ẓāhir [Figure 1.3-01]; therefore, when there is a seemingly opposing view expressed in aẓ-ẓāhir to what we find in an-naṣṣ, an-naṣṣ will take precedence as it is clearer. Moreover, aẓ-ẓāhir is contained in an-naṣṣ.

An example of the seemingly opposite view between aẓ-ẓāhir and an-naṣṣ is if one said to his wife, "Divorce yourself." She replied, "I irrevocably divorce myself." This will result in a revocable divorce and not an irrevocable one. This is because the words of the wife are aẓ-ẓāhir and clear for an irrevocable divorce, as one would understand that upon hearing her words. However, it is an-naṣṣ for revocable divorce. This is because the words of the wife were only possible in the context of what the husband said, as he gave her his right of issuing a divorce. By default, this is a revocable divorce as the words of the husband are aṣ-ṣarīḥ and unequivocal. This means that the context and

QUICK TERMS

المجاز: *al-majāz*

The figurative. A word used for a meaning other than its coined meaning.

الحقيقة: *al-ḥaqīqa*

The literal. A word coined by the lexicon for an item.

الصريح: *aṣ-ṣarīḥ*

The unequivocal. A word or phrase with a clear and palpable meaning.

QUICK DICTIONARY

Curator: *kyoo-rey-ter*
Guardian. Guardian of an incompetent's property.

Emancipate: *ih-man-suh-payt*
To free. To free a slave from bondage and servitude.

Unequivocal: *uhn-i-kwiv-uh-kuhl*
Not ambiguous. Having only one clear meaning or interpretation.

حديث

عن قتادة رضي الله عنه : فأمر لهم رسول الله صلى الله عليه وسلم بذود وراع وأمرهم أن يخرجوا فيه فيشربوا من ألبانها وأبوالها.

عليه الصلاة والسلام

(البخاري: 3956)

QUICK TERMS

النص: *an-naṣṣ*

The clearer. Wording with obvious meaning which is in its context.

الظاهر: *aẓ-ẓāhir*

The clear. Wording with obvious meaning without the need of context.

صاحبين: *ṣāḥibayn*

The Two Colleagues. Imams Abū Yūsuf رحمه الله and Muḥammad رحمه الله

المؤول: *al-muawwal*

The accepted. The dominant and accepted meaning from concurrent meanings.

المفسر: *al-mufassar*

The explained. Wording with a statement of clarity from the issuer.

an-naṣṣ of the wife's words "I irrevocably divorce myself", do not allow for an irrevocable divorce, rather an-naṣṣ only allows for a revocable divorce, which will take precedence and occur.

Another example of the difference in the strength of both aẓ-ẓāhir and an-naṣṣ is evident from the Hadith of the tribe of 'Urayna. This was a tribe who complained of an illness to the blessed Prophet صلى الله عليه وسلم. As a cure they were told to "drink the milk and urine" of camels, which they did and were healed. This narration is an-naṣṣ in stating the cause for cure as that is the context and purpose of the text. It is also aẓ-ẓāhir in stating that it is permissible to drink urine, as that is what someone who hears the words would immediately understand. We can compare this Hadith to another Hadith that states, "Guard against urine", which is an-naṣṣ in stating that it is a requirement to stay away from urine. This means that the Hadith of 'Urayna is aẓ-ẓāhir in suggesting that drinking urine is permitted, however the Hadith we compare it to is an-naṣṣ in stating that urine is prohibited. As an-naṣṣ is stronger in its clarity it is preferred to enact over aẓ-ẓāhir, so we say that consumption of any urine is unlawful.

A final example comparing the superior clarity and preference of an-naṣṣ over aẓ-ẓāhir is taken from a difference of opinion between Imam Abū Ḥanīfa رحمه الله on one hand, and Ṣāḥibayn along with Imam ash-Shāfi'ī رحمه الله on the other hand. Imam Abū Ḥanīfa رحمه الله says that the hadith of the blessed Prophet صلى الله عليه وسلم states that "whatever is naturally irrigated has *al-'ushr*" is an-naṣṣ regarding one-tenth to be given from all produce of the land that is naturally given water from the skies. This would also include vegetables if they were irrigated through rainfall. Ṣāḥibayn say that there are two conditions to be met before any vegetation is deemed liable for *al-'ushr*. Firstly, the produce must have longevity of one year or more, such as wheat, barley and other such grains. Secondly, it must amount to five *al-waṣaq* at least, which is approximately 195 kilograms. They counter Imam Abū Ḥanīfa's position by stating the Hadith, "There is no offering in vegetables". The answer from the Imam's position is that this Hadith contains the word "*aṣ-ṣadaqa*" or offering, which has multiple meanings. It is al-muawwal, so it is not necessarily about *al-'ushr*, as it could be about general charity or about zakah. Yes, the clear meaning of the words is that there are no offerings because the moment someone hears it that is what is clear to them, but this is shown from aẓ-ẓāhir. The Hadith regarding "Whatever is irrigated" is actually about *al-'ushr*, so that is its context and so it is an-naṣṣ in this regard and one-tenth must be given. an-Naṣṣ is clearer and stronger in clarity than aẓ-ẓāhir, and is therefore preferred.

Text and Translation

وإنما يظهر التفاوت بينهما عند المقابلة، ولهذا لو قال لها: طلقي نفسك فقالت: أبنت نفسي يقع الطلاق رجعيا؛ لأنّ هذا نص في الطلاق ظاهر في البينونة فيترجح العمل بالنص، وكذلك قوله عليه السلام لأهل عرينة: اشربوا من أبوالها وألبانها نص في بيان سبب الشفاء وظاهر في إجازة شرب البول، وقوله عليه السلام: استنزهوا من البول فإن عامة عذاب القبر منه نص في وجوب الاحتراز عن البول فيترجح النص على الظاهر فلا يحل شرب البول أصلاً ، وقوله عليه السلام: ما سقته السماء ففيه العشر نص في بيان العشر، وقوله عليه السلام: ليس في الخضراوات صدقة مؤول في نفي العشر؛ لأنّ الصدقة تحتمل وجوهاً فيترجح الأول على الثاني

The difference between them will manifest when contrasting. For this reason were he to say to her: divorce yourself, to which she retorted: I irrevocably divorce myself, only a revocable divorce will occur. This is because it is an-naṣṣ in terms of divorce and aẓ-ẓāhir for an irrevocable divorce. So acting upon the an-naṣṣ takes precedence. Similarly, his instruction, peace and blessings be upon him, to the tribe of 'Urayna: "Drink of their urine and milk", is an-naṣṣ in stating the source of the cure and aẓ-ẓāhir in permitting consumption of urine. And his commanding, peace and blessings be upon him, that: "Guard against urine for the most common punishment of the grave will be due to it", is an-naṣṣ in the necessity of guarding against urine. An-naṣṣ will take precedence over aẓ-ẓāhir so drinking urine will be completely prohibited. His informing, peace and blessings be upon him, that: "One-tenth is due on the naturally irrigated", is an-naṣṣ in defining one-tenth whilst his saying, peace and blessings be upon him, that: "There is no offering in vegetables", is al-muawwal in negating the one-tenth, as the word *aṣ-ṣadaqa* has multiple meanings. So the first is preferred over the second.

❖ ❖ ❖

The next level of clarity after an-naṣṣ is al-mufassar. al-Mufassar is defined as:

حديث

عَنْ أَبِي هُرَيْرَةَ رَضِيَ اللهُ عَنْهُ قَالَ: قَالَ رَسُولُ اَللّٰهِ صَلَّى اللهُ عَلَيْهِ وَسَلَّمَ : اِسْتَنْزِهُوا مِنَ اَلْبَوْلِ فَإِنَّ عَامَّةَ عَذَابِ اَلْقَبْرِ مِنْهُ.

عليه الصلوة والسلام

(اَلدَّارَقُطْنِيّ)

حديث

عن سالم بن عبد الله عن أبيه رضي الله عنه عن النبي صلى الله عليه وسلم قال فيما سقت السماء والعيون أو كان عثريا العشر.

عليه الصلوة والسلام

(البخاري: 1412)

حديث

عن موسى بن طلحة عن أبيه رضي الله عنه أن النبي صلى الله عليه وسلم قال: ليس في الخضروات صدقة.

عليه الصلوة والسلام

(اَلدَّارَقُطْنِيّ: 1888)

QUICK ARABIC

العشر: *al-'ushr*

A tenth. A tithe given to the treasury of the Muslim state, for fruits and produce of the ground.

المفسر: ما ظهر المراد به من اللفظ ببيان من قِبل المتكلم بحيث لا يبقى معه احتمال التأويل والتخصيص

"al-Mufassar is that whose desired word meaning is cleared by a statement of the first person, leaving neither possibility of interpretation nor specification."

The definition of al-mufassar shows that they are words that the originator clarifies. The clarification leaves no room for exemptions nor interpretation. As an example of al-mufassar, verse 30 of Sūrat ul-Ḥijr is used. Allah ﷻ says:

فسجد الملائكة كلهم أجمعون [الحجر: 30]

"Thereupon the angels prostrated, all of them together."

In this verse the word *al-malāika* is common to all angels, it is aẓ-ẓāhir and clear in this meaning. There is, however, a possibility that some of the angels may be exempt from the act of prostration and that those that prostrated were angels but it was not all angels. However, the possibility of an exemption is eliminated when the verse says, *kulluhum*, all of them. This now means that without exception all the angels prostrated. There is still room for interpretation such that it is possible all the angels prostrated individually and not collectively in congregation. The verse adds the word, *ajma'ūn*, together. This closes the interpretation of a series of isolated prostrations, rather they prostrated together in sync.

QUICK TERMS

المفسر: *al-mufassar*

The explained. Wording with a statement of clarity from the issuer.

الظاهر: *aẓ-ẓāhir*

The clear. Wording with obvious meaning without the need of context.

Text and Translation

وأما المفسر فهو ما ظهر المراد به من اللفظ ببيان من قِبل المتكلم بحيث لا يبقى معه احتمال التأويل والتخصيص، مثاله في قوله تعالى: ﴿فسجد الملائكة كلهم أجمعون﴾ فاسم الملائكة ظاهر في العموم إلاّ أنّ احتمال التخصيص قائم فانسد باب التخصيص بقوله: كلهم ثم بقي احتمال التفرقة في السجود فانسد باب التأويل بقوله: أجمعون

As for al-mufassar, it is what clears the intended meaning of a passgae by a statement from the first person, such that no possibility of interpretation or specification remains after it. An example of it from the word of He, Most High, is: "Thereupon the angels prostrated, all of them together." The word for angels is clear for all of them except that there remains a possibility of specification, so this is eliminated with the words for 'all of them'. There still remains the

QUICK ARABIC

الملائكة: *al-malāika*

The angels. A creation of Allah Almighty made of light. They are created in different forms and with different powers.

possibility of isolation in the prostrations so the route to interpretation is removed with the word for 'together'.

❖ ❖ ❖

In the rulings of the Shariah an example of al-mufassar is if someone says, "I married so-and-so for one month for so much". The words ""I married" is clear to mean a legitimate contract of marriage in the Shariah, and it is aẓ-ẓāhir in this respect. There is, however, still a possibility that a time-restraint condition was placed on this marriage contract, thus making it *al-mut'a* marriage and unlawful in the Shariah. Now when the words "for one month" are used, we understand that it is not a legal marriage but *al-mut'a* marriage. These words are clarification from the first person that when he said "I married" it was something *al-ḥarām* and not the legal marriage of *an-nikāḥ*. Whatever the connotations of aẓ-ẓāhir are, we will now act upon al-mufassar, as it is clearer and an explanation from the first person.

Another example of the superior clarity of al-mufassar, even over an-naṣṣ, is given from a case where one said: "I owe so-and-so one thousand for the price of this slave or for the price of this commodity". The words "I owe" are clear to mean that I am compelled to give someone one thousand. The reason for this necessity to give one thousand requires further explanation and clarity, so this is clarified by "for the price of this slave" or "for the price of this commodity". The context and an-naṣṣ of the admission is stating that this person just owes one thousand. The explanation and clarification show that it is for a particular purpose, thus making it al-mufassar. So, this one thousand will not be necessary upon the person, as an-naṣṣ states, unless the slave or the commodity is handed over into to his possession, which is what al-mufassar makes clear. The price of something is only due when possession is surrendered.

Likewise, when someone says, "I owe so-and-so one thousand", it is aẓ-ẓāhir in admitting liability as that is what is understood from the confession. The an-naṣṣ and context would be that the one thousand owed is of the currency that is prevalent in the land, as that is what is normally understood when such a detail is omitted. However, if he adds "from such-and-such currency", the currency will be al-mufassar and fully explained. Now, he will not owe the currency of the land, which was understand from an-naṣṣ, rather al-mufassar will take precedence and he will owe one thousand of the said currency.

QUICK TERMS

النص: *an-naṣṣ*

The clearer. Wording with obvious meaning which is in its context.

QUICK ARABIC

المتعة: *al-mut'a*

Enjoyment. An unlawful marriage contracted for a limited period and for a sum of money.

الحرام: *al-ḥarām*

The unlawful. That which is not permitted in the Shariah, as distinguished from the lawful.

النكاح: *an-nikāḥ*

Conjunction. In legal terms it is the marriage contract.

There are other examples showing the superiority of al-mufassar over an-naṣṣ and aẓ-ẓāhir, but these will suffice.

Text and Translation

وفي الشرعيات إذا قال: تزوجت فلانةً شهراً بكذا فقوله: تزوجت ظاهر في النكاح إلا أن احتمال المتعة قائم، فبقوله: شهراً فسر المراد به فقلنا :هذا متعة وليس بنكاح، ولو قال: لفلان علي ألف من ثمن هذا العبد أو من ثمن هذا المتاع، فقوله: علي ألف نص في لزوم ألف إلاّ أنّ احتمال التفسير باقٍ، فبقوله: من ثمن هذا العبد أو من ثمن هذا المتاع بين المراد به فيترجح المفسر على النص حتى لا يلزمه المال إلاّ عند قبض العبد أو المتاع، وقوله: لفلان علي ألف ظاهر في الإقرار نص في نقد البلد فإذا قال: من نقد بلد كذا يترجح المفسر على النص فلا يلزمه نقد البلد بل نقد بلد كذا وعلى هذا نظائره

In the rulings of the Shariah should one say: I married so-and-so for one month in exchange for so much, his words 'I have married' are aẓ-ẓāhir for marriage except that the possibility of it being *al-mut'a* remains. So his words 'for a month' clarified its meaning. We thus concluded that this is *al-mut'a* and not marriage. If one said: 'I owe so-and-so one thousand for the price of this slave or for the price of this commodity, his words 'I owe' are an-naṣṣ to compel one thousand except that a possibility of clarification remains. So his words 'for the price of this slave or for the price of this commodity' has clarified it. So al-mufassar takes precedence over an-naṣṣ such that the price is only necessary upon possession of the slave or the commodity. Furthermore, his words 'I owe so-and-so one thousand' are aẓ-ẓāhir in acknowledging and an-naṣṣ for the currency of the land. Were he to say, 'from such-and-such currency', al-mufassar would be preferred to an-naṣṣ so the currency of the land will not be necessary rather the such-and-such currency will. Other examples are based on this.

❖❖❖

The highest level of clarity is al-muḥkam. It is defined as:

المحكم: ما ازداد قوةً على المفسر بحيث لا يجوز خلافه أصلا

"al-Muḥkam is that which is greater in strength than al-mufassar, such that it cannot be opposed at all."

QUICK TERMS

المفسر: *al-mufassar*

The explained. Wording with a statement of clarity from the issuer.

النص: *an-naṣṣ*

The clearer. Wording with obvious meaning which is in its context.

الظاهر: *aẓ-ẓāhir*

The clear. Wording with obvious meaning without the need of context.

المحكم: *al-muḥkam*

The unalterable. Wording which has no doubt in its meaning and cannot be controverted.

QUICK ARABIC

المتعة: *al-mut'a*

Enjoyment. An unlawful marriage contracted for a limited period and for a sum of money.

This means that al-muḥkam is similar to al-mufassar in clarity except that it cannot accept abrogation or change. Abrogation, *an-naskh*, may not be possible due to the content of a statement telling a universal truth that cannot be changed, or it may be due to the Legislator's ﷺ time. Two examples of al-muḥkam, due to the content, are cited in verses of the blessed Quran:

﴿إن الله بكلِّ شيءٍ عليم﴾ [الأنفال :75]

"Allah has full knowledge over all things."

﴿إن الله لا يظلم الناس شيئاً﴾ [يونس :44]

"Allah does not wrong people at all."

The fact that Allah Almighty's knowledge is all-encompassing and will not cease to be means that this verse cannot be abrogated or changed. Similarly, Allah جل جلاله is The Just; no one is to be wronged by Him جل جلاله.

An example of al-muḥkam from the rulings is the same as the one cited in the example of al-mufassar. If one confessed, "I owe so-and-so one thousand for the price of this slave", the underlining reason for the words "I owe" are numerous. It could be due to liability for a loan, damages, purchasing another item other than the slave, or even for the slave. However, when the words "for the price of this slave" are added, it becomes al-muḥkam as a confession of owing one thousand for the price of the slave. It should be clarified that this statement is actually al-mufassar and what leads it to become al-muḥkam is that once a confession is recorded the orator cannot overturn it. The only one who has the right to excuse it, is the one to whom the money is owed. In this regard the statement in this case moves beyond al-mufassar in its clarity and becomes al-muḥkam.

Finally, the ruling of both al-mufassar and al-muḥkam is that they both are to be enacted and applied under all circumstances due to the strength in their clarity.

حكم المفسر والمحكم: لزوم العمل بهما لا محالة

"The ruling of al-mufassar and al-muḥkam is the necessity to enact both by all means."

QUICK TERMS

النسخ: *an-naskh*

Abrogation. Replacing a ruling from a passage with a ruling revealed afterwards.

Text and Translation

وأما المحكم فهو ما ازداد قوةً على المفسر بحيث لا يجوز خلافه أصلا، مثاله في الكتاب ﴿إن اللهِ بكلِّ شيءٍ علِيم و﴿إن الله لا يظلم الناس شيئا﴾ وفي الحكميات ما قلنا في الإقرار: إنه لفلان على ألف من ثمن هذا العبد فإنّ هذا اللفظ محكم في لزومه بدلاً عنه وعلى هذا نظائره، وحكم المفسر والمحكم لزوم العمل بهما لا محالة

As for al-muḥkam, it is that which has greater magnitude than al-mufassar such that it cannot be opposed at all. An example from the Quran is: "Allah has full knowledge over all things", and "Allah does not wrong people at all". In the rulings of Shariah what we have mentioned about acknowledging: 'I owe so-and-so one thousand for the price of this slave.' These words are al-muḥkam in obliging it in exchange for the other. Other examples are based on this. The ruling on al-mufassar and al-muḥkam is of necessary enacting of both by all means.

QUICK TERMS

المحكم: *al-muḥkam*

The unalterable. Wording which has no doubt in its meaning and cannot be controverted.

المفسر: *al-mufassar*

The explained. Wording with a statement of clarity from the issuer.

❖ ❖ ❖

Ḥanafī Principles (8)

MEMORISE

	Term	Definition	Ruling	An Example
13	الظاهر	كل كلام ظهر المراد به للسامع بنفس السماع من غير تأمل	وجوب العمل به	وَ أحل الله البيع وحرم الربا [البقرة : ٢٧٥]
14	النص	ما سيق الكلام لأجله	وجوب العمل به	وَ أحل الله البيع وحرم الربا [البقرة :٢٧٥] في جواب إنما البيع مِثل الربا [البقرة :٢٧٥]

15	المفسر	ما ظهر المراد به من اللفظ ببيان من قِبل المتكلم بحيث لا يبقى معه احتمال التأويل والتخصيص	لزوم العمل به لا محالة	﴿فسجد الملائكة كلهم أجمعون﴾ [الحجر : ٣٠]
16	المحكم	ما ازداد قوةً على المفسر بحيث لا يجوز خلافه أصلا	لزوم العمل به لا محالة	﴿إن اللهَ بكلِّ شيءٍ عليم﴾ [الأنفال: ٧٥]

❖ ❖ ❖

Summary Of al-Mutaqābilāt - Clarity

1. al-Mutaqābilāt are eight opposite terms of clarity and obscurity. The four terms of clarity are:

2. Details of aẓ-ẓāhir:
   i) Definition:
   كل كلام ظهر المراد به للسامع بنفس السماع من غير تأمل
   "Any words with a clear meaning for the hearer, in the same instance and without further thought".
   ii) Example: The verse وأحل الله البيع وحرم الربا .
   iii) Ruling: وجوب العمل به عام كان أو خاص مع احتمال إرادة الغير
   "Necessary to enact whether it is al-'āmm or al-khāṣṣ, with the possibility of another understanding". The possibility is because interpretations and exemptions are still possible.

3. Details of an-naṣṣ:
   i) Definition: كل كلام ظهر المراد به للسامع وسيق الكلام لأجله
   "Any words with a clear meaning for the hearer and it is the underlying purpose for the statement".
   ii) Example: The verse وأحل الله البيع وحرم الربا when it has been stated to make a differentiation between trade and usury.

iii) Ruling: وجوب العمل به عام كان أو خاص مع احتمال إرادة الغير
"Necessary to enact whether it is al-'āmm or al-khāṣṣ, with the possibility of another understanding". The possibility is because interpretations and exemptions are still possible.

4. Details of al-mufassar:
   i) Definition: ما ظهر المراد به من اللفظ ببيان من قبل المتكلم بحيث لا يبقى احتمال التأويل والتخصيص
   "The wording with a clear meaning after an explanation provided by the source, leaving no room for interpretations or exemptions".
   ii) Example: فسجد الملائكة كلهم أجمعون
   iii) Ruling: لزوم العمل به لا محالة
   "It must be enacted in all circumstances".

5. Details of al-muḥkam:
   i) Definition: ما ازداد قوة على المفسر بحيث لا يجوز خلافه أصلا
   "The wording that is more permanent than al-mufassar such that it can't be opposed".
   ii) Example: إن اللهِ بكل شيءٍ عليم
   iii) Ruling: لزوم العمل به لا محالة
   "It must be enacted in all circumstances".

1.3.2 al-Mutaqābilāt – Ambiguity

Following the discussions surrounding the terms of clarity, in this section the four terms of ambiguity are presented. The four terms of ambiguity introduced are al-khafīy (the unclear), al-mushkil (the difficult), al-mujmal (the unexplained) and al-mutashābih (the intricate). The summary of how they relate to each other is shown in Figure 1.3.2-01.

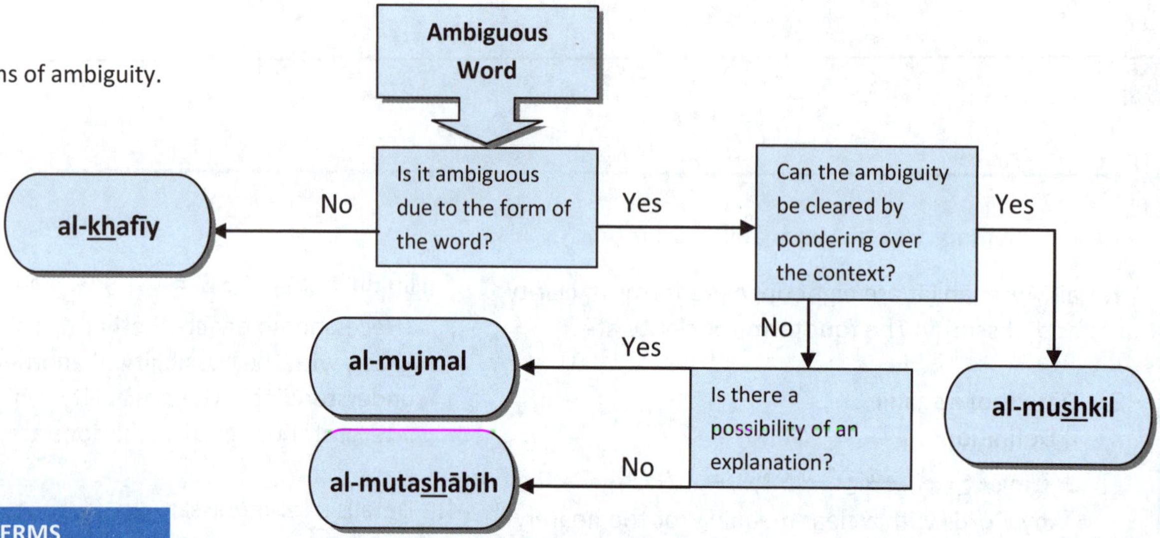

FIGURE 1.3.2-01

A division of terms of ambiguity.

The terms of ambiguity are said to be the opposites of the terms of clarity. Figure 1.3-01 showed that the weakest strength in clarity is that of aẓ-ẓāhir. The opposite of aẓ-ẓāhir and the weakest in ambiguity is al-khafīy. The second weakest in clarity is an-naṣṣ, the opposite of which, in ambiguity, is al-mushkil. In clarity the next in strength is al-mufassar, the opposite of which is al-mujmal. Finally, the clearest is al-muḥkam and its equivalent is the most ambiguous, al-mutashābih. Together these eight terms constitute al-mutaqābilāt, the opposites.

The definition of the first and weakest of the ambiguous terms, al-khafīy, is given as:

الخفي: ما خفي المراد به بعارض لا من حيث الصيغة

"al-Khafīy is the one with an obscure meaning due to an impediment and not the word form itself."

QUICK TERMS

الخفي: *al-khafīy*

The unclear. Wording in which other things are hidden beneath the plain text.

المشكل: *al-mushkil*

The difficult. Wording which requires further enquiry to ascertain its meaning.

المجمل: *al-mujmal*

The unexplained. Wording that requires explanatory statements.

المتشابه: *al-mutashābih*

The intricate. Wording for which it is impossible for man to ascertain its exact meaning.

This definition shows that the reason for the difficulty in understanding the word that is al-<u>kh</u>afīy is due to an external factor and impediment, otherwise the word itself is known and clear. There are three examples provided for al-<u>kh</u>afīy and its ruling follows them. The examples are:

1. It is mentioned in Sūrat ul-Māida, verse 38, regarding a thief:

والسارِقُ والسارِقةُ فاقطعوا أيديهما [المائدة: 38]

"As for the thief, both men and women, cut off their hands..."

This verse is clear and aẓ-ẓāhir regarding *as-sāriq*, the thief, but the question is if the verse also applies to a pickpocket or tomb-raider? The word *thief* is used for the one who steals, especially secretly or without open force, and wrongfully takes the personal goods of another. The ruling of the Shariah is also clear and aẓ-ẓāhir regarding the punishment for the crime, that is the severing of a thief's hand. However, the verse is al-<u>kh</u>afīy with respect to a pickpocket and a tomb-raider because the Arabic speaking world gives both a pickpocket and tomb-raider different names to *as-sāriq*, they are *aṭ-ṭarrār* and *an-nabbā<u>sh</u>*, respectively. If they were all the same then alternative names would not be necessary. This is an external factor and impediment to the words of the verse itself.

After some careful consideration, we find that *aṭ-ṭarrār* has an added intensity than *as-sāriq*. The thief takes others' belongings in secret from a relatively secure location and with no aggression or force, whereas the pickpocket is taking belongings from a very secure place, whilst the victim is momentarily unaware, with a brazen disregard and higher probability of force or aggression. The tomb-raider, *an-nabbā<u>sh</u>*, is called differently to *as-sāriq* because he looks to take the shrouds of the deceased from a very unsecure location and from those who are not going to be threatened with aggression or force. Thus, *aṭ-ṭarrār* takes from a very secure location heightening the possibility of aggression compared to a *as-sāriq*, and *an-nabbā<u>sh</u>* takes from a less secure location and with less aggression than *as-sāriq*. As *aṭ-ṭarrār* is perpetrating a worse crime than *as-sāriq* he is more deserving of the punishment stipulated by

119

al-Mutaqābilāt - Ambiguity

QUICK TERMS

الظاهر :*aẓ-ẓāhir*

The clear. Wording with obvious meaning without the need for context.

النص: *an-naṣṣ*

The clearer. Wording with obvious meaning which is in its context.

المفسر: *al-mufassar*

The explained. Wording with a statement of clarity from the issuer.

المحكم: *al-muḥkam*

The unalterable. Wording which has no doubt in its meaning and cannot be controverted.

QUICK ARABIC

السارق: *as-sāriq*

Thief. Who takes another's items without aggression, in secret and from a secure location.

الطرار: *aṭ-ṭarrār*

Pickpocket. Who takes another's items with possible aggression and from a very secure location.

النباش: *an-nabbā<u>sh</u>*

Tomb raider. Who takes the shroud of the deceased from an unsecure location and without expecting aggression.

the verse regarding the thief. *an-Nabbāsh* is committing a less serious offence to *as-sāriq* so will not be given the same punishment.

2. The second example of al-khafīy is from Sūrat un-Nūr, verse 2.

الزانيةُ والزاني [النور :2]

"The adulteress and the adulterer..."

This verse is aẓ-ẓāhir regarding the adulterer. The Arabs understand the punishment for an adulterer upon hearing the words of the verse. However, whether the verse applies to a sodomite, *al-lūṭī*, is unclear. The ambiguity comes about because the Arabs do not use the same word for both of these sins. So, the verse is said to be al-khafīy with respect to the sodomite because the ambiguity is due to an external factor; a factor and impediment not found in the words of the verse.

After careful deliberations, Imam Abū Ḥanīfa ﷺ expressed a difference between the two acts. In adultery the desire for gratification is found in both participants, whereas in sodomy the cardinal desire to gratify is found only in the penetrator. Therefore, the meaning of *az-zinā* is excessive in comparison to *al-lawāṭa*, thus the punishment of the verse is not applied to the perpetrators of sodomy. Whenever there is even the slightest doubt cast over the application of a divine punishment, it is not applied and other lesser deterrents are utilised.

3. The third example of al-khafīy is if one vowed, "I will not eat a delicacy", using the Arabic word *al-fākiha*. *al-Fākiha* colloquially means fruits, and it is aẓ-ẓāhir in this meaning. Fruits are a food delicacy that are not usually consumed as a main meal. By eating fruits the vow would be broken. However, according to Imam Abū Ḥanīfa ﷺ the vow is not broken by eating grapes or pomegranates. This is because both grapes and pomegranates are consumed as main meals and not as a side delicacy due to their nutritional properties. So, if the concept of delicacy is not applicable to grapes

QUICK TERMS

الخفي: *al-khafīy*

The unclear. Wording in which other things are hidden beneath the plain text.

الظاهر: *aẓ-ẓāhir*

The clear. Wording with obvious meaning without the need for context.

QUICK ARABIC

اللوطي: *al-lūṭī*

Sodomite. The one who commits the act of homosexuality.

الزنا: *az-zinā*

Fornication. Sexual intercourse between two persons not married to each other.

الفاكهة: *al-fākiha*

A delicacy. A choice of food considered with regards to its luxury or enjoyment, such as fruit.

and pomegranates, they are excluded from the vow. Consuming both these items would therefore not invalidate the vow.

The ruling of al-khafīy is:

حكم الخفي: وجوب الطلب حتى يزول عنه الخفاء

"The ruling of al-khafīy is the necessity to pursue it until obscurity is eliminated."

Once an external impediment is encountered, it is necessary to explore the possibilities of eliminating the obscurity caused. If the imposing impediment delivers a meaning more intense than what is understood from aẓ-ẓāhir, what was al-khafīy will be clear and included within the same framework. However, if the impediment delivers a weaker and milder meaning than aẓ-ẓāhir, al-khafīy is excluded from the framework.

Text and Translation

ثم لهذه الأربعة أربعة أخرى تقابلها. فضد الظاهر الخفي وضد النص المشكل وضد المفسر المجمل وضد المحكم المتشابه، فالخفي ما خفي المراد به بعارض لا من حيث الصيغة، مثاله في قوله تعالى: ﴿والسارِق والسارِقة فاقطعوا أيديهما﴾ فإنه ظاهر في حق السارق خفي في حق الطرار والنباش، وكذلك قوله تعالى ﴿الزانيةُ والزاني﴾ ظاهر في حق الزاني خفي في حق اللوطي. ولو حلف لا يأكل فاكهة كان ظاهرا فيما يتفكه به خفيا في حق العنب والرمان وحكم الخفي وجوب الطلب حتى يزول عنه الخفاء.

Then each of these four have their opposites. So the opposite of aẓ-ẓāhir is al-khafīy; for an-naṣṣ it is al-mushkil; for al-mufassar it is al-mujmal; and for al-muḥkam it is al-mutashābih. So al-khafīy is the one with an obscure meaning due to an impediment and not the word itself. An example of it from the Word of the Almighty is: "As for thieves, both men and women, cut off their hands..." It is aẓ-ẓāhir with respect to the thief but al-khafīy with respect to a pickpocket or tomb-raider. Similarly is what He, the Almighty, said: "The adulteress and the adulterer..." It is aẓ-ẓāhir concerning the adulterer but al-khafīy concerning the sodomite. If one was to vow not to eat fruit it would be aẓ-ẓāhir concerning that which is eaten as a delicacy but al-khafīy with respect to grapes and pomegranate. The ruling of al-khafīy is the necessity to pursue it until obscurity is eliminated.

QUICK TERMS

النص: *an-naṣṣ*

The clearer. Wording with obvious meaning which is in context.

المشكل: *al-mushkil*

The difficult. Wording which requires further enquiry to ascertain its meaning.

المفسر: *al-mufassar*

The explained. Wording with a statement of clarity from the issuer.

المجمل: *al-mujmal*

The unexplained. Wording that requires explanatory statements.

المحكم: *al-muḥkam*

The unalterable. Wording which has no doubt in its meaning and cannot be controverted.

المتشابه: *al-mutashābih*

The intricate. Wording for which it is impossible for man to ascertain its exact meaning.

❖❖❖

On the scale of ambiguity, the term that follows al-khafīy is al-mushkil. The definition of al-mushkil is:

المشكل: ما ازداد خفاءً على الخفي

"al-Mushkil is that which is more obscure than al-khafīy."

al-Mushkil literally means the difficult, and it is more obscure than al-khafīy in that not only are the words strange to the one who encounters them, but there is also a confusion of the possible solutions. It requires an exerted effort to explore the words and arrive at an understanding. So, the manner to unravel its meaning would be to first find all the possible meanings of the words and then to apply each of those meanings to the context of the words, to see which one fits. The difference with al-khafīy is that for al-khafīy just to explore the meanings was necessary; however, in al-mushkil the explored meanings need to be applied on a case-by-case basis to see if they are suitable. In this regard, al-mushkil is more obscure than al-khafīy.

An example of al-mushkil from the cases of the Shariah is if one vowed not to eat a sauce, known as *al-īytidām*. It is aẓ-ẓāhir and clear that condiments such as vinegar and syrup are included in this vow. However, it is unclear for cooked meat, eggs or cheese. First, we must find the actual meaning of *al-īytidām* and then explore whether such a meaning is applicable to meat, eggs or cheese. Searching for the meaning of *al-īytidām* reveals that it is a fusion of a preparation with bread, i.e. a sauce. A sauce is a liquid or semi liquid that is eaten as a relish and condiment accompanying food. So, any preparation that fuses with bread in a way that allows the bread to soak it up, will be a sauce and hence the act of *al-īytidām*. Any item consumed without bread or the idea of it being soaked up will be excluded from *al-īytidām*. Vinegar and syrup fuse with bread and are consumed as a condiment, so both will be included in the vow. By eating them, the vow will be broken. However, cooked meat, eggs and cheese do not fuse and soak into bread, and so will not be included in the vow.

Text and Translation

وأما المشكل فهو ما ازداد خفاءً على الخفي كأنه بعدما خفي على السامع حقيقته دخل في أشكاله
وأمثاله حتى لا ينال المراد إلا بالطلب ثم بالتأمل حتى يتميز عن أمثاله، ونظيره في الأحكام إذا حلف

QUICK TERMS

الخفي: *al-khafīy*

The unclear. Wording in which other things are hidden beneath the plain text.

المشكل: *al-mushkil*

The difficult. Wording which requires further enquiry to ascertain its meaning.

الظاهر: *aẓ-ẓāhir*

The clear. Wording with obvious meaning without the need for context.

QUICK ARABIC

الإيتدام: *al-iytidām*

To take a condiment. To enrich bread with some extra flavour using a sauce.

لا يأتدم فإنه ظاهر في الخل والدبس فإنما هو مشكل في اللحم والبيض والجبن حتى يطلب في معنى الائتدام ثم يتأمل أن ذلك المعنى هل يوجد في اللحم والبيض والجبن أم لا

As for al-mushkil, it is that which is more obscure than al-khafīy. It is as though after its actual meaning has become obscure to the listener he contemplates over its possibilities and examples. So much so, that its true meaning can not be found except after pursuing it and then contemplating until it is distinguished from its possibilities. An example of it from the rulings is if one was to vow to not consume a sauce. It is aẓ-ẓāhir for vinegar and syrup, but al-mushkil for meat, eggs and cheese. We would pursue the meaning of 'sauce', then contemplate over whether this meaning is found in meat, eggs and cheese or not.

❖ ❖ ❖

In the scale of ambiguity, the next term is al-mujmal. It is more ambiguous and obscure than al-mushkil. Its definition is:

المجمل: ما احتمل وجوها فصار بحال لا يوقف على المراد به إلا ببيان من قبل المتكلم

"al-Mujmal is that which has many possibilities to such an extent where one meaning cannot be determined except after an explanation from the first person."

This means that, unlike al-mushkil, al-mujmal is not clarified or understood through thought and contemplation alone. Rather it requires a clarifying statement from the one who issued the words in the first place.

An example of al-mujmal from the Shariah is verse 279 of Sūrat ul-Baqara:

﴿حرم الربوا﴾ [البقرة: 279]

"...Allah forbade *ar-ribā*..."

In this verse, we are told *ar-ribā* is unlawful, but the meaning of the word *ar-ribā* remains ambiguous and unclear. If we look at the literal meaning of *ar-ribā,* we find that it is any type of increase. This is clearly not the intent as in the very same verse trading is deemed to be permitted, and trading itself is to increase in profit. So, in this case, not only is the word ambiguous like al-mushkil, moreover

QUICK TERMS

المجمل: *al-mujmal*

The unexplained. Wording that requires explanatory statements.

QUICK ARABIC

الربا: *ar-ribā*

Usury. Excess to the legal standard permitted in a contract of exchange.

it is difficult to begin a thought process or even to contemplate. To unravel this ambiguity an explanatory statement is required.

The explanation of *ar-ribā* comes in the tradition of the blessed Prophet ﷺ: "Wheat for wheat, barley for barley, dates for dates, salt for salt, gold for gold, and silver for silver; should be equal when transferred from one hand to another. Anything in excess is *ar-ribā*." The Hadith mentions that the exchange of six commodities with a similar type must be equal when exchanged in a transaction, otherwise anything extra will constitute *ar-ribā* and is thus unlawful. According to Imam Abū Ḥanīfa رحمه الله the underlining feature of these items is that they are volumetric and weighed. So *ar-ribā* was al-mujmal in the verse and required an explanation. The tradition provided the explanation saying that items that are similar in type, as well as measured volumetrically and in weight, must be exchanged in exact amounts, any disparity will be *ar-ribā*.

Text and Translation

ثم فوق المشكل المجمل وهو ما احتمل وجوها فصار بحال لا يوقف على المراد به إلا ببيان من قبل المتكلم، ونظيره في الشرعيات قوله تعالى: ﴿حرم الربوا﴾ فإن المفهوم من الربا هو الزيادة المطلقة وهي غير مرادة بل المراد الزيادة الخالية عن العوض في بيع المقدرات المتجانسة واللفظ لا دلالة له على هذا فلا ينال المراد بالتأمل

Then beyond al-mushkil is al-mujmal, which is that which has many possibilities to an extent where one meaning cannot be determined except after an explanation from the first person. An example of it from the Shariah is what He Almighty revealed: "...(Allah) forbade *ar-ribā*..." The meaning of *ar-ribā* is mere increase, and that is not intended. Rather what is meant is an increase without a return in a transaction of similar type weights. The word itself has no indication of this, so it can not be arrived at through contemplation.

❖ ❖ ❖

Finally, the last and most obscure of the ambiguous terms is al-mutashābih. al-Mutashābih is defined as:

المتشابه: ما انقطع رجاء معرفة المراد منه في الدنيا بالنسبة إلى الأمة

"al-Mutashābih is whose understanding is lost to the Ummah in this world."

حديث

عن عبادة بن الصامت رضي الله عنه عن النبي ﷺ قال الذهب بالذهب مثلا بمثل والفضة بالفضة مثلا بمثل والتمر بالتمر مثلا بمثل والبر بالبر مثلا بمثل والملح بالملح مثلا بمثل والشعير بالشعير مثلا بمثل فمن زاد أو ازداد فقد أربى.

عليه الصلاة والسلام

(الترمذي: 1240)

QUICK TERMS

المشكل: *al-mushkil*

The difficult. Wording which requires further enquiry to ascertain its meaning.

المجمل: *al-mujmal*

The unexplained. Wording that requires explanatory statements.

QUICK ARABIC

الربا: *ar-ribā*

Usury. Excess to the legal standard permitted in a contract of exchange.

al-Muta<u>sh</u>ābih is so obscure that Muslims as a nation are not required to pursue its meaning in this life. This is because there are no means to a satisfactory explanation. Thus, the ruling of both al-mujmal and al-muta<u>sh</u>ābih is:

حكم المجمل والمتشابه: اعتقاد حقية المراد به حتى يأتي البيان

"The ruling on both al-mujmal and al-muta<u>sh</u>ābih is to believe in the truth of their meaning and await an explanation."

For al-mujmal, the explanation is available from another verse of the blessed Quran or a tradition of the blessed Prophet ﷺ. The example of this passed in the previous segment. For al-muta<u>sh</u>ābih, that possibility is closed too. An example of it are the separated Arabic letters, ḥurūf ul-muqaṭṭa'āt, at the beginning of some chapters of the blessed Quran. Muslims must believe in its truth as a revelation, and leave its exactness to Allah ﷻ and His Beloved ﷺ. Allah ﷻ says in the blessed Quran:

﴿والرسخون في العلم يقولون ءامنا به كل من عند ربنا﴾ [آل عمران: 7]

"...And those who are firmly grounded in knowledge say, "We believe in the Book; the whole of it is from our Lord..."

Text and Translation

ثم فوق المجمل في الخفاء المتشابه، مثال المتشابه الحروف المقطعات في أوائل السور. وحكم المجمل والمتشابه اعتقاد حقية المراد به حتى يأتي البيان

Then after al-mujmal in ambiguity is al-muta<u>sh</u>ābih. Examples of al-muta<u>sh</u>ābih are the staccato-letters at the beginning of chapters. The ruling on both al-mujmal and al-muta<u>sh</u>ābih is to believe in the truth of their meaning and await an explanation.

❖❖❖

Ḥanafī Principles (9)

	Term	Definition	Ruling	An Example
17	الخفي	ما خفي المراد به بعارض لا من حيث الصيغة	وجوب الطلب حتى يزول عنه الخفاء	والسارق والسارقة فاقطعوا أيديهما [المائدة: 38]

125

al-Mutaqābilāt - Ambiguity

QUICK TERMS

المتشابه: *al-muta<u>sh</u>ābih*

The intricate. Wording for which an exact meaning is impossible for people to ascertain.

المجمل: *al-mujmal*

The unexplained. Wording that requires explanatory statements.

QUICK ARABIC

الحروف المقطعات: *al-ḥurūf al-muqaṭṭa'āt*

Staccato letters. Individual letters of the Arabic alphabet at the beginning of 29 chapters of the blessed Quran.

MEMORISE

18	المشكل	ما ازداد خفاءً على الخفي	طلب المراد منه والتأمل فيه	إذا حلف لا يأتدم
19	المجمل	ما احتمل وجوها فصار بحال لا يوقف على المراد به إلا ببيان من قبل المتكلم	اعتقاد حقية المراد به حتى يأتي البيان	﴿حرم الربوا﴾ [البقرة275 :]
20	المتشابه	ما انقطع رجاء معرفة المراد منه في الدنيا بالنسبة إلى الأمة	اعتقاد حقية المراد به حتى يأتي البيان	حروف مقطعات

❖ ❖ ❖

Summary Of al-Mutaqābilāt - Ambiguity

1. Details of al-khafīy:
   i) Definition: ما خفى المراد به بعارض لا من حيث الصيغة
   "The one with an obscure meaning due to an impediment not in the word form".
   ii) Example: والسارِق والسارِقة فاقطعوا أيديهما
   The verse is clear about the thief but ambiguous about the pickpocket and tomb-raider.
   iii) Ruling: وجوب الطلب حتى يزول عنه الخفاء
   "It is necessary to search until the ambiguity is cleared".
2. Details of al-mushkil:
   i) Definition: ما ازداد خفاء على الخفي
   "Wording more ambiguous than al-khafīy".
   ii) Example: if one vowed not to eat a sauce, it would be clear regarding vinegar but not for meat or eggs.
   iii) Ruling: طلب المراد منه والتأمل فيه
   "To search its meaning and then deliberate over it".
3. Details of al-mujmal:
   i) Definition: ما احتمل وجوها ولا يوقف على المراد إلا بالبيان من قبل المتكلم
   "Wording with possibilities, which is only determined with an explanation from the speaker".
   ii) Example: In حرّم الربوا, the word *ar-ribā*
   iii) Ruling: اعتقاد حقيّة المراد به حتى يأتي البيان
   "Believe in its truth and await the explanation".
4. Details of al-mutashābih:
   i) Definition: ما انقطع رجاء معرفة المراد منه في الدنيا
   The meaning of which is lost in this world.
   ii) Example: الحروف المقطعات
   iii) Ruling: اعتقاد حقيّة المراد به حتى يأتي البيان
   "Believe in its truth and await the explanation".

1.4 Abandoning al-Ḥaqīqa

Chapter 1.1 was about word coinage. Chapter 1.2 on word usage followed and then chapter 1.3 on word clarity. Figure 1.0-01 divided the words of the blessed Quran in terms of their impact on rulings into four divisions. Before the final division on Textual Locations, chapter 1.5, Uṣūl ush-Shashī has included this tangential but necessary section on when the literal, al-ḥaqīqa, understanding may be abandoned. It seems more akin to chapter 1.2 that discussed al-ḥaqīqa in some detail, but has been included after chapter 1.3 on levels of clarity.

At first, the section seems misplaced. However, the reason for bringing this discussion here may be that it is related to clarity and ambiguity. Generally speaking, words should be in their literal meaning. In particular, according to Imam Abū Ḥanīfa رحمه الله if al-ḥaqīqa is in use then it takes precedence over al-majāz, even if al-majāz is in use. However, there are occasions when the Aḥnāf entirely abandon the literal meaning and on occasion, they partially abandon it. This can cause confusion and ambiguity. So, to clarify those occasions this section has been included after chapter 1.3 on levels of clarity. The main topic will resume in chapter 1.5 later.

There are five reasons why al-ḥaqīqa may be abandoned. They are:

1. *Dalālat ul-'urf*: indications of customary law;
2. *Dalālat ul-kalām*: indications in the text;
3. *Dalālat us-siyāq*: indications from the context;
4. *Dalālatun min qibal il-mutakallim*: indications from the first person; and,
5. *Dalālatu maḥal il-kalām*: indications from the object of the speech.

The first of them is *dalālat ul-'urf*, or reasons that are established due to customary law. This is when a people popularise a particular meaning for a word, which is other than its coined meaning. The reason this has an impact is that rulings are based upon words, and words gain their meaning from how users choose to use them. When a word has a popular meaning amongst people that is how they would normally use that word. If people are using the words in this manner then the rulings will be a result of these words. This shows that the coined meaning will not be in the consideration of the user, so it cannot be the meaning that is significant in the ruling. It is worth bearing in mind that according to Imam Abū Ḥanīfa رحمه الله *dalālat ul-'urf* only applies when the coined

QUICK TERMS

الحقيقة: *al-ḥaqīqa*

The literal. A word coined by the lexicon for an item.

المجاز: *al-majāz*

The figurative. A word used for a meaning other than its coined meaning.

meaning is no longer prevalent. Otherwise, when the coined meaning is in use, there is no reason to substitute it with an alternative meaning.

An example of *dalālat ul-'urf* is if one vowed not to "buy a head", as this would mean animal heads that are normally bought by people to eat. These would include the likes of cows, goats or buffalos. It would not normally include pigeon heads or sparrow heads. Pigeons and sparrows are bought with their heads attached and not separately due to their small size. Larger animals' parts and limbs are sold separately. After the vow is taken, if the person in question buys a cow, goat or buffalo head, the vow will be violated, and if he went to buy the head of a pigeon or a sparrow the vow would be intact. This is because the "heads" mentioned in the vow would include the former group of animal heads due to *dalālat ul-'urf*, but it would not include the latter group due to the same reason.

Similarly, if one vowed not to 'eat eggs', the vow would only include the eggs that are normally consumed by people. Normally people consume chicken or duck eggs, as these are sold in the common market. Pigeon or sparrow eggs are not normally sold, so they would not come under the vow. Therefore, if the one making the vow were to consume a pigeon or sparrow egg, the vow would remain intact due to *dalālat ul-'urf*.

It is worth noting that the customary law could change over time. Should the custom change in a land then the ruling will also adjust accordingly.

Text and Translation

فصل فيما يترك به حقائق الألفاظ: وما يترك به حقيقة اللفظ خمسة أنواع أحدها: دلالة العرف؛ وذلك لأن ثبوت الأحكام بالألفاظ إنما كان لدلالة اللفظ على المعنى المراد للمتكلم فإذا كان المعنى متعارفا بين الناس كان ذلك المعنى المتعارف دليلا على أنه هو المراد به ظاهرا فيترتب عليه الحكم، مثاله لو حلف لا يشتري رأسا فهو على ما تعارفه الناس فلا يحنث برأس العصفور والحمامة، وكذلك لو حلف لا يأكل بيضا كان ذلك على المتعارف فلا يحنث بتناول بيض العصفور والحمامة

Chapter on reasons to abandon the literal meaning of words: There are five reasons why the literal meaning may be overlooked. The first is *dalālat ul-'urf*. This is because establishing rulings with words is due to a word's indication of

QUICK TERMS

دلالة العرف: *dalālat ul-'urf*

Customary law. Indications due to a meaning popularised by a people.

the speaker's desired meaning. So clearly if a meaning is recognised amongst people it shows that the recognised meaning is what is meant; so rulings will be based upon it. An example of it is if one vows not to buy a head. It will be as people recognise it, so he will not have broken the vow with the head of a sparrow or pigeon. Similarly, if one vowed not to eat eggs, it will be based upon the recognised meaning. So he would not have broken the vow by eating a sparrow or pigeon egg.

❖ ❖ ❖

We also learn from the above discussion that when al-ḥaqīqa is abandoned, as in the examples above, it is not necessary that the replacement is always al-majāz. Rather, it can be replaced by *al-ḥaqīqat ul-qāṣira*, a restricted literal meaning. *al-Ḥaqīqat ul-qāṣira* is a term that means a selection of those things that are included in a coined word are retained, whereas the rest are discarded. Like the use of the words 'heads' and 'eggs' to mean the heads and eggs of selected animals, and not the rest. This shows that al-ḥaqīqa is not only replaced by al-majāz, rather *al-ḥaqīqat ul-qāṣira* may replace al-ḥaqīqa too.

An example of *al-ḥaqīqat ul-qāṣira* is the limiting and restricting of al-'āmm. This was discussed earlier in this book in section 1.1.1, from page 31. In addition to this, when al-muṭlaq is restricted and becomes al-muqayyad, it also is *al-ḥaqīqat ul-qāṣira*. The discussion on al-muqayyad can be read in detail in section 1.1.2, page 36.

Similarly, rather than al-majāz, *al-ḥaqīqat ul-qāṣira* replaces al-ḥaqīqa in the following examples. If one vowed to perform *al-ḥajj*, it would take the meaning of the Hajj that people recognise and understand. That is to say, he would have to make one particular intention to visit and to perform the rituals expected, which is due to *dalālat ul-'urf*. His vow would not mean the literal meaning of *al-ḥajj*, which is simply to make an intention. His vow will be "I vow to *perform the rituals of Hajj*" and not "I vow *to make an intention*". Moreover, if one vowed, "I will walk to the House of Allah", or "I vow to brush my clothes over the Ka'ba", they will mean that he vows to perform the ritual Hajj. This is by way of *dalālat ul-'urf* and it is what people would understand from these statements. It does not mean that he will walk to the House of Allah for another reason like trade or for 'umrah, nor does it mean he will send his clothes with someone else to rub on the walls of the Ka'ba.

QUICK TERMS

المجاز: *al-majāz*

The figurative. A word used for a meaning other than its coined meaning.

الحقيقة القاصرة: *al-ḥaqīqat ul-qāṣira*

The confined literal. A word that indicates a selection of items from the literal meaning.

الحقيقة: *al-ḥaqīqa*

The literal. A word coined by the lexicon for an item.

العام: *al-'āmm*

The general. A word designated for a group.

المطلق: *al-muṭlaq*

The unrestricted. Indicates an entity irrespective of any qualities.

المقيد: *al-muqayyad*

The restricted. Indicates an entity and some of its qualities.

QUICK TERMS

الحقيقة: *al-ḥaqīqa*

The literal. A word coined by the lexicon for an item.

المجاز: *al-majāz*

The figurative. A word used for a meaning other than its coined meaning.

الحقيقة القاصرة: *al-ḥaqīqat ul-qāṣira*

The confined literal. A word that indicates a selection of items from the literal meaning.

عام خص عنه البعض: *'āmmun khuṣṣa 'anhu ul-ba'ḍ*

The general with exemption. A word designated for a group with possible exemptions.

دلالة الكلام: *dalālat ul-kalām*

Textual indications. When the words used intrinsically imply a meaning.

QUICK ARABIC

الحطيم: *al-ḥaṭīm*

The broken. A detached section of the blessed Ka'ba, marked by a short semi-circular wall.

المكاتب: *al-mukātab*

The ransomed. A slave promised freedom by a master in return for money paid.

Text and Translation

وبهذا ظهر أن ترك الحقيقة لا يوجب المصير إلى المجاز بل جاز أن تثبت به الحقيقة القاصرة ومثاله تقييد العام بالبعض وكذلك لو نذر حجا أو مشيا إلى بيت الله تعالى أو أن يضرب بثوبه حطيم الكعبة يلزمه الحج بأفعال معلومة لوجود العرف

From this it is clear that abandoning al-ḥaqīqa doesn't necessitate al-majāz, but it is possible to establish al-ḥaqīqat ul-qāṣira. An example of it is the restricting of al-'āmm khuṣṣa 'anhu al-ba'ḍ. Likewise, if one vowed *al-ḥajj*, to walk to the House of Allah, or to rub his clothes on *al-Ḥaṭīm* of the Ka'ba, the known ritual will become necessary on him due to the customary meaning.

❖❖❖

The second reason why al-ḥaqīqa may be abandoned is due to *dalālat ul-kalām*, which is an indication from the text that points to this. *Dalālat ul-kalām* means that irrespective of the context, the words themselves indicate a particular meaning; a meaning that is intrinsic to the word due to its root word and the letters it consists of. The word designation and coinage may be true for a whole host of individuals but when analysed, the word is precise and accurate for a selection of the group, with the remaining being deficient in that meaning in some way.

An example of this is given with the word 'ownership'. If a master said, "All slaves in my ownership are free", it would exclude those slaves that are *al-mukātab* and those that he partially owns. However, if the master intends their inclusion, they will be included and become free. This is because "slaves in my ownership" gives the impression of being inclusive of all types of slaves, so his intention will be acceptable in this regard. However, when we analyse the words a little closely, we find that 'ownership' when left unqualified would include only those that the master fully owns. Any slave that he can claim sole and complete ownership over would be included. If he is not the sole owner or with complete ownership, it is not accurate for him to say "I own this slave". It is clear that the one he partially owns is not in his sole ownership, so is excluded from the statement announcing freedom. With regards to *al-mukātab*, the master is the sole owner but the ownership is not complete. We know this because the master has no right to interfere with the transactional dealings of *al-mukātab* nor can he legally have intercourse with a female *al-mukātaba*. Had the master complete ownership then these restrictions would not be in place.

To provide a consequence of the fact that the master does not have complete ownership over *al-mukātab* we say that should an *al-mukātab* marry the daughter of his master and the master passed away, *al-mukātab*'s wife and the daughter of the deceased master would become *al-mukātab*'s inheritor in accordance with the agreement of *al-mukātaba*. Furthermore, the marriage will still be valid. If the ownership of the master were complete from the onset, the marriage would be terminated because should one spouse become the owner of the other, the marriage becomes invalid.

This case illustrates that the master does not have complete ownership of an *al-mukātab* slave. It is for this reason that such a slave is not included by default in the earlier statement of freedom.

The situation of the *umm ul-walad* slave-girl and *al-mudabbar* is different to that of *al-mukātab* and the partially owned, *al-mu'taq ul-ba'ḍ*. The *umm ul-walad* and *al-mudabbar* will become free by default when the master states, "All slaves in my ownership are free". This is because the master is the sole owner and his ownership in them is complete. It is for this reason that a master is permitted to have sexual relations with *umm ul-walad* and *al-mudabbara*. Therefore, the ownership of the master is complete in both of these two slave types and so they are included in his statement that frees them.

There remains one question though regarding *umm ul-walad* and *al-mudabbar*, which is that if a master was required to expiate and pay *al-kaffāra*, he is not permitted to free either the *umm ul-walad* or *al-mudabbar*. However, we have just stated that the master has sole and complete ownership over them and so he should be permitted to free them as part of the expiation. This is answered by the fact that the expiation requires a complete expiation of a slave but both *umm ul-walad* and *al-mudabbar* are already promised freedom. This means that they both are partially free in the sense that after the master dies both have a definite free status. The requirement of the expiation is to completely free a slave, and these slaves already have freedom promised, so freeing them is not sufficient to satisfy the terms of expiation. The expiation asks for complete emancipation from serfdom, the *umm ul-walad* and *al-mudabbar* lack in complete serfdom.

QUICK ARABIC

أم الولد: *umm ul-walad*

Mother of offspring. A female slave who gives birth to a master's child.

المدبر: *al-mudabbar*

Free by arrangement. A slave promised freedom that takes effect after the master's death.

العبد المطلق: *al-'abd ul-muṭlaq*

The generic slave. A person who is the property of another irrespective of particulars.

الكفارة: *al-kaffāra*

Expiation. The prescribed atonement for neglected duties.

QUICK DICTIONARY

Emancipate: *ih-man-suh-payt*
To free. To free a slave from bondage or servitude.

Serfdom: *serf-dom*
In slavery. A person in the condition of being the property of another.

بسم الله الرحمن الرحيم

وَالَّذِينَ يُظَاهِرُونَ مِن نِّسَائِهِمْ ثُمَّ يَعُودُونَ لِمَا قَالُوا فَتَحْرِيرُ رَقَبَةٍ (الآية)

صدق الله العظيم

سورة المجادلة: 3

QUICK ARABIC

المكاتب: *al-mukātab*

The ransomed. A slave promised freedom by a master in return for money paid.

المملوك: *al-mamlūk*

The generic slave. A person who is the property of another.

المدبر: *al-mudabbar*

Free by arrangement. A slave promised freedom that takes effect after the master's death.

أم الولد: *umm ul-walad*

Mother of offspring. A female slave who gives birth to a master's child.

المعتق البعض: *al-mu'taq ul-ba'ḍ*

Partial slave. A slave who is partially owned by a master.

الرق: *ar-riq*

Serfdom. The status of a person who is the property of another.

Text and Translation

والثاني: قد تترك الحقيقة بدلالة في نفس الكلام، مثاله إذا قال: كل مملوك لي فهو حر لم يعتق مكاتبوه ولا من أعتق بعضه إلا إذا نوى دخولهم؛ لأن لفظ المملوك مطلق يتناول المملوك من كلّ وجه والمكاتب ليس بمملوك من كل وجه ولهذا لم يجز تصرفه فيه ولا يحل له وطئ المكاتبة ولو تزوج المكاتب بنت مولاه ثم مات المولى و ورثته البنت لم يفسد النكاح وإذا لم يكن مملوكا من كل وجه لا يدخل تحت لفظ المملوك المطلق وهذا بخلاف المدبر وأم الولد فإن الملك فيهما كامل ولذا حل وطئ المدبرة وأم الولد وإنما النقصان في الرق من حيث إنه يزول بالموت لا محالة

The second reason is that sometimes the literal meaning is abandoned due to an indication in the text itself. An example of it is when one said: All slaves in my ownership are free. His *mukātab*-slaves and half-owned slaves will not be free, unless he intends them to be. This is because the word *al-mamlūk* is unrestricted. It means owned in every sense of the word. The *al-mukātab* is not owned in every sense of the word. For this reason the master may not use his services nor is he permitted to have intercourse with a *mukātaba*-slave-girl. If an *al-mukātab* was to marry the daughter of his master and the master was to die, he would be owned by the master's daughter but the marriage will not be dissolved. As he is not owned in every sense of the word, he will not be included under the unrestricted word *al-mamlūk*. This is contrary to the *mudabbar*-slave and the *umm ul-walad*, because ownership in them is complete. For this reason intercourse with a *mudabbar*-slave-girl or *umm ul-walad* is permitted. The incomplete factor is serfdom which will certainly expire at death.

❖ ❖ ❖

Building upon the previous discussion that the master's ownership is complete in both *umm ul-walad* and *al-mudabbar*, but it is incomplete in *al-mukātab* and *al-mu'taq ul-ba'ḍ*, we now learn that serfdom, *ar-riq*, is incomplete in the former two and complete in the latter two. So, when a master says, "All slaves in my ownership are free", *umm ul-walad* and *al-mudabbar* will be free, but *al-mukātab* and *al-mu'taq ul-ba'ḍ* will not be free. This is because ownership is only true when a master is the sole and complete owner. In both *al-mukātab* and *al-mu'taq ul-ba'ḍ* ownership is incomplete due to them being afforded a degree of independence from the master, and therefore they are not included. *Umm ul-walad* and *al-mudabbar* on the other hand are completely in the ownership of the master, having no degree of independence from the master, therefore they are included in the freedom.

As for serfdom, *ar-riq*, it is the opposite to freedom. The status of serfdom and 'being a slave' in *umm ul-walad* and *al-mudabbar* is incomplete and complete in *al-mukātab*. This difference is elaborated upon in the following text in that if one were to break a vow in a case of *al-yamīn* or *aẓ-ẓihār* the expiation would permit the freedom of *al-mukātab* but not *umm ul-walad* or *al-mudabbar*. This is because the verse of expiation requires freeing a slave, *taḥrīru raqaba*. The freeing of a slave means that you take a slave completely out of serfdom, such that the previous status was of a complete slave and the new status is of complete eradication of serfdom. Now, any slave that is a slave in the complete sense can be included in the expiation and any who is not in complete serfdom will not be permitted. *al-Mukātab* is in complete serfdom because his or her agreement with the master is revocable through mutual agreement or if *al-mukātab* realises he cannot raise the funds for his end of the agreement and asks to annul it. His serfdom is complete as his freedom is revocable. However, the reason for freedom in both *umm ul-walad* and *al-mudabbar* is permanent and irrevocable. This is because they will both become free upon the death of the master. Their serfdom is incomplete as their freedom is irrevocable.

Summarising, *umm ul-walad* and *al-mudabbar* have incomplete serfdom so by freeing them as part of the expiation 'a complete freedom' will not occur. Therefore, their freedom is not accepted in the expiation. *al-Mukātab* has complete serfdom so by freeing him as part of the expiation 'a complete freedom' will occur. Therefore, freeing *al-mukātab* is permitted for the expiation. The status of different slaves in summarised in figure 1.4-01.

بســـم الله الرحمن الرحيـــم

فَكَفَّارَتُهُ إِطْعَامُ عَشَرَةِ مَسَاكِينَ مِنْ أَوْسَطِ مَا تُطْعِمُونَ أَهْلِيكُمْ أَوْ كِسْوَتُهُمْ أَوْ تَحْرِيرُ رَقَبَةٍ (الآية)

صدق الله العظيم

سورة المائدة: 89

FIGURE 1.4-01
Statuses of different slaves.

	Master's Ownership	Serfdom
al-'Abd ul-muṭlaq	✓	✓
al-Mu'taq ul-ba'ḍ	½	½
Umm ul-walad	✓	½
al-Mukātab	½	✓
al-Mudabbar	✓	½

Text and Translation

وعلى هذا قلنا: إذا أعتق المكاتب عن كفارة يمينه أو ظهاره جاز ولا يجوز فيهما إعتاق المدبر وأم الولد؛ لأنّ الواجب هو التحرير وهو إثبات الحرية بإزالة الرق فإذا كان الرق في المكاتب كاملاً كان تحريره تحريراً من جميع الوجوه، وفي المدبر وأم الولدَ لما كان الرق ناقصا لا يكون التحرير تحريرا من كل الوجوه.

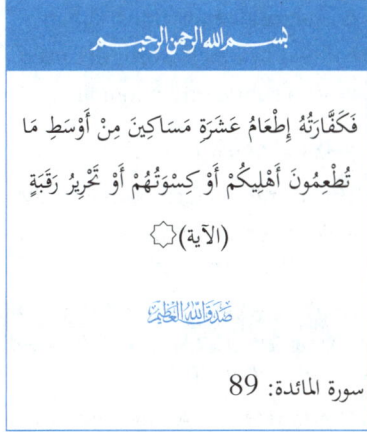

Based on this we have said: it is valid for one to free a *mukātab*-slave as atonement for a vow or for aẓ-ẓihār but invalid to emancipate *al-mudabbar* or *umm ul-walad* in either. This is because emancipation is necessary in all aspects. As serfdom is incomplete in *al-mudabbar* and *umm ul-walad* their emancipation will not be in all aspects.

❖❖❖

The third reason why al-ḥaqīqa may be abandoned is *dalālat us-siyāq* or indications from the context. This means that the words under analysis have a subtle indication that there is a context to be considered alongside the words. The context will point to the fact that the literal meaning is to be abandoned.

Imam Muḥammad ﷫ mentions a few cases in as-Siyar al-Kabīr that are clear examples of how the context is used to abandon al-ḥaqīqa as the operating meaning. If a Muslim calls an enemy, who is besieged in a fort, to descend, it will be to offer him a chance of surrender and protection from death. Should the Muslim call such an enemy to 'descend if he is man enough', it will not be an offer to surrender or an offer of protection. Normally, in the midst of battle when the context is of fighting, and one party gives an instruction that contradicts the idea that each member is trying to fatally wound the other, we would understand that this is an offer to halt the hostilities. Therefore, when the Muslim says 'descend', as an instruction, this is to halt hostilities. If hostilities are halted then the one who acts upon the command is in protection and no fighting can continue. However, when he adds 'if you are man enough', the same instruction of 'descend' no longer means there is an offer to stop hostilities, rather it is confirmation that the fight continues. As the fight continues, there is no protection and no protection. We see from this that indications in the context, *dalālat us-siyāq*, are significant factors and allow al-ḥaqīqa to be abandoned.

Similarly, if the enemy asks for protection, and the Muslim repeats the words, it will mean I accept your plea and grant you protection. However, if the Muslim repeats the words and adds, "You'll see what happens to you tomorrow", the literal meaning of 'protection' changes. Now, if the enemy descends after this exchange there is no protection, as it is clear that the literal instruction is not there to be obeyed but it is a provocation.

QUICK TERMS

دلالة السياق: *dalālat us-siyāq*

Contextual indications. When a context in which words are used gives a subtle understanding.

الحقيقة: *al-ḥaqīqa*

The literal. A word coined by the lexicon for an item.

QUICK ARABIC

المكاتب: *al-mukātab*

The ransomed. A slave promised freedom by a master in return for money paid.

الظهار: *aẓ-ẓihār*

Likening to a mother. A practice in which separation between husband and wife occurs until expiation is made.

المدبر: *al-mudabbar*

Free by arrangement. A slave promised freedom that takes effect after the master's death.

أم الولد: *umm ul-walad*

Mother of offspring. A female slave who gives birth to a master's child.

والثالث: قد تترك الحقيقة بدلالة سياق الكلام، قال في "السير الكبير": إذا قال المسلم للحربي: انزل فنزل كان آمناً، ولو قال: انزل إن كنت رجلاً فنزل لا يكون آمنا ولو قال الحربي: الأمان الأمان فقال المسلم: الأمان الأمان كان أمنا ولو قال: الأمان ستعلم ما تلقى غدا ولا تعجل حتى ترى فنزل لا يكون آمناً

The third is that sometimes the actual meaning is abandoned due to an indication in the context. It is mentioned in as-Siyar al-Kabīr: when a Muslim says to a combatant non-Muslim, "Descend!", and he descends, he will be protected. Had he said, "Descend, if you are man enough!", and he descended, he would not be protected. If the combatant requested, "Protection, Protection", and the Muslim replied, "Protection, protection", he would be protected. If he replied, "Protection? You'll see what happens to you tomorrow, don't hasten to see", and he descended, he will not be protected.

❖ ❖ ❖

Further examples of *dalālat us-siyāq* are:

1. If one made another individual an agent and instructed him to buy a slave-girl so that slave-girl could serve him. If the agent went on to purchase a blind or paralysed slave the instructed will not be liable or responsible to pay. The words, 'buy me a slave', would not mean the literal meaning of buy me any slave, rather the context tells us that the slave girl must be able to serve him. Therefore, it does not indicate any slave, but a slave who is able. Due to the context and *dalālat us-siyāq*, al-ḥaqīqa for 'buy me a slave' is abandoned.

   Similarly, if one instructed an agent to buy him a slave-girl so he could have intercourse with her, and the agent proceeded to buy his sister by suckling, liability will not be on the instructor. He did not instruct nor sanction this purchase. We see that *dalālat us-siyāq* and context does not allow the literal meaning of 'buy me a slave-girl' to mean 'any slave' due to the

QUICK REFERENCE

السير الكبير: *as-siyar al-kabīr*

The major treatise of engagement. The first major Islamic treatise on the law between Muslim and non-Muslim nations by Imam Muḥammad رحمه الله.

indications of, "so I can have intercourse". The al-ḥaqīqa is abandoned due to the indication of the context.

2. The Prophet ﷺ said that should a fly fall in the drink of a person they should immerse it in the liquid and then remove it. The literal instruction seems like it is necessary to do this as part of a legal requirement. However, the explanation of 'for in one of its wings is disease and in the other its cure' there is an indication that the instruction is to cancel the effects of the disease. It is not an instruction that you have to, as a necessary step, fulfil. If you do not wish to drink it, you are entitled not to. The context and *dalālat us-siyāq* has shown that the instruction to 'immerse it' is not literal, so al-ḥaqīqa is abandoned due to it.
3. There are eight categories of individuals who can rightfully receive the compulsory zakah; the poor, the needy, the administrator, whose heart is to be further harmonised, to free the slave, to relieve those in debt, the one struggling in the way of Allah ﷻ, and the traveller.

As the verse of the blessed Quran mentions these categories using plurals and separates them using the conjunction 'and', *al-waw*, some have said that the zakah must be divided amongst a group of each of these categories. Therefore, at least three needy individuals, three poor people and so on, all must take a portion of the zakah. It is their opinion that even if one of the categories is missed, or a group of individuals from each category do not receive the zakah, the zakah is not valid.

The Aḥnāf respond to this by saying that the literal meaning and al-ḥaqīqa of the verse is implying that, but the *dalālat us-siyāq* does not allow the literal understanding. The context of this verse is before the verse of zakah, where it is stated:

﴿ومنهم من يلمزك في الصدقات﴾ [التوبة: 58]

"Among them there are some who find fault with you concerning the zakah..."

حديث

عبيد بن حنين قال سمعت أبا هريرة رضي الله عنه يقول قال النبي صلى الله عليه وسلم إذا وقع الذباب في شراب أحدكم فليغمسه ثم لينزعه فإن في إحدى جناحيه داء والأخرى شفاء.

عليه الصلاة والسلام

(البخاري: 3142)

QUICK TERMS

الحقيقة: *al-ḥaqīqa*

The literal. A word coined by the lexicon for an item.

دلالة السياق: *dalālat us-siyāq*

Contextual indications. When a context in which words are used gives a subtle understanding.

Some of the hypocrites, out of malice and greed, complained that they did not receive wealth and tried to accuse the Just and Noble Beloved ﷺ of partisanship. To curtail and end their wrongful claims Allah ﷻ revealed the verse concerning the different categories of people who's right it is to receive the zakah.

﴿إنما الصدقاتِ للفقراء﴾ [التوبة: 60]

"Zakah is for: the poor..."

The claim of the hypocrites is due to greed and the legitimate claimants of the zakah are these people. This means that in the context of Sūrat ut-Tawba, verse 58, the literal and al-ḥaqīqa meaning of verse 60 is abandoned. One does not need to give to all of these groups of people, but one can give to anyone from these groups of people rather than to the greedy and wrongful hypocrites. Therefore, *dalālat us-siyāq* is used to abandon the application of al-ḥaqīqa.

Text and Translation

ولو قال: اشتر لي جارية لتخدمني فاشترى العمياء أو الشلاء لا يجوز ولو قال: اشتر لي جارية حتى أطاها فاشترى أخته من الرضاع لا يكون عن الموكل، وعلى هذا قلنا في قوله عليه السلام: إذا وقع الذباب في طعام أحدكم فامقلوه ثم انقلوه فإن في إحدى جناحيه داء وفي الأخرى دواء وإنه ليقدم الداء على الدواء دل سياق الكلام على أن المقل لدفع الأذى عنا لا لأمر تعبدي حقا للشرع فلا يكون للإيجاب، وقوله تعالى: ﴿إنما الصدقاتِ للفقراء﴾ عقيب قوله تعالى: ﴿ومِنهم من يلمِزك في الصدقاتِ﴾ يدل على أن ذكر الأصناف لقطع طمعهم من الصدقات ببيان المصارف لها فلا يتوقف الخروج عن العهدة على الأداء إلى الكل.

If one instructed: buy me a slave-girl to serve me, and he bought a blind or paralysed slave, it will not be acceptable. If one instructed: buy me a slave-girl to have intercourse with, and he bought his sister-by-suckling, the appointer is not liable. Based on this we said about his saying, peace and blessings be upon him: "If a fly were to fall in your food, immerse it then remove it, for in one of its wings is disease and in the other its cure; it offers the disease before the cure." The context indicates that immersion is due to neutralising the effect of disease on us and not a legally-binding command, so it is not essential. Furthermore, the word of Allah Almighty: "Zakah is for: the poor...", after the words: "Among them there are some who find fault with you concerning the zakah", shows that mentioning of recipient-categories is to curb their greed for financial welfare by stating the recipient-categories for it. So fulfilling the obligation does not rest on giving to every category.

❖ ❖ ❖

The fourth reason that al-ḥaqīqa may be abandoned is *dalālatun min qibal il-mutakallim* or indications from the first person. This means that there are indications from the eminence or status of the speaker and first person that the literal and al-ḥaqīqa is abandoned for al-majāz. An example of this is Sūrat ul-Kahf, verse 29:

﴿فمن شاء فليؤمن ومن شاء فليكفر﴾ [الكهف: 29]

"...Let him who will, believe; and let him who will, reject it..."

"Let him who will, reject it", *falyakfur*, is a command to disbelieve. A command must be fulfilled; therefore, it would seem that the literal and al-ḥaqīqa is commanding one to disbelieve. The reason why this al-ḥaqīqa is abandoned is an indication from the speaker, our Creator, Allah ﷻ. He is the Most Wise and all His commands are full of wisdom. Disbelief is not a wise choice; rather it is abhorrent and reprehensible. It is unthinkable that the Most Wise ﷻ would command an individual to choose such an act or path to follow. Sūrat ul-A'rāf, verse 28, explicitly says Allah ﷻ does not command what is shameful. Therefore, "let him who will, reject it" is not a command to disbelieve but is literary use of al-majāz to rebuke and say, 'be warned if you choose to disbelieve', for Allah ﷻ has made right and wrong clear, whilst you choose to ignore it.

Indications from the first person can cause al-ḥaqīqa to be abandoned. That is why if one made a person responsible to buy some meat, the status of the instructor and first person will be the governing factor as to whether cooked or uncooked meat is to be purchased. If he is travelling, it will be construed to mean cooked food and if he is resident at home, it will mean uncooked meat.

بسم الله الرحمن الرحيم

وَإِذَا فَعَلُواْ فَاحِشَةً قَالُواْ وَجَدْنَا عَلَيْهَا آبَاءنَا وَاللَّهُ أَمَرَنَا بِهَا قُلْ إِنَّ اللَّهَ لاَ يَأْمُرُ بِالْفَحْشَاء أَتَقُولُونَ عَلَى اللَّهِ مَا لاَ تَعْلَمُونَ

صدق الله العظيم

سورة الأعراف: 28

QUICK TERMS

الحقيقة: *al-ḥaqīqa*

The literal. A word coined by the lexicon for an item.

دلالة المتكلم: *dalālat ul-mutakallim*

First person indications. When a meaning becomes relevant due to the status of the first person.

المجاز: *dalālat us-siyāq*

The figurative. A word used for a meaning other than its coined meaning.

The literal and al-ḥaqīqa of the command will not apply such that the person does not have the right to supply any meat. If the first person is a traveller and stops to rest, his situation and circumstances dictate that he is hungry and would like to eat cooked meat. He would not have the time nor the equipment to cook raw meat. al-Ḥaqīqa is abandoned due to *dalālatun min qibal il-mutakallim* and it is a command to purchase just cooked meat. In a similar fashion, if the first person were resident at home, he would not want the more expensive cooked meat; rather his situation and circumstances dictate that he is able to spend some time cooking the meat. Again, al-ḥaqīqa is abandoned due to *dalālatun min qibal il-mutakallim* and it is a command to purchase just uncooked meat.

Another example of abandoning al-ḥaqīqa due to *dalālatun min qibal il-mutakallim* is the *yamīn ul-fawr*. This is a vow that is expressed impatiently and overemotionally. The vow is only operative in the emotional state and does not apply thereafter. An example of *yamīn ul-fawr* is if someone invites another to come and have breakfast with him. In response, he says, "By Allah, I will not eat breakfast!" This vow will be exclusive to the breakfast he was invited to. If the one who made the vow eats with the same individual later at his home, or has breakfast with another person, the vow will not be broken. The only way the vow would break is if he had the breakfast with the person, on the same day, on that particular occasion. The literal meaning and al-ḥaqīqa of his vow, "I will not eat breakfast", is that he should break this vow by consuming any breakfast, whether it is with that person, another person, on his own, on that day or any other day. However, the *dalālatun min qibal il-mutakallim* or indication from the status of the first person tells us that the literal meaning is not meant and thus abandoned. In other words, due to his overriding emotions the words that the person uses are shortened, otherwise his intention is to strongly decline that particular invitation and nothing more. Therefore, the *yamīn ul-fawr*, will be limited to that invitation, the eating of which will break his vow and no other breakfast will break it.

Similarly, if a woman stands intending to leave the house and the husband says, "If you leave, you are divorced!" This will be restricted to just this occasion. Therefore, if the woman was to leave on that occasion the divorce will come into effect. However, if she does not leave on that occasion but rather allows the emotions of her husband, the first person, to change before leaving, no divorce occurs. The literal meaning and al-ḥaqīqa of his words is that

QUICK ARABIC

يمين الفور: *yamīn ul-fawr*

Current oath. An oath connected to a current reason, implying the present, and not the future.

whenever she leaves the house the divorce should occur, whether on that occasion or any other. The al-ḥaqīqa is abandoned due to *dalālatun min qibal il-mutakallim*, in that in the emotional and angry state he was referring to her leaving on that occasion. Once the emotional state passes, it is no longer his concern. Due to this indication in the situation and circumstances of the first person, al-ḥaqīqa is abandoned.

Text and Translation

والرابع: قد تترك الحقيقة بدلالة من قِبل المتكلم، مثاله قوله تعالى: ﴿فمن شاء فليؤمن ومن شاء فليكفر﴾ وذلك لأن الله تعالى حكيم والكفر قبيح والحكيم لا يأمر به، فيترك دلالة اللفظ على الأمر بحكمة الآمر، وعلى هذا قلنا: إذا وكل بشراء اللحم فإن كان مسافرا نزل على الطريق فهو على المطبوخ أو على المشوي و إن كان صاحب منزل فهو على النيء، ومن هذا النوع يمين الفور مثاله إذا قال: تعال تغد معي فقال: والله لا أتغدى ينصرف ذلك إلى الغداء المدعو إليه حتى لو تغدى بعد ذلك في منزله معه أو مع غيره في ذلك اليوم لا يحنث، وكذا إذا قامت المرأة تريد الخروج فقال الزوج إن خرجت فأنت كذا، كان الحكم مقصورا على الحال حتى لو خرجت بعد ذلك لا يحنث

The fourth is that sometimes the literal meaning is abandoned due to an indication from the first person. An example of it is His word, the Most High: "Let him who will, believe; and let him who will, reject it". This is because Allah Almighty is Wise and disbelief is abhorrent; the Wise does not command it. So the words as a command will be abandoned due to the wisdom of the Instructor. Based on this we have said: when one delegated another to buy meat, if he was a traveller on his journey, it would be cooked meat, or broiled; whereas if he was resident it would be raw. The *yamīn al-fawr* is from this type. An example of it is when one said: Come, dine with me, and he replied: By Allah! I will not dine. This will refer to the invited dinner such that if after this he were to dine at his residence or with someone else on the same day, he would not have broken the vow. Similarly, if a woman stood intending to leave and the husband said to her: if you leave you are like that. The ruling will be restricted to the situation such that if she was to leave after that, he would not have broken the vow.

❖❖❖

QUICK TERMS

الحقيقة: *al-ḥaqīqa*

The literal. A word coined by the lexicon for an item.

دلالة محل الكلام: *dalālatu maḥal il-kalām*

Indications from the object. When the object of some words indicates a particular understanding.

QUICK ARABIC

يمين الفور: *yamīn ul-fawr*

Current oath. An oath connected to a current reason, implying the present, and not the future.

The fifth and last reason al-ḥaqīqa may be abandoned is *dalālatu maḥal il-kalām* or indications from the object of the words. This is where the words used are not suited to the literal meaning because of whom or what they were meant to be true for. The example provided for this is that if a free-woman says to a man, "I sell myself to you" and the man accepts, it is al-majāz for marriage, whilst the literal meaning is abandoned. The literal meaning would imply that a free-woman is being sold into serfdom and this is not permitted, as she cannot be subjected to this as a free-woman. Therefore, these words will be al-majāz and in the meaning of marriage. It is a similar case if the free-woman uses words such as, 'I gift myself', 'I give myself into your ownership', or 'I donate myself to you', and the man accepts. In all these cases al-ḥaqīqa will be abandoned due to *dalālatu maḥal il-kalām*, as she is not suited to any of these meanings. The literal meaning will be replaced with al-majāz, and so marriage will occur in each case.

Lastly, if a master says, "This is my son", to his slave who has a known lineage to someone other than the master, it is al-majāz for emancipation and freedom. This is because the master's words are not suited to the slave as his lineage is known, and the master's words would be claiming something different. Due to *dalālatu maḥal il-kalām* the literal meaning is abandoned and al-majāz is used. The slave will be free in the opinion of Imam Abū Ḥanīfa رحمه الله because al-majāz replaces al-ḥaqīqa in the words according to him. Ṣāḥibayn on the other hand render these words meaningless because in their opinion al-majāz replaces al-ḥaqīqa after application. This difference was previously discussed in detail in section 1.2.1, on page 76.

Text and Translation

والخامس: قد تترك الحقيقة بدلالة محل الكلام بأن كان المحل لا يقبل حقيقة اللفظ، ومثاله انعقاد نكاح الحرة بلفظ البيع والهبة بأن قالت وهبت والتمليك والصدقة، وقوله لعبده وهو معروف النسب من غيره: هذا إبني وكذا إذا قال لعبده وهو أكبر سنا من المولى: هذا إبني كان مجازا عن العتق عند أبي حنيفة رضي الله عنه خلافا لهما بناء على ما ذكرنا أن المجاز خلف عن الحقيقة في حق اللفظ عنده وفي حق الحكم عندهما

The fifth is that sometimes the meaning is abandoned due to an indication from the object of the words, such that the object cannot accept the actual meaning

QUICK TERMS

المجاز: *al-majāz*

The figurative. A word used for a meaning other than its coined meaning.

صاحبين: *ṣāḥbayn*

The Two Colleagues. Imams Abū Yūsuf رحمه الله and Muḥammad رحمه الله

QUICK ARABIC

النكاح: *an-nikāḥ*

Conjunction. In legal terms it is the marriage contract.

Abandoning al-Ḥaqīqa

QUICK TERMS

الحقيقة: *al-ḥaqīqa*

The literal. A word coined by the lexicon for an item.

المجاز: *al-majāz*

The figurative. A word used for a meaning other than its coined meaning.

of the word. An example of it is conducting *an-nikāḥ* of a free-woman with the word for purchasing, gifting - such that she said: I gift myself - ownership or charity. Also one saying to his slave whilst his lineage is known from someone else: "This is my son!" Or similarly if he said to his slave who was more senior in age than the master: "This is my son!" This will be a metaphor for freedom according to Imam Abū Ḥanīfa, Allah be pleased with him, contrary to the Two Colleagues, based upon what we discussed earlier regarding al-majāz replacing al-ḥaqīqa in word according to him and in meaning according to them both.

❖❖❖

Summary Of Abandoning al-Ḥaqīqa

There are five reasons why al-ḥaqīqa may be abandoned. They are:

1. *Dalālat ul-'urf* or indications of customary law.
   An example of this is if one vows to 'buy a head'. It will mean the heads of animals that are normally bought separately to eat, such as a cow, goat or sheep.

2. *Dalālat ul-kalām* or indications in the text.
   An example of this is if a master said, "All slaves in my ownership are free". It will exclude *al-mukātab* and *mu'taq ul-ba'ḍ*, because ownership in them is incomplete.

3. *Dalālat us-siyāq* or indications from the context.
   An example of this is if a Muslim calls an enemy to 'descend', it will be to offer a chance of protection. Should the Muslim call an enemy to 'descend, if he is man enough', it will not be an offer of protection.

4. *Dalālatun min qibal il-mutakallim* or indications from the first person.
   An example of this is the verse of Sūrat ul-Kahf, verse 29:
   ﴿فمن شاء فليؤمن ومن شاء فليكفر﴾ [الكهف: 29]
   "...Let him who will, believe; and let him who will, reject it..."
   The Most Wise would not give instructions for an abhorrent act such as disbelief. The literary style is to rebuke and warn.

5. *Dalālatu maḥal il-kalām* or indications from the object of the speech.
   An example of this is if a free-woman says to a man, "I sell myself to you" and the man accepts. It is al-majāz for marriage because the literal meaning would imply that a free-woman is being sold into serfdom and this is not permitted.

1.5 Text Locations

In chapter 1.0, Figure 1.0-01 divided the words of al-kitāb into four. Chapters 1.1, 1.2 and 1.3 discussed the first three divisions namely coinage, usage and clarity, respectively. In this chapter the last division of text locations, *muta'allaqāt un-naṣṣ*, is discussed.

The term muta'allaqāt un-naṣṣ refers to those locations in a text from which a piece of evidence is extracted. So, this chapter is concerned with the same words that have previously been under discussion throughout the book so far, however, now we are looking to see where the evidence of a given case is located. It is as though there are key sites and anchors in a text where a jurist will look for evidence. In this regard, there are four locations in and around a text and these are the four primary terms introduced. There is 'ibārat un-naṣṣ (the script of the text), ishārat un-naṣṣ (the indication of the text), dalālat un-naṣṣ (the supporting of the text), and iqtiḍā un-naṣṣ (the essentials of the text). Section 1.5.1 discusses the first two terms whereas the latter two are discussed later in section 1.5.2. This division of text locations is summarised in Figure 1.5-01:

QUICK TERMS

متعلقات النص: *muta'allaqāt un-naṣṣ*

Text locations. The part of a text from which evidence is extracted.

FIGURE 1.5-01

A division of the text locations in and around a text.

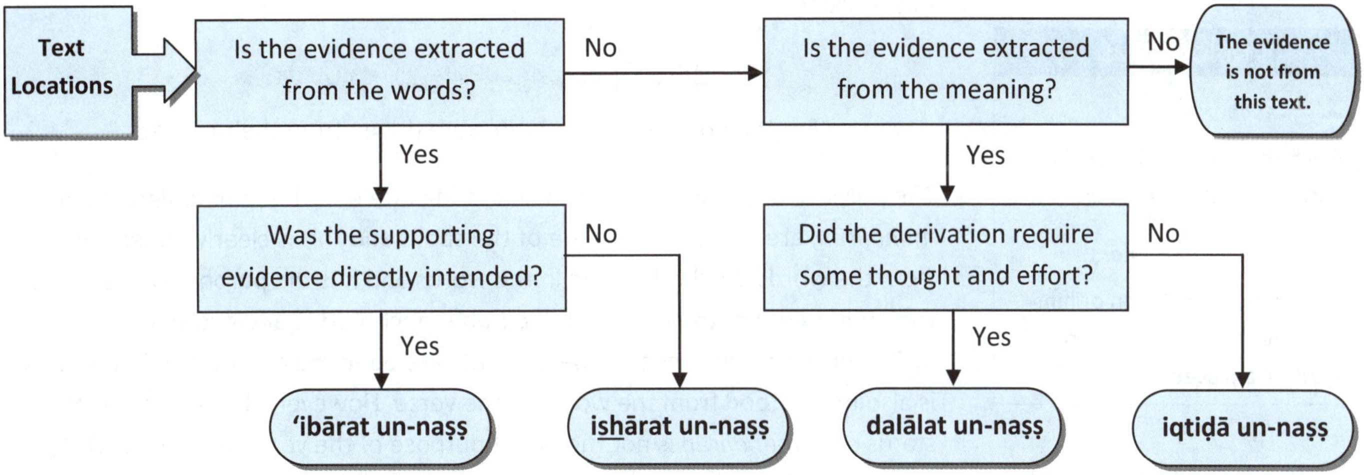

Text and Translation

فصل في متعلقات النصوص نعني بها: عبارة النص وإشارته ودلالته واقتضاؤه

Chapter on muta'allaqāt un-nuṣūṣ: what we mean by it is 'ibārat un-naṣṣ, ishārat un-naṣṣ, dalālat un-naṣṣ and iqtiḍā un-naṣṣ.

‘Ibārat un-naṣṣ, Ishārat un-naṣṣ

1.5.1 ‘Ibārat un-naṣṣ and Ishārat un-naṣṣ

The first two text locations or points in a text that are used to derive solutions and to provide evidence as support for a case are ‘ibārat un-naṣṣ and ishārat un-naṣṣ. They are defined as:

عبارة النص: ما سيق الكلام لأجله وأريد به قصدا

“‘**Ibārat un-naṣṣ** is what the wording has been issued and intended for.”

اشارة النص: ما ثبت بنظم النص من غير زيادة وهو غير ظاهر من كل وجه ولا سيق الكلام لأجله

“**Ishārat un-naṣṣ** is what is established by the words in the passage without any addition; it is not clear on all accounts nor is the wording issued for it.”

These definitions imply that both 'ibārat un-naṣṣ and ishārat un-naṣṣ are concerned with the visible words of the passage. The meaning that makes up the purpose of a text and is clear from its words is 'ibārat un-naṣṣ, whereas any other indirect meanings that are understood from the same text, which may not even be immediately obvious at first, are said to be ishārat un-naṣṣ.

The example provided to understand the two terms is from Sūrat ul-Ḥashr, verse 8:

﴿للفقراء المهاجِرين اللذين أخرِجوا مِن دِيارِهِم﴾ [الحشر:8]

“For the poor emigrants who were driven from their homes..."

The purpose of the words of this verse is to state that the poor emigrants, *al-muhājirūn*, are entitled to a share of the spoils and this is clearly understood from the words. As this is found in the words and it is the purpose of the verse, the entitlement of the poor *al-muhājirūn* is anchored in and extracted from ‘ibārat un-naṣṣ. The fact that the migrants are poor and do not own large sums is also understood from the words of the verse. However, stating the financial status of *al-muhājirūn* is not the direct purpose of the verse. As their poverty is understood from the words of the verse, but it is not the purpose of the verse to state this, we say their poverty is established from ishārat un-naṣṣ.

The implication of describing *al-muhājirūn* as poor is that they do not own anything, as that is the meaning of poverty. However, many of them were wealthy before they migrated to al-Madinah al-Munawwarah from al-Makkah al-Mukarramah. This means that their migration stripped them of their previous

QUICK TERMS

عبارة النص: *‘ibārat un-naṣṣ*

Words of the text. The plain words used in a given text.

إشارة النص: *ishārat un-naṣṣ*

Hint of the text. A sign or hint given by the order in which words are placed.

QUICK ARABIC

المهاجرون: *al-muhājirūn*

The Migrants. The first converts to Islam who fled al-Makkah at the time of the migration to al-Madinah.

wealth. They were once wealthy but by choosing to migrate, they now no longer own that wealth and are hence described as poor. By stating that they are poor, the verse is hinting at the idea that a non-believer who takes possession of a Muslim's wealth and lays claim to it after the Muslim's migration, will become its owner. This means the migrant Muslim is no longer owner of the wealth left behind and is categorised as poor, whereas the now ownerless-property is taken by the non-believer, who becomes its owner. If this transfer of ownership were not accepted it would mean that the migrant Muslim is still the owner of the property, which would categorise him as wealthy and that in turn would be contradicting ishārat un-naṣṣ.

In summary, it is established that the poor *al-muhājirūn* are entitled to the spoils by way of 'ibārat un-naṣṣ, their poverty is established by way of ishārat un-naṣṣ. This implies that they no longer own previously earned wealth, therefore the ownership may legitimately transfer to a non-Muslim.

There are many individual rulings that stem from the implications of verse 8, of Sūrat ul-Ḥashr.

1. When a non-believer takes possession of a Muslim's wealth, and transfers that wealth to non-Muslim lands, the non-believer is the rightful owner. This is because the verse implies that the possession of a non-believer over the wealth of a Muslim establishes the non-believer's ownership.
2. If a tradesman was to purchase this former property of a Muslim from the non-believer, the tradesman will be the rightful owner. This is because the tradesman has purchased it from its owner, and therefore it is a legitimate transaction. The tradesman is then within his rights to dispose of the property as he wills. He is permitted to sell it on, gift it or to free it if it is a slave.
3. If Muslims were to conquer the land of non-believers and to recapture property that once belonged to a Muslim but was taken by a non-believer, it will be included in the spoils of war like the rest of the property captured. It will be distributed to the rightful amongst the soldiers and they will become the legitimate owners of it. The Muslim who owned the property before it fell into the hands of the non-believers cannot lay claim to it.

Many other cases can be evidenced in a similar manner.

Text and Translation

فأما عبارة النص فهو ما سيق الكلام لأجله وأريد به قصدا، وأما إشارة النص فهي ما ثبت بنظم النص من غير زيادة وهو غير ظاهر من كل وجه ولا سيق الكلام لأجله، مثاله في قوله تعالى: ﴿لِلفقراء المهاجِرِين اللذِين أخرِجوا مِن دِيارِهِم﴾ الآية فإنه سيق لبيان استحقاق الغنيمة فصار نصا في ذلك وقد ثبت فقرهم بنظم النص فكان إشارة إلى أن استيلاء الكافر على مال المسلم سبب لثبوت الملك للكافر؛ إذ لو كانت الأموال باقية على ملكهم لا يثبت فقرهم، ويخرج منه الحكم في مسئلة الاستيلاء وحكم ثبوت الملك للتاجر بالشراء منهم وتصرفاته من البيع والهبة والإعتاق وحكم ثبوت الاستغنام وثبوت الملك للغازي وعجز المالك عن انتزاعه من يده وتفريعاته

'Ibārat un-naṣṣ is that which the wording has been issued for and is intended for. As for ishārat un-naṣṣ, it is what is established by the words in the passage without any addition; it is not clear on all accounts nor is the wording issued for it. An example is in the Almighty's word: "For the poor emigrants who were driven from their homes..." It has been revealed to state who is a rightful recipient of the spoils, so in this regard it is 'ibārat un-naṣṣ. The words of the passage establish their poverty hence in this regard it is an allusion, to an extent where the capture of a Muslim's wealth by a non-believer establishes the non-believer's ownership because had the wealth remained in their ownership, their poverty would not be established. From this we extrapolate the rulings of seizure, establishing ownership for a tradesman by purchasing from them, his right to sell, gift or emancipate, for it to become war-booty, ownership of the conqueror and the owner's inability to retrieve it from him, as well as other derivations.

❖ ❖ ❖

QUICK TERMS

عبارة النص: *'ibārat un-naṣṣ*

Words of the text. The plain words used in a given text.

إشارة النص: *ishārat un-naṣṣ*

Hint of the text. A sign or hint given by the order in which words are placed.

QUICK ARABIC

الغسل: *al-ghusl*

Ritual bathing. Washing the whole body after a major legal impurity.

Similar to the case of the poor migrants there is another example of ishārat un-naṣṣ. The example is from Sūrat ul-Baqara, verse 187.

﴿أُحِلَّ لَكُمْ لَيْلَةَ الصِّيَامِ الرَّفَثُ إِلَىٰ نِسَآئِكُمْ هُنَّ لِبَاسٌ لَّكُمْ وَأَنتُمْ لِبَاسٌ لَّهُنَّ عَلِمَ اللهُ أَنَّكُمْ كُنتُمْ تَخْتَانُونَ أَنفُسَكُمْ فَتَابَ عَلَيْكُمْ وَعَفَا عَنكُمْ فَالآنَ بَاشِرُوهُنَّ وَابْتَغُواْ مَا كَتَبَ اللهُ لَكُمْ وَكُلُواْ وَاشْرَبُواْ حَتَّىٰ يَتَبَيَّنَ لَكُمُ الْخَيْطُ الأَبْيَضُ مِنَ الْخَيْطِ الأَسْوَدِ مِنَ الْفَجْرِ ثُمَّ أَتِمُّواْ الصِّيَامَ إِلَى الَّيْلِ..الآية﴾ [البقرة:187]

"It is made lawful for you to go to your wives on the night of the fast. They are your apparel and you are apparel for them. Allah is aware that you were deceiving yourselves in this respect and He has turned in mercy toward you and relieved you. So have intercourse with them and seek that which Allah has ordained for you, and eat and drink until the white thread becomes distinct to you from the black thread of dawn. Then strictly observe the fast till nightfall..."

The direct and primary purpose of the verse is to inform that the one fasting can eat, drink and have sexual relations during the nights of the fasting period. This ruling is extracted from 'ibārat un-naṣṣ. The verse also has indirect consequences due to the words used in the passage. One such ruling is that the state of major ritual impurity, requiring *al-ghusl*, is consistent with being in the state of fasting, if the one fasting started the fast in that state. Requiring *al-ghusl* does not invalidate the fast. This is because 'ibārat un-naṣṣ of the verse permits eating, drinking and intercourse until the end of the night, whilst the 'ibārat un-naṣṣ then states "then complete the fast until nightfall." There is not sufficient time to perform *al-ghusl* between the permitted time of intercourse – just before the first moment of dawn – and the start of the fast – the first moment of dawn. The words indicate that intercourse is permitted until dawn, which means that *al-ghusl* will be necessary. However, immediately at dawn the fast has started due to the words of the verse, so the one fasting has begun his fast in the state of *al-janāba*, and thus requiring *al-ghusl*. The words of the verse make this scenario inevitable, though it is not the direct and primary purpose of the passage. Therefore, we make the ruling that the state of *al-janāba* is not inconsistent and at odds with keeping a fast. This ruling was derived from ishārat un-naṣṣ because it is not the primary purpose of the text, nor is it immediately clear from the text.

Furthermore, it is necessary to rule that one is permitted to rinse the mouth and nostrils with water in the state of sawm. This is because the fast has started in the state of *al-janāba* by ishārat un-naṣṣ, and to pray the one fasting needs to attain purity. The ritual purity from *al-janāba* is unattainable without rinsing both the mouth and the nostrils. Therefore, in the state of fasting one is permitted to rinse the mouth and nostrils to attain ritual purity, to be in an acceptable state to carry out other necessary worship.

Text and Translation

وكذلك قوله تعالى: ﴿أُحِلَّ لَكُمْ لَيْلَةَ الصِّيَامِ الرَّفَثُ﴾ إلى قوله تعالى: ﴿ثُمَّ أَتِمُّوا الصِّيَامَ إِلَى اللَّيْلِ﴾

QUICK ARABIC

الجنابة: *al-janāba*

Major legal impurity. The state of uncleanliness from the likes of menses and after ejaculation.

فالإمساك في أول الصبح يتحقق مع الجنابة؛ لأن من ضرورة حل المباشرة إلى الصبح أن يكون الجزء الأول من النهار مع وجود الجنابة، والإمساك في ذلك الجزء صوم أمر العبد بإتمامه فكان هذا إشارة إلى أن الجنابة لا تنافي الصوم، ولزم من ذلك أن المضمضة والاستنشاق لا ينافي بقاء الصوم

Likewise is His word, the Most High: "On the night of the fast it is lawful for you to have sexual relations with your wives...", to, "...then complete the fast until nightfall." Abstinence at early dawn will coincide with major ritual impurity. By necessity, if intercourse is permitted till dawn then the first part of the day will be with impurity whilst abstinence at that time is the fast that the subject has been instructed to complete. This shows that major ritual impurity is not at odds with fasting. Furthermore, this means that rinsing the mouth or nostrils are not inconsistent with the continuation of the fast.

❖ ❖ ❖

Based on the understanding that rinsing the mouth and nostrils does not invalidate the fast, we can extend the understanding to include tasting something during the fast, provided that one does not swallow the thing. We conclude this because if the water used for *al-ghusl* is salty, the taste will be sensed when rinsing the mouth out. This would not invalidate the fast even though something was tasted.

Furthermore, the commandment of Allah ﷻ in Sūrat ul-Baqara verse 187, which permits sexual intercourse, eating and drinking until dawn, and then instructs to immediately "continue the fast until nightfall", implies that nocturnal emissions, cupping and applying oil do not invalidate the fast either. This is because Allah ﷻ has stated that abstinence from three things, sexual intercourse, eating and drinking, is fasting. Therefore, these three things are the real essence of fasting and constitute all that is required for the fast to be valid. Had anything else been necessary it would have been stated alongside these three things. Nothing else is included, therefore we can conclude that practices such as cupping and applying oil will not invalidate the fast, nor will non-intimate ejaculation such as nocturnal emissions.

Moreover, the same verse of Sūrat ul-Baqara is used to decide the case of *at-tabyīt*. *at-Tabyīt* is the question of whether the intention for the fasts of Ramadan can be after the onset of dawn or not. It is stated in our books of Fiqh

بسم الله الرحمن الرحيم

أُحِلَّ لَكُمْ لَيْلَةَ الصِّيَامِ الرَّفَثُ إِلَى نِسَآئِكُمْ هُنَّ لِبَاسٌ لَّكُمْ وَأَنتُمْ لِبَاسٌ لَّهُنَّ عَلِمَ اللهُ أَنَّكُمْ كُنتُمْ تَخْتانُونَ أَنفُسَكُمْ فَتَابَ عَلَيْكُمْ وَعَفَا عَنكُمْ فَالآنَ بَاشِرُوهُنَّ وَابْتَغُواْ مَا كَتَبَ اللهُ لَكُمْ وَكُلُواْ وَاشْرَبُواْ حَتَّى يَتَبَيَّنَ لَكُمُ الْخَيْطُ الأَبْيَضُ مِنَ الْخَيْطِ الأَسْوَدِ مِنَ الْفَجْرِ ثُمَّ أَتِمُّواْ الصِّيَامَ إِلَى الَّليْلِ وَلاَ تُبَاشِرُوهُنَّ وَأَنتُمْ عَاكِفُونَ فِي الْمَسَاجِدِ تِلْكَ حُدُودُ اللهِ فَلاَ تَقْرَبُوهَا كَذَلِكَ يُبَيِّنُ اللهُ آيَاتِهِ لِلنَّاسِ لَعَلَّهُمْ يَتَّقُونَ ۝

صدق الله العظيم

سورة البقرة: 187

QUICK ARABIC

الغسل: *al-ghusl*

Ritual bathing. Washing the whole body after a major legal impurity.

that the intention can be made even after the onset of dawn. The evidence for allowing the intention after dawn is the commandment in the verse, "...eat and drink until the white thread of dawn appears to you distinct from its black thread; then complete the fast..." The necessity to obey Allah Almighty's command can only occur after He has given the command. The command to '*then complete the fast*' occurs after dawn. So, the task of fasting is due after dawn, therefore it makes sense to make the intention when the commandment asks you. This would mean that after dawn you are required to fast, so after dawn you make the intention to do so. Before dawn, there is no command to fast, so the intention to fast in not necessary before dawn.

Text and Translation

ويتفرع منه أن من ذاق شيئا بفمه لم يفسد صومه، فإنه لو كان الماء مالحا يجد طعمه عند المضمضة لا يفسد به الصوم، وعلم منه حكم الاحتلام والاحتجام والادهان؛ لأن الكتاب لما سمى الإمساك اللازم بواسطة الانتهاء عن الأشياء الثلاثة المذكورة في أول الصبح صوما علم أن ركن الصوم يتم بالانتهاء عن الأشياء الثلاثة، وعلى هذا يخرج الحكم في مسئلة التبييت فإن قصد الإتيان بالمأمور به إنما يلزمه عند توجه الأمر والأمر إنما يتوجه بعد الجزء الأول لقوله تعالى: ﴿ثُمَّ أَتِمُّوا الصِّيَامَ إِلَى اللَّيْلِ﴾

It will be derived from this that whoever tasted something with their tongue will not have invalidated the fast, for if the water is salty it would be sensed when rinsing the mouth and it would not invalidate the fast. From this we also learn the ruling of nocturnal emissions, cupping and applying oil, for when al-kitāb states the necessary abstaining - by ceasing the three mentioned actions in the first part of dawn - as a fast, it is known that the ritual of fasting is complete with the halting of the three things. Based on this the ruling of *at-tabyīt* is derived as the intention to execute the command is necessary upon receiving the command; and the command is directed after the first part as He most High says: "...then complete the fast until nightfall."

❖❖❖

QUICK ARABIC

الكتاب: *al-kitāb*

The book. The inspired final word of Allah ﷻ. The Quran.

Ḥanafī Principles (10)

MEMORISE

	Term	Definition	Ruling	An Example
21	**عبارة النص**	ما سيق الكلام لأجله وأريد به قصدا	– يفيد فائدة القطعية إذا يخلو عن العوارض – وعند المعارضة ترجح على إشارة النص	﴿للفقراء المهاجِرين اللذِين أخرجوا مِن دِيارِهم﴾ [الحشر:8]
22	**اشارة النص**	ما ثبت بنظم النص من غير زيادة وهو غير ظاهر من كل وجه ولا سيق الكلام لأجله	– يفيد فائدة القطعية إذا يخلو عن العوارض – وعند المعارضة العمل بعبارة النص أولى	فقر المهاجرين في ﴿للفقراء المهاجِرين اللذِين أخرجوا مِن دِيارِهم﴾ [الحشر:8]

Summary Of ʻIbārat un-naṣṣ and Ishārat un-naṣṣ

1. Rulings can be derived from four locations or anchors in and around a text. They are: 'ibārat un-naṣṣ, ishārat un-naṣṣ, dalālat un-naṣṣ and iqtiḍā un-naṣṣ.

2. Details of 'ibārat un-naṣṣ:
   i) Definition: ما سيق الكلام لأجله وأريد به قصدا
   "Wording that is purposefully presented and its meaning is intentional".
   ii) Example: The verse
   للفقراء المهاجرين الذين أخرجوا من ديارهم
   is revealed to state that the migrants have a share of the spoils of Jihad.
   iii) Ruling: يفيد فائدة القطعية إذا يخلو عن العوارض وعند المعارضة ترجح على إشارة النص
   "It gives a definitive meaning when there is no impediment and will take precedence over ishārat un-naṣṣ is."

3. Details of ishārat un-naṣṣ:
   i) Definition: ما ثبت بنظم النص من غير زيادة وهو غير ظاهر من كل وجه ولا سيق الكلام لأجله
   "What is established by the text without increasing it, whilst it is not immediately clear nor is it purposely presented."
   ii) Example: The words of the verse
   للفقراء المهاجرين الذين أخرجوا من ديارهم came for a purpose as explained in 'ibārat un-naṣṣ. They also tell us that the migrants are *poor*. Many of them were wealthy before their migration. So, the verse says they are now poor which means they have lost ownership of their wealth accumulated before migration. Now if non-believers possessed the wealth, their ownership of it would be recognised. So, ishārat un-naṣṣ stipulates that non-Muslims may take ownership of Muslims' property.
   iii) Ruling: يفيد فائدة القطعية إذا يخلو عن العوارض وعند المعارضة العمل بعبارة النص أولى
   "It gives a definitive meaning when there is no impediment and will be ignored when opposing ishārat un-naṣṣ."

1.5.2 Dalālat un-naṣṣ and Iqtiḍā un-naṣṣ

The discussion in chapter 1.5 is on text locations, muta'allaqāt un-naṣṣ. Figure 1.5-01 showed the connection between the four locations in a text. 'Ibārat un-naṣṣ, the plain script of the text, and ishārat un-naṣṣ, the indications of the text, were both discussed in section 1.5.1. In this section the remaining two locations, dalālat un-naṣṣ, the deduction of the text, and iqtiḍā un-naṣṣ, the requirement of the text, are discussed.

The definition of dalālat un-naṣṣ is:

دلالة النص: ما علم علة للحكم المنصوص عليه لغة لا اجتهادا ولا استنباطا

"Dalālat un-naṣṣ is what is linguistically known to be the effective cause for an outcome in the text, but not by deduction or inference."

This means that purely from an Arabic language perspective we recognise a cause for a particular outcome based on our understanding of the verse. It is not the meaning of the verse, as that would be 'ibārat un-naṣṣ, rather it is an outcome of the meaning. By saying it is a cause found through meaning dalālat un-naṣṣ also becomes distinct from ishārat un-naṣṣ, which is part of the words. The cause should be an outcome of the meaning of the words and not understood through reasoning or based on the Shariah. If a cause is based on reasoning, it is called al-qiyās and if it is based on the definitive Shariah, it will be iqtiḍā un-naṣṣ, details of which will follow.

An example of dalālat un-naṣṣ is from verse 23 of Sūrat ul-Isrā. Allah ﷻ commands:

﴿فلا تقل لهما أف ولا تنهرهما﴾ [الإسراء: 23]

"..do not say "ugh!" to them, and do not be harsh with them.."

The one who understands Arabic will recognise immediately that to say "ugh!" is forbidden because it is an offensive and harsh response to parents. The prohibition of saying "ugh!" to parents is found in 'ibārat un-naṣṣ and a necessary outcome of this is that striking, swearing or harming the parents is also forbidden. There is no need to resort to reasoning to arrive at this conclusion. Thus, we say that striking, swearing and other forms of harming parents are prohibited through dalālat un-naṣṣ. This leads us to state that the ruling of dalālat un-naṣṣ is:

QUICK TERMS

دلالة النص: *dalālat un-naṣṣ*

Argument of the text. An argument deduced from the use of the words in a text.

عبارة النص: *'ibārat un-naṣṣ*

Words of the text. The plain words used in a given text.

إشارة النص: *ishārat un-naṣṣ*

Hint of the text. A sign or hint given by the order in which words are placed.

اقتضاء النص: *iqtiḍā un-naṣṣ*

Requirement of the text. A deduction which demands certain conditions to be applicable.

القياس: *al-qiyās*

Analogy. The reasoning of the learned.

حكم دلالة النص: عموم الحكم المنصوص عليه لعموم علته

"The ruling on dalālat un-naṣṣ is the generality of the outcome in the text coincides with the generality of the effective cause."

This means that wherever we will encounter the cause, we will stipulate the same outcome that we found in the recorded text. Therefore, to say "ugh!" to parents is deemed forbidden from the verse due to the cause of offense through harshness. What follows is that any other harshness to them should also be forbidden, as it would contain the same cause of offending them. So striking them is forbidden as it causes offense; swearing at them is forbidden as it causes offense; taking their services as labour is forbidden as it is degrading and causes offense; to imprison them due to an outstanding loan owed to their child is forbidden as it is degrading and offensive; and if they were to unlawfully murder their child, it would be forbidden to carry out *al-qiṣāṣ* as it would be degrading and offensive. In all these cases, the source of anguish and harshness is the child, so it would be forbidden to carry out any of them.

Text and Translation

وأما دلالة النص فهي ما علم علة للحكم المنصوص عليه لغة لا اجتهادا ولا استنباطا مثاله في قوله تعالى: ﴿فلا تقل لهما أف ولا تنهرهما﴾ فالعالِم بأوضاع اللغة يفهم بأول السماع أن تحريم التأفيف لدفع الأذى عنهما، وحكم هذا النوع عموم الحكم المنصوص عليه لعموم علته، ولهذا المعنى قلنا: بتحريم الضرب والشتم والاستخدام عن الأب بسبب الإجارة والحبس بسبب الدين أو القتل قصاصا

As for dalālat un-naṣṣ, it is what is linguistically known to be the effective cause for an outcome in the text, but not by deduction or inference. An example of it in His, the Most High, words is: "..do not say "ugh!" to them, and do not be harsh with them.." Upon the first hearing the one familiar with the language understands that the prohibition of grumbling is to avoid offending them both. The ruling regarding this type is the generality of the outcome in the text conincides with the generality of the effective cause. For this reason we state that it is forbidden to beat, swear, exploit the services of a father for work, have him detained due to debt or to subject him to al-qiṣāṣ.

❖❖❖

QUICK TERMS

دلالة النص: *dalālat un-naṣṣ*

Argument of the text. An argument deduced from the use of the words in a text.

QUICK ARABIC

القصاص: *al-qiṣāṣ*

Retaliation. The legal route afforded to the next of kin in case of murder and to the afflicted in loss short of murder.

In terms of its strength and significance, dalālat un-naṣṣ is as good as the text itself. Just as a clear and unambiguous text would be sufficient for punishments such as in cases of *al-kaffāra*, dalālat un-naṣṣ would also be sufficient. Based on this concept, the Aḥnāf have said that expiation for invalidating the fast by engaging in sexual intercourse is proven through 'ibārat un-naṣṣ and expiation of invalidating it by eating and drinking is proven through dalālat un-naṣṣ. This is because Abū Ḥurayra رضي الله عنه says that he was in the company of the blessed Prophet صلى الله عليه وسلم when a man came to him and informed that he was ruined because he had had sexual relations with his wife during the fast. The blessed Prophet صلى الله عليه وسلم informed him of the expiation for the fast. As the Hadith, in its text, mentions the expiation for the invalidating of the fast due to sexual encounters, we extract this from 'ibārat un-naṣṣ. The words of the Hadith, by necessity, also imply that this expiation is due to the purposeful invalidation of the fast and this is the cause of the expiation. This is extracted from dalālat un-naṣṣ. Now, as per the ruling of dalālat un-naṣṣ, wherever we find this cause of purposefully invalidating the fast, we will apply the outcome of the necessity of offering the expiation. Therefore, if one invalidated the fast by purposefully eating or drinking, expiation will be necessary by way of dalālat un-naṣṣ.

One of the implications of the strength of dalālat un-naṣṣ is that on occasion, it may return a solution that seems to contradict the text, but in reality, it is the very purpose of the text. To highlight this point, Qadi Abū Zayd رحمه الله has stated that if a people considered the words 'ugh!' an expression of honour and esteem, rather than offensive, then it would not be forbidden for them to use it. This is what it means by 'the ruling revolves around the cause'. Apparently, it seems to contradict the text, however, in reality the text is asking for the parents to be respected and honoured. That honour and respect is ensured by the dalālat un-naṣṣ.

Another example of the ruling revolving around the cause is from verse 9 of Sūrat ul-Jumu'a:

﴿يأيها الذين آمنوا إذا نودي﴾ الآية [الجمعة: 9]

"O believers! When you are called..."

Allah جل جلاله has commanded the believers to make their way towards the central masjid upon hearing *al-ādhān* of *al-Jumu'a* and to leave their financial dealings. This is an understanding anchored in 'ibārat un-naṣṣ. The meaning also

حديث

فعَنْ أبي هُريرة رضي الله عنه قَال: بَينماَ نَحن جُلُوس عِنْدَ النبي صلى الله عليه وسلم إذ جَاءه رَجلٌ، فقَالَ: يَا رَسولَ الله، هَلَكتُ! فقال: مَالكَ؟ قال: وَقَعْتُ على امْرَأتِي، وأنا صائمٌ. فقالَ رَسُولُ الله صلى الله عليه وسلم: هَلْ تَجِدُ رَقَبَةً تعتقها؟ (الحديث)

عليه الصلاة والسلام

(البخاري: 1936، المسلم 1111)

QUICK TERMS

عبارة النص: *ibārat un-naṣṣ*

Words of the text. The plain words used in a given text.

QUICK ARABIC

الكفارة: *al-qiṣāṣ*

Expiation. The prescribed atonement for neglected duties.

الآذان : *al-ādhān*

The call. The ritual summons to public congregational prayers.

الجمعة: *al-jumu'a*

Friday. The day or the particular prayer offered on the day.

necessitates the understanding that the cause of prohibition from financial dealings is because it prevents a person from making their way to the masjid, which is what the verse requires a believer to do. Thus, the cause of prohibition of the financial dealing is that it prevents from the required action. This means that dalālat un-naṣṣ says that anything that prevents from allowing a person to go to the masjid is prohibited, and anything that does not stop him would still be permitted. Therefore, if we consider a transaction that does not require the believer to halt his advance to the masjid, such as on board a ship that is moving towards the masjid whilst the transaction takes place, it is permitted.

Text and Translation

ثم دلالة النص بمنزلة النص حتى صح إثبات العقوبة بدلالة النص، قال أصحابنا: وجبت الكفارة بالوقاع بالنص وبالأكل والشرب بدلالة النص. وعلى اعتبار هذا المعنى قيل: يدار الحكم على تلك العلة، قال الإمام القاضي أبو زيد: لو أن قوما يعدون التأفيف كرامة لا يحرم عليهم تأفيف الأبوين، وكذلك قلنا في قوله تعالى: ﴿يا أيها الذين آمنوا إذا نودي﴾ الآية؛ ولو فرضنا بيعا لا يمنع العاقدين عن السعي إلى الجمعة بأن كانا في سفينة تجري إلى الجامع لا يكره البيع

Then, dalālat un-naṣṣ is equivalent to the text, such that punishments are valid through dalālat un-naṣṣ. Our scholars say: sexual intercourse necessitates expiation by way of an-naṣṣ and by dalālat un-naṣṣ for eating and drinking. Taking this meaning into consideration it is said: the ruling revolves around the cause. Imam Qāḍī Abū Zayd says: if a people consider uttering "ugh" as respect it will not be forbidden to say it to the parents. Similarly we said in the words of the Most High: "O believers! When you are called...", if we consider a transaction that does not prevent the parties from advancing to the *Jumu'a* such that they are on board a ship that is moving towards the central masjid, it will not be disliked.

❖ ❖ ❖

Based on the concept of dalālat un-naṣṣ providing a cause that becomes pivotal in assessing the outcome of a case, jurists have said that if one vows not to strike his wife, but then pulls her hair, bites her or strangles her, the vow will be dishonoured if the action was intended to hurt. This is because the vow not to strike means that he intends not to physically hurt her; therefore, all those

QUICK TERMS

عبارة النص: *'ibārat un-naṣṣ*

Words of the text. The plain words used in a given text.

دلالة النص: *dalālat un-naṣṣ*

Argument of the text. An argument deduced from the use of the words in a text.

courses of action that lead to the husband hurting his wife will contravene his vow. Any course of action that does not hurt her is excluded from the vow, such that after the vow not to strike, if he playfully strikes her or pulls her hair the vow will still be in place, as the meaning of hurt is not found.

Similarly, if one vowed not to strike someone, then proceeded to strike him after his death, the vow will not be broken. This is because, the reason to strike is to cause pain and get a negative reaction, however this meaning would be lost once someone has passed away. Furthermore, if one vowed not to speak to someone, then proceeded to talk to his corpse after his death, the vow will not be broken. This is because the purpose of the vow is not to converse with the individual and the concept of a conversation has been lost with the person's death, therefore the vow will not be broken.

For the same reason, that the outcome is dependent upon the presence of the cause or the lack of it, if one vowed not to eat meat, and proceeded to eat fish or locusts, the vow would not be broken. However, if he ate swine or human flesh the vow would be broken. This is because anyone who understands the language will recognise that what is meant by 'meat' is that which has a reddish colour due to the high content of myoglobin, a protein found in muscle tissue that gives the reddish colour. Human flesh and swine are both meats of this type, so they will be included in the vow, whilst fish and locusts do no not have this type of meat so are not included. The outcome of whether the vow remains intact revolves around the cause.

Text and Translation

وعلى هذا قلنا: إذا حلف لا يضرب امرأته فمد شعرها أو عضها أو خنقها يحنث إذا كان بوجه الإيلام ولو وجد صورة الضرب ومد الشعر عند الملاعبة دون الإيلام لا يحنث ومن حلف لا يضرب فلانا فضربه بعد موته لا يحنث لانعدام معنى الضرب وهو الإيلام، وكذا لو حلف لا يتكلم فلانا فكلمه بعد موته لا يحنث لعدم الإفهام باعتبار هذا المعنى يقال: إذا حلف لا يأكل لحما فأكل لحم السمك أو الجراد لا يحنث ولو أكل لحم الخنزير أو الإنسان يحنث؛ لأن العالم بأول السماع يعلم أن الحامل على هذا اليمين إنما هو الاحتراز عما ينشأ من الدم فيكون الاحتراز عن تناول الدمويات فيدار الحكم على ذلك

QUICK DICTIONARY

Myoglobin: *mahy-uh-gloh-bin*
Blood in muscles. The oxygen-carrying pigment of red blood cells that gives them their red colour.

Based on this we have said: if one vowed not to beat his wife, then pulled her hair, bit her or strangled her, he has dishonoured the vow if it is to harm her. If a scenario arises whereby beating and pulling the hair is in jest and not to hurt, he has not dishonoured the vow. If one vowed not to beat someone and then beat him after his death, the vow will not be dishonoured as the purpose of beating is lost which is to cause pain. Similarly, if one vowed he would not speak to someone and then spoke to him after his death, he would not have dishonoured the vow as there is no comprehension. Considering this meaning it is said: if one vowed not to eat meat and then ate fish or locust, it will not be dishonoured. Should he eat swine or human it will be dishonoured. This is because the one familiar with language, will from the first instance know that the intent of this vow is to abstain from that which is born of red blood so this will be abstinence from red-blood related products and the ruling will revolve around this.

❖❖❖

The last and final location and placeholder from which a jurist could evidence a ruling is iqtiḍā un-naṣṣ. This is defined as:

اقتضاء النص: زيادة على النص لا يتحقق معنى النص إلا به

"Iqtiḍā un-naṣṣ is an extension to the text that is vital to establish coherence."

al-Muqtaḍa, the vital words added to a text, are important because without them the text would be incoherent and not make sense. It is the text that requires and demands the additional words, otherwise the words issued would themselves be legally null and without point. An example of this from the Shariah is if a husband says to his wife, "You are divorced". She is described as divorced, which intrinsically means that a divorce must have been issued earlier. The word 'divorced', *aṭ-ṭāliq*, is an *ism fā'il* or active participle which is used as a descriptor. Such a word must contain within its meaning the *al-maṣdar* or root word, *aṭ-ṭalāq*, meaning 'divorce'. In other words, the one for whom divorce was issued is described as 'divorced'. Therefore, we say that when a husband says to his wife, "You are divorced", it is vital that a divorce is established by way of al-iqtiḍā, though it is not found in the words explicitly, because she would not be divorced if a divorce had not been issued.

A further more elaborate example of this al-iqtiḍā is if an individual says to another, "Free your slave on my behalf for 1000 dirham". The person replies, "I have freed him". This freedom will be due to the one who initiated the

QUICK TERMS

اقتضاء النص: *iqtiḍā un-naṣṣ*

Requirement of the text. A deduction which demands certain conditions to be applicable.

المقتضى: *al-muqtaḍā*

Essential addition. The vital words added to a text for coherency.

QUICK ARABIC

الطلاق: *aṭ-ṭalāq*

Divorce. A release from the marriage tie, it can be revocable or irrevocable.

QUICK GRAMMAR

الاسم الفاعل: *al-ism ul-fā'il*

Active participle. The thing that carries out the designated action.

المصدر: *al-maṣdar*

The infinitive. Root and origin of an Arabic word group.

process by issuing a command, and so he will owe 1000 dirham. If the one who made the proposal carried the intention of freeing a slave for expiation, this would suffice for the expiation too. This is all possible because his proposal of, "Free your slave on my behalf for 1000 dirham", is actually a proposal to purchase the slave from the owner. It is as though he is saying, "Sell the slave to me, *then be my representative in* freeing my purchased slave on my behalf". These additional words are necessary because for this individual to free the slave legally he must own the slave first. Therefore, the initial proposal of "free him on my behalf" would necessarily require that ownership would have to transfer first. The transfer of ownership can occur if the owner agrees to sell the slave to the proposer, and the stating of "for 1000 dirham" certainly points to a financial transaction. This would mean that the sale of the slave is additional to the initial words of, "Free your slave on my behalf for 1000 dirham". If they are additional words, they are termed al-muqtaḍā and the sale is thus evidenced from iqtiḍā un-naṣṣ.

There is an additional question upon this example, which is that a legitimate sale requires a proposal and acceptance of that proposal. We understand that the proposal of the sale is in the iqtiḍā un-naṣṣ of the words of the one who asked for the slave to be free but where is the acceptance of the sale? Both proposal and acceptance are necessary for the validity of the sale. The answer is that when the owner of the slave accepts the idea of freeing the slave by saying, "I have freed him", the al-iqtiḍā and extended words of this reply contain the acceptance of the sale. So, just as the proposal of the sale was an extension of the words of the initiator of the command, the acceptance of the sale is found in the extended words of the one who freed the slave. Both proposal and acceptance are in the iqtiḍā un-naṣṣ.

Text and Translation

وأما المقتضى فهو زيادة على النص لا يتحقق معنى النص إلا به كأنّ النص اقتضاه ليصح في نفسه معناه، مثاله في الشرعيات قوله: أنت طالق. فإن هذا نعت المرأة إلا أن النعت يقتضي المصدر فكأن المصدر موجود بطريق الاقتضاء، وإذا قال: أعتق عبدك عني بألف درهم فقال: أعتقت. يقع العتق عن الآمر فيجب عليه الألف ولو كان الآمر نوى به الكفارة يقع عما نوى؛ وذلك لأنّ قوله: أعتقه عني

بألف درهم يقتضي معنى قوله: بعه عني بألف ثم كن وكيلي بالإعتاق فأعتقه عني فيثبت البيع بطريق الاقتضاء فيثبت القبول كذلك؛ لأنه ركن في باب البيع

As for al-muqtaḍā it is an extension to the text that is vital to establish coherence. It is as though the text demands it to make sense of its own meaning. An example of it from the Shariah is one saying: you are divorced. This is an adjective of the woman and an adjective requires the root word, so it is as though the root word is present by way of al-iqtiḍā. When one says: free your slave on my behalf for 1000 dirham, and he replies: I have freed him. The emancipation will be due to the instructor and so he will have to pay the 1000, even if he were to intend it for expiation it would occur as he intended. This is because him saying: free him on my behalf for 1000 requires the meaning of his command to be: sell him to me for 1000 and then be my agent in granting freedom and free him from me. So the financial transaction is established by al-iqtiḍā and the acceptance is the same because it is integral in the chapter of financial transactions.

❖❖❖

Extending the concept presented in the example above regarding a sale conducted in iqtiḍā un-naṣṣ, Imam Abū Yūsuf رحمه الله has said that if one did not propose a sale but said, "Free your slave on my behalf for nothing", and the person replied, "I have freed him", the slave will be free. The freedom is, as before, due to the one who issued the command. The iqtiḍā un-naṣṣ will support the idea of a gifting followed by representation rather than a sale followed by a representation. The expanded version of the statement will read, "Gift me your slave and then represent me in freeing the slave."

Normally, when a gifting takes place, one would expect the gift to be given to the beneficiary and until the possession of the item has not taken place, the process cannot be classed as a gifting. In the example above, there is no physical possession so this should not count as a gifting. There are two answers provided for this. Firstly, the gifting occurs in iqtiḍā un-naṣṣ, therefore *al-qabḍ*, possession, also occurs in iqtiḍā un-naṣṣ, much like the proposal and acceptance in the previous example. Secondly, a much more compelling answer than the first is that a sale requires a proposal and acceptance as vital components, so they are necessarily existent. However, taking possession of a

QUICK TERMS

المقتضى: *al-muqtaḍā*

Essential addition. The vital words added to a text for coherency.

اقتضاء النص: *iqtiḍā un-naṣṣ*

Requirement of the text. A deduction which demands certain conditions to be applicable.

QUICK ARABIC

القبض: *al-qabḍ*

Taking possession. For the purchaser to take control of the merchandise.

gift is not a vital component of the process of gifting rather it is a condition. Therefore, the two cases are different and thus not comparable. In the case of the sale, acceptance is a component, *ar-rukn*, so when the sale is necessarily added due to iqtiḍā un-naṣṣ, it is effectively saying both acceptance and proposal are present. Whereas in the case of the gifting, possession is not a component, so when the gifting is mentioned in iqtiḍā un-naṣṣ, taking possession is not necessarily there, and is not required to be.

Text and Translation

ولهذا قال أبو يوسف رحمه الله: إذا قال: أعتق عبدك عني بغير شيء فقال: أعتقت. يقع العتق عن الآمر ويكون هذا مقتضيا للهبة والتوكيل ولا يحتاج فيه إلى القبض؛ لأنه بمنزلة القبول في باب البيع ولكنا نقول: القبول ركن في باب البيع فإذا أثبتنا البيع اقتضاء أثبتنا القبول ضرورة بخلاف القبض في باب الهبة فإنه ليس بركن في الهبة ليكون الحكم بالهبة بطريق الاقتضاء حكما بالقبض

For this reason Imam Abū Yūsuf, Allah have mercy on him, says: when one says free your slave on my behalf for nothing, and he replies: "I have freed him", the emancipation occurs from the one commanding. It will require a gifting and agent-appointing, and possession is not a requirement. This is because it is like acceptance in the chapter of financial transactions. Moreover we say: acceptance is integral to the financial transaction. If we show the transaction by al-iqtiḍā then acceptance is thereby necessity. This is different to possession in the chapter of gifting as it is not integral to gifting such that to stipulate gifting by al-iqtiḍā is a stipulation of possession.

❖ ❖ ❖

The ruling of iqtiḍā un-naṣṣ is:

حكم اقتضاء النص: يثبت بطريق الضرورة فيقدر بقدر الضرورة

"The ruling on iqtiḍā un-naṣṣ is that it is established by necessity, so it is limited to what is necessary."

The iqtiḍā un-naṣṣ is a necessary extension to the text and the words are there because they are vital, without them, the text would not make sense. However, the extended part cannot go beyond the vitally necessary. This means that the bare minimum that is required to make the words make sense is permitted.

QUICK ARABIC

الركن: *ar-rukn*

Chief element. An essential and vital part, the absence of which would undermine the item.

Nothing in excess of this is allowed. Thus, the extended words are limited to only what is necessary and no more.

In accordance with this ruling, if a man said to his wife, "You are divorced", and he intended three divorces, it is not permitted. Only one divorce will occur. This is because the divorce that occurs from his description of his wife as 'divorced' is by way of the root word that is necessarily existent in iqtiḍā un-naṣṣ. If the root word was not present, she could not have been described as 'divorced'. The divorce is thus established by iqtiḍā un-naṣṣ, and now must be limited to the bare minimum that is required as per the ruling. For the woman to be divorced, she is only required to be divorced once, as that is the bare minimum. Nothing extra is permitted in these words. Therefore, one divorce will occur. This is the case even if he intends to issue three with the words. This is because the words that were uttered do not have the capacity to mean anything more than the bare minimum. Therefore, his intention is not taken into consideration.

Furthermore, if one was to vow that his slave, for example, is free "if I eat", and he intended some foods but not others. It will not be accepted, such that he will have broken his vow by eating the very smallest of morsels. This is because his words "if I eat" will require food to be eaten; otherwise, it will not be considered as eating. This means that out of necessity and by iqtiḍā un-naṣṣ there is food mentioned in his statement. As it is by way of al-iqtiḍā it is limited to the minimum amount that is necessary to allow it to make sense. That minimum is a single entity of any food such as a single morsel. Now this is the meaning that is established. It is as though he says, "if I eat *any little bit of what you can call food*". As this implies any one entity of food, he cannot make exceptions and exemptions from it, by intending one food type and not another. The words do not have the capacity to allow this meaning. Therefore, his intention is ignored and the vow will be broken with any food item.

QUICK TERMS

اقتضاء النص: *iqtiḍā un-naṣṣ*

Requirement of the text. A deduction which demands certain conditions to be applicable.

Another example of only allowing the bare minimum and necessary in iqtiḍā un-naṣṣ is if one said to his wife with whom he had already consummated his marriage, "Start counting!", whilst intending divorce. One revocable *ar-raj'ī* divorce would occur through al-iqtiḍā. This is because his words could initially mean numerous things, such as count your blessings, the days to a specific event, the days of the end of the grace period of a divorce or anything else. His intention will determine which meaning fits and as he intended divorce, the

QUICK ARABIC

الرجعي: *ar-raj'ī*

The revocable. A divorce after which the husband has permission to return to the marriage.

meaning is of counting the days to the end of the grace period, *al-'idda*. However, the actual words used, 'start counting', do not include a mention of the grace period but it is still necessary as the words would not make sense without this. The extended words, 'the days of the grace period after divorce', are from iqtiḍā un-naṣṣ and must only include necessary components, enough to make the initial words make sense. The divorce is thus taken from iqtiḍā un-naṣṣ to make, 'Start counting!', make sense, and must be by default a revocable *ar-raj'ī* divorce. Anything more than this will be unnecessary and excessive. So, adding that it is an irrevocable *al-bāin* divorce or that multiple divorces have occurred through iqtiḍā un-naṣṣ is not permitted as it is over and beyond the bare minimum. Only one revocable *ar-raj'ī* divorce will occur even if the intention is otherwise.

Text and Translation

وحكم المقتضى أنه يثبت بطريق الضرورة فيقدر بقدر الضرورة، ولهذا قلنا: إذا قال: أنت طالق. ونوى به الثلاث لا يصح؛ لأن الطلاق يقدر مذكورا بطريق الاقتضاء فيقدر بقدر الضرورة والضرورة ترتفع بالواحد فيقدر مذكورا في حق الواحد، وعلى هذا يخرج الحكم في قوله: إن أكلت ونوى به طعاما دون طعام لا يصح؛ لأن الأكل يقتضي طعاما فكان ذلك ثابتا بطريق الاقتضاء فيقدر بقدر الضرورة والضرورة ترتفع بالفرد المطلق ولا تخصيص في الفرد المطلق؛ لأن التخصيص يعتمد العموم، ولو قال بعد الدخول: اعتدي ونوى به الطلاق فيقع الطلاق اقتضاء؛ لأن الاعتداد يقتضي وجود الطلاق فيقدر الطلاق موجودا ضرورة ولهذا كان الواقع به رجعيا؛ لأن صفة البينونة زائدة على قدر الضرورة فلا يثبت بطريق الاقتضاء ولا يقع إلا واحد لما ذكرنا.

The ruling of al-muqtaḍā is that it is established by necessity and only what is necessary is determined. For this reason we said: when one said: you are divorced, and intended three divorces, it is not correct. This is because divorce is present by way of al-iqtiḍā and only what is necessary is established. The necessity is fulfilled with just one, so it is determined to have just one stated. Based on this the verdict is extrapolated when one said: if I eat, and made an intention of some foods and not others that it is not correct. This is because eating requires food which is established by way of al-iqtiḍā so it is determined as what is necessary and necessity is achieved by any morsel. There is no specifying for an absolute particle, as specification requires generality. If after

QUICK TERMS

المقتضى: *al-muqtaḍā*

Essential addition. The vital words added to a text for coherency.

QUICK ARABIC

العدة: *al-'idda*

The term. The three-month period after a divorce.

البائن: *al-bāin*

The irrevocable. A divorce after which the husband is not permitted to unilaterally return to the marriage.

QUICK TERMS

اقتضاء النص: *iqtiḍā un-naṣṣ*

Requirement of the text. A deduction which demands certain conditions to be applicable.

consummation one said: "Count!" And intended divorce by it, the divorce would occur by way of al-iqtiḍā because counting requires the existence of a divorce. Divorce is determined through necessity and so one revocable divorce is established. It is because a non-revocable is more than the necessarily required so it is not established by al-iqtiḍā. Only one will be established for the reason we have mentioned.

❖ ❖ ❖

MEMORISE

Ḥanafī Principles (11)

	Term	Definition	Ruling	An Example
23	**دلالة النص**	ما علم علة للحكم المنصوص عليه لغة لا اجتهادا ولا استنباطا	– عموم الحكم المنصوص عليه لعموم علته	﴿فلا تقل لهما أف ولا تنهرهما﴾ [الإسراء: 23]
24	**اقتضاء النص**	زيادة على النص لا يتحقق معنى النص إلا به	– يثبت بطريق الضرورة فيقدر بقدر الضرورة	إذا قال: أنت طالق

❖ ❖ ❖

Summary Of Dalālat un-naṣṣ and Iqtiḍā un-naṣṣ

1. Details of dalālat un-naṣṣ:
   i) Definition:
   ما علم علة للحكم المنصوص عليه لغة لا اجتهادا ولا استنباطا
   "What is linguistically recognised as the cause of the stipulated ruling, not reasoned or derived".
   ii) Example: In the verse فلا تقل لهما أف ولا تنهرهما, the one who understands the language will immediately know that uttering "*Ugh*" to parents is prohibited, as it is hurtful to them. To derive from this that you cannot strike them as it is also hurtful, is from dalālat un-naṣṣ. Hurt is the common cause found in both cases.
   iii) Ruling: عموم الحكم المنصوص عليه لعموم علته
   "The stipulated ruling revolves around the cause".

2. Details of iqtiḍā un-naṣṣ:
   i) Definition: زيادة عن النص لا يتحقق معنى النص إلا به
   "An addition to the text, essential to complete its meaning".
   ii) Example: One said, "You are divorced". To be described as 'divorced' the divorce must have been issued to the wife earlier. The divorce is found in al-iqtiḍā.
   iii) Ruling: يثبت بطريق الضرورة ويقدر بقدر الضرورة
   "It is necessarily established and kept to a bare minimum".

1.6 Introduction to al-Amr

Chapters 1.1 through to 1.5 detailed the primary terminology associated with al-Kitāb. In total, there were twenty terms. These terms were summarised in Figure 1.0-01. Additionally, we introduced important secondary terms in their respective places. In this chapter, we revisit the term al-khāṣṣ generally, but in particular, a special type of al-khāṣṣ called al-amr. The full discussion on al-khāṣṣ is on page 12.

al-Amr is a high frequency al-khaṣṣ. This means that it is one of the most often used methods in the Shariah to deliver instruction. In this regard, it is extremely important and as a result demands special attention with a separate chapter. Figure 1.6-01 summarises five matters that we will discuss in detail regarding al-amr:

1. al-Āmir or the Commander, who issues the command. In the case of al-kitāb, the al-āmir is Allah ﷻ.Without the Commander there would be no command; we will discuss this in further detail as a part of section 1.6.1, al-Amr ul-muṭlaq.
2. The word form of al-amr, which is the manner in which the Commander issues the instruction and what it entails; this is discussed partly in section 1.6.1 and also in 1.6.2, Functions of al-amr.
3. al-Mamūr fīhi or the timescale in which the command must be carried out. We will discuss this in 1.6.3, The types of al-mamūr bihī.
4. al-Mamūr bihī or the task itself. This is what the subject of the command has been instructed to do. We will discuss this in section 1.6.4, The excellence of al-mamūr bihī.
5. al-Mamūr or the subject of the command and the one responsible for carrying it out. In other words, at whom the instruction is directed. This is the one who is obliged to carry out the task. Details of what he or she must do are in section 1.6.5 and 1.6.6, al-adā and al-qaḍā.

QUICK TERMS

الكتاب: *al-kitāb*

The book. The inspired final word of Allah ﷻ. The Quran.

الخاص: *al-khāṣṣ*

The specific. A word designated for a singular specific concept.

QUICK GRAMMAR

الأمر: *al-amr*

The imperative. A word form that informs of a demanded act.

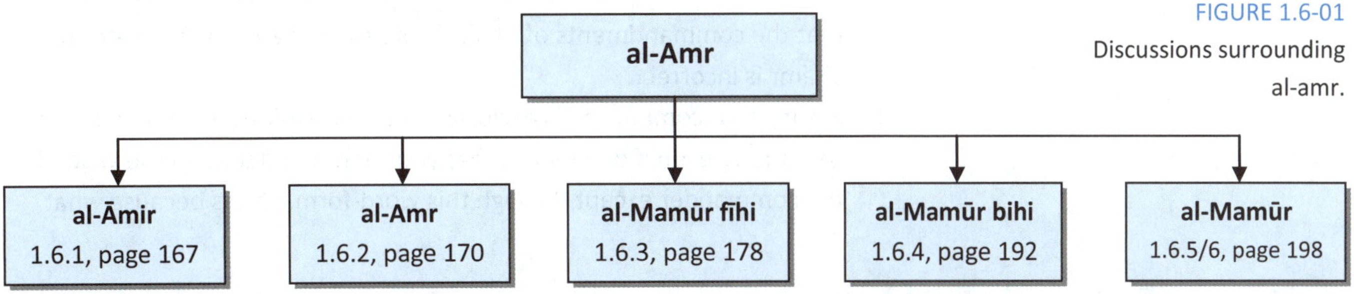

FIGURE 1.6-01

Discussions surrounding al-amr.

A linguistic definition of al-amr and a legal definition from the Shariah are:

الأمر في اللغة: قول القائل لغيره افعل

"al-Amr, linguistically, is an instruction to act and is directed at another".

الأمر في الشرع: تصرف إلزام الفعل على الغير

"al-Amr in the Shariah is to oblige the enacting of a task onto another."

The linguistic definition tells us that if one says to another individual, "Do it!" using the Arabic word-form *i-f-'a-l* it will be called al-amr. The definition as far as the Shariah is concerned tells us that when a task is given to another individual in a manner that it is an obligation and must be carried out, it is called al-amr.

Some scholars have opined that the word-form of al-amr requires the compulsion to carry out a task and that this meaning is exclusive to this word-form. This means that compelling someone to carry out a task can only occur using the word-form designated for al-amr, no other means may be used. There are two primary objections to this point of view:

1. Stating that compulsion is exclusive to the word-form of al-amr cannot be correct; especially if it means that a word is to be issued. This is because it is the belief of the Ahlus Sunnati wal-Jamā'a that Allah ﷻ is al-Mutakallim, The Speaker, from eternity. His speech is commandments, prohibitions, discourse and information. If the issuing of commands that give compulsion was exclusive to word-forms of al-amr it would mean that these words existed from eternity, as they would be used by The Almighty to issue commands. However, it is impossible for this word-form to exist in eternity as all words are perishing entities. Whether spoken or written, one part of a word needs to conclude and perish before the next one is delivered. Something that perishes and ceases to exist cannot be eternal. Therefore, concluding that the commandments of Allah ﷻ are exclusive to the word-form of al-amr is incorrect.
2. Stating that compulsion is exclusive to the word-form of al-amr cannot be correct, even if one means that you cannot understand the wish of the commander except through this word-form. This is because what

the commander wants from the subject by issuing al-amr is to be obliged and compelled to carry out a task. However, there are matters that one is obliged and compelled to carry out without ever hearing a word. For example, if there are a people so remote from civilisation who have never heard of the invitation of Islam it is still necessary for them to believe in a Supreme Being, as long as they have had time to consider this. The opinion of Imam Abū Ḥanīfa رحمه الله supports this concept and idea as he has stated that had Allah جل جلاله not sent any messengers it would still be required of intelligent members of a community to conclude that there is a Supreme Creator through their intellect alone and for them to believe in Him جل جلاله. They would arrive at this conclusion by looking at the beautiful creation around them and looking at their own existence. The point to note is that they would be compelled to believe in Allah جل جلاله, yet no word-form would have reached them. This means that compulsion is not exclusive to the word-form of al-amr, but is possible in other ways.

Both these issues are solved by understanding that Allah جل جلاله is not dependent upon these word-forms to issue His divine commands, rather it is the subjects that require the word-forms to understand what is required of them. Furthermore, this only concerns matters of practice and what to do; not matters of belief. So, when it comes to belief in Allah جل جلاله or other matters of belief they are not only found in word-forms of al-amr. In the practices of the Shariah, for the clarity of the subjects and those that are duty-bound, the word-form of al-amr denotes compulsion to carry out a task.

Another point in this chapter concerns the difference between the acts of the blessed Prophet صلى الله عليه وسلم and his words. When the Prophet صلى الله عليه وسلم issues an instruction, it denotes something that must be carried out. It is necessary and the one instructed is obliged to carry it out. However, the act of the blessed Prophet صلى الله عليه وسلم does not hold the same weight. This is because the word-form of al-amr is for obliging a person to carry out a task. However, the action of the blessed Prophet صلى الله عليه وسلم does not have this word-form and thus will not be for compulsion by default. The question that then arises is that why are some acts of the blessed Prophet صلى الله عليه وسلم regarded as al-wājib and necessary? The reason some sunna acts are al-wājib is that the blessed Prophet صلى الله عليه وسلم carried them out regularly and persistently. Moreover, this persistence is coupled with the absence of evidence that the matter is exclusive to the blessed Prophet صلى الله عليه وسلم. An

QUICK TERMS

الواجب: *al-wājib*

The necessary. The non-observance of which is sinful, but denial does not lead to disbelief.

example of an act persistently carried out by the blessed Prophet ﷺ but did not become necessary upon the rest of the ummah is the at-Tahajjud prayers. Although the Prophet ﷺ prayed them without fail, there is evidence to say that they were only necessary for him ﷺ and not the rest of the ummah.

Text and Translation

فصل في الأمر: الأمر في اللغة قول القائل لغيره افعل، وفي الشرع تصرف إلزام الفعل على الغير، وذكر بعض الأئمة أن المراد بالأمر يختص بهذه الصيغة واستحال أن يكون معناه أن حقيقة الأمر يختص بهذه الصيغة فإن الله تعالى متكلم في الأزل عندنا وكلامه أمر ونهي وإخبار واستخبار، واستحال وجود هذه الصيغة في الأزل واستحال أيضا أن يكون معناه أن المراد بالأمر للآمر يختص بهذه الصيغة، فإن المراد للشارع بالأمر وجوب الفعل على العبد وهو معني الابتلاء عندنا وقد ثبت الوجوب بدون هذه الصيغة أليس أنه وجب الإيمان على من لم تبلغه الدعوة بدون ورود السمع قال أبو حنيفة رحمه الله: لو لم يبعث الله تعالى رسولا لوجب على العقلاء معرفته بعقولهم، فيحمل ذلك على أن المراد بالأمر يختص بهذه الصيغة في حق العبد في الشرعيات حتى لا يكون فعل الرسول بمنزلة قوله: افعلوا ولا يلزم اعتقاد الوجوب به، والمتابعة في افعاله عليه السلام إنما تجب عند المواظبة وانتفاء دليل الاختصاص

Chapter on al-amr: linguistically al-amr is an instruction to act, directed at another individual. In the Shariah it is to oblige the enacting of a task onto another. Some scholars have mentioned that the meaning of al-amr is exclusive to this word-form. However, it is impossible for this to mean that the reality of al-amr is specific to this form because Allah Almighty is al-Mutakallim from eternity according to us. His Word is in command, prohibition, discourse and information. It is impossible for this word-form to have eternally existed, as it is also impossible that this means that the Commander is limited to this word-form to give a command. For the Legislator al-amr means to compel an action on the subject which according to us, is a trial. Compulsion has been shown without this word-form: is it not that believing is mandatory even on those who have not been invited through transmission. Imam Abū Ḥanīfa, Allah have mercy on him, said: Had Allah Almighty not sent a single messenger it would still be necessary for the intelligent to acknowledge Him through their intellect. So what is meant by this is that al-amr is specific to this word-form for the subjects only in matters of Shariah such that the words of the Messenger will not be in

QUICK GRAMMAR

الأمر: *al-amr*

The imperative. A word form that informs of a demanded act.

QUICK ARABIC

التهجد: *at-tahajjud*

The Night Prayer. A voluntary prayer performed at night, consisting of two to eight units.

المتكلم: *al-mutakallim*

The Speaker. Although this is not an explicit Divine Name, it is true for Allah ﷻ, for He Speaks with Divine Speech, al-Kalām.

the same bracket as his command of: Do! Nor will this necessitate a belief of the act's compulsion. Pursuing his actions, peace be upon him, is only necessary when persisted upon and the lack of evidence of exclusivity.

❖ ❖ ❖

1.6.1 al-Amr al-Muṭlaq

al-Amr ul-muṭlaq is a command that is not restricted or bound by any indications of whether the instruction is compulsory or not. There are two examples provided from the blessed Quran of an instruction that is void of any signs of compulsion. Firstly, from Sūrat ul-A'rāf, verse 204, and secondly, Sūrat ul-Baqara, verse 35. Allah جل جلاله says:

﴿وإذا قرئ القرآن فاستمعوا له وَ أنصِتوا لعلكم ترحمونَ ﴾ [الأعراف: 204]

"When the Quran is recited pay attention to it and listen quietly so that hopefully you will gain mercy."

﴿ولاَ تقربا هـذِهِ الشجرةَ فتكونا مِن الظالمين﴾ [البقرة: 35]

"But do not approach this tree or you will both become wrongdoers."

'Pay attention', 'listen quietly', and 'do not approach', are all examples of commands that do not have any signs indicating compulsion or the lack of compulsion. On such occasions, the scholars differ whether the instruction is a recommendation or a mandatory requirement, merely an advisable act or something else. Some scholars have given up to twenty-one different possibilities for al-amr, stating that one should look out for evidence indicating one of the meanings before stating what the word means. The majority opinion of the Ḥanafī scholars and the adopted opinion is that al-amr is for compulsion by default.

The opinion that al-amr is for compulsion is attached to the condition that there is no indication in the text pointing to an alternative meaning such as a sign of recommendation or of being an advisable act. If such a piece of evidence is present, al-amr is construed to have that meaning. If no such evidence is present, al-amr will be for compulsion by default. This is because ignoring a command is disobedience, whilst fulfilling it is seen as obedience. Words such as disobedience are only used to describe a situation where a necessary task has been ignored. If someone is given a recommendation and they choose to ignore it, it is not seen as disobedience.

The adopted opinion of the madhhab is supported by a couplet from the Dīwān of al-Ḥamāsa. The couplet of Abū 'Alī al-Marzūqī has equated, *al-īytimār*, carrying out a command of al-amr, to obedience and it has equated the unfulfilling of a command to disobedience. Disobedience only results from not fulfilling a necessary duty and not by ignoring a recommendation or an optional task. It is accepted that matters appointed by the Shariah as responsibilities and duties hold such significance that disregard for them carries a penalty of reprimand and punishment. It is also accepted that punishment is reserved for failing to fulfil necessary tasks and not optional ones. Thus, equating abandoning of al-amr to disobedience and punishment being necessary for ignoring al-amr of the Shariah, are both ample proof that al-amr must be fulfilled and that is what is understood from just its word-form.

Furthermore, the degree of importance of al-amr is directly related to the authority of the one issuing the command. If the commander is of the highest authority, the weight of importance in fulfilling the command is equally of the highest significance and would thus be al-wājib and necessary. If the issuer of the command is of equal authority to the recipient, al-amr will be a recommendation rather than essential. And if the issuer is inferior to the recipient, al-amr is neither necessary nor a recommendation, rather it is a suggestion and fulfilling it is an option for the superior. Clearly, the significance of al-amr in importance is dependent upon the one issuing it. Bearing this in mind we see that when a command is issued to a superior it may be ignored with no repercussions, and if it is issued to an inferior such as a slave or employee, it must be fulfilled. Ignoring it purposefully and without reason will result in a reprimand and penalty, customarily and legally.

Once it is established that the authority of the issuer lends weight to the importance of fulfilling the command of al-amr, we know that Allah ﷻ has absolute authority over all His creation. No part of the creation is excluded from His authority or ownership. When we have accepted that a master, with his deficient ownership, can reprimand his slave for not fulfilling a command, then make your own judgment regarding the absolute Sovereign ﷻ Who brought you forth from non-existence into existence, and then showered you with a multitude of blessings. When He commands, it is necessary for it to be fulfilled and disobeying it will most definitely deserve punishment. Therefore, when the Shariah issues al-amr it is al-wājib and necessary to fulfill it. This will remain the case until there is a contradictory indication.

QUICK TERMS

الواجب: *al-wājib*

The necessary. The non-observance of which is sinful, but denial does not lead to disbelief.

QUICK ARABIC

المذهب: *al-madhhab*

School of fiqh. A system of practices according to mujtahids.

QUICK REFERENCE

الحماسة: *al-ḥamāsā*

Valour. It is an anthology of poetry compiled by Abū Tammām Ḥabīb bin Aws aṭ-Ṭāī [788 – 845 CE]. The work is one of the early sources of Arabic poetry. It is considered one of the greatest pieces of Arabic literature ever compiled.

فصل في الأمر المطلق: اختلف الناس في الأمر المطلق أي: المجرد عن القرينة الدالة على اللزوم وعدم اللزوم، نحو قوله تعالى: ﴿وإذا قرئ القرآن فاستمعوا له وَ أنصِتوا لعلكم ترحمونَ﴾ وقوله تعالى: ﴿ولاَ تقربا هذِهِ الشجرةَ فتكونا مِن الظالِمين﴾ والصحيح من المذهب أن موجبه الوجوب إلا إذا قام الدليل على خلافه؛ لأن ترك الأمر معصية كما أن الايتمار طاعة، قال الحماسي:

أطعت لآمريك بصرم حبلي مريهم في أحبّتهم بذاك

فهم إن طاوعوكِ فطاوعِيهم وإن عاصوكِ فاعصِي من عصاكِ

والعصيان فيما يرجع إلى حق الشرع سبب للعقاب، وتحقيقه أن لزوم الايتمار إنما يكون بقدر ولاية الآمر على المخاطب ولهذا إذا وجهت صيغة الأمر إلى من لا يلزمه طاعتك أصلا لا يكون ذلك موجبا للايتمار وإذا وجهتها إلى من يلزمه طاعتك من العبيد لزمه الايتمار لا محالة حتى لو تركه اختيارا يستحق العقاب عرفا وشرعا، فعلى هذا عرفنا أن لزوم الايتمار بقدر ولاية الآمر، إذا ثبت هذا فنقول: إن لله تعالى ملكا كاملا في كل جزء من أجزاء العالم وله التصرف كيف ما شاء وأراد، وإذا ثبت أن من له الملك القاصر في العبد كان ترك الايتمار سببا للعقاب فما ظنك في ترك أمر من أوجدك من العدم وأدر عليك شآبيب النعم

Chapter on al-amr al-muṭlaq: Scholars differed regarding al-amr al-muṭlaq. In other words, the one free of an indication signifying necessity or nonnecessity, such as in the word of the Almighty: "When the Quran is recited pay attention to it and listen quietly so that hopefully you will gain mercy", and "But do not approach this tree or you will both become wrongdoers". The adopted position in the school is that it necessitates compulsion except when there is proof to the contrary, because ignoring a command is disobedience just as fulfilling it is obedience. The al-Ḥumāsī couplet reads:

"You obeyed your instructors in breaking my bond;
Command them of the same for their lovers.

QUICK TERMS

الأمر المطلق: *al-amr ul-muṭlaq*

The unrestricted imperative. A word-form that informs of a demanded act, irrespective of any qualities.

For if they obey you, you then obey them;
If they disobey you, disobey those who disobey you".

Disobedience in matters concerning the Shariah evokes punishment. An explanation of this is that the necessity to obey a command is in accordance with the degree of authority the command-giver has over the addressee. For this reason if you were to direct the command towards one who is not obliged to obey you at all, such a command does not necessitate an undertaking. Should you direct it at a slave who must obey you, he certainly would have to obey it, to an extent where if he intentionally disobeys he would be culpable in custom and in Shariah. From this we learn that the necessity to obey is proportional to the authority of the command-giver. As this is established we then say: Allah Almighty has absolute authority in all parts of the universe and can dispose however He wills and wants. As it is established that for whomsoever has temporary ownership of a slave, disobedience of his command causes liability, so what do you think about disobedience of the command of the One Who brought you into existence and showered a deluge of blessings on you.

❖ ❖ ❖

1.6.2 Functions of al-Amr

The previous section discussed the necessity demanded by al-amr to carry out a task. In this section we discuss whether al-amr seeks repetition or not. There are several opinions prevalent amongst the jurists regarding this but the preferred opinion of the Aḥnāf is that al-amr does not demand repetition nor does it have the possibility of repetition. That is to say whether one intends repetition using al-amr or does not intend it, the task it demands only needs to be carried out once by the duty-bound individual.

As an example, if one was to grant another individual the responsibility to divorce his wife saying, "Divorce my wife", and the representative, exercising this responsibility, divorces her. Now, should the issuer of the command remarry the same woman again, the representative does not have the right to divorce the woman again under the directive of the first al-amr. This is clearly because the command and al-amr to 'divorce my wife' does not demand the necessity or the possibility to repeatedly carry out the task. The representative is only duty-bound to divorce the wife once and not repeat the task time after time. Similarly, if one was to instruct another to, "marry me to a woman", it will

QUICK GRAMMAR

الأمر: *al-amr*

The imperative. A word form that informs of a demanded act.

not include repetition. In other words, the representative has the right to enter him into one marriage contract and not into a second or third contract. On a similar note, if a master instructs his slave to marry using the al-amr word-form, it is an instruction to marry just once. The slave is not permitted to marry a second time.

These examples all go to show that the Aḥnāf do not consider repetition a factor in al-amr in any circumstance. They substantiate this by stating that al-amr is actually a shortened manner of asking for an act to be carried out. It is like when one commands, "Strike!" One is actually saying, "Carry out the task of a strike", but in a much more elaborate way than the very concise, 'strike!'. When a statement is short or expanded it still provides the same meaning and results in the same outcome. This is because the point of shortening a statement is to deliver the same result as the lengthy statement but in fewer words, the point is not to change or alter its meaning. This means that al-amr, for example 'strike!', is a shortened version of asking for a task, 'to strike', to be carried out. The expanded version of al-amr therefore contains al-maṣdar or a root word and by extension the shorter al-amr word-form also contains the same al-maṣdar; the shortened statement is demanding the very same thing as the lengthier statement. It is established that al-maṣdar is singular and is not made up of numerous occurrences. If it is not made of multiple occurrences then it cannot have repetition as only then will it truly be singular.

Summarising the above, it all means that the al-amr word-form is a shortened version of a statement that contains al-maṣdar, al-maṣdar is singular and thus cannot contain multiple occurrences. Multiple occurrences and repetition are one of a kind, therefore the al-amr word-form does not constitute repetition.

The command 'strike!' is demanding a task of a particular kind, *al-jins*. In other words, it is asking for the task of striking to occur, where striking is *al-jins*. One of the features of *al-jins* is that when no intention or indication is present it constitutes the least amount, and with an intention or an indication it can constitute the whole amount. *al-Jins* therefore has only two possible meanings: it can mean 'one individual', applying the understanding of the least amount, or it can mean 'every individual', applying the understanding of the whole amount. It is worth bearing in mind that the default meaning of *al-jins* is the least

QUICK ARABIC

الجنس: *al-jins*

Genus. A class or group. A group of closely related things.

QUICK GRAMMAR

المصدر: *al-maṣdar*

The infinitive. The root and origin of an Arabic word group.

amount, it would require an intention or a piece of evidence to take it from the default meaning to the possible meaning of the whole amount.

As an example of this, without any intention if one said, "By God, I will not drink water", the person will have breached the vow by drinking just a single drop of water. This is because a single drop of water is the amount required for the default meaning of drinking. It is the least amount for *al-jins* of drinking to take place and as it is the default, it does not require an intention. However, if one intends the drinking of all the water of the world as the whole amount, the intention will be valid and this individual will not ever break his vow as one is unable to consume all the water in the world. If one was to intend an amount between the minimum 'one drop' and the maximum 'all the water of the world', like a jug of water for example, the intention will be invalid. This is because *al-jins* does not have the capacity of anything but the minimum or maximum amounts.

al-Amr does not demand repetition, so it is inevitable that without a specific intention in mind if a husband says to his wife, "Divorce yourself", to which she replies, "I am divorced", she will be divorced just the once. If the husband intended all three divorces, all three would occur. But if he intended two, the intention will be invalid and it will default to one divorce. Similarly, if one instructed another individual with respect to his own wife to, "Divorce her", without an intention it will default to one divorce and the representative will have permission to issue just one divorce. If the husband intended three then that would also be valid. If the husband intended two, it will default back to one, as the words do not have the capacity to mean anything but the minimum or maximum amount and there is no repetition in al-amr itself.

Should the wife be a slave, there is a possibility of intending two divorces, because in her case the maximum number of divorces is two. This will be the whole *al-jins* for her. For the free-woman the whole amount was three and for the slave the whole amount is two. Three in the case of the free woman was permitted as it is the whole *al-jins* and two is permitted for the slave as it is also the whole *al-jins*.

Furthermore, if a master grants his slave permission to marry saying, "Marry!", this command will be for him to marry one woman by default. This is in the case where the master has not made a specific intention. If the master intends for the slave to marry twice, it is valid. This is because the total number

QUICK ARABIC

الجنس: *al-jins*

Genus. A class or group. A group of closely related things.

QUICK GRAMMAR

الأمر: *al-amr*

The imperative. A word-form that informs of a demanded act.

of marriages permitted for a slave at one time is two; this is the whole amount. As this is the whole amount and intending the whole amount is permitted in al-amr, the intention will stand and the slave will have permission to marry twice.

Text And Translation

فصل الأمر بالفعل لا يقتضي التكرار: ولهذا قلنا: لو قال: طلق امرأتي. فطلقها الوكيل ثم تزوجها الموكل ليس للوكيل أن يطلقها بالأمر الأول ثانيا، ولو قال: زوجني امرأة. لا يتناول هذا تزويجا مرة بعد أخرى، ولو قال لعبده: تزوج. لا يتناول ذلك إلا مرة واحدة؛ لأن الأمر بالفعل طلب تحقيق الفعل على سبيل الاختصار، فإن قوله: اضرب. مختصر من قوله: افعل فعل الضرب والمختصر من الكلام والمطول سواء في الحكم، ثم الأمر بالضرب أمر بجنس تصرف معلوم، وحكم اسم الجنس أن يتناول الأدنى عند الإطلاق ويحتمل كل الجنس وعلى هذا قلنا: إذا حلف لا يشرب الماء، يحنث بشرب أدنى قطرة منه، ولو نوى به جميع مياه العالم صحت نيته، ولهذا قلنا إذا قال لها: طلقي نفسك فقالت: طلقت يقع الواحدة، ولو نوى الثلاث صحت نيته، وكذلك لو قال لآخر: طلقها يتناول الواحدة عند الإطلاق، ولو نوى الثلاث صحت نيته ولو نوى الثنتين لا يصح إلا إذا كانت المنكوحة أمة فإن نية الثنتين في حقها نية بكل الجنس، ولو قال لعبده :تزوج. يقع على تزوج امرأة واحدة، ولو نوى الثنتين صحت نيته؛ لأن ذلك كل الجنس في حق العبد.

Chapter on repetition not being a function of al-amr: for this reason we say: if one instructed: “Divorce my wife”, so the agent divorced her, then the appointer remarried her; it is not for the agent to divorce her due to the first command for a second time. If one instructed: “Marry me to a woman”. This would not entail one marriage after another. If one said to his slave: “Marry”. This would only mean once. This is because al-amr seeks an action with utmost brevity. So one commanding: “Strike!” Is brief for: ‘perform the act of striking’. Concise wording is the same as detailed wording in terms of its function. Furthermore, the command to strike is a command to undertake a known generic action. The ruling regarding a generic-noun is that it means the minimum component when unrestricted and has the capacity to mean the whole genus. Based on this we said: if one vows not to drink water, he will have broken the vow by consuming the tiniest drop of it. And if he intended all the world's water his intention would be valid. Also for this reason we said: if one said to his wife: “Divorce yourself”, she replied: “I divorced”, one divorce will occur. Had he intended three, his intention would be valid and had he intended two it would not be correct except if the married woman is a slave for in her case the intention of two would be all the genus. If one said to his slave: “Marry!” It would mean marry one woman and if he had intended two his intention would be accepted. This is because in a slave's case this is all the genus.

❖ ❖ ❖

The question that arises here is that by saying al-amr does not demand repetition or have the possibility of repetition, how then are five daily prayers necessary from the command:

﴿وَأَقِيمُواْ الصَّلاَةَ﴾ [البقرة: 43]

“Establish worship.”

The command is delivered with an al-amr word-form and it is the command that makes the five daily prayers necessary for the rest of one's life. However, by suggesting that al-amr has no repetition it should be sufficient to pray just once in your lifetime to fulfil this command. Similarly, despite the command:

﴿وَآتُواْ الزَّكَاةَ﴾ [البقرة: 43]

“Pay the poor-due.”

A command in the al-amr word-form, zakah is compulsory yearly, whilst al-amr does not demand repetition. Furthermore:

﴿فَمَن شَهِدَ مِنكُمُ الشَّهْرَ فَلْيَصُمْهُ﴾ [البقرة: 185]

“Whomsoever of you is present, let him fast the month.”

This is also a command in the al-amr word-form. It should require fulfilment on one occasion as it does not demand repetition, however fasting occurs yearly. These examples are enough to suggest that al-amr demands repetition.

The answer to this is that the repetition that occurs in acts of worship such as salah, zakah and sawm, is not due to al-amr but due to their respective causes. The cause of salah is time, the cause of zakah is the minimum quota and the cause of sawm is the presence of the month of Ramadan. As the respective

QUICK GRAMMAR

الأمر: *al-amr*

The imperative. A word-form that informs of a demanded act.

causes repeat, so does the obligation to perform each type of worship. As the cause of Hajj is *al-Bayt* and that does not repeat, the obligation of the Hajj does not repeat and is necessary only once in a lifetime. Further details of causes of various worship, *al-asbāb*, is in chapter 5.2, page 428.

It is one thing for a task to be compulsory, but another for it to be necessary to perform. A task becomes compulsory from its cause but the obligation of performing it becomes necessary upon the command of al-amr. An example of this is when a cashier tells a customer "Pay for the merchandise!" Payment is necessary due to the purchase, but the necessity to pay is realised upon the command to pay. Thus, the cause of the necessity to pay is the purchase, and the necessity to fulfil the demand of the payment is upon the command of the cashier. Similarly, the maintenance of the wife becomes necessary from the marriage agreement, but in the case of a husband denying this right to his wife, the necessity to pay will be realised when the judge demands it saying, "Pay the maintenance!" Like this, worship becomes necessary from its relative cause, *as-sabab*, and it becomes a duty to be fulfilled following al-amr. It is as though al-amr reminds the subject that a particular type of worship has become necessary upon you.

Every time a new cause comes about a new al-amr reminds that the worship is to take place. This means that when the first ever time of aẓ-Ẓuhur salah arrived for an adult Muslim, all aẓ-Ẓuhur of a lifetime became necessary. This is the worship becoming necessary. Thus, the maximum amount of aẓ-Ẓuhur became necessary. Now every day aẓ-Ẓuhur salah time arrives, and with it al-amr reminds the adult Muslim to pray once for aẓ-Ẓuhur on that particular day. This is the necessity to fulfil the obligation. A similar system occurs at al-'Aṣr salah and so forth in the remaining prayers. On the very first eligible moment the cause of the worship makes all the worship of that type, *al-jins*, necessary. Whenever all the conditions are met for worship, the al-amr word-form reminds the individual that that type of worship needs to be fulfilled once. Thus, al-amr does not have repetition even though salah is repeated daily, zakah is repeated periodically, and so and so forth.

Text And Translation

ولا يتأتى على هذا فصل تكرار العبادات، فإن ذلك لم يثبت بالأمر بل بتكرار أسبابها التي يثبت بها

QUICK TERMS

السبب: *as-sabab*

(جـ) الأسباب: (pl.) *al-asbāb*

The channel. The route and way in which the means attains the end.

الجنس: *al-jins*

Genus. A class or group. A group of closely related things.

QUICK ARABIC

البيت: *al-bayt*

The House. The building in the courtyard of the masjid in al-Makkah al-Mukarramah; the House of Allah ﷻ.

الظهر: *aẓ-ẓuhr*

The afternoon. The time of day or the prayer performed after the sun begins to decline after noon.

العصر: *al-'aṣr*

The late-noon. The time of day or the prayer performed before the sun sets.

الوجوب والأمر لطلب أداء ما وجب في الذمة بسبب سابق لا لإثبات أصل الوجوب، وهذا بمنزلة قول الرجل: أد ثمن المبيع وأد نفقة الزوجة، فإذا وجبت العبادة بسببها فتوجه الأمر لأداء ما وجب منها عليه، ثم الأمر لما كان يتناول الجنس يتناول جنس ما وجب عليه، ومثاله ما يقال: إن الواجب في وقت الظهر هو الظهر، فتوجه الأمر لأداء ذلك الواجب، ثم إذا تكرر الوقت تكرر الواجب فيتناول الأمر ذلك الواجب الآخر ضرورة تناوله كل الجنس الواجب عليه صوما كان أو صلاة، فكان تكرار العبادة المتكررة بهذا الطريق لا بطريق أن الأمر يقتضي التكرار

At this juncture do not bring forth the chapter of repetition in worship, for it is not established through al-amr but because of a repetition of the cause that makes it necessary. al-Amr demands the performance of the necessary act due because of a preceding cause, it is not to prove the actual necessity. This is like a man saying: "Pay the price of the purchase", or "Pay up the expenses of the wife". When a worship becomes necessary due to its cause, al-amr directs one to perform what is due because of it. Moreover, because al-amr is generic it includes the genus of what is necessary. An example of it is what is said: the necessary task in the time of aẓ-Ẓuhur is the aẓ-Ẓuhur prayer. So al-amr engages to demand the performance of that necessary act. Then as the time repeats the necessary act repeats so al-amr engages for this different necessary act. This is inevitable as it contains all the genus of the neccesary act, whether it is sawm or salah. So the cycle of repeated worship is in this manner and not due to al-amr functioning with repetition.

❖ ❖ ❖

QUICK ARABIC

الظهر: *aẓ-ẓuhr*

The afternoon. The time of day or the prayer performed after the sun begins to decline after noon.

QUICK GRAMMAR

الأمر: *al-amr*

The imperative. A word-form that informs of a demanded act.

Ḥanafī Principles (12)

MEMORISE

	Term	Definition	Ruling	An Example
25	الأمر	في اللغة قول القائل لغيره افعل وفي الشرع تصرف إلزام الفعل على الغير	وجوب الايتمار إلا إذا قام الدليل على خلافه	﴿وإذا قرء القرآن فاستمعوا له وأنصتوا﴾ [الإسراء: 23]

❖ ❖ ❖

Summary Of al-Amr

1. The definition of al-amr:
في اللغة قول القائل لغيره افعل وفي الشرع تصرف إلزام الفعل على الغير
"Linguistically it is to say to the other, "Do!", and in the Shariah, it is to delegate the necessity of a task to the other."

2. An example of al-amr:
In the verse وإذا قرء القرآن فاستمعوا له وأنصتوا لعلكم ترحمون we are commanded to listen and remain silent when the blessed Quran is recited.

3. The orthodox Ḥanafī position is that without context al-amr is for necessity. The evidence for this is that ignoring a command is seen as disobedience. If ignoring is disobedience and a sin when it concerns the Shariah, then obeying is necessary. Therefore, al-amr is for necessity.

4. The ruling of al-amr is:
وجوب الايتمار إلا إذا قام الدليل على خلافه
"Obeying is necessary unless its necessity is disproved".

❖ ❖ ❖

1.6.3 al-Mamūr Bihī

The duty necessary upon a subject is of two types: al-māmūr bihī muṭlaqun 'an il-waqt, time-independent duties and al-māmūr bihī muqayyadun bil-waqt, time-dependant duties. Figure 1.6.3-01 shows this division. al-Māmūr bihī muṭlaqun 'an il-waqt is that duty that is time-independent, where the Shariah has not determined a set time frame for it to be delivered. Examples of such tasks include the giving of zakah, the ṣadaqa tul-fiṭr and al-'ushr. Once they are obligatory, they can be fulfilled at any time. al-Māmūr bihī muqayyadun bil-waqt, on the other hand, is that duty that is time-dependant and must be completed within a time-frame. Examples of such duties are the compulsory salah and the sawm of Ramadan. These duties must be carried out and completed within the given time-frame set by the Shariah.

The ruling on al-māmūr bihī muṭlaqun 'an il-waqt is that it can be fulfilled at the most convenient time and without any urgency. The condition, though, is that it must be carried out within a person's lifetime and not missed

QUICK TERMS

المأمور به: *al-mamūr bihī*

The duty. The task that is necessary upon a subject. It can be time-dependant or independent of time.

QUICK ARABIC

صدقة الفطر: *ṣadaqat ul-fiṭr*

Alms of fast breaking. Alms given on the conclusion of the month of Ramadan.

العشر: *al-'ushr*

A tenth. A tithe given to the treasury of the Muslim state for fruit and produce of the ground.

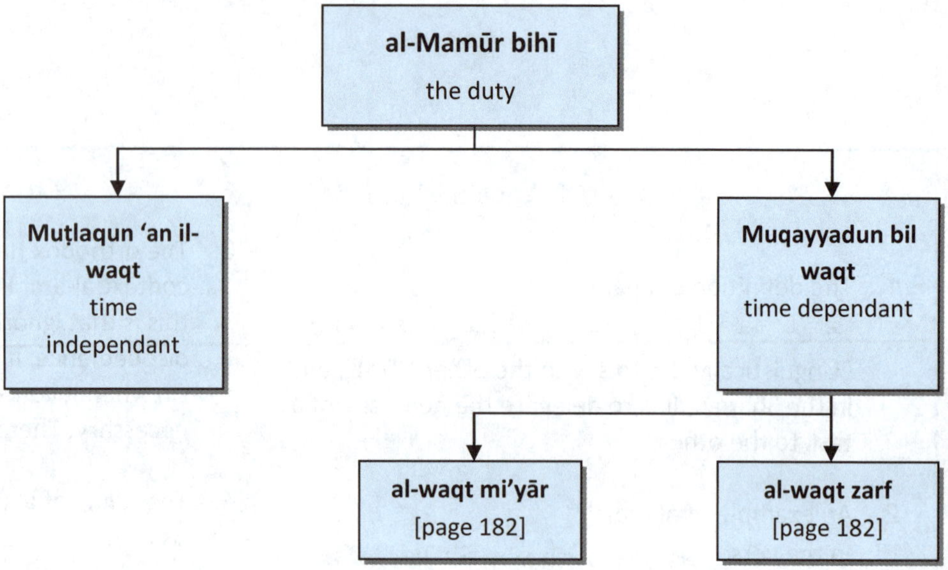

FIGURE 1.6.3-01
Division of duties, al-mamūr bihī.

QUICK ARABIC

صدقة الفطر: *ṣadaqat ul-fiṭr*

Alms of fast breaking. Alms given on the conclusion of the month of Ramadan.

العشر: *al-'ushr*

A tenth. A tithe given to the treasury of the Muslim state.

الاعتكاف: *al-i'tikāf*

Seclusion. The act of isolating oneself in the masjid for veneration of Allah ﷻ.

المذهب: *al-madhhab*

School of fiqh. A system of practices according to mujtahids.

QUICK REFERENCE

الجامع الكبير: *al-jāmi' al-kabīr*

The Great Collection. A collection of narrations that Imam Muḥammad رحمه الله compiled directly from Imam Abū Ḥanīfa رحمه الله

entirely. Whenever it is carried out, it will be considered complete and there is no sin attached to delaying it either. If the whole life is spent pondering on when to perform it and the person is unable to perform it, the individual will be sinful. Based on this ruling, Imam Muḥammad رحمه الله has stated in al-Jāmi' al-Kabīr that if one vows to sit secluded in *al-i'tikāf* for one month, it is up to the person to choose which month to fulfil it in, and if one were to vow a month of fasting, it would be their choice as to which month to fast.

It is the adopted position of the Ḥanafī madhhab that in delaying the delivery of zakah, ṣadaqat ul-fiṭr and al-'ushr the individual is not sinful. This means that after the minimum term was complete zakah was not paid, the fiṭr was not paid on the day of Eid and the al-'ushr was not given once the produce of the land was obtained. Rather in each case the individual delayed the delivery, the person will not be sinful. This is because each of these duties is time-independent and can be fulfilled at the individual's convenience. As this is the ruling regarding such duties, then the person is not sinful by exercising a right.

To highlight this point, the case is put forth that should any zakah-deductible wealth perish after the minimum period has lapsed and before the zakah was paid, there would be no payment due. This is because this person has not slacked in delivering his dues because the Shariah has permitted delaying the payment of zakah. Similarly, if all the produce harvested was to perish and the owner was unable to pay al-'ushr from it, it would no longer be due.

It should be noted, contradictory to what the text of Uṣūl ush-Shāshī implies, if ṣadaqat ul-fiṭr is not paid on the day of Eid it remains necessary even if the one liable is to become poor and lose all their wealth later. The reason for this is that zakah and 'ushr are significantly different to al-fiṭr, in that they have conditions of ease attached to them. A whole term must pass with the wealth in the possession of the individual for the zakah to be obligatory, and even upon giving only a small portion of the excess wealth is to be given. This points to an element of ease from the Shariah. As for al-'ushr, simply owning the land to harvest is a sign of wealth, and upon giving only one-tenth is to be given and nine-tenths are to be retained by the owner. This also shows an element of ease for the owner. As the Shariah has given ease in these two cases, that ease is retained and the person is not asked to pay the dues once the wealth has perished. However, the ṣadaqat ul-fiṭr does not have such ease attached to it. It becomes necessary on the morning of Eid ul-Fiṭr on the one who is wealthy enough to have the minimum quota on just that day. There is no condition of allowing a whole term to pass, nor is there a percentage to pay. Rather, a fixed amount is to be paid. As there is no sign of ease for the ṣadaqat ul-fiṭr, even if it is to perish, it is to be paid and the individual will remain liable until it is. One will not be sinful if it is paid within their lifetime and it can be paid at convenience, but by not paying at all one will be sinful.

Another example of the ruling on al-māmūr bihī muṭlaqun 'an il-waqt is when one breaks a vow, they are at first liable for a financial penalty. If they are unable to compensate financially then they are liable to fast. Allah ﷻ has said in Sūrat ul-Māida, verse 89:

﴿فَكَفَّارَتُهُ إِطْعَامُ عَشَرَةِ مَسَاكِينَ مِنْ أَوْسَطِ مَا تُطْعِمُونَ أَهْلِيكُمْ أَوْ كِسْوَتُهُمْ أَوْ تَحْرِيرُ رَقَبَةٍ فَمَن لَّمْ يَجِدْ فَصِيَامُ ثَلَاثَةِ أَيَّامٍ﴾

[المائدة: 89]

"...for expiation, feed ten poor persons, on a scale of the average for the food of your families; or clothe them; or give a slave his freedom. If that is beyond your means, fast for three days."

In this verse, the financial expiation is time-independent and muṭlaqun 'an il-waqt. This means that if the one liable delays payment, despite having the means to pay immediately, the individual will not be sinful. If all the wealth is

QUICK TERMS

المأمور به: *al-mamūr bihī*

The duty. The task that is necessary upon a subject. It can be time-dependant or independent of time.

consumed in the meantime, the person is then duty-bound to fast as he has now become poor. This expiation by fasting will be valid because the duty is muṭlaqun 'an il-waqt and thus delaying it is not a sin. When taking circumstances at the time of delivery of the duty into consideration, he is poor, so expiation through fasting is valid.

Following the principle that al-māmūr bihī muṭlaqun 'an il-waqt can be delayed, we say that making up missed prayers in al-makrūh times is not permitted. This is because when one does not offer a salah in its correct time, it becomes al-qaḍā, and so it is now necessary to make it up. There is no time allocated by the Shariah for missed prayers, so al-qaḍā salah is al-māmūr bihī muṭlaqun 'an il-waqt. The cause for making al-qaḍā salah necessary is the completely missed time allocated to that salah, which was its true and correct place. Now that it was missed, it collectively became the cause of the al-qaḍā. As the period that is the cause is al-kāmil and complete, the resultant duty must also be al-kāmil and complete. By delivering the duty deficient, it will not be acceptable. The al-makrūh times are all nāqiṣ and deficient. Therefore, performing a complete duty in a deficient time is not permitted. Simply put, this is saying that al-qaḍā is necessary independently of time, so it is necessary to fulfil it in the complete time. As this is the case, the duty-bound subject is not permitted to perform it in the deficient al-makrūh time.

Furthering this idea, when the sunlight weakens at sunset, the al-'Aṣr prayer for that day is permitted but al-qaḍā of al-'Aṣr for a previous day is not. Today's prayer is permitted because when one begins the prayer in the weakened sunlight, the prayer's cause will be the moment immediately preceding the prayer. As that moment is deficient due to the weakened sunlight and being al-makrūh, the prayer that is required can also be performed deficient. Performing a deficient duty due to a deficient cause is satisfactory. The al-qaḍā of previous al-'Aṣr prayers will not be acceptable at this same al-makrūh time because when one missed it initially, the whole of the complete and al-kāmil time of al-'Aṣr became the cause of the al-qaḍā. As the cause in this case is complete, its delivery must also be complete. On a subsequent day, at sunset, when this person attempts to pray the al-qaḍā of al-'Aṣr, the attempt is to deliver it in al-makrūh and deficient time. To deliver a complete and al-kāmil duty in a deficient and an-nāqiṣ manner is not acceptable, and thus it will not be sufficient to pray it in this time.

QUICK TERMS

المأمور به: *al-mamūr bihī*

The duty. The task that is necessary upon a subject. It can be time-dependant or independent of time.

المكروه: *al-makrūh*

The disliked. An act disliked due to a discrepancy.

القضاء: *al-qaḍā*

To settle. To settle and make up a missed obligatory observance.

الكامل: *al-kāmil*

Complete. Executed as required and without any deficiency.

الناقص: *an-nāqiṣ*

Deficient. Executed in an improper manner.

QUICK ARABIC

العصر: *al-'aṣr*

The late-noon. The time of day or the prayer performed before the sun sets.

The ruling of al-māmūr bihī muṭlaqun 'an il-waqt according to the majority of Ḥanafī jurists is that it is necessary at the earliest convenience, however, Imam Karkhī ﷺ says the delivery must be immediate. It is necessary for the subject to fulfil the duty immediately to the extent that should one delay it, one will be sinful. However, the sin will be temporary in that as soon as the delayed duty is complete no sin will remain. The difference of opinion between the majority and Imam Karkhī ﷺ is about whether it is essential and necessary to fulfil the duty immediately or at the earliest convenience, otherwise they all unanimously agree that early delivery and performance is desirable and best.

Text And Translation

فصل: المأمور به نوعان: مطلق عن الوقت ومقيد به، وحكم المطلق أن يكون الأداء واجبا على التراخي بشرط أن لا يفوته في العمر، وعلى هذا قال مُحَمَّد عليه الرحمة في "الجامع": لو نذر أن يعتكف شهرا له أن يعتكف أي شهر شاء ولو نذر أن يصوم شهرا له أن يصوم أي شهر شاء، وفي الزكاة وصدقة الفطر والعشر المذهب المعلوم أنه لا يصير بالتأخير مفرطا، فإنه لو هلك النصاب سقط الواجب، والحانث إذا ذهب ماله وصار فقيرا كفر بالصوم، وعلى هذا لا يجب قضاء الصلاة في الأوقات المكروهة؛ لأنه لما وجب مطلقا وجب كاملا فلا يخرج عن العهدة بأداء الناقص، فيجوز العصر عند الاحمرار أداء ولا يجوز قضاء، وعن الكرخي رحمه الله: أن موجب الأمر المطلق الوجوب على الفور والخلاف معه في الوجوب ولا خلاف في أن المسارعة إلى الايتمار مندوب إليها

Chapter: necessary tasks are of two types: temporally unrestricted and temporal. The ruling of the unrestricted is that its performance is necessary at convenience, provided that one does not miss it in a lifetime. Based on this Imam Muḥammad, mercy be upon him, states in al-Jāmi': if one vowed to observe devoted seclusion for a month, he may do so for any month. If one vowed to fast a month, he may do so for any month. Regarding zakah, ṣadaqat ul-fiṭr and al-'ushr, the known opinion is that one will not be a sinner by delaying. So if the minimum quota was to be destroyed the duty would cease. When the violator of a vow loses all his wealth, becoming poor, he can expiate through fasting. Based on this it is not necessary to make up lost prayers in disliked times because as it became necessary unrestrictedly, it is necessary to complete it wholly. So one would not sufficiently fulfil the task by performing it deficient. So the performance of al-'Aṣr is permitted at the reddening but cannot

QUICK ARABIC

صدقة الفطر: *ṣadaqat ul-fiṭr*

Alms of fast breaking. Alms given on the conclusion of the month of Ramadan.

العشر: *al-'ushr*

A tenth. A tithe given to the treasury of the Muslim state.

be made-up. al-Karkhī, Allah have mercy on him, says: unrestricted al-amr demands the necessity of immediate performance. The difference with him is in its compulsion and there is no disagreement that hastening to fulfil the command is recommended.

❖ ❖ ❖

The second type of al-māmūr bihī is al-māmūr bihī muqayyadun bil-waqt, time-dependant duty, and it is itself of two types. The first is when time acts as a container, *aẓ-ẓarf*, for the duty. The task itself is to exist within the time given, that is to say it is contained within it. This means that the time is more expansive than the task. An example of this is a salah, such that if one were to pray it according to the sunna, it would not engage the whole time allocated for it. The second type of al-māmūr bihī muqayyadun bil-waqt, is that time-dependant task which takes up all the time allocated, *al-mi'yār*, in which the task is to be performed. An example of this is sawm as it takes up every moment of daylight in which it is to be performed. The details of this type will come in the next segment.

There are three rulings regarding the first type of al-māmūr bihī muqayyadun bil-waqt, where time is *aẓ-ẓarf*:

The first ruling is that it is possible for another similar type of task to be necessary in the exact same time. In other words, it is possible to have two similar duties in that time, that must both be undertaken. This is like it is necessary to pray aẓ-Ẓuhr salah in the time of aẓ-Ẓuhr as well as the additional salah one has vowed to pray in that time. Both are necessary and both are to be performed within the same time-frame. The reason for this is that the whole time allocated for aẓ-Ẓuhr salah will not be spent in the aẓ-Ẓuhr salah, rather only a portion of it will, so it is possible to undertake other similar necessary acts in the same time.

The second ruling is that if one salah is necessary in a given time, it does not prevent another salah legitimately occupying that time. This means that a salah was necessary for example the compulsory aẓ-Ẓuhur salah in the time of aẓ-Ẓuhur. However, the whole time was spent in another salah that is not the obligatory aẓ-Ẓuhur, this other prayer will be valid even though the person will be sinful for missing the obligatory prayer.

QUICK TERMS

المأمور به: *al-mamūr bihī*

The duty. The task that is necessary upon a subject. It can be time-dependant or independent of time.

الظرف: *aẓ-ẓarf*

Container. The time in which a certain type of worship is contained; it is more expansive than the act.

المعيار: *al-mi'yār*

Span. The time to which a certain type of worship is equal to; the length of the worship expands and contracts with the time span.

QUICK ARABIC

الظهر: *aẓ-ẓuhr*

The afternoon. The time of day or the prayer performed after the sun begins to decline after noon.

النية: *an-nīya*

Intention. A vow and non-verbal understanding present before an act.

The third ruling is that the duty will only be acceptable with a valid intention, *an-niyyah*. This is because in the given time-frame, just like that specific duty is necessary and possible, other similar worship is also permitted and possible. This means that there are multiple possibilities that are potentially going to be offered, so without determining which one is actually being offered, there is none selected by default. Therefore, it will be necessary to have an intention to specify which salah is actually being offered in that instance. This ruling is still operational even if the time left to perform the necessary act is extremely tight. For example, in the time of aẓ-Ẓuhur the time left is only sufficient for performing four units of aẓ-Ẓuhur, still the intention is necessary. This is because an intention to identify the exact worship is necessary when there are contenders and possibilities. Whilst the time is tight, there are still multiple acts that could occupy and contend for that time, in that if someone were to engage the whole of that time in voluntary prayers or in a vowed salah, that performed salah would be valid as we explained in the second ruling. Thus, if there are multiple contending acts possible in a time-frame, an intention is required to specify the duty being delivered. Without this intention the task is not valid.

Text And Translation

وأما الموقت فنوعان: نوع يكون الوقت ظرفا للفعل حتى لا يشترط استيعاب كل الوقت بالفعل كالصلاة، ومن حكم هذا النوع أن وجوب الفعل فيه لا ينافي وجوب فعل آخر فيه من جنسه حتى لو نذر أن يصلي كذا وكذا ركعة في وقت الظهر لزمه، ومن حكمه أن وجوب الصلاة فيه لا ينافي صحة صلاة أخرى فيه حتى لو شغل جميع وقت الظهر لغير الظهر يجوز، وحكمه أنه لا يتأدى المأمور به إلا بنية معينة؛ لأن غيره لما كان مشروعا في الوقت لا يتعين هو بالفعل وإن ضاق الوقت؛ لأن اعتبار النية باعتبار المزاحم وقد بقيت المزاحمة عند ضيق الوقت

As for the temporal it is of two types: one type is that for which time contains the action such that it is not a condition for the whole of the time to be taken up by the act, like salah. The ruling of this type is that the necessity of an act in it does not prevent the necessity of another act of a similar genus in it, such that if one vowed to pray a number of units of salah in the time of aẓ-Ẓuhr, they would become necessary. And from its rulings is that the necessity of a salah in it does not oppose the validity of another salah in it, such that if one spent all the time of aẓ-Ẓuhr in other than aẓ-Ẓuhr salah it would be valid. And its ruling is that the necessary task is only validly performed with a specific intention because whilst another act is legally permitted in the same time, it is not specified merely by performance even if the time is tight. The intention is considered in terms of other contenders and contenders still remain when the time is short.

❖❖❖

The second type of al-māmūr bihī muqayyadun bil-waqt is the duty that is time-dependant and time is *al-mi'yār* for it. This means that the time allocated for that duty is as expansive as the duty itself. After one delivers the duty there is no excess time to offer anything else. If the allocated time increases, the worship also increases in equal measure, and if the time decreases, the duty follows suit. An example of this type of duty is sawm as it is tied to the length of the day in a manner that if the day extends the fast length also increases, and if the day decreases the length of the fast also decreases.

The time which is *al-mi'yār* is either specified for a duty by the Shariah or it is not specified for it at all. The ruling for the specified *al-mi'yār* is that when the Shariah has specified it for that duty, it is not possible to make any other similar duty necessary in the same time-frame. An example of this is the fasts of Ramadan. If one was to vow to fast other fasts during Ramadan, it will not be a valid vow. This is because the time does not have the capacity to occupy two fasts, as it is not possible to have two simultaneous fasts on the same day. As this is not possible, to vow to fast in these days is vowing an impossible feat. It is also not possible for the subject to alter the Shariah, demote the necessity of the Ramadan fast, and replace it with a sawm vowed by oneself. As this is also not a possibility, the only fast that will be necessary on such an occasion is the fast of Ramadan as determined by the Shariah. It follows that it would not be possible to deliver any other fast in Ramadan other than the fast of Ramadan, given that the verse states:

﴿فَمَن شَهِدَ مِنكُمُ الشَّهْرَ فَلْيَصُمْهُ﴾ [البقرة: 185]

"... whoever from you is present in that month, should fast it..."

And the Hadith states: "When Sha'bān draws to an end there is no fast but that of Ramadan". Both these texts support this position.

حديث

عن أبي هريرة رضي الله عنه أن رسول الله صلى الله عليه وسلم قال: إذا انتصف شعبان فلا تصوموا.

وعن أبي هريرة رضي الله عنه قال: قال رسول الله صلى الله عليه وسلم: لا تقدموا رمضان بصوم ولا يومين إلا رجل كان يصوم صوما فليصمه.

عليه الصلاة والسلام

(الترمذي: 738 والبخاري: 1914)

QUICK TERMS

المأمور به: *al-mamūr bihī*

The duty. The task that is necessary upon a subject. It can be time-dependant or independent of time.

المعيار: *al-mi'yār*

Span. The time to which a certain type of worship is equal to; the length of the worship expands and contracts with the time span.

A cited case of how no other sawm is permitted in the month of Ramadan is if a resident in good health offers a fast with the intention of al-qaḍā or al-kaffāra in Ramadan, the fast will still be for Ramadan and not for the other necessary fast. This is because the Shariah has specified a time-frame for a duty that is al-mi'yār, covering all the allocated time, and also the Shariah specified a particular attribute for that worship, that it is a fast of Ramadan, so the subject is not able to alter or change this attribute on his or her own accord.

In the cited case, the one fasting is described as a resident, *al-muqīm*, and in good health, *aṣ-ṣaḥīḥ*. This is to avoid the cases of a traveller or the ill during the month of Ramadan. According to Imam Abū Ḥanīfa ﷺ if either of these two individuals were to intend to fast another necessary sawm, like a previously missed sawm or for expiation, it will be valid for that necessary fast and not the fast of Ramadan.

As the al-māmūr bihī muqayyadun bil-waqt that is al-mi'yār takes up all the allocated time and does not leave the possibility of any other duty, there remains no contenders for that time. Without other contending duties, there is no requirement for an intention specifying an exact attribute for the worship. A specific intention was only required when there were a number of possibilities, but as the fast of Ramadan is the only duty that can occupy that time it will be selected by default. One is not required to intend for the fast of Ramadan, rather a simple unattributed intention of a sawm would suffice. Of course, this does not mean that it is possible to fast without an intention because mere abstinence from eating, drinking and intercourse does not constitute fasting in the Shariah. Rather, intentionally abstaining from these three acts during daylight hours will be a fast and sawm in the view of the Shariah. This means a fast requires three things:

a) Abstinence from the three acts;
b) Abstinence during daylight hours; and
c) Intentional abstinence.

If any one of these conditions is missing, it may be a fast in word and act but will not be a divinely rewarded fast in the view of the Shariah. Therefore, the fast of the month of Ramadan will still require an intentional abstinence to technically be a sawm. The only difference is that the intention does not have to be of an attributed sawm as the Shariah has already allocated this time for a specifically attributed fast, which is that of Ramadan.

QUICK TERMS

القضاء: *al-qaḍā*

To settle. To settle and make up a missed obligatory observance.

QUICK ARABIC

الكفارة: *al-kaffāra*

Expiation. The prescribed atonement for neglected duties.

المقيم: *al-muqīm*

The resident. Someone who has not intended to travel in excess of three days' distance and is still in the vicinity of the home town.

الصحيح: *aṣ-ṣaḥīḥ*

The sound. Someone who is well and considered able to perform a worship without a valid excuse.

The duty for which time is *al-mi'yār* is either given a specific time by the Shariah or it is left to the subject to decide when to perform it. Details of the Shariah specified duty, like fasting of Ramadan, is detailed above. This leaves that duty which is al-mi'yār but the Shariah has not specified when this time-dependant duty needs to begin. An example of this is the missed al-qaḍā fasts of Ramadan. Each fast is time-dependant in that it must expand the length of a day. It is also necessary to make it up at some point as it is a duty set by the Shariah and was not delivered on time, so it must be made up. However, the Shariah does not give a specific set of days in which these fasts are to be made up. It is unlike the fasts of Ramadan as they have a specific month. The missed Ramadan fasts however do not have such a set of Shariah specified days in which they must be made up. Such duties, even though the subject specified a day for them are not essential and necessary to deliver on the said day. In other words, if one set aside a few days to make up missed fasts of Ramadan, but on the day decided not to fast or to fast for any other purpose like a voluntary sawm or sawm of expiation, they are all valid. Just as the make up fast of Ramadan is possible, so are the other fasts or not fasting at all. The evidence of this is in the verse 185 of Sūrat ul-Baqara:

﴿وَمَن كَانَ مَرِيضًا أَوْ عَلَى سَفَرٍ فَعِدَّةٌ مِّنْ أَيَّامٍ أُخَرَ﴾ [البقرة: 185]

"...but he that is ill, or on a journey, the prescribed period is on other days..."

The time for making up the fasts is al-muṭlaq and not specified. If a person wants to specify a time for it, it will contradict the unspecified nature of the verse. The person's specification will not be considered binding, rather it is just an option, and thus al-muṭlaq of the verse remains unaltered.

QUICK TERMS

المعيار: *al-mi'yār*

Span. The time to which a certain type of worship is equal to; the length of the worship expands and contracts with the time span.

القضاء: *al-qaḍā*

To settle. To settle and make up a missed obligatory observance.

المطلق: *al-muṭlaq*

To unrestricted. Indicates an entity irrespective of any qualities.

Text And Translation

والنوع الثاني ما يكون الوقت معيارا له، وذلك مثل الصوم فإنه يتقدر بالوقت وهو اليوم، ومن حكمه أن الشرع إذا عين له وقتا لا يجب غيره في ذلك الوقت ولا يجوز أداء غيره فيه حتى أن الصحيح المقيم لو أوقع إمساكه في رمضان عن واجب آخر يقع عن رمضان لا عما نوى، وإذا اندفع المزاحم في الوقت سقط اشتراط التعيين، فإن ذلك لقطع المزاحمة ولا يسقط أصل النية؛ لأن الإمساك لا يصير صوما إلا بالنية، فإن الصوم شرعا هو الإمساك عن الأكل والشرب والجماع نهارا مع النية، وإن لم يعين الشرع له

وقتا فإنه لا يتعين الوقت له بتعيين العبد حتى لو عين العبد أياما لقضاء رمضان لا تتعين هي للقضاء،
ويجوز فيها صوم الكفارة والنفل ويجوز قضاء رمضان فيها وغيرها

The second type is when time encompasses the whole act. This is like sawm for it is measured to a time-frame, which is daylight. A ruling of it is that when the Shariah has specified a time for it, other than it are not necessary in that time nor is it permitted to perform other than it; such that if an able resident was to abstain in the month of Ramadan due to another necessary act, it will be an observance of Ramadan and not of what he intended. As there is no possibility of contenders in this time, specifying is not a condition for that is to avoid possibilities, but the basic intention remains. This is because abstinence only becomes a sawm through intention. Sawm in the Shariah is abstinence from eating, drinking and sexual intercourse throughout the day with an intention. When the Shariah does not allocate a time for it, it can not be allocated by a subject such that if a subject allocated a few days to make up missed fasts of Ramadan, they will not be restricted to the missed fasts. Fasts for expiation and voluntary fasts would be permitted in them, as would missed Ramadan fasts, in them and in other days.

❖ ❖ ❖

The ruling for this type of al-māmūr bihī muqayyadun bil-waqt is that an intention is required for it to be valid. This means that on the day that the missed Ramadan fast is to be made up, the person must intend to keep that particular sawm and not just any fast, as was the case with the fasts of Ramadan. The reason is that this time has many contenders, ranging from the voluntary fast to the necessary. As there are many possibilities, to eliminate the possibility of others an intention must be made, specifying which fast is being delivered.

The point raised regarding a person assigning a time for a task and it not being necessary at that particular time, seems contradictory to the idea that if one makes something necessary on themselves, it normally becomes binding. If one is to make a whole task necessary upon themselves, then why can they not specify particulars such as time, for that same task? In response we say that people are permitted to make something necessary on themselves, however it should be without altering the Shariah. As the Shariah has kept the command of

QUICK TERMS

المأمور به: *al-mamūr bihī*

The duty. The task that is necessary upon a subject. It can be time-dependant or independent of time.

المقيد: *al-muqayyad*

To restricted. Indicates an entity and some of its qualities.

al-qaḍā sawm unrestricted and al-muṭlaq as stated in verse 185 of Sūrat ul-Baqara, the person has no right to alter this ruling on his or her own accord. So, if one was to vow to fast on a particular day, it will be necessary to deliver it. However, on the day he decided to fast a missed fast of Ramadan or a fast of expiation, those fasts would be permitted instead. If for an instance we say that both of these fasts are not correct on that day, we would be implying that al-qaḍā sawm and fasts of expiation are not al-muṭlaq with any time but al-maqayyad and restricted to particular times. This is altering the Shariah and thus is not permitted. Of course, if one was to break a vow, the expiation would be necessary, but the self-allocated sawm for that day will be valid.

There is another point of contention that the Shariah has prescribed voluntary worship as al-muṭlaq just like missed fasts of Ramadan and fasts of expiation. There are no days set aside for these types of worship. Now, a person vows to fast on a particular day but on the day decides to fast voluntarily and not for the vowed fast. It is stated that the fast will be for the vowed fast and not the voluntary fast, which the person intended. Does this not contradict the previous point made that al-muṭlaq cannot be changed to al-maqayyad, because the voluntary fast was permitted on any day, however you have made an exception for the day that was vowed by not allowing the voluntary fast on that day? This is a verdict that follows the rule that a voluntary fast is the right of a person as one is permitted to fast it or leave it as a choice. The fasts of missed Ramadan and expiation are the right of the Shariah. People are not permitted to alter the ruling of the Shariah but it is within one's remit to alter their own decision. Therefore, a vow to fast on a particular day is binding on the individual with respect to his or her own choices but cannot have an impact on matters established by the Shariah. The vow for a particular day's fast will annul the validity of a voluntary fast on the same day, as both of these fasts are one's own choice. However, the vowed fast is necessary to fulfil whereas the voluntary fast is not. Therefore, the vowed sawm will take precedence. In summary, on a day that one vowed to fast, if the individual chose to fast a voluntary fast, the voluntary fast will be invalid and the fast will count as the vowed fast. If on the day of the vowed fast, the individual decided to fast a missed fast of Ramadan or a fast of expiation, the fast of Ramadan or expiation will be valid, and the vowed fast will be invalid.

The fact that a person can affect their own decision in this manner but not the stipulations of the Shariah is further illustrated by a particular verdict of

QUICK TERMS

المطلق: *al-muṭlaq*

The unrestricted. Indicates an entity irrespective of any quality.

المقيد: *al-muqayyad*

To restricted. Indicates an entity and some of its qualities.

the Aḥnāf. In a case of *al-khul'* if the couple agree that during the *al-'idda* waiting period, the husband does not have to provide residence nor maintenance, it will be valid for the maintenance but not the residence. This is because the condition of providing the residence is a stipulation of the Shariah. Allah جل جلاله has said in verse 1 of Sūrat uṭ-Ṭalāq:

﴿لَا تُخْرِجُوهُنَّ مِن بُيُوتِهِنَّ﴾ [الطلاق: 1]

"... and turn them not out of their houses, nor shall they leave..."

The verse forbids men to force their wives to leave nor are the wives allowed to leave on their own accord during this period. This shows that residing at the residence of the husband and the same house is a right afforded by the Shariah. As it is a right of the Shariah, the couple do not have a right to overrule it even if it is mutually agreed. Consequently, the husband must provide the residence. This is different to the right of maintenance, as the Shariah does not stipulate it in the same manner. Rather, it is the right of the wife as she has foregone her ability to earn in order to look after the couple's home and children. She has a right to maintenance and if she agrees to forego this right, it is her choice to stipulate this. This example shows how a person can influence his or her own rights and choices, but not the rights of the Shariah.

Text And Translation

ومن حكم هذا النوع أنه يشترط تعيين النية لوجود المزاحم، ثم للعبد أن يوجب شيئا على نفسه موقتا أو غير موقت وليس له تغيير حكم الشرع، مثاله إذا نذر أن يصوم يوما بعينه لزمه ذلك، ولو صامه عن قضاء رمضان أو عن كفارة يمينه جاز؛ لأنّ الشرع جعل القضاء مطلقا فلا يتمكن العبد من تغييره بالتقييد بغير ذلك اليوم، ولا يلزم على هذا ما إذا صامه عن نفل حيث يقع عن المنذور لا عما نوى؛ لأن النفل حق العبد؛ إذ هو يستبد بنفسه من تركه وتحقيقه فجاز أن يؤثر فعله فيما هو حقه لا فيما هو حق الشرع، وعلى اعتبار هذا المعنى قال مشايخنا: إذا شرطا في الخلع أن لا نفقة لها ولا سكنى سقطت النفقة دون السكنى، حتى لا يتمكن الزوج من إخراجها عن بيت العدة؛ لأن السكنى في بيت العدة حق الشرع فلا يتمكن العبد من إسقاطه بخلاف النفقة

A ruling regarding this type is that it is a condition to exact the intention due to the existence of contenders. Furthermore, it is fine for a subject to make

QUICK ARABIC

الخلع: *al-khul'*

Divorce. An agreement to divorce after compensation is paid by the wife.

العدة: *al-'idda*

The term. The three-month period after a divorce.

something necessary upon himself, temporal or not, but he can not change the ruling of the Shariah. An example of this is that if one vowed to fast for a particular day, it would be necessary for him. Were he to fast on the day for a missed Ramadan fast or for expiation of a vow, it is permitted, because the Shariah left the missed fast unrestricted. So the subject cannot change that by limiting it to other than that day. This cannot be countered with one fasting voluntarily, it would be sufficient to be the vowed fast and not voluntary, because a voluntary fast is the right of the subject. He it is who squanders or establishes it for himself, so his actions can impact his rights but not the requirements of the Shariah. Considering this meaning our scholars have said: if in the case of *al-khul'* both parties agree that she is not to receive maintenance nor residence; maintenance would be forfeited but not the residence. The husband would not be able to expel her from the waiting-residence. This is because dwelling in the waiting-residence is a requirement of the Shariah so, unlike the maintenance, the subject is unable to overturn it.

QUICK ARABIC

الخلع: *al-khul'*

Divorce. An agreement to divorce after compensation is paid by the wife.

❖ ❖ ❖

Ḥanafī Principles (13)

MEMORISE

	Term	Definition	Ruling	An Example
26	**مأمور به مطلق عن الوقت**	لا يقرر له وقت حيث إن لم يتأدى فيه المأمور به يقضى	الأداء واجب على التراخي	الزكاة؛ العشر؛ صدقة الفطر؛ الحج
27	**مأمور به مقيد بالوقت: الظرف**	يقرر له وقت والوقت ظرفا للفعل	– وجوب الفعل فيه لا ينافي وجوب فعل آخر فيه من جنسه – وجوب الصلاة فيه لا ينافي صحة صلاة أخرى فيه – لا يتأدى المأمور به إلا بنية معينة	صلاة الظهر
28	**مأمور به مقيد بالوقت: المعيار**	يقرر له وقت والفعل يتقدر بالوقت	– الشرع إذا عين له وقتا لا يجب غيره في ذلك الوقت ولا يجوز غيره فيه – يشترط تعيين النية لوجود المزاحم	الصوم

Summary Of al-Mamūr Bihī

1. In terms of time, the duties set by al-amr are of two types:
i) Muṭlaqun 'an il-waqt; and
ii) Muqayyadun bil-waqt.

2. Definition of muṭlaqun 'an il-waqt:
لا يقرر له وقت حيث إن لم يتأدى فيه المأمور به يقضى
"No time-frame is set for it, such that if left it would be necessary to make it up".

3. Examples of muṭlaqun 'an il-Waqt are: zakah, al-'ushr, ṣadaqat ul-fiṭr, and Hajj. They can all be made up at any time in life. They will never be considered to be al-qaḍā.

4. The ruling for muṭlaqun 'an il-waqt is:
الأداء واجب على التراخي
"Performance is necessary at convenience".

5. Definition of muqayyadun bil-waqt:
يقرر له وقت حيث إن لم يتأدى فيه المأمور به يقضى
"A time-frame is set for it, such that if left it would be necessary to make it up".

6. Examples of muqayyadun bil-waqt:
"The five daily salah and the fasts of Ramadan".

7. There are two types of muqayyadun bil-waqt duties. when:
i) Time is aẓ-ẓarf, container, for the worship; and
ii) Time is al-mi'yār, exact span, of the worship.

8. Details of aẓ-ẓarf:
i) The duty doesn't require all the time to be engaged in performance, hence is contained within it.
ii) An example of it is the aẓ-Ẓuhr salah as it requires a handful of minutes from the whole expansive time.
iii) The ruling is:
a) وجوب الفعل فيه لا ينافي وجوب فعل آخر فيه من جنسه
"The necessity of a task in it doesn't obstruct the necessity of another similar task in it".
b) لا يتأدى المأمور به إلا بنية معينة
"The duty is not performed without an intention".

9. Details of *al-mi'yār*:
i) The performance of the duty encompasses the whole allowable time.
ii) An example is a fast of Ramadan, which shortens in the winter months and lengthens in the summer months.
iii) The ruling is:
الشرع إذا عين له وقتا لا يجب غيره في ذلك الوقت ولا يجوز غيره فيه
"When the Shariah specifies a time for it, no other similar worship is necessary nor permitted in the time".

❖ ❖ ❖

1.6.4 The excellence in al-Mamūr Bihī

al-Māmūr bihī is a duty and is a thing of excellence. This is because the One ﷻ demanding it is the Most Wise ﷻ, and the wise always command that which is good. Anything that is commanded by the Most Wise ﷻ must necessarily be excellent. The al-amr word-form makes it clear that the duty mentioned is something that should be performed, and as it should be performed it must also be an excellent thing as the Most Wise ﷻ demanded it.

In terms of excellence, *al-ḥusn*, al-māmūr bihī is of two types: ḥasan li-dhātihī and ḥasan li-ghayrihī. Ḥasan li-dhātihī means that the excellence is intrinsic and integral to that duty. In other words, the duty itself is worthy and excellent. Ḥasan li-ghayrihī, on the other hand, is a duty that is excellent due to something else. The excellence is not necessarily in the task itself, but something external is lending it the excellence. Examples of ḥasan li-dhātihī are belief in Allah Almighty ﷻ and His Attributes, gratitude to a benefactor, honesty, being just, and all types of worship. All of these tasks are al-māmūr bihī as they have been demanded by Allah ﷻ, and they are ḥasan li-dhātihī because the excellence in each is intrinsic and a part of the exact thing that has been prescribed. The division is shown in Figure 1.6.4-01.

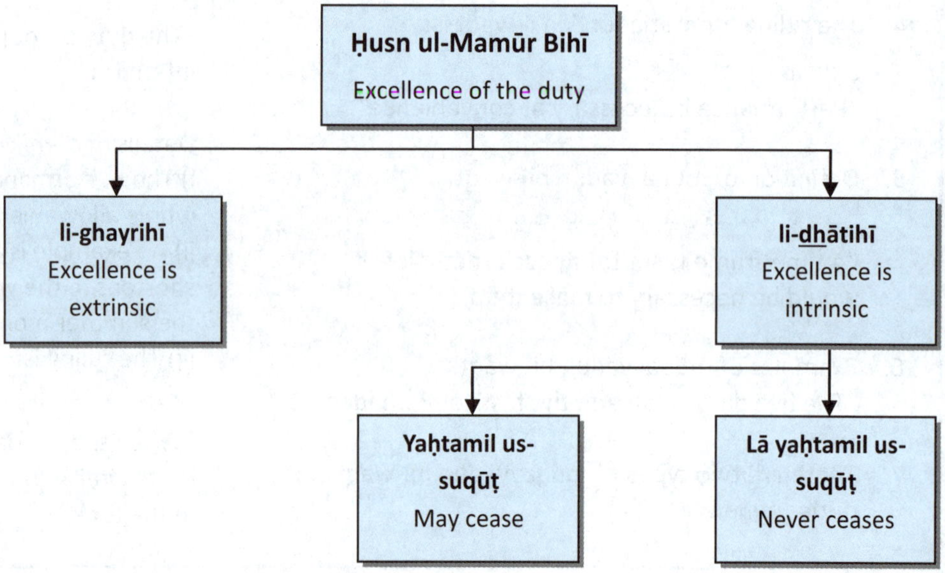

FIGURE 1.6.4-01
Division in terms of excellence of the duty, al-mamūr bihī.

QUICK TERMS

حسن لذاته: *ḥasan li-dhātihī*

Intrinsically excellent. The duty itself is a worthy act and a thing of beauty.

حسن لغيره: *ḥasan li-ghayrihī*

Extrinsically excellent. The duty is excellent due to an external factor.

There are two rulings connected to ḥasan li-dhātihī because such duties are of two types. Those duties that are excellent and must always be maintained, never ceasing. Once they are delivered, they must remain in that state and will never be removed. The other type is the duty that is excellent intrinsically and is sometimes present and on other occasions not. An example of the first is belief, as when one becomes a believer it will never be annulled nor cancelled. One will be required to be in a state of belief constantly. An example of the latter type is the duty to pray or fast. The ruling on the first type is that it has to be delivered by the individual, for the individual to be obedient. There is no other option for it. The ruling on the second type is that one can abide by it in one of two ways, by delivering it or by exemption of the Shariah. It is due to the ruling on this second type that the Aḥnāf say that salah becomes necessary at the onset of the prayer time and leaves the subject with only two viable options. The first is delivery of the duty by performing the prayer, and the second is to be excused due to insanity, menstrual bleeding or post-natal bleeding. These are excuses validated by the Shariah and thus the duty is no longer a responsibility demanded from the individual.

If the prayer time is tight, there is a lack of water or a lack of clothes, performance of the prayer will still be required as these factors are not excused by the Shariah. Performance must occur even after the time of delivery has lapsed by performing *at-tayammum* if there is no water, and in a state of nakedness in the absence of adequate clothing.

Text And Translation

فصل: الأمر بالشيء يدل على حسن المأمور به إذا كان الآمر حكيما؛ لأن الأمر لبيان أن المأمور به مما ينبغي أن يوجد فاقتضى ذلك حسنه، ثم المأمور به في حق الحسن نوعان: حسن بنفسه وحسن لغيره، فالحسن بنفسه مثل: الإيمان بالله تعالى وشكر المنعم والصدق والعدل والصلاة ونحوها من العبادات الخالصة، فحكم هذا النوع أنه إذا وجب على العبد أداؤه لا يسقط إلا بالأداء وهذا فيما لا يحتمل السقوط مثل: الإيمان بالله تعالى، وأما ما يحتمل السقوط فهو يسقط بالأداء أو بإسقاط الآمر، وعلى هذا قلنا: إذا وجبت الصلاة في أول الوقت سقط الواجب بالأداء أو باعتراض الجنون والحيض والنفاس في آخر الوقت باعتبار أن الشرع أسقطها عنه عند هذه العوارض ولا يسقط بضيق الوقت وعدم الماء واللباس ونحوه

Chapter: the command of an action indicates its excellence when the command-giver is wise. This is because al-amr is to state that the necessary task is essential therefore this demands its excellence. In terms of excellence the essential task is of two types: Ḥasan bi-nafsihī and Ḥasan lighayrihī. Examples of Ḥasan bi-nafsihī are the likes of belief in Allah Almighty, gratitude towards a

QUICK TERMS

حسن بنفسه: *ḥasan bi-nafsihī*

Intrinsically excellent. The duty itself is a worthy act and a thing of beauty. This is the same as ḥasan li-dhātihī.

المأمور به: *al-mamūr bihī*

The duty. The task that is necessary upon a subject. It can be time-dependant or time-independent.

QUICK ARABIC

التيمم: *at-tayammum*

Dry ablution. The ritual ablution performed without water.

benefactor, honesty, justice, salah and its likes from sincere worship. The ruling regarding this type is that once necessary upon a subject it only ceases once performed. This is for those matters that remain constant like faith in Allah Almighty. As for those that may be waived, they will be so by performance or by the command-giver. Based on this we said: when salah became necessary at the start time, the task will be complete upon performance or at the onset of insanity, menstrual bleeding or postnatal bleeding at the end of the time considering that the Shariah has waived it from the person during these occurrences. It will not be waived due to shortage of time, lack of water or clothes or the likes.

❖ ❖ ❖

The second type of al-māmūr bihī in terms of excellence is ḥasan li-ghayrihī. This is when the excellence is not in the duty itself but due to an external factor. An example of this is moving towards the congregation on Friday. It is a duty as Allah ﷻ has commanded in verse 9 of Sūrat ul-Jumu'a:

﴿إِذَا نُودِي لِلصَّلَاةِ مِن يَوْمِ الْجُمُعَةِ فَاسْعَوْا إِلَى ذِكْرِ اللَّهِ﴾ [الجمعة: 9]

"...when the call to prayer is sounded on the day of congregation, hasten to the remembrance of God..."

Another example is performance of ablution for prayers from the commandment in verse 6 of Sūrat ul-Māida:

﴿إِذَا قُمْتُمْ إِلَى الصَّلاَةِ فاغْسِلُواْ وُجُوهَكُمْ﴾ [المائدة: 6]

"...when you rise up for prayer, wash your face..."

Both moving and washing are not intrinsically excellent, rather they are neutral. However, when the movement is for the purpose of the congregation it becomes excellent, as it is leading to worship. Therefore, the movement is excellent due to the congregation and hence it is categorised as ḥasan li-ghayrihī. Similarly, the washing is to allow us to pray salah; hence, ablution is also ḥasan li-ghayrihī.

The ruling on ḥasan li-ghayrihī is that if the purpose of the task is annulled, the task is also annulled. Therefore, if one is not required to attend the congregation on a Friday, such as a traveller, then hastening towards the congregation will not be required from him. Similarly, the one who is not

QUICK TERMS

المأمور به: *al-mamūr bihī*

The duty. The task that is necessary upon a subject. It can be time-dependant or time-independent.

حسن لغيره: *ḥasan li-ghayrihī*

Extrinsically excellent. The duty is excellent due to an external factor.

required to pray need not perform ablution for it. It is for this reason that when the one required to attend the Jumu'a is making his way to it but is held up temporarily and then released before the prayer; he must continue to make his way to the Jumu'a. It is not sufficient for him to say I have already hastened before I was held up, so I have fulfilled the task. Rather, the first attempt at hastening did not achieve the purpose and it is the purpose that is required. Equally, if one is already present at the place of the congregation of Jumu'a, like the one in *al-i'tikāf*, he need not hasten to the congregation as the duty will be null for him. The purpose of attending the congregation is already achieved without requiring any movement. In a similar way, if one performed ablution for prayer but invalidated it before praying, the ablution would have to be performed again. It is not sufficient to say that the prayer required me to perform ablution and that was done. Rather, the purpose of the first ablution was not achieved so it was as though it has not been performed, so the ablution was required for a second time. Equally, if one was already with ablution at the time of a prayer, the ablution will not be required again. These examples go to show that the excellence is in the purpose of the task and not in the task itself.

al-*Ḥudūd*, al-*qiṣāṣ* and jihad can also be seen as ḥasan li-ghayrihī. al-*ḥudūd* is the penal system, which looks to punish and reprimand people; it is not a thing of excellence in itself. However, the penal system may act as a deterrent for many who may be inclined to commit a crime. Prevention from crime is a good thing, so it becomes the reason for *al-ḥudūd* to be classed as ḥasan li-ghayrihī. Similarly, *al-qiṣāṣ* is to give capital punishment to an individual, which in itself is not an excellent thing. However, its acting as a deterrent to reduce criminals from murdering is a good thing. This means that *al-qiṣāṣ* becomes ḥasan li-ghayrihī, as its purpose is excellent. Jihad is much the same, in that it can result in the destruction of lands and people, which is not excellence. As jihad contributes to repel the aggressions of non-believers and raise the Command of the Lord Almighty ﷻ it becomes ḥasan li-ghayrihī. Raising the Name of Allah ﷻ and putting a stop on the encroachment of disbelieve are good purposes. If the good purposes mentioned in *al-ḥudūd*, *al-qiṣāṣ* and jihad were absent, then these acts will no longer be prescribed. Thus, if crime did not occur, there would be no *al-ḥadd*, if murder did not occur, there would be no *al-qiṣāṣ*, and if menacing disbelief did not exist, there would be no jihad.

QUICK ARABIC

الجمعة: *al-jumu'a*

Friday. The day or the particular prayer offered on the day.

الاعتكاف: *al-i'tikāf*

Seclusion. The act of secluding oneself in the masjid for veneration of Allah ﷻ.

الحدود: *al-ḥudūd*

Defined punishment. Punishments that are defined in the Quran and Hadith.

القصاص: *al-qiṣāṣ*

Retaliation. The route afforded to the next of kin in the case of murder and to the afflicted in loss short of murder.

النوع الثاني ما يكون حسنا بواسطة الغير وذلك مثل: السعي إلى الجمعة والوضوء للصلاة، فإن السعي حسن بواسطة كونه مفضيا إلى أداء الجمعة والوضوء حسن بواسطة كونه مفتاحا للصلاة، وحكم هذا النوع أنه يسقط بسقوط تلك الواسطة، حتى أن السعي لا يجب على من لا جمعة عليه ولا يجب الوضوء على من لا صلاة عليه، ولو سعى إلى الجمعة فحمل مكرها إلى موضع آخر قبل إقامة الجمعة يجب عليه السعي ثانيا، ولو كان معتكفا في الجامع يكون السعي ساقطا عنه وكذلك لو توضأ فأحدث قبل أداء الصلاة يجب عليه الوضوء ثانيا، ولو كان متوضئا عند وجوب الصلاة لا يجب عليه تجديد الوضوء، والقريب من هذا النوع الحدود والقصاص والجهاد، فإن الحد حسن بواسطة الزجر عن الجناية، والجهاد حسن بواسطة دفع شر الكفرة وإعلاء كلمة الحق ولو فرضنا عدم الواسطة لا يبقى ذلك مأمورا به فإنه لولا الجناية لا يجب الحد ولولا الكفر المقضي إلى الحراب لا يجب عليه الجهاد.

The second type is that which is excellent due to another. Examples of it are progressing to the Friday congregation and ablution for salah. Progressing is excellent due to it leading to the performance of Jumu'a and ablution is excellent as it is a condition for salah. The ruling regarding this type is that it is waived when that end is not required, such that progressing is not necessary for the one who is not required to perform Jumu'a and ablution is not necessary for the one who isn't required to perform salah. If one was progressing towards Jumu'a and was forced to another location before the performance of Jumu'a, progress to it would be necessary again. If one was observing *al-i'tikāf* in the central masjid progression would be waived for him. Similarly, if one performed ablution and then invalidated it before the salah, ablution would be necessary again. If he were to be in the state of purity when salah became necessary, he need not perform a fresh ablution. Close to this type are *al-ḥudūd*, *al-qiṣāṣ* and jihad; for punishments are excellent due to being a deterrent to crime, jihad is excellent due to repelling the evil of disbelief and honouring the truth. If we hypothesised the lack of the end product, these actions would not remain necessary. So were there no crime, punishment would not be necessary; were there no disbelief that required war, jihad would not be necessary.

❖❖❖

QUICK ARABIC

الجمعة: *al-jumu'a*

Friday. The day or the particular prayer offered on the day.

الاعتكاف: *al-i'tikāf*

Seclusion. The act of secluding oneself in the masjid for veneration of Allah ﷻ.

الحدود: *al-ḥudūd*

Defined punishment. Punishments that are defined in the Quran and Hadith.

القصاص: *al-qiṣāṣ*

Retaliation. The route afforded to the next of kin in the case of murder and to the afflicted in loss short of murder.

	Term	Definition	Ruling	An Example
29	مأمور به حسن بنفسه	الحسن فيه من حيث الذات	- إذا وجب لا يسقط إلا بالأداء فيما لا يحتمل السقوط - يسقط بالأداء أو بإسقاط الآمر فيما يحتمل السقوط	الإيمان بالله تعالى وشكر المنعم والصدق والعدل والصلاة
30	مأمور به حسن لغيره	الحسن فيه بواسطة الغير	يسقط بسقوط الواسطة	السعي إلى الجمعة والوضوء للصلاة

MEMORISE

Summary Of Excellence in al-Mamūr Bihī

1. There are two types of *al-ḥusn* or excellence in duties:
   i) ḥasan li-dhātihī;
   ii) ḥasan li-ghayrihī.

2. Details of ḥasan bi-nafsihī:
   i) Definition: الحسن فيه من حيث الذات
   "The excellence is in the task itself".
   ii) Examples: Belief in Allah ﷻ, honesty, Justice and salah.
   iii) Ruling: لا يسقط إلا بالأداء
   "It is only removed by performance".

3. Details of *ḥasan li-ghayrihī*:
   i) Definition: الحسن فيه بواسطة الغير
   "The excellence is a result of association to another".
   ii) Examples: wuḍū, progressing to Jumu'a.
   iii) Ruling: يسقط بسقوط تلك الواسطة
   "It is removed with disassociation to the other".

❖ ❖ ❖

1.6.5 al-Adā

The al-amr word-form tells of a duty that is necessary to deliver. The duty's accomplishment and delivery can be categorised into two types, al-adā and al-qaḍā. al-Adā is to deliver the exact matter as required by al-amr, whilst al-qaḍā is to deliver something that resembles what al-amr required. Figure 1.6.5-01 shows this division. al-Qaḍā is discussed in the following section, 1.6.6 and al-Adā is discussed here.

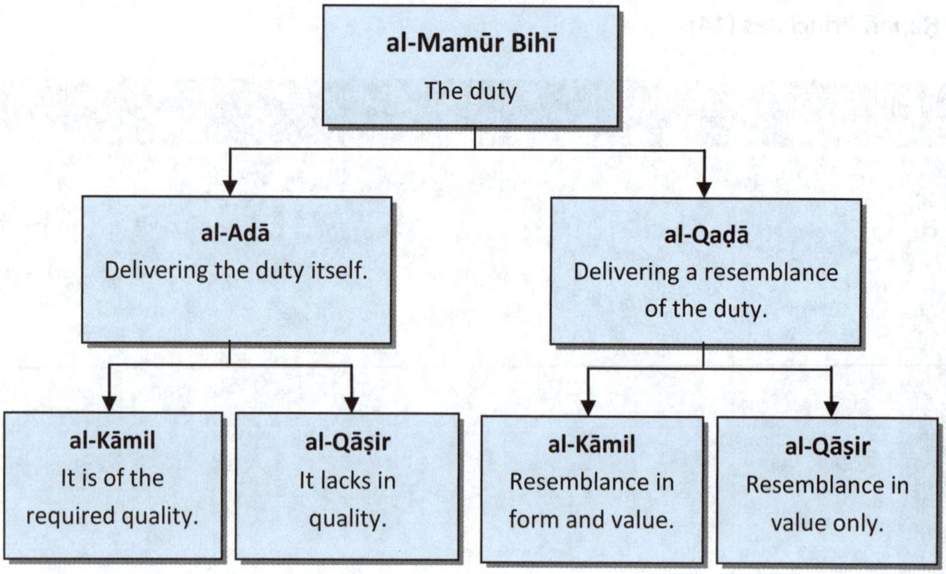

FIGURE 1.6.5-01
Types of delivery and observance of the duty, al-mamūr bihī.

al-Adā subdivides into two, al-kāmil and al-qāṣir. al-Adā ul-kāmil is the delivery of the task exactly as the Shariah intended it. al-Adā ul-qāṣir on the other hand is to deliver the task but different to the way it was intended. An example of al-adā ul-kāmil is the compulsory prayers for they must be performed on time and in congregation. Another example is circumambulation of the Ka'ba with ablution. These two tasks have been prescribed in this manner and if they are delivered in that manner, they are complete exactly as they should be. In general dealings, an example of this would be for a seller to hand over merchandise of the quality and specifications expected by the purchaser, or for a usurper to return the usurped to the owner exactly as it was taken.

The ruling for al-adā ul-kāmil is that by executing the task by al-adā ul-kāmil one will be exonerated, the task complete and the individual free from that responsibility. Based on this we say that when a usurper sells the usurped back to the owner, leaves it as security with him, or gifts it back to him, by handing it over in the exact state it was taken, the usurper is ruled to have returned the usurped. This is because the owner has in his possession his things without any loss or change to it. This will be judged as returning the right of the owners exactly as it was intended. The language used by the usurper, 'I sold you it' or 'I gifted you it', will be void. This is because the usurper was never the owner of the item, so the right to sell the item or to gift it has no meaning when it is said by him. He has no right to dispose of it in any way, therefore the wording is void. However, it is the right of the owner to receive what is rightfully

QUICK ARABIC

البيع الفاسد: *al-bay' ul-fāsid*

Invalid sale. Where a sale is deemed illegal due to various impermissible causes and circumstances.

QUICK DICTIONARY

Usurp: *yoo-zurp*

To seize. To hold or use something by force without legal right or authority.

Exonerate: *ig-zon-uh-reyt*

To clear. To free from an accusation, blame or guilt.

his, which has now been delivered even though the wording used to deliver it is void. The important fact is that the item is returned. Similarly, if one usurped another's raw foodstuff and had the owner consume it without prior knowledge that it was actually his, or one usurped some cloth and had the owner wear it without realising it was his, it will be considered al-adā ul-kāmil. Equally, in an invalid *al-bay' ul-fāsid* if the buyer has the merchandise in his possession but 'lends' it, leaves it as 'security', 'leases' it, 'sells' it, or 'gifts' it back to the seller who went on to actually take possession of it, this will be returning it as al-adā ul-kāmil. This is because the transaction was invalid and its ruling is that it had to be reversed by returning the items. The items were returned in the same state they should have been, so al-adā ul-kāmil has occurred.

Text And Translation

فصل الواجب بحكم الأمر: نوعان أداء وقضاء، فالأداء عبارة عن تسليم عين الواجب إلى مستحقه، والقضاء عبارة عن تسليم مثل الواجب إلى مستحقه، ثم الأداء نوعان: كامل وقاصر فالكامل مثل: أداء الصلاة في وقتها بالجماعة أو الطواف متوضئا وتسليم المبيع سليما كما اقتضاه العقد إلى المشتري وتسليم الغاصب العين المغصوبة كما غصبها، وحكم هذا النوع أن يحكم بالخروج عن العهدة به، وعلى هذا قلنا: الغاصب إذا باع المغصوب من المالك أو رهنه عنده أو وهب له وسلمه إليه يخرج عن العهدة ويكون ذلك أداء لحقه ويلغو ما صرح به من البيع والهبة، ولو غصب طعاما فأطعمه مالكه وهو لا يدري أنه طعامه، أو غصب ثوبا فألبسه مالكه وهو لا يدري أنه ثوبه يكون ذلك أداء لحقه، والمشتري في البيع الفاسد لو أعار المبيع من البائع او رهنه عنده أو آجره منه أو باعه منه أو وهبه له وسلمه يكون ذلك أداء لحقه ويلغو ما صرح به من البيع والهبة ونحوه .

Chapter on what becomes necessary with the ruling of al-amr: this is of two types, al-adā and al-qaḍā. al-Adā is a term to express the delivery of the necessary to its rightful and al-qaḍā is a term to express the delivery of a likeness of the necessary to its rightful. Then al-adā is of two types: al-kāmil and al-qāṣir. So examples of al-kāmil are performance of salah on time in congregation, circumambulating with ablution, delivery of merchandise as the agreement warranted to the buyer and the usurper returning the usurped as it was taken. The ruling regarding this type is that by performing it the duty will be executed. Based on this we said: when the usurper sells the usurped to the owner, deposits it with him, gifts it to him or returns it to him, he has fulfilled

QUICK TERMS

الأمر: *al-amr*

The imperative. A word-form that informs of a demanded act.

الأداء: *al-adā*

To deliver. To observe a duty that is required.

القضاء: *al-qaḍā*

To settle. To settle and make up a missed obligatory observance.

الأداء الكامل: *al-adā ul-kāmil*

Complete delivery. To observe a duty as per the requirement.

الأداء القاصر: *al-adā ul-qaṣir*

Deficient delivery. To observe a duty in a manner that is lacking.

the necessary and this will be al-adā to the rightful. The expression of purchasing or gifting will be void. If one usurped food and fed it to the owner whilst he did not know it is his, or usurped clothes and clothed the owner with them whilst he did not recognise his clothes, this will be deliverance of his right. If a purchaser in a void transaction was to lend the purchased item to the seller, deposit, hire, sell or gift it to him, and hand it over, it will be deliverance of his right. Any mention of transactions, gifting or the likes will be void.

❖❖❖

al-Adā al-qāṣir is to deliver the required task but with a deficiency in its quality. The deficiency must not be in the task itself, but the manner in which it is delivered. The following five examples illustrate this.

1. To pray without steadiness in the postures of salah, which means that if one hastily goes through the motions of prayer, the worship will be accepted but it will be deficient.

2. Circumambulation of the Ka'ba without ablution, this would count as being aṭ-ṭawāf but deficient in an additional quality.

3. For a seller to hand over merchandise to the purchaser that has incurred a debt or is sought for a crime. An example of this is a slave who whilst in the custody of the seller damaged someone's property and thus the slave will be liable to pay for that damage. Alternatively, another situation would be if the slave, whilst in the custody of the seller committed a crime, which would be compensated for by loss of limb or life, is then handed over to the purchaser. The handing over of the slave, with these added liabilities, is delivery of the exact item but it is deficient in the quality as there is a liability attached to it.

4. A usurper usurped a slave free of deficiency and the slave went on to kill purposefully another individual while in the custody of the usurper, or committed an act with a liability. The slave may now be killed in retaliation or has incurred a debt. After this, the usurper returns the slave with the deficiency, it will be al-adā al-

QUICK TERMS

الأداء القاصر: *al-adā ul-qaṣir*

Deficient delivery. To observe a duty in a manner that is lacking.

QUICK ARABIC

الطواف: *aṭ-ṭawāf*

Circumambulation. The ritual of encircling the Ka'ba seven times.

QUICK DICTIONARY

Usurp: *yoo-zurp*

To seize. To hold or use something by force without legal right or authority.

qāṣir because the exact slave has been returned but he is now deficient.

5. Someone who owes silver dirhams but returns dirhams of a lower purity and the creditor was unaware of it. The reason for stating that the owner is unaware of the impurity is to avoid the scenario in which the creditor was aware of the impurity and still accepted the dirhams as repayment. In such a case, the delivery will be considered to be al-adā al-kāmil.

Text And Translation

وأما الأداء القاصر فهو تسليم عين الواجب مع النقصان في صفته نحو: الصلاة بدون تعديل الأركان أو الطواف محدثا و رد المبيع مشغولا بالدين أو بالجناية ورد المغصوب مباح الدم بالقتل أو مشغولا بالدين أو الجناية بسبب عند الغاصب وأداء الزيوف مكان الجياد إذا لم يعلم الدائن ذلك

As for al-adā al-qāṣir it is deliverance of the necessary but with a deficient quality, like salah without balanced postures, aṭ-ṭawāf without ablution, return of the merchandise riddled with debt or liability, return of the usurped guilty of the death penalty, riddled with debt or liability, due to a cause occurring in the custody of the usurper. Or returning counterfeit in place of originals when the creditor did not know this.

❖ ❖ ❖

The ruling on al-adā al-qāṣir is that if it is possible to compensate for the deficiency with something similar, then it should be compensated for. The compensation is sometimes rational and on other occasions irrational. Compensation that is rational will resemble the deficiency in either appearance or in value. If it is not possible to compensate then there will be no requirement to do so except that the individual will be sinful for allowing the deficiency.

An example of al-adā al-qāṣir is if one was not steady in the postures of salah. It is not possible to compensate for 'steadiness' so the individual will be sinful for missing it but will not be able to compensate for it. The reason it cannot be compensated for is that the person either will have to perform individual postures with steadiness by themselves or will need to repeat the

QUICK TERMS

الأداء الكامل: *al-adā ul-kāmil*

Complete delivery. To observe a duty as per the requirement.

whole prayer with steadiness. Isolated postures are not considered prayer and if one repeats the whole prayer it will be the equivalent of saying that a deficiency in delivery has rendered the whole task invalid. The ruling, however, is that the task has been accomplished, it is just that it was deficient in a particular quality. One cannot invalidate the whole task due to a single quality of the task. Therefore, the one who is not steady in the postures of the prayer has performed the prayer, but it is deficient and the deficiency cannot be made up, so there is sin attached to it solely.

Another example is if one misses a salah in the days following Eid al-Aḍḥā or the days of *at-tashrīq*. If one is making up the salah later on other days of the year the *takbīrāt ut-tashrīq*, glorification of the days of *at-tashrīq*, will not be repeated, as they are only necessary on those specific days. There is no requirement or evidence to suggest making them up on other days. This can be contrasted with the understanding that if those prayers are made up within the days of *at- tashrīq*, and in congregation, the glorification will be repeated aloud as it is the correct occasion for them. This shows that if it is possible to make up a deficiency it is necessary to do so, however if it is not possible it has to be forgone and the sin will remain for the Hereafter.

Another example to highlight the point that if a deficiency can be made up it will be made up, but if that is not possible then there is nothing further that can be done, is if one was to miss the recitation of al-Fātiḥa, al-qunūt, or at-tashahhud in salah, or *at-takbīrāt ul-Eid*. Each of these acts will be made up with *sajdat us-sahw*. This is because the Shariah has allocated the *sajdat us-sahw* as the equivalent and appropriate atonement for the missing of al-wājib and necessary component of salah. As the aforementioned acts are all al-wājib in salah, by accidentally missing them in prayer, the worshipper is permitted to make up the deficiency with *sajdat us-sahw*. Similarly, if one was to perform *ṭawāf uz-ziyāra* without al-ablution, the deficiency can be atoned for by sacrificing an animal such as a goat. This is because the Shariah has likened theal-wājib components of Hajj to a sacrifice. Since the Shariah has appointed this as atonement, it can be made up in this manner.

The principle of making up a deficiency if at all possible, gives rise to the case that should one return impure coins to a lender and the coins were to be destroyed whilst in the possession of the lender, there would be nothing further necessary upon the indebted. This is because according to Imam Abū Ḥanīfa رحمه الله

QUICK TERMS

الواجب: *al-wājib*

The necessary. The non-observance of which is sinful, but denial does not lead to disbelief.

QUICK ARABIC

التشريق: *at-tashrīq*

Drying flesh. The three days following sacrifices during Hajj.

تكبيرات التشريق: *takbīrāt ut-tashrīq*

Expressions of Allah's greatness. This is after the compulsory prayers from the 9th of Dhul-Ḥijjah to the 13th afternoon.

القنوت: *al-qunūt*

Supplication. A supplication that forms part of the third unit of the al-witr prayer.

التشهد: *at-tashahhud*

The testimony. A declaration made during the sitting phase of the prayer or the sitting itself.

تكبيرات العيد: *takbīrāt ul-ʿīd*

Expressions of Allah's greatness during Eid prayers. Six extra glorifications performed during congregational Eid prayers.

there is no alternative or substitute for 'quality of products'. There is no substitute in appearance because quality is a feature and characteristic, so it does not have its own presence; it must always exist with something else. There is also no symbolic substitute because it would mean the value of 'quality' and there is no value for quality as the Prophet ﷺ said: "the pure and the impure are equal". Therefore, as there is no equivalent to quality it cannot be made up.

Furthermore, if one was to usurp a slave and whilst in his possession the slave committed a crime, which allows his blood to be spilt for murdering someone. Then the usurper returns the slave to the owner. It will be ruled that the usurper returned the usurped. Alternatively, in another scenario, after the completion of a trade, whilst the slave was in transit from the seller to the buyer, the slave committed a crime, which meant he could be sentenced to death. The buyer would still have to pay for the transaction. Both of these cases will be because what was required was delivered in the form of the very slave that was usurped or bought. As the item required was delivered, the cost of the transaction will be necessary and the ruling on the usurper will be that he has returned the item. However, if the said slave is to be killed as part of al-qiṣāṣ for the crime committed whilst in the custody of the seller or usurper, the seller or usurper will have to pay the cost of the slave to the buyer or owner. This is because it is as though they have not delivered what was necessary upon them in the first place. al-Qiṣāṣ occurred due to a reason connected to the custody of the seller and usurper, so they failed to deliver the necessary and so will have to compensate by paying for it.

If a usurper returned a slave-girl pregnant due to a cause in the custody of the usurper and she died giving birth whilst back in the custody of the owner, the usurper will be liable and will need to compensate for the loss of the slave-girl, according to Imam Abū Ḥanīfa رحمه الله This is because the cause of the death of the slave-girl is the birth and that was caused by the pregnancy, which occurred in the custody of the usurper. Therefore, it will be as though the usurper did not return the usurped at all and it was necessary for him to do that. Now that the slave-girl has died, he cannot give her back as was necessary so he must pay the owner the cost.

Text And Translation

وحكم هذا النوع أنه إن أمكن جبر النقصان بالمثل ينجبر به وإلا يسقط حكم النقصان إلا في الإثم،

حديث

قال ﷺ: جيدها ورديئها سواء.

عليه الصلاة والسلام

(نصب الراية: 4/37 حديث غريب)

QUICK ARABIC

سجدة السهو: *sajdat us-sahw*

Prostration of forgetfulness. Two prostrations made if al-wājib is missed during the salah.

طواف الزيارة: *ṭawāf uz-ziyāra*

Circumambulation of the visit. The encircling of the Ka'ba performed by the pilgrim on the 10th of Dhul-Ḥijja.

الوضوء: *al-wuḍū*

Ablution. The ritual cleaning to attain purity.

القصاص: *al-qiṣāṣ*

Retaliation. The route afforded to the next of kin in the case of murder and to the afflicted in loss short of murder.

QUICK DICTIONARY

Usurp: *you-zurp*
To seize. To hold or use something by force without legal right or authority.

وعلى هذا إذا ترك تعديل الأركان في باب الصلاة لا يمكن تداركه بالمثل؛ إذ لا مثل له عند العبد فسقط، ولو ترك الصلاة في أيام التشريق فقضاها في غير أيام التشريق لا يكبر؛ لأنه ليس له التكبير بالجهر شرعا، وقلنا في ترك قراءة الفاتحة والقنوت والتشهد وتكبيرات العيدين: إنه ينجبر بالسهو ولو طاف طواف الفرض محدثا ينجبر ذلك بالدم وهو مثل له شرعا، وعلى هذا لو أدى زيفا مكان جيد فهلك عند القابض لا شيء له على المديون عند أبي حنيفة رحمه الله؛ لأنه لا مثل لصفة الجودة منفردة حتى يمكن جبرها بالمثل، ولو سلم العبد مباح الدم بجناية عند الغاصب أو عند البائع بعد البيع فان هلك عند المالك أو المشتري قبل الدفع لزمه الثمن وبرئ الغاصب باعتبار أصل الأداء وإن قتل بتلك الجناية استند الهلاك إلى أول سببه فصار كأنه لم يوجد الاداء عند أبي حنيفة، والمغصوبة إذا ردت حاملا بفعل عند الغاصب فماتت بالولادة عند المالك لا يبرأ الغاصب عن الضمان عند أبي حنيفة رحمه الله.

The ruling regarding this type is that if it is possible to make up the deficiency with something like it, it will be enforced, otherwise the concept of deficiency will be dropped except in terms of sin. Based on this if one was not balanced in postures in the chapter of salah, it can't be made up like-for-like, as there is no equivalent available to the worshiper, so it is dropped. If one misses salah in the days of *tashrīk* and makes them up in other days he will not recite *takbīr* as there is no *takbīr* recited aloud for them in the Shariah. We say regarding missing the recitation of al-Fātiḥa*, al-qanūt*, *at-tashahhud* or *takbīrāt ul-'Īdayn*, that they are made up by *as-sahw*. If one performed the compulsory ṭawāf without ablution it is to be made up with a sacrifice, as it is an equivalent for it in the Shariah. Based on this if one gave counterfeit in place of originals and they perished in the hands of the possessor, the lender will not have to compensate according to Imam Abū Ḥanīfa, Allah have mercy on him, because there is no equivalent of quality alone such that it can be made up like-for-like. If a slave was returned with a death sentence due to the guilt of a crime committed in the possession of the usurper or the seller after the sale, then if he is executed when with the owner or the purchaser before payment, the price will be necessary and the usurper will be exonerated for the actual delivery. If there is an execution due to that crime, the execution will be connected to the first cause. It will be as though there was no delivery according to Imam Abū Ḥanīfa. If a usurped is returned pregnant due to an act in the custody of the

QUICK ARABIC

التشريق: *at=tashrīq*

Drying flesh. The three days following sacrifices during Hajj.

تكبيرات التشريق: *takbīrāt ut-tashrīq*

Expressions of Allah's greatness. This is after the compulsory prayers from the 9th of Dhul-Ḥijjah to the 13th afternoon.

القنوت: *al-qunūt*

Supplication. A supplication that forms part of the third unit of the al-witr prayer.

التشهد: *at-tashahhud*

The testimony. A declaration made during the sitting phase of the prayer or the sitting itself.

تكبيرات العيد: *takbīrāt ul-'īd*

Expressions of Allah's greatness during Eid prayers. Six extra glorifications performed during congregational Eid prayers.

السهو: *as-sahw*

Prostration of forgetfulness. Two prostrations made if al-wājib is missed during the salah.

الطواف: *aṭ-ṭawāf*

Circumambulation. The encircling of the Ka'ba performed by the pilgrim on the 10th of Dhul-Ḥijja.

usurper, and she dies at childbirth when in the custody of the owner, the usurper will be liable for compensation according to Imam Abū Ḥanīfa.

❖ ❖ ❖

When delivering what is necessary the default is al-adā, whether it is al-kāmil or al-qāṣir. This means that one cannot resort to al-qaḍā whilst al-adā is still possible. Only when al-adā is not a realistic possibility is one permitted to turn to its alternative al-qaḍā. This is because al-adā is the actual requirement and whilst it remains possible, there is no need of an alternative. How we deal with a deposit, representation or usurped item is based upon this principle, because each of these things will be defined and exact. For example, if one was to deposit some money, a defined and exact item is deposited. Similarly, if one appointed another as a representative to sell or trade, or one was to usurp money of another, the money is known and specific. Therefore, if the entrusted, representative or usurper wants to replace them with other money, even if it is of equal value, it will not be permitted to do so. This is because al-adā - delivery of the exact thing - is possible, and whilst it is possible, one cannot opt to turn to the alternative al-qaḍā.

If one was to sell an item and hand it over to the buyer, who then went on to discover a deficiency because of an event that occurred whilst the item was in the possession of the seller, the purchaser will have just two options. The transaction can be validated and the item is kept, or the transaction is invalidated and the item is returned for the return of the payment. The buyer does not have the right to uphold the transaction and insist that the seller pays a separate amount to compensate for the deficiency. This is because the seller handing over the deficient item is al-adā al-qāṣir. As the delivery was deficient, the purchaser has a right to refuse it, and because the delivery was delivered, the seller has fulfilled what was necessary. The buyer has the option of validating the transaction. These two options do not leave a third possibility in the context of the original transaction, so the third option of compensating for the deficiency is not permitted.

Under the rule that al-adā is the default, Imam ash-Shāfa'īy ﷺ says that the usurper must return the exact item usurped even if the item is significantly deficient beyond recognition. The deficiency will need to be compensated for at the same time. The Aḥnāf, however, say that if the deficiency is to a degree where the item is unrecognisable to a point that it has a different name and a

QUICK TERMS

الأداء الكامل: *al-adā ul-kāmil*

Complete delivery. To observe a duty as per the requirement.

الأداء القاصر: *al adā ul qāṣir*

Deficient delivery. To observe a duty in a manner that is lacking in quality.

القضاء: *al-qaḍā*

To settle. To settle and make up a missed obligatory observance.

QUICK DICTIONARY

Usurp: *you-zurp*

To seize. To hold or use something by force without legal right or authority.

different value, the ownership of the owner is annulled and the usurper becomes it's new owner, but with the responsibility to compensate for the loss to the original owner.

A number of rulings on cases will stem from the aforementioned. If one usurped some wheat and then ground it, a wooden beam and then built upon it, a goat and sacrificed it or cooked it, a bunch of grapes and juiced them, or some wheat and planted them to yield crops, then Imam ash-Shāfa'īy ﷺ says that the usurped thing must be returned. This is because despite an extreme and drastic change the original item is still available and so it remains in the ownership of the owner. If there is a loss incurred due to the change, it must also be made up by the usurper. The Aḥnāf say in all of the cases that due to the extreme nature of the change it is as though the original item is no longer available. We even give it a different name. Its usage and the benefit derived from it have also changed. Therefore, the item now belongs to the usurper and the usurper owes the owner for the loss of the item.

Text And Translation

ثم الأصل في هذا الباب هو الأداء كاملا كان أو ناقصا وإنما يصار الى القضاء عند تعذر الأداء، ولهذا يتعين المال في الوديعة والوكالة والغصب ولو أراد المودع والوكيل والغاصب أن يمسك العين ويدفع ما يماثله ليس له ذلك، ولو باع شيئا وسلمه فظهر به عيب كان المشتري بالخيار بين الأخذ والترك فيه، وباعتبار أن الأصل هو الأداء يقول الشافعي: الواجب على الغاصب رد العين المغصوبة وإن تغيرت في يد الغاصب تغيرا فاحشا ويجب الأرش بسبب النقصان وعلى هذا لو غصب حنطة فطحنها أو ساجة فبنى عليها دارا أو شاة فذبحها وشواها أو عنبا فعصرها أو حنطة فزرعها ونبت الزرع كان ذلك ملكا للمالك عنده، وقلنا: جميعها للغاصب ويجب عليه رد القيمة

Then the principle in this chapter is to deliver, whether al-kāmil or al-qāṣir. Turning to al-qaḍā is when al-adā is difficult. That is why money is defined in deposit, agency or usurpation. Should the keeper, agent or usurper want to retain the actual and return something similar he can not. If one sold something and delivered it, then a defect was found in it, the buyer has a choice of keeping it or returning it. Considering the priority is al-adā, Imam ash-Shāfa'ī y says: it is necessary for the usurper to return the actual usurped item even if it is grossly tampered with in the custody of the usurper, whilst a penalty will be due for the

QUICK TERMS

الأداء الكامل: *al-adā ul-kāmil*

Complete delivery. To observe a duty as per the requirement.

الأداء القاصر: *al-adā ul-qāṣir*

Deficient delivery. To observe a duty in a manner that is lacking in quality.

القضاء: *al-qaḍā*

To settle. To settle and make up a missed obligatory observance.

QUICK DICTIONARY

Usurp: *you-zurp*

To seize. To hold or use something by force without legal right or authority.

damage. Based on this if one usurped, wheat and ground it into flour, an oak and built a house on it, a goat and sacrificed it then broiled it, grapes and juiced them or wheat and planted it and the harvest grew; all according to him will belong to the owner. We say: all of it is the usurper's and he must repay the cost.

❖ ❖ ❖

There are however a few exceptions to the rule according to Imam Abū Ḥanīfa ﷺ Despite the drastic and unrecognisable change, an item will on occasion remain in the ownership of the original owner. It will be necessary for the usurper to return the item despite the extreme deficiency. The underlying reason for this is that for something to be significantly changed beyond its original state Imam Abū Ḥanīfa ﷺ says three things must happen. Firstly, the name of the item must change along with its primary purposes; secondly, for the item to be so changed that the process is irreversible to separate it without contamination of unrelated items; and thirdly, for it to be connected and separable but separating it would cause extended difficulty, such as removing a single usurped beam from a structure that is built around it. Though it is extractable, it would cause more difficulty.

In each of the aforementioned cases there has been change caused by the usurper, but each change is not too drastic. The minting of silver to dirhams or of gold to dinars has changed the original item but it has not changed it to an extent where you stop calling them silver and gold. Therefore, if the name has not changed, they must be the same item. If they are the same item, they must be returned to the original owner and the change is not significant enough to annul the previous ownership. Similarly, by slaughtering a goat there has been change, but the change is not drastic. This is because after the slaughter, it retains the name 'goat'. One would still call it goat's meat. By slaughtering it, the goat has not shed its name, and as it has not shed its name, the previous ownership has not changed as the change is not drastic enough to warrant it. The usurper must return the meat and is not permitted to substitute it with the cost. It is a similar narrative with usurped wool. If it was spun, or the spun wool was woven, there has been change but the change is not drastic enough. A primary purpose of fleece is to spin it, which is what was done. Moreover, a primary purpose of spun wool is to weave it, which was done. By achieving a primary purpose of an item, one has not changed it drastically. Therefore, by spinning or weaving wool the usurper has not changed it enough to diminish the ownership of the owner, so it is necessary for the usurper to return it rather than pay the cost of it.

The rule learnt previously that when a usurped item is drastically changed by the usurper, the ownership transfers from the original owner to the usurper, and the usurper is liable to pay its cost, is directly in opposition to the opinion of Imam ash-Shāfa'īy رحمه الله. According to him, the usurped will return to the ownership of the owner even after a major alteration and complete change. This difference gives rise to the different verdicts on cases involving liabilities. The Aḥnāf have said that the price must be given, whereas ash-Shawāfi' say the item must be returned in any condition. Imam ash-Shāfa'īy رحمه الله says that if one usurped another's slave and the slave escaped, the usurper would have to pay the price of the slave. Later, if the slave is then found, he will belong to the original owner and the original owner would pay back the amount paid by the usurper. The Aḥnāf say that once the usurper has paid for the runaway slave, the ownership of the original owner is no longer valid. The slave now belongs to the usurper. When the slave is found and returned, he will go to the usurper as he has already compensated the owner with al-qaḍā. After al-qaḍā was executed, there is no reverting back to adā, therefore returning the slave after payment will not be necessary.

Text And Translation

ولو غصب فضة فضربها دراهم أو تبرا فاتخذها دنانير أو شاة فذبحها لا ينقطع حق المالك في "ظاهر الرواية"، وكذلك لو غصب قطنا فغزله أو غزلا فنسجه لا ينقطع حق المالك في "ظاهر الرواية"، ويتفرع من هذا مسئلة المضمونات ولذا قال: لو ظهر العبد المغصوب بعد ما أخذ المالك ضمانه من الغاصب كان العبد ملكا للمالك والواجب على المالك رد ما أخذ من قيمة العبد

If one usurped silver and minted it into dirhams, ingots and shaped them into dinars or a goat and sacrificed it, according to Ẓāhir ur-Riwāya the right of the owner is not forfeited. Similarly, if one usurped cotton and spun it, or spun cotton and wove it, the right of the owner does not cease according to Ẓāhir ur-Riwāya. Issues of liabilities branch out from this and so a jurist said: if a usurped slave appeared after the owner has taken his liability from the usurper, the slave

QUICK TERMS

الأداء: *al-adā*

To deliver. To observe a duty as per the requirement.

القضاء: *al-qaḍā*

To settle. To settle and make up a missed obligatory observance.

QUICK REFERENCE

ظاهر الرواية: *ẓāhir ur-riwāya*

The Manifest Narrations. A compendium of legal opinions of the Ḥanafī school of fiqh collected by Imam Muḥammad in six collection: al-Jāmi' al-Kabīr, al-Jāmi' aṣ-Ṣaghīr, as-Siyar al-Kabīr, as-Siyar aṣ-Ṣaghīr, al-Mabsūṭ (al-Aṣl), and az-Ziyādāt.

QUICK DICTIONARY

Usurp: *you-zurp*

To seize. To hold or use something by force without legal right or authority.

will belong to the owner and the owner would have to return the amount he received for the slave.

❖ ❖ ❖

Ḥanafī Principles (15)

MEMORISE

	Term	Definition	Ruling	An Example
31	الاداء الكامل	أداء المأمور به بجميع أوصافه	الخروج عن العهدة به –	الصلاة بالجماعة في وقتها؛ تسليم المبيع سليما
32	الاداء القاصر	تسليم عين الواجب مع النقصان في صفته	أمكن جبر النقصان بالمثل ينجبر به وإلا يسقط حكم النقصان إلا في الإثم	الصلاة بدون تعديل الأركان؛ رد المبيع مشغولا بالدين

❖ ❖ ❖

Summary Of al-Adā

1. It is important that al-adā is performed before al-qaḍā is even considered.

2. Definition of al-adā: تسليم عين الواجب إلى مستحقه
"Delivery of the necessary task to its rightful."

3. There are two types of al-adā: al-kāmil and al-qāṣir.

4. Details of al-adā ul-kāmil:
i) Definition: أداء المأمور به بجميع أوصافه
"Execution of the duty with all its correct qualities".
ii) Examples: Performing the salah in congregation and on time; Handing over the merchandise as per a contract.
iii) Ruling: الخروج عن العهدة به
"The required task is fulfilled".

5. Details of al-adā ul-qāṣir:
i) Definition: تسليم عين الواجب مع النقصان في صفته
"Delivery of the necessary task with a deficiency in its quality".
ii) Examples: salah without steady postures; Handing over merchandise with liabilities.
iii) Ruling:
إذا أمكن جبر النقصان بالمثل ينجبر به وإلا يسقط حكم النقصان إلا في الإثم
"If the deficiency can be made up with a like-for-like it will be, otherwise ignored except in sin".

1.6.6 al-Qaḍā

Similar to al-adā, al-qaḍā also has two types. Figure 1.6.5-01 showed both types. One is al-qaḍā al-kāmil and the other is al-qaḍā al-qāṣir. al-Qaḍā al-kāmil is the delivery of something that resembles the task and responsibility in form and value. For example, if a person usurped a measure of wheat and it perished, it would be necessary to give a similar measure of wheat to the owner. This measure of wheat is not the exact one that was usurped; rather it resembles the usurped, both in appearance and in value. Therefore, this is al-qaḍā al-kāmil. This ruling will be valid for all volumetric and weighed items.

al-Qaḍā al-qāṣir is the delivery of something that does not resemble the task and responsibility in appearance, but it is the equivalent in value. For example, if one usurped a goat and the goat perished, the usurper will be liable to pay for the goat. The payment does not resemble the goat in appearance but it is its equivalent in value. There is a resemblance between the usurped and the payment because the value of goats is measured by the price that is to be paid for them. Other goats are not considered to be of the same resemblance because each animal has its own pedigree and its own grazing history.

From the two types of al-qaḍā, al-kāmil is the priority. This means that liability for things that have been destroyed or lost is first made up by finding something that resembles the lost thing in appearance and in value. This will ensure that the rightful are given their right in the best possible way.

QUICK TERMS

الأداء: *al-adā*

To deliver. To observe a duty as per the requirement.

القضاء: *al-qaḍā*

To settle. To settle and make up a missed obligatory observance.

القضاء الكامل: *al-qaḍā al-kāmil*

Wholesome settlement. Delivery of a resemblance of a duty, with a likeness in form and value.

القضاء القاصر: *al-qaḍā al-qāṣir*

Minimal settlement. To deliver a resemblance of a duty in value only.

QUICK DICTIONARY

Usurp: *you-zurp*

To seize. To hold or use something by force without legal right or authority.

Text And Translation

وأما القضاء فنوعان: كامل وقاصر فالكامل منه تسليم مثل الواجب صورة ومعنى كمن غصب قفيز حنطة فاستهلكها ضمن قفيز حنطة ويكون المؤدى مثلا للأول صورة ومعنى، وكذلك الحكم في جميع المثليات، وأما القاصر فهو ما لا يماثل الواجب صورة ويماثل معنى كمن غصب شاة فهلكت ضمن قيمتها، والقيمة مثل الشاة من حيث المعنى لا من حيث الصورة

As for al-qaḍā, it is of two types: al-kāmil and al-qāṣir. al-Kāmil from it is to deliver something resembling the necessary in appearance and value. Like if one usurped a measure of wheat and it was consumed, he would be liable for a measure of wheat. The returned will resemble the first in appearance and in value. A similar ruling applies to all items with similarity. As for al-qāṣir it does not resemble the necessary in form but resembles it in value. Like if one usurped a goat and it perished, he is liable for its price. The price resembles the goat in value not in appearance.

❖❖❖

al-Qaḍā al-qāṣir will only be permitted when al-qaḍā al-kāmil is no longer an option. For this reason, Imam Abū Ḥanīfa ؓ says that if one usurps a replaceable item that is then destroyed, but similar items are now not available in the market place, the usurper will be liable for the cost. The price will be set from the day the court hearing takes place and the judge delivers a verdict. This is because the inability to deliver the replica equivalent is known fully only when the investigation into finding an exact replica has been completed. Once the judge has decided that an equivalent replica cannot be found, it will be final that there is no chance of it being offered. Before this date, the possibility remained of finding the item, as it is the norm in the markets for things to trend from time to time, and on other occasions become unavailable. However, once the judge has decreed that the item is no longer available, it is the first time we know that the item is no longer available. Therefore, that will be the day the cost equivalent will be calculated. Before the hearing at court, it was a possibility to find al-qaḍā al-kāmil, so resorting to the cost was not permitted. At the time of the hearing, the inability to replace the item like-for-like became clear and so al-qaḍā al-qāṣir became necessary. As this is the time it became necessary, it is also the time from where the price calculation will begin. The day of the usurping or the day of the lack of availability will not be considered for pricing.

Text And Translation

والأصل في القضاء الكامل، وعلى هذا قال أبو حنيفة عليه الرحمة: إذا غصب مثليا فهلك في يده وانقطع ذلك عن أيدي الناس ضمن قيمته يوم الخصومة؛ لأنّ العجز عن تسليم المثل الكامل إنما يظهر عند الخصومة، فأما قبل الخصومة فلا لتصور حصول المثل من كل وجه

The priority in al-qaḍā is al-kāmil. Based on this Imam Abū Ḥanīfa, mercy be upon him, said: if one usurped a mass-produced item and it perished in his hands; when it became unavailable amongst people, he would be liable for its cost on the day of the lawsuit. This is because the inability to deliver a completely similar item would become apparent on the day of the lawsuit. As for before the lawsuit, it would not, because obtaining a completely similar item would be plausible.

❖ ❖ ❖

As for those items or things that have no exact equivalent, by neither al-qaḍā al-kāmil nor al-qāṣir, there is no al-qaḍā necessary for them. This means that once al-qaḍā is necessary, al-qaḍā al-kāmil will be required; whilst it is possible, nothing else is acceptable. If al-qaḍā al-kāmil is not possible then al-qaḍā al-qāṣir will be required in the form of the cost of the item. If a value cannot be placed on an item, there is nothing suitable to compensate for it. The only thing is that the one who finds themselves liable for such an item will be sinful and held to account in the court of Allah ﷻ. For this reason, the Aḥnāf say that loss of use of an item cannot be compensated. If someone was able to restrict the usage of something for the owner, the one restricting it will be sinful but not liable to pay for the potential usage. This is because the manner of use employed by different people differs greatly and thus cannot be given an equivalent value. When a value cannot be assigned to it, al-qaḍā al-qāṣir is not possible, so there is nothing else to resort to. One cannot even provide a similar item for the usage of the other to gain parity because an item and how it is used are not comparable either.

An example of the above dilemma is if one usurped the slave of another and used his services for one month, or if one usurped someone's house and resided in it for one month. The usurper is instructed to return the slave or the house. This is al-adā al-qāṣir, as the item is returned but with a little wear and tear from usage whilst being wrongly possessed. Now, compensation for the usage is in question. This cannot be compensated for as we only have two options. Firstly, to compensate usage with usage which is unfair as one individual uses an item differently to another. One person may instruct a slave to perform light work whilst the other uses him in strenuous work. Similarly, a house may be occupied without causing much wear and tear, whilst others would use it extensively. Therefore, usage cannot be compensated by allowing the other to use the perpetrator's things in return. Secondly, there is an option to compensate usage by an item. This option would not be compensation of like-for-like and therefore rejected.

QUICK TERMS

القضاء: *al-qaḍā*

To settle. To settle and make up a missed obligatory observance.

القضاء الكامل: *al-qaḍā al-kāmil*

Wholesome settlement. Delivery of a resemblance of a duty, with a likeness in form and value.

القضاء القاصر: *al-qaḍā al-qāṣir*

Minimal settlement. To deliver a resemblance of a duty in value only.

الأداء القاصر: *al-adā al-qāṣir*

Deficient delivery. To observe a duty in a manner that is lacking.

QUICK DICTIONARY

Usurp: *you-zurp*

To seize. To hold or use something by force without legal right or authority.

This would mean that if we tried to compensate for a month-long usurped house by giving the perpetrator's house to the victim for a month, it would be unfair as the way the perpetrator used the house would be distinctly different to how the victim would use the house. Therefore, this is not like for like. Usage cannot be compensated for by something tangible. That is because usage is intangible and therefore a tangible physical item will not be like for like. The conclusion of this is that usage cannot be adequately compensated for in either way, so in the case of loss of such a thing, no liability can be placed on the perpetrator, other than assigning blame and knowing that the sin will be compensated for in the Hereafter.

Imam ash-Shāfa'īy رحمه الله differs with the Aḥnāf in this matter. He considers there to be compensation for usage, likening it to a rental agreement. So, as is a rental agreement the benefits are compensated for by monetary payments, in the case of usurping the usage will be compensated for financially. The Aḥnāf respond to this by saying that the agreement of renting, although mutually agreed, is not logical and to form another legal analogy based on something that is not logical is not valid [see chapter 4.2, Conditions for the authenticity of al-qiyās on page 376].

Text And Translation

فأما ما لا مثل له لا صورة ولا معنى لا يمكن إيجاب القضاء فيه بالمثل، ولهذا المعنى قلنا: إن المنافع لا تضمن بالإتلاف؛ لأن إيجاب الضمان بالمثل متعذر وإيجابه بالعين كذلك؛ لأن العين لا تماثل المنفعة لا صورة ولا معنى كما إذا غصب عبدا فاستخدمه شهرا أو دارا فسكن فيها شهرا ثم رد المغصوب إلى المالك لا يجب عليه ضمان المنافع خلافا للشافعي، فبقي الإثم حكما له وانتقل جزاؤه إلى دار الآخرة

As for that which has no resemblance, neither in appearance nor in value, al-qaḍā of something similar cannot be necessary for it. For this reason we said: usage has no liabilities, because to necessitate the liability with something similar is difficult, and necessity of liability with the item itself is just as difficult. This is because two benefits cannot resemble each other in appearance nor in value. Like, if one usurped a slave and worked him for a month, or a house and resided in it for a month, and then returned the usurped to the owner. No liability will be necessary on the usage; contradicting the view of Imam ash-

QUICK TERMS

القضاء: *al-qaḍā*

To settle. To settle and make up a missed obligatory observance.

القضاء الكامل: *al-qaḍā al-kāmil*

Wholesome settlement. Delivery of a resemblance of a duty, with a likeness in form and value.

القضاء القاصر: *al-qaḍā al-qāṣir*

Minimal settlement. To deliver a resemblance of a duty in value only.

القضاء الشرعي: *al-qaḍā ush-shar'īy*

Legal settlement. A non-resembling equivalent set by the Shariah.

QUICK ARABIC

الفدية: *al-fidya*

Ransom. An expiation for sin or for unperformed duties.

الشيخ الفاني: *ash-shaykh ul-fānī*

A senile person. Someone who reaches old age, where health is unlikely to return.

قتل الخطأ: *qatl ul-khaṭa*

Homicide by misadventure. Killing by either an error in intention or an error in the act.

Shāfa'īy. The ruling for it will be of sin and its judgement transferred to the Hereafter.

❖ ❖ ❖

On the principle that if there is no al-qaḍā al-kāmil or al-qāṣir possible, and there is also no al-qaḍā in benefits derived from usage; the Aḥnāf present the case of two witnesses testifying. They testify that a person issued three divorces to his wife after consummation of the marriage, and a judge separated the couple on this basis stating that the bridal gift is to be paid by the husband. Then the witnesses retracted their statements. The false witnesses will not be liable to pay for the losses incurred by the husband, according to the Aḥnāf. Imam ash-Shāfa'īy رحمه الله on the other hand holds that the false witnesses are liable with respect to the bridal gift too. Similarly, if one murdered the wife of another, the murderer will not be liable for the bridal gift paid by the husband. In the same manner, if one had intercourse with another man's wife, the sinner is not liable to pay for the loss suffered by the husband.

In most circumstances, where there is no equivalent there is no material liability. However, if the Shariah has specified something as an equivalent even though it does not resemble the actual item in appearance nor value, then that will be a valid equivalent. Therefore, al-qaḍā will be possible through what the Shariah has deemed an equivalent. The perpetrator will need to make up the al-qaḍā ash-shar'īy. One example of this is an elderly individual, *ash-shaykh al-fānī*, who is unable to keep his fasts. For such an individual to pay *al-fidya* as redemption rather than fast is al-qaḍā ash-shar'īy. There is no resemblance in appearance or in value between a fast and money. That is evident. However, the Shariah has stated that the money is al-qaḍā ash-shar'īy in this case. Another such example is of accidental killing, *qatl ul-khaṭa*, where blood money is an equivalent for a life. The money does not resemble the life in appearance nor in value but it is still al-qaḍā ash-shar'īy and will be necessary to pay.

Text And Translation

ولهذا المعنى قلنا: لا تضمن منافع البضع بالشهادة الباطلة على الطلاق ولا بقتل منكوحة الغير ولا
بالوطيء حتى لو وطئ زوجة إنسان لا يضمن للزوج شيئا إلا إذا ورد الشرع بالمثل مع أنه لا يماثله صورة

ومعنى فيكون مثلا له شرعا فيجب قضاؤه بالمثل الشرعي، ونظيره ما قلنا: إن الفدية في حق الشيخ الفاني مثل الصوم، والدية في القتل خطأ مثل النفس مع أنه لا مشابهة بينهما.

For this reason we said: false testimony of divorce will not be liable for pleasures of marriage, nor by the murder of another's wife, nor by intercourse such that if one had sexual intercourse with the wife of another person no liability will be granted to the husband. The exception is if the Shariah has assigned an equivalent despite no resemblance in appearance or value. It will be an equivalent for it in the Shariah and its al-qaḍā will be with the Shariah equivelent. An example of it is what we have said: monetary redemption for a very old person resembles sawm and blood-money in accidental murder is the equivalent of a life despite no resemblance between the two.

❖ ❖ ❖

Ḥanafī Principles (16)

MEMORISE

	Term	Definition	Ruling	An Example
33	القضاء الكامل	أداء مثل المأمور به صورة ومعنى	الخروج عن العهدة به	غصب قفيز حنطة فاستهلكها ضمن قفيز حنطة
34	القضاء القاصر	ما لا يماثل الواجب صورة بل يماثله معنى	الأصل في القضاء هو الكامل فإن لم يمكن فالقاصر	غصب شاة فهلكت ضمن قيمتها
35	المثل الشرعي	ما ورد الشرع بالمثل مع انه لا يماثله صورة ولا معنى	الخروج عن العهدة به	الفدية في حق الشيخ الفاني مثل الصوم

❖ ❖ ❖

Summary Of al-Qaḍā

1. Definition of al-qaḍā: تسليم مثل الواجب إلى مستحقه
"Delivery of a resemblance of the necessary duty to its rightful".

2. There are two types of al-qaḍā: al-kāmil and al-qāṣir.

3. Details of al-qaḍā al-kāmil:
i) Definition: أداء مثل المأمور به صورة ومعنى
"Delivery of a resemblance of the duty that resembles both in form and in value".
ii) Example: If one usurped some wheat and it was destroyed. Replacing it with wheat of equal measure, would mean a replica in form and value.
iii) Ruling: الخروج عن العهدة به
"Fulfilment of the required agreement".

4. Details of al-qaḍā al-qāṣir:
i) Definition: ما لا يماثل الواجب صورة بل يماثله معنى
"What does not resemble the required in form but resembles it in value.
ii) Example: Paying the monetary price of a usurped item.
iii) Ruling: الأصل في القضاء هو الكامل فإن لم يكن فالقاصر
"The requirement in al-qaḍā is al-kāmil, only when it is not possible al-qāṣir is to be delivered".

5. Once something is al-qaḍā, if it has no equivalent monetary value, it cannot be made up.

6. Details of al-mithl (al-qaḍā) ash-shar'īy:
i) Definition:
ما ورد الشرع بالمثل مع انه لا يماثله صورة ولا معنى
"An equivalent determined by the Shariah despite no resemblance in form nor value".
ii) Example: The compensation for homicide by misadventure set by the Shariah. It does not resemble the murdered in form nor is it an equivalent value of a human life.
iii) Ruling: الخروج عن العهدة به
"Fulfilment of the responsibility".

1.7 an-Nahī

Following chapter 1.6 about al-amr, a high frequency al-khaṣṣ, this chapter introduces another high frequency al-khaṣṣ, termed an-nahī. The full discussion on al-khāṣṣ has passed on page 11.

al-Nahī is a high frequency al-khaṣṣ and is from amongst the most often used methods in the Shariah of delivering prohibition. We learnt previously that al-amr is employed to give an instruction of command, and in this chapter, we will learn that an-nahī is used to give an instruction of prohibition. The prohibition is applicable to two scenarios and these scenarios constitute its types.

an-Nahī means prohibition in the lexicon. As far as terminology is concerned, an-nahī is to demand an act is not performed by someone inferior. It is issued by someone assuming superiority by directing the word-form *lā taf'al* – Don't do it! - to another. Similar to al-amr, an-nahī has a range of meanings it may cover, however, the literal al-ḥaqīqa meaning is of prohibition and disliking, whereas other meanings are the metaphorical al-majāz.

an-Nahī is of two types, as shown in Figure 1.7-01:

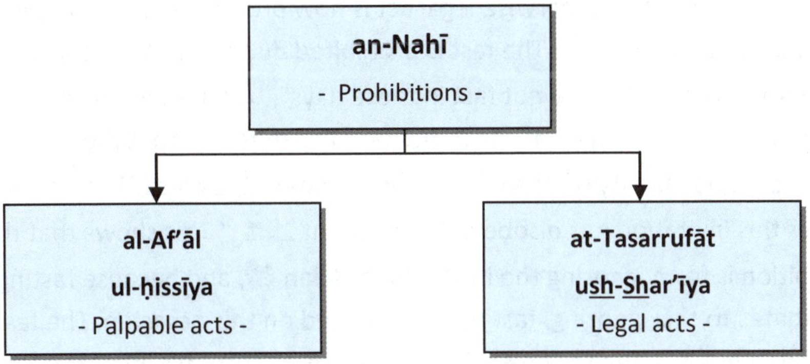

FIGURE 1.7-01
Types of an-nahī.

1) an-Nahī 'an il-af'āl il-ḥissīya, prohibitions from palpable acts such as fornication, consuming wine, lying or oppression, and

2) an-Nahī 'an taṣarrufāt ush-shar'īyya, prohibitions from religious acts such as fasting on Eid day, praying at disliked times or exchanging one dirham for two.

QUICK TERMS

الأمر: *al-amr*

The imperative. A word-form that informs of a demanded act.

الخاص: *al-khāṣṣ*

The specific. A word designated for a singular specific concept.

النهي: *an-nahī*

The prohibition. A word-form that informs of a prohibited act.

الحقيقة: *al-ḥaqīqa*

The literal. A word coined by the lexicon for an item.

المجاز: *al-majāz*

The figurative. A word used for a meaning other than its coined meaning.

By palpable, al-af'āl ul-ḥissiyya, we mean all actions that can be sensed and are tangible. The disliking of such acts is not limited to evidence from the Shariah because they are recognised as abhorrent before the arrival of the Shariah and remained so upon its arrival. Religious acts, on the other hand, are dependent upon the Shariah. Acts such as prayer and fasting were not known in the form they are in currently before the Shariah described them, thus they are dependent upon it.

The ruling on the first type, an-nahī 'an il-af'āl ul-ḥissīya, is that the prohibited thing is the exact thing upon which the prohibition has been issued, therefore it is inherently abhorrent and disliked. The prohibited thing is termed qabīḥ li-'aynihī or inherently abhorrent and it refers to something which is disliked in itself and not due to an external factor or circumstance. Under no circumstance will a kabīh li-'aynihī be legal, it may however be excused in extreme situations. An example of such an act is disbelief or to sell a free individual. Both these acts are abhorrent and disliked in themselves and will never be permitted.

The ruling on the second type, an-nahī 'an taṣarrufāt ush-shar'īyya, is that the prohibited thing is other than the act that has been prohibited. This means that the act itself is not abhorrent; rather the manner and circumstances surrounding it are disliked. It is due to the connection to the abhorrent circumstance that this otherwise legal act is now prohibited. An example of this is fasting on the day of Eid. The fast is prohibited due to the Messenger of Allah ﷺ informing: "Listen, do not fast in these days", but the underlying prohibition is not because fasting is disliked. The reason is that the one fasting is ignoring the hospitality of Allah جل جلاله, as the Prophet ﷺ said, "The one who refuses this invitation has disobeyed Abū Qāsim ﷺ!" This shows that the prohibition is from ignoring the invitation of Allah جل جلاله, and because fasting contributes to this ignoring, fasting is prohibited on this occasion. The fasting is prohibited but it is due to something else that is abhorrent and as the fasting is associated with it, it too becomes disallowed. Intrinsically, the fast is a good thing, ḥasan li-dhātihī, but it has abhorrence due to another factor, ignoring the invitation of Allah جل جلاله, so it becomes kabīḥ li-ghayrihī.

حديث

فعَنْ أبي هُريرة رضي الله عنه أن رَسُولَ الله ﷺ بعث عبد الله بن حذافة رضي الله عنه يطوف في منى (أن لا تصوموا هذه الأيام، فإنها أيام أكل وشرب وذكر الله عز وجل)

عليه الصلاة والسلام

(رواه أحمد)

حديث

فعَن أبي هُريرة رضي الله عنه أنه كان يقول: ومن ترك الدعوة فقد عصى الله ورسوله ﷺ

عليه الصلاة والسلام

(البخاري: 4882)

Text And Translation

فصل في النهي: النهي نوعان: نهي عن الأفعال الحسية كالزنا وشرب الخمر والكذب والظلم ونهي عن

التصرفات الشرعية كالنهي عن الصوم في يوم النحر والصلاة في الأوقات المكروهة وبيع الدرهم بالدرهمين، وحكم النوع الأول أن يكون المنهي عنه هو عين ما ورد عليه النهي فيكون عينه قبيحا فلا يكون مشروعا أصلا، وحكم النوع الثاني أن يكون المنهي عنه غير ما أضيف إليه النهي فيكون هو حسنا بنفسه قبيحا لغيره ويكون المباشر مرتكباً للحرام لغيره لا لنفسه

Chapter on an-nahī: an-Nahī is of two types: prohibition from al-af'āl al-ḥissīya like adultery, drinking wine, lying and oppression; and prohibition from at-taṣarrufāt ush-Shar'īya like fasting on the day of Eid ul-Adha, salah in disliked-times and selling one dirham for two. The ruling on the first type is that prohibition is directly due to the prohibited act, so it is in itself abhorrent and not ever prescribed. The ruling on the second type is that the prohibition is directed at something other than the prohibited act, so it is excellent in itself but abhorrent due to the other. The one engaged with it is committing a haram for another thing, not for it itself.

❖ ❖ ❖

As the prohibition from taṣarrufāt ush-shar'īyya are ḥasan li-dhātihī and qabīḥ li-ghayrihī, our jurists have established that such a prohibition affirms the act itself. This means that the prohibition demands that the prohibited act itself is legal before and after the prohibition. To understand this point it is important to note the difference between prohibition, *an-nahī*, and negation, *an-nafi*. If one is able to do something and is told to refrain from it, it will be a prohibition. On the other hand, when one is unable to do something, stating they cannot do it, it is a negation. The difference being that in a prohibition one can do it if they intend to, and in a negation, the individual cannot do it even if they intended to. Furthermore, in the context of the Shariah if an act is considered permitted it is said that the individual is *able* to do it legally and if the Shariah forbids an act it is said the individual is *unable* to do it legally. However, it might be actually possible for the person to perform it physically even though the Shariah deems it unable. Bearing these two points in mind, if we say that an act within the Shariah is no longer legal after the issuing of an-nahī, and then this would imply that the individual is now legally unable to perform it in the future even though physically one may be able to. Now after the an-nahī is issued, as the individual is continually unable to perform this otherwise legal act, it will mean that an-nahī is now issued for a person unable to do something. To issue a prohibition

QUICK TERMS

النهي: *an-nahī*

The prohibition. A word-form that informs of a prohibited act.

التصرفات الشرعية: *at-taṣarrufāt ush-shar'īya*

Legal acts. Acts that are prescribed by the Shariah.

حسن لذاته: *hasan li-dhātihī*

Intrinsically excellent. The duty itself is a worthy act and a thing of beauty.

قبيح لغيره: *qabīḥ li-ghayrihī*

Externally disliked. Acts that are abhorrent due to external factors.

الأفعال الحسية: *al-af'āl ul-ḥissīya*

Palpable acts. Acts that can be sensed and are tangible.

QUICK GRAMMAR

النفي: *an-nafi*

Negation. The absence of something that is actual or affirmative.

for someone who is unable to do something is futile in that it is just like prohibiting a blind man from seeing. For the Shariah to instruct something futile is impossible. This situation was created by considering an act continually illegal after an-nahī, so it is understood that after an-nahī the act is not continually illegal. Rather, it remains legal in itself but it may not be possible to perform it due to other factors or circumstances.

The explanation above highlights that al-af'āl ul-ḥissīya are different to taṣarrufāt ush-shar'īyya. After the issuance of an-nahī, if the taṣarrufāt ush-shar'īyya also remain continually forbidden it will result in prohibiting the unable, as is explained above, whereas issuance of an-nahī upon al-af'āl ul-ḥissīya keeps them prohibited without resulting in the impossible scenario of prohibiting the unable. This is because the person is always physically able to perform the acts even after the Shariah has prohibited them.

Text And Translation

وعلى هذا قال أصحابنا النهي عن التصرفات الشرعية يقتضي تقريرها ويراد بذلك أن التصرف بعد النهي يبقى مشروعا كما كان؛ لأنه لو لم يبق مشروعا كان العبد عاجزا عن تحصيل المشروع وحينئذٍ كان ذلك نهيا للعاجز وذلك من الشارع محال. وبه فارق الأفعال الحسية؛ لأنه لو كان عينها قبيحا لا يؤدي ذلك إلى نهي العاجز؛ لأنه بهذا الوصف لا يعجز العبد عن الفعل الحسي

Based on this our jurists have said that prohibition of acts of Shariah affirm their legality. What this means is that the acts, after the prohibition, remain prescribed as they were because if they did not remain prescribed the subject would be unable to perform the legal act. Thus, this will become a prohibition of an unfeasible act, which is impossible from the legislator. In this palpable acts differ, because if they themselves were repulsive it would not lead to prohibition of the unfeasible. In this sense a subject is never incapable of a palpable act.

❖❖❖

A number of cases result from the rule of an-nahī issued upon a matter of the Shariah being excellent in itself and that it is only prohibited and abhorrent due to another reason or quality. Rulings upon cases such as *al-bay'*

QUICK TERMS

النهي: *an-nahī*

The prohibition. A word-form that informs of a prohibited act.

QUICK ARABIC

البيع الفاسد: *al-bay' ul-fāsid*

Invalid sale. Where a sale is deemed illegal due to various impermissible causes and circumstances.

الإجارة الفاسدة: *al-ijārat ul-fāsida*

Invalid hire. Where the hiring is deemed illegal due to various impermissible causes and circumstances.

ul-fāsid, *al-ijārat ul-fāsida* and vowing to fast on the day of Eid, all fall under this category.

An example of *al-bay' ul-fāsid*, an invalid transaction, is if one sold a slave on the condition that the slave would be still serving him for a period of time. *al-Ijārat ul-*fāsida, an invalid lease, would occur if the property owner rented out an accommodation on the condition that he would occupy it for himself for a period of time. Both these cases are prohibited because the blessed Prophet ﷺ forbade a transaction with such a condition. The prohibition through an-nahī is not because transactions are prohibited but because placing a condition, which conflicts with the transaction, is disliked. Due to the presence of the invalid condition, both the sale and rental agreements are invalid. This does not mean that the agreements did not take place; there was a proposal and acceptance, therefore the transactions in themselves did take place. This then implies that should there have been an exchange in possession at this point, ownership of the item also transferred, as the transaction did occur and an outcome of a transaction is the transfer of ownership from one party to the other. As soon as the invalid condition becomes known, the transaction is annulled as it is an unlawful transaction, but it is important to note that it can only be annulled if it was established in the first place.

Similarly, the invalid lease or other such matters of the Shariah that are accompanied by an-nahī will be established in themselves but annulled due to the prohibition of external factors. Therefore, fasting on any day of Eid is legal in itself, so if one vows to fast on the day of Eid the vow is valid. It is made up of an intention to refrain from eating, drinking and conjugal relations, which are all valid. However, it is abhorrent and unlawful because of the day it is to be established, a day of Allah Almighty's invitation. This is what makes it unlawful and so it will be unlawful to fast on the day despite the validity of the vow.

There is an objection to the aforementioned rule. The statement of the Aḥnāf that an-nahī upon the matters of the Shariah implies that the act itself is legal and the external factor renders it unlawful, is problematic when it comes to cases such as marriage to idolatrous women where Allah جل جلاله has forbidden it, or marriage to the spouse of a father which is also forbidden by Allah جل جلاله. You can add to these two cases, marriage to a woman in her waiting period before her previous marriage is over; such a woman is similar to a woman in someone

حديث

عن عبد الرحمن بن عبد الله بن مسعود رضي الله عنهما عن أبيه قال نهى رسول الله صلى الله عليه وسلم عن صفقتين في صفقة واحدة.

عليه الصلاة والسلام

(مسند الإمام أحمد: 3774)

else's marriage. It is forbidden for such a person to marry in this state due to the command of Allah جل جلاله. Similarly, a marriage conducted without witnesses is also forbidden due to a narration of the blessed Prophet صلى الله عليه وسلم. In these cases, *an-nikāḥ*, an act of Shariah, is prohibited whilst at the same time these acts will never be prescribed. They are in themselves abhorrent and the circumstances surrounding them are also abhorrent. The previous rule stated that prohibition from such acts establishes them but here this is clearly not the case.

In reply, it is stated that we can only establish such acts when it is possible to do so, whereas in these cases it is not possible. The outcome of *an-nikāḥ* is the legality of intimacy and intercourse, whilst the prohibition in these cases is from the exact same thing. There is a contradiction between the two points in that the very same thing cannot be legal and illegal. In the stated cases, this is the position, so we have said that the texts are not for prohibition but for negation. Negation does not hold the same function as prohibition; therefore, the negated matters are never established. This ultimately means that the objection no longer stands because the objection was on an-nahī whereas in the stated cases we have negation, an-nafī, which does not function in a similar way.

As for *al-bay' ul-fāsid*, an-nahī is not deemed to be an-nafī because keeping it as an-nahī does not result in an impossible outcome. The transaction, *al-bay'*, results in ownership and the prohibition, an-nahī, disallows bringing it into usage. It is not impossible for both of these matters to be together. The transaction allows the ownership of an item to transfer to the purchaser but the prohibition disallows the person from using it, like in the case of a Muslim who prepares a grape juice. It naturally ferments into an intoxicating alcoholic beverage, which results in the Muslim being the legal owner of it but it is forbidden for him to use it by consuming or selling it. This clearly shows that ownership and prohibition on usage can be found together. When two things can coexist, they do not result in an impossible outcome. As this is also proposed as the outcome of *al-bay' ul-fāsid* by keeping an-nahī as an-nahī, there is no impossible scenario to contend with. It is needless to try to divert an-nahī to a meaning of negation.

Text And Translation

ويتفرع من هذا حكم البيع الفاسد والإجارة الفاسدة والنذر بصوم يوم النحر وجميع صور التصرفات

حديث

عن ابن عباس رضي الله عنهما أن النبي صلى الله عليه وسلم قال البغايا اللاتي ينكحن أنفسهن بغير بينة... والعمل على هذا عند أهل العلم من أصحاب النبي صلى الله عليه وسلم ومن بعدهم من التابعين وغيرهم قالوا لا نكاح إلا بشهود

عليه الصلاة والسلام

(الترمذي: 1103)

QUICK TERMS

النهي: *an-nahī*

The prohibition. A word-form that informs of a prohibited act.

القضاء: *al-qaḍā*

To settle. To settle and make up a missed obligatory observance.

QUICK GRAMMAR

النفي: *an-nafī*

Negation. An absence of something that is actual or affirmative.

الشرعية مع ورود النهي عنها، فقلنا: البيع الفاسد يفيد الملك عند القبض باعتبار أنه بيع ويجب نقضه باعتبار كونه حراما لغيره، وهذا بخلاف نكاح المشركات ومنكوحة الأب ومعتدة الغير ومنكوحته ونكاح المحارم والنكاح بغير شهود؛ لأن موجب النكاح حل التصرف وموجب النهي حرمة التصرف فاستحال الجمع بينهما فيحمل النهي على النفي، فأما موجب البيع ثبوت الملك وموجب النهي حرمة التصرف وقد أمكن الجمع بينهما بأن يثبت الملك ويحرم التصرف أليس أنه لو تخمر العصير في ملك المسلم يبقى ملكه فيها ويحرم التصرف

Rulings branch off from this regarding an imperfect transaction, an imperfect rental, a vow to fast on the day of Eid ul-Adha and all those acts of Shariah that have prohibitions concerning them. So we said: an imperfect transaction transfers ownership at the exchange, considering it is a transaction but we must annul it as it is forbidden for another reason. This differs from marriage to idolatrous women, to stepmothers, to another's wife in her waiting period, to another's wife, to those closely related and without witnesses. This is because marriage necessitates permission to use, whereas an-nahī is prohibition of use, so combining both is impossible. So prohibition will be considered to mean negation. As for transactions they necessitate establishment of ownership and an-nahī prohibition of use. It is possible to combine both such that we establish ownership but disallow use. Is it not that if juice fermented whilst in the ownership of a Muslim, it would remain his property but he would not be permitted to use it?

❖ ❖ ❖

The principle of 'an-nahī upon matters of the Shariah establishes them' results in numerous verdicts. Based on it, our jurists have said that if one vowed to fast on the day of Eid ul-Aḍḥa and two days of *at-tashrīk* following it, the vow is valid. This is because it is abhorrent to fast on these days due to ignoring Allah Almighty's invitation but in itself, the act of fasting is legal. As it is intrinsically legal and the individual has vowed to do something legal, the vow is valid. It is worth noting that the individual should not fast on those days, rather the vowed fasts should be made up by way of al-qaḍā on days that one is permitted to do so. If one happened to fast on the original days, the vow would be complete and the responsibility will be lifted.

QUICK ARABIC

النكاح: *an-nikāḥ*

Conjunction. In legal terms it is a marriage contract.

البيع الفاسد: *al-bay' ul-fāsid*

Invalid sale. Where a sale is deemed illegal due to various impermissible causes and circumstances.

التشريق: *at-tashrīq*

Drying flesh. The three days following sacrifices during the Hajj.

Similarly, if one vowed to pray in disliked, *al-makrūh*, times, the vow will be valid. The reasoning, as before, is that the vow is for an intrinsically legal act. A vow of an act that is legal in itself is valid and so it is upheld. If the individual prayed in those times, the vow will be fulfilled and the responsibility lifted. Both the examples above, fasting on prohibited days and praying at prohibited times, are legal because of the ruling that 'an-nahī, prohibition, of matters of the Shariah establish the acts'.

Due to the same principle voluntary prayers started in the disliked times still remain necessary to complete. This means that the individual must stop praying at the disliked time and after the time has lapsed, they must be performed as al-qaḍā. If the prayer was not stopped in the disliked time and completed, the responsibility and burden of performing it is fulfilled however, the person will be sinful. The reason for this is that though the prayer in these times is not permitted, it is still legal in itself. This means that beginning the voluntary prayer is permitted at any time and once they have been started completion is also necessary. This does not mean that an illegal and forbidden act is being encouraged when we say the prayer must be completed even though the time is disliked. al-Ḥarām is not encouraged because if the worshiper simply waits a short while until the disliked time passes by the rising, declining or setting of the Sun, the permitted time of prayer would begin again and without objection one would be able to complete the prayer and al-ḥarām would be avoided. Hence, when there is nothing illegal advocated, then by beginning the prayer in disliked times and maintaining that they must be completed, is valid. This ruling of the prayer is different to the completion of the fast on the day of Eid because by beginning the prayer in disliked times they must be completed later, but according to Ṭarafayn by beginning a voluntary fast on Eid it need not be completed. Imam Abū Yūsuf رحمه الله says it also must be completed by way of al-qaḍā. He likens the case of the voluntary prayer to the voluntary fast by way of al-qiyās. The other two jurists, however, maintain that by stating completion is necessary for prayers, a legal outcome is suggested but when completion is stipulated for the fast it stipulates a forbidden and al-ḥarām act by design. This is because fasting by definition is abstaining from eating, drinking and intercourse from true morning until sunset, but doing this on the day of Eid would directly involve rejecting Allah Almighty's hospitality, which is forbidden. Therefore, an instruction to complete the fast of Eid would be an instruction to commit an illegal act, as completing it without abhorrence is not

QUICK TERMS

المكروه: *al-makrūh*

Disliked. An act disliked due to a discrepancy.

الحرام: *al-ḥarām*

The unlawful. That which is not permitted in the Shariah, as distinguished from the lawful.

طرفين: *ṭarafayn*

The two parties. Imams Abū Ḥanīfa رحمه الله and Muḥammad رحمه الله

القضاء: *al-qaḍā*

To settle. To settle and make up a missed obligatory observance.

القياس: *al-qiyās*

Analogy. The reasoning of the learned.

possible. This is why by starting the voluntary fast one is not instructed to complete it at any point.

Text And Translation

وعلى هذا قال أصحابنا: إذا نذر لصوم يوم النحر وأيام التشريق يصح نذره؛ لأنه نذر بصوم مشروع وكذلك لو نذر بالصلاة في الأوقات المكروهة يصح؛ لأنه نذر بعبادة مشروعة لِما ذكرنا أن النهي يوجب بقاء التصرف مشروعا ولهذا قلنا: لو شرع في النفل في هذه الأوقات لزمه بالشروع، وارتكاب الحرام ليس بلازم للزوم الإتمام فإنه لو صبر حتى حلت الصلاة بارتفاع الشمس وغروبها ودلوكها أمكنه الإتمام بدون الكراهة وبه فارق صوم يوم العيد فإنه لو شرع فيه لا يلزمه عند أبي حنيفة ومحمّد عليهما الرحمة؛ لأن الإتمام لا ينفك عن ارتكاب الحرام

Based on this our scholars said: if one vowed to fast the Day of Sacrifice and the days of at-tashrīq, his vow is valid because it is a vow of a legal fast. Similarly, if one vowed to perform salah in disallowed times, it is valid because he vowed a legal worship based on what we mentioned that prohibition necessitates the validity of continuity of performance. For this reason we said: if one began voluntary salah in these times, it will be necessary for him due to starting. Committing a prohibition is not inevitable by the necessity to complete because had he waited until salah was permitted with the rising, setting or declining of the Sun, he could complete it without undesirability. By this, sawm on the Day of Sacrifice is different because if he begins it, completion is not necessary according to Imam Abū Ḥanīfa and Imam Muḥammad, mercy be on them both, because completion can not be separated from committing al-ḥarām.

❖ ❖ ❖

At this juncture, a query can be raised and duly answered. It is established that a prohibition from al-af'āl ul-ḥissiyya means that the prohibited act is intrinsically abhorrent and is not legal at all. However, we find that intercourse is such an act and it is prohibited when a women is in her days of bleeding, but you still class it as qabīḥ li-ghayrihi, and not inherently abhorrent. It is prohibited due to *al-adhā*, impurity. In reply, intercourse in such circumstances is classed like this because the exception to the rule is that when there is evidence to support that an act is qabīḥ li-ghayrihi despite its status as a

QUICK TERMS

الأفعال الحسية: *al-af'āl ul-ḥissīya*

Palpable acts. Acts that can be sensed and are tangible.

قبيح لغيره: *qabīḥ li-ghayrihī*

Externally disliked. An act that is abhorrent due to an external factor.

QUICK ARABIC

التشريق: *at-tashrīq*

Drying flesh. The three days following sacrifices during the Hajj.

الأذى: *al-adhā*

Damage. The impurity, damage and harm caused due to intercourse during menstrual bleeding.

prohibited palpable act of the al-af'āl ul-ḥissiyya, it will be deemed qabīḥ li-ghayrihi in accordance with the evidence at hand. The evidence at hand is that the reason for its abhorrence is stated as *al-adhā*, or impurity. Allah ﷻ has stated in verse 222 of Sūrat ul-Baqara:

﴿ويسألونك عنِ المحِيضِ قل هوَ أذى فاعتزلوا النساء فِي المحِيضِ ولاَ تقربوهن حتى يطهرن﴾ [البقرة: 222]

"They ask you about menstruation. Say, 'it is an impurity, so keep apart from women during menstruation. Do not approach them until they are cleansed..."

This understanding yields numerous verdicts. As the abhorrence is not intrinsic and is due to another cause, we say that, we will validate consequences of having intercourse during a woman's period. If it is the first time that intercourse has taken place then the individuals will no longer be classed as virgins. They may be sentenced to death for fornication thereafter. The details of this case are that if a fornicator is not a virgin, the punishment for fornicating is *ar-rajm*, or death by stoning. If the perpetrator is a virgin then the punishment is lashings. The conditions for the punishment of a non-virgin fornicator are being free, mature, sane, Muslim and has had intercourse with his wife in a permitted manner. If a person was to marry and on the first occasion of intimacy have intercourse with his wife when she was in her period, he will still be considered a non-virgin. This is because intercourse is forbidden due to a non-intrinsic reason, which is *al-adhā*. Even though it is not permitted and illegal, it is due to an external reason, whilst the act in itself is intrinsically permitted. This means that the individual had intercourse in a normally permitted manner and so his status as a non-virgin is established. This means having intercourse with a woman in her period, though forbidden, will still change the status of the individuals.

In another similar verdict, if a woman was divorced three times and after waiting the required time, she marries another man. The second husband has intercourse with her on her period and then divorces her. This woman will now be eligible to marry the first husband again, she will also have to spend a whole term in *al-'idda* as any other divorcee and the husband issuing the divorce will owe her, her complete bridal gift, as well as take on the responsibility of her costs during the whole duration of her *al-'idda*.

Furthermore, if intercourse takes place during a woman's period and after the bleeding has stopped, she then refuses the husband on the grounds

QUICK TERMS

قبيح لغيره: *qabīḥ li-ghayrihī*

Externally disliked. An act that is abhorrent due to an external factor.

QUICK ARABIC

الأذى: *al-adhā*

Damage. The impurity, damage and harm caused due to intercourse during menstrual bleeding.

الرجم: *ar-rajm*

Lapidation. To stone to death.

العدة: *al-'idda*

The term. The three-month period after a divorce.

that he has not paid her bridal gift, she is considered *an-nā<u>sh</u>iza* according to the Ṣāḥibayn and so will not be eligible for maintenance costs. This verdict is exactly the same for the one who refuses her husband, after intercourse took place outside the bleeding period. The background to this is that the bridal gift is the right of the wife, like a payment for any merchandise. As the product can be held back from the buyer until payment is received, the wife can withhold herself from the husband until he pays the bridal gift. In the case of the merchandise, once the seller has handed over the product to the seller without taking payment, the right to demand non-usage of the item until payment is forfeited. It is as though the seller has given his right up. Once a right is given up and is no longer applicable it cannot be restored. Similarly, by allowing the first intercourse to take place, though it was in her period, she has forfeited her right to withhold herself from the husband on the next occasion. As the forfeit is from her part, and she then refuses, she will be the disobedient *an-nā<u>sh</u>iza* and thus not rightful for maintenance costs from the husband.

Imam Abū Ḥanīfa ﷺ maintains that she is still eligible for the maintenance. Whilst an act may be forbidden and al-ḥarām, it does not prevent its consequences. For example, divorcing a woman in her period is forbidden but it will be established and she will have to begin her *al-'idda*. Similarly, performing ablution with usurped water is forbidden but the prayer performed with such an ablution is valid, and handling a copy of the Quran is also permitted. Moreover, hunting with a usurped bow is forbidden but the meat of the catch will be permitted. Additionally, slaughtering with a usurped knife, praying on usurped land, buying and selling after the call for al-Jumu'ah, are all forbidden, but the consequences are valid. The slaughtered is legally edible, the prayer is valid and the merchandise is owned and fully legal to use. So, in a similar fashion, intercourse during the period is forbidden but the consequences are still established.

Text And Translation

ومن هذا النوع وطئ الحائض فإن النهي عن قربانها باعتبار الأذى لقوله تعالى: ﴿ويسألونك عنِ المحِيضِ قل هوَ أذى فاعتزِلوا النساء فِي المحِيضِ ولاَ تقربوهن حتى يطهرن﴾ ولهذا قلنا: يترتب الأحكام على هذا الوطيء فيثبت به إحصان الواطئ وتحل المرأة للزوج الأول ويثبت به حكم المهر والعدة والنفقة، ولو امتنعت عن التمكين لأجل الصداق كانت ناشزة عندهما فلا تستحق النفقة، وحرمة الفعل لا تنافي

QUICK TERMS

صاحبين: *ṣāḥibayn*

The two colleagues. Imams Abū Yūsuf ﷺ and Muḥammad ﷺ

QUICK ARABIC

الناشزة: *an-nā<u>sh</u>iza*

Recalcitrant. A woman who resists the obligations of her marriage contract.

الحرام: *al-ḥarām*

The unlawful. That which is not permitted in the Shariah, as distinguished from the lawful.

الجمعة: *al-jumu'a*

Friday. The day or the particular prayer offered on the day.

QUICK DICTIONARY

Usurp: *you-zurp*

To seize. To hold or use something by force without legal right or authority.

ترتب الأحكام كطلاق الحائض والوضوء بالمياه المغصوبة والاصطياد بقوس مغصوبة والذبح بسكين مغصوبة والصلاة في الأرض المغصوبة والبيع في وقت النداء فإنه يترتب الحكم على هذه التصرفات مع اشتمالها على الحرمة

From this type is intercourse with a menstruating woman. Prohibition of approaching her is due to the Almighty saying: "They ask you about menstruation. Say,'it is an impurity, so keep apart from women during menstruation. Do not approach them until they are cleansed..." For this reason we said: consequences are established due to this intercourse, so virginity of the participants, permissibility for the woman to remarry an ex-husband, matters of bridal gift, waiting-periods and maintenance, are established. If a woman denies intercourse due to the bridal gift she will be considered disobedient by Both Colleagues and thus is not eligible for maintenance. The prohibition of an act does not prevent consequent rulings like divorce of a woman in menstruation, ablution with usurped water, hunting with a usurped bow, slaughter with a usurped knife, salah on usurped land and transaction at the time of the call. So rulings will follow each of these acts despite each constituting al-ḥarām.

❖❖❖

Bearing the rule in mind, that an-nahī upon al-af'āl ush-shar'īya demands that the act remains legal in itself, we say there is evidence that sinners have a right to testify, from Sūra an-Nūr, verse 4:

﴿وَ لا تقبلوا لهم شهادةً أبدًا﴾ [النور: 4]

"Don't accept their testimony ever."

For example, if a marriage ceremony took place in the presence of two sinful men as witnesses, the marriage is considered valid. This is because the prohibition in the verse is from accepting their testimony and acceptance of a testimony with the right to testify is impossible. It is only when a testimony comes forth that it can then be dismissed and rejected; if one does not have that right from the onset then there is no question of rejecting it. With this in mind, those who are reprimanded and sinful in cases of *al-qadhaf* will still have a testimony; it is just that their testimony will not be accepted. This is because there is an issue with their delivery and a possibility of falsehood, and so it is ineligible for admission. This is the underlying reason why such individuals are

QUICK TERMS

النهي: *an-nahī*

Prohibition. A word-form that informs of a prohibited act.

الأفعال الشرعية: *al-af'āl ush-shar'īya*

Legal acts. The same as *at-tasarrufāt ush-shar'īya* – acts that are prescribed by the Shariah.

QUICK ARABIC

القذف: *al-qadhaf*

Accusation. A false accusation of a married person with adultery.

not subject to *al-li'ān* either. The whole concept of *al-li'ān* is to give testimony and a sinner is not eligible to give testimony, so it goes without saying that it is not necessary for him. However, in some other cases such as marriage, their witnessing is upheld.

To elaborate upon the case of *al-li'ān*, if a man accuses his wife of adultery or denied fathering her child, the upright woman in turn demands him to prove her infidelity by invoking the consequence of *al-qadhaf*, a false accusation. If infidelity remains unproven then *al-li'ān* becomes necessary on the husband. This means that he must swear four times that he is truthful in the claim and on the fifth occasions invoke the wrath of Allah ﷻ if he is lying. The woman then swears four times that he is false in his claim and on the fifth occasion she invokes the wrath of Allah ﷻ upon herself if he is truthful. After such an episode, the man has the status of one who is reprimanded for the false accusation of *al-qadhaf* and the woman has the status of one reprimanded for adultery. The marriage is untenable and thus the man must issue a divorce or the judge forcibly ends the marriage. The involvement of the husband in the process of *al-li'ān* is only if he is not a sinful *al-fāsiq* and unable to prove the adultery.

Text And Translation

وباعتبار هذا الأصل قلنا في قوله تعالى: ﴿وَ لا تقبلوا لهم شهادةً أبدًا﴾ إن الفاسق من أهل الشهادة فينعقد النكاح بشهادة الفساق؛ لأن النهي عن قبول الشهادة بدون الشهادة محال، وإنما لم تقبل شهادتهم لفساد في الأداء لا لعدم الشهادة أصلا وعلى هذا لا يجب عليهم اللعان؛ لأن ذلك أداء الشهادة ولا أداء مع الفسق

Based on this rule we say about Allah Almighty's word: "...and accept not their testimony ever afterwards...", the sinners have a testimony. So their witnessing is valid for marriage, as it is impossible to have prohibition from accepting their testimony, when they do not have one. Their testimony is not accepted due to a flaw in delivery not because they do not have the actual right. For this reason *al-li'ān* is not necessary on them as this concerns testimony directly and this can not be performed with sin.

❖ ❖ ❖

QUICK ARABIC

اللعان: *al-li'ān*

Mutual cursing. A procedure of divorce after accusations of adultery.

الفاسق: *al-fāsiq*

Reprobate person. An individual who neglects Islamic values and decorum in dress and behaviour.

QUICK DICTIONARY

Usurp: *you-zurp*
To seize. To hold or use something by force without legal right or authority.

an-Nahī

MEMORISE

	Term	Definition	Ruling	An Example
36	النهي	قول القائل لغيره لا تفعل على سبيل الاستعلاء	– عن الأفعال الحسية: المنهي عنه هو ما ورد عليه النهي فيكون عينه قبيحا – عن التصرفات الشرعية: المنهي عنه هو غير ما أضيف اليه النهي فيكون هو حسنا بنفسه قبيحا لغيره	– الزنا وشرب الخمر والكذب والظلم – الصوم في يوم النحر والصلاة في الأوقات المكروهة وبيع الدرهم بالدرهمين

❖❖❖

Summary Of an-Nahī

1. Definition of an-nahī:
   قول القائل لغيره لا تفعل على سبيل الاستعلاء
   "The directing of a prohibition to the other by a superior".

2. There are two types of an-nahī:
   i) an-Nahī 'an il-af'āl ul-ḥissīya; and
   ii) an-Nahī 'an it-taṣarrufāt ush-shar'īya.

3. Details of an-nahī 'an il-af'āl al-ḥissīya:
   i) These are prohibitions from palpable matters universally understood before the Shariah and do not require the Shariah to define them.
   ii) Examples: The prohibition of fornication, wine consumption and deceit. These are matters universally accepted as having immoral elements attached to them.
   iii) Ruling: المنهي عنه هو ما ورد عليه النهي فيكون عينه قبيحا
   "The prohibited act is directly prohibited and so is abhorrent in itself".

4. Details of an-nahī 'an it-taṣarrufāt ash-shar'īya:
   i) These are prohibitions from matters prescribed by and normally permitted by the Shariah.
   ii) Examples: Fasting on the day of Eid or praying salah during prohibited times.
   iii) Ruling: المنهي عنه هو غير ما أضيف اليه النهي فيكون هو حسنا بنفسه قبيحا لغيره
   "The prohibited is other than what the prohibition is directed at, and so is excellent in itself but abhorrent due to the other".

1.8 Techniques to understand a text

This chapter is an addendum to the four primary divisions of al-kitāb made earlier [Figure 1.0-01]. Chapter 1.1 was about word coinage, 1.2 about word usage, 1.3 about clarity, 1.4 about reasons to abandon the literal al-ḥaqīqa and 1.5 about textual locations. Then chapters 1.6 and 1.7 revisited particular types of al-khāṣṣ directly involved in the delivery of rulings, namely al-amr and an-nahī. The aim of this chapter, chapter 1.8, is to look at some practical steps that help unravel the true meaning and purpose of texts. One can employ numerous techniques to make the understanding of a text simpler. Some of the techniques included here are:

1) Preference of the literal over the metaphorical;
2) Preference of the unrestricted over the restricted; and
3) Inclusion of variation from different recitations or different reports.

❖ ❖ ❖

The first technique is when a word is used both literally and metaphorically; it is preferred to enact the literal meaning rather than the metaphorical. This preference is not a choice; rather it is al-wājib and necessary. An example of this is a girl born out of wedlock. Our jurist categorically state that an-nikāḥ of the girl is forbidden to the one who committed az-zinā and she was the resultant offspring. It is claimed Imam ash-Shāfa'īy رحمه الله says otherwise. The difference stems from the argument of whether the girl born out of wedlock falls under verse 23 of Sūrat un-Nisā:

﴿حُرِّمَتْ عَلَيْكُمْ أُمَّهَاتُكُمْ وَبَنَاتُكُمْ﴾ [النساء: 23]

"Forbidden to you (in marriage) are your mothers and your daughters..."

Imam ash-Shāfa'īy رحمه الله says that the daughter born out of wedlock is not included and so an-nikāḥ is permitted. The Aḥnāf argue that the illegitimate daughter is also included in this verse as any other daughter would be, and so marriage to her is forbidden. The ash-Shāfa'īy viewpoint is that the verse refers to those women with established lineages to their fathers, however a woman born out of wedlock will not have a recognised and established lineage to the man so will not be subject to this verse. The Aḥnāf counter that the Arabic word for daughter, *al-bint*, is coined for a biological daughter whether a recognised

QUICK TERMS

الكتاب: *al-kitāb*

The book. The inspired final word of Allah جل جلاله.

الحقيقة: *al-ḥaqīqa*

The literal. A word coined by the lexicon for an item.

الخاص: *al-khāṣṣ*

The specific. A word designated for a singular specific concept.

الأمر: *al-amr*

The imperative. A word-form that informs of a demanded act.

النهي: *an-nahī*

The prohibition. A word-form that informs of a prohibited act.

الواجب: *al-wājib*

The necessary. The non-observance of which is sinful, but denial does not lead to disbelief.

QUICK ARABIC

النكاح: *an-nikāḥ*

Conjunction. In legal terms it is the marriage contract.

الزنا: *az-zinā*

Fornication. Sexual intercourse between parties not married to each other.

lineage is established or not. The metaphorical meaning of the word *al-bint*, however, is for a daughter whose lineage is recognised and established. It is the preferred position to take the literal al-ḥaqīqa meaning before the metaphorical al-majāz, so the aforementioned verse includes any type of daughter whether lineage is established or not. The biological daughter is thus forbidden for an-nikāḥ. This is further confirmed in that a female child born out of wedlock is called the parents' daughter both technically and in common understanding, and so will be within the instruction of the verse.

The difference gives rise to different verdicts to particular cases. According to ash-Shāfa'īy رحمه الله the marriage to a person born from one's own seed out of wedlock would be permitted and the bridal gift would be necessary. Furthermore, maintenance would be necessary and matters of inheritance will be established as they are between a husband and wife. The man would also have the right to control the movements of his wife. The Aḥnāf do not recognise the marriage, so they disallow intercourse, do not deem bridal gift or maintenance necessary, nor do they recognise the distribution of inheritance between them as husband and wife or the restrictions upon movement.

Text And Translation

فصل في تعريف طريق المراد بالنصوص: اعلم أن لمعرفة المراد بالنصوص طرقا، منها أن اللفظ إذا كان حقيقة لمعنى ومجازا لآخر فالحقيقة أولى، مثاله ما قال علماؤنا عليهم الرحمة: البنت المخلوقة من ماء الزنا يحرم على الزاني نكاحها، وقال الشافعي رحمه الله: يحل والصحيح ما قلنا؛ لأنها بنته حقيقة فتدخل تحت قوله تعالى: ﴿حرمت عليكم أمهاتكم وبناتكم﴾ ويتفرع منه الأحكام على المذهبين من حل الوطيء ووجوب المهر ولزوم النفقة وجريان التوارث وولاية المنع عن الخروج والبروز

Chapter on recognition of techniques to understand the text: know that there are techniques to recognise the purpose of texts. Amongst them is that if a word has a literal and a metaphorical meaning, the literal is given prevalence. An example of it is what our jurists, mercy be on them, have said that the marriage of a girl born out of wedlock is forbidden to the perpetrator. Imam ash-Shāfa'ī, Allah have mercy on him, says it is permitted but our view is correct because she is his daughter in reality. She will be governed by the verse of the Almighty: "Forbidden upon you are your mothers, and your daughters..." Branching from this are the rulings of both schools regarding permissibility of intercourse,

QUICK TERMS

الحقيقة: *al-ḥaqīqa*

The literal. A word coined by the lexicon for an item.

المجاز: *al-majāz*

The figurative. A word used for a meaning other than its coined meaning.

QUICK ARABIC

النكاح: *an-nikāḥ*

Conjunction. In legal terms it is the marriage contract.

necessity of bridal gift, necessity of maintenance, matters of inheritance and the authority of granting permission to enter or to leave.

❖ ❖ ❖

The second technique to help understand the text is that if a text has two possible meanings where one meaning requires further limits to make it practical and the other does not, in such a case, the unrestricted al-muṭlaq meaning is preferred. An example of this is the words *lāmastum un-nisā* from verse 43 of Sūrat un-Nisā:

﴿أَوْ لَامَسْتُمُ النِّسَاءَ﴾ [النساء: 43]

"...or you have cohabited with [touched] a woman..."

This could mean to have intercourse with a woman or it could mean to simply touch and come into direct contact with a woman. The Aḥnāf take the view that it means intercourse and the ash-Shāfa'īy school takes the meaning of touch. ash-Shāfa'īy ﷺ states that touching is the literal and al-ḥaqīqa of the word whereas intercourse is metaphorical and al-majāz, so al-ḥaqīqa will take precedence. Under this rule the verse will mean that if one comes into physical contact with women ablution will become invalid and it will be necessary to make it up once again. The Aḥnāf state that *al-mulāmasa* can be both touching and intercourse as stated but taking the meaning of intercourse is better as it gives the added advantage of not requiring any further *at-takhṣīṣ* and limitations. This is because intercourse will render both types of purity, *as-sughrā* and *al-kubrā*, invalid and the text will thus be unrestricted and comprehensive. However, if we were to take *al-mulāmasa* to mean physical contact it would mean further limitations would be required. Therefore, we would be saying, physical contact with a woman invalidates the ablution but not when the female is a *al-maḥram* or an infant. This is also true in the understanding of Imam ash-Shāfa'īy ﷺ This would mean that the text in question does not cover all cases of *al-mulāmasa*, rather further limitations are required to exclude close relatives and young children. Now, our rule states that it is better to construe the text to mean a more comprehensive meaning where further limitations are not required. This is achieved through the meaning of intercourse and is the ideal understanding.

QUICK TERMS

المطلق: *al-muṭlaq*

The unrestricted. Indicates an entity irrespective of any quality.

QUICK ARABIC

الملامسة: *al-mulāmasa*

Touching. The metaphorical meaning is sexual intercourse.

التخصيص: *at-takhṣīṣ*

Specification. Exempting using an attached yet independent clause.

الحدث الأكبر: *al-ḥadath ul-akbar*

Major impurity. The state of the one who has not bathed.

الحدث الأصغر: *al-ḥadath ul-aṣghar*

Minor impurity. The state of the one who is not performed ablution.

المحرم: *al-maḥram*

Unlawful. A near relative with whom marriage is not permitted.

A few different verdicts come because of the aforementioned difference. For example, if a man with ablution touched a woman with his hand it will still be permitted for him to pray with a previous ablution or to handle the blessed Quran, there would be no restrictions on him entering the vicinity of the masjid or on becoming the imam of a congregation. This is according to the Aḥnāf as according to them the man's purity is still intact. ash-Shāfa'īy رحمه الله on the other hand consider his ablution invalid, so praying, handling the blessed Quran, entering the masjid without *al-karāha* and leading the congregation are all unacceptable. Similarly, if a man with ablution touched a woman or recalled during a prayer that he had touched a woman after performing ablution, and this man was at present unable to use water, in both cases Imam ash-Shāfa'īy رحمه الله would rule that *at-tayammum* necessary and the Aḥnāf would permit him to continue ,as he is still with purity.

Text And Translation

ومنها أن أحد المحملين إذا وجب تخصيصا في النص دون الآخر فالحمل على ما لا يستلزم التخصيص أولى، مثاله في قوله تعالى: ﴿أو لامستم النساء﴾ فالملامسة لو حملت على الوقاع كان النص معمولا به في جميع صور وجوده ولو حملت على المس باليد كان النص مخصوصا به في كثير من الصور، فإن مس المحارم والطفلة الصغيرة جدا غير ناقض للوضوء في أصح قولي الشافعي، ويتفرع منه الأحكام على المذهبين من إباحة الصلاة ومس المصحف ودخول المسجد وصحة الإمامة ولزوم التيمم عند عدم الماء وتذكر المس في أثناء الصلاة

From them is that if one possibility requires restriction whilst the other does not, then the one that does not require it is given preference. An example of it from the word of the Most High, is: "...or you have touched a women..." If 'touch' is taken as intercourse the text will be sufficient in all instances and if it is taken as touch of the hand it will have to be limited in many scenarios. Touching a close-relative or very young child does not invalidate the ablution in the most correct of Imam ash-Shāfa'īy's two opinions. Branching from this are the rulings of both schools regarding permissibility of salah, touching a copy of the Quran, entering the masjid, permissibility of leading the salah, necessity to perform at-tayammum in the absence of water and remembering contact during the prayer.

QUICK ARABIC

الكراهة: *al-karāha*

Disliked. An act disliked due to a discrepancy.

التيمم: *at-tayammum*

Dry ablution. The ritual ablution performed without water.

❖ ❖ ❖

Another technique of understanding the text is that if a verse of the blessed Quran has two variations in recitation or a narration has two variants reported, it should be enacted in a manner where both variants are independent cases and both are thus enacted independent of the other. For example, in the verse of ablution, verse 6 of Sūrat ul-Māida:

﴿وَامْسَحُواْ بِرُؤُوسِكُمْ وَأَرْجُلَكُمْ إِلَى الْكَعْبَينِ﴾ [المائدة: 6]

"...and rub your heads and (wash) your feet up to the ankles..."

One consideration is to connect the feet to the ruling of the faces, if the recitation is in the accusative state of *an-naṣb, arjulakum*. This would mean the feet are to be washed. The other lesser known recitation is to connect the feet to the ruling of the head, that is if the recitation is in the genitive state of *al-jarr, arjulikum*, and in which case the feet are to be wiped. We rule that the washing of feet concerns the situation where feet are bare, and the wiping of the feet is when they are covered with a leather or extremely thick sock. Because of this ruling for the wiping of the leather-clad feet, some scholars insist on the proof of such an act being derived directly from the verses of the blessed Quran. Others have said it is proven through narrations and not the blessed Quran.

In the lesser known recitation, the justification for the genitive state of the word *arjuli* in the verse is due to its close proximity to the genitive *rūsikum* and not due to its connection to the ruling of wiping the head.

Another example of two different recitations of a verse of the blessed Quran resulting in two different cases is verse 222 of Sūrat ul-Baqara:

﴿وَلاَ تَقْرَبُوهُنَّ حَتَّىَ يَطْهُرْنَ﴾ [البقرة: 222]

"...and do not go to them till they are cleansed..."

One is not to have intercourse with a woman who is on her period. There are two enunciations for the word for cleanliness, *yaṭṭahharna* and *yaṭhurna*. *Yattahharna* gives a meaning of exaggeration whilst *yaṭhurna* does not. For a woman in her period the norm is to bathe when the bleeding stops, but in the case in question the bleeding stops but she has not yet bathed. This means she is clean but has not exaggerated her cleanliness by bathing yet. This suggests that the recitation with *Yattahharna* means that between the delay from the

QUICK GRAMMAR

النصب: *an-naṣab*

Accusative. When nouns are used as object in a verbal sentence, and their modifying adjectives.

الجر: *al-jarr*

Genitive. When nouns occur after prepositions or as a second word in appositions.

bleeding halting and the bathing, intercourse will not be permitted for her, as she has to 'exaggerate' her cleanliness before intercourse is permitted.

The second recitation with *yaṭhurna* means that exaggerating is not required, so intercourse would be permitted in the delay between the bleeding coming to a halt and bathing. There is a clear difference between the requirements of both recitations.

When applying both of these recitations we say that the exaggerated recitation refers to a case where the bleeding concludes before the threshold of ten days and the non-exaggerated recitation is for the case where bleeding ceases upon or after ten days. Based on this our scholars have ruled that if a woman's bleeding ceases before ten days it is not permissible for the husband to have intercourse with her, as complete cleanliness still needs to be obtained through the exaggerated meaning. If the bleeding ceases after the maximum limit of ten days then intercourse is permitted with her before the bathing because simple cleanliness, without the exaggeration of bathing, is required and that was obtained when the bleeding ceased.

Furthermore, we add that if the bleeding ceased upon ten days towards the end of a particular prayer time, the prayer will become necessary. This is true even if the time is extremely tight or insufficient to bathe and complete the prayer within the time. It will be necessary and will be made up as al-qaḍā later. This is because the restriction in eligibility to pray was due to the absence of purity due to *al-ḥayḍ* and that purity was restored by the process of the bleeding passing; an exaggerated purity was not required to obtain it. Now that she was eligible to pray at the last moment, the prayer became necessary. On the other hand, if the bleeding ceases within the ten days and at the end of a prayer time, there has to be sufficient time for her to complete the exaggerated purity to restore eligibility. Therefore, if there was insufficient time for her to bathe and enter the prayer with *al-takbīr* before the conclusion of that prayer time, it will not be necessary on her and she need not make it up later. If there was ample time to bathe and enter the prayer, it will need to be performed in this case too.

QUICK TERMS

المطلق: *al-muṭlaq*

The unrestricted. Indicates an entity irrespective of any quality.

QUICK ARABIC

الحيض: *al-ḥayḍ*

The menses. A woman's periodic blood flow from the uterus.

التكبير: *at-takbīr*

Expression of greatness. Expressing Allah's ﷻ greatness at the beginning or during prayer, as well as out of prayer.

Text And Translation

ومنها أن النص إذا قرئ بقراءتين أو روي بروايتين كان العمل به على وجه يكون عملا بالوجهين أولى،

مثاله في قوله تعالى: ﴿وَ أرجلكم﴾ قرئ بالنصب عطفا على المغسول وبالخفض عطفا على الممسوح، فحملت قراءة الخفض على حالة التخفف وقراءة النصب على حالة عدم التخفف، وباعتبار هذا المعنى قال البعض: جواز المسح ثبت بالكتاب، وكذلك قوله تعالى: ﴿حتى يطهرنَ﴾ قرئ بالتشديد والتخفيف فيعمل بقراءة التخفيف فيما إذا كان أيامها عشرة، وبقراءة التشديد فيما إذا كان أيامها دون العشرة، وعلى هذا قال أصحابنا: اذا انقطع دم الحيض لأقل من عشرة أيام لم يجز وطئ الحائض حتى تغتسل؛ لأن كمال الطهارة يثبت بالاغتسال ولو انقطع دمها لعشرة أيام جاز وطئها قبل الغسل؛ لأن مطلق الطهارة ثبت بانقطاع الدم، ولهذا قلنا: اذا انقطع دم الحيض لعشرة أيام في آخر وقت الصلاة تلزمها فريضة الوقت وان لم يبق من الوقت مقدار ما تغتسل فيه، ولو انقطع دمها لأقل من عشرة أيام في آخر وقت الصلاة إن بقي من الوقت مقدار ما تغتسل فيه وتحرم للصلاة لزمته الفريضة وإلا فلا

From them is that if the text is recited in two readings or reported in two narrations then acting by incorporating both is given prevalence. An example of it in His word, the Most High, is: "...and your feet...". The final consonant is pronounced with an 'a' connecting it to the washed or it's final consonant is with an 'i' connecting it to the wiped. The 'i' reading incorporates the ruling of leather socks and the 'a' reading for when no leather socks are worn. Considering this meaning, some have said that permissibility of wiping is established by the Quran. Similar is His word, the Most High: "...until they achieve purity..."; recited with a stress and without. The non-stress is being adhered to when her days are ten and the stressed reading is for when her days are less than ten. Based on this our jursits have said: when the blood of menses stops in less than ten days intercourse is not permitted with the woman before al-ghusl because the completion of the purity is established by the bathing. And if the blood stopped on ten days, intercourse with her is permitted before al-ghusl because absolute purity is achieved by the ceasing of the blood. For this reason we said: if the blood of menses ceases on ten days at the concluding time of salah it becomes compulsory on her even if it does not allow enough time to bathe. If her blood ceased in less than ten days at the concluding time of salah, the salah is only necessary if enough time remains to bathe and enter the salah with *at-takbīr*.

❖ ❖ ❖

QUICK ARABIC

الغسل: *al-ghusl*

Ritual bathing. Washing the whole body after a major legal impurity.

Summary Of Understanding the Text

1. There are several basic techniques a jurist can employ to understand the true meaning of a text. Three of them are:
   i) Literal over metaphorical;
   ii) Unrestricted over the restricted; and
   iii) Inclusion of variation.

2. Details of literal over metaphorical:
   i) If a word has both a literal and metaphorical meaning in use, the literal meaning will take precedence.
   ii) Example: Female offspring born out of wedlock will be a recognised daughter of the biological father. Allah Almighty says: حُرِّمَتْ عَلَيْكُمْ أُمَّهَاتُكُمْ وَبَنَاتُكُمْ This means that parentage is established even if the girl is illegitimate. Being a legitimately born daughter is a metaphorical understanding. The literal will take precedence and she will be his daughter legally. Therefore, they are not permitted to marry each other.

3. Details of general over limited:
   i) If two meanings are possible for a word, but one meaning will result in further restrictions and limiting, it is preferable to take the broader general meaning.
   ii) Example: Allah Almighty says: أو لامستم النساء. If *al-mulāmasa* is a metaphor for intercourse it will apply in all cases, and if it is in its literal meaning of *touching,* we would have to make exemptions such as touching a child or *al-maḥram*; the likes of which would not invalidate the ablution. So, the metaphorical meaning would be preferred as it will remain unrestricted.

4. Details of inclusion of variation:
   i) When there are two readings of a text of the blessed Quran or two variants in a tradition, an approach that incorporates both would be preferred if possible.
   ii) Allah Almighty says: وامسحوا برءوسكم وأرجلكم. The accusative (نصب) and the genitive (جر) readings are possible for the word *arjul*. The subjunctive will result in a connection to the washed parts and the genitive reading would connect the word to the wiped part. Both are incorporated by deriving two distinct rulings; the first refers to washing the bare feet whilst the latter refers to wiping over the leather socks. Thus, both readings are applied.

1.8.1 Some Weak Extractions

The following are a series of weak extractions of rulings from their sources. The purpose of discussing them here is to lay bare the nature of these errors and their cause. It is a direct result of not comprehensively understanding the text, and then using it to issue rulings.

The first is from a tradition that states: "He ﷺ vomited and did not perform his ablution." Imam ash-Shāfa'īy رحمه الله deduces from this that vomiting does not invalidate the ablution as the tradition states that the blessed Prophet ﷺ vomited and did not perform his ablution. If it were to invalidate the ablution then the blessed Prophet ﷺ would have performed it. His not performing the ablution is evidence of it not being invalidated. This evidencing is weak because this Hadith merely shows that ablution is not immediately necessary after vomiting. There is no difference of opinion in this regard. The question we differ in is whether the ablution is invalid due to vomiting or not. If one was to pray after such an episode, could they do it without performing ablution first or not? We say that this tradition says it is not immediately necessary to perform ablution. Furthermore, another tradition reported by Lady Aisha رضي الله عنها states: "Whomsoever vomited, had a nose bleed or excreted pre-ejaculate should leave his prayer and perform ablution and then continue his prayer so long as he has not spoken in this time." In another narration, Abū Dardā رضي الله عنه said: "The Prophet ﷺ vomited and performed his ablution."

حديث

روي أنه ﷺ قاء ولم يتوضأ.

عليه الصلاة والسلام

(رواه الدارقطني)

حديث

عن عائشة رضي الله عنها عن النبي ﷺ قال: إذا قاء أحدكم في صلاته، أو رعف، أو قلس فلينصرف وليتوضأ، ثم يبني على ما مضى من صلاته، مالم يتكلم.

عليه الصلاة والسلام

(سنن الكبرى)

حديث

عن أبي الدرداء رضي الله عنه أن رسول الله ﷺ قاء فأفطر فتوضأ، فلقيت ثوبان في مسجد دمشق فذكرت ذلك له، فقال :صدق، أنا صببت له وضوءه.

عليه الصلاة والسلام

(سنن الترمذي)

Text And Translation

ثم نذكر طرقا من التمسكات الضعيفة ليكون ذلك تنبيها على موضع الخلل في هذا النوع، منها إن التمسك بما روي عن النبي ﷺ: أنه قاء فلم يتوضأ لإثبات أن القيء غير ناقض ضعيف؛ لأن الأثر يدل على أن القيء لا يوجب الوضوء في الحال، ولا خلاف فيه وإنما الخلاف في كونه ناقضا

Then, we recall some techniques of failed substantiation to caution against possible pitfalls of this type. Amongst them is, to provide evidence from the report of the Prophet, peace and blessings be upon him: that he vomited but did not perform ablution. It is weak to prove that vomiting does not invalidate the ablution. This is because the report shows that vomiting does not warrant immediate ablution. There is no disagreement in this, rather it is in it being an invalidator.

❖ ❖ ❖

A second example of weak evidencing is that some amongst the followers of ash-Shāfa'īy رحمه الله have stated that if a fly falls in water, the water is impure and cannot be consumed. They validate this by providing verse 3 of Sūrat ul-Māida:

﴿حُرِّمَتْ عَلَيْكُمُ الْمَيْتَةُ﴾ [المائدة: 3]

"Forbidden for you are carrion..."

The generality of the word *al-mayta* would include the fly and it is forbidden due to its impurity rather than its honour. It is worth bearing in mind that there is a rule stated by the Shawāfi' that says, if consumption of something is not forbidden due to its honour, then it is forbidden due to impurity. This rule leaves two possible reasons for the impermissibility, namely honour of the thing or its impurity. The water in which the fly, al-*mayta*, is found will also be impure as the fly was impure, and thus it is forbidden to consume the water. We say this is weak evidencing because this verse merely shows that carrion is forbidden and no one disagrees with this. The point of contention is whether water in which a fly has fallen is forbidden or not. We say it is not impure and the Shawāfi' claim is that it is impure. We find that consuming soil is forbidden but the impermissibility is not due to honour, at the same time soil is not impure. This means it is forbidden to consume but both honour and impurity are not causing this ruling. Moreover, fish that has died and floats on the surface is impermissible to consume, but its impermissibility is not due to honour nor is it impure. We thus say everything that is forbidden to consume for a reason other than honour is not automatically forbidden due to impurity, rather it could be due to impurity or that it is flesh and blood that causes it to be forbidden for consumption. This condition is absent in a fly as insects do not have blood from the onset, so the dead fly is forbidden but not impure. Therefore, if the fly is not impure, the water in which it is found is also not impure.

QUICK ARABIC

الميتة: *al-mayta*

Carrion. Halal animals that die naturally without slaughter. They are prohibited for consumption.

Text And Translation

وكذلك التمسك بقوله تعالى: ﴿حرمت عليكم الميتة﴾ لإثبات فساد الماء بموت الذباب ضعيف؛ لأن النص يثبت حرمة الميتة ولا خلاف فيه، وإنما الخلاف في فساد الماء

Similarly to present His word, the Most Highy: "Forbidden for you are carrion...", to prove that a fly falling in water spoils the water, is weak. This is because the text proves the prohibition of carrion and there is no disagreement regarding it. The disagreement is about the spoiling of water.

❖❖❖

The third example of weak evidencing is to use the saying of the blessed Prophet ﷺ to rule that vinegar does not eliminate impurity. Imam ash-Shāfa'īy رحمه الله says that the blessed Prophet ﷺ said to one of his wives that the manner to cleanse dried blood on a cloth is to first rub it with something coarse, then to scratch it with finger nails to remove the finer parts and finally to wash it with water. In the narration the washing is restricted, al-muqayyad, to water which indicates that it is necessary to wash the blood with water. If anything, other than water is permitted to cleanse the blood, the enacting of the Hadith would be redundant and this is not permitted. The Aḥnāf respond by saying this evidencing is weak because the Hadith makes it necessary to wash the blood with water in the situation where blood is on the cloth, and there is no disagreement in this. The disagreement is when one has removed the blood from the cloth with vinegar and whether the cloth is then clean or not. We say it is clean and they say it is not. Our evidence is that vinegar visibly removes the body of the impurity and removal of impurity is by definition purity. This means that removing the blood from the cloth will leave it pure as the impure blood is no longer there. The Hadith is not concerned with this issue.

Text And Translation

وكذلك التمسك بقوله عليه السلام: حتيه ثم اقرصيه ثم اغسليه بالماء لإثبات أن الخل لا يزيل النجس ضعيف؛ لأن الخبر يقتضي وجوب غسل الدم بالماء فيتقيد بحال وجود الدم على المحل ولا خلاف فيه، وإنما الخلاف في طهارة المحل بعد زوال الدم بالخل

Similarly to present his statement, peace and blessings be upon him: "Scratch it, peel it and then wash it with water", to prove that vinegar does not remove impurity, is weak. This is because the narration implies the necessity to wash blood with water in a situation where there is blood in an area. There is no disagreement regarding this, rather the disagreement is regarding the purity of the area after the blood is removed with viniger.

حديث

عن أسماء بنت أبي بكر رضي الله عنهما أن امرأة سألت النبي ﷺ عن الثوب يصيبه الدم من الحيضة فقال رسول الله ﷺ حتيه ثم اقرصيه بالماء ثم رشيه وصلي فيه.

عليه الصلاة والسلام

(سنن الترمذي: 138)

QUICK ARABIC

المقيد: *al-muqayyad*

The restricted. Indicates an entity and some of its qualities.

❖❖❖

The fourth example of weak evidencing is when Imam ash-Shāfa'īy ﷺ says for every forty goats one must be given as zakah. If one were to give money equivalent in value instead of a goat, it would not be acceptable. To support this there is the tradition in which the blessed Prophet ﷺ said, "From forty goats there is one goat." There is an explicit mention of a goat so the right of the poor is the goat. To exchange that right for an alternative such as money is to violate the right of the poor and is thus disallowed. The Aḥnāf say this evidencing is weak because this tradition only shows that one goat is necessary from forty and we do not disagree with this. The disagreement is if one gave money instead of the goat, is the zakah accepted? They say it is not acceptable, but we say it is. Our evidence is that the tradition does not concern the issue of whether the goat can be replaced with its monetary value or not. We see that the purpose of zakah is to fulfil the need of the poor, which is better served by giving them money. As the purpose is achieved, there is no need to disqualify the manner in which it is attached.

Text And Translation

وكذلك التمسك بقوله عليه السلام: في أربعين شاة شاة لإثبات عدم جواز دفع القيمة ضعيف؛ لأنه يقتضي وجوب الشاة ولا خلاف فيه، وإنما الخلاف في سقوط الواجب بأداء القيمة

Similarly to present his statement, peace and blessings be upon him: "For forty goats, there is one goat", to invalidate payment with money, is weak. This is because it implies the necessity of one goat and there is no disagreement in this. The disagreement is in whether by paying money the necessary task is accomplished.

❖❖❖

The fifth example of weak evidencing is that Imam ash-Shāfa'īy ﷺ deems the initial performance of 'Umra to be wājib and necessary, whereas the Aḥnāf consider it as-sunna. The evidence to say it is necessary from the beginning is that Allah ﷻ has established the performance of both Hajj and Umrah using the word-form of al-amr, *atimmū*, in verse 196 of Sūrat ul-Baqara:

حديث

عن سالم عن أبيه رضي الله عنهما أن رسول الله صلى الله عليه وسلم كتب كتاب الصدقة... وفي الشاء في كل أربعين شاةٍ شاةٌ إلى عشرين ومائة...

عليه الصلاة والسلام

(سنن الترمذي: 621)

QUICK TERMS

الواجب: *al-wājib*

The necessary. The non-observance of which is sinful but denial does not lead to disbelief.

﴿وَأَتِمُّوا الْحَجَّ وَالْعُمْرَةَ لِلَّهِ﴾ [البقرة: 196]

"Perform the Hajj and 'Umrah for Allah..."

Both Hajj and Umrah would thus have the same ruling which should be of necessity to perform. The Aḥnāf say that this is weak evidencing because the verse is asking to *complete* the Umrah and completion of something can only occur when the thing has commenced in the first place. From the verse one can say completion of the Umrah is necessary once it has begun, but one cannot say it makes Umrah necessary when one is not actually performing it. No one disagrees that once Umrah is being performed, the performer must necessarily complete it. For the Aḥnāf even a voluntary worship becomes necessary to complete once it is started.

Text And Translation

وكذلك التمسك بقوله تعالى: ﴿وأتموا الحج والعمرةَ لله﴾ لإثبات وجوب العمرة ابتداء ضعيف؛ لأن النص يقتضي وجوب الإتمام وذلك إنما يكون بعد الشروع ولا خلاف فيه، وإنما الخلاف في وجوبها ابتداء

Similarly to present His word, the Most High: "Complete Hajj and Umrah for Allah...", to prove the initial necessity of Umrah, is weak. This is because the text implies the necessity to complete which can only be after commencing it. There is no disagreement in this, rather disagreement is in its initial necessity.

❖ ❖ ❖

The sixth example of weak evidencing is the question of whether in a *al-fāsid* and invalid transaction the buyer becomes the owner of the merchandise after taking possession of it or not? The Aḥnāf say that ownership is transferred in *al-bay' ul-fāsid* after the purchaser has taken possession of the merchandise, whereas the adherents of Imam ash-Shāfa'īy رحمه الله disagree. They support their view through the tradition of the blessed Prophet ﷺ to not exchange one dirham for two, nor one measure of *aṣ-ṣā'* for two. His ﷺ forbidding it makes this a void, *al-bay' al-fāsid*, transaction and thus al-ḥarām and forbidden. Ownership on the other hand is a blessing, so how can a forbidden act lead to a blessing? This can be likened to stealing being an impermissible act and resulting in the ownership of the thief! We say this evidencing is weak because

حديث

عن ابن عمر رضي الله عنهما قال: قال رسول الله ﷺ: "لا تبيعوا الدينار بالدينارين، ولا الدرهم بالدرهمين ولا الصاع بالصاعين، فإني أخاف عليكم الرمآء".

عليه الصلاة والسلام

(مسند أحمد بن حنبل: 5725)

QUICK ARABIC

الأمر: *al-amr*

The imperative. A word-form that informs of a demanded act.

البيع الفاسد: *al-bay' ul-fāsid*

Invalid sale. When a sale is deemed illegal due to various impermissible causes and circumstances.

the tradition in question only states that *al-bay' ul-fāsid* is forbidden and we do not disagree with this. The point of contention is whether transfer of ownership, a direct consequence of transactions, occurs or not. The tradition does not talk about this and so is not a suitable piece of evidence. We support the idea of transfer of ownership in *al-bay' ul-fāsid* based on a previously stated principle that prohibition of an otherwise legal act requires the act itself to be legitimate [1.7 an-Nahī, page 219]. *al-Bay' ul-fāsid* is a prohibited legal act and is thus permitted in itself. As it is permissible in itself, any consequences of it will also be established and as transfer of ownership is one of its consequences, it will occur.

Text And Translation

وكذلك التمسك بقوله عليه السلام: لا تبيعوا الدرهم بالدرهمين ولا الصاع بالصاعين لإثبات أن البيع الفاسد لا يفيد الملك ضعيف؛ لأن النص يقتضي تحريم البيع الفاسد ولا خلاف فيه، وإنما الخلاف في ثبوت الملك وعدمه

Similarly to present his saying, peace be upon him: "Do not sell one dirham for two nor one measure for two", to prove that an invalid transaction does not give ownership, is weak. This is because the text implies the prohibition of the invalid transaction and there is no disagreement in that. The disagreement is about establishing ownership or not.

❖ ❖ ❖

The seventh and final example of weak evidencing is whether a vow to fast on the forbidden days of Eid is permitted or not. Imam ash-Shāfa'īy رحمه الله says that such a vow is not valid whereas the Aḥnāf say that the vow is binding, except it will not be carried out. Imam ash-Shāfa'īy رحمه الله substantiates his stance using the tradition that prohibits fasting on these days because they are days of feasting, drinking and intimacy. The prohibition makes it clear that should one fast on these occasions, they are disobedient and vowing to be disobedient is not correct. The command of the blessed Prophet صلى الله عليه وسلم is clear: "There is no vow in the disobedience of Allah Almighty". We respond that this is weak evidencing because the tradition states that fasting is prohibited on these days. There is no objection to this point. The difference of opinion is about whether a prohibited act can result in a legal ruling or not. Our opinion is that it can, so in

QUICK ARABIC

الصاع: *aṣ-ṣā'*

A cubic measure. An ancient measure which equates to approximately 2.035 Kg.

الحرام: *al-ḥarām*

The unlawful. That which is not permitted in the Shariah, as distinguished from the lawful.

البيع الفاسد: *al-bay' ul-fāsid*

Invalid sale. When a sale is deemed illegal due to various impermissible causes and circumstances.

line with this the vow will be correct. When the days pass the one making the vow must make up for missing them, and in the case that the days themselves were spent in fast, the vow will be fulfilled though the perpetrator will be sinful. Imam ash-Shāfa'īy رحمه الله deems the vow invalid and so no fast needs to be made up once the days have passed. As for the cited tradition, it does not speak about this case and so is not suited to extract the correct ruling.

There is a need to clarify how an impermissible act can lead to a ruling in the Shariah and how both can coexist. We see a similar coexistence in numerous other cases. Firstly, if a man had intercourse with his son's slave-girl and impregnated her, the act is forbidden. However, the father will become the owner of the slave and will be required to pay the cost of the slave. It is evident that an impermissible act leads to a ruling of the Shariah where ownership is transferred. Secondly, if one slaughtered a goat with a usurped knife, the act is impermissible. However, the meat is al-ḥalāl and its consumption is permitted. Thirdly, if one cleansed an impure cloth with usurped water the cloth would become pure despite the act of usurping water remaining forbidden. Fourthly, if one had intercourse with his wife during her period, it is forbidden. The forbidden act will however result in a change of status from virgin to non-virgin. Furthermore, if a woman had been divorced three times by a former husband, she will be permitted to remarry the former husband once again, providing the current husband divorces her. Therefore, despite the illegal act of intercourse during the period occurring, consequences of the Shariah still remain. In a similar fashion, we say that though a fast on the day of Eid is not permitted, a vow for a fast on that day will still yield consequences.

Text And Translation

وكذلك التمسك بقوله عليه السلام: ألا لا تصوموا في هذه الأيام فإنها أيام أكل وشرب وبعال لإثبات أن النذر بصوم يوم النحر لا يصح ضعيف؛ لأن النص يقتضي حرمة الفعل ولا خلاف في كونه حراما، وإنما الخلاف في إفادة الأحكام مع كونه حراما وحرمة الفعل لا تنافي ترتب الأحكام، فإن الأب لو استولد جارية ابنه يكون حراما ويثبت به الملك للأب، ولو ذبح شاة بسكين مغصوبة يكون حراما ويحل المذبوح، ولو غسل الثوب النجس بماء مغصوب يكون حراما ويطهر به الثوب، ولو وطئ امرأة في حالة الحيض يكون حراما ويثبت به إحصان الواطئ ويثبت الحل للزوج الأول.

حديث

عن عائشة رضي الله عنها عن النبي صلى الله عليه وسلم قال: من نذر أن يطيع الله فليطعه ومن نذر أن يعصي الله فلا يعصه".

عليه الصلاة والسلام

(البخاري: 6696)

QUICK ARABIC

الحلال: *al-ḥalāl*

The lawful. That which is permitted in the Shariah, as distinguished from the unlawful.

QUICK DICTIONARY

usurp: *you-zurp*

The seize. To hold or use something by force without legal right or authority.

Similarly presenting his statement, peace be upon him: "Listen! Do not fast in these days for they are days of feasting, drinking and intimacy", to prove the invalidity of vowing to fast on the Day of Sacrifice, is weak. This is because the text implies the prohibition of the act and there is no disagreement that it is forbidden. The disagreement is in establishing rulings despite its prohibition and that prohibition of an act doesn't prevent consequent rulings. So, if a father impregnates his son's slave, it will be forbidden but it will establish ownership of the father. If one sacrificed a goat with a usurped knife it would be forbidden, yet the sacrifice would be permitted. If one washed an impure cloth in usurped water it would be forbidden, however it would cleanse the cloth. If one had intercourse with a woman in her period it would be forbidden but the sexual activity of the perpetrator would be established and remarrying an ex-husband would be permitted.

حديث

عن أبي هريرة رضي الله عنه أن رسول الله صلى الله عليه وسلم بعث عبد الله بن حذافة يطوف في منى أن: لا تصوموا هذه الأيام؛ فإنها أيام أكل وشرب وذكر الله عز وجل.

عليه الصلاة والسلام

(سنن الدارقطني: 33/2255)

❖❖❖

Ḥurūf ul-Ma'ānī
- Significant Particles -

al-'Āṭifa
- Conjunctions –

1. الواو (al-wāw) page 247
2. الفاء (al-fā) page 253
3. ثم (thumma) page 262
4. بل (bal) page 265
5. لكن (lākin) page 268
6. أو (aw) page 273
7. حتى (ḥattā) page 279

al-Jārra
- Prepositions –

8. إلى (ilā) page 285
9. على ('alā) page 288
10. في (fī) page 290
11. الباء (al-bā) page 296

FIGURE 1.9-01
Types of al-ḥurūf ul-ma'ānī and where they have been disucussed.

1.9 Ḥurūf ul-Ma'ānī

This chapter is about ḥurūf ul-ma'ānī or particles that have significant consequences in rulings due to the implications of their relative meanings. Chapters 1.1 through to 1.7 were about important terms of uṣūl ul-fiqh, and chapter 1.8 was an addendum that presented some practical steps to help unravel the true meaning and purpose of texts. The previous chapter also highlighted some weak and incorrect techniques resulting in incorrect rulings from a text.

al-Ḥurūf ul-ma'ānī are of a great deal of importance. A ruling can hinge upon the presence of a particular particle or the absence of it. There are two types of ḥurūf ul-ma'ānī*:* al-ḥurūf ul-'āṭifa*,* particles of conjunction, and al-ḥurūf ul-jārra, particles of preposition. There are eleven in total mentioned in Uṣūl ush-Shāshī, seven of which are conjunctions and four are prepositions. Figure 1.9-01 shows this division and where each particle is discussed in this book.

The first discussion is on the conjunctions because in the Arabic language they combine with both verbs and nouns, whereas the use of prepositions is with nouns only. As conjunctions are more general and far-reaching, they come first. From the conjunctions, the particle al-*wāw* is discussed first as it is used for an unrestricted and unconditioned meaning, so it takes precedence over the remaining conjunctions.

1.9.1 al-Wāw

The particle *al-wāw* (الواو) is for mere conjoining which means the part of the sentence preceding the particle and the part following it are together in the ruling. However, there is no consideration for the order, proximity or delay by which they are subject to that ruling. This means that a sentence such as, "Zayd and(*wa*) 'Amar came", does not give any indication to the order in which they came. It simply states that they are both subject to the idea of *coming*. They could have come separately, together one after the other, or even in reverse order. The particle gives no indication of the additional detail. Contrast this with the view of Imam ash-Shāfa'īy رحمه الله who holds that the particle *al-wāw* is for conjoining with an order too. It is for this reason he states that the ablution must be performed in order, as the verse of ablution, sūrat ul-Māida verse 6, separates face, arms, head and feet with the particle *al-wāw*. As the particle is

QUICK TERMS

أصول الفقه: uṣūl ul-fiqh

Principles of jurisprudence. Rules that systematically allow a jurist to derive rulings.

QUICK DICTIONARY

حروف المعاني: ḥurūf ul-ma'ānī

Meaningful particles. These parts of speech hold specific and significant meanings.

الحروف العاطفة: al-ḥurūf ul-'āṭifa

Conjunctions. These particles are used to connect clauses in coordination or subcoordination.

الحروف الجارة: al-ḥurūf ul-jārra

Prepositions. Particles that are followed by nouns, making them genitive.

for conjoining and order according to him, it would follow that they must all be part of the ablution and at the same time must be performed in order of appearance.

Based on our standpoint that *al-wāw* is merely for conjoining under one ruling, if one said to his wife, "If you speak to Zayd and(*wa*) 'Amar, you are divorced", and she went on to talk to 'Amar first and then Zayd, reversing the order, the divorce will still occur. There will be no consideration for the order in which she spoke to them or for any delay that may occur. Similarly, if one said to his wife, "If you enter this house and(*wa*) this house, you are divorced", while she entered the second house first and the first house last, the divorce will still occur. This is because the particle is for merely joining both preceding and proceeding under one ruling, and that has occurred irrespective of order, so the divorce will occur.

Imam Muḥammad ﷺ says that if one said to his wife, "If you enter the house and(*wa*) you are divorced", the divorce will occur immediately. The divorce will not be dependent upon her entering the house. This example clearly shows that the particle *al-wāw* is not for establishing an order. Had it demanded an order, entering the house would be a condition for the divorce. For this to be an immediate divorce, as Imam Muḥammad ﷺ has stated, it must not contain any order but simply the preceding part is subject to the same that the proceeding part is subject to, though each are independent of the other.

Text And Translation

فصل في تقرير حروف المعاني: الواو للجمع المطلق، وقيل: إن الشافعي جعله للترتيب، وعلى هذا أوجب الترتيب في باب الوضوء، قال علماؤنا رحمهم الله: إذا قال لامرأته: إن كلمت زيدا وعمرا فأنت طالق، فكلمت عمرا ثم زيدا طلقت، ولا يشترط فيه معنى الترتيب والمقارنة، ولو قال: إن دخلت هذه الدار وهذه الدار فأنت طالق، فدخلت الثانية ثم دخلت الأولى طلقت، قال مُحَمَّد رحمه الله: إذا قال: إن دخلت الدار وأنت طالق، تطلق في الحال ولو اقتضى ذلك ترتيبا لترتب الطلاق به عند الدخول ويكون ذلك تعليقا لا تنجيزا

Chapter on the assignment of significant particles: the particle *al-wāw* is for mere combining. It is said that Imam a<u>sh</u>-<u>Sh</u>āfa'īy considers it for sequence. For this reason he necessitates sequence in the chapter of ablution. Our scholars, Allah have mercy on them, said: if one says to his wife: "If you speak to Zayd and(*wa*) 'Amar, you are divorced". If she spoke to 'Amar then to Zayd, she is divorced. There is no consideration in it for order or sequence. If one said: "If you enter this house and(*wa*) this house, you are divorced", and she entered the second one then the first one, she will be divorced. Imam Muḥammad, Allah have mercy on him, said: if one said: "If you enter the house and(*wa*) you are divorced", she will be divorced immediately. Had it implied sequence the divorce would follow the entering because of it, and this would be deferred and not immediate.

❖ ❖ ❖

Sometimes the particle *al-wāw* is used metaphorically. In such a case, it forms a circumstantial phrase, where the circumstance *al-ḥāl* is conjoined with the individual. The phrase functions as a conditional sentence because the circumstance, *al-ḥāl*, acts as a limiter and restriction for the individual, *dhū ul-ḥāl*, much like a condition, *ash-sharṭ*, is to its final clause, *al-jazā*. As an example of this, a sentence such as "Give me one thousand and(*wa*) you are free", when said to a slave who has permission to earn, *al-madhūn*, giving one thousand becomes the condition for his freedom. It is as though we can restructure the sentence to a conditional by saying, "If you give me one thousand, you are free". The two sentences have the same meaning. Now, if the slave gives one thousand, he becomes free, otherwise not.

Imam Muḥammad ﷺ says in as-Siyar al-Kabīr that should a Muslim leader instruct non-believers, "Open the gates and(*wa*) you are safe", they will not be safe without opening the gate. The leader's words will mean that on the condition that you open the gate, you will be safe, and should you choose not to open the gate, you will not be safe. Similarly, if the leader says to a combatant, "Descend and(*wa*) you are safe", the combatant will be safe only by descending from his position. The words will mean that on the condition that you descend, you are safe, otherwise not.

For the particle *al-wāw* to take on the metaphorical *al-ḥāl* meaning it must fulfil two conditions. Firstly, that the words should have the flexibility to be a suitable circumstance, and secondly that there should be an indicator present that suggests the literal meaning is to be abandoned and replaced by the metaphorical. These conditions are met in the previous example where the

QUICK ARABIC

المأذون: *al-madhūn*

Authorised slave. A slave given legal rights to trade.

QUICK GRAMMAR

حال: *ḥāl*

State. A circumstantial statement, expression or phrase, said of noun.

ذو الحال: *dhū ul-ḥāl*

Conditional noun. The noun which is expressed with a circumstance.

الشرط: *ash-sharṭ*

The condition. The first clause in a conditional sentence.

الجزاء: *al-jazā*

The return. The second and final clause in a conditional sentence.

QUICK REFERENCE

السير الكبير: *as-siyar al-kabīr*

The major treatise on engagement. The first major Islamic treatise on the law between Muslim and non-Muslim nations by Imām Muḥammad ash-Shaybānī ﷺ

master says to the slave, "Give me one thousand, and(*wa*) you are free". The suitability and indicator here is that a financial compensation is a suitable condition for the emancipation of a slave, whilst the slave has already been granted independence to earn his own money. This takes away the possibility of the literal meaning of *al-wāw* of mere conjoining. If the particle was for mere conjoining the first part of the sentence would be independent of the second, so it would read 'give me one thousand' and separately, 'you are free'. For the master to ask for a slave who already earns him money, to give him money is pointless in itself and then to add to that he would also be freeing him. This clearly is not the case. In short, taking the literal meaning of the particle *al-wāw* is problematic and needs to be abandoned. The words have the capacity to become a circumstantial sentence, so we say that the words now read, 'on the condition that one thousand is given by the slave, he is free', as per our earlier explanation.

Text And Translation

وقد يكون الواو للحال فتجمع بين الحال وذي الحال، وحينئذٍ تفيد معنى الشرط، مثاله ما قال في المأذون إذا قال لعبده: أد إلي ألفا وأنت حر يكون الأداء شرطا للحرية، وقال محمَّد في "السير الكبير": إذا قال الإمام للكفار: افتحوا الباب وأنتم آمنون لا يأمنون بدون الفتح، ولو قال للحربي: انزل وأنت آمن لا يأمن بدون النزول، وإنما تحمل الواو على الحال بطريق المجاز فلا بد من احتمال اللفظ ذلك وقيام الدلالة على ثبوته، كما في قول المولى لعبده: أد إلي ألفا وأنت حر، فإن الحرية يتحقق حال الأداء وقامت الدلالة على ذلك فإن المولى لا يستوجب على عبده مالا مع قيام الرق فيه، وقد صح التعليق به فحمل عليه.

Sometimes *al-wāw* is used for circumstantial expression and so it combines the circumstance to its referent noun. In this form it will give the meaning of a condition. An example of it is what is mentioned regarding *al-madhūn* that if one said to his slave: "Give me one thousand and(*wa*) you are free"; giving will be a condition for emancipation. Imam Muḥammad says in as-Siyar al-Kabīr that if an Imam says to the disbelievers: "Open the gates and(*wa*) you are safe", they would not be safe without opening. If he said to the combatant: "Descend and(*wa*) you are safe", he would not be safe without descending. The meaning of circumstance for *al-wāw* will be metaphorical so it is vital that the words have

QUICK ARABIC

المأذون: *al-madhūn*

Authorised slave. A slave given legal rights to trade.

QUICK REFERENCE

السير الكبير: *as-siyar al-kabīr*

The major treatise on engagement. The first major Islamic treatise on the law between Muslim and non-Muslim nations by Imām Muḥammad ash-Shaybānī ﷺ

the capacity for it and there must be evidence to support it, like a master saying to his slave: "Give me a thousand and(*wa*) you are free". Emancipation will occur when payment is made, and evidence supports this because the master need not impose wealth on his slave whilst he is a slave. Deferring is correct for it, so it will be considered so.

❖ ❖ ❖

The condition to take the particle *al-wāw* out of the literal meaning and into the metaphorical is that the literal must not be feasible, and where it is feasible, the metaphorical is not possible. As an example, if one said to his wife, "You are divorced and(*wa*) you are ill" or "You are divorced and(*wa*) you are praying", the divorce will occur immediately in accordance with the literal meaning of two independently conjoined sentences, as this is a valid possibility. Whilst the literal meaning is valid, there is no cause to abandon it for the metaphorical. As both sentences are independent, the first will be applied and the divorce will be established, whilst the second sentence remains unconnected. At the time of uttering the words, if the man intended to construct the sentence as the metaphorical conditional sentence, as the words do have this capacity too, the intention will be valid in the court of Allah ﷻ but not valid before the judge. The judge's rejection will be based on the fact that the intention is diverting the literal meaning and in the chapter of divorce, this is not possible. In the court of Allah ﷻ he may be correct, as it is He Who is truly aware of intentions, and the words can also be construed to mean this.

Furthermore, if one said to another, "Take this one thousand in *al-muḍāraba* and(*wa*) work with it in textiles". The work will not be limited to textiles, rather the partnership will be in general and in any trade. This is because the textile industry does not have the capacity to be *ḥāl* for a joint venture with one thousand because the one thousand will be given before the business begins. This means that *ḥāl* is coming before the thing that it is supposed to be a circumstance for, and this is not possible as they should be present together. Due to this, we say that in this example the words do not have the capacity to be part of a circumstantial phrase, so they are two separate sentences by default. When the sentences are independent in this manner, it is not possible to connect *al-muḍāraba* to the one thousand, so it is not a condition for it.

QUICK ARABIC

المضاربة: *al-muḍāraba*

Co-partnership. An agreement whereby co-partners are entitled to profit, one as proprietor of the stock and the other on account of labour.

QUICK GRAMMAR

حال: *ḥāl*

State. A circumstantial statement, expression or phrase, said of a noun.

Text And Translation

ولو قال: أنت طالق وأنت مريضة أو مصلية تطلق في الحال ولو نوى التعليق صحت نيته فيما بينه وبين الله تعالى؛ لأن اللفظ وإن كان يحتمل معنى الحال إلا أن الظاهر خلافه وإذا تأيد ذلك بقصده ثبت، ولو قال: خذ هذه الألف مضاربة واعمل بها في البز لا يتقيد العمل في البز ويكون المضاربة عامة؛ لأن العمل في البز لا يصلح حالا لأخذ الألف مضاربة فلا يتقيد صدر الكلام به

If one said: "You are divorced when(*wa*) you are ill or praying", she will be divorced immediately and if he intended it to be deferred, the intention will be valid between him and Allah Almighty. This is because although the words have the capacity to be circumstantial except that the apparent meaning is against it and when this is confirmed with his intention, it is established. If one said: "Take this one thousand in partnership and(*wa*) trade in textiles, it will not be limited to textiles and the partnership will be general. This is because working in textiles does not have the capacity to act as a circumstance for the one thousand in partnership, so the earlier sentence will not be restricted to it.

❖❖❖

If a phrase cannot be circumstantial, the default meaning of *al-wāw* is operative, so if a woman says to her husband, "Divorce me and(*wa*) you have a thousand", and the husband responds by giving her a divorce, there will be nothing to pay for the woman. The reasoning is that the woman's conditioning the divorce with one thousand has no bearing on the act of the man, which is the issuance of the divorce. The statement belongs to the woman and the act of issuing the divorce is the husband's act. The one thousand cannot be *al-ḥāl* when the man independently issues the divorce. As this is the case, the two statements are stand-alone statements without interfering with each other. The issuance of the divorce will stand once the husband issues it, and it will remain unconnected to any conditions. Therefore, as there is no condition to the divorce, no money in necessary once it has been issued. This is different to when one says to a porter, "Pick up this luggage and(*wa*) you have a dirham". Though the statement is from one person and the act of picking is from the other person, the act is not independent of the instruction. The issuance of divorce is originally independent and not for financial gain from the husband but carrying a load is dependent upon the instruction. There is also an indicator to

QUICK ARABIC

الإيجار: *al-ījār*

To hire. The use and enjoyment of property for a time, in exchange for a sum.

QUICK GRAMMAR

حال: *ḥāl*

State. A circumstantial statement, expression or phrase, said of noun.

this connection, which are the surroundings of *al-ījār* or offering of a service. Therefore, in the case of hiring someone to pick a load, the words have the flexibility to be *al-ḥāl* and there is an indicator too. This means that it is not correct to refuse to pay for the service by saying they are unconnected, rather once the service is complete, the payment will be necessary. On the other hand, issuing divorce is not for money by default, and there is no indicator to change *al-wāw* from the default meaning. This shows that both cases are different.

Text And Translation

وعلى هذا قال أبو حنيفة: إذا قالت لزوجها: طلقني ولك ألف فطلقها لا يجب له عليها شيء؛ لأن قولها: ولك ألف لا يفيد حال وجوب الألف عليها، وقولها: طلقني مفيد بنفسه فلا يترك العمل به بدون الدليل بخلاف قوله: احمل هذا المتاع ولك درهم؛ لأن دلالة الإجارة يمنع العمل بحقيقة اللفظ.

Based on this Imam Abū Ḥanīfa said: if one said to her husband: "Divorce me and(*wa*) you have a thousand", he divorced her, she does not owe him anything. This is because her saying: 'and you have a thousand', does not have the capacity to be a circumstance for the one thousand to be necessary upon her. And her saying: 'divorce me', is enough by itself so we shall not abandon acting upon it without evidence. This not like one saying: "Carry this load and(*wa*) you have a dirham", because evidence of renting prevents enacting the literal meaning.

❖ ❖ ❖

1.9.2 al-Fā

The second particle from the conjunctions is *al-fā*, which comes for sequence and immediate order. This means that the clause proceeding the particle follows immediately after the preceding clause and without a delay or gap between the two. So, what is after *al-fā* comes after what is before *al-fā* in order and the two are immediately together. Due to this immediate order found with the particle *al-fā* it attaches to the final apodosis clause, *al-jazā*, of a conditional sentence. This is because the *al-jazā* is expressing the consequence in a conditional sentence, and it must follow the protasis, which is the clause expressing the condition. The consequence immediately follows the condition. An example of this is if one said to his wife, "If you enter the house, then(*fa*) you

QUICK GRAMMAR

الجزاء: *al-jazā*

The return. The second and final clause in a conditional sentence.

QUICK DICTIONARY

apodosis: *uh-pod-uh-sis*

Consequence. The clause expressing the consequence in a conditional sentence.

protasis: *prot-uh-sis*

Condition. The clause expressing the condition in a conditional sentence.

are divorced". She will be divorced immediately upon entering the house. This shows the immediate effect of the particle in a conditional sentence.

Another example is when one says, "I sell this slave on your behalf for one thousand", and the person replies, "Then(*fa*) he is free". The reply is an implicit and hidden acceptance of the sale of the slave and upon the completion of the sale, it expresses the slave's freedom. It is as though the expanded reply is, 'I accept the sale of the slave for one thousand on my behalf, and I as the new owner of the slave, set him free.' The reason for this expanded text is that freedom of the slave cannot occur from the one who granted it unless he is the actual owner. Based on the actual words uttered, there must be an implicit and concealed acceptance of the sale as a requisite for the viability of the actual reply, 'then he is free'. If he did not accept the sale, how could the reply make any sense? This means that the reply contains the acceptance of the sale of the slave for one thousand, and then it is followed by the new owner emancipating the slave.

This situation should be contrasted with a scenario in which the reply is issued without the particle *al-fā*. The particle *al-fā* gives a meaning of immediate continuation, whereas other particles such as *al-wāw* do not have this meaning. So, if the reply to the initial proposal of "I sell this slave on your behalf for one thousand', is 'and(*wa*) he is free' or without a particle, 'he is free', there is a possibility that this is a refusal of the proposal to sell. The wording with *al-wāw* or without a particle has two possibilities; first, the responder is informing the proposer that the slave you are selling is a free man, and so I am not permitted to buy him and thus refuse the sale. Second, the responder could be accepting the sale and freeing the slave, which is only possible if he has accepted the implicit and hidden sale proposal in the first place. In the first possibility, there is a refusal of the proposal and in the second possibility, there is acceptance. This brings doubt in establishing the sale, as the situation is al-mushtarak between acceptance and refusal. A transaction cannot be complete with any element of doubt. Therefore, the response will be deemed a refusal of the sale, and as the sale is refused, the freedom is also not valid.

QUICK TERMS

المشترك: *al-mushtarak*

The concurrent. A word coined for two or more inherently different meanings.

QUICK DICTIONARY

emancipate: *ih-man-suh-payt*

To free. To free a slave from bondage or servitude.

Another example of the particle *al-fā* is if a customer approached a tailor and asked him to look at a cloth, asking, "Is this sufficient for my garment?" The tailor said it would be sufficient, so the customer instructed, "Then(*fa*) cut it". The tailor went ahead and cut the cloth but it turned out to be far less than the required amount. The tailor will be responsible for the mistake. This is because the instruction, "Then(*fa*) cut it" contains the particle *al-fā*, which implies that the instruction to cut was immediately after and based upon the tailor saying it would be sufficient. It is as though the customer is saying, 'if the cloth is enough for my garment *then* go ahead and cut it, otherwise don't'. Now that the cloth was insufficient, the tailor's cutting the cloth is not in accordance with the customer's instruction. As the tailor has acted on his own accord and not upon the customer's instruction, the tailor is responsible for the act. The outcome would be different if the customer had used the particle *al-wāw* or no particle at all, 'and cut it' or 'cut it'. These instructions do not show an immediate connection or explicit ordering after the advice of the tailor that the cloth will be sufficient. Rather, these latter two instructions are independent of the earlier conversation and stand-alone instructions from the customer and what follows is entirely the customer's responsibility.

An example of a similar nature is if one said, "I have sold this cloth on your behalf for ten, so then(*fa*) cut it". Without any further dialogue, the one instructed went ahead and cut the cloth. His act of cutting will be the completion of a transaction, because the meaning of the seller's words when expanded will be, 'if you accept the sale of this cloth for ten, go ahead and cut it'. When the buyer cuts the cloth, he shows that he accepts the proposal of the seller. The acceptance of the sale will be implicitly present in his act. With the presence of both a proposal from the seller and acceptance from the purchaser, the transaction is complete.

The function of *al-fā* is also evident if one said to his wife, "If you enter this house, then(*fa*) this house, you are divorced." For the divorce to occur the wife must first enter the first house and then immediately after that enter the second house. Should the wife enter the second house first and then the first house, the order would be lost and the divorce would not occur. Furthermore, should she enter the first house first but then only enter the second house after a period of time had lapsed, the divorce would still not occur because although the order is still intact, the two acts are not immediately together. For the divorce to occur promptness and order must both be established when the particle *al-fā* is used.

Text And Translation

فصل: الفاء للتعقيب مع الوصل ولهذا تستعمل في الأجزيةِ لما أنها تتعقب الشرط، قال أصحابنا رحمهم

الله: إذا قال: بعت منك هذا العبد بألف فقال الآخر: فهو حر يكون ذلك قبولا للبيع اقتضاء ويثبت العتق منه عقيب البيع بخلاف ما لو قال: وهو حر أو هو حر فإنه يكون ردا للبيع، وإذا قال للخياط: انظر إلى هذا الثوب أيكفيني قميصا فنظر فقال: نعم! فقال صاحب الثوب: فاقطعه فقطعه، فإذا هو لا يكفيه كان الخياط ضامنا؛ لأنه إنما أمره بالقطع عقيب الكفاية بخلاف ما لو قال: اقطعه أو واقطعه فقطعه فإنه لا يكون الخياط ضامنا، ولو قال: بعت منك هذا الثوب بعشرة فاقطعه فقطعه ولم يقل شيئا كان البيع تاما، ولو قال: إن دخلت هذه الدار فهذه الدار فأنت طالق فالشرط دخول الثانية عقيب دخول الأولى متصلا به حتى لو دخلت الثانية أولا أو آخرا لكنه بعد مدة لا يقع الطلاق

Chapter: The particle *al-fā* (الفاء) is for immediate continuation and for this reason it is used for a apodosis clause as it follows a condition. Our scholars, Allah Almighty have mercy on them, say: when one said: “I sell you this slave for one thousand”. The responder replies: “so(*fa*) he is free”. This will be acceptance of the purchase implicitly. The emancipation is established after the purchase. This is contrary to if he said: “and(*wa*) he is free” or “he is free”. This would be a rejection of the purchase. If one said to the tailor: “Look at this cloth, will it suffice for my tunic?” He looks and replies: “Yes”. The cloth-owner instructs: “so(*fa*) cut it,” and he cuts it. If it is not sufficient the tailor will be responsible, because his instruction followed the suitability. This is contrary to his instruction of: “cut it” or “and(*wa*) cut it”, and then he cuts it; as the tailor will not be responsible. If one said: “I buy this cloth from you for ten so(*fa*) cut it”, so he cuts it without saying a word, the transaction is complete. If one said: “If you enter this house then(*fa*) this house, you are divorced”, it is on the premise that she enters the second immediately after entering the first, such that if she entered the second one first or second but after a while, the divorce will not occur.

❖ ❖ ❖

Sometimes the particle *al-fā* is used to state and highlight a root cause. The cause could be before the particle or after it, as is the customary use of the word amongst the Arabs. However, there is a condition that validates placing the particle *al-fā* with the cause, which is that the cause must remain after the effect just as it was before it. It would not be correct to allow the particle *al-fā* to accompany the cause unless this condition is met. This condition shows how

QUICK DICTIONARY

apodosis: *uh-pod-uh-sis*
Consequence. The clause expressing the consequence in a conditional sentence.

the particle *al-fā* enables its accompanying words to immediately follow and continue. It is not possible for the effect to be before the cause, so it is established that the cause will bring about the effect but at the same time remain in place after the effect has come about. Bearing this in mind, an example of the particle *al-fā* being used for a cause is when a master says to his slave, "Give me a thousand, as(*fa*) you are free'. The slave will be free immediately. This is because in the example, the particle *al-fā* is appearing on the cause and the effect is before it. The cause is that 'you are free O slave', now give a thousand as a result and effect of your freedom. The cause is present before the effect as well as remaining thereafter, therefore freedom is present before the one thousand is given and even remains after it. In short, freedom is the cause, giving one thousand is the effect, and as the cause is before the effect, freedom will occur immediately when the master utters the words.

The reason we have diverted from using the literal meaning of the particle *al-fā* is that the literal is unfeasible as the sentence that precedes the particle is *al-jumla al-inshāiyya* and the sentence that follows it is *al-jumla al-khabarīya*. To join them with a conjunction is not correct, so we revert to the figurative meaning of stating the cause, *bayān ul-'illa*.

A second example of the particle *al-fā* being used to state and highlight a cause is when a Muslim says to a combatant, "Descend, as(*fa*) you are safe". In this case, the combatant is safe whether he descends or he does not. This is because the particle *al-fā* is not a conjunction because the sentence before it is *al-jumla al-inshāiyya* and the sentence after it is *al-jumla al-khabarīya*. Having a conjunction between two different types of sentence is not permitted. As the particle is not in its literal meaning the metaphorical meaning is taken, which is that it is to state the cause. The meaning of the sentence will be, 'due to the cause of your safety, you should descend'. The safety is present whether the individual descends or he does not.

To reiterate the point, the particle *al-fā* may appear with the cause or with the effect. The previous examples show the particle *al-fā* with the cause. An example for the particle appearing with the effect are taken from the work of Imam Muḥammad رحمه الله, al-Jāmi' al-Kabīr. If a man appointed another as his representative in granting divorce saying, "My wife's matter is in your hands, so(*fa*) divorce her", the particle *al-fā* is for *bayān ul-'illa* because the sentence before the particle is *al-jumla al-khabarīya* and the sentence following it is *al-*

QUICK TERMS

بيان العلة: *bayan ul-'illa*

Expressing the means. A statement that identifies the root cause of an effect.

QUICK ARABIC

التفويض: *at-tafwīḍ*

To empower. To authorise by delegating a responsibility to another.

QUICK GRAMMAR

جملة إنشائية: *jumla inshāīya*

Non-informative sentence. A sentence that does not permit the issuer to be categorised as either a liar or truthful.

جملة خبرية: *jumla khabarīya*

Informative sentence. A sentence that permits the issuer to be categorised as either a liar or truthful.

QUICK REFERENCE

الجامع الكبير: *al-jāmi' al-kabīr*

The Great Collection. A collection of narrations that Imam Muḥammad ash-Shaybānī رحمه الله compiled directly from Imam Abū Ḥanīfa رحمه الله.

jumla al-inshāiyya. The two differing sentence structures cannot be merely conjoined with *al-fā*, so the literal meaning of the particle is abandoned. This means the cause in the sentence is the 'matter is in your hands' and the effect is 'divorce'. The sentence effectively says 'give my wife a divorce because I have given you the choice'. If the representative gives his wife a single divorce in the same sitting, one irrevocable divorce will occur. The reason for adding the condition of 'in the same sitting' is that this is *at-tafwīḍ*, delegation of responsibility. *at-Tafwīḍ* is only permitted in the same setting and so if the sitting changes, the instruction no longer remains. The divorce issued will be irrevocable because the instructor's words, "matter is in your hand", is al-kināya. Using such words to issue a divorce results in an irrevocable divorce.

In the instruction, the words "so divorce her", is not an independent stand-alone instruction. Two divorces will not occur once the representative issues a divorce as well as the instruction of the husband. Rather, what is meant by this part of the instruction is the same divorce that the representative is given the choice for with the words "matter is in your hands". Had the particle *al-fā* taken its literal meaning, then no doubt two divorces would have been issued.

Compare the aforementioned to if a husband says, "Divorce her, as(*fa*) I have placed her matter in your hands", as only one revocable divorce will occur if the representative gives a divorce in the same sitting. This is because the instruction to divorce is explicit and not the figurative, al-kināya. This means that the delegation of responsibility, *at-tafwīḍ*, is in explicit form so the resulting divorce will be revocable. The words "I have placed her matter in your hands" will be the explanation and further details of the previously stated divorce.

If a husband said to someone, "Divorce her, and(*wa*) I have placed her matter in your hands", and the representative gave the divorce in the same sitting, two divorces will be established and both will be irrevocable. There are two divorces issued because the particle *al-wāw* does not have the meaning of highlighting a cause like the particle *al*-fā, and so the particle will function literally. This means both parts are independent and the instruction is to give two divorces, one derived from the statement "Divorce her" and the second derived from, "I have placed her matter in your hands". Once the representative says he has divorced her, he executes both divorces that he has been made representative for. The first part of the statement is explicit so the resulting

QUICK TERMS

الكناية: *al-kināya*

The concealed. A word or phrase that has a concealed and hidden meaning. A metaphor.

QUICK ARABIC

التفويض: *at-tafwīḍ*

To empower. To authorise by delegating a responsibility to another.

divorce is revocable, and the second part is figurative, so the resulting divorce is irrevocable. However, when a revocable and an irrevocable divorce are established together, they both become irrevocable. This happens because the revocable divorce requires the possibility of the husband returning to the wife whilst the irrevocable divorce disallows the exact same thing. When applying them together, the irrevocable will always be dominant as it expresses the real purpose of issuing the divorce, which is to form a separation. A true separation can only occur if the irrevocable overrides the revocable divorce, thus both issuances become irrevocable.

Similarly, if a husband says, "Divorce her, and(*wa*) separate her", or, "Separate her and(*wa*) divorce her", and the representative gives the divorce in the very same sitting, in both cases two irrevocable divorces will be established. This is because the particle *al-wāw* is for conjoining two independent sentences and thus two divorces. When the representative executes the command, he executes both divorces. As one of the sentences issued by the husband is al-kināya, "separate her", it results in an irrevocable divorce. Though the "divorce her" instruction is explicit and results in a revocable divorce, when combined with an irrevocable divorce, both divorces become irrevocable. Thus, we concluded that the representative has issued two irrevocable divorces.

Text And Translation

وقد يكون الفاء لبيان العلة، مثاله إذا قال لعبده: أد إلي ألفا فأنت حر كان العبد حرا في الحال وإن لم يؤد شيئا، ولو قال للحربي انزل فأنت آمن كان آمنا وإن لم ينزل، وفي "الجامع" ما إذا قال: أمر امرأتي بيدك فطلقها فطلقها في المجلس طلقت تطليقة بائنة ولا يكون الثاني توكيلا بطلاق غير الأول فصار كأنه قال: طلقها بسبب أن أمرها بيدك، ولو قال: طلقها فجعلت أمرها بيدك فطلقها في المجلس طلقت تطليقة رجعية، ولو قال: طلقها وجعلت أمرها بيدك وطلقها في المجلس وقعت تطليقتان

Sometimes the particle *al-fā* is to express the root cause. An example of it is if one said to his slave: “Give me a thousand as(*fa*) you are free”, he is immediately free even if he has not given anything. If one said to a combatant: “Descend as(*fa*) you are protected,” he will be protected even if he does not descend. In al-Jāmi' it says that if one said: “My wife's matter is in your hands so(*fa*) divorce her”, so he divorces her on the same occasion, one irrevocable divorce will occur. The second (sentence) will not be permission to divorce other than the first. It is as though he said: "Divorce her as her matter is in your hands". If one said: "Divorce her so(*fa*) I have put her matter in your hands'. So he divorces her on the same occasion. She will have one revocable divorce. If one said: "Divorce her and(*wa*) her matter is in your hands", and he divorced her on the same occasion, she will have two divorces.

❖ ❖ ❖

Based on the principle that the particle *al-fā* can accompany both the cause and effect, our scholars have said that when a married slave-girl is freed, she has the freedom to choose to continue or to annul her previous marriage with her husband whether he is a slave or freeman. The evidence for this is that the blessed Messenger ﷺ said to the Companion Barīra رضي الله عنها after her emancipation, "You own your body, so(*fa*) you choose." In this narration the Legislator ﷺ, has given Barīra رضي الله عنها a choice that is the effect, and the cause is her emancipation. The particle *al-fā* is accompanying the effect, which means that when a married slave-girl is in ownership of herself, the cause, she will have the choice to annul her marriage, the effect. This will hold true irrespective of whether her husband is a slave or freeman himself. Imam ash-Shāfa'īy رحمه الله differs in this regard. He says if the husband is a slave, the married former slave-girl has a choice to annul the marriage, but if the husband is a freeman, she does not have this choice.

The aforementioned tradition, "so(*fa*) you choose", contains a particle to express the cause. There are a number of implications of this usage when put into practice. It implies that the number of allowable divorces is dependent upon the status of the woman and not the status of the husband. Bear in mind that the number of allowable divorces is reduced in servitude, where a freeman can give up to three divorces and a slave can issue only two. This is agreed upon by all jurists, however, disagreement arises in whether the cause of this reduction is due to the status of the man or the status of the woman. The Aḥnāf maintain that the determining factor is the status of the woman and Imam ash-Shāfa'īy رحمه الله considers the status of the man. According to the Aḥnāf, if the wife is a slave the husband has the right to issue two divorces and if the wife is a free woman, he has the right to issue up to three divorces. The husband's own status is not taken into consideration. Imam ash-Shāfa'īy رحمه الله says that if the husband is free, he can issue three divorces and if he is a slave, he can issue just two. The difference is highlighted in a case where a freeman has a slave wife. The Aḥnāf

حديث

عن عائشة رضي الله عنها في قصة بريرة رضي الله عنها قالت كان زوجها عبدا فخيرها رسول الله ﷺ فاختارت نفسها ولو كان حرا لم يخيرها.

عليه الصلوة والسلام

(سنن أبي داوود: 2233)

say there is a right to issue two divorces due to the status of the woman, and Imam a<u>sh</u>-<u>Sh</u>āfa'īy ﷺ says there is a right to issue three divorces due to the status of the man. If the case were that the husband is a slave and the wife is free, the reverse would be true for both schools.

The view of the Aḥnāf is derived from the aforementioned tradition in that it is agreed by all that the right over a married slave-girl is in the ownership of the husband, and the act of a master freeing the slave-girl does not diminish that ownership. If the ownership were to diminish, the slave-girl would not even have the choice to continue the marriage. Rather a new marriage contract would be required. As no one has stated that a marriage renewal is required in such a case, it is clear that all jurists agree that merely by the freedom of the slave-girl, the ownership of the husband remains. What follows is that through the freedom of the slave-girl wife, the ownership of the husband has increased from the right of two divorces to three divorces. This has an impact on the stake of the wife who entered the marriage contract with the knowledge that the husband will only have the right of two divorces, but the increase means that she is set to take a loss. It is therefore necessary to give her a choice either to accept this loss or to annul it. Therefore, if she wishes she may continue the marriage and should she wish, she can annul it. In short, the aforementioned tradition is showing that the number of divorces allowed is dependent upon the status of the woman and not upon the status of the man, in terms of emancipation and serfdom.

Text And Translation

وعلى هذا قال أصحابنا إذا أعتقت الأمة المنكوحة ثبت لها الخيار سواء كان زوجها عبدا أو حرا؛ لأن قوله عليه السلام لبريرة: حين أعتقت: ملكت بضعك فاختاري، أثبت الخيار لها بسبب ملكها بضعها بالعتق، وهذا المعنى لا يتفاوت بين كون الزوج عبدا أو حرا، ويتفرع منه مسئلة اعتبار الطلاق بالنساء فإن بضع الأمة المنكوحة ملك الزوج ولم يزل عن ملكه بعتقها فدعت الضرورة إلى القول بازدياد الملك بعتقها حتى يثبت له الملك في الزيادة ويكون ذلك سببا لثبوت الخيار لها، وازدياد ملك البضع بعتقها معنى مسئلة اعتبار الطلاق بالنساء، فيدار حكم مالكية الثلاث على عتق الزوجة دون عتق الزوج كما هو مذهب الشافعي رحمه الله تعالى.

Based on this our jurists have said: when a married slave-girl is emancipated, she has a choice, irrespective of whether her husband is a slave or a freeman. This is because he, peace and blessings be upon him, said to Barīra when she was freed: "You own your self, so choose". Her choice is established due to her owning her self from emancipation. This status is indifferent to the husband being a slave or a freeman. Branching from this is the problem of divorce based on the women. The married slave-girl's private parts are in the ownership of the husband. Despite her freedom his ownership remains in that , so there is a need to increase his ownership due to her freedom so that he may have a right in the added status. This is the cause of her right of choice. The increase in ownership of the private parts due to her emancipation is what is meant by the problem of divorce initiated by women. So the ruling on owning all three depends on the freedom of the wife and not the freedom of the husband, as is the school of ash-Shāfa'īy, Allah Almighty have mercy on him.

❖ ❖ ❖

1.9.3 Thumma

The third particle from the connectors is *thumma*. The particle is for mitigation by reducing the impact of an act by delaying it and allowing a respite. So, if one was to say, "Zayd and then (*thumma*) 'Amar came", it means there is a delay and separation between the arrivals of both Zayd and 'Amar, even though both are together in undertaking the act. All of our jurists agree that this is the correct function of the particle *thumma*, however they disagree if the function is to be enforced when the word is uttered or when the content of the words occur. Imam Abū Ḥanīfa holds that the mitigation occurs in both the words and their application, whereas the Ṣāḥibayn regard the mitigation only upon occurrence. The difference in the two approaches is highlighted in cases such as if one was to say to his wife with whom he had not previously consummated the marriage, "Should you enter the house, (*fa*)you are divorced, then(*thumma*) divorced, and then(*thumma*) divorced." According to Imam Abū Ḥanīfa the first divorce will be connected to entering the house, the second will occur immediately and the third will be void. This is because the first is immediately connected to entering the house as a conditional sentence, so without entering the house, the first divorce will not occur. The second and third divorces are connected to this sentence through the particle *thumma*. Imam Abū Ḥanīfa considers this to be for mitigation in words, which means it is as though the

QUICK TERMS

صاحبين: *ṣāḥibayn*

The two colleagues. Imams Abū Yūsuf and Muḥammad

QUICK ARABIC

العدة: *al-'idda*

The term. The three-month period after a divorce.

QUICK DICTIONARY

emancipate: *ih-man-suh-payt*

To free. To free a slave from bondage and servitude.

serfdom: *serf-dom*

In slavery. A person in the condition of being the property of another.

person stopped after the first sentence and then waited before delivering the second sentence, which simply says, 'you are divorced', therefore this is not connected to the condition of entering the house and thus occurs immediately. The third divorce is void because the woman in question has not consummated the marriage with her husband and is only subject to one divorce which will be irrevocable and she does not have to wait for *al-'idda* waiting period either. That irrevocable divorce was issued by the second divorce, so she now is not subject to any more divorces, therefore the third divorce is void. Ṣāḥibayn say that all three divorces are connected to the condition of entering the house. Once the woman enters the house, the words are applied, all three divorces will occur in order and with mitigation. So, the first will be a valid irrevocable divorce as the marriage was not consummated and the wife was subject to just one divorce. The second and third divorces will be void as the wife is not subject to them. The reason Ṣāḥibayn are applying these divorces upon the wife entering the house and not when the words are uttered is because they believe the particle *thumma* only mitigates upon occurrence of the content of the words. All three jurists agree that one divorce has occurred but how it occurs is different. Imam Abū Ḥanīfa ﷺ has said it is the second divorce when the words are said, and Ṣāḥibayn say it is the first divorce but only when the condition is actually triggered by the wife entering the house.

A second example, which highlights the difference of opinion, is if the husband was to leave the conditional part of the sentence to the end by saying, "You are divorced, then(*thumma*) divorced, and then(*thumma*) divorced if you enter the house". In this example, both opinions state that one divorce will occur. Imam Abū Ḥanīfa ﷺ says it will be the first one and it will take effect immediately without entering any house, whilst the second and third divorces will be void. This is because the particle *thumma* is for mitigation and delay in both words and occurrence according to him. It is as though the sentence is broken into separate parts. The husband has said 'you are divorced' and then became silent. He then added 'you are divorced' and then became silent. Finally, he added, 'you are divorced if you enter the house'. This means the first divorce will occur immediately as it is unconnected to the condition and the second and third divorces will be void because the marriage is not consummated and she is only subject to one allowable divorce. Ṣāḥibayn also say the first divorce will occur but only when the woman enters the house. This is because they do not allow for mitigation in the words when they are uttered, rather they factor it in upon the occurrence of the contents of the words. This means at the point of utterance all three divorces are connected to the condition of entering the house, and once the entrance has occurred, they will come into effect in order. Therefore, the first divorce will occur upon entering and the latter two will be void because the woman in question is only subject to one allowable divorce.

A third and final example to highlight the two different opinions is if the marriage has been consummated and the wife is subject to all three divorces. If the condition was brought to the fore by the husband, such that he said, "If you enter the house (*fa*)you are divorced, then(*thumma*) divorced, and then(*thumma*) divorced", Imam Abū Ḥanīfa says the first will be deferred to the entering but the latter two will occur immediately. This is because the particle *thumma* has mitigated and separated the latter two from the condition and so they are independent and occur immediately. The woman is subject to three divorces, so two of them can and will occur.

In the aforementioned scenario if the condition was mentioned at the end, such that the husband said, "You are divorced, then(*thumma*) you are divorced and then(*thumma*) you are divorced if you enter the house', the first and second divorce will occur immediately and the third will be deferred to the entering. This is because the particle *thumma* is causing the sentence to mitigate and separate. So, the first and second part is not connected to the condition and is an issuance of two separate divorces. These will occur immediately. The final one connected to the condition will only occur if the wife enters the house. This is according to Imam Abū Ḥanīfa. Ṣāḥibayn will say that the particle *thumma* does not allow for mitigation in the words but will allow it only when the event occurs, so all three divorces are deferred to entering the house. Once the entering occurs, all three divorces will be enforced in order.

QUICK TERMS

صاحبين: *ṣāḥibayn*

The two colleagues. Imams Abū Yūsuf and Muḥammad

Text And Translation

فصل: ثم للتراخي لكنه عند أبي حنيفة يفيد التراخي في اللفظ والحكم وعندهما يفيد التراخي في الحكم، وبيانه فيما إذا قال لغير المدخول بها: إن دخلت الدار فأنت طالق ثم طالق ثم طالق فعنده يتعلق الأولى بالدخول وتقع الثانية في الحال ولغت الثالثة وعندهما يتعلق الكل بالدخول، ثم عند الدخول يظهر الترتيب فلا يقع إلا واحدة، ولو قال: أنت طالق ثم طالق ثم طالق إن دخلت الدار فعند أبي حنيفة وقعت الأولى في الحال ولغت الثانية والثالثة، وعندهما يقع الواحدة عند الدخول لما ذكرنا وإن كانت

المرأة مدخولا بها، فإن قدم الشرط تعلقت الأولى بالدخول ويقع ثنتان في الحال عند أبي حنيفة وإن أخر الشرط وقع ثنتان في الحال وتعلقت الثالثة بالدخول وعندهما يتعلق الكل بالدخول في الفصلين

Chapter: the particle *thumma* (ثُمَّ) is for mitigation. However, according to Imam Abū Ḥanīfa it mitigates in both word and ruling, and according to the Two Colleagues it mitigates in the ruling. Its explanation is when one says to his wife in an unconsummated marriage: "If you enter the house, you are divorced, then(*thumma*) divorced, then(*thumma*) divorced". According to him the first will be connected to the entrance, the second will occur instantly and the third will be void. According to them both, all will be connected to the entrance; then when there is entrance the order will become apparent so only one will occur. If one said: "You are divorced, then(*thumma*) divorced, then(*thumma*) divorced, if you enter the house", according to Imam Abū Ḥanīfa the first will occur instantly, and the second and third will be void. According to the Two Colleagues the first will occur upon entrance because of what we mentioned. If the woman is in a consummated marriage, bringing the condition first will connect the first to the entrance, and the two will occur instantly according to Imam Abū Ḥanīfa. Placing the condition at the end will establish two instantly and the third will be connected to the entrance. According to the Two Colleagues, all will occur upon entrance in both scenarios.

❖ ❖ ❖

1.9.4 *Bal*

The fourth particle from the connectors is *bal*. It is used for correcting an error in what precedes the particle by replacing it with what follows it. The particle can act as a connector for both positive and negative sentences. It is as though one says the first part of the sentence and realises that that was not what was meant to be communicated. So simply by adding the particle *bal* the correct information is then relayed with an aim to replace what came before the particle. For example, if one said, "Zayd helped, rather(bal) 'Amar did. The person only wanted to communicate that 'Amar helped, and the mention of Zayd was a mistake. This rule only applies when it is possible to take back a statement. If a statement does not have the capacity to be replaced, such as a non-informative, *al-inshā*, sentence, the particle *bal* will act as a mere connector and lose the function of replacing what preceded it. Both the preceding and the

QUICK GRAMMAR

جملة إنشائية: *jumla inshāīya*

Non-informative sentence. A sentence that does not permit the issuer to be categorised as either a liar or truthful.

proceeding parts will be considered independent and will be merely joined together in utterance. As an example, if a husband says to a wife with whom the marriage has not yet been consummated, "You are divorced once, rather(*bal*) twice", only one divorce will occur. This is because his words, 'rather twice', have replaced his word, 'once', and as the wife is only subject to one divorce, because the marriage has not been consummated, one irrevocable divorce will occur. She is not a subject to more than one divorce, so all additional instances of divorce will be void. If the case in question occurs with a wife with whom the marriage has been consummated, all three divorces mentioned will occur. This is because the first divorce issued cannot be repealed once it has been issued, so when the husband adds the words after the particle *bal*, the effect is that the single divorce is conjoined to two further divorces. As the wife in question is subject to three possible divorces and all three have been issued, they will all be enacted.

The aforementioned case of divorce is very different to a case of confession. By saying to a woman with whom a marriage has been consummated, "You are divorced once, rather(*bal*) twice", all three divorces will occur, but confessing, "I owe so-and-so one thousand, rather(*bal*) two thousand", will not leave the individual liable for three thousand. The individual will owe just two thousand. Imam Zufar رحمه الله disagrees with this and states that such a confession will result in a liability of three thousand.

Our evidence for not owing three thousand is that the particle *bal* is designated to replace the error made earlier. This is not allowed in a confession because by its very nature a confession is admitting something, but in the very same sentence, one cannot be making an error, as that will render it a non-confession. This will mean that we must keep the one thousand as a confession. The part after the particle must now be independent and at the same time hold true too, as it also forms part of the confession. This is achieved by extending a thousand upon the first confessed thousand and so the independent sentence also holds true. The net result will be that this is a confession of one thousand owed, with an additional one thousand confessed too. In total, this will be two thousand. Imam Zufar رحمه الله likens this case to that of the case of the divorces earlier. He says that just as in that case the one thousand will be conjoined with a further two thousand, and a total of three thousand will be owed.

QUICK GRAMMAR

جملة إنشائية: *jumla inshāīya*

Non-informative sentence. A sentence that does not permit the issuer to be categorised as either a liar or truthful.

Furthermore, the case of the confession is also different to the example of the divorces issued to a wife with whom the marriage was not consummated. In the confession, we state that two thousand becomes necessary but, in the divorces, we do not say that two divorces occur. The difference is that issuing a divorce is a non-informative *al-inshā* sentence, which brings a previously non-existent matter to the realm of existence. There was no divorce before the utterance of these words, and once they were uttered, the divorce came into being, whereas the confession is an informative *al-khabar* sentence. This is relaying information that was already in existence prior to the words. The words merely validate a previously existing matter. It is possible for the one confessing to say I lied and the truth is like this. In short, it is possible to negate a lie and replace it with a truth when informing, but in *al-inshā,* as there is no element of error, and so one is unable to replace it with a correction. Once one has brought something into existence, it cannot return to non-existence. One can make an error when informing but not otherwise, so when an error is possible its correction is also possible but when there is no room for error, there is no correction either.

We say that in the confession, the confessor has given information so we are able to say he made a mistake by saying 'I owe one thousand' and made up the error by adding 'rather two thousand'. This resulted in two thousand becoming necessary. As the case of the divorces is non-informative, we have said that when the husband says 'you are divorced once' to the wife with whom the marriage is not consummated, one divorce occurs instantly. His words are in fact bringing about the existence of a divorce. This cannot be corrected, even if it is uttered by mistake. Now, when he adds 'rather twice', it will be void in this case as the wife is only subject to one divorce because her marriage is not consummated. It is worth noting that if a divorce is delivered in a manner where it becomes informative, such that one says, "I have divorced you once yesterday, rather(*bal*) twice", this will be the issuance of two divorces. This is exactly as we stated for the case of the confession above.

QUICK GRAMMAR

جملة خبرية: *jumla khabarīya*

Informative sentence. A sentence that permits the issuer to be categorised as either a liar or truthful.

Text And Translation

فصل: بل لتدارك الغلط بإقامة الثاني مقام الأول فإذا قال لغير المدخول بها: أنت طالق واحدة لا بل ثنتين وقعت واحدة؛ لأن قوله: لا بل ثنتين رجوع عن الأول بإقامة الثاني مقام الأول ولم يصح رجوعه

فيقع الأول فلا يبقى المحل عند قوله: ثنتين ولو كانت مدخولا بها يقع الثلاث، وهذا بخلاف ما لو قال: لفلان علي ألف لا بل ألفان حيث لا يجب ثلاثة آلاف عندنا، وقال زفر: يجب ثلاثة آلاف؛ لأن حقيقة اللفظ لتدارك الغلط بإثبات الثاني مقام الأول ولم يصح عنه إبطال الأول فيجب تصحيح الثاني مع بقاء الأول وذلك بطريق زيادة الألف على الألف الأول، بخلاف قوله: أنت طالق واحدة لا بل ثنتين؛ لأنّ هذا إنشاء وذلك إخبار والغلط إنما يكون في الإخبار دون الإنشاء فأمكن تصحيح اللفظ بتدارك الغلط في الإقرار دون الطلاق حتى لو كان الطلاق بطريق الإخبار بأن قال: كنت طلقتك أمس واحدة لا بل ثنتين يقع ثنتانِ لما ذكرنا

Chapter: The particle *bal* (بل) is to retract an error, by replacing the first with the second. So, if one said to her in an unconsummated marriage: "You are divorced once, no rather(*bal*) twice", one divorce would occur. This is because his words: 'no rather twice' is a retraction from the first by placing the second in the place of the first. However, his retraction is not valid so one will occur. Then she will no longer be a subject when he says: 'twice'. If the marriage is consummated all three would occur. This is different to if one said to another: "I owe a thousand, no rather(*bal*) two thousand", because three thousand will not be necessary according to us. Imam Zufar says: three thousand are necessary because the reality of the words is to retract the mistake by replacing the first by the second, and the annulling of the first is not permitted by him. So the second is established whilst the first remains by adding a thousand to the first thousand. This is contrary to one saying: "You are divorced once, no rather(*bal*) twice", as this is a non-informative statement and that is an informative statement. A mistake occurs in a informative and not in the non-informative, so it is possible to correct the words by retracting the mistake in a confession and not in divorce. However, if the divorce takes the form of the informative by one saying: "I divorced you once yesterday, no rather(*bal*) twice", two would occur because of what we have stated.

❖ ❖ ❖

1.9.5 Lākin

The fifth particle from the conjunctions is *lākin* and it functions just like the verb-like particle *lākinna.* The particle comes to clarify a possible preceding misconception and will always appear after a negation. Appearing after a negation makes the particle *lākin* different to the previously discussed particle *bal*, which can appear after negative or positive sentences. Furthermore, the function of *lākin* is that it only concerns the part that proceeds it and does not look to negate what precedes it. Rather the negation of the part of the sentence that comes before *lākin* is clearly visible in the words in the form of a particle of negation; the negation is not because of the particle *lākin*. The particle *bal* on the other hand, is in itself a particle of negation for what comes before it and a particle of establishing what comes after it. The particle *lākin* will act as a connector only when the two parts connected to it are actually beside each other, as well as the fact that the negation concerns one thing whilst the positive aspect concerns a different thing. If either of these conditions is missing, the two parts will be independent of each other and unconnected.

An example of the two parts, before and after, *lākin* being beside each other is what Imam Muḥammad رحمه الله says in al-Jāmi' al-Kabīr that should one confess, "I owe so-and-so one thousand as a loan," repayment, and so-and-so replies, "No, but(*lākin*) it was usurped". In such a case, the confession will be upheld and the one thousand will be payable. This is because the one who is owed says his statement, 'No, but(*lākin*) it was usurped', with the negative 'no' immediately beside the positive 'it was usurped', where the negation concerns the loan and the affirmation concerns usurping. Therefore, the two conditions are met. The statement of the one owed is coherent because both parts of his statement, before and after the particle *lākin*, are beside each other and the positive and negative parts concern two different matters. This means that both the confessor and the one confessed for, are agreeing that one thousand is owed, but they disagree with the cause of why it is owed. The confessor says it was a loan and the one owed says it was usurped. The negation in the sentence of the one owed is not a denial of being owed one thousand, it is a denial for the reason given for it. So, if there is no dispute in what is owed, the confession will stand and the money will be owed.

If one was to confess, "I owe so-and-so one thousand as payment of this slave-girl", to which so-and-so replied, "No, the slave-girl is yours, but(*lākin*) you do owe me one thousand". This will be an acknowledgment of the confession of owing one thousand and the money will become necessary on the confessor. This is because the one owed is only disputing the cause and not the actual amount owed. As both parties agree to the amount, it is undisputed and is due.

QUICK DICTIONARY

Usurp: *you-zurp*

To seize. To hold or use something by force without legal right or authority.

QUICK REFERENCE

الجامع الكبير: *al-jāmi' al-kabīr*

The Great Collection. A collection of narrations that Imam Muḥammad ash-Shaybānī رحمه الله compiled directly from Imam Abū Ḥanīfa رحمه الله.

فصل: لكن للاستدراك بعد النفي فيكون موجبه إثبات ما بعده فأما نفي ما قبله فثابت بدليله والعطف بهذه الكلمة إنما يتحقق عند اتساق الكلام فإن كان الكلام متسقا يتعلق النفي بالإثبات الذي بعده وإلا فهو مستأنف، مثاله ما ذكره مُحَمَّد عليه الرحمة في "الجامع": إذا قال: لفلان علي ألف قرض فقال فلان: لا ولكنه غصب لزمه المال؛ لأن الكلام متسق فظهر أن النفي كان في السبب دون نفس المال، وكذلك لو قال: لفلان علي ألف من ثمن هذه الجارية فقال فلان: لا، الجارية جاريتك ولكن لي عليك ألفا يلزمه المال فظهر أن النفي كان في السبب لا في أصل المال

Chapter: the particle *lākin* (لكن) is for correction after a negation. It necessitates the affirmation of what proceeds it. As for the negation of what preceded it, it is self evident. Using the particle as a connector is when the statement is conjoined. If the statement is conjoined the negation is connected to the affirmation otherwise it is a new sentence. An example of it is as Imam Muḥammad, mercy be on him, mentioned in al-Jāmi': if one said: "I owe so-and-so one thousand as a loan", and that individual says: "no, rather(*lākin*) it was usurped", the money will be necessary. This is because the statements are conjoined, so it is clear that the negation concerns the cause and not the actual amount. Similarly, if one said: "I owe so-and-so one thousand for this slave girl", but that individual says: "no, the slave-girl is yours but(*lākin*) you owe me one thousand". The money will be owed as it is clear that the negation is in the cause and not in the money itself.

❖ ❖ ❖

When in possession of a slave, one announced, "This belongs to so-and-so", and so-and-so said, "He's never been mine, but(*lākin*) he belongs to another". If this second statement was stated together without separation between what comes before the particle *lākin* and what follows it, the statement is valid, and it means the negation for his personal ownership and the establishment of ownership is for another individual. There is no contradiction in this and so the owner of the slave will be the other individual. Had this statement been separated, such that he first said, "He's never been mine", and then fallen silent, only to add later, "But(*lākin*) he belongs to another", it will be considered a separate sentence. This means he is denying any knowledge of ownership and effectively disputing the words of the one who claimed the slave to be his. Furthermore, he is providing an alternative to the suggestion of the one who had possession of the slave. This will be a rejection of the claim of the first individual and a challenge against his word. The statement following the silence, "But(*lākin*) he belongs to another", is unconnected to the first part and is independent. Its purpose is to establish evidence against the one who had possession of the slave by opposing his claim and providing evidence that the slave is not mine but belongs to another individual. This would mean that the one who made the claim is lying that it belongs to me. The slave will be treated as though he belongs to the one in whose possession the slave was found and ownership will not transfer by mere claims.

An important matter to note in the construct of the particle *lākin* is that it should not negate and establish the same thing. As an example, if a slave-girl was to marry without the consent of her master and agree to a bridal gift of one hundred dirham, whilst the master said, "I don't permit the marriage for one hundred but(*lākin*) for one hundred and fifty I do", it will invalidate the marriage conducted by the slave-girl. This is because the statement of the master is not coherent, as coherency is achieved by negating a different thing to the thing that is established. Here, the negation is for the marriage and immediately after the particle, the establishment is of the same marriage too. It is not permitted for both of these opposites to become part of one sentence. This means the condition has not been fulfilled and as it is not fulfilled, the two parts of the sentence are not connected. The two parts are considered independent and separate sentences. Thus, the words of the master now indicate that he has refused the marriage with the first part, "I don't permit the marriage for one hundred", and with the second part, "But for one hundred and fifty, I do", is a new proposal for a marriage on behalf of the slave-girl. For a marriage to be finalised there must be a proposal and acceptance. As no new acceptance is present with just the master's words, there is no marriage established. However, with this new proposal a new acceptance can be sought.

Similarly, if the master had used alternative words such as, "I don't accept it, but(*lākin*) I accept it if you increase fifty upon the one hundred", the marriage contract of the slave-girl is void. This is because the first part before the particle *lākin* cancelled the previous marriage and the second part following the particle *lākin* is a new proposal. It will be upon the groom-to-be to accept or reject this. Similar to the previous example, in this example the negation concerns the same thing that is then established; therefore, the statement is said to be incoherent and unconnected. Furthermore, it cannot even be considered as an explanation in this case because of the directly opposing structures of 'I don't accept it' and ' but I accept it'. The second part is not connected nor an explanation of the first part, so it is independent and unrelated to the first part. Thus, this new proposal from the master will require an acceptance to form a new marriage contract.

Text And Translation

ولو كان في يده عبد فقال: هذا لفلان، فقال فلان: ما كان لي قط ولكنه لفلان فإن وصل الكلام كان العبد للمقر له الثاني؛ لأن النفي يتعلق بالإثبات وإن فصل كان العبد للمقر الأول فيكون قول المقر له ردا للإقرار، ولو أن أمة تزوجت نفسها بغير إذن مولاها بمائة درهم فقال المولى: لا أجيز العقد بمائة درهم ولكن أجيزه بمائة وخمسين بطل العقد؛ لأن الكلام غير متسق فإن نفي الإجازة وإثباتها بعينها لا يتحقق فكان قوله: لكن أجيزه إثباته بعد رد العقد، وكذلك لو قال: لا أجيزه ولكن أجيزه إن زدتني خمسين على المائة يكون فسخا للنكاح لعدم احتمال البيان؛ لأن من شرطه الاتساق ولا اتساق

If one was in possession of a slave and he said: "This belongs to so-and-so", that person says: "He has never been mine rather(*lākin*) it's another's"; so if the statements were conjoined the salve would belong to the second implicated person, as the negation is connected to the affirmation. Had it been delayed, the slave would belong to the first implicated person because the statement of the second-implicated would be a refusal of the confession. If a slave-girl married herself without the permission of her master for one hundred dirham and the master said: "I do not permit the contract for one hundred dirham but(*lākin*) I permit it for one hundred and fifty", the contract will be void. This is because the statement is not conjoined as refusing permission and accepting it simultaneously cannot occur. So him saying: "but(*lākin*) I permit it", is acceptance after refusing the contract. It is the same had he said: "I don't accept it but(*lākin*) I accept it if you add fifty to the one hundred". This would annul the marriage as there is no scope for explanations. A condition of it is conjunction and there is not a conjunction.

❖❖❖

The sixth particle from the connectors is the particle *aw*. The function of the particle is to say that the matter at hand concerns one of two mentioned things, but without specifying which one. The choice will be left with the originator of the words to indicate which one is selected. The general view of linguists and jurists is that the particle *aw* can connect between two words, so one can be selected, or it can connect between sentences, so one of the sentences is to be enforced.

An example is if a master points to two of his slaves and says, "This one or(*aw*) this one is free". This is effectively the master saying 'one of them is free' and it will be the master's choice to pinpoint which one. Once the master has informed of the free one, the freedom will shift in his favour from the other. Before this choice is stated neither will be free and emancipation will only commence after a clear choice is made.

Another example of the particle *aw* offering a choice is if someone appointed two agents to sell his slave saying, "I appoint him or(*aw*) him to sell this slave". In this case, one of the two will be the agent. Before the master makes the choice clear, both agents have a right to act on his behalf. However, only one of them will prevail in securing the agency, such that if the sold slave happens to be acquired by the same master later, the other agent no longer has any agency to sell based on that previous instruction.

Imam Zufar رحمه الله says that structurally two sentences, one regarding divorce and the other an oath of silence, are the same and will yield a similar verdict. The statement of divorce is if one says to his three wives, "This one is divorced or this one, and this one". One of the first two wives is divorced, along with the third wife. The oath of silence is said regarding three men, "I will not speak to this one or this one, and this one". By speaking to one of the first two and the third one, the vow will be broken. The Three Imams رحمهم الله say that the two cases are not similar as Imam Zufar رحمه الله has stated. The divorce case is as stated; however, the oath will be violated if the individual speaks to the first man only. It is also violated if he speaks to both the second and third man, but it will not be violated by speaking to just one of the second or third men.

The Three Imams رحمهم الله substantiate their position by stating that the particle *aw* requires a choice between two mentioned things, whilst the choice

QUICK TERMS

الأئمة الثلاثة: *al-aimma ath-thalātha*

The three imams. The three grand Ḥanafī jurists, Imams Abū Ḥanīfa رحمه الله, Abū Yūsuf رحمه الله and Muḥammad رحمه الله

QUICK DICTIONARY

emancipate: *ih-man-suh-payt*

To free. To free a slave from bondage and servitude.

is as yet undetermined. An undetermined thing is in the category of being an indefinite, *an-nakira*, article. When an indefinite article is subject to a negation, *an-nafī*, it brings about a generality, *al-'umūm*, in individuals. This means that in the said case each individual is subject to the negation individually. Therefore, if he speaks to the first man, he violates the vow, and if he speaks to both the latter two, he also violates the vow. This reflects the generality of the negation. However, if he speaks to just one of the latter two only, the vow remains intact. The explanation of Imam Zufar ﷺ does not allow this general negation as he says only one of the first two is negated along with the third. This implies that one of the first is not negated and thus the generality of the structure is ignored, even though an indefinite article after a negation should be general. The Three Jurists ﷺ say that it is sufficient for the man to have broken his oath by speaking to either of the latter two because they have been grouped together with the particle *al-waw*. The particle allows the third individual to be included under the negation with the second; it is as though the individual said, "I shall not speak to this one, or these two". This shows clearly that speaking to just the first one invalidates the vow, or speaking to both the second and third will invalidate it, along with the fact that just speaking to one of the latter two will not invalidate it. Contrast this to the case of the divorces and one sees that the particle *aw* is asking for one of the two unspecified items mentioned but the sentence structure is positive. A positive sentence with a negation does not demand that an indefinite article allows the meaning of generality. When the sentences in the two cases are differently structured, they cannot be used to support each other in terms of the resulting verdict.

Another example of the particle *aw* is if one pointed to his two slaves and said, "Sell this slave, or(*aw*) this one", the agent has a choice as to which one he will sell. This is because the statement uses a word of *al-amr, which* is in the meaning of *at-ta<u>kh</u>yīr,* granting a choice. The choice is granted to the agent to choose which slave to sell.

Expanding upon the application of the particle *aw*, if a woman was to marry and the bridal gift was mentioned with *aw*, such that it was said, "I marry you for one thousand or(*aw*) two thousand", the bridal gift will revert to the default, *al-mahr ul-mi<u>th</u>l*, according to Imam Abū Ḥanīfa ﷺ. This is because the particle *aw* is used to indicate one of the two amounts, however it is not known which amount. It is established that the default bridal gift in any marriage is *al-mahr ul-mi<u>th</u>l*, because it is like the price in any other financial contract, and it

QUICK ARABIC

العموم: *al-'umūm*

Generalities. Indefinite, unspecific and undetailed words and statements.

التخيير: *at-ta<u>kh</u>yīr*

To grant a choice. To be given a number of possibilities from which a preference is selected.

المهر المثل: *al-mahr ul-mi<u>th</u>l*

Standard bridal gift. A bridal gift that is equivalent to the position and status of the bride.

التشهد: *at-ta<u>sh</u>ahhud*

The testimony. A declaration made during the sitting phase of the prayer, or the sitting itself.

QUICK GRAMMAR

النكرة: *an-nakira*

Indefinite noun. A noun that refers to non-specific beings, objects or places.

النفي: *an-nafī*

Negation. The absence of something that is actual or affirmative.

can only be superseded by a stated amount greater than it. As the particle *aw* in this case does not state any single amount greater than the default, it remains undefined and so the issue reverts to the default bridal gift.

Based on the same rule that the particle *aw* is used to select one of two mentioned items the Hadith regarding *at-ta<u>sh</u>ahhud* is understood. Ibn Mas'ūd ﷺ was told by the Messenger of Allah ﷺ, "When you have recited this or(*aw*) done this, your prayer is complete." Here, the first 'this' refers to the recital of *at-ta<u>sh</u>ahhud* and the second 'this' refers to the sitting of *al-qa'da*. As the two are grouped together with the particle *aw*, we say that the completion of the necessary part of the prayer is dependent upon one of the two matters, either the recital or the sitting. As only one of them is essential for the completion of the prayer, only one of them can be *ar-rukn*, and an integral component of the salah. There is a unanimous agreement amongst the jurists that the final sitting of *al-qa'da* is compulsory and integral, so it is determined and thus the recital in *at-ta<u>sh</u>ahhud* is not compulsory for the prayer, as the Hadith only requires 'one of the two mentioned' to be essential for the completion of salah. If we determine both to be compulsory, the function of the particle *aw* becomes redundant.

Text And Translation

فصل: أو لتناول أحد المذكورين ولهذا لو قال: هذا حر أو هذا كان بمنزلة قوله: أحدهما حر حتى كان له ولاية البيان، ولو قال: وكلت ببيع هذا العبد هذا أو هذا كان الوكيل أحدهما ويباح البيع لكل واحد منهما ولو باع أحدهما ثم عاد العبد إلى ملك الموكل لا يكون للآخر أن يبيعه، ولو قال لثلاث نسوة له: هذه طالق أو هذه وهذه طلقت إحدى الأولين وطلقت الثالثة في الحال لانعطافها على المطلقة منهما ويكون الخيار للزوج في بيان المطلقة منهما بمنزلة ما قال: إحداكما طالق وهذه وعلى هذا قال زفر: إذا قال لا أكلم هذا أو هذا وهذا كان بمنزلة قوله: لا أكلم أحد هذين وهذا فلا يحنث ما لم يكلم أحد الأولين والثالث، وعندنا لو كلم الأول وحده يحنث ولو كلم أحد الآخرين لا يحنث مالم يكلمهما، قال: بع هذا العبد أو هذا كان له أن يبيع أحدهما أيهما شاء، ولو دخل أو في المهر بأن تزوجها على هذا أو على هذا يحكم مهر المثل عند أبي حنيفة؛ لأن اللفظ يتناول أحدهما والموجب الأصلي مهر المثل فيترجح ما يشابهه، وعلى هذا قلنا: التشهد ليس بركن في الصلاة؛ لأن قوله عليه السلام: إذا قلت هذا

حديث

عن عبد الله بن مسعود ﷺ أن رسول الله ﷺ أخذ بيد عبد الله فعلمه التشهد في الصلاة فذكر مثل دعاء حديث الأعمش إذا قلت هذا أو قضيت هذا فقد قضيت صلاتك إن شئت أن تقوم فقم وإن شئت أن تقعد فاقعد.

عليه الصلاة والسلام

(سنن أبي داؤد: 970)

QUICK ARABIC

القعدة: *al-qa'da*

Sitting. The sitting posture in prayer, where at least the testimony is recited or the time lapses.

الركن: *ar-rukn*

Chief element. An essential and vital part, the absence of which would undermine the item.

أو فعلت هذا فقد تمت صلوتك علق الإتمام بإحداهما فلا يشترط كل واحد منهما وقد شرطت القعدة بالاتفاق فلا يشترط قراءة التشهد

Chapter: The particle aw (أو) is to utilise one of two mentioned items. For this reason if one said: "This one is free or(*aw*) this one", it is the same as him saying: "One of them is free", such that he even has the authority to explain. If one said: "For the sale of this slave, I appoint this one or(*aw*) this one", the appointee will be one of them and both of them are permitted to sell. If one of them sold him and the slave returned to the appointer, the other cannot resell him. If one said to his three wives: "This one is divorced, or(*aw*) this one and this one", one of the first two will be divorced and the third one instantly, as she is conjuncted to the one divorced of the (first) two. The choice will be for the husband to specify which of the two are divorced. This is like saying: "One of you two is divorced and this one." Based on this Imam Zufar says: when one said: "I shall not talk to this one or(*aw*) this one, and this one", it is just like saying: "I will not talk to one of these two and this one", so he will not have broken the vow as long as he does not converse with either of the first two and the third. According to us, if he talks to the first alone he breaks the vow and if he converses with one of the last two he does not break the vow so long as he does not talk to both of them. Someone instructed: "Sell this slave or this one." He can sell any one of them he wants. If the particle *aw* is used for the bridal gift such that one marries her for this or(*aw*) this, the standard bridal gift will be set according to Imam Abū Ḥanīfa, as the text means one of them and the required default is the standard bridal gift, so preference will be for the one that equates to it. Based on this we said: *at-tashahhud* is not a requisite of prayer, because of the words of the Prophet, peace and blessings be upon him: "When you have recited this or(*aw*) completed this, your prayer is complete". Completion is dependant upon one of them so both are not necessary. The *al-qa'da* is mutually agreed to be compulsory, so the recital of *at-tashahhud* is not a condition.

❖ ❖ ❖

When the particle *aw* appears in a negative structure, it negates both mentioned items. If one said, "I shall not speak to him or(*aw*) him", it means he will not speak to either of the two individuals. In the case of a vow if he spoke to either of the men, the vow would be broken. The reason for this is that 'one of

QUICK ARABIC

التشهد: *at-tashahhud*

The testimony. A declaration made during the sitting phase of the prayer, or the sitting itself.

two mentioned' remains undetermined and is as though it is indefinite. An indefinite article under negation gives rise to the generality of the negation, which includes all options stated. Therefore, speaking to either of them will result in a broken vow.

In a positive structure, only one of the options is engaged and the choice to determine is left to the speaker. The concept of choice necessitates that all choices are permitted. It is not that one choice has a preference over the other, as that would negate the concept of unbiased choice. To support this there is verse 89 of Sūrat ul-Māida:

﴿فَكَفَّارَتُهُ إِطْعَامُ عَشَرَةِ مَسَاكِينَ مِنْ أَوْسَطِ مَا تُطْعِمُونَ أَهْلِيكُمْ أَوْ كِسْوَتُهُمْ أَوْ تَحْرِيرُ رَقَبَةٍ﴾ [المائدة: 89]

"...it must be atoned for by feeding ten needy persons with more or less the same food as you give to your own families, or by clothing them, or by freeing a human being from bondage..."

Allah ﷻ has mentioned three things to compensate for a vow; feeding ten poor individuals, clothing ten poor individuals, and freeing a slave. Each choice is separated with the particle *aw*. There is agreement that the expiation will be valid whichever of the three possible choices the person makes. There is no preference of one over the other, as the verse is showing that all choices are permitted equally.

Metaphorically, the particle *aw* can have the same meaning as the particle *ḥattā*. This occurs when the literal meaning is not possible. An example of this is from the verse 128 of Sūrah Āali ʻImrān:

﴿لَيْسَ لَكَ مِنَ الأَمْرِ شَيْءٌ أَوْ يَتُوبَ عَلَيْهِمْ أَوْ يُعَذِّبَهُمْ فَإِنَّهُمْ ظَالِمُونَ﴾ [آل عمران: 128]

" Not for you is the decision: whether(*aw*) He turn in mercy to them, or punish them; for they are indeed wrong-doers."

Here, the blessed Prophet ﷺ is told that the matter is not for him to decide, until Allah ﷻ decides to accept their repentance or to punish them. The literal usage of the particle *aw* is not possible because the word following the particle, *yatūba*, is a present tense verb and grammatically it is conjoined with either the word *shay* or the word *laysa*. The first is a noun and the latter a verb in the past tense. Conjoining a present tense verb with either a noun or a past tense verb is incorrect, therefore the particle cannot be in its literal meaning as a

QUICK DICTIONARY

expiation: *ek-spee-ey-shuh n*
Atonement. The act of atoning and making amends for legal mistakes.

conjunction. If it is not in its literal meaning the possibility arises for the metaphorical meaning, which is the same as the particle *ḥattā* [1.9.7 page 279].

As an example of the particle *aw* in its metaphorical meaning Ḥanafī jurists say that if one vowed, "I shall not enter this house until(*aw*) I enter this house", it means I shall not enter the first house until I have not first entered the second house. If this individual enters the first house first, he will have violated the vow, and should he enter the first house last, the vow would be intact. In a similar fashion, if one said, "I shall not leave you until(*aw*) you repay my loan", the particle *aw* is in the meaning of the particle *ḥattā*. It means that the limit at which I will leave you is when you repay me. If this was a vow and the one who made the vow left after receiving the repayment the vow is intact, and if he left before the repayment the vow would be broken.

Text And Translation

ثم هذه الكلمة في مقام النفي يوجب نفي كل واحد من المذكورين حتى لو قال: لا أكلم هذا أو هذا يحنث إذا كلم أحدهما وفي الإثبات يتناول أحدهما مع صفة التخيير، كقولهم: خذ هذا أو ذلك ومن ضرورة التخيير عموم الإباحة قال الله تعالى: ﴿فكفارته إطعام عشرةِ مساكِين مِن أوسطِ ما تطعِمون أهلِيكم أو كِسوتهم أو تحرِير رقبةٍ﴾ وقد يكون أو بمعنى حتى قال الله تعالى: ﴿ليس لك مِن الأمرِ شيءٌ أو يتوب عليهم﴾ قيل: معناه حتى يتوب عليهم قال أصحابنا: لو قال لا أدخل هذه الدار أو أدخل هذ الدار يكون أو بمعنى حتى، حتى لو دخل الأولى أولا حنث ولو دخل الثانية أولا بر في يمينه، وبمثله لو قال: لا أفارقك أو تقضي ديني يكون بمعنى: حتى تقضي ديني

Then this word in a place of negation will negate both mentioned items. Such that if one said: "I will not speak to him or(*aw*) him", he will have broken the vow if he speaks to either of the two. In an the affirmative it would entail one of them with a right to choose. Like they say: "Take this or(*aw*) that." From the consequences of choice is general permissibility; Allah Almighty says: "...for expiation, feed ten needy persons, on a scale of the average for the food of your families; or clothe them; or free a slave". Sometimes, *aw* takes the meaning of *ḥattā*. Allah Almighty says: "Not for you is the decision: whether(aw) He turn in mercy to them, or punish them; for they are indeed wrong-doers...". It is said that it means "*ḥattā*(whether) He forgives them". Our jurists say: if one said: "I will not enter this house until(*aw*) I enter this house", *aw* will be in the meaning of *ḥattā*. Such that if he enters the first house first he will have broken the vow and should he enter the second house first, the vow will be in tact. Similar to this is if one said: "I will not leave you until(*aw*) you repay my loan". It will be in the meaning of '*ḥattā* you repay my loan'.

❖ ❖ ❖

1.9.7 Ḥattā

The seventh particle of conjunction is *ḥattā*. The particle has a similar meaning to *ilā*, which is to denote an end [1.9.8 page 285]. It shows the limit and boundary for a thing. The word that follow *ḥattā* shows the end, *al-g͟hāya*, and conclusion of the words mentioned before the particle, *al-mug͟hayyā*. Two conditions allow the particle *ḥattā* to function in this capacity. Firstly, the thing before the particle must be able to extend and continue, so it is feasible for it to come to an end. If a thing is not of this quality such that it appears and ends instantly, it does not require anything to denote its end and conclusion. Secondly, the part after the particle *ḥattā* should be a suitable and appropriate end to the preceding thing. When these two conditions are met, the particle *ḥattā* functions in its literal meaning, otherwise it is metaphorical.

An example of the literal meaning of *ḥattā* is the statement of Imam Muḥammad رحمه الله عليه that if one said, "My slave is free if I don't beat you until so-and-son interjects for you" or "until you cry out" or "until you don't plead before me" or "until night falls", the particle *ḥattā* is in its literal meaning. This is because the part before the particle, the beating, can continue to each of these endings and each ending is a recognised ending for such an act. Should the one vowing cease to beat the individual before any of these stated endings, the slave will be free.

Similarly, if one vowed not to separate from his debtor before receiving payment and then separated before the payment, the vow will be broken. This is because pursuing and not separating allows for being extended and prolonged, and the repayment is a suitable conclusion to this. As both conditions are present, the particle *ḥattā* is in the literal meaning, and should the individual separate before payment the vow is broken.

Should there be a reason, such as *al-'urf* and common understanding, the literal meaning of *ḥattā* may be abandoned for the metaphorical. For

QUICK ARABIC

الغاية: *al-g͟hāya*

Limit. The end point and boundary of a process.

المغيا: *al-mug͟hayyā*

The limited. Words before a limiting particle, determining the item to be confined.

العرف : *al-'urf*

Custom. A habitual practice, usual way and collective manner of a people.

example, if one vowed, "I will beat you until(*ḥattā*) you die" or "until I kill you", though the beating can be prolonged and the ending is a possible outcome, however the literal will not be taken into account due to common understanding. Rather, the metaphorical meaning of 'severe beating' will be applied. It will be as though the person vowing is saying 'I vow to severely beat you'. In such a case if he severely beats the individual and stops before he kills his victim, the vow will be in tact even though the stated outcome was not literally achieved.

Text And Translation

فصل: حتى للغاية كـ إلى فإذا كان ما قبلها قابلا للامتداد وما بعدها يصلح غاية له كانت الكلمة عاملة بحقيقتها، مثاله ما قال مُحَمَّد رحمه الله: إذا قال: عبدي حر إن لم أضربك حتى يشفع فلان أو حتى تصيح أو حتى تشتكي بين يدي أو حتى يدخل الليل كانت الكلمة عاملة بحقيقتها؛ لأن الضرب بالتكرار يحتمل الامتداد، وشفاعة فلان وأمثالها تصلح غاية للضرب فلو امتنع عن الضرب قبل الغاية حنث، ولو حلف لا يفارق غريمه حتى يقضيه دينه ففارقه قبل قضاء الدين حنث، فإذا تعذر العمل بالحقيقة لمانع كالعرف، كما لو حلف أن يضربه حتى يموت أو حتى يقتله حمل على الضرب الشديد باعتبار العرف

Chapter: the particle *ḥattā* (حتى) is to show an end, like the particle *ilā*. If what precedes it accepts continuation and what proceeds it is a suitable end for it, the word will function in its literal meaning. An example of it is as Imam Muhammad, Allah have mercy on him, said: when one said, "My slave is free if I don't strike you till(*ḥattā*) so-and-so intercedes or you scream or you plead before me or till night falls", the word will function literally. This is because repeated striking can be continued, and someone's intercession and the likes, are a suitable end to the striking. So if he stops striking before the end is reached, he will have broken his vow. If one vowed not to part from his debtor until the recovery of the loan, and then parted from him before the payment of the loan, he will have broken the vow. If enforcing the literal meaning is unfeasible due to an impediment like common usage like if one vowed to beat someone till(*ḥattā*) death or till(*ḥattā*) he murdered him, it will mean a severe beating based on common usage.

❖❖❖

If the part before the particle *ḥattā* does not have the capacity to be prolonged or extended, or the part after the particle is not a suitable conclusion, it will mean that a vital condition for enforcing the literal meaning of *ḥattā* will be missing. In such a case, the literal meaning of *ḥattā* will be abandoned. If the preceding and proceeding parts can be constructed as conditionals, then the metaphorical meaning of *ḥattā* will be of *lāmu kay*. The part preceding the particle will be the condition and the part following it will be its result. As an example, Imam Muhammad عليه رحمة الله said that if a master announced, "My slave is free if I don't come to you and(*ḥattā*) you feed me breakfast", and the master proceeded to go to the individual but was not fed. The master will not be in violation of the vow and the slave will not go free. This is because the particle *ḥattā* is not to demonstrate an ending of a process, as what comes before the particle is not a prolonged and extended event. It is simply the arrival of a person. Furthermore, what follows the particle, the feeding, is not a sensible conclusion as it does not conclude or end the arrival. At the most, it is an incentive to come. The particle *ḥattā* in this example does not fulfil the conditions to be in its literal meaning so it takes up the metaphorical meaning of *lāmu kay*, which is used to justify something. The meaning of the statement will be 'If I don't come to you after which I am fed, my slave is free'. When the master arrives and the host does not feed him, arrival has still occurred and it is only that the justification of the arrival is not realised. The freeing of the slave was concerned with not coming, and as the master came, the slave is not free.

If it is problematic to construct a conditional meaning for the particle *ḥattā* such that there is no condition before the particle or that there is no outcome after it, the particle *ḥattā* will be for mere conjunction alone. In such a case, *ḥattā* will be like the particle *al-fa* or *thumma*, as both of these particles are a follow-up and a connected addition to the previous sentence. This is very similar to a meaning of 'end and conclusion'. As an example there is the statement of Imam Muḥammad عليه رحمة الله that if a master said, "My slave is free if I don't come to you, then(*ḥattā*) I breakfast at yours today", or "My slave is free if you don't come to mine, then(*ḥattā*) you breakfast with me today", the slave will be free if he doesn't break fast. This is because in both examples, 'coming' and 'breaking fast' are the action of one person, and the actions of one person cannot be a condition and outcome for one another. So, this would mean that there is a significant problem in constructing a conditional sentence and in such a case, the particle *ḥattā* is used for conjunction only. Thus, the statement will read, 'if I don't come to you and then eat at yours, my slave is free', this will

QUICK GRAMMAR

لام كي (لِ): *lāmu kay*

So that. The Arabic letter *lām* which is in a genitive state and has the meaning of the Arabic word *kay*, 'so that'.

render both the arrival and the eating to collectively become the condition. Now, if he does both acts of coming and eating, the condition is met and the slave is not free. It follows that if he comes but does not eat, or does not come at all, the condition is not met and the slave will be free.

Text And Translation

وإن لم يكن الأول قابلا للامتداد والآخر صالحا للغاية وصلح الأول سببا والآخر جزاء يحمل على الجزاء مثاله ما قال محمد رحمه الله: إذا قال لغيره: عبدي حر إن لم آتك حتى تغديني فأتاه فلم يغده لا يحنث؛ لأن التغذية لا يصلح غايةً للإتيان بل هي داعٍ إلى زيادة الإتيان وصلح جزاء فيحمل على الجزاء فيكون بمعنى لام كي فصار كما لو قال: إن لم آتك إتياناً جزاؤه التغذية، وإذا تعذر هذا بأن لا يصلح الآخر جزاء للأول حمل على العطف المحض، مثاله ما قال محمد رحمه الله: إذا قال: عبدي حر إن لم آتك حتى أتغدي عندك اليوم، أو إن لم تأتني لأنه لما أضيف كلّ واحد من الفعلين إلى ذات واحد لا يصلح أن يكون فعله جزاء لفعله فيحمل على العطف المحض فيكون المجموع شرطا للبر

When the preceding cannot be continued whilst the proceeding can be an end, and the preceding can be a cause and the latter an effect, it will be considered to be so. An example of it is as Imam Muḥammad, Allah have mercy on him, said: when one said to another, 'My slave is free if I don't come to you and(*ḥattā*) you feed me'. If he comes to him and he doesn't feed him, the vow is not broken. This is because feeding is not an end to coming but rather it is an incentive to come. It does have the capacity to be an outcome so it will be considered so and take the meaning of *lām ul-kay*. It will be as though he said: 'If I don't come to you with the reward of a feast." When this is impeded such that the latter cannot be an outcome for the former, it will be a simple connector. An example of it is what Imam Muḥammad, Allah have mercy on him, said: if one said, 'My slave is free if I don't come to you until(*ḥattā*) I feast with you today or if you don't come." This is because both actions are connected to the same individual, so it is not possible for one action to be an outcome for his other action. So it will be considered to be a simple connector and collectively it will be a precondition to be vindicated.

❖❖❖

QUICK GRAMMAR

لام كي (لِ): *lāmu kay*

So that. The Arabic letter *lām* which is in a genitive state and has the meaning of the Arabic word *kay*, 'so that'.

Summary Of Significant Particles (1)

1. These are the parts of speech that are particles and have a meaningful contribution to rulings. There are 11 of them in total; 7 are connectors and 4 are genitives.

Summary of the Connectors

2. Details of the particle *al-wāw*: it has two functions.
i) It can be used for mere conjoining with no regard for order. For example, جاء زيد وعمرو this has no indication as to who was first and who was second.
ii) It may be used for a circumstantial phrase where it joins the circumstance to the individual. It will function like a conditional. For example, Imam Muḥammad ﷬ says if one said: أدّ إليّ ألفا وأنت حر the 1000 dirham will be a condition for emancipation.

3. Details of the particle *al-fā*: it has two functions.
i) It can be used for immediate order, where the noun that follows it is second but is immediately second. That is a reason why in a conditional construct this particle is used on the apodosis, *al-jazā*. For example, if one said to his wife إن دخلت الدار فهذا الدار فأنت طالق the divorce will occur only if both the order in the statement is observed and it is done immediately one after the other.
ii) Sometimes it is used to highlight the cause. The word following it will be the cause of what precedes it. For example, a master says to his slave أدّ إليّ ألفا فأنت حر The slave will immediately be free even though he has not paid the money. This is because freedom is a permanent status that is not dependent upon a payment, however the debt will remain.

4. Details of the particle <u>th</u>*umma*.
It is to show delay which signifies a separation between the preceding and proceeding parts. For example, if one said to his virgin wife, إن دخلت الدار فأنت طالق ثم طالق ثم طالق, the first divorce is connected to the condition. So, when she enters the house the divorce will be enforced. The second will have occurred immediately. The third will be void as she is not eligible for it. Being an as yet virgin she is entitled to one divorce and does not need to wait for the *al-'idda* period.

5. Details of the particle *bal*:
The word corrects an error in the preceding statement. The proceeding statement replaces the preceding. For example, if one said to a virgin wife, أنت طالق واحدة لا بل ثنتين the first part before the *bal* is replaced with the words after it. It is a different matter that in this case the first words are irrevocable.

6. Details of the particle *lākin*: it has two functions.
i) After a negative, it clarifies a possible misconception. For example:
لفلان علي ألف قرض فقال فلان لا ولكنه غصب
The money will become necessary because the statements are conjoined, so it is clear that the negation concerns the cause and not the actual amount.

** The condition for *lākin* to be in meaning (i) is that the statement should be connected and the positive and negative parts of the sentence must be distinct.

(...continued)

Summary Of Significant Particles (1)
(...continued)

ii) A new sentence may begin with it. In this case it is unrelated to the previous sentence and has no bearing on it. An example is if a slave marries herself for 100 dirhams without the consent of her master. Upon hearing of it the master says: لا أجيز العقد بمائة درهم لكن أجيزه بمائة وخمسين
The particle *lākin* will not be a mere connector and it will nullify the contract, as the master is rejecting the 100-dirham contract and gives permission for a new contract of 150 dirham.

* Note: *lākin* and *lākinna* both function as above.

7. Details of the particle *aw*: it has two functions.
i) It may come for the inclusion of only one of two things. For example, if a master delegates the sale of his two slaves saying, بع هذا أو هذا the agent has a choice as to which one he will sell.
* In a negative sentence it will mean neither of the options.
ii) It may function as the word *ḥattā*. For example, Allah ﷻ says: ليس لك من الأمر شيء أو يتوب عليهم. Here, the *aw* will be in the meaning of *ḥattā*.

8. Details of the particle *ḥattā*: it has three functions.
i) In its coinage *ḥattā* is like the particle *ilā* with the condition that the preceding statement is extendable and what proceeds it can be a valid end for it. For example, Imam Muḥammad رحمه الله says, if one said عبدي حر إن لم أضربك حتى يشفع فلان hitting can be a prolonged activity and the intermediary is a possible end to it. So, the word *ḥattā* will be in the meaning of *ilā*.
ii) If one or both conditions are not met, and the preceding and proceeding statements are able to be in a conditional construct then *ḥattā* will be for the apodosis. This means it will take the meaning of *lām ul-kay*. For example, Imam Muḥammad رحمه الله said, if a master says عبدي حر إن لم آتك حتى تغدّيني. Because feeding is not a suited end to arrival, as arrival is not prolonged, and the conditional construct is possible, the *ḥattā* will take the meaning of *lām ul-kay*.
iii) If the conditional construct is not possible either, the word will be a connector only. For example, Imam Muḥammad رحمه الله says, if one said: عبدي حر إن لم آتك حتى أتغدى عندك اليوم. Here, there is mere connection as it is not a conditional construct as both actions concern one individual.

After the conjunctions, the first of the prepositions is the particle *ilā*. The particle *ilā* is to signify the end to a distance. The part preceding the particle is referred to as *al-mughayyā*, the restricted, and the part proceeding is known as *al-ghāya*, the limit. In some cases, the particle *ilā* allows the matter under discussion, *al*-mughayyā, to extend up to the limit, and on other occasions, it stops and restricts *al*-mughayyā at the limit. If the particle is used to extend up to the limit, it will not include the limit, and if the particle is used to stop and restrict, the limit will be included.

An example of the particle used to extend the ruling up to the limit is if one said, "I purchased this plot up to(*ilā*) this wall", the wall will not be included in the purchase. This is because the word 'plot' can be the smallest of areas and the word's meaning is extended using the particle *ilā* up to the wall, so all the area can be included in the purchase. As the particle *ilā* is extending the purchase, the limit is not included.

An example of the particle *ilā* restricting and stopping the ruling at the limit is if one said, "I sold it with the choice to return it up to and including(*ilā*) three days". The third day will be included in the returns period. This is because the limit is restricting the otherwise open-ended right to return. If the option to return the item was left unrestricted it would nullify the purchase, as the meaning of transfer of ownership would not exist in such an arrangement, whereas the whole purpose of purchasing is to transfer ownership. By stating the limit, a restriction to the ruling has been applied, and as such a restriction using a limit placed by the particle *ilā* includes the limit. Therefore, the third day will also be part of the grace period. Another example of a limit of restriction is if one announced, "By Allah I will not speak to so-and-so for(*ilā*) one month". The particle *ilā* is for a restricting limit because the individual not speaking is unrestricted and would be forever, however by using the particle *ilā* a limit is placed, which cuts short that period and restricts it to one month. As the limit is a restriction, it will be included in the ruling of the period of not speaking.

Text And Translation

فصل: إلى لانتهاء الغاية ثم هو في بعض الصور يفيد معنى امتداد الحكم وفي بعض الصور يفيد معنى الإسقاط، فإن أفاد الامتداد لا تدخل الغاية في الحكم وإن أفاد الإسقاط تدخل، نظير الأول: اشتريت

QUICK ARABIC

الغاية: *al-ghāya*

Limit. The end point and boundary of a process.

المغيا: *al-mughayyā*

The limited. Words before a limiting particle, determining the item to be confined.

هذا المكان إلى هذا الحائط، لا يدخل الحائط في البيع، ونظير الثاني: باع بشرط الخيار إلى ثلاثة أيام
وبمثله لو حلف لا أكلم فلانا إلى شهر كان الشهر داخلا في الحكم وقد أفاد فائدة الإسقاط ههنا

Chapter: The particle *ilā* (إلى) is for the end limit. Then in some cases it gives a meaning of extending the ruling and in some cases it gives a meaning of exclusion. If it is for extension, the limit will not be included and if it is for exclusion the limit will be included. An example of the first is: "I purchased this house to(*ilā*) this wall". The wall will not be included in the purchase. The example of the second is if one purchased with the right to return for(*ilā*) three days, and likewise if one vowed: "I will not speak to so-and-so for(*ilā*) a month". The month is included in the ruling and it has given the benefit of exclusion here.

❖ ❖ ❖

The rule stated that the particle *ilā* denotes a restricting limit when the preceding part to the particle is unrestricted and as such, the limit is included within the ruling. Based on this, the Aḥnāf say both elbows and ankles are included in the ablution as stated in verse 6 of Sūrat ul-Māida:

﴿فاغْسِلُواْ وُجُوهَكُمْ وَأَيْدِيَكُمْ إِلَى الْمَرَافِقِ وَامْسَحُواْ بِرُؤُوسِكُمْ وَأَرْجُلَكُمْ إِلَى الْكَعْبَينِ﴾ [المائدة: 6]

"...so wash your faces and your arms to(*ilā*) the elbows and wipe your heads, and wash your feet to(*ilā*) the ankles"

This is because the word for arms, *aydī*, is unrestricted to include the whole of the limb to the shoulder. The verse is asking for it to be washed. Using the particle *ilā* this washing has been stopped and limited at the elbow. Had the verse not included this limit, it would be necessary to wash the whole of the arm. Furthermore, the elbow is included in the washing, as the particle is denoting a restricting limit. Similarly, the ankles are denoting a restricting limit for the word for legs, *arjul*. If the particle *ilā* was not mentioned the prescribed washing would be necessary for the whole leg. As the particle is restricting the washing to the ankle, the ankle is included in the washing for the same reasons stated before.

This rule for *ilā* also applies to the Hadith concerning the necessary covering of the knees. The narration states, "A man's necessary cover is from

حديث

عن عمر بن شعيب عن أبيه عن جده رضي الله عنهم قال: قال رسول الله صلى الله عليه وسلم: فإن ما أسفل من سرته إلى ركبتيه من عورته.

عليه الصلاة والسلام

(مسند أحمد: 6717)

beneath the navel to(*ilā*) the knee". The particle *ilā* is to denote a restrictive limit. This is because the initial statement is that the cover is all what appears beneath the navel, so this would include the legs and feet, to the ground. However, the particle comes to restrict and stop this at the knees. The limit of the covering is set at the knee; therefore, the knee is also included as it is a restrictive limit. Consequently, it becomes necessary for men to cover the knee at all times.

When the particle *ilā* is used with time, it delays the ruling to the stated limit. As an example, if without a particular intention in mind one said to his wife, "You are divorced in(*ilā*) a month", the divorce will not occur instantly, rather it will occur after the stated one month. If the intention was to issue it immediately, the intention will be taken into account and the remainder of the utterance, 'in a month', will be void. Imam Zufar رحمه الله disagrees with this. He says, with or without the clear intention, the divorce occurs immediately. Our position is that 'one month' is neither an extendable nor an unrestricted thing, and these are the only two possibilities with the literal understanding of the particle *ilā*. The context of divorce however allows for a meaning of deferring and delaying, as it is an accepted rule that *al-isqāṭāt* such as divorce and emancipation, can be deferred, whereas *al-ithbātāt* such as trade, may not be. Therefore, it is possible to defer a divorce. So rather than render a part of a statement as void, the deferred and delayed meaning is adopted. The statement will thus read, 'you are divorced after a month', and so after a month passes the divorce will be enacted.

Text And Translation

وعلى هذا قلنا: المرفق والكعب داخلان تحت حكم الغسل في قوله تعالى: ﴿إلى المرافِقِ﴾ لأن كلمة إلى ههنا للإسقاط فإنه لولاها لاستوعبت الوظيفة جميع اليد، ولهذا قلنا: الركبة من العورة ؛لأن كلمة إلى في قوله عليه الصلاة والسلام: عورة الرجل ما تحت السرة إلى الركبة تفيد فائدة الإسقاط فتدخل الركبة في الحكم، وقد تفيد كلمة إلى تأخير الحكم إلى الغاية، ولهذا قلنا: إذا قال لامرأته: أنت طالق إلى شهر ولا نية له لا يقع الطلاق في الحال عندنا خلاف الزفر؛ لأنّ ذكر الشهر لا يصلح لمد الحكم والإسقاط شرعا والطلاق يحتمل التأخير بالتعليق فيحمل عليه

QUICK ARABIC

الإسقاطات: *al-ithqāṭāt*

Projected matters. Matters that are devised or planned, often requiring a major undertaking.

الإثباتات: *al-ithbātāt*

Substantiated matters. Matters that are evidently in existence.

Based on this we said: the elbow and the ankle are included in the ruling of washing from the word of Allah Almighty: "to(*ilā*) the elbows". This is because the word *ilā* here is for exclusion. Were it not there, the task would have encompassed the whole arm. For this reason we say the knee is part of *al-'awra*, because of the word *ilā* in his saying, peace and blessings be upon him: "The covering of a man is from beneath the navel to(*ilā*) the knee". It is for exclusion so the knee is within the ruling. Sometimes the particle *ilā* is to delay the ruling to a limit. For this reason we said when one says to his wife: "You are divorced till(*ilā*) a month", and he has no intention, the divorce will not occur immediately according to us but differing with Imam Zufar. This is because a month cannot be an extension for the ruling nor an exclusion for it legally. Divorce can be deferred in a conditional, so it will be considered so.

❖❖❖

1.9.9 *'Alā*

The second significant preposition is the particle *'alā*. It gives a meaning of superiority and elevation above another. In the Shariah, it denotes the compulsion and necessity of something upon someone. For this reason, if one said, "I owe(*'alā*) so-and-so one thousand", it will be a repayment of a loan, because owing someone implies an obligation to give or return a thing, and that obligation is felt when the thing actually belongs to another. This differs with one stating, "I have(*`indī*) one thousand for so-and-so" or "so-and-so's one thousand is with(*qibalī*) me". In these cases, it does not default to a loan, as the particle for obligation, *'alā*, is not used.

It is due to the meaning of obligation in the particle *'alā* that Imam Muḥammad ﷺ states in as-Siyar al-Kabīr, that if the commander of a fort asks the Muslims, "Grant me safety upon(*'alā*) ten men in the fort", and the Muslims granted the safety, it will be ten individuals in addition to the commander. Furthermore, the choice of which individuals will be at the commander's discretion. This is because the commander has sought safety for himself in addition to ten others using the particle *'alā* which gives a sense of superiority and being above and over. The commander is thus saying that he requires safety for himself and ten others whilst maintaining his own superiority over them. So, by granting him the choice to choose the ten, his superiority is maintained. Had the commander asked with different particles, such that he said, "Grant me safety and(*wa*) ten", "Grant me safety, then(*fa*) ten others", or "Grant me safety

QUICK ARABIC

العورة: *al-'awra*

Area of bodily privacy. Area of the body from beneath the navel up to and including the knee.

QUICK REFERENCE

السير الكبير: *as-siyar al-kabīr*

The Major Treatise on Engagement. The first major Islamic treatise on the law between Muslim and non-Muslim nations by Imam Muḥammad ash-Shaybānī ﷺ

and then(*thumma*) ten others", and the Muslims granted it, all eleven will be granted safety. However, the choice of who the ten others are is at the discretion of the one granting the safety. This is because there is no indication of superiority in any of these words and so it need not be granted to the commander.

Metaphorically, the particle *'alā* may be used in the meaning of the particle *al-bā* [1.9.11 page 296]. It will thus take the meaning of joining and attaching. As an example, if one said, "I sold you this for(*'alā*) one thousand", the particle *'alā* is functioning as *al-bā* because the sentence is clearly discussing an exchange. Where the context has provided a reason to bypass the literal meaning, the context also provides the appropriate metaphorical meaning of 'attachment', as in any exchange an item is attached to its price.

When there is a difficulty in producing the literal meaning of obligation for the particle *'alā* in a sentence, it may be in a conditional construction. An example of this is from verse 12 of Sūrat ul-Mumtaḥina:

﴿يُبَايِعْنَكَ عَلَى أَن لَّا يُشْرِكْنَ بِاللَّهِ شَيْئًا﴾ [الممتحنة: 12]

"...taking an oath of allegiance to you providing(*'alā*) they will ascribe nothing as partner to Allah..."

The particle *'alā* is functioning as a conditional. For this reason, Imam Abū Ḥanīfa ﷺ says if a wife says to her husband, "Divorce me thrice on the proviso(*'alā*) of one thousand", and the husband only gives one, the one thousand will not become necessary on the wife. This is because the particle *'alā* is a conditional in this structure. It would be necessary for the condition of three divorces to be met before the one thousand can become necessary upon the wife. As three divorces were not issued, nothing is owed.

Text And Translation

فصل: كلمة على للإلزام وأصله لإفادة معنى التفوق والتعلي، ولهذا لو قال: لفلان علي ألف يحمل على الدين بخلاف ما لو قال: عندي أو معي أو قبلي، وعلى هذا قال في "السير الكبير": إذا قال رأس الحصن: آمنوني على عشرة من أهل الحصن ففعلنا فالعشرة سواه وخيار التعيين له، ولو قال: آمنوني وعشرة أو فعشرة أو ثم عشرة ففعلنا، فكذلك وخيار التعيين للآمن، وقد تكون على بمعنى الباء مجازاً

QUICK DICTIONARY

proviso: *pruh-vahy-zoh*

Stipulation. A clause by which a condition is introduced.

حتى لو قال: بعتك هذا على ألف يكون على بمعنى الباء لقيام دلالة المعاوضة، وقد يكون على بمعنى الشرط قال الله تعالى: ﴿يبايعنك على أن لا يشركن بالله شيئاً﴾ ولهذا قال أبو حنيفة: إذا قالت لزوجها: طلقني ثلاثاً على ألف فطلقها واحدة لا يجب المال؛ لأنّ الكلمة ههنا تفيد معنى الشرط فيكون الثلاث شرطا للزوم المال.

Chapter: the particle *'alā* (على) is to obligate and is originally to denote a meaning of superiority and loftiness. For this reason if one said: "I owe(*'alā*) so-and-so a thousand", it will be considered as debt unlike if one said: "I have(*'indī*), I have(*ma'ī*) or with me(*qibalī*). Based on this it is stated in as-Siyar al-Kabīr: when the leader of a fort says: "Protect me with(*'alā*) ten inhabitants of the fort", and we accepted, the ten will exclude him and he has a right to choose. Should he say: "Protect me and(*wa*) ten", "then(*fa*) ten" or "then(*thumma*) ten", and we accepted, it would be the same and the choice will be for the protector. Sometimes, *'alā* is used metaphorically in the meaning of *al-bā*, such that if one said: "I have sold you this for(*'alā*) one thousand", the *'alā* will be in the meaning of *al-bā* due to the present sense of exchange. Sometimes, *'alā* gives a meaning of condition. Allah Almighty says: " ...taking an oath of allegiance to you, providing(*'alā*) they will ascribe nothing as partner to Allah...". For this reason Imam Abū Ḥanīfa says: if a woman said to her spouse: "Divorce me thrice for(*'alā*) one thousand", and he divorced her once, no money will be owed because the particle here is in the conditional meaning, so three is a condition for the necessity of money.

❖ ❖ ❖

1.9.10 *Fī*

The third preposition *fī* is for containment, *aẓ-ẓarfīya*. The words after the particle *fī* indicate the container in which the words before *fī* are contained. It is due to this meaning of containment that the jurists have said if one admitted, "I usurped cloth in(*fī*) a kerchief", or "I usurped dates in(*fī*) a case", both the cloth and the kerchief are to be returned, as well as both the dates and the case. The usurpers words mean I have seized the contents with the container.

QUICK GRAMMAR

الظرفية: *aẓ-ẓarfīya*

Containment. The notion that something is held or included within a volume, area or scope.

QUICK DICTIONARY

usurp: *you-zurp*

To seize. To hold or use something by force without legal right or authority.

QUICK REFERENCE

السير الكبير: *as-siyar al-kabīr*

The Major Treatise on Engagement. The first major Islamic treatise on the law between Muslim and non-Muslim nations by Imam Muḥammad ash-Shaybānī رحمه الله.

The particle *fī* can be used with time, space or to give an infinitive, *al-maṣdarī*, meaning. An example of it being used with time is if one said, "You are divorced on(*fī*) the morrow". The Ṣāḥibayn state that it makes no difference if one states the preposition *fī* or omits it from a sentence. So, the previous example could be "you are divorced tomorrow", and it would function in the same manner, which is that the divorce will occur at the onset of the following morning. Imam Abū Ḥanīfa رحمه الله says there is a difference in the ruling when one states or omits the preposition *fī*. If it is omitted the divorce will occur in the morning of the following day. So, if one said, "You are divorced tomorrow", as soon as the first moment of tomorrow arrives the divorce occurs. Furthermore, if he intends the divorce to occur at the end of the day, it will not be valid. However, if one was to state the preposition *fī* by saying, "You are divorced on(*fī*) the morrow", the preposition will be showing the container in which the contents, the divorce in this case, will be found. This could be in the beginning, middle or end of the day. Now, if the person had not made any intention the divorce would occur in the morning, as soon as morning arrived. If he intends any other part of the day, such as the final moment, the intention will be taken into consideration because it will help settle the matter from the many moments of the day that were in contention. Any one of the moments was able to be the container that contained the divorce as its contents, but the intention has assigned the event to one of them. The words allow the intended moment to be the moment of divorce, so it will be valid.

To help understand the significance of stating and omitting the preposition *fī* further, an example can be used. If one said, "If you fast a month, you are divorced", the divorce will be realised once a whole month of fasting is concluded, and if she was short of a month of fasts, no divorce would occur. On the other hand, if one said, "If you fast in(*fī*) the month, you are divorced", a moment's withdrawal from eating and drinking with the intention of an act of worship will bring about the divorce. This is because if the fast is found in any part of the month, be it the smallest of parts, the condition will be met and the divorce will occur.

QUICK TERMS

صاحبين: *ṣāḥibayn*

The Two Colleagues. Imams Abū Yūsuf رحمه الله and Muḥammad رحمه الله

QUICK GRAMMAR

المصدري: *al-maṣdarī*

Infinitive. Pertaining to the root and origin of an Arabic word-group.

Text And Translation

فصل: كلمة في للظرف وباعتبار هذا الأصل قال أصحابنا: إذا قال غصبت ثوبا في منديل أو تمرا في قوصرة لزماه جميعا، ثم هذه الكلمة تستعمل في الزمان والمكان والفعل، أما إذا استعملت في الزمان بأن

> يقول: أنت طالق غدا، فقال أبو يوسف ومحمّد: يستوي في ذلك حذفها و إظهارها حتى لو قال: أنت
> طالق في غد كان بمنزلة قوله: أنت طالق غدا يقع الطلاق كما طلع الفجر في الصورتين جميعا، وذهب
> أبو حنيفة رحمه الله إلى أنها إذا حذفت يقع الطلاق كما طلع الفجر وإذا أظهرت كان المراد وقوع
> الطلاق في جزء من الغد على سبيل الإبهام فلو لا وجود النية يقع الطلاق بأول الجزء لعدم المزاحم له،
> ولو نوى آخر النهار صحت نيته، ومثال ذلك في قول الرجل: إن صمت الشهر فأنت كذا فإنه يقع
> على صوم الشهر ولو قال: إن صمت في الشهر فأنت كذا يقع ذلك على الإمساك ساعة في الشهر

Chapter: the particle fī (في) is for containment. Based on this principle our jursits have said: if one confessed, "I usurped a cloth in(*fī*) a towel", or "dates in(*fī*) a container", both would be necessary upon him. This particle is used for place, time and acts. As for when it is used for time, such that one said: "You are divorced tomorrow", Imams Abū Yūsuf and Muḥammad say omitting or including it are the same. So if one said: "You are divorced on(*fī*) the morrow", it will be like saying: "You are divorced tomorrow". The divorce would occur as the morning arrives in both cases. Imam Abū Ḥanīfa, Allah have mercy on him, has inclined towards divorce occurring as morning arrives if it is omitted and when it is included it means that divorce is at an unspecified moment of tomorrow. So if there was no intention the divorce would occur at the first moment as there is no contention. Should he intend the end of the day, his intention is valid. The example of this is when a man says: "If you fast a month, you will be like that", it will occur upon a month of fasting. And if he said: "If you fast in(*fī*) the month, you are like that", it will occur upon abstinence of a single moment of the month.

❖❖❖

If the preposition *fī* is used spatially like if one said, "You are divorced in(*fī*) the house" or "You are divorced in(*fī*) Makkah", by attaching the divorce to a location, the divorce will occur immediately and will not be restricted to the place. The divorce will be established in all places, so it will be upheld in the house and outside the house, as it will be upheld in al-Makkah al-Mukarramah or in any other city.

Taking into consideration the idea of *aẓ-ẓarfīyya* and being spatiotemporally connected, if a verb is connected to a space or time, the

QUICK GRAMMAR

الظرفية: *aẓ-ẓarfīya*

Containment. The notion that something is held or included within a volume, area or scope.

QUICK DICTIONARY

usurp: *you-zurp*
To seize. To hold or use something by force without legal right or authority.

spacio-temporal: *spey-sio-temp-pruh l*
Related to time and space. A parameter in which all physical qualities may be located.

transitive: *tran-si-tiv*
Involving transition. A verb indicating a complete action only with a direct object.

intransitive: *in-tran-si-tiv*
Not involving transition. A verb indicating a complete action without a direct object.

transitive and intransitive characteristic of the verb impacts verdicts. In the case of an intransitive verb the time and location of the subject is considered, and if the verb is transitive the time and location of the object is considered. In an intransitive verb the effect of the act is limited to what the subject does and so the subject alone matters. In a transitive verb, the subject's acts take effect on an object, so the object's circumstance becomes the determining factor. Imam Muḥammad ﷺ says in al-Jāmi' al-Kabīr that if one vowed, "If I swear at you in(*fī*) the masjid, my slave is free", and then proceeds to swear at the individual whilst in the masjid but with the recipient out of the masjid, the vow will be violated. This is because uttering the profanity is intransitive and the verb will be complete with just the act. The governing circumstances are that of the subject, who at the time of the act was inside the masjid, so the condition is met and the slave will be free. If the subject was outside the masjid whilst the recipient was inside, the vow will not be violated and the slave will not be free. If one vowed, "If I strike you in the masjid, my slave is free", or "If I argue with you in the masjid, my slave is free", it will be necessary for the object to be in the masjid for the freedom to occur. So, if the one he is arguing with or beating is present in the masjid, whilst the one vowing was inside or outside, the slave will be free. This is because the verbs are transitive and require an effect to be realised by the object, who should be in the masjid to meet the condition. If the one vowing was inside whilst striking or arguing and the object was outside, the condition will not be met and the freedom will not occur.

If one said, "If I kill you on(*fī*) Thursday, my slave is free", and injured the person before Thursday, the object then succumbed to his injuries on Thursday, the condition will be met. However, if he managed to injure him on Thursday, but the death occurred on Friday, the condition will not be met and the vow will not be violated.

QUICK REFERENCE

الجامع الكبير: *al-jāmi' al-kabīr*

The Great Collection. A collection of narrations that Imam Muḥammad ash-Shaybānī ﷺ compiled directly from Imam Abū Ḥanīfa ﷺ.

Text And Translation

وأما في المكان فمثل قوله: أنت طالق في الدار و في مكة يكون ذلك طلاقا على الإطلاق في جميع الأماكن، وباعتبار معنى الظرفية قلنا: إذا حلف على فعل وأضافه إلى زمان أو مكان فإن كان الفعل مما يتم بالفاعل يشترط كون الفاعل في ذلك الزمان أو المكان، وإن كان الفعل يتعدى إلى محلّ يشترط كون المحلّ في ذلك الزمان والمكان لأنّ الفعل إنما يتحقق بأثره وأثره في المحل. قال مُحَمَّد رحمه الله في

"الجامع الكبير": إذا قال: إن شتمتك في المسجد فكذا فشتمه وهو في المسجد والمشتوم خارج المسجد يحنث ولو كان الشاتم خارج المسجد والمشتوم في المسجد لا يحنث، ولو قال: إن ضربتك أو شججتك في المسجد فكذا يشترط كون المضروب والمشجوج في المسجد ولا يشترط كون الضارب والشاج فيه، ولو قال: إن قتلتك في يوم الخميس فكذا فجرحه قبل يوم الخميس ومات يوم الخميس يحنث ولو جرحه يوم الخميس ومات يوم الجمعة لا يحنث

As for when it is used for place it will be like one's statement: "You are divorced in(*fī*) the house" or "in(*fī*) Makkah". This will be an unconditional divorce for all places. Considering the spatio-temporal dimension we say: if one vowed an act and associated it to a time or location and the verb was non-transitive, it is a precondition that the subject must be in that time or place. And if the verb extends to an object, the object must be in that time or place as the act will be achieved with his effort and its affect on the object. Imam Muḥammad, Allah have mercy on him, says in al-Jāmi' al-Kabīr: when one vowed: "If I curse you in the masjid then that will happen." So he curses him when he is in the masjid and the recipient is outside, he will be in violation. And if the curser was outside the masjid and the recipient inside the masjid, he will not be in violation. If one vowed: "If I strike you or injure you in the masjid then that will happen". It will depend on the stricken or the injured being in the masjid and it is not a condition for the striker or the injurer being in it. If one vowed: "If I kill you on Thursday then that will happen", so he injured him before Thursday and he died on Thursday, he'll be in violation. If he injured him on Thursday and he died on Friday, he'll not be in violation.

❖ ❖ ❖

When the preposition *fī* is used with a root word, *al-maṣdar*, it results in a conditional sentence and the ruling will be dependent upon the root verb. As an example, if one said to his wife, "You are divorced upon(*fī*) entering the house", it is the same as the conditional sentence 'if you enter the house, you are divorced'. The divorce will occur once the condition of entering the house is met, before this no divorce occurs. In a similar way, if one said to his wife who was experiencing the monthly bleeding, "You are divorced in(*fī*) your period", the divorce will occur immediately as the condition will be present. If she is not

QUICK GRAMMAR

المصدر: *al-maṣdar*

The infinitive. The root and origin of an Arabic word-group.

QUICK REFERENCE

الجامع الكبير: *al-jāmi' al-kabīr*

The Great Collection. A collection of narrations that Imam Muḥammad ash-Shaybānī رحمه الله compiled directly from Imam Abū Ḥanīfa رحمه الله.

currently in that phase of the cycle the divorce will occur once the next bleeding begins and not before it.

Furthermore, it is stated in al-Jāmi' al-Kabīr that if one said to his wife, "You are divorced upon(*fī*) the arrival of day", the occurrence of the divorce will depend upon the arrival of day. Therefore, as soon as the morning of the following day arrives the divorce will occur and not before it. If the husband said, "You are divorced on(*fī*) the passing of the day", it will depend on whether the statement was made during the day or the night. If it was made at night, the divorce will occur once the Sun has set on the following day, as that is when the condition of the passing of the day will be realised. If the statement was made during daylight hours, the divorce will occur at exactly the same time the following day. This is because the condition requires the passing of a day and that cannot occur if the sunset of the same day is considered as the moment, only a few hours of daylight will have passed and the condition will not be met. By the same moment the following day, however, a whole day's worth of daylight will have passed and thus the condition will be met.

It is mentioned in az-Ziyādāt that if one was to say to his wife, "You are divorced in(*fī*) the decree of Allah" or "You are divorced in(*fī*) the will of Allah", both sentences are conditionals, as that is how the preposition *fī* functions with a root word. As they are conditionals and the Will and Decree of Allah ﷻ cannot be known regarding this matter of divorce, the condition is not met and the divorce does not occur.

Text And Translation

ولو دخلت الكلمة في الفعل تفيد معنى الشرط، قال مُحَمّد رحمه الله: إذا قال: أنت طالق في دخولك الدار فهو بمعنى الشرط فلا يقع الطلاق قبل دخول الدار، ولو قال: أنت طالق في حيضتك إن كانت في الحيض وقع الطلاق في الحال وإلا يتعلق الطلاق بالحيض، وفي "الجامع" لو قال: أنت طالق في مجيء يوم لم تطلق حتى يطلع الفجر، ولو قال: في مضي يوم إن كان ذلك في الليل وقع الطلاق عند غروب الشمس من الغد لوجود الشرط وإن كان في اليوم تطلق حين تجيء من الغد تلك الساعة، وفي "الزيادات" لو قال: أنت طالق في مشيئة الله تعالى أو في إرادة الله تعالى كان ذلك بمعنى الشرط حتى لا تطلق.

QUICK REFERENCE

الزيادات: *az-ziyādāt*

The Additions. Written after al-Jāmi' al-kabīr this work of Imam Muḥammad ash-Shaybānī رحمه الله served as a continuum of the previous book. It contains 12 chapters on various legal rulings .

If the particle *fī* is used with an act it will provide the meaning of a condition. Imam Muḥammad, Allah have mercy on him, says: when one said "You are divorced on(*fī*) entering the house", it will be a conditional so divorce will not occur before entering the house. Had one said, "You are divorced on(*fī*) your period", and she was in her period the divorce would occur immediately otherwise the divorce will be attached to the period. It is in al-Jāmi': should one say: "You are divorced on(*fī*) the arrival of day", she will not be divorced until the morning comes. Should one say: "on(*fī*) the passing of the day", if it was at night, the divorce would occur on the setting of the Sun on the following day as the condition is met. And if it was in the daytime then the divorce would occur at the same moment the following day. It is in az-Ziyādāt: if one said: "You are divorced in(*fī*) Divine Will" or "in(*fī*) Divine Decree", it is a conditional and the divorce will not occur.

❖ ❖ ❖

1.9.11 *al-Bā*

The prepositions also include *al-bā*, which gives the meaning of adhering and attaching. When one item adheres to another it stays attached to it and sticks to it. By the consensus of linguists, this is the literal meaning of *al-bā*. It is for this reason that *al-bā* accompanies the price in transactions. This can be better understood by breaking a transaction down in to two components: an item for sale and the price of that item that must be exchanged for it to transfer ownership. The base of the deal is the item and its set price is the condition that must be met in order for the transaction to complete successfully. Now the jurists say that if the purchaser has not yet taken the item into possession and the item was to be destroyed whilst with the seller, the transaction will be null because the base of the transaction no longer exists. Contrast this with the buyer losing the price of the item before possession and we will simply say replace the price with something similar, like the same value in money, and the transaction will continue. This is because the price is a condition that must be met for the transaction to complete. Destroying it or losing it will not void the transaction but we will simply say bring something else that satisfies the condition of the transaction.

As the item is the base of the transaction and the price is its condition, we say that the price is attached to the item and not the other way around. So, when the preposition *al-bā* is seen in a transaction it denotes the price, and it is

QUICK REFERENCE

الجامع الكبير: *al-jāmi' al-kabīr*

The Great Collection. A collection of narrations that Imam Muḥammad ash-Shaybānī ﷺ compiled directly from Imam Abū Ḥanīfa ﷺ.

الزيادات: *az-ziyādāt*

The Additions. Written after al-Jāmi' al-kabīr this work of Imam Muḥammad ash-Shaybānī ﷺ served as a continuum of the previous book. It contains 12 chapters on various legal rulings.

understood that the price is secondary and attached to the other item. As an example, if one said, "I buy this slave from you for(*bā*) a volume of wheat", and then described the quality of the wheat, the slave will be the base and item for sale, whilst the wheat will be the price. The buyer will be permitted to bring any wheat that meets the quantity and quality mentioned before the exchange, and not necessarily specific wheat set aside. This is because the wheat is the price and condition of the transaction.

Should the transaction be worded, "I buy a volume of wheat from you for(*bā*) this slave", followed by a description of the quality of the wheat, the wheat will be the base and item for sale, whilst the slave will be the price and condition. This transaction is categorised as *bay' as-salam*. In such a transaction, the item is delivered later and so the wheat may be delivered later. It is *bay' as-salam* because the item for sale is 'a volume of wheat' and not a specific one. As it is unspecified, it becomes a loan due and a liability. In any transaction if the item and base is a loan the transaction is named *bay' as-salam* and must satisfy its conditions to be lawful.

Text And Translation

فصل: حرف الباء للإلصاق في وضع اللغة ولهذا تصحب الأثمان وتحقيق هذا أن المبيع أصل في البيع والثمن شرط فيه، ولهذا المعنى هلاك المبيع يوجب ارتفاع البيع دون هلاك الثمن، إذا ثبت هذا فنقول: الأصل ملصِقا بالتبع، فإذا دخل حرف الباء في البدل في باب البيع دل ذلك على أنه تبع ملصق بالأصل فلا يكون مبيعا فيكون ثمنا، وعلى هذا قلنا إذا قال: بعت منك هذا العبدِ بكر من الحنطة ووصفها يكون العبد مبيعا والكر ثمنا فيجوز الاستبدال به قبل القبض، ولو قال: بعت منك كرا من الحنطة و وصفها بهذا العبد يكون العبد ثمنا والكر مبيعا ويكون العقد سلما لا يصح إلا مؤجلا.

Chapter: the particle *al-bā* (الباء) is for attachment in it's lexical coinage and this is why it affixes prices. The detail of this is that the item subject to sale is the base of the transaction and the price is a condition. For this reason destruction of the item necessitates the annulment of the transaction, and not the price. When this is established, we say: the attachment is affixed to the base. So when the article *bā* enters on the exchange in the chapter of transactions it shows that it is an affixed attachment to the base and so it is not the sale item rather it is the payment. Based on this we said when one says: "I've sold you this slave

QUICK ARABIC

بيع السلم: *bay' us-salam*

An advance sale. A sale in which the price is advanced for the goods to be delivered at a future fixed time. Only things of similar class can be sold in this way.

for(*bā*) a measure of wheat", and he described it, the slave will be the sale item and the wheat payment. So the exchange will be permitted before possession. Had he said: "I've sold you a measure of wheat", and he describes it, "for(*bā*) this slave", the slave will be payment and the measure the sale item. The contract will be *as-salam* and only permitted through deferral.

❖ ❖ ❖

If a master says to his slave, "If you inform me of(*bā*) so-and-so's arrival, you are free", it will depend on a true account of the person's arrival. If the slave wrongfully informed of the arrival, he will not be free. This is because the informing is attached to the arrival using the particle *bā*, so the two must be together for the freedom to occur. If the slave now falsely informs the master, the arrival and the informing are not together, so the slave will not be free. Arrival and informing will be together once the person arrives, and in such a case, the slave will be free. Contrast this to the master saying, "If you inform me that so-and-so came, you are free", without *al-bā*. It will depend on merely informing, such that should the slave falsely inform of the arrival, he will still be free. This is because omitting *al-bā* means the information need not be attached to the arrival, so it will not be a condition for the emancipation. The only requirement for freedom is to inform of an arrival, and whether it is true or false is not considered.

If a husband said to his wife, "If you leave the house, except with(*bā*) my permission, you are divorced", every time she needs to leave the house, she must seek permission to avoid the divorce. This is because the exception is attached to the permission using *al-bā*. This implies that the leaving that is exempt from the divorce will always be attached to seeking permission. The husband's words mean that do not leave the house except for when you have sought my permission. Should she leave the house on any occasion without this permission, the divorce will take effect. Contrast this with the husband saying, "If you leave the house, except if I permit you, you are divorced", without the use of *al-bā*. In this case, the permission will only need to be sought on the single occasion. This is because by omitting *al-bā*, the leaving need not be attached to the permission on every occasion. Having the permission granted on one occasion would be sufficient and if the woman was to leave the house on another occasion without permission, it will not bring the divorce into effect.

QUICK DICTIONARY

emancipate: *ih-man-suh-payt*
To free. To free a slave from bondage and servitude.

QUICK REFERENCE

الزيادات: *az-ziyādāt*
The Additions. Written after al-Jāmi' al-kabīr this work of Imam Muḥammad ash-Shaybānī رحمه الله served as a continuum of the previous book. It contains 12 chapters on various legal rulings .

It is stated in az-Ziyādāt that if one said to his wife, "You are divorced with(*bā*) the Decree of Allah", or "You are divorced with(*bā*) the Will of Allah", the divorce will not occur. This is because the statements attach the divorce to Divine Decree and to Divine Will with *al-bā,* and Divine Decree and Will cannot be known by us and so the divorce will never be realised.

Text And Translation

وقال علماؤنا رحمهم الله: إذا قال لعبده: إن أخبرتني بقدوم فلان فأنت حر فذلك على الخبر الصادق ليكون الخبر ملصقا بالقدوم فلو أخبر كاذبا لا يعتق، ولو قال: إن أخبرتني أن فلانا قدم فأنت حر فذلك على مطلق الخبر فلو أخبره كاذبا عتق، ولو قال لامرأته: إن خرجت من الدار إلا بإذني فأنت كذا تحتاج إلى الإذن كل مرة؛ إذ المستثنى خروج ملصق بالإذن فلو خرجت في المرة الثانية بدون الإذن طلقت. ولو قال: إن خرجت من الدار إلا أن آذن لك فذلك على الإذن مرة حتى لو خرجت مرة أخرى بدون الإذن لا تطلق، وفي "الزيادات" إذا قال: أنت طالق بمشيئة الله تعالى أو بإرادة الله تعالى أو بحكمه لم تطلق

Our jurists, Allah have mercy on them, have said: when one said to his slave: "If you inform me of(*bā*) the arrival of so-and-so, you are free", it will be based on true information so that the information is affixed to the arrival. Should he inform him falsely, he will not be free. If one said: "Should you inform me that so-and-so has arrived, (*fa*)you are free," this will be based on mere information. If he falsely informs him, he'll be free. If one said to his wife: "If you leave the house except with(*bā*) my permission, you are like that", she'll require permission every time. The exceptional leave is affixed to permission, so if she leaves the second time without permission she is divorced. If one said: "If you leave the house except that I permit you," this will be permission for the once, such that if she leaves another time without permission she isn't divorced. az-Ziyādāt includes, when one said: "You are divorced with(*bā*) Divine Will", "with(*bā*) Divine Decree" or "with(*bā*) His Command", she's not divorced.

❖ ❖ ❖

Summary Of Significant Particles (2)

Summary of the Prepositions

1. Details of the particle *ilā*:
It comes to show the limit or boundary of something and it has two functions.
i) Sometimes it comes to extend the locus of the ruling. For example, اشتريت هذا المكان إلى هذا الحائط The purchase extends from the house to the said wall. The wall will not be included in the purchase. On other occasions it comes to limit the locus of the ruling. For example, لا أكلم فلانا إلى شهر. The period of no communication will be set and limited to one month. The last moments of the month will be included within the ruling.
ii) Sometimes it delays a ruling to a later point. For example, of one says to his wife, أنت طالق إلى شهر. If he had no intention at the time of saying the words the divorce process will begin after the completion of one month.

2. Details of the particle *'alā*:
It has three functions.
i) To show that something is necessary. For example, لفلان عليّ ألف. This compels the payment of 1000.
ii) Metaphorically it can come in the meaning of the particle *al-bā*. For example, if one said بعتك هذا على ألف. Here it is in the meaning of *al-bā*, as there is an exchange involved.
iii) Sometimes it is used as a conditional. For example, يبايعنك على أن لا يشركن بالله شيئا. The path of allegiance is conditional.

3. Details of the particle *fī*:
It has two functions.
i) For containment or *aẓ-ẓarfīya*. For example, غصبتُ ثوبا في منديل would be a confession of taking both contents and container. The word may be used for time or space, and it could be omitted from or included in the words.
a) An example of usage with time is if one said to his wife أنت طالق في غد or أنت طالق غداً; both are for temporal containment.
b) An example of spatial usage is if one said to his wife أنت طالق في الدار وفي مكة. The divorce will universally apply to all places and the *fī* is for spatial containment.
ii) Sometimes it is used with a root noun, *al-maṣdar*. It will result in a conditional statement. For example, Imam Muḥammad رحمه الله says when one said to his wife, أنت طالق في دخولك الدار it is a conditional construct.

4. Details of the particle *al-bā*:
It is for conjoining and connecting. All other meanings of it are metaphorical. For example, if one says to his slave إن أخبرتني بقدوم فلان فأنت حر it will mean a correct and true communication. So, upon giving false information he will not be free.

1.10 Types of al-Bayān

This chapter deals with al-bayān, statements. The various types of al-bayān are an essential component of al-Kitāb just like the other terms introduced throughout this book. Linguistically al-bayān or statements are to communicate an idea with added clarity. In terms of al-uṣūl and principles, it is to take an ambiguity from its ambiguous state into a state of clarity. In the Shariah, this is achieved through words as well as through actions. On numerous occasions, the blessed Prophet ﷺ has asked the Companions رضي الله عنهم to observe his actions in order to learn religious practices. The chapter deals with seven types of al-Bayān; namely, bayān ut-taqrīr (Affirmation), bayān ut-tafsīr (Clarification), bayān ut-taghyīr (Change), bayān uḍ-ḍarūra (Implied), bayān ul-ḥāl (Silent), bayān ul-'aṭf (Explanatory Apposition), and bayān ut-tabdīl (Abrogation).

Text And Translation

فصل في وجوه البيان: البيان على سبعة أنواع: بيان تقرير وبيان تفسير وبيان تغيير وبيان ضرورة وبيان حال وبيان عطف وبيان تبديل

Chapter on the types of al-bayān: al-Bayān is of seven types: at-taqrīr, at-tafsīr, at-taghyīr, aḍ-ḍarūra, al-ḥāl, al-'atf and at-tabdīl.

❖ ❖ ❖

1.10.1 Bayān ut-Taqrīr and Bayān ut-Tafsīr

Bayān ut-taqrīr is the statement that affirms what was previously said. This statement is used when a word is clear in a meaning but has a possibility of an alternate meaning. For example, a word is used in a literal sense and is understood to be so, but still carries the possibility of a metaphorical meaning. When the speaker makes a statement clarifying the clear and already understood meaning, we say that the statement is bayān ut-taqrīr, or a statement of affirmation. It affirms and maintains the truth of what we already understood.

An example of bayān ut-taqrīr is if one confesses, "I owe(*'alā*) so-and-so a measure of wheat, by the measure of this city", or "I owe(*'alā*) so-and-so one thousand, of the currency of this city". Both statements, 'the measure of this

QUICK TERMS

البان: *al-bayān*

Statements. Something declared in speech, writing or the lack thereof, that sets forth facts or particulars.

الكتاب: *al-kitāb*

The book. The inspired final word of Allah ﷻ. The Quran.

الأصول: *al-uṣūl*

Principles. The accepted fundamental rules of deriving matters of fiqh.

بيان التقرير: *bayan ut-taqrīr*

Affirmation. A statement that confirms a previously understood meaning.

بيان التفسير: *bayan ut-tafsīr*

Clarification. A statement that clears up the meaning of a previous statement.

city' and 'the currency of this city', are bayān ut-taqrīr. This is because when the confessions do not include these two extensions we would, by default, understand it to be of the same city in which the confession is made. By the confessor stating what we already understood, he has simply affirmed what we already suspected. However, there was always a possibility that in each case he may have been referring to the measure or currency of another land. This remote possibility was eliminated by his affirming statement of bayān ut-taqrīr.

Similarly, if one said, "I have(*'inda*) so-and-so's one thousand in safekeeping", we will understand before the extended words of 'in safekeeping' that the Arabic word *'inda* suggests something in safekeeping that it is to be returned. That is the default understanding from the words used. When the speaker added 'in safekeeping', it only affirmed what we already knew. However, there was a remote possibility that he could 'have' the amount with him for a number of other reasons such as a loan. The speaker eliminated the other remote possibilities and affirmed what we already knew by the words 'in safekeeping', so this is bayān ut-taqrīr, a statement of affirmation.

Text And Translation

أما الأول فهو أن يكون معنى اللفظ ظاهرا لكنه يحتمل غيره فبين المراد بما هو الظاهر فيتقرر حكم الظاهر ببيانه، ومثاله إذا قال: لفلان علي قفيز حنطة بقفيز البلد أو ألف من نقد البلد فإنه يكون بيان تقرير؛ لأن المطلق كان محمولا على قفيز البلد ونقده مع احتمال إرادة الغير، فإذا بين ذلك فقد قرره ببيانه، وكذلك لو قال: لفلان عندي ألف وديعة فإن كلمة عندي كانت بإطلاقها تفيد الأمانة مع احتمال إرادة الغير فإذا قال: وديعة فقد قرر حكم الظاهر ببيانه

The first is that the meaning of the word is evident but has the possibility of another, and the interpretation is stated to be the evidently clear. So the evident is affirmed through the statement. An example of it is when one said: "I owe so-and-so a measure of wheat of the city" or "one thousand of the city's currency". This will be bayān at-taqrīr because the unqualified was the city's measure and its currency, with the possibility of intending another. So when he states it, he confirms it with his statement. Similarly, if one said: "I have so-and-so's one thousand in safekeeping", the words 'I have' default to 'in trust' with the possibility of intending something else. So when he states 'in safekeeping', he affirms the evident with his statement.

QUICK TERMS

بيان التقرير: *bayan ut-taqrīr*

Affirmation. A statement that confirms a previously understood meaning.

❖ ❖ ❖

The second type is bayān ut-tafsīr. It is brought about by an ambiguity in the initial words of the speaker, such that *al-mujmal* or *al-mushtarak* was initially used. By issuing a statement that clears that ambiguity, the speaker is issuing bayān ut-tafsīr, a statement of clarification. As an example, if one said, "I owe so-and-so something", and then went on to name what that 'something' is, we would say that the naming is a clarification of the ambiguity which was present when the statement was simply left at 'something'. Similarly, if one said, "I owe ten and some(*nayyif*) dirham", the word *nayyif* is ambiguous in that it can be anywhere between one and three. When the speaker makes the exact amount clear, the statement of clarification is known as bayān ut-tafsīr. Furthermore, if one said, "I owe dirham", and then went on to say 'ten' for example, to specify the amount, it is bayān ut-tafsīr.

The ruling of both bayān ut-taqrīr and bayān ut-tafsīr is that they are valid as explanatory statements when stated alongside the speaker's initial statements as well as when offered later.

Text And Translation

وأما بيان التفسير فهو ما إذا كان اللفظ غير مكشوف المراد فكشفه ببيانه، مثاله إذا قال: لفلان علي شيء ثم فسر الشيء بثوب أو قال: علي عشرة دراهم ونيف ثم فسر النيف، أو قال: علي دراهم وفسرها بعشرة مثلا، وحكم هذين النوعين من البيان أن يصح موصولا ومفصولا

As for bayān ut-tafsīr it is if the word is not evidently clear so it is cleared by his statement. An example of it is when one said: "I owe so-and-so something", then explains the thing to be a garment. Or he said: "I owe ten and a bit dirham", then clarified the 'bit'. Or one said: "I owe dirhams", and stated them to be ten for example. The ruling for both of these types of al-bayān is that they are valid together or separate.

❖ ❖ ❖

1.10.2 Bayān ut-Taghyīr

The third type of bayān is bayān ut-taghyīr. This is when a statement changes the meaning and direction of the initial statement. This can occur when

QUICK TERMS

المجمل: *al-mujmal*

The unexplained. Wording that requires explanatory statements.

المشترك: *al-mushtarak*

The concurrent. A word coined for two or more inherently different meanings.

بيان التفسير: *bayan ut-tafsīr*

Clarification. A statement that clears up the meaning of a previous statement.

بيان التغيير: *bayan ut-taghyīr*

Change. A statement that changes the direction and understanding of a previous statement.

a speaker uses a word as the metaphorical al-majāz instead of the literal al-ḥaqīqa, or by using a general al-'āmm word and then applying a restriction to it and effectively changing it to al-'ām khuṣṣa 'anhu. These are all examples of bayān ut-taghyīr, or statement of change.

Deferrals, *at-ta'līq*, and exceptions, *al-istithnā*, are also types of bayān ut-taghyīr. If we consider a deferral such as, "You are free if you enter the house", the initial statement 'you are free' would emancipate the slave immediately. However, by adding 'if you enter the house' the emancipation does not occur immediately, rather only when the condition is met. It is as though this condition has changed the meaning and direction of the initial statement. Similarly, in cases of exemptions, "I owe so-and-so one thousand less(*illā*) one hundred", initially states that a whole one thousand is owed. However, by adding the exception of one hundred, the value of the amount owed is changed. It now becomes nine hundred and not the initial one thousand.

Jurists have differed regarding the manner in which both deferrals and exceptions are applied. The Aḥnāf say in the case of deferrals by way of conditions, the initial words only become a cause when the condition is realised and not before it, whereas Imam ash-Shāfa'īy عليه رحمة الله says the words are a cause immediately when spoken and only the condition not being met prevents applying the words. Rather, the mechanism of application is disputed. If for example one said, "You are divorced if you enter the house", Imam ash-Shāfa'īy عليه رحمة الله would say, had the deferral not been uttered the divorce would occur immediately. The words are a cause for divorce in that very instance. Now, because a condition of entering a house is attached to defer the divorce, he says that the condition is acting as a preventive for the occurrence of the divorce. Once the condition of entering the house occurs, the preventive is no longer in place and so the divorce occurs. The Aḥnāf present the mechanism at work differently. They maintain that the whole deferral sentence is ineffective in the instance it is stated and it is not a cause for anything. It is as though the words are not uttered. It is only when the condition of entering the house occurs, that the whole statement becomes effective and it is as though it is now being uttered. So, before the condition of entering the house occurs there is no effective statement, but when the entering occurs the words are effectively there and the divorce occurs.

QUICK TERMS

المجاز: *al-majāz*

The figurative. A word used for a meaning other than its coined meaning.

الحقيقة: *al-ḥaqīqa*

The literal. A word coined by the lexicon for an item.

عام خص عنه البعض: *'āmmun khuṣṣa 'anh ul-ba'ḍ*

The general with exemptives. A word designated for a group with possible exemptions.

بيان التغيير: *bayan ut-taghyīr*

Change. A statement that changes the direction and understanding of a previous statement.

QUICK ARABIC

التعليق: *at-ta'līq*

Suspension. To defer and postpone a matter.

الاستثناء: *al-istithnā*

Exemption. To exclude and leave out individual(s).

The consequence of the different mechanisms is highlighted in particular cases. One such case is if one said to a female stranger, "If I marry you, you are divorced", or to another individual's slave, "If I come to own you, you are free". In both cases the Aḥnāf say the deferral is valid, whereas Imam ash-Shāfa'īy رحمه الله says it is invalid. The Aḥnāf are thus saying that when the individual marries the woman a divorce will take effect and when the individual buys the said slave, the slave will be free. In the view of Imam ash-Shāfa'īy رحمه الله the marriage will not result in the issuance of a divorce, nor will the slave become free upon purchase. The ash-Shāfi'ī evidence is that deferrals will be checked for validity when they are uttered. At the point of utterance of the initial statement, both marriage and ownership are a cause for their respective outcomes, divorce and freedom. As both causes are not suitable because the recipient is neither a spouse nor an owned slave, the effect in both cases is prevented. The cause is not valid so the effect becomes invalid, and the statements are null and void. In the future when the marriage and purchase occur, the previous statements have been annulled and so the marriage goes ahead without a divorce, and the purchase goes ahead without emancipation. The Aḥnāf understand that both utterances are valid deferrals. This is because the effect of the cause is not considered at the point of utterance. Rather, the effect only becomes active when the condition has been realised. Now, when the individual marries the woman and purchases the slave, the condition is realised and so respective causes, marriage and purchase, result in their outcome, divorce and marriage, respectively.

Text And Translation

فصل: و أما بيان التغيير فهو أن يتغير ببيانه معنى كلامه ونظيره التعليق والاستثناء، وقد اختلف الفقهاء في الفصلين فقال أصحابنا: المعلق بالشرط سبب عند وجود الشرط لا قبله وقال الشافعي رحمه الله: التعليق سبب في الحال إلا أن عدم الشرط مانع من حكمه، وفائدة الخلاف تظهر فيما إذا قال لأجنبية: إن تزوجتك فأنت طالق أو قال لعبد الغير: إن ملكتك فأنت حر، يكون التعليق باطلا عنده؛ لأن حكم التعليق انعقاد صدر الكلام علة والطلاق والعتاق ههنا لم ينعقد علة لعدم إضافته إلى المحل فبطل حكم التعليق فلا يصح التعليق، وعندنا كان التعليق صحيحا حتى لو تزوجها يقع الطلاق؛ لأن كلامه إنما ينعقد علة عند وجود الشرط والملك ثابت عند وجود الشرط فيصح التعليق

Bayān ut-Taghyīr

Chapter: As for bayān ut-taghyīr it is that one's statement alters the meaning of one's words. The example of it are conditional deferrals and exceptions. Jurists have differed regarding both. Our jurists say: a conditional is an effective cause when the condition is operational and not earlier. Imam ash-Shāfa'īy, Allah have mercy on him, said: a conditional is effective immediately, except the absence of the condition prevents it's outcome. The differing opinions manifest when one says to a strange woman: "If I marry you, you are divorced" or one says to another's slave: "If I come to own you, you are free". According to him the conditional is void because the functioning of a conditional is by engaging the protasis - dependent clause - as a cause. Divorce and emancipation, here, are not causes as they are inapplicable to the situation, so the function of the conditional is void and the conditional is not permitted. According to us, the conditional is correct to a point that were he to marry her, the divorce would occur. This is because his words will be engaged as a cause when the condition is met. Ownership is established when the condition is met so the conditional is correct.

❖ ❖ ❖

As the deferred only becomes effective when the cause is realised, and not before it, it follows that the deferral must be directly linked to ownership itself or to the cause of ownership, and nothing else. For example, if one said to a female stranger, "If you enter the house, you are divorced", the cause is marriage, the effect is divorce, and the condition is entering the house. However, the cause is not mentioned in the statement and so the condition is not directly connected to it. As the condition is not connected directly to the cause, i.e. marriage, the statement is invalid as it is spoken to a stranger, who is not bound to the instruction of this individual. The statement thus becomes void. Later, when the stranger marries this individual and enters the house, divorce will not occur because the previous statement was void. Thus, the statement remains ineffective.

Furthermore, the case of *ṭawl ul-ḥurra*, having the means to marry a free woman, can be understood through the same concept. The case is that Allah ﷻ says in verse 25 of Sūrat un-Nisā:

﴿وَمَن لَّمْ يَسْتَطِعْ مِنكُمْ طَوْلاً أَن يَنكِحَ الْمُحْصَنَاتِ الْمُؤْمِنَاتِ فَمِن مَّا مَلَكَتْ أَيْمَانُكُم مِّن فَتَيَاتِكُمُ الْمُؤْمِنَاتِ﴾

[النساء: 25]

QUICK TERMS

بيان التغيير: *bayan ut-taghyīr*

Change. A statement that changes the direction and understanding of a previous statement.

QUICK ARABIC

طول الحرة: *ṭawl ul-ḥurra*

Capability upon the freewoman. The financial ability to marry a free-woman.

"And whoso is not able to afford to marry free, believing women, let them marry from the believing maids whom you own..."

In this verse, the marriage of slaves is deferred to the inability to marry free women. Due to this deferral Imam ash-Shāfa'īy رحمه الله says that ability to marry a free woman prevents from marrying a slave. So according to him, whilst you are able to marry a free woman the condition of 'unable to marry a free woman' is not fulfilled and whilst the condition is not met, it will prevent the permission to marry a slave. Similarly, Imam ash-Shāfa'īy رحمه الله says that an irrevocably divorced woman need not be paid maintenance during her waiting in *al-'idda*. The exception to this is when she is pregnant. The reason is verse 6 of Sūrat uṭ-Ṭalāq:

﴿وَإِن كُنَّ أُولَاتِ حَمْلٍ فَأَنفِقُوا عَلَيْهِنَّ حَتَّىٰ يَضَعْنَ حَمْلَهُنَّ﴾ [الطلاق: 6]

"...and if they are with child, then spend for them till they deliver..."

Here, Allah جل جلاله has deferred the payment of maintenance in cases of pregnancy, therefore with a pregnancy the husband must pay and when the condition of pregnancy is not met, he need not pay. The absence of the condition is preventing the ruling.

In both previous cases, ability to marry a free woman and of maintenance, the Aḥnāf say that one is permitted to marry a slave even if he has the means to marry a free woman, and when there is no pregnancy, maintenance is still necessary upon the husband. The evidence is that the mention of a condition governs the situation where such a condition is present, but it is silent on cases where the condition is not present, as it is not to be thought of as a preventive. In other words, when the condition is present, the ruling must be applied. However, when the condition is not present, it does not automatically follow that the ruling will also cease to be. When the condition is not found, this text is silent on the matter, neither allowing nor prohibiting it. It is possible that the case without the condition is discussed in another text altogether.

In short, marriage to any owned slave despite ability to marry a free woman will be permitted through verse 24 of Sūrat un-Nisā:

﴿وَأُحِلَّ لَكُم مَّا وَرَاءَ ذَٰلِكُمْ﴾ [النساء: 24]

"...Lawful for you are all beyond those mentioned..."

QUICK ARABIC

العدة: *al-'idda*

The term. The three-month period after a divorce.

Furthermore, the unrestricted verse 3 of Sūrat un-Nisā, also allows the aforementioned marriage:

﴿فَانكِحُواْ مَا طَابَ لَكُم مِّنَ النِّسَاء مَثْنَى وَثُلاَثَ وَرُبَاعَ﴾ [النساء: 4]

"...marry of the women, who seem good to you, two or three or four..."

The necessity to maintain a divorcee despite no pregnancy will be established from verse 2 of Sūrat ul-Baqara, and from the ruling of verse 6 of Sūrat uṭ-Ṭalāq:

﴿وَعلَى الْمَوْلُودِ لَهُ رِزْقُهُنَّ وَكِسْوَتُهُنَّ بِالْمَعْرُوفِ﴾ [البقرة: 233]

"...the duty of feeding and clothing nursing mothers in a seemly manner is upon the father of the child..."

﴿فَأَنفِقُوا عَلَيْهِنَّ﴾ [الطلاق: 6]

"...then spend for them...."

Text And Translation

ولهذا المعنى قلنا: شرط صحة التعليق للوقوع في صورة عدم الملك أن يكون مضافا إلى الملك أو إلى سبب الملك حتى لو قال لأجنبية: إن دخلت الدار فأنت طالق ثم تزوجها ووجد الشرط لا يقع الطلاق وكذلك طول الحرة يمنع جواز نكاح الأمة عنده؛ لأن الكتاب علق نكاح الأمة بعدم الطول فعند وجود الطول كان الشرط عدما وعدم الشرط مانع من الحكم فلا يجوز، وكذلك قال الشافعي رحمه الله: لا نفقة للمبتوتة إلا إذا كانت حاملا؛ لأن الكتاب علق الإنفاق لقوله تعالى: ﴿وإن كن أولات حمل فأنفقوا عليهن حتى يضعن حملهن﴾ فعند عدم الحمل كان الشرط عدما وعدم الشرط مانع من الحكم عنده، وعندنا لما لم يكن عدم الشرط مانعا من الحكم جاز أن يثبت الحكم بدليله فيجوز نكاح الأمة ويجب الإنفاق بالعمومات

For this reason we say: the requirement for the validity of the conditional to be functional in the case of non-ownership is that it should be attached to the ownership or the cause of ownership. Such that if one said to a strange woman: "If you enter the house, you are divorced". He then married her and the condition is fulfilled but the divorce will not occur. Similarly, capability upon a free-woman obstructs permissibility of marriage to a slave-girl, according to him, because the Book defers the marrying of slaves to incapability. So when there is capability, the condition is not met and the absence of the condition prevents the ruling, so it is not permitted. Similarly, Imam ash-Shāfa'īy, Allah have mercy on him, said there is no maintenance for the housebound-woman except when she is pregnant, because the Book conditions the maintenance. Allah Almighty says: "...and if they are with child, then spend for them till they deliver..." So when there is no pregnancy the condition is not met, and the lack of a condition obstructs the ruling according to him. According to us, due to the lack of a condition not being a preventive from the ruling, the ruling may be established with its own evidence. So marrying a slave-girl is permitted and maintenance is necessary due to the generality.

❖ ❖ ❖

The topic of the attributed noun, *al-mawṣūf*, follows the topic of deferrals by condition. That is because an attribute is like a condition, in that the ruling only applies when the condition is met and the ruling will only apply when the attribute is present. The same difference is observed between the views of the Aḥnāf and Imam ash-Shāfa'īy رحمه الله as was discussed in deferrals by condition. Imam ash-Shāfa'īy رحمه الله says in the absence of the attribute, the ruling will be reversed just as in the absence of the condition the ruling was reversed. The Aḥnāf assert that just as the absence of the condition does not mean the ruling is reversed, the absence of the attribute will not reverse the ruling either. Bearing this in mind, Imam ash-Shāfa'īy رحمه الله has said that marrying a slave-girl from the Ahl ul-Kitāb is not permitted because Allah جل جلاله says in verse 25 of Sūrat un-Nisā:

﴿مِّن فَتَيَاتِكُمُ الْمُؤْمِنَاتِ﴾ [النساء: 25]

"...from the believing maids whom your right hands possess..."

The slave-girls have been attributed with belief and so the ruling is that you are permitted to marry them. However, if the attribute is removed, the ruling will be reversed. So, the slave-girls of the Ahl ul-Kitāb are not believers and marriage to them is impermissible. The Aḥnāf contend that just as one is permitted to marry a believing slave-girl, a slave-girl of the Ahl ul-Kitāb may be married. This is because the absence of the attribute of belief does not translate to the reversing of the ruling, just as it did not in deferrals by condition.

QUICK ARABIC

اهل الكتاب: *ahl ul-kitāb*

People of the book. Jews and Christians, who are believers in a revealed religion.

QUICK GRAMMAR

الموصوف: *al-mawṣūf*

The described. The item depicted or detailed by an attribute.

ومن توابع هذا النوع ترتب الحكم على الاسم الموصوف بصفة فإنه بمنزلة تعليق الحكم بذلك الوصف عنده، وعلى هذا قال الشافعي رحمه الله: لا يجوز نكاح الأمة الكتابية؛ لأن النص رتب الحكم على أمة مؤمنة لقوله تعالى: ﴿من فتياتكم المؤمنات﴾ فيتقيد بالمؤمنة فيمتنع الحكم عند عدم الوصف فلا يجوز نكاح الأمة الكتابية

Subsequent to this type, is the ruling of an attributed noun with its attribute. It is in the place of a conditional ruling with that attribute, according to him. Based on this Imam ash-Shāfa'īy, Allah have mercy on him, said marrying a slave-girl of the People of the Book is not permitted, because the text has based the ruling on a believing slave-girl. He Almighty says: "...from your believing maids..." So it is conditioned with believing and so it prevents the ruling when the condition is not met, hence marrying a slave-girl of the People of the Book is not permitted.

❖ ❖ ❖

The other method of deferrals in bayān ut-taghyīr is by *al-istithnā*, exceptions. There is a difference between the Aḥnāf and Imam ash-Shāfa'īy رحمه الله regarding the mechanism by which exceptions are applied. The Aḥnāf say that after the exception is applied, the remainder are subject to the ruling only and the ruling is silent regarding those that are exempt. For example, if one said, "I owe one thousand less(*illa*) one hundred". We say that once the exception has been applied the sentence only concerns the nine hundred that remain; it is what is owed. This statement has no bearing on the exempt one hundred; this statement is silent regarding them. The equivalent of this is to say, 'I owe nine hundred'. Imam ash-Shāfa'īy رحمه الله holds that the sentence is to be thought of in two parts, one part before the exception, and the second with the exception. The part before the exception is all necessary, and is thus owed. However, the exception prevents the latter part from being necessary, effectively making the whole one thousand necessary but only requiring a payment of nine hundred, as the one hundred is prevented from inclusion.

An example of the difference of opinion is in the tradition of the blessed Prophet صلى الله عليه وسلم, "Don't trade food for food, except in parity". Imam ash-Shāfa'īy رحمه الله reads from this that the initial statement before the exception states that

حديث

عن معمر بن عبد الله رضي الله عنه كنت أسمع رسول الله صلى الله عليه وسلم يقول الطعام بالطعام مثلا بمثل.

عليه الصلاة والسلام

(صحيح مسلم: 1592)

QUICK TERMS

بيان التغيير: *bayan ut-taghyīr*

Change. A statement that changes the direction and understanding of a previous statement.

QUICK ARABIC

الاستثناء: *al-istithnā*

Exemption. To exclude and leave out individual(s).

trading food for food is prohibited. This implies that it is prohibited in small quantities and in large quantities. A small quantity is one that is not easily measured, and a large quantity is one that has an easily measurable amount. In any case, trading food for food is prohibited regardless. Then the exception of parity - when the amounts are equal - prevents this case from being part of the prohibition, and is thus permitted. So, trading food for food by estimating the amounts will be prohibited, as this would have the possibility of both amounts being unequal and thus prohibited. It follows that one handful of food will not be permitted to be exchanged for two handfuls. The Aḥnāf say the case of trading one handful of food for two is not discussed in this Hadith because this tradition concerns parity in trade being permitted and non-parity being forbidden. Parity and inequality can only be factors in measurable items, and items that are too small to measure individually are not subject to measurement so how can parity and inequality be factors in their trade? One or two handfuls of foodstuff, which are lighter than the readily available weight measures, would not be governed by this tradition; this tradition only concerns items that are measurable. Thus, exchanging one handful of food for two, in measures that are small, is permitted and not forbidden.

Text And Translation

ومن صور بيان التغيير الاستثناء. ذهب أصحابنا إلى أن الاستثناء تكلم بالباقي بعد الثنيا كأنه لم يتكلم إلا بما بقي، وعنده صدر الكلام ينعقد علة لوجوب الكل إلا أن الاستثناء يمنعها من العمل بمنزلة عدم الشرط في باب التعليق، ومثال هذا في قوله عليه السلام: لا تبيعوا الطعام بالطعام إلا سواء بسواء فعند الشافعي رحمه الله صدر الكلام انعقد علة لحرمة بيع الطعام بالطعام على الإطلاق، وخرج عن هذه الجملة صورة المساواة بالاستثناء فبقي الباقي تحت حكم الصدر، ونتيجة هذا حرمة بيع الحفنة من الطعام بحفنتين منه، وعندنا بيع الحفنة لا يدخل تحت النص؛ لأن المراد بالمنهي يتقيد بصورة بيع يتمكن بالحفنتين لأن المراد بالمنهي يتقيد بصورة بيع يتمكن العبد من إثبات التساوي والتفاضل فيه كيلا يؤدي إلى نهي العاجز فما لا يدخل تحت المعيار المسوى كان خارجا عن قضية الحديث

Of the forms of bayān ut-taghyīr is al-istithnā. Our jurists hold the view that *al-istithnā* speaks of the remainder after the exception; it is as though nothing is said except regarding the remainder. According to him, the initial sentence will be a cause of enacting the whole except that *al-istithnā* prevents it from functioning, like the lack of a condition in the chapter of conditionals. An example of this is in his saying, peace and blessings be upon him: "Don't sell foodstuff for foodstuff except like for like. So according to Imam ash-Shāfa'īy, Allah have mercy on him, the initial sentence is the cause of absolute prohibition of selling foodstuff for foodstuff. The scenario of parity is exempted from this sentence with al-istithnā, so the remainder remains under the function of the initial. This results in the prohibition of selling a handful of foodstuff for two handfuls. According to us, the selling of handfuls does not concern this text because the prohibition is limited to that exchange which is possible with handfuls. This is because the prohibition concerns that exchange in which the subject is able to establish parity and excess, so that it does not lead to prohibiting the implausable. So whatever is not included in the standard of parity is out of the discussion of the Hadith.

❖ ❖ ❖

Some other examples of bayān ut-taghyīr include if one said, "I owe(*'alayya*) so-and-so one thousand from safekeeping". The word 'owe' gives the impression of a necessary and obligatory returning which means it is a loan that is to be repaid. However, when the words 'from safekeeping' are used, it changes the meaning to an entrusted amount that is to be returned. It is the equivalent of one saying that I am not in debt by one thousand, rather it was entrusted to me and I am going to return it.

Another example is if one said, "You gave me one thousand but I didn't take possession of it". The words 'you gave me' imply that the item given was received and possession changed hands in the process. The item could not have been 'given' if the other did not take possession. However, by adding 'I didn't take possession', it changes the meaning of the previous part. It now means you verbally gave me the one thousand but I did not physically take possession of it.

Furthermore, if one said, "You advanced me one thousand but I didn't take possession of it", we typically understand from 'you advanced me' that possession would have occurred in the form of *bay' as-salam*. However, by adding that possession did not take place, the transaction becomes void as it is a condition for *bay' as-salam* for the capital to be exchanged.

QUICK TERMS

بيان التغيير: *bayan ut-taghyīr*

Change. A statement that changes the direction and understanding of a previous statement.

QUICK ARABIC

الاستثناء: *al-istithnā*

Exemption. To exclude and leave out individual(s).

بيع السلم: *bay' us-salam*

An advance sale. A transaction in which the price is advanced for the goods to be delivered at a future fixed time. Only things of similar class can be sold in this manner.

In each of the aforementioned examples, 'I didn't take possession' is bayān ut-taghyīr because it changes the direction and default understanding of the statement.

It is also bayān ut-taghyīr when one says, "I owe you one thousand in counterfeit". The first part gives the impression that one thousand is actually owed, as is the norm that people deal in genuine items and currency. However, by adding 'counterfeit' it changes the meaning of the initial statement.

The ruling of bayān ut-taghyīr is that it is permitted *muttaṣil*, when it immediately follows the initial statement, but it is not permitted *munfaṣil*, when there is a significant gap between the initial statement and the explanatory statement. This is because it is as though the speaker is revoking the previous statement and replacing it with the new element, and this is only permitted immediately.

Jurists disagree on whether the case falls in the category of bayān ut-taghyīr or in the category of bayān ut-tabdīl in a few cases. In bayān ut-taghyīr the cases would be permitted when delivered immediately but not separately, and in bayān ut-tabdīl they would not be permitted in either situation. Further details of such cases will follow later in the discussion of bayān ut-tabdīl. [Chapter 1.10.6, page 320]

Text And Translation

ومن صور بيان التغيير ما إذا قال: لفلان علي ألف وديعة فقوله: علي يفيد الوجوب وهو بقوله: وديعة غيره إلى الحفظ، وقوله: أعطيتني أو أسلفتني ألفا فلم أقبضها من جملة بيان التغيير، وكذا لو قال: لفلان علي ألف زيوف. وحكم بيان التغيير أنه يصح موصولا ولا يصح مفصولا، ثم بعد هذا مسائل اختلف فيها العلماء أنها من جملة بيان التغيير فتصح بشرط الوصل أو من بيان التبديل فلا تصح، وسيأتي طرف منها في بيان التبديل.

From the forms of bayān ut-taghyīr is if one said: "I owe(*'alā*) so-and-so one thousand held in trust". Him saying 'I owe' signifies necessity but his saying 'held in trust' changes it to safekeeping. And one saying: "You gave me", or "You lent me a thousand but I didn't take possession' are from bayān ut-taghyīr. Similarly, if one said: "I owe so-and-so one thousand in counterfeit". The ruling of bayān

QUICK TERMS

بيان التبديل: *bayan ut-tabdīl*

Abrogation. A statement that repeals and replaces a previous statement.

QUICK ARABIC

متصل: *muttaṣil*

Adjoining. Items located next to each other.

منفصل: *munfaṣil*

Detached. Not joined or connected to one another.

ut-taghyīr is that it is valid together but not valid separate. Then following this there are some issues in which the jurists have differed as to include them in bayān ut-taghyīr - so they would be valid together - or in bayān ut-tabdīl - so they would be invalid. A part of the discussion will come in bayān ut-tabdīl.

❖❖❖

1.10.3 Bayān uḍ-Ḍarūra

The fourth type of bayān is bayān uḍ-ḍarūra, an implied statement. This is a statement without actual words and comes about as the consequence of the words of a speaker. A particular point becomes inevitable and implied, though not stated. For example, verse 11 of Sūrat un-Nisā:

﴿فَإِن لَّمْ يَكُن لَّهُ وَلَدٌ وَوَرِثَهُ أَبَوَاهُ فَلِأُمِّهِ الثُّلُثُ﴾ [النساء: 11]

"...and if he has no son and his parents are his heirs, then to his mother is one third..."

In the verse, the portion of the father is not stated in the words, but the constraints placed in the verse inevitably state the portion of the father without stating it. If the inheritors are only the parents and the mother's part is one third, it inevitably leaves the remainder to the father. This is not stated in the words of the verse, so we say the statement of the father's portion is obtained by bayān uḍ-ḍarūra, through the statement is directly concerning the mother.

In a similar way, in an arrangement of *al-muḍāraba*, if either of the two partners' shares is explicitly stated, the other share is inevitably specified too. In an *al-muḍāraba* arrangement one partner, *rabb ul-māl*, provides the capital, whilst the other partner, *al-muḍārib*, manages the business. The profits and losses are shared by both partners in accordance with their initial agreed share in the business. For such an arrangement to be valid, both partners' share must be determined from the onset, otherwise it would be invalid. For example, in the setup of the business two partners agreed that one would provide the capital as a silent partner and the other would run the day-to-day affairs, whilst the capital investor would own 40% of the company. If the share of the other partner is not mentioned, it is still inevitably stated as 60%; this is implied through bayān uḍ-ḍarūra. Similarly, if the share of *al-muḍārib* is set and the agreement's words are silent on the portion of the capital investor, the capital investor's portion is still defined by way of bayān uḍ-ḍarūra.

QUICK TERMS

بيان الضرورة: *bayan uḍ-ḍarūra*

Implied. A statement understood intrinsically from within a statement.

QUICK ARABIC

المضاربة: *al-muḍāraba*

Co-partnership. An agreement whereby co-partners are entitled to profit, one as proprietor of the stock and the other on account of labour.

رب المال: *rabb ul-māl*

Proprietor. The owner and capital investor in a co-partnership.

المضارب: *al-muḍārib*

Labourer. A worker who invests bodily strength, skill and training in a co-partnership, for a share of the profit.

المزارعة: *al-muzāra'a*

Sharecropping. A temporary contract whereby a tenant farmer pays as rent a share of the crop.

The arrangement of *al-muzāra'a* is similar to *al-muḍāraba*. It involves the land of one partner and the labour of another, whilst both share the profit from the yield. When the arrangement is set up, both partners' share is to be mutually agreed. If only one of the partners' share is actually cited, the other's is silently stated by way of bayān uḍ-ḍarūra. The arrangement is thus valid.

Further examples of bayān uḍ-ḍarūra include if someone bequeathed one thousand to two people and proceeded to mention the allocation of one of them. The other individual's allocation is inevitably accounted for too. This is through bayān uḍ-ḍarūra. Similarly, if one divorced one of his two wives without specifying which one, an explanation would be required from him. If he was to then proceed to have intercourse with one of them, it is deemed an explanatory statement. By way of bayān uḍ-ḍarūra the other wife will be the one divorced because one does not give divorce in order to have intercourse! As there is no verbal explanation and one of the two wives is divorced, the one who he has not cohabited with will be specified as the divorced.

Imam Abū Ḥanīfa ﷺ has stated that if a master was to state that one of two slave-girls is free and then to have intercourse with one of them, it does not necessarily lead to the other one becoming free. This intercourse will not be bayān uḍ-ḍarūra for freedom. This is because intercourse is permitted with slave-girls in two ways, by ownership or by freeing and marrying her. Just because intercourse has occurred, it does not clearly pinpoint one outcome. It could be that the one he had intercourse with still remains a slave and the other is free, or it could mean that the one he had intercourse with is free and he has married her. The point is that merely by intercourse we do not have a conclusive explanation of which one is free. As the explanation is not conclusive, it cannot be classed as bayān uḍ-ḍarūra. The master will be required to make it clear which one is free.

Text And Translation

فصل: وأما بيان الضرورة فمثاله في قوله تعالى: ﴿وورِثه َ أبواه فلأُمهِ الثلثُ﴾ أوجب الشركة بين الأبوين ثم بين نصيب الأم فصار ذلك بيانا لنصيب الأب، وعلى هذا قلنا: إذا بينا نصيب المضارب وسكتا عن نصيب رب المال صحت الشركة، وكذلك لو بينا نصيب رب المال وسكتا عن نصيب المضارب كان بيانا وعلى هذا حكم المزارعة، وكذلك لو أوصى لفلان وفلان بألف ثم بين نصيب احدهما كان

ذلك بيانا لنصيب الآخر، ولو طلق إحدى امرأتيه ثم وطىء إحداهما كان ذلك بيانا للطلاق في الأخرى بخلاف الوطيء في العتق المبهم عند أبي حنيفة؛ لأن حل الوطيء في الإماء يثبت بطريقين فلا يتعين جهة الملك باعتبار حل الوطيء.

Chapter: As for bayān uḍ-ḍarūra its example is in the Almighty's saying: "...and his parents are his heirs , then to his mother is one third...". The share is necessitated for both parents, then the portion of the mother is stated. Therefore, this is a statement for the portion of the father. Based on this we say: when they state the share of the managing-partner and remain muted regarding the capital-investor, the partnership is valid. Similarly, if they state the share of the capital-investor and muted regarding the share of the managing-partner, it is stated. Based on this are the rulings on sharecropping. Also, if one bequeathed one thousand for so-and-so and so-and-so, and stated the share of one of them, it will be a statement of the share of the other. If one divorced one of his two wives and then had intercourse with one of them, it will be a statement of divorce with respect to the other; contrary to intercourse in an unspecified emancipation, according to Imam Abū Ḥanīfa, due to permissibility of intercourse with slaves in two circumstances. So the ownership slant will not be established through consideration for permissibility of intercourse.

❖ ❖ ❖

1.10.4 Bayān ul-Ḥāl

The fifth type of bayān is bayān ul-ḥāl. It is a statement of approval by remaining silent. Numerous examples exist for such a silent approval.

Firstly, when the blessed Prophet صلى الله عليه وسلم saw anyone doing something and did not comment, his blessed silence is a statement. It states that this act is permitted in the Shariah, because it is the duty of the Beloved Prophet صلى الله عليه وسلم to make such matters clear if they contradict it. If it was not permitted, Allah's Messenger صلى الله عليه وسلم would have certainly said so. His silence on the matter is his stated approval through bayān ul-ḥāl.

A second example is the silence of *ash-shafī'*, the one with the first right of refusal, when he knew of a sale of a property and remained silent. When one has a right to be the first to enter into negotiations with an owner of a property,

QUICK TERMS

بيان الحال: *bayan ul-ḥāl*

Silent. The silence of the concerned party that takes the place of a statement.

QUICK ARABIC

الشفيع: *ash-shafī'*

Pre-empter. The holder of the right to establish a prior right to buy before someone else.

no one else can buy the said property. However, the one with this right must make their intent of purchasing clear by speaking up once the property is up for sale. When such a person opts to remain silent despite knowing of the sale, and being in a position to purchase, it is clear that the silence is making a statement of lack of interest. This statement is made through silent approval of the sale to go ahead without their personal interest to purchase it. This is understood through bayān ul-ḥāl.

A third example is if a previously unmarried adult woman has an agreement of marriage made by her guardian and *al-walī*, she has the right to go ahead with it or to refuse it. If upon hearing of the marriage agreement she remains silent and does not refuse it, it is a statement in silence. It denotes her approval, as she has every right to voice her refusal if she disapproved. This statement is by bayān ul-ḥāl.

A fourth example is if a master sees his slave trading in the marketplace and remains silent, it denotes that the master approves of the act of the slave. It would be the master's right to voice his disapproval but he chooses not to. His silence is bayān ul-ḥāl to show the slave is permitted to trade.

A fifth example is an individual who claimed that another person owed him one thousand but was unable to produce a witness in a court of law. The claimant makes a demand of *al-qasam* but the defendant refuses. The defendant's refusal to go ahead with *al-qasam* is a statement. He is in a place where he is required to defend himself if at all possible. His refusal is a statement and so he will owe the one thousand. The Ṣāḥibayn say that this is a statement that is equivalent to a confession. It is as though he has confessed to owing one thousand by remaining silent. However, Imam Abū Ḥanīfa ﷺ considers it to be by way of *al-ba<u>dh</u>l*, forfeit. It is that the defendant is not confessing that he owes the money but he wants to avoid the swearing due to its significance and he feels it is not an appropriate thing to do for something as trivial as money.

In summary, all these cases show that when a statement is required from someone who is able and in need to make it, remaining silent is a statement in itself. It is for this same reason that when a group of scholars voice their opinion on a pressing matter whilst others remain silent, it is considered an agreement by consensus. Had any of the scholars disagreed, they would have

QUICK TERMS

صاحبين: *ṣāḥibayn*

The Two Colleagues. Imams Abū Yūsuf ﷺ and Muḥammad ﷺ

QUICK ARABIC

الولي: *al-walī*

Guardian. A male who is entrusted by law with the care of a person and their property.

القسم: *al-qasam*

Oath. An appeal to Allah Almighty to witness one's determination in an act.

البذل: *al-ba<u>dh</u>l*

Forfeiture. The loss of a right regrading a matter.

voiced their opposition, as that is what their office entails. Their silence states their approval of the prevalent view.

Text And Translation

فصل: وأما بيان الحال فمثاله فيما إذا رأى صاحب الشرع أمرا معاينة فلم ينه عن ذلك كان سكوته بمنزلة البيان أنه مشروع، والشفيع إذا علم بالبيع وسكت كان ذلك بمنزلة البيان بأنه راضٍ بذلك، والبكر البالغة إذا علمت بتزويج الولي وسكتت عن الرد كان ذلك بمنزلة البيان بالرضاء والإذن، والمولى إذا رأى عبده يبيع ويشتري في السوق فسكت كان ذلك بمنزلة الإذن فيصير مأذونا في التجارات، والمدعى عليه إذا نكل في مجلس القضاء يكون الامتناع بمنزلة الرضاء بلزوم المال بطريق الإقرار عندهما و بطريق البذل عند أبي حنيفة رحمه الله، فالحاصل أن السكوت في موضع الحاجة إلى البيان بمنزلة البيان وبهذا الطريق قلنا: الإجماع ينعقد بنص البعض وسكوت الباقين.

Chapter: As for bayān ul-ḥāl, it's example is when the legislator ﷺ sees a specific matter and does not prohibit it. His ﷺ silence is in the place of a statement that it is permitted. When a holder of the first right of refusal knows of the sale and remains silent, it will be in the place of a statement of his acceptance of it. When a mature virgin knows of her guardian marrying her off and she remains silent from responding, it will be classed as a statement of acceptance and permission. When a master sees his slave buying and selling in the marketplace and remains silent, it is classed as permission and he is permitted to trade. When the defendant refuses to testify in court, the refusal will be classed as acceptance of liability for the money by confession according to Ṣāḥibayn, and by forfeiture according to Imam Abū Ḥanīfa, Allah have mercy on him. In summary, silence at a time when a statement is required, is a statement. In this way we have stated that consensus is established with the words of some and the silence of the rest.

❖❖❖

1.10.5 Bayān ul-'Aṭf

The sixth type of explanatory statements is bayān ul-'aṭf, the explanatory apposition. It is an explanatory expression that occurs due to a statement being consecutively after and having the same function as an earlier

QUICK TERMS

بيان الحال: *bayan ul-ḥāl*

Silent. The silence of the one concerned with a matter, that takes the place of a statement.

بيان العطف: *bayan ul-'aṭf*

Explanatory apposition. A statement that occurs due to qualifying a previous word by being placed next to it.

صاحبين: *ṣāḥibayn*

The Two Colleagues. Imams Abū Yūsuf رحمه الله and Muḥammad رحمه الله

text. It seeks to supplement and identify the first part. For example, a cubic or weighted thing is consecutively conjoined on an otherwise unqualified quantity. The cubic and weighted thing will be bayān ul-'aṭf for the unqualified quantity. If one said, "I owe so-and-so one hundred and a dirham", or "I owe so-and-so one hundred and a measure of wheat", the words 'a dirham' and 'a measure of wheat' are conjunctional and consecutive to 'one hundred', which in turn is unqualified. It is for this reason called bayān ul-'aṭf. The overall understanding will be that the two conjoined items are of the same kind, so the person is confessing he owes 'one hundred and one dirham' and 'one hundred and one measures of wheat'. Similarly, if one said, "one hundred and three cloths", "one hundred and three dirham", or "one hundred and three slaves", both conjunctions are of the same type of thing. In the first case the 'one hundred' is of the same thing as the 'three cloths', in the second case 'one hundred' is of the same thing as the 'three dirham', and in the third case the 'one hundred' is of the same thing as the 'three slaves'. It is the same as when one says, *"aḥadun wa 'ishrūna dirhaman"*, or twenty-one dirham. It is understood that just as the 'twenty' are dirham, the 'one' is also a dirham.

Ṭarafayn are of the opinion that if one said, "one hundred and a cloth" or "one hundred and a goat", it will not be understood as bayān ul-'aṭf and the conjoined items are not of the same type. Rather, in this case the issuer of the words will be asked to qualify the 'one hundred'. This is because according to them such a structural arrangement is only a valid explanatory conjunction, bayān ul-'aṭf, when the item conjoined is either a cubic or weighted thing, or a number. If it is none of these, the conjoined will not be an explanation of the first part. This is because they say it is commonplace in dealings for people to omit such repeated qualifying for brevity and ease. And it is widespread that people's dealings are in numbers or items that are measured, items that can be *daynan fī dh-dhimma*, personal liabilities. So, they limit this word structure of bayān ul-'aṭf to these items only. As neither 'cloth' nor 'goat' is cubic, weighed or a number, they are not considered suitable qualifiers for the 'one hundred'. As it is not a qualifier, the speaker will need to explain what he meant by the 'one hundred'.

Imam Abū Yūsuf رحمه الله does not make any distinction. He considers non-cubic and non-weighted items suitable in this bayān ul-'aṭf structure too. So according to him, 'one hundred and one cloths' and 'one hundred and one

QUICK TERMS

طرفين: *ṭarafayn*

The Two Parties. Imams Abū Ḥanīfa رحمه الله and Abū Yūsuf رحمه الله

goats', will be necessary in these examples, due to the same reason discussed above for 'one hundred and three cloths'.

Text And Translation

فصل: وأما بيان العطف فمثل أن تعطف مكيلا أو موزونا على جملة مجملة يكون ذلك بيانا للجملة المجملة، مثاله إذا قال: لفلان علي مئة ودرهم أو مئة وقفيز حنطة كان العطف بمنزلة البيان أن الكل من ذلك الجنس، وكذا لو قال: مائة وثلاثة أثواب أو مائة وثلاثة دراهم أو مائة وثلاثة أعبد فإنه بيان أن المائة من ذلك الجنس بمنزلة قوله: أحد وعشرون درهما بخلاف قوله: مئة وثوب أو مائة وشاة حيث لا يكون ذلك بيانا للمائة، واختص ذلك في عطف الواحد بما يصلح دينا في الذمة كالمكيل والموزون، وقال أبو يوسف رحمه الله: يكون بيانا في مائة وشاة ومائة وثوب على هذا الأصل.

Chapter: as for bayān ul-'aṭf, its example is the conjunction of a cubic measure or weight upon an unqualified sentence. It will become a statement for the unqualified sentence. An example of it is if one said: "I owe so-and-so one hundred and a dirham" or "One hundred and a measure of wheat". The conjunction will be in the place of a statement that the whole amount is of that type. Similarly, if one said: "One hundred and three cloths", "One hundred and three dirhams" or "One hundred and three slaves", it will be a statement that the hundred is of that type. It is like one saying: "Twenty-one (*aḥad uw-wa 'ishrūn*) dirhams"; whilst it is contrary to saying: "One hundred and a cloth" or "One hundred and a goat", as it will not be a statement for the one hundred. This is reserved for one conjoining that which is appropriate to become one's liable debt, like a measured or weighted item. Imam Abū Yūsuf, Allah have mercy on him, said: it will be a statement in "One hundred and a goat", and in "One hundred and a cloth", based on this principle.

❖❖❖

QUICK TERMS

بيان العطف: *bayan ul-'aṭf*

Explanatory apposition. A statement that occurs due to qualifying a previous word by being placed next to it.

بيان التبديل: *bayan ut-tabdīl*

Abrogation. A statement that repeals and replaces a previous statement.

1.10.6 Bayān ut-Tabdīl

The seventh type of bayān is bayān ut-tabdīl. This is abrogation and effectively annulling a previous statement. Abrogating is only permitted from the Legislator of the Shariah and is not permitted by people. It is for this reason that when extending the scope of exceptions based on a text, we are not permitted to carry on exempting to a point where no one is left under the ruling. It would simply mean that the ruling of the Shariah is abrogated, as no one would be left to apply it on. [see Chapter 1.1.1, page 31]This is not permitted for people. Furthermore, confessions, divorces and emancipation are not reversible once issued. If reversing them were permitted, it would effectively mean that their respective rulings are non-existent. The Shariah however has stated rulings in each of them, so by reversing them, the Shariah's rulings would be abrogated and people are not permitted to do this.

There are a number of cases in which jurists disagree whether the case is to be treated as bayān ut-taghyīr or bayān ut-tabdīl.

The first example of such a case is if one confessed, "I owe so-and-so one thousand in loans" or "for a purchase", and then added "in counterfeit currency". Ṣāḥibayn say that it becomes bayān ut-taghyīr, because there are two types of dirham, genuine and counterfeit, where the counterfeit is impure and not accepted as tender amongst tradesman. Genuine dirham is more prevalent and the tender by which people commonly conduct their dealings. In this sense, the genuine dirham is the literal and al-ḥaqīqa, whereas counterfeit dirham is al-majāz. When the individual confessed about owing, it would have been understood to be the prevalent and al-ḥaqīqa, but when he added 'counterfeit' it changed the meaning and direction of the statement from the first understanding. Thus, the statement has become bayān ut-taghyīr. The ruling of it will follow that this will be permitted if added immediately but not accepted if added later.

Imam Abū Ḥanīfa رحمه الله, on the other hand, considers this bayān ut-tabdīl, and consequently does not permit it whether added immediately or later. This is because all transactions are only valid with genuine legitimate items in full working order. Counterfeit is admittance of impurity, and that the item is not in an acceptable full working order. So, when one confessed to owing, one has confessed to a genuine item without fault, but by adding 'counterfeit' it contradicts the legitimacy of the transaction and is thus an abrogation. The result is that one has contradicted their own statement by issuing a bayān ut-tabdīl, and so the ruling follows that this is not valid whether added immediately or after a while.

A second example is if one said, "I owe so-and-so one thousand for the price of a slave-girl that was sold to me and I didn't take possession", whilst there is no sign of the slave-girl and she is an unknown. According to Imam Abū

QUICK TERMS

بيان التغيير: *bayan ut-taghyīr*

Change. A statement that that changes the direction and understanding of a previous statement.

صاحبين: *ṣāḥibayn*

The Two Colleagues. Imams Abū Yūsuf رحمه الله and Muḥammad رحمه الله

الحقيقة: *al-ḥaqīqa*

The literal. A word coined by the lexicon for an item.

المجاز: *al-majāz*

The figurative. A word used for a meaning other than its coined meaning.

Ḥanīfa رحمه الله, the words 'I didn't take possession ' render this in the category of bayān ut-tabdīl. This is because when merchandise is lost, any confession of owing would imply that possession had occurred. This is necessary because had the merchandise been lost before possession the transaction would be void. So, by saying 'I owe' he implies that possession had taken place and to complete the transaction he now needs to pay the price. After this, if he now claims 'I didn't take possession', it is an abrogation and bayān ut-tabdīl. The ruling follows, that it is not a valid statement if made immediately or even later. The one thousand will be payable. The Ṣāḥibayn say that this is bayān ut-taghyīr and merely changing the prevalent understanding of the statement. So, if the buyer says these words immediately after the initial statement, it is acceptable and he will not be liable to pay the one thousand, however, if said later it will not be valid. The confession will be in place and one thousand will be owed.

Text And Translation

فصل: وأما بيان التبديل وهو النسخ فيجوز ذلك من صاحب الشرع ولا يجوز ذلك من العباد، وعلى هذا بطل استثناء الكل عن الكل؛ لأنه نسخ الحكم ولا يجوز الرجوع عن الإقرار والطلاق والعتاق؛ لأنه نسخ وليس للعبد ذلك، ولو قال: لفلان علي ألف قرض أو ثمن المبيع وقال: وهي زيوف كان ذلك بيان التغيير عندهما فيصح موصولا وهو بيان التبديل عند أبي حنيفة رحمه الله فلا يصح و إن وصل، ولو قال: لفلان علي ألف من ثمن جارية باعنيها ولم أقبضها والجارية لا أثر لها كان ذلك بيان التبديل عند أبي حنيفة رحمه الله؛ لأنّ الإقرار بلزوم الثمن إقرار بالقبض عند هلاك المبيع؛ إذ لو هلك قبل القبض ينفسخ البيع فلا يبقى الثمن لازما.

Chapter: as for bayān ut-tabdīl, it is abrogation. It is permitted from the legislator and not permitted from subjects. Based on this exemption of the whole from the whole is not permitted as it removes the ruling. Retracting a confession, divorce or emancipation is not permitted, as it is abrogation and that is not for the subject. If one said: "I owe('ala) so-and-so one thousand as debt or payment of a purchase", then added: "it is counterfeit", it is bayān ut-taghyīr according to them both, therefore permitted immediately. It is bayān ut-tabdīl according to Imam Abū Ḥanīfa, Allah have mercy on him, therefore not valid even if it is immediate. If one said: "I owe so-and-so one thousand for the price of a salve-girl sold to me, but I didn't take possession of her", whilst there

QUICK TERMS

بيان التبديل: *bayan ut-tabdīl*

Abrogation. A statement that repeals and replaces a previous statement.

صاحبين: *ṣāḥibayn*

The Two Colleagues. Imams Abū Yūsuf رحمه الله and Muḥammad رحمه الله

بيان التغيير: *bayan ut-taghyīr*

Change. A statement that that changes the direction and understanding of a previous statement.

is no sign of the salve-girl, it will be considered bayān ut-tabdīl according to Imam Abū Ḥanīfa, Allah have mercy on him. This is because acknowledging the price is due, is acknowledgment of possession when the the purchase perishes because had it perished before possession the transaction would be void, so the price would not be due.

❖ ❖ ❖

Summary Of al-Bayān

1. Definition of al-bayān:
البيان: إظهار المتكلم بقوله أو فعله أو حالته ما في ضميره بحيث يفهمه المخاطب
"It is that statement which makes the purpose of the speaker clearer by word, action or circumstance, to the recipient".
There are seven types of al-bayān:

2. Details of bayān ut-taqrīr (affirmation):
i) Definition: وهو تقرير كلامه
"It confirms his previous words".
The words are clear but could be construed to mean something else. The statement that spells out the clearly understood meaning is bayān ut-taqrīr.
ii) Example: Someone said لفلان عندي ألف. This clearly shows that the money was placed in trust, however it could be a loan or gift. When he adds the word وديعة it confirms the clear understanding of being in trust. So وديعة is bayān ut-taqrīr.
iii) Ruling: يصح موصولا ومفصولا
"It is permitted when both initial words and statement come together, and also when separate".

3. Details of bayān ut-tafsīr (clarification):
i) Definition: وهو شرح المتكلم معنى كلامه الغير الواضح
"It is a statement of the orator explaining his previous unclear words".
When the words are not clear and a statement from the person clarifies them.
ii) Example: in someone's confession لفلان علي شيء, the understanding of what exactly the *thing* is, is unclear. So, when the person clarifies it saying الثوب, this is a statement of clarification that makes it clear what the *thing* is.
iii) Ruling: يصح موصولا ومفصولا
"It is permitted when both initial words and statement come together, and also when separate".

4. Details of bayān ut-taghyīr (change):
i) Definition: وهو أن يتغير ببيانه معنى كلامه
"It is a statement that changes the direction of the previous words".
This would be by adding a condition, exception etc

(continued...)

Summary Of al-Bayān (continued)

ii) Example: If one said لفلان علي ألف, it would imply that he owes 1000 as a loan. But if he was to add the word وديعة it changes it to a deposit in trust. An example of a conditional change is أنت حر إن دخلت الدار. And an example of change by way of exception would be: كل من عبادي حر إلا زيدا.

iii) Ruling: يصح موصولا ولا يصح مفصولا
"It is permitted when both initial words and statement are together, but not when separate".

5. Details of bayān uḍ-ḍarūra (Implied):
i) Definition: وهو بيان يفهمه المخاطب من فحوى الكلام ويقع بغير كلام
"It is a statement understood by the recipient intrinsically from the words and it occurs without wording".
ii) Example: Allah ﷻ said: وورثه أبواه فلأمه الثلث.
When the parents are sole inheritors the mother is given a third of the inheritance in the verse. The father's share is set at two thirds by the same verse without any additional words.

6. Details of bayān ul-ḥāl (Silent):
i) Definition: وهو السكوت الذي يقع بيانا بدلالة حال المتكلم
"It is the silence that becomes a statement due to the circumstance of the orator".
Where a statement is required but the orator chooses to remain silent.
ii) Example: When someone with first right to buy learns that a neighbour is selling but doesn't put an offer in and remains quiet. It will mean he relinquishes his right and agrees to the sale to another party. The silence is his statement.
iii) The ruling is: إن السكوت في موضع الحاجة إلى البيان بمنزلة البيان
"Silence at a time when a statement is required is in itself a statement".

7. Details of bayān ul-'aṭf (explanatory apposition)
i) Definition: وهو بيان يقع بسبب العطف
"It is a statement which occurs due to apposition".
It is when an abstract idea is qualified with a weight or measure by way of explicative apposition.
ii) Example: When one says لفلان علي مائة وثلاثة دراهم, the 100 is qualified as money by being side by side with 3 dirham.

8. Details of bayān ut-tabdīl (abrogation):
i) Definition: رفع حكم شرعي بدليل شرعي متأخر عنه بجعل الشيء مقام شيء آخر
"It is to repeal a ruling of the Shariah with legal evidence made available at a later time; by replacing one thing with another".
This is abrogation, which is the repealing and replacement of a law. This can only be done by the Legislator and not people.
ii) Example: if anyone gives a divorce, confesses or emancipates, they have no right to revoke it as the Shariah has established it.

as-Sunna

PART 2

2.0 Introduction to as-Sunna

The second principle of the four uṣūl is as-Sunna. The literal meaning of sunna is way and manner. In the Shariah, it is a voluntary worship upon which a person is rewarded, whilst there is no reprimand if one chooses to leave it. As far as principles are concerned, the as-Sunna is that which is given by the Messenger ﷺ and it is not the blessed Quran. This could be in the form of sayings, actions or approval.

Approval means that an act was carried out or words were spoken in the presence of the Prophet ﷺ and he remained silent regarding it or did not forbid it. According to jurists, the difference between Hadith and as-Sunna is that Hadith only refers to the speech of the Prophet ﷺ whilst as-Sunna implies his speech, action and approval. Additionally, Sunna includes the speech and actions of the Companions رضي الله عنهم. The scholars of Hadith, *al-muḥaddit͟hūn*, do not distinguish between as-Sunna, al-ḥadīt͟h or al-k͟habar; the words are synonymous for them. Some have said that the term Hadith can be used for *al-marfū'* or *al-mawqūf* narrations, whereas an *al-maqṭū'* narration is called *al-at͟har.* Some have said that there is a difference between al-ḥadīt͟h and al-k͟habar in that the former is transmitted from the Prophet ﷺ, Companions رضي الله عنهم

QUICK TERMS

الأصول: *al-uṣūl*

Principles. The accepted fundamental rules of deriving matters of fiqh.

السنة: *as-sunna*

The practice. The sayings, doings and approval of the blessed Prophet ﷺ.

المحدثون: *al-muḥaddit͟hūn*

Scholars of tradition. Scholars concerned with the sciences of prophetic tradition.

and Successors ﷺ regarding themselves. However, if it is transmitted from them and concerns parables of the past then it is al-khabar. An *al-marfū'* narration is a continuous transmission from the Prophet ﷺ. An *al-Mawqūf* narration is not connected to the Prophet ﷺ, but instead stops at a Companion after a continuous chain. If continuity is broken lower in the chain of narration it is termed *al-maqṭū'*. The jurists are only concerned with a connection of a narration to the Prophet ﷺ and not how the connection comes about. Therefore, they simply use the term as-Sunna. The *al-muḥaddithūn* however, are concerned with manners of transmission, narrator profiles and conditions, and so employ different terminology.

QUICK TERMS

المرفوع: *al-marfū'*

Elevated. A narration that has a chain with an explicit beginning from the Prophet ﷺ.

الموقوف: *al-mawqūf*

Stopped. A narration that starts its chain of transmission from a Companion رضي الله عنهم.

المقطوع: *al-maqtū'*

Severed. A narration that starts its chain of transmission from a Successor رحمهم الله.

الأثر: *al-athar*

Narration. Any narration whether beginning with the blessed Prophet ﷺ, a Companion رضي الله عنهم or a Successor رحمهم الله

الخبر: *al-khabar*

Singular tradition. Traditions related by single narrator chains.

الكتاب: *al-muḥaddithūn*

The book. The inspired final word of Allah جل جلاله. The Quran.

Text And Translation

البحث الثاني في سنة رسول الله ﷺ

وهي أكثر من عدد الرمل والحصى

Discussion two on the sunna of the Messenger of Allah, peace and blessings of Allah be upon him. They number more than sand and stone.

❖ ❖ ❖

2.1 Types of al-khabar

This chapter is about the types of al-khabar. The word al-khabar denotes that this chapter is about the speech and words of the blessed Prophet ﷺ. In terms of granting knowledge and for purposes of obedience, al-khabar of the Messenger of Allah ﷺ is like al-Kitāb. As it is necessary to believe in the Book of Allah جل جلاله and to have a firm belief in it, it is necessary to also have a similar belief about the speech and word of the Messenger of Allah ﷺ, as well as to carry it out in practice. The importance of both is the same. The evidence for this is that obeying the Messenger of Allah ﷺ is obeying Allah جل جلاله. The blessed Quran says in verse 80 of Sūrat an-Nisā and verses 3-4 of Sūrat an-Najm:

﴿مَّنْ يُطِعِ الرَّسُولَ فَقَدْ أَطَاعَ اللَّهَ﴾ [النساء: 80]

"Whoso obeys the messenger obeys Allah..."

﴿وَمَا يَنطِقُ عَنِ الْهَوَى ۝ إِنْ هُوَ إِلَّا وَحْيٌ يُوحَى﴾ [النجم: 4-3]

"Nor does he speak of (his own) desire. It is only inspired revelation."

In other words, a prophet only instructs and prohibits what Allah ﷻ asks. So, as this is the case, obedience to the Messenger ﷺ is obedience to Allah ﷻ. Similarly, the Almighty ﷻ says in verse 7 of Sūrat ul-Ḥashr:

﴿وَمَا آتَاكُمُ الرَّسُولُ فَخُذُوهُ وَمَا نَهَاكُمْ عَنْهُ فَانتَهُوا﴾ [الحشر: 7]

"...and whatsoever the messenger gives you, take it. And whatsoever he forbids, abstain (from it)..."

It is clear from this that narrations of the Messenger ﷺ are legal sources just as al-Kitāb is. Therefore, the twenty or so terminologies and their respective discussions valid for al-Kitāb are also valid for as-Sunna. That terms and their discussions do not need repeating.

It is true that there is no doubt in narrations per se, as they are definitive like al-Kitāb, but doubt is cast from two considerations. Firstly, whether the narration is actually from the Messenger ﷺ and if so, what is its status. And secondly, whether it has a continuous line of transmission or is it broken. Due to the possibilities arising from these considerations al-khabar is three types: al-mutawātir, which is a sound narration and the chain of narrators connects to the Messenger ﷺ without any doubt; al-mashhūr, which has an element of doubt; and khabar ul-wāḥid, which has a possibility of not being connected to him ﷺ.

Text And Translation

فصل في أقسام الخبر: خبر رسول الله ﷺ بمنزلة الكتاب في حق لزوم العلم والعمل به فإن من أطاعه فقد أطاع الله فما مر ذكره من بحث الخاص والعام والمشترك والمجمل في الكتاب فهو كذلك في حق السنة إلا أن الشبهة في باب الخبر في ثبوته من رسول الله ﷺ واتصاله به ولهذا المعنى صار الخبر على ثلاثة أقسام: قسم صح من رسول الله صلى الله عليه وسلم وثبت منه بلا شبهة وهو المتواتر وقسم فيه ضرب شبهة وهو المشهور وقسم فيه احتمال وشبهة وهو الآحاد

Chapter on the types of al-khabar: The khabar of the Messenger of Allah, peace and blessings of Allah be upon him, is ranked with al-Kitāb in respect to the

QUICK TERMS

السنة: *as-sunna*

The practice. The sayings, doings and approval of the blessed Prophet ﷺ.

المتواتر: *al-mutawātir*

Uninterrupted mass transmission. A narration with an unbroken chain and related by many in every generation.

المشهور: *al-mashhūr*

Popular tradition. A narration that started as a singular and later gained popularity.

الخبر الواحد: *al-khabar ul-wāḥid*

Singular tradition. Traditions related by single narrator chains.

الخاص: *al-khaṣṣ*

The specific. A word designated for a singular specific concept.

العام: *al-'āmm*

The general. A word designated for a group.

المشترك: *al-mushtarak*

The concurrent. A word coined for two or more inherently different meanings.

المجمل: *al-mujmal*

The unexplained. Wording that requires explanatory statements.

necessity of knowledge and its application. The one who obeyed him, has obeyed Allah. So what has been mentioned in the discussions of al-khāṣṣ, al-'āmm, al-mushtarak and al-mujmal from al-Kitāb is the same regarding as-Sunna. Except doubt is cast in the chapter of al-khabar in establishing it from the Messenger of Allah, peace and blessings of Allah be upon him, and its transmission from him. For this reason al-khabar is of three types: one type which is sound from the Messenger of Allah, peace and blessings be upon him, and is established from him without doubt. It is called al-mutawātir. One type has a shade of doubt; it is al-mashhūr. And one type has possibility and doubt; it is al-aḥād.

❖ ❖ ❖

al-Mutawātir is defined as a narration that is transmitted by a group of individuals to another, generation after generation. The group is large enough to eliminate possibilities of collusion upon falsehood, and the numbers remain large throughout each subsequent transmission. If there is a generation in between that does not have sufficient numbers to fit these criteria, the narration is not classed as al-mutawātir. Examples of this class of narration include the transmission of the verses of the blessed Quran, the number of units in each salah and the thresholds of zakah. From the time of the blessed Prophet ﷺ until today, the masses that have confirmed these details are so numerous that their agreement upon falsehood is not rationally acceptable.

al-Mashhūr is a narration that began as a singular al-aḥād narration with not many reporters. In the time of the Companions رضي الله عنهم it did not receive any level of popularity nor amounted to any kind of *at-tawātur* but in consequent generations of either the Successors رحمهم الله or their Understudies رحمهم الله, it gained popularity to a degree that it gained acceptance from the Ummah in general. So, after the second generation, it became similar to a al-mutawātir and the number of people reporting it subsequently increased to numbers large enough for them not be able to collude upon falsehood. This state remained until the last reporter in the chain. Any narration gaining popularity after the first three generations of Islam, *al-qurūn ath-thalātha*, do not hold the same weight or authority, because every narration has gained in popularity after those times. The factor taken into consideration is the beginning of the chain of narration. Examples of al-mashhūr narrations include the narration of wiping over the leather socks and the narration of *ar-rajm*.

QUICK TERMS

المتواتر: *al-mutawātir*

Uninterrupted mass transmission. A narration with an unbroken chain and related by many in every generation.

المشهور: *al-mashhūr*

Popular tradition. A narration that started as a singular and later gained popularity.

الأحاد: *al-aḥād*

Singular traditions. Traditions related by single narrator chains.

التواتر: *at-tawātūr*

Uninterrupted mass transmission. Narrating with an unbroken chain and related by many in every generation.

القرون الثلاثة: *al-qurūn uth-thalātha*

The three generations. The first three generations after the blessed Prophet ﷺ.

الخبر الواحد: *al-khabar ul-wāḥid*

Singular tradition. Traditions related by single narrator chains.

Narrations classed as al-mutawātir are definitive, *al-qaṭ'ī*. Their falsehood is entirely eliminated, so disbelief in them is tantamount to disbelief, *al-kufr*. Narrations that are al-mashhūr are reliable and trustable, *at-tumānīna*, whilst the one who disbelieves what they contain is an innovator; their actions are rejected as *al-bid'a*. It is necessary to enact both al-mutawātir and al-mashhūr; there is no disagreement amongst jurists in this. However, the status of khabar ul-wāḥid is contested.

Khabar ul-wāḥid is a narration in which a singular narrator reports from an individual, a group reports from an individual, or a group reports from a group, but the groups are not large enough for the report to be considered al-mashhūr. Khabur ul-wāḥid is valid for issuing rulings in the Shariah and it is necessary to obey its contents so long as certain conditions are met. These conditions are that the narrators are Muslim, of high integrity, with sound memory, intelligent and part of a continuous unbroken chain reaching back to the blessed Messenger of Allah ﷺ. Khabar ul-wāḥid gives neither certain nor significantly reliable information, but is necessary to follow in matters of rulings.

Text And Translation

فالمتواتر ما نقله جماعة عن جماعة لا يتصور توافقهم على الكذب لكثرتهم واتصل بك هكذا، مثاله: نقل القرآن وأعداد الركعات ومقادير الزكاة والمشهور ما كان أوله كالآحاد ثم اشتهر في العصر الثاني والثالث وتلقته الأمة بالقبول فصار كالمتواتر حتى اتصل بك، وذلك مثل حديث المسح على الخف والرجم في باب الزنا، ثم المتواتر يوجب العلم القطعي ويكون رده كفرا والمشهور يوجب علم الطمأنينة ويكون رده بدعة ولا خلاف بين العلماء في لزوم العمل بهما، وإنما الكلام في الآحاد فنقول: خبر الواحد هو ما نقله واحد عن واحد أو واحد عن جماعة أو جماعة عن واحد ولا عبرة للعدد إذا لم تبلغ حد المشهور وهو يوجب العمل به في الأحكام الشرعية بشرط إسلام الراوي وعدالته وضبطه وعقله واتصاله بك ذلك من رسول الله عليه الصلاة والسلام بهذا الشرط.

al-Mutawātir is the one transmitted by a group from a group, whose agreement upon a false notion is inconceivable due to their numbers, and it has reached you like this. An example of it is the transmission of the Quran, the number of units of prayer and the amounts of zakah. al-Mashhūr was first like al-aḥād then became popular in the second and third generation and the Ummah received it

QUICK TERMS

القطعي: *al-qaṭ'ī*

The definitive. Most reliable and certain.

QUICK ARABIC

الرجم: *ar-rajm*

Lapidation. To stone to death.

الكفر: *al-kufr*

Disbelief. The refusal or inability to accept the truth of Islam.

الطمأنينة: *at-ṭumanīna*

Reassuring. The state of being with peace of mind regarding a matter.

البدعة: *al-bid'a*

Innovation. A novelty act in Islam that contravenes an established sunnah.

with acceptance. It became like al-mutawātir whence it reached you. It is like the Hadith of wiping the leather sock or stoning in the chapter of adultery. Then al-mutawātir necessitates a definitive knowledge and its rejection is disbelief. al-Mashhūr necessitates an assured knowledge and its rejection is innovation. There is no contention amongst jurists in the necessity of enforcing both. The discussion is in al-aḥād. We say: Khabar ul-wāḥid is the one transmitted one-to-one, by an individual from a group, or by a group from one individual. There is no consideration for the number so long as it doesn't reach the limit of al-mashhūr. It is necessary to enforce it in rulings of the Shariah on the condition that the reporter is a Muslim, just, rigorous and intelligent, and that it reaches you from the Messenger of Allah, peace and blessings be upon him, with this condition.

❖❖❖

Summary Of as-Sunna and Types of al-Khabar

1. The linguistic definition of as-Sunna is *way* or *path*. And the juristic definition is:
   كل ما صدر عن رسول الله ﷺ من قول أو فعل أو تقرير
   "All what is experienced from the Messenger of Allah ﷻ, whether in verse, in motion or acceptance".
2. Its ruling is: بمنزلة الكتاب في حق لزوم العلم والعمل به
   "It is like the Quran in providing necessity in information and in enacting".
3. Allah ﷻ says: من يطع الرسول فقد أطاع الله
   "Whoever obeys the messenger has obeyed Allah".
4. However, not every narration is proven to have definitely come from the Messenger of Allah ﷺ. So, narrations are of various types.
5. In terms of transmission there are three types of narration: al-mutawātir, al-mashhūr and khabar ul-wāḥid.
6. Details of *al-mutawātir*:
   i) Definition: ما نقله جماعة عن جماعة لا يتصور توافقهم على الكذب لكثرتهم واتصل بك هكذا
   "The tradition transmitted to one group from another whose agreement upon a lie is unimaginable due to their number, and it is transmitted to you like this".
   ii) Example: The number of verses of the blessed Quran, amounts in zakah and the number of units of salah.
   iii) Ruling: يوجب علم قطعي وردّه كفر ولزوم العمل به
   "It necessitates a definitive knowledge, its rejection is disbelief and it must be enacted".
7. Details of al-mashhūr:
   i) Definition: ما كان أوله كالآحاد ثم اشتهر في العصر الثاني والثالث وتلقته الأمة بالقبول فصار كالمتواتر حتى اتصل بك
   "The tradition which began as singular al-aḥād, then became popular in the second and third generations. The Ummah openly accepted it and it became like al-mutawātir until it was transmitted to you like this".
   ii) Example: The Hadith of stoning the married adulterer and the wiping of leather footwear.
   iii) Ruling: يوجب علم الطمأنينة ورده بدعة ولزوم العمل به
   "It necessitates an assured knowledge, its rejection is innovation and it must be enacted".

Summary Of as-Sunna and Types of al-Khabar

8. Details of khabar ul-wāḥid:

i) Definition: ما نقله واحد عن واحد أو واحد عن جماعة أو جماعة عن واحد

"The narration transmitted one-to-one, by an individual from a group, or a group from an individual".

ii) Example: The Hadith إنما الأعمال بالنيات

"Actions are based on intentions".

iii) Ruling: يوجب العمل به في الأحكام الشريعة بشرط إسلام الراوي وعدالته وضبطه وعقله واتصاله بك ذلك من رسول الله ﷺ بهذا الشرط

"It necessitates enacting it in rulings of the Shariah on the proviso that the narrator is a Muslim, just, thorough and intelligent. It must be transmitted to you from the Messenger of Allah ﷺ in this condition".

2.1.1 Types of Reporters

Reporters of narrations from the blessed Prophet ﷺ are of two types. Firstly, there are those known for their knowledge and rigour in judgement, like the Four Rightly-guided Caliphs, 'Abdullāh Ibn Mas'ūd, 'Abdullāh Ibn 'Abbās, 'Abdullāh Ibn 'Umar, Zayd Ibn Thābit, Mu'ādh Ibn Jabal and the likes رضي الله عنهم. When this category of Companion رضي الله عنه narrates from the blessed Prophet of Allah ﷺ and it arrives with a sound chain to us, it is better to enact it over al-qiyās and analogy. Such narrations will be given priority over our own thinking. This is because we hold that the Companions رضي الله عنهم themselves opted to relate and narrate the Hadith rather than give their own personal opinion. This shows the importance with which they regarded the narration despite the knowledge and rigour they were known for. It is for this reason that Imam Muḥammad رحمه الله penned numerous verdicts consistent with narrations, rather than al-qiyās. Four examples are as follows:

1. In the case of laughter, *al-qahqaha*, in salah. In a narration, it states that the blessed Prophet ﷺ was leading the prayer when a Companion رضي الله عنه with an ailment in his eye came and stumbled into a pit. Some Companions رضي الله عنهم, seeing this, could not control their laughter whilst in prayer. After the prayer concluded, the blessed Prophet ﷺ informed them that whosoever had laughed in prayer was required to renew their ablution and to repeat the prayer. The narration implies that laughter in prayer annuls the ablution as well as the prayer. al-Qiyās on the other hand would dictate that the ablution should not be affected, as it is only annulled when impurity

حديث

عن أبي المليح بن أسامة عن أبيه، قال: بينما نحن نصلي خلف رسول الله ﷺ إذ أقبل رجل ضرير البصر، فوقع في حفرة، فضحكنا منه، فأمرنا رسول الله ﷺ بإعادة الوضوء كاملا، وإعادة الصلاة من أولها.

عليه الصلاة والسلام

(سنن الدارقطني: 1/160،161)

QUICK TERMS

القياس: *al-qiyās*

Analogy. The reasoning of the learned.

QUICK ARABIC

القهقهة: *al-qahqaha*

To guffaw. An audible burst of unrestrained laughter.

is emitted. Laughter does not fit this condition and should therefore not annul the ablution. Despite this understanding, the verdict is in accordance with the narration, which is reported by the scholarly and rigorous Abū Muṣā al-Ash'arī ؓ, and al-qiyās is ignored.

2. In the case of a woman standing parallel to a man, *al-muḥādhā*, in salah: The grand jurist and companion 'Abdullāh Ibn Mas'ūd ؓ narrates that the Messenger of Allah ﷺ said to arrange the rows of the women at the rear of the congregation as Allah ﷻ has placed them. This is a reference to the creation of woman after the first man. Now if a woman was to stand next to a man, or a man was to join the row of women, the man will be at fault for ignoring an obligation. This is because the narration instructs men to arrange the rows of women at the rear and not in line with men. As this instruction, directed at men, is ignored by the man in question, his prayer is deemed invalid. al-Qiyās on the other hand holds that his prayer remains valid. This is because standing in parallel to another individual is not a cause of invalidating a prayer, as the woman's prayer, in the very same case, remains unaffected. If we liken his prayer to her prayer, both prayers should still be valid. However, due to the knowledge and rigour of the narrator al-qiyās is abandoned in favour of the narration.

3. In the case of vomiting in salah invalidating the ablution: Mother of Believers, Lady 'Āisha ؓ reports that the Messenger of Allah ﷺ informed that if one regurgitated or had a nose bleed during prayer, he or she can leave the prayer, perform ablution and return to complete the prayer from where it was left. This is so long as a word is not spoken during this time. This narration implies that regurgitation invalidates the ablution. al-Qiyās is that it should not invalidate the ablution because it is a surge of undigested food and is thus not considered impure. If indeed it is impure, it follows that no impurity has been emitted, and thus ablution should still be valid. The authority, knowledge and rigour of the narrator, however, take precedence and al-qiyās is side-lined for the narration.

حديث

عن أبي معمر عن ابن مسعود أنه كان يقول: أخروهن حيث أخرهن الله.

عليه الصلاة والسلام

(مصنف عبد الرزاق: 5115)

حديث

عن عائشة رضي الله عنها قالت: قال رسول الله صلى الله عليه وسلم من أهابه قيئ أو رعاف أو قلس أو مذي فلينصرف فليتوضأ ثم ليبن على صلاته وهو في ذلك لا يتكلم.

عليه الصلاة والسلام

(سنن ابن ماجة: 1221)

QUICK TERMS

القياس: *al-qiyās*

Analogy. The reasoning of the learned.

QUICK ARABIC

المحاذاة: *al-muḥādhā*

Draw parallel. In the state of congregational prayer, for a woman to pray directly beside or in front of a man.

4. In the case of *sajdat us-sahw* following the conclusion of salah: Ibn Mas'ūd رضي الله عنه has reported that for every major mistake in the prayer two prostrations of neglect must be performed, after the prayer is concluded. al-Qiyās would dictate that this prostration should occur before the prayer is concluded because it is to make up for a mistake within the prayer and therefore should be rectified within the prayer. It can only be within the prayer if it is performed before the prayer is concluded. The Hadith is preferred over al-qiyās due to the authority and standing of the narrator, and the prostration is to be performed after the prayer is concluded with *as-salām*.

Text And Translation

ثم الراوي في الأصل قسمان: معروف بالعلم والاجتهاد كالخلفاء الأربعة وعبد الله بن مسعود وعبدالله بن عباس وعبدالله بن عمر وزيد بن ثابت ومعاذ بن جبل وأمثالهم رضي الله عنهم، فإذا صحت عندك روايتهم عن رسول الله عليه الصلاة والسلام يكون العمل بروايتهم أولى من العمل بالقياس، ولهذا روى مُحَمَّد رحمه الله حديث الأعرابي الذي كان في عينه سوء في مسئلة القهقهة وترك القياس به، وروى حديث تأخير النساء في مسئلة المحاذاة وترك القياس به، وروى عن عائشة حديث القيء وترك القياس به، وروى عن ابن مسعود رضي الله عنه حديث السهو بعد السلام وترك القياس به

Then, the reporter is actually of two types: recognised for knowledge and rigour, like the Four Caliphs, 'Abdullah bin Mas'ūd, 'Abdullah bin 'Abbās, 'Abdullah bin 'Umar, Zayd bin Thābit, Mu'ādh bin Jabal and the likes, Allah be pleased with them all. When their authenticated report from the Messenger of Allah, peace and blessings be upon him, reaches you, it will be better to act upon their report than acting upon al-qiyās. For this reason Imam Muḥammad, Allah have mercy on him, reports the Hadith of the Bedouin who had an impairment of the eye, with respect to the case of laughter and he abandons al-qiyās for it. He reports the Hadith of holding back the women in the case of *al-muḥādhā* and abandons al-qiyās for it. He reports from Lady 'Āisha رضي الله عنها the Hadith of vomiting and abandons al-qiyās for it. And he reports from Ibn Mas'ūd, Allah be pleased with him, the Hadith of forgetting after *as-salām* and abandons al-qiyās for it.

❖ ❖ ❖

حديث

عن عبد الله رضي الله عنه أن رسول الله صلى الله عليه وسلم صلى الظهر خمسا فقيل له أزيد في الصلاة فقال وما ذاك قال صليت خمسا فسجد سجدتين بعد ما سلم.

عليه الصلاة والسلام

(صحيح البخاري: 1168)

QUICK ARABIC

سجدة السهو: *sajdat us-sahw*

Prostration of forgetfulness. Two prostrations made if a necessary act is missed during the salah.

السلام: *as-salām*

Declaration of peace. Turning the head to the right and then to the left invoking the peace of Allah جل جلاله, to conclude the prayer.

The second type of narrator is the one who is renowned for strength of memory and integrity, but not for their rigour in verdicts. This includes the likes of Abū Hurrayra, Anas bin Mālik and 'Uqba bin 'Āmir, Allah Almighty be pleased with them all. If the narration from the likes of these Companions reaches us with a sound chain of narrators, and it is in accordance with al-qiyās, it is to be adhered to. If it does not comply with al-qiyās, it will be side-lined and the verdict will be in line with al-qiyās. An example of such a narration is that Abū Hurrayra narrates that consuming food cooked over flames invalidates the ablution. When 'Abdullāh Ibn 'Abbās heard this he responded by asking if it was necessary to repeat ablution with 'normal' water if one had performed it with heated water? The point raised was that if one was with ablution and happened to perform an ablution with heated water, would this mean that he would have to perform his ablution yet again because the heated water had rendered it invalid. Abū Hurrayra remained quiet upon hearing this. Ibn 'Abbās had used al-qiyās to respond to the narration as he deemed this a suitable counter. Had Ibn 'Abbās known of another narration that countered the narration of Abū Hurrayra, he would have surely presented it. The response was left at al-qiyās and it was deemed a valid and suitable response.

Furthermore, another example of the superior authority of al-qiyās over the narration of a non-jurist Companion is the case of *al-muṣarrā*. This relates to a narration in which the Messenger of Allah ﷺ instructed people not to avoid milking their camels and small cattle. If one was to buy such an animal, they had a choice either to accept the purchase or to reject it. If the buyer chose to reject it, he could return it with a measure of dates. *al-Muṣarra* refers to the practice of not milking animals so their udders seem fuller, this in turn would drive up the price of the animal because any potential buyer would assume that the animal produced a significantly large quantity. Once purchased and milked for the first time it would give abundantly, but after this, the amount would gradually decrease. The tradition narrated by Abū Hurrayra suggests that the purchaser has the choice to continue with the sale or to return the animal. However, the milk that the purchaser benefitted from over the few days he had possession needs to be compensated for, and so he can give a measure of dates to the seller and take his money back for the animal. Imam Abū Ḥanīfa says this is not rational. This is because making up a loss is valid in one of two ways. Either a similar item is returned or a price is paid for the loss. If the item lost can be compensated for by an equivalent, like wheat and grain for

حديث

عن أبي هريرة رضي الله عنه قال: سمعت رسول الله ﷺ يقول: توضؤوا مما مست النار.

عليه الصلاة والسلام

(صحيح مسلم: 352)

حديث

قال أبو هريرة رضي الله عنه عن النبي ﷺ لا تصروا الإبل والغنم فمن ابتاعها بعد فإنه بخير النظرين بعد أن يحتلبها إن شاء أمسك وإن شاء ردها وصاع تمر.

عليه الصلاة والسلام

(صحيح البخاري: 2041)

QUICK TERMS

القياس: *al-qiyās*

Analogy. The reasoning of the learned.

QUICK ARABIC

المصراة: *al-muṣarrā*

To withhold. To hold back milking of an animal, giving the impression of fuller udders during a sale.

example, then that is what is required. If this is not an option due to significant differences from one item to the next, like replacing an animal with another, the price must be paid. As for the milk being compensated for by dates, it is neither compensation of like-for-like in appearance nor in value by paying the price in money. This means that the tradition is not granting a rational solution to the problem. The narrator for the tradition is not known for his knowledge or rigour, so the suggested compensation is ignored, and the buyer is given the choice to return the animal only.

Text And Translation

والقسم الثاني: من الرواة هم المعروفون بالحفظ والعدالة دون الاجتهاد والفتوى كأبي هريرة وأنس بن مالك فإذا صحت رواية مثلهما عندك فإن وافق الخبر القياس فلا خفاء في لزوم العمل به وإن خالفه كان العمل بالقياس أولى، مثاله ما روى أبو هريرة الوضوء مما مسته النار فقال له ابن عباس: أرأيت لو توضأت بماء سخين أكنت تتوضأ منه، فسكت، وإنما رده بالقياس؛ إذ لو كان عنده خبر لرواه، وعلى هذا ترك أصحابنا رواية أبي هريرة في مسئلة المصراة بالقياس

The second type: is of reporters known for their memory and integrity rather than rigour and verdict, like Abū Hurayra ﵁ and Anas bin Mālik ﵁. When an authentic narration from the likes of them both reaches you, and the narration agrees with al-qiyās then it is quite obvious to strictly act upon it. Should it oppose it, acting upon al-qiyās is better. An example of it is what Abū Hurayra ﵁ reports of ablution performed with 'water that touches fire'. Ibn 'Abbās ﵄ said to him: 'Do you think that were you to perform wuḏū with hot water, would you be cleansed with it?' He remained quiet. He had replied with al-qiyās; were he to have a narration he would have reported it. Based on this our scholars have abandoned the report of Abū Hurayra ﵁ in the case of *al-musarrā* for al-qiyās.

❖ ❖ ❖

Summary Of Types of Reporters

There are two types of reports in terms of reporters' natural ability:

1. Those that are known for their knowledge and rigour.
   i) For example, the Four Rightly Guided Caliphs, 'Abdullah bin Mas'ūd, 'Abdullah bin 'Abbas, 'Abdullah bin 'Umar, Zayd bin Thābit and Mu'ādh bin Jabal رضي الله عنهم.
   ii) Ruling: العمل بروايتهم أولى من العمل بالقياس
   "Enacting their reports is preferred over al-qiyās".

2. Those reporters not known for their knowledge and rigour.
   i) For example, Abū Hurayra رضي الله عنه, Anas bin Mālik رضي الله عنه
   ii) Ruling:
   a) إن وافق الخبر القياس فالعمل به باللزوم
   If the narration agrees with al-qiyās it is necessary to enact it.
   b) إن خالف الخبر القياس فالعمل بالقياس أولى
   If the narration contradicts al-qiyās, enacting al-qiyās is preferred.

2.1.2 Criteria for Accepting Khabar ul-Wāḥid

The circumstances of narrators differ. Due to these differences the criteria for accepting khabar ul-wāḥid is that it should not oppose the blessed Quran, the popular traditions nor rational thought. If one of these fundamental sources is contradicted, khabar ul-wāḥid will not be enacted. This criterion is cited because the blessed Prophet ﷺ informed that after his departure from the physical world we would encounter many traditions attributed to him and should we hear of such an attributed tradition we are to hold it to the standard of the blessed Quran. If the tradition is compliant with the blessed Quran, we are to accept it, and if it contradicts it, we are to refuse it. These words explicitly make it clear how a tradition is to be received from the blessed Prophet ﷺ. It also implicitly states that it should not contradict what is popularly known to be from the blessed Prophet ﷺ and what is common sense.

Due to the narrators' varying circumstances narrations have to be compared to the Book of Allah جل جلاله. This view is supported by an explanation provided by Sayyidunā 'Ali رضي الله عنه, Allah Almighty honour his noble personage, that reporters are of three kinds. Firstly, there are those who were true and honest believers. They accompanied the blessed Messenger ﷺ and understood the exact application of his blessed words and movements. Secondly, there was a group of well-wishing Bedouins. They would travel from their tribes and lands to the blessed Prophet ﷺ, heard his blessed wisdom, and on occasion missed

حديث

قال عبد الله بن عمر رضي الله عنهما أنه ﷺ قال: ستفشو عني أحاديث فما أتاكم من حديثي فأقرئوا كتاب الله فاعتبروه فما وافق كتاب الله فأنا قلته وما لم يوافق كتاب الله فلم أقله.

عليه الصلاة والسلام

(الطبراني: 12/316)

QUICK TERMS

خبر الواحد: *khabar ul-wāḥid*

Singular tradition. Traditions related by single-narrator chains.

some vital points. Sometimes they did not even fully grasp the context of a particular instruction. The Bedouin would then return to his people, transmit what he heard from the blessed Prophet ﷺ in his own words, and unwittingly change the meaning. Thirdly, there were the hypocrites whose hypocrisy and disobedience was not widely known. Without hearing from the blessed Prophet ﷺ, he would just fabricate a saying and falsely attribute it to him ﷺ. Some people would hear this from the hypocrite's mouth and assuming no foul play would transmit the fabricated saying to others. That narration then gained traction amongst people.

From these three distinctly different narrations, the first is authentic and reliable, but the second and third are not to be trusted. It is due to this variation amongst narrators that any singular-chained Hadith must first be compared to the Book of Allah ﷻ and the body of established narrations.

Text And Translation

وباعتبار اختلاف أحوال الرواة قلنا: شرط العمل بخبر الواحد ألا يكون مخالفا للكتاب والسنة المشهورة وألا يكون مخالفاً للظاهر، قال عليه السلام: تكثر لكم الأحاديث بعدي فإذا روي لكم عني حديث فاعرضوه على كتاب الله فما وافق فاقبلوه وما خالف فردوه وتحقيق ذلك فيما روي عن علي بن أبي طالب أنه قال: كانت الرواة على ثلاثة أقسام: مؤمن مخلص صحب رسول الله ﷺ وعرف معنى كلامه. وأعرابي جاء من قبيلة فسمع بعض ما سمع ولم يعرف حقيقة كلام رسول الله صلى الله عليه وسلم فرجع إلى قبيلته فروى بغير لفظ رسول الله ﷺ فتغير المعنى وهو يظن أن المعنى لا يتفاوت. ومنافق لم يعرف نفاقه فروى مالم يسمع وافترى فسمع منه أناس فظنوه مؤمنا مخلصا فرووا ذلك واشتهر بين الناس. فلهذا المعنى وجب عرض الخبر على الكتاب والسنة المشهورة

Taking into consideration the difference in reporters' circumstances we say: the condition of acting upon a singular narration is that it should not oppose al-kitāb, the popular Sunna and that it shouldn't oppose the obvious. He, peace and blessings be upon him, said: 'Narrations will increase for you after me. So if a narration is narrated to you of me, compare it to the Book of Allah. Whatever matches, accept it and whatever opposes reject it.' The detail of this is in what is reported of 'Alī bin Abī Tālib رضي الله عنه that he said: 'Reporters were of three types: Sincere believers who accompanied the Messenger of Allah, peace and blessings

QUICK TERMS

الكتاب: *al-kitāb*

The book. The inspired final word of Allah ﷻ. The Quran.

السنة: *as-sunna*

The practice. The sayings, doings and approvals of the blessed Prophet ﷺ.

be upon him, and understood his words. The Beduin who came from a tribe, heard some of what he heard and did not truly understand the words of the Messenger, peace and blessings be upon him. He returned to his tribe and reported in alternative words to the Messenger of Allah, peace and blessings be upon him. The meaning changed and he thinks the meaning has not altered. And the hypocrite whose hypocrisy was not known. He reports what he did not hear and fabricated. People heard it from him and considering him a true believer report from him the same and it became popular amongst the people.' For this reason it is necessary to compare al-khabar to al-kitāb and popular as-Sunna.

❖ ❖ ❖

Summary Of Criteria for Enacting Khabar ul-Wāḥid

1. Due to a variance in the quality of reporters, the khabar ul-wāḥid must fulfil the following criteria:
   i) It should not contradict a verse of the blessed Quran;
   ii) It should not oppose a popular al-mashhūr or al-mutawātir narration;
   iii) It should not be ambiguous and oppose the obvious.

2. The reason behind these conditions is the Prophet ﷺ saying: After me there will be many narrators. So, when you hear of such, measure it against the blessed Quran. If it corresponds accept it, if not, reject it.

3. The reasons are similar to what 'Alī bin Abī Ṭālib رضي الله عنه, Allah Almighty honour him, said: Reporters are of three types:
   i) The sound believer who accompanied the Messenger of Allah ﷺ and reported the words and transferred the true spirit of the message.
   ii) The Bedouins who visited the Messenger of Allah ﷺ and heard some of what is said but not all. Upon returning to their tribe they informed their tribe honestly but could not transfer the true concept in their own words.
   iii) The hypocrites whose hypocrisy was not well known. They falsely attributed things to the blessed Prophet ﷺ. Sound believers heard their words and assumed them to be true.

Due to these reasons, khabar ul-wāḥid should be contrasted with stronger sources.

2.1.3 Contrasting Khabar ul-Wāḥid With Other Sources

Khabar ul-wāḥid is a vital source of rulings in the Shariah. However, when it opposes stronger sources it is not enacted. This chapter highlights cases where a stronger piece of evidence is used to derive a ruling and khabar ul-wāḥid is not utilised.

An example of khabar ul-wāḥid being compared to the blessed Quran, and then being side-lined, is that it is attributed to the Messenger of Allah that he ﷺ said whoever touches his private parts invalidates his ablution. We compare this narration to verse 108 of Sūrat ut-Tawba:

﴿فِيهِ رِجَالٌ يُحِبُّونَ أَن يَتَطَهَّرُواْ﴾ [التوبة: 108]

"...wherein are men who love to purify themselves..."

We find that the narration opposes this verse. The verse was revealed for al-Anṣār of Qubā, who were in the habit of cleaning themselves with water, in addition to stones, after answering the call of nature. The verse praises them for this vigilance and care in personal hygiene. The praiseworthy act of washing the private area with water is not possible without physically handling the sensitive area, whereas the tradition is implying that physically touching the area is unclean and a violation of ablution. The tradition requires the act to be disallowed due to its impurity, whereas the verse is praising it as an act of purity and cleanliness. For this contradiction with the blessed Quran, al-khabar is set aside and not enacted.

Another example of not enacting a narration in favour of the blessed Quran is the narration which states that any woman marrying herself without the permission of her guardian has void her marriage. It gives the impression that no woman may marry on her own accord. Verse 232 of the Sūrat ul-Baqara says:

﴿فَلاَ تَعْضُلُوهُنَّ أَن يَنكِحْنَ أَزْوَاجَهُنَّ﴾ [البقرة: 232]

"...place not difficulties in the way of their marrying their husbands..."

The verse implies that women are marrying themselves and it is without anyone's permission. As the previous narration is contradicting this verse, the narration is side-lined and the verdict is given that women are permitted to marry themselves without the explicit permission of guardians.

حديث

عن بسرة بنت صفوان رضي الله عنها أنها سمعت رسول الله ﷺ يقول: من مس ذكره فليتوضأ.

عليه الصلاة والسلام

(ابو داوود: 181)

حديث

عن عائشة رضي الله عنها قالت: قال رسول الله ﷺ: أيما امرأة نكحت بغير إذن وليها فنكاحها باطل، فنكاحها باطل، فنكاحها باطل.

عليه الصلاة والسلام

(الترمذي: 1102)

QUICK TERMS

خبر الواحد: *khabar ul-wāḥid*

Singular tradition. Traditions narrated by single-narrator chains.

QUICK ARABIC

الأنصار: *al-ansār*

The helpers. The Companions of the blessed Prophet ﷺ who were the early converts of al-Madina.

قبا: *qubā*

Dwelling of Quba. A place three miles from al-Madinah, wherein is the first masjid of Islam.

An example of comparing khabar ul-wāḥid to a popular al-mashhūr narration is a narration in which Abū Hurrayra ﵁ says that the Prophet of Allah ﷺ permitted a judgement with one witness supported by an oath. The popular al-mashhūr tradition of Ibn 'Abbās ﵁ on the other hand states that the burden of proof is on the claimant and the oath is for the defendant. If one alleged that another person committed a crime and only produced one credible witness instead of the required two, the singular-tradition is suggesting that the lack of a witness can be made up by the individual swearing that he is telling the truth. The popular tradition is stating that an oath is reserved for the one defending himself, and it is not available for the one making the claim. The claimant is required to bring two witnesses only. When he is unable to do that, he will not be asked to make an oath based on the lesser known narration. The khabar ul-wāḥid is suggesting that one witness and an oath can be used by the claimant, but the al-mashhūr narration is stating that the oath is reserved for the defendant. The khabar ul-wāḥid will be side-lined in favour of al-mashhūr.

Text And Translation

ونظير العرض على الكتاب في حديث مس الذكر فيما يروي عنه: من مس ذكره فليتوضأ فعرضناه على الكتاب فخرج مخالفا لقوله تعالى: ﴿فِيهِ رِجَالٌ يحبون أن يتطهروا﴾ فإنهم كانوا يستنجون بالأحجار ثم يغسلون بالماء ولو كان مس الذكر حدثا لكان هذا تنجيسا لا تطهيرا على الإطلاق، وكذلك قوله عليه السلام: أيما امرأة نكحت نفسها بغير إذن وليها فنكاحها باطل باطل باطل خرج مخالفا لقوله تعالى: ﴿فلاَ تعضلوهنَ أن ينكِحنَ أزواجهن﴾ فإن الكتاب يوجب تحقيق النكاح منهن؛ ومثال العرض على الخبر المشهور رواية القضاء بشاهد و يمين فإنه خرج مخالفا لقوله عليه السلام: البينة على المدعي واليمين على من أنكر.

The example of contrasting it with al-Kitāb is the Hadith of touching the private organ, about which it is narrated from him, peace and blessings be upon him: "Whosoever touches his private organ should perform ablution". We contrast it to al-kitāb and it infringes the word of He, Almighty: "Wherein are men who love to purify themselves."They used to perform *al-istinjā* with stones, then wash with water. If touching the private organ was impure, this would be severe impurity and not purity at all. Similarly, his saying, peace and blessings be upon him: "The marriage of any woman - marrying on her own accord without the

حديث

عن أبي هريرة ﵁ قال: قضى رسول الله ﷺ باليمين مع الشاهد الواحد.

عليه الصلاة والسلام

(سنن الدارقطني: 214/4)

QUICK TERMS

خبر الواحد: *khabar ul-wāḥid*

Singular tradition. Traditions narrated by single-narrator chains.

المشهور: *al-mashhūr*

Popular tradition. Traditions that started as singular traditions and later gained popularity.

الكتاب: *al-kitāb*

The book. The inspired final word of Allah ﷻ. The Quran.

consent of her guardian - is void void void." It infringes upon the word of He Almighty: "...do not obstruct them women from marrying their husbands..." al-kitāb necessitates establishing the marriage from them. An example of contrasting it with the al-khabar al-mashhūr is the narration of judicial cases with a witness and an oath. It infringes his saying, peace and blessings be upon him: "Burden of proof is for the claimant and an oath is for the defendant".

❖ ❖ ❖

As there is a variance in the quality of narrators, the Aḥnāf also check the authenticity of khabar ul-wāḥid by checking to see if the contents are sensible. One such measure is that khabar ul-wāḥid gives a ruling regarding a matter of common concern, or a widespread phenomenon. It is not reasonable for such a ruling to remain confined to a few individuals. In the first generations, at a time when Muslims exerted every effort to abide by the practice of the blessed Prophet ﷺ, for a narration to remain obscure despite a widespread need defies comprehension. When there is a common concern and people are inquiring about a matter to see if there is an established way, for that way to still remain unpopular is unreasonable. It clearly indicates that al-khabar was rejected by the Companions رضي الله عنهم and their Successors رحمهم الله, and thus it did not gain any popularity despite the need. Had the narration been credible and authentic, the popularity of the matter and the common concern would have elevated the tradition to popularity too. It is unfathomable that the Companions رضي الله عنهم and their Successors رحمهم الله would have ignored or not sought a precedent set by the practice of the Messenger of Allah ﷺ on such an occasion of need.

If any singularly reported khabar ul-wāḥid, in general, contradicts common sense, it will be sidelined. An example of this from general dealings is a a man entering a marriage contract with a young girl who then drank the milk of her husband's mother. If a credible man informs the husband that his wife had drunk his mother's milk, it would be sufficient for the man to rely upon this singular report and annul the contract. Thus, it would also be feasible for him to marry the sister of his now former wife. This is because this singular report is credible and stands to reason. However, if someone was to inform that a long-term marriage is invalid because the wife had, in her infancy, drank the husband's mother's milk and was thus a foster-sister, the singular report from the individual will not be admitted. It will thus follow that the husband is not permitted to marry the sister of his wife, because marrying two sisters at one

حديث

عن ابن عباس رضي الله عنهما قال قال رسول الله ﷺ: البينة على من ادعى واليمين على من أنكر.

عليه الصلاة والسلام

(مسند الربيع بن حبيب: 576)

QUICK ARABIC

الإستنجاء: *al-istinjā*

Abstersion. The cleaning of the private parts from filth.

time is not permitted. The marriage will not become invalid because it does not stand to reason and defies common norms. It is the norm that any marriage becomes well known in a community and many guests attend such ceremonies. If the wife was a foster-sister to the husband it would be common knowledge and someone would have spoken up during the marriage ceremony. As no one had spoken up at that time, despite the need to, a singular report on the contrary will not be sufficient to overturn the apparent. Therefore, the marriage will remain valid.

Similarly, if a woman is informed by a single account that her husband has died or has issued divorce three times, whilst the husband is absent, it will be accepted as it does not oppose the apparent. The account is relied upon by the woman accepting it, spending her days of *al-'idda* and then remarrying.

If the direction of the qibla is not clear to a worshipper and an individual informed him that it is in a particular direction, it will be necessary for the worshipper to obey this account. This is because this account does not oppose the apparent situation. Furthermore, if one was to stumble upon some water and not know of its purity, and an individual informed that the water is impure, the information will be accepted. This is because it does not oppose the apparent and so it is not permitted for the individual to perform ablution with that water; rather he would have to perform *at-tayammum* in order to proceed with salah.

Text And Translation

وباعتبار هذا المعنى قلنا: خبر الواحد إذا خرج مخالفا للظاهر لا يعمل به ومن صور مخالفة الظاهر عدم اشتهار الخبر فيما يعم به البلوى في الصدر الأول والثاني؛ لأنهم لا يتهمون بالتقصير في متابعة السنة فإذا لم يشتهر الخبر مع شدة الحاجة وعموم البلوى كان ذلك علامة عدم صحته، ومثاله في الحكميات إذا أخبر واحد أن امرأته حرمت عليه بالرضاع الطاري جاز أن يعتمد على خبره ويتزوج أختها ولو أخبر أن العقد كان باطلاً بحكم الرضاع لا يقبل خبره، وكذلك إذا أخبرت المرأة بموت زوجها أو طلاقه إياها وهو غائب جاز أن تعتمد على خبرها وتتزوج بغيره، ولو اشتبهت عليه القبلة فأخبره واحد عنها وجب العمل به، ولو وجد ماء لا يعلم حاله فأخبره واحد عن النجاسة لا يتوضأ به بل يتيمم.

QUICK ARABIC

العدة: *al-'idda*

The term. The three-month period after a divorce.

التيمم: *at-tayammum*

Dry ablution. The ritual ablution performed without water.

Taking this meaning into consideration we say: when khabar ul-wāḥid infringes upon the obvious it will not be enacted. A case of infringing upon the obvious is the lack of popularity of al-khabar in a matter of public commotion during the first and second generations. This is because they are not accused of slacking when following the sunna. So when al-khabar did not gain popularity despite the greater need and general interest, it is a sign of it lacking authenticity. An example of it in the rulings is when one informs that his wife is unlawful for him due to common suckling. It is valid to depend on his testimony and he to marry her sister. If one informed that the marriage was invalid due to suckling, his testimony is unacceptable. Similarly, if a woman is informed of the death of her husband or him divorcing her, whilst he is not present, her depending upon the testimony is permitted and she may marry another. If the qibla becomes unclear to someone and someone else informs of it, acting upon it is necessary. If one found water and does not know of its state, and someone informs of its impurity, he must not perform ablution with it but perform *at-tayammum*.

❖ ❖ ❖

QUICK TERMS

خبر الواحد: *khabar ul-wāḥid*

Singular tradition. Traditions narrated by single-narrator chains.

الخبر: *al-khabar*

Singular tradition. Traditions narrated by single-narrator chains.

Summary Of Contrasting Khabar ul-Wāḥid

1. Khabar ul-wāḥid should be contrasted with stronger sources, before it is admitted for deriving rulings.

2. Example of khabar ul-wāḥid contradicting al-kitāb:
   A tradition says: من مس ذكره فليتوضأ whereas the blessed Quran says: فيه رجال يحبّون أن يتطهروا. al-khabar suggests that touching the private parts is impurity. The verse tells of people who cleaned themselves with stones as being lovers of purity. They must have touched the private parts in the process, so al-khabar is side-lined.

3. Example of khabar ul-wāḥid contradicting al-mashhūr:
   al-khabar says: القضاء بشاهد ويمين whereas a al-mashhūr tradition says: البينة على المدعي واليمين على من أنكر. Allowing the prosecution to use an oath as evidence contradicts the exclusivity of the defence using it in the absence of witnesses.

4. Khabar ul-wāḥid contradicting common sense: Any tradition that reports from an event where there are masses present. Despite it being well attended the information remains restricted to individuals. Its popularity should be inevitable. However, when Companions ﷻ and Successors ﷺ have not made such a report common knowledge, despite their eagerness to emulate and pass on the sunna, means it is clear there is an issue with the report.

2.2 Admitting Khabar al-Wāḥid

Some examples in the previous chapter looked at singular reports in general dealings. In this chapter the discussion is about the four scenarios in which a general khabar ul-wāḥid is legally valid. This validity is for any account that does not reach the popularity or robustness of al-mashhūr and al-mutawātir. It includes accounts of two or four witnesses, as their accounts have not gained enough traction to merit authenticity on their own.

The four scenarios are: firstly, a right of Allah ﷻ that is not a punishment. Punishments require certainty. Any degree of doubt will jeopardise the administration of a punishment and as khabar ul-wāḥid has an element of doubt attached to it, it cannot be alone in proving guilt in punishments. Secondly, a right of an individual which includes liabilities. Thirdly, a right of an individual without any liabilities. And lastly, a right of an individual with an element of a liability. The details of each scenario are as follows:

When it is a matter that concerns the right of Allah ﷻ only, such as salah, sawm, and aṣ-ṣadaqa, khabar ul-wāḥid is a valid source because the blessed Prophet ﷺ accepted the testimony of a Bedouin man in citing the moon and the commencing of the new Islamic month. On such an occasion, if a singular account was not permitted, the blessed Prophet ﷺ would not have accepted it. It was accepted, so in matters concerning Allah ﷻ only, such a report is admissible.

In a matter concerning people, where there is a liability and an accusation on another, there are two conditions for the acceptance of khabar ul-wāḥid. The first is multiplicity, by having two accounts from males, or one account from a male and two from females. The second is integrity, in that both testimonies come from credible individuals. The condition of multiplicity is from the words of the Almighty ﷻ in verse 282 of Sūrat ul-Baqara, and the evidence of their integrity is from verse 2 of Sūrat ut-Talāq:

﴿وَاسْتَشْهِدُوا شَهِيدَيْنِ من رِّجَالِكُمْ﴾ [البقرة: 282]

"...and call to witness, from among your men, two witnesses...."

﴿وَأَشْهِدُوا ذَوَيْ عَدْلٍ مِّنكُمْ﴾ [الطلاق: 2]

"...And let two persons of integrity from amongst your own witness..."

حديث

عن ابن عباس رضي الله عنهما أن اعرابيا جاء إلى النبي ﷺ فقال: رأيت الهلال، قال: أتشهد ألا إله إلا الله وأن مُحَمَّدا عبده ورسوله، قال: نعم، قال: يا بلال أذن في الناس فليصوموا غدا.

عليه الصلاة والسلام

(أبو داوود والنسائي والترمذي)

QUICK TERMS

خبر الواحد: *khabar ul-wāḥid*

Singular tradition. Traditions narrated by single-narrator chains.

المشهور: *al-mashhur*

Popular tradition. Traditions that started as single traditions and later gained popularity.

المتواتر: *al- mutawātir*

Uninterrupted mass transmission. A narration that is an unbroken tradition and related by many in every generation.

QUICK ARABIC

الصدقة: *aṣ-ṣadaqa*

Almsgiving. Provisions given voluntarily to the needy.

This scenario plays out in financial disputes. For example, if there is a dispute over the buying or selling of merchandise, where one claims he is owed by the other party. In such a case the claimant needs to prove his position by bringing forth two credible witnesses, which will ensure multiplicity of the khabar ul-wāḥid as well as the integrity of the individuals.

Matters that are between people but do not involve liability may be established through khabar ul-wāḥid. There is no stipulation for the integrity of the individuals, so it may be the account of a credible person or of a sinner, a Muslim or otherwise. This scenario is found in general dealings amongst people. For example, if one person informs another that so-and-so has appointed an individual to represent him, or so-and-so has permission to trade on behalf of another. The evidence of this is that the blessed Prophet ﷺ accepted the gifts of just individuals as well as sinners. When a person of integrity informed that an item was not charity, he accepted it, and if a sinner told him the same, he accepted it, Allah Almighty's choicest peace and blessings be upon him and his family.

Rights of people that have an element of liability in them may be supported by khabar ul-wāḥid, but require either multiplicity or integrity. This means that two individuals of unknown character may support the case, or one individual of credibility may support it. An example of this is found in hiring and firing. If, for example, a couple of people informed another that so-and-so has revoked your right to act on his behalf, or one individual of reputable standing was to inform of the same thing, it would be accepted as the truth. There is an element of accusation in this in that if the individual continues to act on behalf of the other after receiving the accounts, he will be responsible for his own actions thereafter. There is also the idea that liability does not play a part because it was at the discretion of the individual to appoint an individual to represent him, just as it is at his discretion to cease that permission. It is just like general dealings. Bearing in mind that it is like general dealings without liability in one sense and like liabilities in another sense, it follows that the condition is either multiplicity or integrity.

Text And Translation

فصل: خبر الواحد حجة في أربعة مواضع: خالص حق الله تعالى ما ليس بعقوبة، وخالص حق العبد ما فيه إلزام محض، وخالص حقه ما ليس في إلزام، وخالص حقه ما فيه إلزام من وجه، أما الأول فيقبل

فيه خبر الواحد فإن رسول الله ﷺ قبل شهادة الأعرابي في هلال رمضان، وأما الثاني فيشترط فيه العدد والعدالة، ونظيره المنازعات وأما الثالث فيقبل فيه خبر الواحد عدلاً كان أو فاسقا، ونظيره المعاملات وأما الرابع فيشترط فيه إما العدد أو العدالة عند أبي حنيفة رضي الله عنه ونظيره: العزل والحجر.

Chapter: A singular narrative is valid in four places: an absolute right of Allah Almighty whilst not a punishment; an absolute right of a person with accusation; absolute right of a person with no accusation; and the absolute right of a person with an element of accusation. The first will be accepted by a single narrative as the Messenger of Allah, peace and blessings be upon him, accepted the testimony of a Beduin for the Ramadan crescent. The second will require multiplicity and integrity. The example of it is disputes. The third will be accepted by a single narrative whether of an honest or dishonest individual. An example of it is social settings. As for the fourth, it requires either multiplicity or integrity according to Imam Abū Ḥanīfa, Allah be pleased with him. An example of it is dismissal and limitation of legal competence.

❖ ❖ ❖

Summary Of Admission of Khabar ul-Wāḥid

Singularly reported accounts are admissible as evidence in four scenarios:

1. When it concerns a matter that is the right of Allah ﷻ alone, and is not related to a punishment. For example, the Prophet ﷺ accepted the testimony of a Bedouin with respect to the sighting of the crescent of Ramadan.

2. When it solely concerns a right of a person, where there is an accusation, such as in a financial dispute. Here al-khabar has to be from a reporter of sound character and multiple accounts (at least two).

3. When it concerns a right of a person with no element of accusation. For example, in general dealings. There is no condition of any sort on the character of the reporter.

4. When it concerns the right of a person and has a degree of accusation. For example, in dismissals based on breaches of contract, or restrictions based on legal competence.

al-Ijmā'

PART 3

3.0 Introduction to al-Ijmā'

The third discussion is on al-ijmā' and it follows the discussion on as-Sunna. Lexically al-ijmā' means agreement or firm intention. In Shariah terminology al-ijmā' denotes a particular type of agreement. This is a consensus and agreement regarding an event or matter reached by the noble jurists and scholars of the Ummah of the blessed Prophet ﷺ in a given generation. This consensus can be verbal, practical or even doctrinal. The silence of a scholar regarding such matters is also considered their tacit approval, as it would be necessary for a scholar to voice their opposition on a matter of importance.

There are numerous pieces of evidence that highlight the validity of al-ijmā' as a principle of jurisprudence. Amongst the evidence is the word of the Almighty جل جلاله in verse 115 of Sūrat un-Nisā:

﴿وَمَن يُشَاقِقِ الرَّسُولَ مِن بَعْدِ مَا تَبَيَّنَ لَهُ الْهُدَى وَيَتَّبِعْ غَيْرَ سَبِيلِ الْمُؤْمِنِينَ نُوَلِّهِ مَا تَوَلَّى وَنُصْلِهِ جَهَنَّمَ وَسَاءَتْ مَصِيرًا﴾

[النساء: 115]

"And whoso opposes the messenger after the guidance is clear for him, and follows other than the believers' path, We will grant him where he treads, and expose him to Hell, what a terrible end!"

QUICK TERMS

الإجماع: *al-ijmā'*

Consensus. The unanimous consent of the mujtahids.

السنة: *as-sunna*

The practice. The sayings, doings and approval of the blessed Prophet ﷺ.

In the verse there is a strong reprimand for the one who opposes the way of the Messenger of Allah ﷺ and for the one who takes a path different to that of the believers. Those matters that carry a reprimand are forbidden and conversely their opposition is necessary and sought. This shows that treading the path of the believers is necessary and al-wājib. Treading the path believers choose as a collective is the very purpose of al-ijmā' becoming a valid base and foundation of legal issues in the Shariah. When all jurists and scholars have agreed on a matter, all Muslims follow suit, and thus when one takes this opinion, they safeguard themselves from the punishments outlined in the blessed Quran. There are many other examples from both Quran and the Sunna that support al-ijmā' as a valid source.

The consensus and al-ijmā' of this Ummah is a valid source of the Shariah, but not the agreement of the nations of the past. This is because this Ummah is blessed and honoured by Allah ﷻ, more so than nations of the past. As a manifestation of that blessing, the collective agreement of the Ummah is an authority. It is an authority after the lifetime of the beloved Messenger of Allah ﷺ and not during it. Whilst he ﷺ was on Earth it was necessary to seek his approval in all matters, peace and blessings of Allah Almighty be upon him and his family. Furthermore, al-ijmā' is an authority in applied, *al-far'ī*, matters and not in the fundamental tenants, *al-uṣūl*, such as *at-tawḥīd* and *an-nubuwwa*. Fundamental matters are supported by both textual and rational evidence, so there is no need to rely on al-ijmā' for them.

FIGURE 3.0-01

Types of al-Ijmā’.

al-Ijmā’
- Consensus –

3.1 as-sanadī [page 349]

1. Textually evidenced from the Companions رضي الله عنهم of unanimous agreement.
2. Evidence of some Companions by text and silence of others رضي الله عنهم.
3. Agreement of jurists رحمهم الله of a latter generation on a matter Companions رضي الله عنهم were silent on.
4. An agreement of a latter generation of jurists رحمهم الله on an opinion of a Companion رضي الله عنه.

3.2 al-madhhabī [page 351]

1. al-murakkab
   - ‘adam ul-qāili bil faṣl
2. ghayr ul-murakkab

al-Ijmā' is of two types: al-ijmā' as-sanadī and al-ijmā' al-madhhabī. al-Ijmā' as-sanadī is the consensus reached by scholars of the whole Ummah, irrespective of an alliance to any *al-madhhab* or school. It is an agreement on an issue across the board. al-Ijmā' al-madhhabī is a consensus with a consideration for alliances to a *madhhab* and school. Details of this type of al-ijmā' will follow.

Text And Translation

البحث الثالث في الإجماع

فصل: إجماع هذه الأمة بعد ما توفي رسول الله ﷺ في فروع الدين حجة موجبة للعمل بها شرعا كرامة لهذه الأمة

Chapter: Consensus of this Ummah after the departure of the Messenger of Allah, peace and blessings be upon him, in applied religious matters is authoritative, legally necessitating application as an honour for this Ummah.

❖ ❖ ❖

3.0.1 Types of al-ijmā' as-Sanadī

al-Ijmā' as-sanadī is a source of evidence and its particulars must be obeyed and enacted. There are four types of this al-ijmā':

1. The consensus of the noble Companions ﷺ on a matter of concern. This may be based on a transmitted text that reads "all the Companions ﷺ agreed" or for them to have practically acted as a whole. An example of this is the selection of the noble Abū Bakr aṣ-Ṣiddīque ﷺ as the first Caliph of Islam by swearing allegiance to him.

2. By some of the Companions ﷺ voicing their approval of a matter, whilst the others remained silent. An example of this is the delivery of three divorces in one sitting accounting for all three divorces and not one. This was voiced by the noble 'Umar ﷺ whilst other Companions ﷺ remained silent on the matter. Their silence reflects their agreement to the consensus on the matter.

3. When the Companions ﷺ have not voiced anything regarding a matter, but the elite jurists, *al-mujtahidūn*, of a later generation such as the Successors, at-Tābi'īn, have agreed upon an issue.

4. When an opinion of a Companion ﷺ is taken up by a later generation, and in that generation a consensus is achieved.

The strength of each of these types of al-ijmā' varies. The first type is like the Book of Allah ﷻ and the strongest in authority. The one who opposes it is out of the fold of Islam. The second is like an al-mutawātir tradition, which must be enacted, but the one who opposes does not necessarily become a non-Muslim, as its authority is weaker than the first type. The third type is like an al-mashhūr tradition, which is weaker than the second type, and lastly the weakest

QUICK TERMS

الإجماع السندي: *al-ijmā' as-sanadī*

Strengthened consensus. The agreement of all eligible scholars of a generation on a matter.

الإجماع المذهبي: *al-ijmā' al-madhhabī*

Consensus in a school. When adherents to a school of fiqh agree on a matter.

الفرعي: *al-far'ī*

Subsidiary. The branches of fiqh concerning religious ceremonial and civil practices.

الأصول: *al-uṣūl*

Primary. The main and root matters of fiqh, concerning theological matters.

QUICK ARABIC

التوحيد: *at-tawḥīd*

Unity of God. The fundamental basis of Islam regarding the oneness of Allah Almighty.

النبوة: *an-nubūwwa*

Prophecy. The office and work of the prophets of Allah Almighty.

المذهب: *al-madhhab*

School of fiqh. A system of practices according to mujtahids.

is the fourth type, which is the equivalent of <u>kh</u>abar ul-wāḥid. Whilst all four types must be enacted, the first two are definitive, *al-qaṭ'ī*, and the latter two are presumptive, *a<u>dh</u>-<u>dh</u>annī*.

In any al-ijmā' the consensus and agreement of *al-mujtahidūn* is taken into account. The views of the public and the *al-mutakallimūn* are not considered, nor are the opinions of the non-jurist *al-muḥaddi<u>th</u>ūn*. The public includes those scholars who are not versed in jurisprudence. al-Mutakallimūn are those whose primary concern is to discuss doctrinal matters and al-muḥaddi<u>th</u>ūn are those that are primarily concerned with texts of Hadith and chains of narrations. These categories of scholars are not specialised in matters of jurisprudence and are consequently not considered in al-ijmā. Those that are considered are al-mujtahidūn, who are concerned with deriving practical solutions from verses of the Blessed Quran and the vast body of prophetic tradition.

Text And Translation

ثم الإجماع على أربعة أقسام: إجماع الصحابة ﷺ على حكم الحادثة نصا. ثم إجماعهم بنص البعض وسكوت الباقين عن الرد. ثم إجماع من بعدهم فيما لم يوجد فيه قول السلف. ثم الإجماع على أحد أقوال السلف. أما الأول فهو بمنزلة آية من كتاب الله تعالى ثم الإجماع بنص البعض وسكوت الباقين فهو بمنزلة المتواتر، ثم إجماع من بعدهم بمنزلة المشهور من الأخبار ثم أجماع المتأخرين على أحد أقوال السلف بمنزلة الصحيح من الآحاد، والمعتبر في هذا الباب إجماع أهل الرأي والاجتهاد فلا يعتبر بقول العوام والمتكلم والمحدث الذي لا بصيرة له في أصول الفقه

Then al-ijmā' is of four types: the consensus of the Companions, Allah be pleased with them, on a matter expressively. Then their concensus expressed by some and the silence of the rest in responding. Then the concensus of a latter generation to them in a matter not expressed by the predecessors. Then the concensus upon a viewpoint of a predecessor. The first is like a verse of the Book of Allah. al-Ijmā' expressed by some and the silence of the rest is like al-mutawātir. al-Ijmā' of latter generations is like al-ma<u>sh</u>hūr from the Hadith and al-ijmā' of latter generations upon a viewpoint of the predecessors is like a sound <u>kh</u>abar ul-wāḥid. In this chapter the authoritative consensus is that of the

QUICK TERMS

خبر الواحد: *<u>kh</u>abar ul-wāḥid*

Singular tradition. Traditions related by single-narrator chains.

القطعي: *al-qaṭ'ī*

The definitive. Most reliable and certain.

الظني: *a<u>dh</u>-<u>dh</u>annī*

The speculative. Reached after careful consideration.

الإجماع: *al-ijmā'*

Consensus. The unanimous agreement of the mujtahids.

QUICK ARABIC

المتكلمون: *al-mutakallimūn*

Scholastic theologians. Scholars concerned with matters of Islamic creed.

المحدثون: *al-muḥaddi<u>th</u>ūn*

Scholars of traditions. Scholars concerned with the science of prophetic traditions.

المجتهدون: *al-mujtahidūn*

The strivers. The exerter of effort in attaining a high position of scholarship and learning in matters of fiqh.

judicious and legist. The view of the general public, a theologian or al-muḥaddith who has no insight into the principles of Fiqh, are not considered.

❖❖❖

3.0.2 Types of al-Ijmā' al-Madhhabī

The second type of al-ijmā' is al-ijmā' al-madhhabī. It is when a group of scholars come to an agreement, bearing in mind their adherence to a particular school and *madhhab*. This type of consensus is further divided into ghayr ul-murakkab, the simple, and al-murakkab, the complex. The simple consensus is when the thoughts of the jurists from different schools come to a ruling based on one cause, and in accordance with their respective schools. For example, both the Aḥnāf and the Shawāfi' agree that a person who breaks wind invalidates his ablution. The cause of the invalidation in both schools is also the same, the exiting of an impurity. Both schools, independent of each other, have come to this ruling based on their respective principles. As they agree upon the ruling and the cause of the ruling, it is a simple consensus, al-ijmā ghayr ul-murakkab. al-Ijmā ul-murakkab, the complex consensus, on the other hand, is a ruling upon which the jurists agree but the agreement is due to different causes. For example, in the state of ablution if one was to vomit and come into physical contact with a woman, his ablution will become invalid. Both the Aḥnāf and the Shawāfi' agree to this ruling. However, the Aḥnāf say the cause of invalidation is the vomiting, whilst the Shawāfi' say it is due to the contact. The fact is that they agree on the ruling but disagree on the cause, making this a complex consensus, al-ijmā' ul-murakkab.

In al-ijmā ul-murakkab should any of the different causes become problematic; the consensus no longer remains credible. Hypothetically, if it became clear that vomiting does not invalidate the ablution, the Aḥnāf would alter their verdict and proclaim that the ablution is still valid even though the individual may have had physical contact with a woman. The cause and basis of their previous ruling no longer applies so their verdict changes. Equally, if it becomes clear through valid evidence that physical contact with a woman does not invalidate the ablution, the Shawāfi' will change their ruling and say the ablution is still valid. The cause of invalidation in their opinion will no longer apply and so the verdict will change. In either case, if one party withdraws from the consensus, the consensus is no longer applicable and if it is not a consensus, it is no longer a credible legal source in the Shariah.

QUICK TERMS

المتواتر: *al-mutawātir*

Uninterrupted mass transmission. A narration that is an unbroken tradition and related by many in every generation.

المشهور: *al-mashhūr*

Popular tradition. Traditions that start as singular traditions and later gain popularity.

الإجماع المذهبي: *al-ijmā' al-madhhabī*

Consensus in a school. When adherents to a school of fiqh agree on a matter.

الإجماع المركب: *al-ijmā' al-murakkab*

Complex consensus. Were jurists agree on a ruling based on differing causes.

الإجماع غير المركب: *al-ijmā' ghayr ul-murakkab*

Simple consensus. Where jurists of different schools come to the same conclusion based on their own respective principles.

QUICK ARABIC

المذهب: *al-madhhab*

School of fiqh. A system of practices according to mujtahids.

A difference of opinion is usually presented from one party upon the other, but in the case of al-ijmā' ul-murakkab the fickle nature of the consensus means that weakness in the cause is a possibility from both sides. Just as it is possible that each party could be wrong in identifying their own cause correctly, it is equally possible for the party to be incorrect in dismissing the other party's cause. For example, the Aḥnāf could be correct in saying that physical contact does not invalidate but mistaken in identifying vomiting as the cause. In such a circumstance, the stated cause would be incorrect. It is equally possible that a<u>sh</u>-<u>Sh</u>awāfi' are correct in identifying that vomiting does not invalidate the ablution but wrong in that physical contact with a woman invalidates it. In this circumstance, the stated cause would also be incorrect. In short, when it is possible for one of both schools to be correct as well as incorrect, the exact reason for being incorrect remains indeterminate and when being incorrect is just a possibility, and not a reality, it does not affect the credibility of the consensus.

After the invalidity of a cause becomes actual, the consensus no longer remains credible and authoritative. This is very different to al-ijmā' <u>gh</u>ayr ul-murakkab because that consensus does not include the suspicion of an error. As there is no suspicion of an error, there is no need to say it will no longer remain authoritative because if there is no suspicion by extension an actual error is even more remote. al-Ijmā' ul-murakkab may have an error in its composition and so can become invalid if such an error becomes apparent, but al-ijmā <u>gh</u>ayr ul-murakkab does not have even the suspicion of error in its formation, so it will not become invalid either.

QUICK TERMS

الإجماع المركب: *al-ijmā’ al-murakkab*

Complex consensus. Were jurists agree on a ruling based on differing causes.

الإجماع غير المركب: *al-ijmā’ <u>gh</u>ayr ul-murakkab*

Simple consensus. Where jurists of different schools come to the same conclusion based on their own respective principles.

Text And Translation

ثم بعد ذلك الإجماع على نوعين، مركب وغير مركب فالمركب ما اجتمع عليه الآراء على حكم الحادثة مع وجود الاختلاف في العلة، ومثاله الإجماع على وجود الانتقاض عند القيء ومس المرأة، أما عندنا فبناء على القيء وأما عنده فبناء على المس، ثم هذا النوع من الإجماع لا يبقى حجة بعد ظهور الفساد في أحد المأخذين حتى لو ثبت أن القيء غير ناقض فأبو حنيفة عليه الرحمة لا يقول بالانتقاض فيه ولو ثبت أن المس غير ناقض فالشافعي عليه الرحمة لا يقول بالانتقاض فيه لفساد العلة التي بني عليها الحكم، والفساد متوهم في الطرفين لجواز أن يكون أبو حنيفة رحمه الله مصيبا في مسئلة المس مخطئا في

مسئلة القيء والشافعي مصيبا في مسئلة القيء مخطئا في مسألة المس، فلا يؤدي هذا إلى بناء وجود الإجماع على الباطل، بخلاف ما تقدم من الإجماع، فالحاصل أنه جاز ارتفاع هذا الإجماع لظهور الفساد فيما بني هو عليه

Then after that, al-ijmā' is of two types: complex and simple. The complex al-murakkab is the one upon which opinions have gathered regarding a ruling on a matter, despite a difference in the cause. An example of it is al-ijmā' upon invalidity after vomiting and physical contact with a woman. According to us it is based upon vomiting and according to him it is based upon contact. Then, this type of al-ijmā' no longer remains authoritative on the appearance of wrongness in one of the sources. So if it is proven that vomit does not void, then Abū Ḥanīfa, Allah have mercy on him, would not rule it void. If it were proven that contact does not void, then ash-Shāfa'ī, Allah have mercy on him, would not rule it void due to the voidness of the cause that the ruling was based upon. Because the wrongness is imaginable from both parties – as it is possible that Abū Ḥanīfa, Allah have mercy on him, is right about the contact case but wrong about the vomiting case, and ash-Shāfa'ī is right about the vomiting case but wrong about the contact case – this will not lead to basing the existence of al-ijmā' upon falsehood; unlike what has passed from al-ijmā'. In short, it is possible for this al-ijmā to cease due to the appearance of wrongness in what it is based upon.

❖ ❖ ❖

When a cause is wrongly identified the resulting ruling is also invalidated, so it follows that if a judge made a judgement based on evidence and testimony that was later found to be falsified or retracted for any other reason, the judgement will also be retracted. The foundation upon which the judgement was made was wrong, so the resulting verdict would also be wrong. It is worth noting that in such a miscarriage of justice if a financial penalty was issued by the judge on the defendant it will not be reversed. This is because the verdict is invalid with respect to the defendant and witnesses, which does not automatically mean that the decision is in favour of the claimant. It just means there was an error in giving the said judgement due to the false testimony, and as such, this reversal is not a judgement in favour of the other party. At the time of the first verdict, the penalty was levied legally based on evidence so it will remain. As for the loss incurred by the defendant due to the false testimony of the witnesses, it will be made up through compensation levied on those witnesses.

Another example of the absence of a cause resulting in an invalidated ruling is found in the categories of zakah recipients. Those attracted to Islam, *muallafat ul-qulūb*, no longer qualify as recipients as the cause is no longer there. The non-believing leaders amongst the tribes of the Arabs were inclined towards Islam and their acceptance would give Islam strength. To facilitate this process, zakah was permitted for them so they would not incur any financial loss by converting, rather they would be better off. However, once Allah جل جلاله blessed Islam with its own dominance and strength, there was no need for any additional incentive to facilitate conversions. As this cause no longer remained valid, the ruling was also rescinded and they no longer remain a valid category for receiving zakah.

Furthermore, the *<u>dh</u>aw il-qurbā* have lost their allocation from the spoils due to the absence of a cause. In the time of the beloved Prophet صلى الله عليه وسلم, the spoils of battle were divided into five and the recipients included the near relatives of the Prophet صلى الله عليه وسلم. They were entitled because they assisted the Messenger of Allah صلى الله عليه وسلم in matters of the religion. After the passing of the Messenger صلى الله عليه وسلم the Aḥnāf hold that only three of the five recipient categories are still active. The portion allocated to the Messenger of Allah صلى الله عليه وسلم is not required nor that of his inner circle of relatives because the cause that entitled them, assistance of the Messenger of Allah صلى الله عليه وسلم, no longer applies. This is supported by the narration, "From them the *<u>dh</u>aw il-qurbā* are relevant in my lifetime, and not after it." It is worth noting that the near relatives of the Messenger of Allah صلى الله عليه وسلم may still qualify for a share if they fall into one of the other eligible categories, such as the category of the poor, the orphan or the wayfarer, but will not be eligible due to their kinship.

The lifting of a cause resulting in the lifting of the ruling is further illustrated by the case in which an impure cloth is washed by vinegar or any other pure non-water liquid, which resulted in the removal of the physical impurity. The Aḥnāf rule that the cloth becomes pure. This is because the cause that created the impurity in the cloth is removed, so the ruling of the impurity of the cloth is also removed. As the cloth is no longer impure, it is ruled to be pure.

QUICK ARABIC

مؤلفة القلوب: *muallafat ul-qulūb*

Encouraged persons. Influential people for whom financial support would assist Islam's progress.

ذوي القربى: *<u>dh</u>aw il-qurbā*

Kinsfolk. Relatives who are connected to an individual through blood or marriage.

النجاسة الحكمية: *an-najāsat ul-ḥukmīya*

Legal impurity. Not a physical impurity but the state of requiring either ablution or bathing.

النجاسة الحقيقية *an-najāsat ul-ḥaqīqīya*

Physical impurity. An actual impure substance, the removal of which is required for purity.

The removal of impurity is a cause for purity. This highlights the difference between ritual impurities, *an-najāsat ul-ḥukmīya*, and physical impurities, *an-najāsat ul-ḥaqīqīya*. Other than water, any clean liquid such as vinegar may be used to remove a physical impurity but would be insufficient to remove a ritual impurity. Ritual impurity may only be removed by a purifying agent, which is water. The difference is clear because for a cloth to be pure from a physical impurity it merely requires the cause, the body of the impurity, to be removed. That is achieved by using any pure flowing liquid. The liquid will carry the impurity away leaving the cloth in a state of purity. Purity after a ritual impurity is different. A ritual impurity, such that requires ablution or a bath, is not removed by simply washing away a physical impure body, rather it is stipulated by the Shariah that ritual impurity is removed by washing with water only. As this is expressed by the Shariah, it means that the only way to remove ritual impurity is by washing with water, which is an agent of purity, and not using any other liquid even if it is pure.

Text And Translation

ولهذا إذا قضى القاضي في حادثة ثم ظهر رق أو كذبهم بالرجوع بطل قضاؤه وإن لم يظهر الشهود ذلك في حق المدعي وباعتبار هذا المعنى سقطت المؤلفة قلوبهم عن الأصناف الثمانية لانقطاع العلة، وسقط سهم ذوي القربى لانقطاع علته، وعلى هذا إذا غسل الثوب النجس بالخل فزالت النجاسة يحكم بطهارة المحل لانقطاع علتها وبهذا ثبت الفرق بين الحدث والخبث، فإن الخل يزيل النجاسة عن المحل، فأما الخل لا يفيد طهارة المحلّ وإنما يفيدها المطهر وهو الماء.

Due to this, when a judge rules in a case and then serfdom or deceit by retraction surfaces, the judgement is voided, even if the witnesses do not surface in favour of the claimant. Considering this meaning, muallafat ul-qulūb, are omitted from the eight recipients as the cause has ceased. The share of the relatives is omitted as the cause has ceased. Based on this, when one washed an impure cloth with vinegar and the filth was removed, the location is ruled as pure as its cause is no longer. With this the difference between *al-ḥadath* and *al-khubuth* is established. The vinegar removes the filth from the place, but the vinegar does not achieve purity in the place. That can be achieved by the cleanser, which is water.

❖ ❖ ❖

حديث

عن أم هاني رضي الله عنها قالت: أن فاطمة رضي الله عنها أتت أبا بكر رضي الله عنه تسأله سهم ذوي القربى فقال لها أبو بكر رضي الله عنه سمعت رسول الله صلى الله عليه وسلم يقول: سهم ذوي القربى لهم في حياتي وليس لهم بعد موتي.

عليه الصلوة والسلام

(كنز العمال: 367/5)

QUICK ARABIC

الحدث: *al-ḥadath*

Ritual impurity. An act or occurrence that necessitates either ablution or bathing.

الخبث: *al-khubuth*

Physical impurity. An actual impure substance, the removal of which is necessary for purity.

QUICK DICTIONARY

Serfdom: *serf-dom*

In slavery. A person in the condition of being the property of another.

Summary Of al-Ijmā'

1. Linguistic meaning: firm intention or agreement.
Definition:
هو اتفاق المجتهدين من أمة محمد ﷺ في عصر من العصور على حكم شرعي بعد وفاته عليه الصلاة والسلام
"It is the generational agreement of jurists of the Ummah of the blessed Prophet ﷺ upon a legal matter of the Shariah after his passing".

2. Types: fundamentally it has two types:
i) al-Ijmā' as-sanadī; and
ii) al-Ijmā' al-madhhabī.

3. Details of al-ijmā' as-sanadī:
i) Definition: ما اتفق عليه جميع علماء أمة محمد ﷺ في عصر من العصور
"What is agreed upon by all the jurists of the Ummah of the Prophet ﷺ, in one generation".
ii) Types: there are four types of this al-ijmā'.
a) Agreement of the Companions رضي الله عنهم upon a new matter with a clear text. Its ruling is:
بمنزلة آية من كتاب الله تعالى في لزوم العمل به والاعتقاد به
"It is like a verse of al-kitāb in the necessity to enact it and believe in it".
b) The clear text of some of the Companions رضي الله عنهم and the silence of the rest. Its ruling is:
بمنزلة المتواتر
"It is like an al-mutawātir narration".
c) The agreement of successors رحمهم الله on a matter, where no collective position is known for the Companions رضي الله عنهم. Its ruling is:
بمنزلة المشهور من الأخبار
"It is like a al-mashhūr narration".
d) The agreement of successors رحمهم الله on one opinion of a Companion رضي الله عنه. Its ruling is:
بمنزلة الصحيح من الأحاد
"It is like a sound khabar ul-wāḥid from the narrations".

*Agreement includes jurists and men of the discipline, not laymen, theologians or non-jurists.

4. Details of al-ijmā' al-madhhabī:
i) Definition: إجماع بعض المجتهدين على حكم
"Agreement of a group of jurists on a ruling".
ii) Types: there are two types:
a) al-Murakkab; and
b) Ghayr ul-murakkab.

5. Details of al-murakkab:
i) Definition: اتفاق المجتهدين على حكم جديد بالاختلاف في علّته
"Agreement of the jurists on a new ruling, with a disagreement on its cause".
ii) Example: When a man vomits a mouthful and touches a woman. Both Aḥnāf and ash-Shāfa'īy رحمه الله agree that his ablution is invalid but the cause is different. For the Aḥnāf it is the vomit that invalidates it, and for ash-Shāfa'īy رحمه الله it is touching that invalidates.

6. Details of ghayr ul-murakkab:
i) Definition: اتفاق المجتهدين على حكم جديد وعلى علّته
"Agreement of the jurists on a new ruling and agreement upon its cause".
ii) Example: Marriage to a grandmother is prohibited due to their honour and respect. The ruling and cause are unanimously agreed upon.

3.1 'Adam ul-Qāili bil-Faṣl

Another form of al-ijmā' al-murakkab is termed 'adam ul-qāili bil-faṣl, which literally reads as 'no proposal for separation'. This comes about when there are two cases under review. One party accepts both cases for a particular ruling and the other party denies the ruling in both cases. There happens to be no one who holds a third opinion, such that one case accepts the ruling and the other case does not. Either both cases are accepted by a party or both are rejected by a party. There is no proposal from any quarter to disconnect and separate the two cases. If a party were able to show the ruling in one of the cases, it would follow that they accept it in the other case. If the party object to the ruling in one case, it would follow that they reject it in the other case too. This type of consensus is further divided in two: firstly, that there is just one cause for accepting or rejecting both cases, and secondly, there are different causes in both cases. The first type is legal evidence and the second type is not.

Examples of the first type are present in any two cases that stem from the same principle. For example, a principle established in the Ḥanafī school is 'a prohibition issued on an otherwise legal matter retains the legality of the matter' [see chapter 1.7 an-Nahi, page 219]. This means that when an otherwise permitted act is subject to a prohibition in a given circumstance, the prohibition is in fact establishing that the matter itself is legal and permitted. Based on this principle, we say that a vow to fast on the day of Eid al-Aḍḥa is valid and in an invalid transaction, once the purchaser takes possession of the merchandise his ownership is established. Both fasting and purchasing are legal acts, however there is a prohibition issued for fasting on the day of Eid al-Aḍḥa and from partaking in an invalid purchase. Accordingly, we say that the prohibition issued on both legal acts shows their basic legality. If they are legal, then a vow to fast is valid and transfer of ownership is established. The vow is permitted but on the day of Eid al-Aḍḥa by actually fasting the hospitality of the Almighty ﷻ will be shunned and thus it is prohibited and al-ḥarām. To carry out the fast on the day will be halted and a make up fast will be required on an alternative day. Similarly, entering a transaction is a legal act, which in this instance happens to be invalid due to a condition and is thus prohibited. Based on the principle that prohibition establishes its legality, the transaction is completed. This means that just as the purchaser takes possession of the merchandise his ownership over it comes into effect, but as the deal has an invalid clause, which the Shariah has prohibited, the merchandise is to be returned immediately thus reversing the

QUICK TERMS

الإجماع المركب: *al-ijmā' al-murakkab*

Complex consensus. Were jurists agree on a ruling based on differing causes.

عدم القول بالفصل: *'adam ul-qawli bil-faṣl*

Bipartisan. When jurists fall into two parties over a matter, whilst all agree that a third option is invalid.

الحرام: *al-ḥarām*

The unlawful. That which is not permitted in the Shariah, as distinguished from the lawful.

transaction. The rulings in both cases stem from the very same principle. In the Shāfi'īy school the same principle is not held, rather a prohibition would establish the illegality of the matter at hand. This means that the Aḥnāf hold that both cases are established, such that the vow to fast is upheld and the invalid transaction still enables transfer of ownership, but the Shawāfi' disallow both matters, such that the vow is invalid and there is no transfer of ownership. Both these cases are connected and there is no proposal from anyone to disconnect them. If one is accepted, the other is accepted. If one is dismissed, the other is dismissed. It is because the cause of the difference is based on one principle.

Another illustration of this is the difference between the Aḥnāf and the Shawāfi' when considering the point at which the cause for a deferral becomes effective [see chapter 1.10.2 bayān ut-taghyīr, page 303]. The Aḥnāf hold that the cause of the deferral becomes effective when the condition is realised and the Shawāfi' opine that it becomes effective immediately upon utterance. The root from which the difference between the two schools stems is one, which is the point at which a deferral becomes effective.

As the deferral becomes effective when the condition is present, the Aḥnāf say divorce and emancipation may be deferred to the condition of ownership or to its cause. Moreover, as the deferral is effective immediately, ash-Shawāfi' do not allow divorce and emancipation to be deferred to ownership or to its cause. An example of it being deferred to ownership is if one says to the slave of someone else, "If I come to own you, you are free". An example of deferring to the cause of ownership is if one said to a stranger, "If I happen to marry you, you are divorced", or if one said to the slave of another, "If I purchase you, you are free". The Aḥnāf say that as the deferral is effective when the condition is met, it is permissible to defer in both cases of divorce and emancipation. The Shawāfi' say that as the deferral is effective immediately neither divorce nor emancipation can be deferred in this manner. Deferral is either permitted for both or denied for both. There is no opinion that disconnects the two matters and so it is termed 'adam ul-qāili bil-faṣl.

Continuing the same idea that two cases based on one principle will either be accepted together or rejected together, when a ruling is placed on a noun with a descriptor the Aḥnāf and the Shawāfi' disagree whether the ruling is attached to the description or not [chapter 1.10.2 bayān ut-taghyīr, page 309]. If

QUICK TERMS

عدم القول بالفصل: *'adam ul-qawli bil-faṣl*

Bipartisan. When jurists fall into two parties over a matter, whilst all agree that a third option is invalid.

the Aḥnāf succeed in showing that the ruling is not necessarily attached to the description then being able to marry a free woman is no obstacle to the permissibility of marrying a slave-girl. ash-Shawāfi' contend this. Allah Almighty said in verse 25 of Sūrat un-Nisā:

﴿وَمَن لَّمْ يَسْتَطِعْ مِنكُمْ طَوْلاً أَن يَنكِحَ الْمُحْصَنَاتِ الْمُؤْمِنَاتِ فَمِن مَّا مَلَكَتْ أَيْمَانُكُم﴾ [النساء: 25]

"And whoso is not able to afford to marry free, believing women, let them marry from the believing maids whom your right hands possess."

The verse defers the permissibility of marrying a slave-girl to the inability in marrying a free woman. Accordingly, the Aḥnāf say when a person is able to marry a free woman, this deferral using a description does not prevent him from marrying a slave-girl. ash-Shawāfi' do not agree to this.

Some scholars have pointed out that Imam ash-Shāfa'īy رحمه الله did not base this opinion on the cited principle of 'a ruling on a noun and its description defers the ruling to the description'. Rather he based it on another principle that states, 'absence of a condition results in the absence of the ruling bound to the conditioned", where he has likened a description to a condition. That is why, according to him, whilst being able to marry a free woman, marriage to a slave girl is not permitted. This idea is extended by him to not being permitted to marry a slave-girl from the Ahl ul-Kitāb, as the verse describes the slave-girl as a 'believer'. In response to the point raised by these scholars, others have cited authentic early Shāfi'īy sources that base the question of marriage to a slave-girl whilst able to marry a free woman on the principle of 'a ruling on a noun and its description defers the ruling to the description'.

In short, if one shows that a ruling upon an attributed noun does not defer the ruling to the adjective, it will establish the fact that ability to marry a free woman does not prevent one marrying a slave-girl. Furthermore, if we show that marriage to a believing slave-girl is permitted despite ability to marry a free woman, then due to 'adam ul-qāili bil-faṣl one can also marry a slave girl from the Ahl ul-Kitāb. This is because those that allow marriage to a believing slave-girl despite ability to marry a free woman also allow it to one of the Ahl ul-Kitāb; there is no one who calls for the two cases to be different and unconnected.

An example of this passed previously in the chapter of bayān ut-taghyīr, where the absence of a condition does not imply absence of the ruling

QUICK ARABIC

أهل الكتاب: *ahl ul-kitāb*

People of the book. Jews and Christians, who are believers in a revealed religion.

according to the Aḥnāf, but according to ash-Shāfa'īy ﵀ it does. It was mentioned that Allah Almighty says in verse 6 of Sūrat uṭ-Ṭalāq:

﴿وَإِن كُنَّ أُولَاتِ حَمْلٍ فَأَنفِقُوا عَلَيْهِنَّ حَتَّىٰ يَضَعْنَ حَمْلَهُنَّ﴾ [الطلاق: 6]

"...and if they are with child, then spend for them till they deliver their pregnancy..."

When an irrevocably divorced woman's maintenance payment is conditioned to a pregnancy, both schools agree that the maintenance is necessary upon the husband until the delivery. However, when there is no pregnancy ash-Shawāfi' maintain that no maintenance is necessary as the lack of a condition means the ruling is reversed too. The Aḥnāf say that the absence of a condition does not imply the absence of the ruling, so despite the lack of pregnancy the maintenance is still necessary upon the husband.

Text And Translation

فصل: ثم بعد ذلك نوع من الإجماع وهو عدم القائل بالفصل وذلك نوعان أحدهما: ما إذا كان منشأ الخلاف في الفصلين واحدا والثاني: ما إذا كان المنشأ مختلفا والأول حجة والثاني ليس بحجة، مثال الأول فيما خرج العلماء من المسائل الفقهية على أصل واحد، ونظيره إذا أثبتنا أن النهي عن التصرفات الشرعية يوجب تقريرها، قلنا: يصح النذر بصوم يوم النحر والبيع الفاسد يفيد الملك لعدم القائل بالفصل، ولو قلنا: إن التعليق سبب عند وجود الشرط قلنا: تعليق الطلاق والعتاق بالملك وسبب الملك صحيح، وكذا لو أثبتنا أن ترتب الحكم على اسم موصوف بصفة لا يوجب تعليق الحكم به، قلنا: طول الحرة لا يمنع جواز نكاح الأمة؛ إذ صح بنقل السلف أن الشافعي رحمه الله فرع مسألة طول الحرة على هذا الأصل ولو أثبتنا جواز نكاح الأمة المؤمنة مع الطول جاز نكاح الأمة الكتابية بهذا الأصل، وعلى هذا مثاله مما ذكرنا في ما سبق

Chapter: after this there is a type of al-ijmā' that is 'adam ul-qāili bil-faṣl. It is of two types: the first of the two is when the point of contention in two cases is the same. The second is when the point of contention is different. The first is a proof and the second is not. An example of the first are the derivations of the scholars in cases of fiqh based on one principle. Examples of it are when we establish that prohibition from legal matters necessitates their enactment. We

QUICK TERMS

بيان التغيير: *bayan ut-taghyīr*

Change. A statement that changes the direction and understanding of a previous statement.

الإجماع: *al-ijmā'*

Consensus. The unanimous agreement of the mujtahids.

عدم القول بالفصل: *'adam ul-qawli bil-faṣl*

Bipartisan. When jurists fall into two parties over a matter, whilst all agree that a third option is invalid.

said: vowing a fast on the day of Sacrifice is valid and an invalid transaction establishes ownership, because no one separates. If we said: that deferral is a cause when the condition is met, we would say: conditioning divorce or emancipation with ownership or a cause of ownership, is valid. Similarly, if we establish that forming a ruling on a descriptive noun does not necessitate conditioning the ruling to it, we would say: capacity to marry a free-woman does not prevent marriage to a slave, as it is correctly cited from the predecessors that Shāfi'īy, Allah have mercy on him, based the case of marriage to a free-woman upon this principle. If we were to prove the permissibility of marriage to a believing woman whilst having the capacity, marrying a woman of the Ahl ul-Kitāb would be permitted based on this principle. Based on this is what we have mentioned previously.

❖ ❖ ❖

An example of the second type of 'adam ul-qāili bil-faṣl – where despite being connected, at the core of the two issues there are different causes – is that the Aḥnāf say vomiting invalidates the ablution and that an invalid transaction allows for the transfer of ownership. This is an example because no one proposes anything different. Those who agree to these two rulings, the Aḥnāf, agree to them both, and those that disagree with the rulings, the Shawāfi', disagree to both. There is no one who holds one ruling true and the other ruling false. However, it is clear that the two rulings in question are unconcerned with each other. The Aḥnāf insist that vomiting invalidates the ablution because of the tradition: "Whoever vomits, has a nose bleed, regurgitates, or ejaculates should leave and perform ablution." Whilst they also say ownership transfers in an invalid transaction due to the principle 'a prohibition from legal matters retains their legality'.

Similarly, the Shawāfi' would say as vomiting does not invalidate ablution, contact with a woman will invalidate it, because no one dissociates the two. Those who agree to one case, like the Shawāfi', agree to the other, and those that disagree to one, like the Aḥnāf, disagree to the other. For the reason of 'adam ul-qāili bil-faṣl the Shawāfi' will say as vomiting does not invalidate the ablution, contact with a woman will invalidate it.

This second type of 'adam ul-qāili bil-faṣl is not a legally valid proof. This is because though each ruling may be valid and true to its source independently, it has no bearing on the validity of the source of the other ruling. It does not

حديث

عن عائشة رضي الله عنها قالت: قال رسول الله صلى الله عليه وسلم من أهابه قيئ أو رعاف أو قلس أو مذي فلينصرف فليتوضأ ثم ليبن على صلاته وهو في ذلك لا يتكلم.

عليه الصلاة والسلام

(سنن ابن ماجة: 1221)

support the possibility of adding further cases to its validity. In other words, the ruling that vomiting invalidates the ablution may be true and valid due to its source in the Hadith, but it has no bearing on the principle upon which you ruled that an invalid transaction permits the transfer of ownership. As both rulings are independent of each other at the principle level, they are unconnected; one cannot be proven by the other.

Text And Translation

ونظير الثاني إذا قلنا: إن القيء ناقض فيكون البيع الفاسد مفيداً ا للملك لعدم القائل بالفصل أو يكون موجب العمد القود لعدم القائل بالفصل وبمثل هذا القيء غير ناقض فيكون المس ناقضا وهذا ليس بحجة؛ لأنّ صحة الفرع وإن دلت على صحة أصله ولكنها لا توجب صحة أصل آخر حتى تفرعت عليه المسئلة الأخرى.

The example of the second is what we said that vomit invalidates so an invalid transaction suffices ownership, as no one differentiates; or intentional murder necessitating retaliation, as no one differentiates. Like this, vomiting does not invalidate so touching invalidates. This is not proof because the correctness of the ruling - despite exhibiting the correct principle – does not necessitate the correctness of another principle, such that another case can be derived from it.

❖❖❖

QUICK TERMS

عدم القول بالفصل: *'adam ul-qawli bil-faṣl*

Bipartisan. When jurists fall into two parties over a matter, whilst all agree that a third option is invalid.

Summary Of 'Adam ul-Qāili bil-Faṣl

1. This type of al-ijmā' is a type of al-ijmā' al-murakkab in which the validation of one contentious issue necessitates the validity of another, as each party would either disagree or agree with both.

2. 'Adam ul-qāili bil-faṣl has two types:
i) Both cases are connected to a single fundamental principle. For example, a vow to fast on 10 Dhul Hijjah is valid and secondly, an invalid transaction transfers ownership upon exchange. The origin of agreement to both these seemingly random cases is one. Both the fast and transaction are not permitted. Its ruling is: أنه حجة that "it is valid evidencing".
ii) Both cases are based on separate principles. For example, vomiting invalidates the fast, and an invalid transaction enables a transfer of ownership. The principles are different in both cases. Its ruling is: أنه ليس بحجة that "it is invalid evidencing".

al-Qiyās

PART 4

4.0 Duty of the Mujtahid

This chapter serves as an introduction to the section on al-qiyās. It details the circumstances that lead to the necessity of al-qiyās. When a mujtahid is faced with producing a legal ruling on a case, the first step is to seek the matter in the book of Allah جل جلاله. The Book of Allah جل جلاله is the strongest of the sources and no evidence is superior. Due to this superiority if a case is found in it, there is no need to seek any other supporting evidence. If the ruling for the case is not found in the Book of Allah جل جلاله then the next source is the Sunna of the Messenger of Allah صلى الله عليه وسلم. If the ruling on the case is found in any of the textual locations of the Book of Allah جل جلاله and the Sunna of the Messenger صلى الله عليه وسلم there is no need to resort to al-qiyās. Whilst it is possible to act upon a transmitted text, one is not permitted to enact a personal judgement through al-qiyās. This is illustrated by the fact that when one is unsure of the direction of the qibla and an individual informs that it is in a particular direction, the worshipper is not permitted to ignore the informant and attempt to guess the direction on his own. A guess is the equivalent to personal judgment and al-qiyās, whilst the information supplied is like a transmitted text. The personal judgement is to be discarded when there is information already present. In a similar illustration, if one was to stumble across water whose degree of purity

QUICK TERMS

القياس: *al-qiyās*

Analogy. Traditions narrated by single-narrator chains.

was unknown. If a just individual informed that the water was indeed impure, the water cannot be used for ablution on the basis that water is naturally a pure substance and, on this occasion, it must be pure too. Rather, the worshipper will need to perform *at-tayammum* due to the impurity of the water.

Text And Translation

فصل: الواجب على المجتهد طلب حكم الحادثة من كتاب الله تعالى ثم من سنة رسول الله صلى الله عليه وآله وسلم بصريح النص أو دلالته على ما مر ذكره، فإنه لا سبيل إلى العمل بالرأي مع إمكان العمل بالنص، ولهذا إذا اشتبهت عليه القبلة فأخبره واحد عنها لا يجوز له التحري ولو وجد ماء فأخبره عدل أنه نجس لا يجوز له التوضي به بل يتيمم

Chapter: It is necessary for the mujtahid to seek the ruling of a case from the Book of Allah Almighty, then the Sunna of the Messenger of Allah, peace and blessings be upon him and his family, from the wording of the text or its indications as mentioned earlier. There is no scope for enacting an opinion when enacting a text is possible. For this reason if the Qibla is obscure for someone and an individual informs him of it, he is not permitted to further make inquiries about it. If one finds water and a trustable individual informs him that it is impure, he is not permitted to perform ablution with it. Rather he is to perform *at-tayammum.*

❖ ❖ ❖

ash-Shubha, uncertainty, occurs when a matter resembles an established fact but in itself, it is not proven. The uncertainty may arise in the application, *ash-shubha fī il-maḥal*, or in the thought process, *ash-shubha fī iẓ-ẓann*. Uncertainty in application means that a legal ruling is established in approving or prohibiting a matter but a preventive is obstructing it from being realised. It is as though that preventive is causing uncertainty in the ruling. An example of this is the narration, "You and your wealth belong to your father". The ruling gives the impression that the father's ownership extends to all the wealth of his son, including the son's slave-girls. This would imply that the father is permitted to cohabit with those slave-girls, but the ruling is in fact that he cannot. The preventive is creating uncertainty. An example of uncertainty in thought is if one thinks that a piece of information is the correct evidence to

QUICK TERMS

الشبهة في المحل: *ash-shubha fī il-maḥal*

Uncertainty in application. When a ruling is not enforced due to a doubt arising in a particular situation.

الشبهة في الظن: *ash-shubha fī iẓ-ẓann*

Doubt in thought. When a ruling is not enforced due to a doubt arising in the thought process.

QUICK ARABIC

التيمم: *at-tayammum*

Dry ablution. The ritual ablution performed without water.

الحد: *al-ḥadd*

A defined punishment. A punishment that is set out in the Quran and Hadith.

الشبهة: *ash-shubha*

Uncertain. Something that is not clearly defined and carries an element of doubt.

support an act when in fact it is not. The two types of uncertainty differ in that there is no consideration for intentions in *ash-shubha fī il-maḥal*, but in *ash-shubha fī iẓ-ẓann*, the intention is considered.

Keeping the aforementioned in mind, and based on our understanding that enacting our own judgment is inferior to enacting a transmitted text, we say that uncertainty in application is superior to uncertainty in thought. Uncertainty in application does not take an intention into account but uncertainty in thought does. An illustration of this is if a father cohabits with his son's slave-girl. The punishment of *al-ḥadd* will not be administered whether he acknowledges prior knowledge of its unlawfulness or not. The lineage of a child born because of this intercourse will also be directly linked to the father. This is supported by the narration, "You and your wealth belong to your father". This narration creates an uncertain possibility that the father is owner of his son's entire wealth including the slave-girl. The father has simply cohabited with a slave-girl he himself owns, because what belongs to his son belongs to him. Cohabitation with one's own slave-girl does not draw the punishment of *al-ḥadd* and so it will not be administered. As for acknowledging that he, the father, knew it was unlawful, it will have no bearing because the uncertainty created by the narration is in application, *ash-shubha fī il-maḥal*, where there is a degree of uncertainty if the evidence includes slave-girls or not. There are many texts that show that the son owns his own slaves and there is al-ijmā' established in this matter too. Though it is established that the father does not own his son's slave-girl, the tradition "You and your wealth belong to your father", still places an element of doubt in this ruling. As there is doubt in the case, there cannot be a punishment of *al-ḥadd* administered. Furthermore, this doubt in ownership does not affect the parentage of the child so the new-born will be the child of the perpetrating father.

Contrast this with a case in which a son cohabits with a slave-girl owned by his father. If he acknowledged that he knew it was impermissible, *al-ḥadd* will be administered, but if he expresses ignorance of its impermissibility, *al-ḥadd* will not be administered. This is because the son's ownership of his father's wealth is not supported by any text; rather any suspicion of the sort is due to an understanding that there is a degree of fluidity between the wealth of a father and son. It is this point that casts a doubt over the possibility that maybe the son has ownership over his father's slave-girl. This is a doubt in the thought process, *ash-shubha fī iẓ-ẓann*, and as such, the intent will be taken into

حديث

عن جابر بن عبد الله رضي الله عنه أن رجلا قال يا رسول الله إن لي مالا وولدا وإن أبي يريد أن يجتاح مالي. فقال صلى الله عليه وسلم أنت ومالك لأبيك.

(سنن ابن ماجة: 2291)

QUICK TERMS

الإجماع: *al-ijmā'*

Consensus. The unanimous agreement of the mujtahids.

QUICK ARABIC

الزنا: *az-zinā*

Fornication. Sexual intercourse between two persons not married to each other.

consideration. His knowing that it is forbidden will result in the punishment, and his ignorance of it will avert it. The new-born's parentage will not be established to the son even if he claims it because this cohabitation is due to az-zinā and az-zinā is insufficient in establishing parentage.

a<u>sh</u>-<u>Sh</u>ubha fī il-maḥal and *a<u>sh</u>-<u>sh</u>ubha* fī iẓ-ẓann are thus different. The doubt cast by *<u>sh</u>ubha fī il-maḥal* was the result of a transmitted tradition and consequently remained a factor despite a contradicting intent; this shows its strength. The doubt of *a<u>sh</u>-<u>sh</u>ubha fī iẓ-ẓann* was the result of inappropriate application and consequently remained dependent upon the intention. The doubt was not a factor when the intention was made clear, but whilst the intention was unclear the doubt remained.

Text And Translation

وعلى اعتبار أن العمل بالرأي دون العمل بالنص قلنا: إن الشبهة بالمحل أقوى من الشبهة بالظن حتى سقط اعتبار ظن العبد في الفصل الأول ومثاله في ما إذا وطئ جارية ابنه لا يحد وان قال: علمت أنها علي حرام ويثبت نسب الولد منه؛ لأن للأب شبهة الملك له تثبت بالنص في مال الابن، قال عليه الصلاة والسلام: أنت ومالك لأبيك فسقط اعتبار ظنه في الحل والحرمة في ذلك ولو وطئ الابن جارية أبيه يعتبر ظنه في الحل والحرمة حتى لو قال: ظننت أنها علي حرام يجب الحد، ولو قال: ظننت أنها علي حلال لا يجب الحد؛ لأنّ شبهة الملك في مال الأب لم يثبت له بالنص فاعتبر رأيه ولا يثبت نسب الولد وإن ادعاه.

Considering that enacting an opinion is inferior to enacting a text we said: doubt in the application supersedes the doubt in thought such that the subject's thought is rendered void in the former. An example of it is if one cohabited with his son's salve-girl, he will not be administered *al-ḥadd*; even if he says I knew it to be unlawful for me. The lineage of the newborn will be from him. This is because for the father there is doubt in ownership established by a text regarding a son's wealth. He, peace and blessings be upon him, said: "You and your wealth are your father's". So consideration of his opinion in permissibility or impermissibility is void in this matter. If a son cohabited with his father's salve-girl, his notion of permissibility and impermissibility will be considered. Such that if one said: "I thought she's not permitted for me", *al-ḥadd* will be necessary. If he said: "I thought she's permitted for me", *al-ḥadd* will not be

حديث

عن جابر بن عبد الله رضي الله عنه أن رجلا قال يا رسول الله إن لي مالا وولدا وإن أبي يريد أن يجتاح مالي. فقال صلى الله عليه وسلم أنت ومالك لأبيك.

عليه الصلاة والسلام

(سنن ابن ماجة: 2291)

QUICK ARABIC

الحد: *al-ḥadd*

A defined punishment. A punishment that is set out in the Quran and Hadith.

QUICK DICTIONARY

Chronology: *kruh-nol-uh-jee*

Order. The sequential order in which past events occur.

necessary. This is because doubt of ownership in the wealth of the father is not established for him from a text. So his opinion will be considered and the lineage of the newborn will not be established, even if he claims it.

❖ ❖ ❖

When there seems to be a contradiction between two pieces of evidence of equal authority, such that one cannot be reconciled with the other without changes, then first an attempt must be made to determine their chronology. The earlier legal evidence will be ignored in favour of the latter piece. If chronology cannot be determined, then the next attempt is to determine a reason for preference. Once a reason for preference is established, the superior evidence will be preferred over the inferior. If preference cannot be determined between the two equally matched pieces, then evidence of a lesser authority will be leaned upon for support.

The hierarchy and order of authority will be as follows: if two verses of al-kitāb are seemingly contradictory, supporting evidence from as-sunna will be sought. If it is two traditions that are seemingly contradictory, then support will be sought from the practice of the Companions رضي الله عنهم and from the sound analogy of al-qiyās. If there seems to be a contradiction between two positions of the Companions رضي الله عنهم or between two pieces of al-qiyās, the jurist will point out a reason for preference, and then select the superior of the two due to his reasoning. If no clear reasoning can be determined, then it is necessary to make a choice between them. A perceived contradiction does not render two pieces of evidence invalid; rather it is necessary to enact one of them, as there is no lower legal source to resort to after al-qiyās.

Enacting al-qiyās and personal judgement is only valid when there is no other legal evidence available. It follows that a traveller with two containers of water, and no recollection of which one of the two is pure and which is impure, is not permitted simply to make a choice between them in order to perform ablution. Rather, *at-tayammum* is to be performed in order to continue to the prayer. This is because making a choice for him is in the category of al-qiyās and it is only permitted when there is no other legal ruling. However, in this case the higher legal ruling is that soil is a suitable replacement for water to attain purity and so in the absence of pure water or the presence of unattainable pure water, performing dry ablution with soil is prescribed. If the aforementioned traveller is

QUICK TERMS

الكتاب: *al-kitāb*

The book. The inspired final Word of Allah جل جلاله. The Quran.

السنة: *as-sunna*

The practice. The sayings, doings and approval of the blessed Prophet صلى الله عليه وسلم.

القياس: *al-qiyās*

Analogy. The reasoning of the learned.

QUICK ARABIC

التيمم: *at-tayammum*

Dry ablution. The ritual ablution performed without water.

faced with making a choice as to which container to drink from, a choice can be made. This is because there is no replacement for water when it is required for drinking. Therefore, in the absence of any other water, he can make a choice as to which of the two containers he will use to quench his thirst; this will be permitted.

Text And Translation

ثم إذا تعارض الدليلان عند المجتهد فإن كان التعارض بين الآيتين يميل الى السنة وان كان بين السنتين يميل الى آثار الصحابة رضي الله تعالى عنهم والقياس الصحيح، ثم إذا تعارض القياسان عند المجتهد يتحرى ويعمل بأحدهما لأنه ليس دون القياس دليل شرعي يصار إليه، وعلى هذا قلنا: إذا كان مع المسافر إناءان طاهر ونجس لا يتحرى بينهما بل يتيمم

Then if two pieces of evidence are contradictory before the mujtahid and the contradiction is between two verses he should turn to as-sunna; if it is between two traditions of as-sunna he should turn to customs of the Companions, Allah be pleased with them all, and to sound al-qiyās. If two pieces of al-qiyās contradict before the mujtahid he should contemplate and enact one of them, as there is no legal evidence below it for him to turn to. Based on this we said: when a traveller has two containers, one pure and one impure. He cannot contemplate over them, rather he should perform *at-tayammum*.

❖❖❖

Moreover, if a traveller had two garments, one pure and the other impure, and he did not know which is which, he is permitted to choose one of them to wear for prayer. This is because there is no legal replacement for clothes that he can resort to. It shows that personal choice and al-qiyās is permitted when there is no other legal avenue.

There is an additional rule to bear in mind here. Where the traveller chose one of two garments, considering it to be without impurity, and proceeded to perform a prayer in it, the choice strengthens through this very act. It now becomes a choice that is supported by an act. As such, merely another change of opinion and a new choice will not be strong enough to invalidate it. For example, if a traveller made a choice between two garments and performed the aẓ-Ẓuhr prayer with it. Then at the time of the al-'Aṣr he just

QUICK TERMS

القياس: *al-qiyās*

Analogy. The reasoning of the learned.

QUICK ARABIC

الظهر: *aẓ-ẓuhr*

The afternoon. The time of day or the prayer performed after the sun declines after noon.

العصر: *at-'aṣr*

The late-noon. The time of day or the prayer performed before the sun sets.

التيمم: *at-tayammum*

Dry ablution. The ritual ablution performed without water.

happened to think he'd wear the other garment; it will not be permitted. This is because the first choice is now not merely a choice, but a choice strengthened and supported by an act, the act of a aẓ-Ẓuhr prayer. The second choice at the al-'Aṣr prayer time is merely a choice, and not supported by any act. As the use of the first garment is strengthened, it must be used again for the al-'Aṣr prayer as it was used for the aẓ-Ẓuhr prayer; replacing it with the other garment is not permitted.

The rule that choice supported by an act is stronger than a choice alone, gives rise to an objection. When one does not know of the direction to face for prayer, a personal choice and guess is permitted. Once the person has prayed in a particular direction, he then changes his mind and selects a different direction for a following prayer. The ruling is that the second prayer is to be prayed in the new direction and not the first direction. If the aforementioned rule were to be followed, this change of choice would not be permitted as the earlier choice was followed up with an act. It should result in the first direction having added surety in comparison to the new direction.

This objection is settled because there is a substantial difference between a choice made for a pure garment and the choice of the direction of prayer. The direction of the qibla can readily change with respect to the location of the worshipper. As the worshipper moves location, he needs to monitor his positioning constantly with respect to the qibla. Even within one locality, the position of the qibla Is fluid. It is as though; on the second instance he has reassessed his positioning and concluded that the newly selected direction is the correct one. The previous direction will be abrogated and the new direction will take its place. However, in the case of the garments the impurity is not fluid or transferable, such that it jumps from one garment to the other. When it is established that only one of the garments is impure, and a choice has been supported with an act to determine which garment is pure, the impurity is stationary and will not transfer, and so it need not be constantly monitored. As the impure garment has been selected with relatively stronger evidence, there is no reason to change that merely with weaker evidence. The comparison of the choice of direction in prayer and the choice of one garment shows that where there is a constant change, the choice may be renewed, but if there is no possibility of change then a choice strengthened with an act will not be invalidated by a mere choice.

Text And Translation

ولو كان معه ثوبان طاهر ونجس يتحرى بينهما؛ لأن للماء بدلا وهو التراب وليس للثوب بدل يصار إليه، فثبت بهذا أنّ العمل بالرأي إنما يكون عند انعدام دليل سواه شرعا ثم إذا تحرى وتأكد تحريه بالعمل لا ينتقض ذلك بمجرد التحري وبيانه فيما إذا تحرى بين الثوبين وصلى الظهر بأحدهما ثم وقع تحريه عند العصر على الثوب الآخر لا يجوز له أن يصلي العصر بالآخر؛ لأن الأول تأكد بالعمل فلا يبطل بمجرد التحري وهذا بخلاف ما إذا تحرى في القبلة ثم تبدل لأن القبلة مما يحتمل الانتقال فأمكن نقل الحكم بمنزلة نسخ النص

If one had two pieces of cloth, one pure and one impure, he may contemplate over them. This is because water has a substitute, which is soil, but clothes do not have a substitute for him to turn to. This establishes that enacting an opinion is only when there is lack of alternative evidence of the Shariah. Then, when he has contemplated and ascertained his thought through action, it can not be voided by mere thought. Explanation of it is that if he contemplated two cloths and prayed aẓ-Ẓuhur in one of them. Then a thought came to him at the time of al-'Aṣr regarding the other cloth. He is not permitted to pray al-'Aṣr in the other cloth because the first is strengthened through action, so mere thought will not nullify it. This is different to one contemplating the qibla and then changing it because the qibla has a possibility of changing. So it is possible to alter the ruling just like abrogating a text.

❖❖❖

FIGURE 4.1-01

The process of al-qiyās, showing two cases connected by a common cause(العلة).

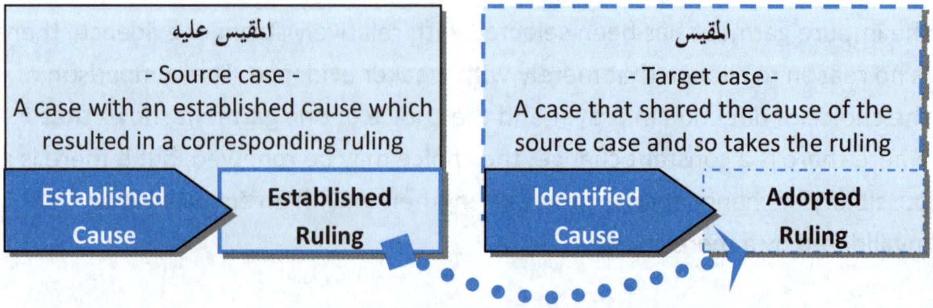

QUICK TERMS

القياس: *al-qiyās*

Analogy. The reasoning of the learned.

المقيس: *at-'aṣr*

Analogical target. The target case upon which the analogy is to apply.

المقيس عليه: *al-maqīs 'alayhi*

Analogical source. The source from which the common cause is cited, to deliver the ruling on a target case.

العلة: *al-'illa*

Dry ablution. The ritual ablution performed without water.

الحكم: *al-ḥukm*

The ruling. An authentic decision of the Shariah regarding the level of importance of an act, whether an instruction or prohibition.

الأصول: *al-usūl*

Principles. The accepted fundamental rules of deriving matters of fiqh.

4.1 Validity of al-Qiyās

al-Qiyās literally means to measure and scale something up. In al-uṣūl, it is defined as:

تعريف القياس: تعدية الحكم من الأصل إلى الفرع بعلة متحدة بينهما

Definition of al-qiyās: To transfer a ruling from a source case to a target case due to a common cause.

There are four components to be aware of in al-qiyās:

1) *al-Maqīs*, the target;
2) *al-Maqīs 'alayhi*, the source;
3) *al-'illa*, the cause; and
4) *al-ḥukm*, the ruling.

The new case to be presented and validated in the Shariah is the target, *al-maqīs*. The previously existing case that is already validated and which is to be used to validate the new case is the source, *al-maqīs 'alayhi*. The factor, which is common to the source and the target cases and makes the target case suitable to 'measure and scale up' to the source by giving it the same ruling, is the cause, *al-'illa*. The effect of the common factor is that it results in the source and target cases to be applied and enacted in a similar manner and with the same ruling, *al-ḥukm*. Figure 4.1-01 shows this process.

al-Qiyās is a legal source of rulings in the Shariah when there is no stronger evidence. If a solution is not found using a verse of the blessed Quran, a tradition of the blessed Prophet ﷺ or the consensus of the scholars of this Ummah, it is necessary to enact al-qiyās. There are a few traditions that highlight al-qiyās as a source of rulings. Four are presented here.

The blessed Messenger of Allah ﷺ appointed Mu'ādh bin Jabal رضي الله عنه as a governor of Yemen. Whilst bidding him farewell the Messenger of Allah ﷺ asked how he would resolve people's issues, to which he replied that he would seek a solution from the Book of Allah جل جلاله. The Messenger of Allah ﷺ followed up by asking what he would do if he was unable to find a solution from the Book of Allah جل جلاله. Mu'ādh رضي الله عنه answered that he would find a resolution from the sunna and practice of the beloved Messenger ﷺ. The Messenger of Allah ﷺ further questioned what he would do if he were unable to find it there

حديث

عن أناس من أهل حمص من أصحاب معاذ بن جبل رضي الله عنه أن رسول الله ﷺ لما أراد أن يبعث معاذا إلى اليمن قال كيف تقضي إذا عرض لك قضاء قال أقضي بكتاب الله قال فإن لم تجد في كتاب الله قال فبسنة رسول الله ﷺ فإن لم تجد في سنة رسول الله ﷺ ولا في كتاب الله قال أجتهد رأيي ولا آلو فضرب رسول الله ﷺ صدره وقال الحمد لله الذي وفق رسول رسول الله لما يرضي رسول الله.

عليه الصلاة والسلام

(سنن ابي داوود: 3592)

also. He رضي الله عنه replied that he would then resort to his personal judgement, which is al-qiyās. With this the Messenger of Allah ﷺ thanked Allah ﷻ for enabling his emissary to display an understanding pleasing to Him and His Messenger ﷺ. If al-qiyās were not an acceptable source of rulings the blessed Messenger ﷺ would surely have corrected the noble Companion رضي الله عنه. As he ﷺ did not admonish him, but rather praised him by thanking Allah ﷻ and displayed his own pleasure at his replies, it shows that al-qiyās is a valid source.

Text And Translation

البحث الرابع في القياس

فصل: القياس حجة من حجج الشرع يجب العمل به عند انعدام ما فوقه من الدليل في الحادثة وقد ورد في ذلك الأخبار والآثار قال عليه الصلاة والسلام لمعاذ بن جبل حين بعثه الى "اليمن" قال: بم تقضي يا معاذ؟ قال: بكتاب الله تعالى، قال: فان لم تجد، قال: بسنة رسول الله ﷺ، قال: فإن لم تجد، قال أجتهد برأيي، فصوبه رسول الله ﷺ، فقال: الحمد لله الذي وفق رسول رسولِ الله على ما يحب ويرضاه

Discussion Four on al-Qiyās

Chapter: al-Qiyās is a proof of the Shariah which must be enacted when there is no proof stronger than it in an event. That is as is reported in the narrations and traditions. He, peace and blessings be upon him, said to Mu'ādh bin Jabal when he sent him to Yemen: "O Mu'ādh, how will you judge?" He said: "Using the Book of Allah Almighty." He ﷺ probed: "If you don't find it?" He replied: "With the sunna of the Messenger of Allah, peace and blessings be upon him." He, peace and blessings be upon him, furthered: "If you don't find it?" He answered, "I will give my informed opinion." The Messenger of Allah, peace and blessings be upon him, acknowledged it and supplicated: "All praise is for Allah who has blessed the messenger of the Messenger of Allah with what He loves and is pleased with."

❖❖❖

The Companion Asmā bint 'Umays رضي الله عنها of the Khath'am tribe came to the Messenger of Allah ﷺ and told of the Hajj necessary upon her elderly father.

حديث

عن عبد الله بن عباس رضي الله عنهما قال كان الفضل رديف النبي ﷺ فجاءت امرأة من خثعم فجعل الفضل ينظر إليها وتنظر إليه فجعل النبي يصرف وجه الفضل إلى الشق الآخر فقالت: يا رسول الله ﷺ، إن فريضة الله على العباد في الحج أدركت أبي شيخا كبيرا لا يستطيع أن يثبت على الرحلة أفأحج عنه؟ قال ﷺ: أرأيت لو كان على أبيك دين فقضيته عنه؟ قالت: نعم. قال ﷺ: فذاك ذاك.

عليه الصلاة والسلام

(مسند الربيع بن حبيب: 385)

QUICK TERMS

القياس: *al-qiyās*

Analogy. The reasoning of the learned.

Her father was so aged that he was unable to sit upright on a ride. She asked whether she was permitted to perform the obligation on his behalf. The blessed Messenger ﷺ asked her if it would be sufficient for her to pay her father's financial debt on his behalf, should he have accrued it? She replied that it would be. To this, the Messenger of Allah ﷺ informed her that a debt owed to Allah جل جلاله is of a higher order than a financial debt and is more worthy of her offering it. The Messenger of Allah ﷺ likened the obligation of Hajj on an ageing old man to a financial right, and highlighted the acceptability of one as the underlining reason for the acceptability of the other. This is the very essence of al-qiyās, to find a common effective factor in two cases with similarities, and to transfer the accepted ruling of one case to the case in question. If al-qiyās were not an accepted source of rulings then the blessed Messenger ﷺ would not educate us with it.

Text And Translation

وروي أن امرأة خثعمية أتت إلى رسول الله ﷺ فقالت: إن أبي كان شيخاً كبيراً أدركه الحج ولا يستمسك على الراحلة أفيجزئني أن أحج عنه، قال عليه السلام: أرأيت لو كان على أبيك دين فقضيته أما كان يجزئك، فقالت: بلى! فقال عليه السلام: فدين الله أحق وأولى، ألحق رسول الله عليه السلام الحج في حق الشيخ الفاني بالحقوق المالية وأشار إلى علة مؤثرة في الجواز وهي القضاء وهذا هو القياس.

It is reported that a woman of the tribe of Khath'am came to the Messenger of Allah, peace and blessings be upon him, and inquired: "My father is very elderly and is required to perform the Hajj. He can no longer ride. Am I permitted to perform Hajj on his behalf?" The Prophet, peace and blessings be upon him, replied: "Do you not think if your father had a debt and you repaid it, you would be permitted to do it?" She replied: "Of course." The Prophet, peace and blessings be upon him, said: "The debt owed to Allah is more rightful and worthy." The Messenger of Allah, peace and blessings be upon him, correlated the Hajj of the senile man with financial rights and pointed out an effective cause in allowing it; which was repayment of debt. This is al-qiyās.

❖ ❖ ❖

حديث

عن قيس بن طلق بن علي عن أبيه قال خرجنا وفدا حتى قدمنا على رسول الله صلى الله عليه وسلم فبايعناه وصلينا معه فلما قضى الصلاة جاء رجل كأنه بدوي فقال يا رسول الله ما ترى في رجل مس ذكره في الصلاة؟ قال عليه السلام: وهل هو إلا مضغة منك أو بضعة منك.

(سنن النسائي: 165)

QUICK TERMS

القياس: *al-qiyās*
Analogy. The reasoning of the learned.

QUICK ARABIC

المهر المثل: *al-mahr ul-mithl*
Standard bridal gift. A marriage gift given by the husband to the bride equivalent to her status.

QUICK REFERENCE

الشامل: *ash-shāmil*
The Comprehensive Treatise. A key piece of work in the ash-Shāfa'īy school by 'Abd us-Sayyid bin Muḥammad al-Baghdādī, Ibn uṣ-Ṣabbāgh.

The Companion Qays bin Ṭalaq bin 'Alī ؓ narrated that a Bedouin man came to the blessed Messenger of Allah ﷺ and asked if one was to touch the private parts after performing ablution, would ablution become invalid. The blessed Messenger ﷺ replied that the private parts were nothing more than another part of the body. The choice of response is showing that just as touching the rest of the body does not invalidate the ablution, touching the private parts will also not invalidate the ablution. The usage of this manner in responding is highlighting the workings of al-qiyās. If al-qiyās were in fact not a source of rulings the blessed Messenger of Allah ﷺ would not have employed this method.

The noble Companion 'Abdullāh Ibn Mas'ūd ؓ was asked if a woman was married without her bridal gift being announced, and her husband was to pass away before the marriage was consummated, would she receive a bridal gift or not? The noble Companion ؓ asked for a whole month to deliberate over the matter, in which time he would employ al-qiyās; if the outcome was correct it would be from Allah ﷻ, and if it was incorrect, he would be solely responsible. He eventually gave the ruling that a customary bridal gift, *al-mahr ul-mithl*, would be necessary, not an ounce more or less. It shows that the Companion ؓ used al-qiyās to come to legal rulings.

There are many more citations possible to show al-qiyās applied, but the above will suffice here.

Text And Translation

وروى ابن الصباغ وهو من سادات أصحاب الشافعي في كتابه المسمى بالشامل عن قيس بن طلق بن علي أنه قال: جاء رجل إلى رسول الله عليه السلام كأنه بدوي فقال: يا نبي الله ما ترى في مس الرجل ذكره بعد ما توضأ فقال: هل هو إلا بضعة منه وهذا هو القياس. وسئل ابن مسعود عمن تزوج امرأة ولم يسم لها مهرا وقد مات عنها زوجها قبل الدخول فاستمهل شهرا، ثم قال: أجتهد فيه برأيي فان كان صوابا فمن الله وإن كان خطأ فمن ابن أم عبد فقال: أرى لها مهر مثل نسائها لا وكس فيها ولا شطط.

Ibn uṣ-Ṣabbāgh, a leading companion of Imam ash-Shāfa'ī, reports in his book titled, ash-Shāmil, on the authority of Qays bin Ṭalaq bin 'Alī ؓ that he says a man came to the Messenger of Allah, peace and blessings be upon him, seemingly a Beduin. He asked: "O Prophet of Allah, what do you say about a man who touches his private parts after performing ablution?" He ﷺ replied: "Is it not just a part of his body?" This is al-qiyās. Ibn Mas'ūd رضي الله عنه was questioned about a man who married a woman without stating the bridal gift. Her husband passed away before consummation. He waited a month, then replied: "I rule in it with my opinion, should it be correct it is from Allah and if it is incorrect it is from a humble servant," adding, "I think she has a bridal gift equivalent to her tribe's women, no less and no more."

❖❖❖

Summary Of Validity of al-Qiyās

1. The definition of al-qiyās is:
   تعدية الحكم من الأصل الى الفرع بعلة متحدة بينهما
   "To reproduce a ruling from a source case to the target case due to a common cause".

2. An example is verse 58 of Sūrat un-Nūr that confirm servants need not seek permission to enter homes because they frequently enter and leave to perform their tasks. Repeatedly seeking permission would be a nuisance. It is based on this that a domestic cat would repeatedly lick bowls and drink water causing a nuisance. Therefore, due to the common cause of nuisance a cat's leftover will be excused. Permissibility is the ruling transferred from one case to the other.

3. Its ruling: يجب العمل به عند انعدام ما فوقه من الدليل في الحادثة
   "You must enact it whilst there is no stronger evidence regarding the matter".

4. Its validity: The blessed Prophet ﷺ sent Mu'ādh bin Jabal رضي الله عنه to Yemen. He ﷺ asked him how he would deal with enquiries. He replied from the Quran, the sunna and then from his own personal analogies. The blessed Prophet ﷺ praised this method.

4.2 Conditions for Authentic al-Qiyās

Five conditions must be met for al-qiyās to be accepted as a legal source for rulings. If it falls short of any one of these conditions it no longer remains valid.

1. al-Qiyās should not oppose an existing text, *an-naṣṣ*. This text could be of the blessed Quran, a tradition from the sunna or the words of a scholarly Companion ﷺ. These texts are definitive and *al-qaṭ'ī*, whereas al-qiyās is speculative and *aẓ-ẓannī*. Definitive texts will always take precedence over speculative ideas.

2. al-Qiyās should not alter the ruling existing in an-naṣṣ. This entails the existing text giving a particular kind of ruling whilst al-qiyās attempts to give an altered version of the ruling in the target case. For example, the source text gives an unrestricted al-muṭlaq ruling whilst al-qiyās is giving a restricted al-muqayyad ruling. This condition, however, is not concerned with the unavoidable fact that the ruling of an-naṣṣ is definitive whilst the al-qiyās ruling is speculative; this difference in the delivered ruling is acceptable.

3. The transferred ruling should be rational. If the ruling in the source text is in itself not understood and it is unknown why it is a suitable ruling in the source, it cannot be transferred to the target case. For example, the thresholds in zakah or forgetfully eating in a fast not invalidating it, are both not rational, but are present in *an-naṣṣ*. As the reasoning in the source is unknown, it cannot be transferred to a target case.

4. The identification of the cause, *al-'illa*, should be for legal reasons and not linguistics. an-Naṣṣ should be shedding light on a matter of the Shariah and not on language because language does not develop by analogy and al-qiyās.

5. The target case must not already be addressed in *an-naṣṣ*. The case in which al-qiyās is utilised should not have an existing *an-naṣṣ* dealing with it already. This is because if al-qiyās is in accordance with the text, there is no need for al-qiyās as it is a weaker source than the existing

QUICK TERMS

القياس: *al-qiyās*

Analogy. The reasoning of the learned.

المطلق: *al-muṭlaq*

The unrestricted. Indicates an entity irrespective of any quality.

المقيد: *al-muqayyad*

The restricted. Indicates an entity and some of its qualities.

القطعي: *al-qaṭ'ī*

The definitive. Most reliable and certain.

الظني: *adh-dhannī*

The speculative. Reached after careful consideration.

النص: *an-naṣṣ*

The text. The plain words used in a verbal or written passage.

العلة: *al-'illa*

The means. The method or instrument used to attain an end.

text, and if al-qiyās is contradictory to the text, it is rejected as per condition number one above.

Text And Translation

فصل: شروط صحة القياس خمسة أحدها: ألا يكون في مقابلة النص، والثاني: ألا يتضمن تغيير حكم من أحكام النص، والثالث: ألا يكون المعدى حكما لا يعقل معناه، والرابع: أن يقع التعليل لحكم شرعي لا لأمر لغوي، والخامس: ألا يكون الفرع منصوصا عليه

Chapter: the conditions for the validity for al-qiyās are five. The first is that it must not be in opposition to a text; secondly, it must not contain a change to a ruling of a text; thirdly, the infringement should not be a ruling whose meaning is not understood; fourthly, the process of finding the cause is for a Shariah ruling and not a lexical concern; and the fifth is that the derivation should not already be in canonical text.

❖ ❖ ❖

An example of al-qiyās failing the first condition of not opposing *an-naṣṣ* is that someone asked Ḥasan bin Zayd رحمه الله if laughing audibly in prayer invalidated the ablution or not. He replied that it did. The enquirer said if one slandered a chaste woman in the prayer, it does not invalidate the ablution even though it is a grave sin and worse in nature. This would mean that a lesser crime, such as laughter in prayer, than slander should not invalidate the ablution too. This al-qiyās contradicts an existing text. The text is of a tradition that states a man with an ailment in his eye fell over a ditch and some Companions رضي الله عنهم laughed audibly in the prayer when they saw it happening before them. After concluding the prayer, the Messenger of Allah صلى الله عليه وسلم instructed them to repeat their ablution and prayers. This narration makes it clear that laughing audibly in prayer will invalidate the ablution. al-Qiyās on the other hand is proposing that laughing aloud is not worse than slandering in the prayer, whilst slandering does not invalidate the ablution, so laughing should not either. al-Qiyās directly contradicts the text. The condition for al-qiyās to be valid is that it should not contradict an existing legal text, an-naṣṣ, and if it does, al-qiyās is invalid.

حديث

عن أبي المليح بن أسامة عن أبيه، قال: بين نحن نصلي خلف رسول الله صلى الله عليه وسلم إذ أقبل رجل ضرير البصر، فوقع في حفرة، فضحكنا منه، فأمرنا رسول الله صلى الله عليه وسلم بإعادة الوضوء كاملا، وإعادة الصلاة من أولها.

عليه الصلاة والسلام

(سنن الدارقطني: 1/160،161)

In a similar manner, it is unanimously agreed that a woman can perform her Hajj with her *al-maḥram*. Imam ash-Shāfa'īy ﷺ has said that a woman can also perform Hajj in the company of a large band of women, because just as *al-maḥram* provides security, a large contingent of pious women would provide it too. This al-qiyās also contradicts a text. The tradition says, "It is unlawful for a woman believing in Allah Almighty and the Last Day to travel more than three days and nights except in the company of her father, husband or *al-maḥram* relative". It states that a woman cannot perform this obligation with anyone other than her *al-maḥram*. al-Qiyās that suggests otherwise is rejected on the basis that it contradicts *an-naṣṣ*.

Text And Translation

ومثال القياس في مقابلة النص فيما حكي أنّ الحسن بن زياد سئل عن القهقهة في الصلاة فقال: انتقضت الطهارة بها قال السائل: لو قذف محصنة في الصلاة لا ينتقض به الوضوء مع أن قذف المحصنة أعظم جناية فكيف ينتقض بالقهقهة وهي دونه فهذا قياس في مقابلة النص وهو حديث الأعرابي الذي في عينه سوء، وكذلك إذا قلنا: جاز حج المرأة مع المحرم فيجوز مع الأمينات كان هذا قياسا بمقابلة النص وهو قوله عليه السلام: لا يحلّ لامرأة تؤمن بالله واليوم الآخر أن تسافر فوق ثلاثة أيام ولياليها إلا ومعها أبوها أو زوجها أو ذو رحم محرم منها

The example of al-qiyās opposing a text is the narration that al-Ḥasan bin Zayād was asked about laughing in salah. He replied that ritual impurity is invalidated by it. The questioner retorted: "If one was to slander the chasitity of an innocent woman in salah it would not invalidate the ablution despite slandering the chaste woman is a more severe sin, so how can it be invalid with laughter whilst it is minor to it!" This is al-qiyās compared to a canonical text, which is the tradition of the Beduin who had an ailment in his eye. Similarly, when we said that the Hajj of a woman is permitted with *al-maḥram*, it should also be permitted with a group of pious women. This is al-qiyās opposing a canonical text, which is his saying, peace and blessings be upon him: "It is unlawful for a woman believing in Allah and the Last Day to travel more than three days and nights except in the company of her father, husband or *al-maḥram* relative."

❖ ❖ ❖

حديث

عن أبي سعيد الخدري رضي الله عنه قال قال رسول الله صلى الله عليه وسلم لا يحل لامرأة تؤمن بالله واليوم الأخر أن تسافر سفرا يكون ثلاثة أيام فصاعدا إلا ومعها أبوها أو أخوها أو زوجها أو ابنها أو ذو محرم منها.

عليه الصلاة والسلام

(سنن الترمذي: 1169)

QUICK TERMS

القياس: *al-qiyās*

Analogy. The reasoning of the learned.

النص: *an-naṣṣ*

The text. The plain words used in a verbal or written passage.

QUICK ARABIC

المحرم: *al-maḥram*

Unlawful. A near relative with whom marriage is unlawful.

التيمم: *at-tayammum*

Dry ablution. The ritual ablution performed without water.

An example of al-qiyās failing the second condition, in that al-qiyās should not alter the ruling of *an-naṣṣ*, is if one said that an intention is a condition for ablution just as an intention is required in *at-tayammum*. This is transferring the ruling of necessity of an intention from *at-tayammum* to the necessity of an intention in ablution. However, such al-qiyās will place a restriction on an existing text concerning ablution. Verse 6 of Sūrat ul-Māida has stated:

﴿فاغْسِلُواْ وُجُوهَكُمْ﴾ [المائدة: 6]

"...so wash your face..."

It is an unrestricted al-muṭlaq command. By making an intention necessary for ablution, al-muṭlaq of the Quran will become al-muqayyad. This is changing the ruling of an existing text, which it is not permitted by al-qiyās.

Similarly, the tradition, "circumambulation of the House is prayer", likens *aṭ-ṭawāf* to salah. If one uses this to analogise that circumambulation must be with ritual purity, *aṭ-ṭahāra*, and it must be performed appropriately covered, *satr ul-'awra*, just as is necessary for prayer, it will alter the text on circumambulation, which is an unrestricted al-muṭlaq. al-Qiyās will cause the aforementioned *an-naṣṣ* to become a restricted al-muqayyad. As al-qiyās is invalid when it alters the ruling of a text, it will be neglected.

Text And Translation

ومثال الثاني: وهو ما يتضمن تغيير حكم من أحكام النص ما يقال: النية شرط في الوضوء بالقياس على التيمم فإن هذا يوجب تغيير آية الوضوء من الإطلاق الى التقييد، وكذلك إذا قلنا: الطواف بالبيت صلاة بالخبر فيشترط له الطهارة وستر العورة كالصلاة كان هذا قياسا يوجب تغيير نص الطواف من الإطلاق الى القيد

An example of the second, which is the one resulting in a change to a ruling of the canonical text, is what is said that the intention is a condition for ablution by al-qiyās with *at-tayammum*. This necessitates changing the verse of ablution from the unrestricted to the restricted. Similarly, if we say circumambulation of the House is salah in a narration, so purity and covering of private parts are a condition for it like the salah. This is al-qiyās, which necessitates changing the canonical text regarding *aṭ-ṭawāf* from unrestricted to restricted.

حديث

عن ابن عباس رضي الله عنهما أن النبي صلى الله عليه وسلم قال: الطواف حول البيت مثل الصلاة إلا أنكم تتكلمون فيه، فمن تكلم فيه فلا يتكلمن إلا بخير.

عليه الصلاة والسلام

(جامع الترمذي: 881)

QUICK TERMS

المطلق: *al-muṭlaq*

The unrestricted. Indicates an entity irrespective of any quality.

المقيد: *al-muqayyad*

The restricted. Indicates an entity and some of its qualities.

QUICK ARABIC

الطواف: *aṭ-ṭawāf*

Circumambulation. The ritual of encircling the Ka'ba seven times.

الطهارة: *aṭ-ṭahāra*

Purification. To make something pure and free from filth.

ستر العورة: *satr ul-'awra*

Covering bodily privacy. Covering the private parts of the body, beneath the navel up to and including the knees for men.

❖❖❖

An example of the third condition, where al-qiyās should occur using a cause that is rational in the source case, is that one is permitted to perform ablution with a date-beverage. This is based on the understanding that 'dates are pure and water is pure'. Some have analogised based on the date-beverage that other beverages are permitted for the performance of ablution. This al-qiyās is invalid. This is because the reason why a date-beverage is permitted for ablution is not in itself understood. What is the underpinning cause that allows such a liquid to be used for ablution? The date-beverage is not water as it has its own distinct name, nor is it considered to be in the bracket of plain water as its longevity is drastically reduced and it does not quench thirst in a comparable manner. The reason why a date-beverage is suitable for ablution is not understood; it is not rational. As it is not rational, it cannot then be used as a source case to construct al-qiyās to transfer its ruling to a target case.

In a similar way, the tradition, "whomsoever vomits, has a nose bleed, or ejaculates in prayer, should perform ablution and return to continue the prayer from where it was disrupted, so long as he has not conversed", is not fully understood. This is because emission of impurities like blood and the contents of the stomach are directly in violation of the prayer, as these impurities do not allow for ritual purity, *aṭ-ṭahāra*, which in turn does not allow salah as it is a condition for it. So, rather than allowing the prayer to continue when these emissions occur, it should be invalidated. Rationally the prayer should be voided but contradictory to this; the text of the tradition says the salah can be continued after ablution, as the prayer is not invalid. As this is irrational and against al-qiyās in itself, using it as the source of another al-qiyās is not permitted. In a similar manner, if one's head wound opens or one becomes mature during the prayer, purity cannot be restored and the prayer continued from where the disruption occurred, based on the tradition. The reasoning in the tradition is not immediately clear and so it cannot be extended to cover these scenarios too.

Another example of this condition of al-qiyās is that the ash-Shawāfi' say that if two pails of impure water are combined, they become pure. According to them a large quantity of water is water in excess of two pails, and an impurity found in a large quantity of water does not impact the status of the water, unless one of the characteristics, taste, colour or odour, of the water

حديث

عن عائشة رضي الله عنها قالت: قال رسول الله صلى الله عليه وسلم من أهابه قيئ أو رعاف أو قلس أو مذي فلينصرف فليتوضأ ثم ليبن على صلاته وهو في ذلك لا يتكلم.

عليه الصلاة والسلام

(سنن ابن ماجة: 1221)

QUICK TERMS

القياس: *al-qiyās*

Analogy. The reasoning of the learned.

QUICK ARABIC

الطهارة: *aṭ-ṭahāra*

Purification. To make something pure and free from filth.

changes. Additionally, a small quantity of water will become impure with an impurity mixing with it, whether a characteristic of the water changes or not. Their reasoning is that whilst the water is in separate pails it is a small quantity and consequently an impurity has rendered the water impure even though characteristics of the water are unchanged. Individually this is true for both pails. However, when one combines them, they become a large quantity and as such, so long as the characteristics of water remain, the water is deemed pure despite the mixing of an impurity. They then continue by saying that if you are to now separate this combined water into two pails once more, both pails of water will now contain pure water because separating water into two containers does not render water impure. Their position is based on al-qiyās upon a text found in a tradition, "When water is two pails in quantity, it is not considered impure". Now, when this pure water is separated into two or more containers it does not lose its purity.

The Aḥnāf respond to this position by making it clear that the text of the tradition used to formulate this upon is in itself not rational. Rationality dictates that when impurity falls in water it renders the water impure. Why then in this case, whilst the quantity of water is still not overly expansive, is the tradition stating that the water remains pure? As the reasoning in the source case is unclear, transferring this to another case is against the conditions of a valid al-qiyās. For this reason, in this case al-qiyās of the ash-Shawāfi' is not accepted.

Text And Translation

ومثال الثالث: وهو ما لا يعقل معناه في حق جواز التوضي بنبيذ التمر فإنه لو قال: جاز بغيره من الأنبذة بالقياس على نبيذ التمر، أو قال: لو شج في صلاته أو احتلم يبني على صلاته بالقياس على ما إذا سبقه الحدث لا يصح؛ لأنّ الحكم في الأصل لم يعقل معناه فاستحال تعديته إلى الفرع، وبمثل هذا قال أصحاب الشافعي عليه الرحمة: قلتان نجستان إذا اجتمعتا صارتا طاهرتين فاذا افترقتا بقيتا على الطهارة بالقياس على ما إذا وقعت النجاسة في القلتين؛ لأنّ الحكم لو ثبت في الأصل كان غير معقول معناه

An example of the third, which is the one whose meaning is not understood, is the permissibility of performing ablution with a date-beverage. So if one said it is permitted with other beverages by analogy to the date-beverage. Or one said:

حديث

عن عبد الله بن عمر رضي الله عنهما أن النبي صلى الله عليه وسلم قال: إذا بلغ الماء قلتين لم ينجسه شيء.

عليه الصلوة والسلام

(سنن ابن ماجة: 517)

if one is injured in his prayer or becomes pubescent, he can resume his prayer by al-qiyās with the case of a preceding invalidation of ablution, would be incorrect. This is because reasoning of the ruling in the source is not understood, so it is not possible to transfer it to the target. Similar to this is what the scholars of ash-Shāfa'īy say, mercy be upon him, two impure bails, when combined become pure. If they are then separated they remain pure by al-qiyās with the impurity falling in two bails. This is because although the ruling is established in the source its reasoning is not understood.

❖❖❖

An example of the fourth condition of al-qiyās not being fulfilled is that lexically *al-khamr* is a grape based beverage in which fermentation has taken place and the liquid has become an intoxicant. Its ruling in the Shariah is that anyone who considers it lawful becomes a nonbeliever and a single drop of it is unlawful for consumption. Anyone who consumes it will be punished whether one is intoxicated because of it or not. Other intoxicants do not hold the same ruling. Someone who says they are permitted to consume other intoxicants remains a believer and consuming an amount that has not intoxicated the individual will not result in the ultimate punishment. The ash-Shawāfi' hold that any heated grape-based-beverage that has become an intoxicant is also classed as *al-khamr* because *al-khamr* is named such because it intoxicates. Now, anything that intoxicates will be likened to the fermented *al-khamr*. Based on the literal meaning of *al-khamr*, that which intoxicates, anything that clouds the mind will be analogised and given the same ruling by way of al-qiyās. The Aḥnāf respond that likening a fermented grape-beverage to a heated grape-beverage based on its name, which happens to indicate it being an intoxicant, is invalid. It is invalid because this is a literal al-qiyās such that the meaning of a word, in this case *al-khamr*, is used to apply the same ruling to all that literally fall in its category. al-Qiyās is a source of the Shariah and not a valid tool in matters pertaining to language; as such, it is only valid when the cause is determined from a source of the Shariah and not due to language.

Another example of transferring a ruling based on linguistics is the ruling on *an-nabbāsh*, the raider of tombs. The Aḥnāf do not consider *an-nabbāsh* to be the same as *as-sāriq*, a thief, in punishment. Where a thief will have his hand severed, the raider of tombs will not. The ash-Shawāfi' disagree and by way of al-qiyās categorise a tomb raider alongside a thief, saying that a

QUICK TERMS

القياس: *al-qiyās*

Analogy. The reasoning of the learned.

QUICK ARABIC

الخمر: *al-khamr*

Wine. A fermented juice of grapes used as a beverage and having an alcoholic content.

النباش: *an-nabbāsh*

Tomb-raider. Who takes the shroud and possessions of the deceased from an unsecure location, and without expected aggression.

السارق: *as-sāriq*

Thief. The one who takes another's belongings without aggression and in secret from a secure location.

thief is one who takes the belongings of another in secret and this is a meaning also found in the tomb-raider as he takes the shroud of the departed. As both are essentially committing the same act, and the thief is to have his hand severed, then so must the tomb-raider. The response is that for al-qiyās to be valid, it must not be based upon linguistics. The cause for likening *an-nabbāsh* to *as-sāriq* is because of the word meaning of *as-sāriq* and this is based on language, which is invalid in al-qiyās. It is clear that even the proponents of this al-qiyās acknowledge that the lexicon itself coined different words for a fermented beverage and for a heated one, as it coined different words for a thief as it did for a tomb-raider. Even the lexicon makes it clear that the two are different.

The invalidity of al-qiyās based on linguistics can be clarified further in two ways. The first is that the Arabs call a black horse *al-adham* due to its colour and a chestnut horse *al-kumayt* due to its colour. Using this we cannot then call a dark-skinned person *al-adham* or a reddish-brown cloth *al-kumayt*, because they both share the respective colours. If al-qiyās were applicable linguistically, this transfer would be permitted as they share a common cause. This reasoning in unanimously rejected in language and so it is not acceptable.

The second way to express the invalidity of al-qiyās based on linguistics is that it would result in the redundancy of causes explicitly mentioned in the Shariah. For example, the Shariah has expressed that *as-sariqa* is the cause for severing the hand. If we were to now say that the cause of severing is not *as-sariqa* but a meaning which is more general, such as 'taking the wealth of another in secret', so it can include *an-nabbāsh* too, it is the equivalent of saying the text has assigned the wrong cause. Rather than severing the hand, being caused by *as-sariqa* its real cause is taking someone else's wealth in secret. This would imply that the Shariah has assigned it wrongly. Similarly, the Shariah has assigned *al-ḥadd* as the punishment for consuming *al-khamr*. If we assign this very punishment to 'any intoxicant', to include weaker beverages that could lead to intoxication, it will be altering the assignment explicitly stipulated by the Shariah. This shows that al-qiyās based on linguistics leads to altering the cause clearly given in the Shariah. As this is not permitted, neither is any type of al-qiyās, which can result in the same outcome.

Text And Translation

ومثال الرابع: وهو ما يكون التعليل لأمر شرعي لا لأمر لغوي في قولهم: المطبوخ المنصف خمر لأنّ

QUICK ARABIC

الأدهم: *al-adham*

Deep black. The name given to a dark coloured breed of horse.

الكميت: *al-kumayt*

Chestnut. The name given to a reddish-brown coloured breed of horse.

الحد: *al-ḥadd*

Defined punishment. Punishments that are defined in the Quran and Hadith.

الخمر إنما كان خمرا؛ لأنه يخامر العقل وغيره يخامر العقل أيضا فيكون خمرا بالقياس، والسارق إنما كان سارقا؛ لأنه أخذ مال الغير بطريق الخفية وقد شاركه النباش في هذا المعنى فيكون سارقا بالقياس وهذا قياس في اللغة مع اعترافه أن الاسم لم يوضع له في اللغة والدليل على فساد هذا النوع من القياس أن العرب يسمي الفرس أدهم لسواده وكميتا لحمرته، ثم لا يطلق هذا الاسم على الزنجي والثوب الأحمر، ولو جرت المقايسة في الأسامي اللغوية لجاز ذلك لوجود العلة؛ ولأن هذا يؤدي الى إبطال الأسباب الشرعية؛ وذلك لأن الشرع جعل السرقة سببا لنوع من الأحكام فاذا علقنا الحكم بما هو أعم من السرقة وهو أخذ مال الغير على طريق الخفية تبين أن السبب كان في الأصل معنى هو غير السرقة، وكذلك جعل شرب الخمر سببا لنوع من الأحكام فإذا علقنا الحكم بأمر أعم من الخمر تبين أنّ الحكم كان في الأصل متعلقا بغير الخمر

An example of the fourth, which is that the effective cause is for a matter concerning Shariah and not a lexical matter, is in their saying: the half fermented is a wine because the wine is what it is, as it clouds the mind. Other than it also cloud the mind, so they are also wine by al-qiyās. The thief is a thief as he takes the valuables of another secretly. The tomb-raider is the same as him in this sense, so he's a thief by analogy. This is lexical analogy despite acknowledging that the word is not coined for it in the lexicon. The proof that this type of analogy is flawed is that the Arabs call a horse *al-adham* for its blackness, and *al-kumayt* for its reddish colour. Then these words are not used for a dark-skinned person or a red cloth. If analogy was applicable in lexicon entries this would be permitted due to the presence of the cause. Moreover, this leads to the annulling of Shariah causes. This is because the Shariah has classed thievery as a cause for particular rulings. If we were to assign the ruling to something more general than thievery - which is taking the valuables of another in secret - it would be clear that the cause was actually something other than thievery. Similar is the assigning of wine consumption as a cause for a particular ruling. So when we assigned it to a ruling more general than wine, it would be clear that the ruling was in actuality associated to other than wine.

❖ ❖ ❖

An example of the fifth condition for al-qiyās, that the ruling for the target case must not already exist in texts, is that it is necessary to free a Muslim

QUICK TERMS

القياس: *al-qiyās*

Analogy. The reasoning of the learned.

slave in the expiation for murder. It will not suffice to free a non-believing slave. This is because verse 92 of Sūrat un-Nisā says:

﴿وَمَن قَتَلَ مُؤْمِنًا خَطَئًا فَتَحْرِيرُ رَقَبَةٍ مُّؤْمِنَةٍ﴾ [النساء: 92]

"...He who has killed a believer by mistake must set free a believing slave..."

In the expiation of a broken vow or in the case of *aẓ-ẓihār* there is no restriction of freeing a Muslim slave, in fact any slave may be freed. This is because verse 89 of Sūrat ul-Māida and verse 3 of Sūrat ul-Mujādila say:

﴿أَوْ تَحْرِيرُ رَقَبَةٍ﴾ [المائدة: 89]

"...or the liberation of a slave..."

﴿وَالَّذِينَ يُظَاهِرُونَ مِن نِّسَائِهِمْ ثُمَّ يَعُودُونَ لِمَا قَالُوا فَتَحْرِيرُ رَقَبَةٍ مِّن قَبْلِ أَن يَتَمَاسَّا﴾ [المجادلة: 3]

"Those who put away their wives by *aẓ-ẓihār* and afterward go back on that which they have said; free a slave before they touch one another..."

In both of these cases, the slave is left without a restriction and so any slave may be freed, believing or non-believing. Imam a<u>sh</u>-<u>Sh</u>āfa'īy رحمه الله likens the emancipation in vows and *aẓ-ẓihār*, to the emancipation for murder, and says that only Muslim slaves may be freed for expiation in all three cases. Accordingly, freeing non-believing slaves will be invalid. The Aḥnāf respond to this saying that this al-qiyās of likening the two cases to that of murder falls short of the fifth condition. The condition is that the target cases, expiation in vows and *aẓ-ẓihār*, already exist in texts. Whilst they already exist in texts, they cannot be subject to al-qiyās.

Another example of this condition is that if the one who committed aẓ-ẓihār expiates his mistake by fasting and then breaks the continuity in the fasts by cohabiting with his wife before completion of two consecutive months, the counting will begin again. Any fasts from before the cohabitation will be void and must be repeated. This is because verse 89 of Sūrat ul-Mujādala says:

﴿فَمَن لَّمْ يَجِدْ فَصِيَامُ شَهْرَيْنِ مُتَتَابِعَيْنِ مِن قَبْلِ أَن يَتَمَاسَّا﴾ [المجادلة: 4]

"And he who does not find, let him fast for two successive months before they touch one another..."

QUICK ARABIC

الظهار: *aẓ-ẓihār*

Likening to a mother. A practice in which separation between husband and wife occurs until expiation is made.

However, if he expiates for *aẓ-ẓihār* by feeding the poor but cohabits before the feeding of sixty individuals is complete, the feeding does not have to start over. This is because the same verse continues:

﴿فَمَن لَّمْ يَسْتَطِعْ فَإِطْعَامُ سِتِّينَ مِسْكِينًا﴾ [المجادلة: 4]

"...and for him who is unable to do so, the feeding of sixty needy ones...."

This command is unrestricted and it does not stipulate that the feeding should be 'before cohabiting'. This means that it will remain al-muṭlaq and unrestricted, so if cohabiting does occur before the feeding is complete, the feeding does not have to restart. Imam ash-Shāfa'īy ﷺ likens the feeding to the fasting in aẓ-ẓihār. So, just as the fasts are to be repeated if their continuity is halted by cohabiting, feeding must also be repeated afresh if the sixty meals are not given before cohabiting. The Aḥnāf respond to this by saying the fifth condition of al-qiyās is not met. The target case of al-qiyās in this case, expiation by feeding, is already found in the text and as such, it cannot be subjected to al-qiyās.

A further example of this fifth condition is that *al-muḥṣar*, the one held back from the performance of Hajj whilst on the way, is to send his sacrificial animal to al-Ḥaram when he is sure that it will be sacrificed on his behalf. He is then free to have his head shaven or hair cut to leave the state of *al-Iḥrām*. If he does not send his sacrificial animal, he will remain in the state of *al-Iḥrām*. This is because Allah Almighty says:

﴿وَلَا تَحْلِقُوا رُءُوسَكُمْ حَتَّىٰ يَبْلُغَ الْهَدْيُ مَحِلَّهُ﴾ [البقرة: 196]

"...and shave not your heads until the sacrifices have reached their destination..."

The shaving of the head is associated with sending the animal. Imam ash-Shāfa'īy ﷺ says that just as the one performing the Hajj of *at-tamattu'* is permitted to fast for three days during the days of Hajj and seven when he returns home, the *al-muḥṣar* is permitted to do the same. The common cause between the two cases for al-qiyās is that they are unable to perform the sacrifice. The Aḥnāf respond saying that for al-qiyās to be valid it must fulfil its fifth condition. That is, that the target case must not have an existing text governing it. In this case, *al-muḥṣar* is given a ruling in the text and so cannot be subject to any al-qiyās.

QUICK TERMS

المطلق: *al-muṭlaq*

The unrestricted. Indicates an entity irrespective of any quality.

QUICK ARABIC

الظهار: *aẓ-ẓihār*

Likening to a mother. A practice in which separation between husband and wife occurs until expiation is made.

المحصر: *al-muḥṣar*

The blockaded. The pilgrim held back from performing the rituals of Hajj.

الحرم: *al-ḥaram*

The sacred land. A sacred land around the blessed Ka'ba, wherein certain acts are unlawful.

الإحرام: *al-iḥrām*

Pilgrim's garb and state. The dress of the pilgrim and the state in which he or she is held to be.

التمتع: *at-tamattu'*

Enjoyment. Enjoying the privilege of both 'Umrah and Hajj in one journey.

Furthermore, another example of the fifth condition of al-qiyās not being met is that the one performing *ḥajj ut-tamattu'* and unable to sacrifice an animal, is to fast on the 7th, 8th and 9th of Dhu al-Ḥijjah, followed by seven more fasts after the days of the Hajj. If the pilgrim did not fast for the three days before the 10th of Dhu al-Ḥijjah then he is not to make up those missed fasts, rather he is to fulfil the penalty only. The reason for this is that a man told Sayyidunā 'Umar ﷺ of this situation, to which the noble Companion ﷺ told him that the penalty of another sacrifice must be paid. He said he did not have one, so Sayyidunā 'Umar ﷺ told him to ask the people of his tribe, to which he said he didn't have any tribesmen at all. The noble Companion ﷺ instructed a servant to donate to the man by which he was able to pay the penalty. The narration shows that a penalty must be paid and the fasts cannot be made up later. Imam ash-Shāfa'īy ﷺ says that such a pilgrim may correctly exit the Hajj and make up the three fasts later, just as one would make up for missed fasts of Ramadan. The Aḥnāf respond to this by saying this likening to the fast of Ramadan is al-qiyās and is not acceptable because the target case already has an authentic text concerning it.

Text And Translation

ومثال الشرط الخامس: وهو ما لا يكون الفرع منصوصا عليه كما يقال: إعتاق الرقبة الكافرة في كفارة اليمين والظهار لا يجوز بالقياس على كفارة القتل، ولو جامع المظاهر في خلال الإطعام يستأنف الإطعام بالقياس على الصوم، ويجوز للمحصر أن يتحلل بالصوم بالقياس على المتمتع، والمتمتع إذا لم يصم في أيام التشريق يصوم بعدها بالقياس على قضاء رمضان

An example of the fifth condition, which is that the target case should not be in canonical text, is like it is said emancipating a non-believing slave as expiation for a vow or for *aẓ-ẓihār* is not permitted by analogy with the expiation for murder. If the one who committed *aẓ-ẓihār* has intercourse during the feeding, the feeding will discontinue by al-qiyās with sawm. The one held back from Hajj is permitted to exit *al-iḥrām* with fasting by analogy with *al-mutamatti'*. When *al-mutamatti'* has not fasted in the days of *at-tashrīq* he can can fast after them by analogy with making up for Ramadan.

❖ ❖ ❖

QUICK ARABIC

المتمتع: *at-mutmatti'*

The enjoyer. The one who enjoys the privilege of both 'Umrah and Hajj in one journey.

التشريق: *at-tashrīq*

Drying flesh. The three days following sacrifices during the Hajj.

Summary Of Conditions for Authentic al-Qiyās

There are five conditions for al-qiyās to be valid.

1. It must not oppose an existing text. For example, Ḥasan bin Zayd رحمه الله was asked about laughing out loudly in salah and he responded in accordance with the Hadith that it invalidates the ablution. The enquirer countered that if one slanders another in the salah, it invalidates the prayer but not the ablution, even though it is worse than laughing as a sin. This reasoning is not al-qiyās as it opposes an existing text.

2. It must not alter a ruling of an existing text. For example, Imam ash-Shāfa'īy رحمه الله says that an intention is necessary for ablution analogising with *at-tayammum*. This would mean altering a verse from al-muṭlaq to *al-muqayyad* to accommodate this analogy which is not permitted.

3. The transferred cause must not be illogical. For example, Imam ash-Shāfa'īy رحمه الله saying two impure pails of water when combined and then separated become pure. This is derived from a tradition that rules that when impurity falls in water amounting to two pots it is not impure. This does not have a clear reasoning.

4. The common cause should be for a purpose based in the Shariah and not for a linguistic purpose. For example, *as-sāriq* is called so because he secretly takes valuables. To analogise on this that a tomb-raider also has a similar quality as this, so he must be punished the same, is linguistic. This is not al-qiyās.

5. The ruling derived is not already stated. For example, to analogise the expiation of murder on the expiation of *aẓ-ẓihār* or vows. Murder expiation only allows freeing a Muslim slave so the other cases must too. This is not valid as the other cases already have their respective rulings.

4.3 Authentic al-Qiyās

al-Qiyās that is acceptable in the Shariah is to provide a ruling in a target case, which has no previous textual existence, by likening it to a source case due to a common effective cause that both cases share. This means that a cause is identified in an existing text and it is associated with a ruling in that text. As the target case shares the same cause as the source case, the ruling is also adopted in the target case. This is al-qiyās in the Shariah. The process is depicted in figure 4.1-01. The validity of an authentic al-qiyās centres on *al-'illa*, the effective cause. This *al-'illa* must be the same in both the source and target cases, and due to it being the same we are able to transfer the ruling of the source case to the target case. The effective cause, *al-'illa*, that is valid is the cause found in al-kitāb, as-sunna, al-ijmā' or from the scholarly efforts of the jurists and from personal derivation.

Text And Translation

فصل: القياس الشرعي هو ترتب الحكم في غير المنصوص عليه على معنى هو علة لذلك الحكم في المنصوص عليه، ثم إنما يعرف كون المعنى علة بالكتاب وبالسنة وبالإجماع وبالاجتهاد وبالاستنباط

Chapter: the legal al-qiyās is to form a ruling on an uncanonised case based on an effective cause for that ruling from a canonised text. Then, an effective cause will be known to be so from al-kitāb, as-sunna, al-ijmā', by scholarly effort and deduction.

❖ ❖ ❖

An example of *al-'illa* taken from the blessed Quran as the source is 'frequenting', *ka<u>th</u>rat uṭ-ṭawāf*, visiting on a regular basis. It is an *al-'illa* because Allah ﷻ has said that a domestic help or servant needs to seek permission to enter any private quarters on three occasions; before the morning prayer, at midday and after the late-night prayers. This is because these three times are the times of relaxation and the likelihood of finding one in an undesirable state is heightened. Therefore, in these three times, permission must be sought to enter, but other than these times, to avoid constant annoyance of repeatedly seeking permission to enter, one need not seek permission. The cause of this ruling of 'not seeking permission' is frequenting and passing through on a regular basis. The command is found in verse 58 of Sūrat un-Nūr:

QUICK TERMS

القياس: *al-qiyās*

Analogy. The reasoning of the learned.

العلة: *al-'illa*

The means. The method or instrument used to attain an end.

الكتاب: *al-kitāb*

The book. The inspired final word of Allah ﷻ. The Quran.

السنة: *as-sunna*

The practice. The sayings, doings and approval of the blessed Prophet ﷺ.

الإجماع: *al-ijmā'*

Consensus. The unanimous agreement of the mujtahids.

QUICK ARABIC

كثرة الطواف: *ka<u>th</u>rat uṭ-ṭawwāf*

Frequenting. A high volume of entering and leaving due to need of access.

﴿لَيْسَ عَلَيْكُمْ وَلَا عَلَيْهِمْ جُنَاحٌ بَعْدَهُنَّ طَوَّافُونَ عَلَيْكُم بَعْضُكُمْ عَلَى بَعْضٍ﴾ [النور: 58]

"...there is no blame on you or on them at other times, when some of you go round attendant upon others..."

You will constantly seek their assistance and they will constantly visit you to serve you, so asking for permission each time is troublesome and annoying. Other than the three stated times, seeking permission is waived and its underlying and effective cause is frequenting. In summary, seeking permission is waived to reduce annoyance due to the frequency of your meetings. This is derived from the verse of the blessed Quran. The Messenger of Allah ﷺ stated this very *al-'illa* when stating the ruling on the remnants and left-over water of a cat. He ﷺ said, "The cat is not impure for it is from those that frequent you". It should be that a cat is impure, as consuming it is not permitted, and it needs to sustain itself with meat too. However, due to it being domestic and frequenting the home its impurity is waived and excused. If it were deemed impure in all circumstances, it would cause much annoyance to the households in which the cats lived. It is for this reason and cause, frequenting, that the Messenger of Allah ﷺ waived the impurity of the cat's left over. Our jurists have further expanded upon the use of this *al-'illa* of frequenting by way of al-qiyās upon the cat, to include domestic animals such as mice and snakes. This would mean that the leftover of these animals would not be considered impure too.

Another example of *al-'illa* from the blessed Quran as the source is verse 185 of Sūrat ul-Baqara:

﴿يُرِيدُ اللهُ بِكُمُ الْيُسْرَ وَلاَ يُرِيدُ بِكُمُ الْعُسْرَ﴾ [البقرة: 185]

"...Allah desires for you ease; He desires not hardship for you..."

The Shariah has permitted an ill person and a traveller to delay the fasting of Ramadan to create ease. It is at their discretion to fast or not to fast. The cause and *al-'illa* to delay the fast for the ill and the traveller is 'ease', which is sourced from the blessed Quran. There is a degree of ease in not fasting in Ramadan for the excused to safeguard their health, as there is also a degree of ease in fasting in Ramadan rather than at a later date, to ensure communal encouragement. Ease can be in fasting on occasions, as ease can be in not fasting on other occasions. Thus, the traveller and the ill, have a choice either to fast or to delay the fast in Ramadan, should they choose. It is for this reason that Imam Abū Ḥanīfa رحمه الله has ruled that it is permitted for a traveller to choose to make up

حديث

عن كبشة بنت كعب بن مالك رضي الله عنهما أن رسول الله ﷺ قال: إنها ليست بنجس إنما هي من الطوافين عليكم أو الطوافات.

عليه الصلاة والسلام

(سنن الترمذي: 92)

QUICK TERMS

القياس: *al-qiyās*

Analogy. The reasoning of the learned.

العلة: *al-'illa*

The means. The method or instrument used to attain an end.

another necessary fast such as fasting for a vow or making up a fast of a previous Ramadan, on the day of travel, rather than fasting for the present Ramadan. This is because the cause of 'ease' from the blessed Quran grants dispensation from fasting for a physical benefit, which is to eat and drink to compensate for physical weakness from travel, so it is more fitting that dispensation from the same fast should be allowed for a religious benefit. There is a choice granted to fast for that day's fast or not, and the individual has chosen to fast for another necessary fast. There is religious benefit in this, in that ease has been achieved by using the dispensation to fulfil another duty that was necessary.

Text And Translation

فمثال العلة المعلومة بالكتاب كثرة الطواف فإنها جعلت علة لسقوط الحرج في الاستئذان في قوله تعالى: ﴿ليس عليكم ولا عليهم جناح بعدهن طوافون عليكم بعضكم على بعضٍ﴾ ثم أسقط رسول الله عليه الصلاة والسلام حرج نجاسة سؤر الهرة بحكم هذه العلة فقال عليه السلام: الهرة ليست بنجسة فإنها من الطوافين عليكم والطوافات فقاس أصحابنا جميع ما يسكن في البيوت كالفارة والحية على الهرة بعلة الطواف، وكذلك قوله تعالى: ﴿يريد الله بكم اليسر ولاَ يرِيد بكم الْعسر﴾ بين الشرع أن الإفطار للمريض والمسافر لتيسير الأمر عليهم ليتمكنوا من تحقيق ما يترجح في نظرهم من الإتيان بوظيفة الوقت أو تأخيره إلى أيام أخر، وباعتبار هذا المعنى قال أبو حنيفة رحمه الله: المسافر إذا نوى في أيام رمضان واجبا آخر يقع عن واجب آخر؛ لأنه لما ثبت له الترخص بما يرجع إلى مصالح بدنه وهو الإفطار فلأن يثبت له ذلك بما يرجع الى مصالح دينه وهو إخراج النفس عن عهدة الواجب أولى

So an example of an effective cause known from al-kitāb is 'persistent rounds', as they are the effective cause for cancelling the annoyance of seeking permission. It is from the Almighty's verse: "...there is no blame on you or on them at other times, when some of you go round attendant upon others." Then the Messenger of Allah, peace and blessings be upon him, relaxed the annoyance of a cat's impure leftover by virtue of this effective cause. So he, peace and blessings be upon him, said: "The cat is not impure as it is of those that roam around you." So our jurists have analogised all domestic animals like rodents and snakes, with cats due to the cause of persistent rounds. Similarly, His saying, the Most High: "Allah wants ease for you and he doesn't want for

QUICK TERMS

الكتاب: *al-kitāb*

The book. The inspired final word of Allah ﷻ. The Quran.

you hardship." The Shariah explains that not fasting for an ill person or a traveller is to ease the duty upon them so they are able to determine their preference of fulfilling the present duty or to defer it to an alternative day. Considering this meaning Imam Abū Ḥanīfa, Allah have mercy on him, says if the traveller intends another necessary fast in the days of Ramadan, it will occur as the other necessary fast, because it is established that he has a concession regarding his physical wellbeing, that is not to fast. So as this is established for him, what concerns his religious wellbeing, which is relieving himself of a necessary act, is of a higher priority.

❖ ❖ ❖

An example of a cause and *al-'illa* sourced from as-Sunna is the command of the Messenger of Allah ﷺ that if one was to sleep whilst standing, bowing or in prostration, ablution is not invalidated. The ablution is necessary for the one who has slept flat because sleeping in such a manner causes the muscles and joints to relax. The tradition identifies the relaxation of joints, *istirkhā ul-mafāṣil*, as the cause and *al-'illa* of invalidation of ablution. This means that sleeping in any posture that allows joints to relax will invalidate the ablution. A person who leans or props himself on a cushion such that hypothetically if that cushion was removed the person would fall over, is not with a rigid structure and the joints must be relaxed. This would mean that sleeping in this manner invalidates the ablution. Furthermore, if one was to become unconscious or intoxicated, control over joints will diminish and thus ablution of such an individual will be deemed invalid too.

Another example of an *al-'illa* present in as-Sunna and used as a source case is that the messenger of Allah ﷺ said to an *al-mustaḥāḍa* woman who had abnormal bleeding, "Make your ablution and pray, even if the drops of blood flow, for this is venous blood". In this tradition, the flowing of venous blood is identified as the cause and *al-'illa* for the need for an ablution. Using the *al-'illa* we can extend the ruling of a need to renew ablution for the one who has undergone cupping or blood-letting, because both procedures also involve flowing of blood.

Text And Translation

ومثال العلة المعلومة بالسنة في قوله عليه الصلاة والسلام: ليس الوضوء على من نام قائما أو قاعدا أو

حديث

عن ابن عباس رضي الله عنهما أن النبي صلى الله عليه وسلم قال:

ليس على من نام ساجدا وضوء حتى يضطجع فإنه إذا اضطجع استرخت مفاصله.

عليه الصلاة والسلام

(مسند أحمد: 2313)

QUICK TERMS

العلة: *al-'illa*

The means. The method or instrument used to attain an end.

QUICK ARABIC

استرخاء المفاصل: *istirkhā ul-mafāṣil*

Relaxed joints. When the body is not forming a stable and controlled posture.

المستحاضة: *al-mustaḥāḍa*

Non-menstrual bleeding. Blood flow seen by a woman that is not originating in the womb.

راكعا أو ساجدا إنما الوضوء على من نام مضطجعا فإنه إذا نام مضطجعا استرخت مفاصله جعل استرخاء المفاصل علة فيتعدى الحكم بهذه العلة الى النوم مستندا أو متكئا إلى شيء لو أزيل عنه لسقط، وكذلك يتعدى الحكم بهذه العلة إلى الإغماء والسكر، وكذلك قوله عليه السلام: توضئي، وصلي، وإن قطر الدم على الحصير فإنه دم عرق انفجر جعل انفجار الدم علة فتعدى الحكم بهذه العلة الى الفصد والحجامة

An example of an effective cause from the Sunna is his saying, peace and blessings be upon him: "Ablution is not necessary for the one who slept whilst standing, sitting, bowing or prostrating. Ablution is for the one who slept flat, for if he slept flat his limbs are relaxed." The relaxing of the limbs is made the effective cause, so the ruling extends due to this cause to sleeping whilst leaning or propped by something such that were it to be removed he would fall. Similarly, the ruling extends due to this cause to unconsciousness and to intoxication. Likewise, his saying, peace and blessings be upon him: "Perform ablution and pray, for the drops of blood on the mat are from a burst vein." The bursting of blood is made the effective cause, so the ruling of this cause extends to venesection and cupping.

❖ ❖ ❖

An example of *al-'illa* sourced from al-ijma' is that the effective cause for a father's guardianship over a son is 'being a minor', *aṣ-ṣighr*. There is a unanimous agreement upon this *al-'illa* amongst both the Aḥnāf and ash-Shawāfi'. The Aḥnāf extend this *al-'illa* to include a daughter too, as she also is a minor. As she is a minor, a father has guardianship over her affairs too. This is al-qiyās using an *al-'illa* of 'being a minor' in the case of a son, as agreed upon by consensus, and then applied to the target case of a daughter who shares the same *al-'illa*. This means the father's guardianship over the daughter is because she is a minor. When a son matures and becomes an adult, the guardianship of the father diminishes and the son becomes responsible for his own affairs; this too is agreed unanimously. In a similar manner, when a daughter matures, the guardianship of the father diminishes and the daughter too becomes responsible for her own affairs, according to the Aḥnāf.

حديث

عن عائشة رضي الله عنها قالت استحيضت فاطمة بنت حبيش رضي الله عنها فسألت النبي صلى الله عليه وسلم فقالت: يا رسول الله صلى الله عليه وسلم إني أستحاض فلا أطهر أفادع الصلاة قال رسول الله صلى الله عليه وسلم: إنما ذلك عرق وليست بالحيضة فإذا اقبلت الحيضة فدعي الصلاة وإذا ادبرت فاغسلي عنك أثر الدم وتوضئي فإنما ذلك عرق وليست بالحيضة.

عليه الصلاة والسلام

(سنن النسائي: 217)

QUICK ARABIC

الصغر: *aṣ-ṣighr*

Juvenility. The state of being young and requiring guardianship over agency.

Additionally, it is unanimously agreed that the *al-mustaḥāḍa* is to renew her ablution with the flow of blood, so wherever there is a flow of blood the ruling that the ablution needs to be renewed will be given.

Text And Translation

ومثال العلة المعلومة بالإجماع فيما قلنا: الصغر علة لولاية الأب في حق الصغير فيثبت الحكم في حق الصغيرة لوجود العلة، والبلوغ عن عقل علة لزوال ولاية الأب في حق الغلام فيتعدى الحكم إلى الجارية بهذه العلة، وانفجار الدم علة الانتقاض للطهارة في حق المستحاضة فيتعدى الحكم الى غيرها لوجود العلة

An example of the effective cause from al-ijmā is our saying: juvenility is the cause for the guardianship of the father over a minor boy, so the ruling is established with respect to the minor girl, due to the presence of the cause. Maturity is the cause of independency from a father with respect to the boy, so the ruling traverses to the girl with this cause. The rupture of blood invalidates purity with respect to the woman with abnormal bleeding, so the ruling traverses to other states with the existence of the cause.

❖❖❖

An example of the *al-'illa* being derived from the effort of the mujtahid through personal deduction and reason is discussed later, [chapter 4.3.1, page 399]. In short, if we have an attribute that is appropriate for a ruling and we find it in a situation that makes the ruling unavoidable, the ruling will be given. It is as though it is commonly understood that such a scenario is associated with that ruling. There is not a canonical text of the Shariah that can be pinpointed where that *al-'illa* appears. Before it is discussed at length, the types of authentic al-qiyās in terms of the connection between the source and target cases are presented.

❖❖❖

4.3.1 Types of Authentic al-Qiyās

When al-qiyās is completed successfully and the ruling is transferred from the source case to the target case, al-qiyās can be categorised into two. The source and target cases are either from the same kind, *an-naw'*, or both

QUICK TERMS

العلة: *al-'illa*

The means. The method or instrument used to attain an end.

القياس: *al-qiyās*

Analogy. The reasoning of the learned.

QUICK ARABIC

المستحاضة: *al-mustaḥāḍa*

Non-menstrual bleeding. Blood flow seen by a woman that is not originating in the womb.

النوع: *an-naw'*

Type. A group of related things that almost exemplify the essential characteristics of a higher group.

الجنس: *al-jins*

Genus. A class or group of similar closely related things.

cases are of the same genus, *al-jins*. An example of both the source and target cases having the same *an-naw'* is that a father is permitted to enter his minor son into a marriage contract, the cause of which is him 'being a minor', *aṣ-ṣighr*. This very cause is also found in a minor daughter, so a father is also permitted to enter her into a marriage. The ruling can be extended to a minor who has previously been married too. The initial source case from where *al-'illa* is taken, 'marriage contract of the minor son', is the same type of case to the target case, 'marriage of the minor daughter' or 'previously married minor'.

Another example of a source and target case being of one kind is that the remnant water of a cat is no longer impure due to *al-'illa* of frequenting, *aṭ-ṭawwāf*. To transfer the ruling of 'no longer impure' to the cases of the remnant water of all domestic animals, is a transfer to a case that is the same in *an-naw'*. Both source and target cases concern the same kind of case, which in this instance is the status of remnant water left by an animal.

A third example is that a father's authority to enter a son into marriage diminishes with the son's maturity. When the *al-'illa* of maturity is also present in a daughter, the father's authority to enter her into a marriage will also diminish. Both the source and target cases are the same kind in that they are both concerned with the same thing, autonomy in marriage.

Text And Translation

ثم بعد ذلك نقول: القياس على نوعين أحدهما: أن يكون الحكم المعدى من نوع الحكم الثابت في الأصل، والثاني: أن يكون من جنسه، مثال الاتحاد في النوع ما قلنا: إن الصغر علة لولاية الإنكاح في حق الغلام فيثبت الإنكاح في حق الجارية لوجود العلة فيها وبه يثبت الحكم في الثيب الصغيرة، وكذلك قلنا: الطواف علة سقوط نجاسة السؤر في سؤر الهرة فيتعدى الحكم الى سؤر سواكن البيوت لوجود العلة، وبلوغ الغلام عن عقل علّة زوال ولاية الإنكاح فيزول الولاية عن الجارية بحكم هذه العلة.

Then after that we say al-qiyās is of two types. The first is that the derived ruling is of the same type as the ruling established in the source. The second is that it is of the same genus. The example of the same type is what we said: that childhood is an effective cause for authority over marriage for a boy so it is established for the marriage of a girl because the cause is found in her; with it the ruling is established for a non-maiden child. Similarly, we said frequenting is

QUICK ARABIC

الصغر: *aṣ-ṣighr*

Juvenility. The state of being young and requiring guardianship over agency.

الطواف: *aṭ-ṭawwāf*

Frequenting. Constant entering and leaving due to need of access.

an effective cause for abandoning the impurity of the leftover, in the leftover of a cat, so the ruling traverses to the leftovers of domestic animals as the cause is present. And the maturing of a boy is cause to diminish authority in marriage, so authority diminishes for the girl with the ruling of this cause.

❖ ❖ ❖

An example of both the source and the target cases being of the same genus, *al-jins*, is that domestic helpers have been instructed to seek permission to enter private quarters at three specified times, before *al-fajr*, at noon and after *al-'ishā*. At other times, they are permitted to enter without seeking permission to avoid repeated annoyance. The ruling allowing for not seeking any permission due to annoyance is because of the cause and *al-'illa* of frequently entering and leaving. Verse 58 of Sūrat un-Nūr states:

﴿لَيْسَ عَلَيْكُمْ وَلَا عَلَيْهِمْ جُنَاحٌ بَعْدَهُنَّ طَوَّافُونَ عَلَيْكُم بَعْضُكُمْ عَلَى بَعْضٍ﴾ [النور: 58]

"...there is no blame on you or on them at other times, when some of you go round attendant upon others..."

This *al-'illa* is also found in cats and other domestic animals. It is for this reason that the impurity of their remnants and left-over water is annulled, due to the repeated annoyance and inconvenience of replacing water due to impurity. Both cases, seeking of permission to enter for attendants and the impurity of the remnant water of domestic animals, are of the same genus because both look to diminish unnecessary annoyance. However, both cases are not of the same kind because one concerns annoyance of seeking permission whilst the other concerns annoyance of impurity.

Similarly, the right of a father to administer the wealth of his daughter is due to her minority. This right will extend to a right over the administration of her personal status. Both of these cases are of the same genus, *al-jins*. They both involve administration, but they are different kinds and different in *an-naw'* because one concerns the administration of wealth and the other concerns administration of the self. Once the minor girl matures, this right of administration is hers and the right of the father diminishes. This ruling also involves both cases, financial and personal, that share the same *al-jins*. They both are the same in that the daughter's maturity diminishes the right of the father in administration, but they are of a different kind because one is a

QUICK TERMS

العلة: *al-'illa*

The means. The method or instrument used to attain an end.

QUICK ARABIC

الجنس: *al-jins*

Genus. A class or group of similar closely related things.

الفجر: *al-fajr*

Dawn. The time of day before sunrise or the prayer performed at this time.

العشاء: *al-'ishā*

Late evening. The time of day when there is darkness or the prayer performed at this time.

النوع: *an-naw'*

Type. A group of related things that almost exemplify the essential characteristics of a higher group.

diminished right in financial affairs and the other is a diminished right of personal status.

Text And Translation

ومثال الاتحاد في الجنس ما يقال: كثرة الطواف علة سقوط حرج الاستئذان في حق ما ملكت أيماننا فيسقط حرج نجاسة السؤر بهذه العلة فإن هذا الحرج من جنس ذلك الحرج لا من نوعه، وكذلك الصغر علة ولاية التصرف للأب في المال فيثبت ولاية التصرف في النفس بحكم هذه العلة وإن بلوغ الجارية عن عقل علة زوال ولاية الأب في المال فيزول ولايته في حق النفس بهذه العلة

An example of the same genus is what is said that frequenting is a cause to abandon the nuisance of seeking permission with respect to our slaves so the nuisance of the impurity of leftovers of a cat are abandoned with this cause. This nuisance is of the same genus to that nuisance; not from the same type. Similarly, childhood is an effective cause of authority for the father in finance, so authority is established for the self too with the ruling of this cause. The mental maturity of the girl is a cause to diminish authority of the father in wealth, so his authority diminishes for the self with this cause.

❖ ❖ ❖

It is vital that when the source and target case are connected by *al-jins* that the connection be general and far-reaching. This is called *tajnīs ul-'illa*. The generality and far-reaching nature of *al-'illa* should allow it to include both the textual source case and the target al-qiyās case. As an example, a minor girl is unable to manage and administer her own affairs. It is for this reason that the Shariah has given the right to her father to manage her financial matters. This would allow her to not stall in life or lose out when an opportunity arises. The administration of the father allows her beneficial matters to progress. The minor girl is also unable to manage her personal contracts. Her father has been appointed as her administrator in this regard too. The cause and *al-'illa* of the guardianship is 'inability to administer', which is a general term and includes both financial matters and personal matters. It is for this reason the father's right to administer includes both of these issues. There are many more examples of this connecting of the source and target cases through *tajnīs ul-'illa* which you can explore in advanced uṣūl ul-fiqh texts.

QUICK TERMS

تجنيس العلة: *tajnīs ul-'illa*

Generalising the cause. Identifying a general cause that includes both a source and target case in al-qiyās.

القياس: *al-qiyās*

Analogy. The reasoning of the learned.

أصول الفقه: *uṣūl ul-fiqh*

Principles of fiqh. The accepted fundamental rules of deriving matters of fiqh.

The ruling of al-qiyās of *an-naw'* is that it is not invalidated with a simple difference. This means that if one was to find simple differences between the source case and the target case, al-qiyās will still apply, because al-qiyās does not require both cases to be the same in every aspect. It is only necessary for the source and target to be the same in the major aspects. When differences are highlighted, the validity is still not affected. The main underlying reason for this is that because the effective cause and *al-'illa* in both cases is the same; the ruling will be the same too.

The ruling of al-qiyās of *al-jins* is that if a particular type of difference can be highlighted between the source and the target in *tajnīs ul-'illa*, it will invalidate the al-qiyās. An example of this is if, for instance, one objected that the administration of a father in the life-matters of a minor is based on al-qiyās upon the administration of the father in financial matters, whereas there is a major difference between the two. A minor is more in need of financial administration, like for living expenses such as clothes, food and accommodation, which are essential and immediate needs. A minor is unable to fulfil these functions, so a father is responsible on behalf of the minor. The need for management of personal status, however, is not an immediate and pressing issue. The minor is not in pressing and immediate need of entering any contract that will secure a future, so there is little use of delegating this non-essential right to another individual. This shows that the minority of the individual is more of an issue in financial matters than it is in personal contractual matters, and thus there is a major difference between the source and target cases that were connected by *al-jins* at first. This results in declaring that al-qiyās of one matter on the other is not acceptable.

QUICK TERMS

القياس: *al-qiyās*

Analogy. The reasoning of the learned.

تجنيس العلة: *tajnīs ul-'illa*

Generalising the cause. Identifying a general cause that includes both a source and target case in al-qiyās.

QUICK ARABIC

النوع: *an-naw'*

Type. A group of related things that almost exemplify the essential characteristics of a higher group.

الجنس: *al-jins*

Genus. A class or group of similar closely related things.

Text And Translation

ثم لا بد في هذا النوع من القياس من تجنيس العلة بأن تقول: إنما يثبت ولاية الأب في مال الصغيرة؛ لأنها عاجزة عن التصرف بنفسها فأثبت الشرع ولاية الأب كيلا يتعطل مصالحها المتعلقة بذلك وقد عجزت عن التصرف في نفسها فوجب القول بولاية الأب عليها، وعلى هذا نظائره، وحكم القياس الأول: أن لا يبطل بالفرق؛ لأن الأصل مع الفرع لما اتحد في العلة وجب اتحادهما في الحكم وإن افترقا في غير هذه العلة، وحكم القياس الثاني: فساده بممانعة التجنيس والفرق الخاص وهو بيان أن تأثير الصغر في ولاية التصرف في المال فوق تأثيره في ولاية التصرف في النفس.

Then it is necessary in this type of al-qiyās to make a genus of the cause such that you say that authority of the father is established in the wealth of a girl because she is unable to administer affairs on her own. So the Shariah establishes the father's authority so that her affairs are not stalled by that. She is unable to administer her own affairs so it is necessary to acknowledge the authority of the father over her. Other examples are based on this. The ruling of the first al-qiyās is, it is not invalid with a difference because the source and the target, share the the cause so they must share the ruling, even if they differ in other than this cause. The ruling of the second al-qiyās is invalidity when creating a genus is prohibited and with a specific difference. That is the explanation of the effect of childhood in authority to administer wealth as superior to its effect on authority to administer personal affairs.

❖ ❖ ❖

After discussing the types of al-qiyās in terms of the connection of the source case to the target case, we now return to close the topic of authentic al-qiyās from chapter 4.3 page 394.

The al-qiyās which is based upon an *al-'illa* that is neither sourced from the textual form of al-kitāb or as-sunna, nor from al-ijmā', is the third type of al-qiyās. It is recognised through a degree of insight and experience, and it is easily understood. It is when we see that a particular feature or quality is appropriate for a ruling, and that quality is making the ruling necessary when immediately observed. This is more so when on other previous occasions, in similar circumstances, the ruling has already been noted and recorded. On such an occasion, due to the similarities between the source and target cases, and the presence of a particular feature and quality, we will rule that the feature is an *al-'illa* for a particular ruling.

Text And Translation

وبيان القسم الثالث: وهو القياس بعلة مستنبطة بالرأي والاجتهاد ظاهر، وتحقيق ذلك إذا وجدنا وصفا مناسبا للحكم وهو بحال يوجب ثبوت الحكم ويتقاضاه بالنظر إليه وقد اقترن به الحكم في موضع الإجماع يضاف الحكم إليه للمناسبة لا لشهادة الشرع بكونه علة

The explanation of the third type, which is al-qiyās by an effective cause derived through reason and deduction, is clear. The detail of that is that if we have an

QUICK TERMS

الكتاب: *al-kitāb*

The book. The inspired final word of Allah ﷻ. The Quran.

السنة: *as-sunna*

The practice. The sayings, doings and approval of the blessed Prophet ﷺ.

الإجماع: *al-ijmā'*

Consensus. The unanimous agreement of the mujtahids.

attribute that is appropriate for a ruling and is in a situation which necessitates establishing the ruling and it demands it when viewed. A ruling has attached to it on agreed occasions, the ruling will be connected to it due to appropriateness not due to the evidence of the Shariah of it being a cause.

❖ ❖ ❖

An example of such an *al-'illa* is as we see someone giving a coin to another individual who looks poor. We will interpret this to reflect what we normally observe. It is most likely an act of charity to alleviate the suffering of the poor individual and to gain reward in the Hereafter. We can summarise this process by saying we have seen a particular quality and act, that results in the suitable conclusion and ruling of 'giving in charity'. A similar ruling has been associated with such an act, quality or circumstance on many occasions before. There are countless examples of this in the texts and through consensus, as well as personal experiences. This all makes it likely that such a quality results in a particular ruling; this quality becomes an *al-'illa* for that ruling. The increased likelihood, *aẓ-ẓann ul-ghālib*, of a matter necessitates application in the Shariah. It is worth bearing in mind that *aẓ-ẓann ul-ghālib* is only applicable in the Shariah when there is no stronger evidence available. If al-kitāb, as-sunna or al-ijmā' supply evidence then *aẓ-ẓann ul-ghālib* will be ignored. This is just like a traveller on his travels who suspects with an increased likelihood, *aẓ-ẓann ul-ghālib*, that water is in the vicinity, he is not permitted to perform *at-tayammum.* All cases that grant a choice are similar to this and based upon *aẓ-ẓann ul-ghālib*.

The ruling of al-qiyās based on an *al-'illa* determined by insight and experience is that if there is a difference highlighted between the source and target cases with respect to the quality that binds the two cases together, the al-qiyās will be invalid. This means that if another appropriate quality were identified, whilst the new quality is different to the previous one, it would result in the source case al-qiyās being invalid as a source, as it was based on a different quality. This is because whilst the second quality identified is associated with a ruling, the *aẓ-ẓann ul-ghālib* that allowed for the first al-qiyās is now no longer due to an 'increased likelihood' because the second quality has cast doubt over the first identified quality. This would mean that the first al-qiyās is wrong.

QUICK TERMS

القياس: *al-qiyās*

Analogy. The reasoning of the learned.

العلة: *al-'illa*

The means. The method or instrument used to attain an end.

الكتاب: *al-kitāb*

The book. The inspired final word of Allah ﷻ. The Quran.

السنة: *as-sunna*

The practice. The sayings, doings and approval of the blessed Prophet ﷺ.

الإجماع: *al-ijmā'*

Consensus. The unanimous agreement of the mujtahids.

QUICK ARABIC

الظن الغالب: *aẓ-ẓann ul-ghālib*

Dominant thought. Where one thought or idea becomes more likely from a group of possibles.

التيمم: *at-tayammum*

Dry ablution. The ritual ablution performed without water.

Summarising, we can differentiate between the three types of al-qiyās through an analogy. The first type, where *al-'illa* is sourced from a text of al-kitāb or as-sunna, is like a witness who is first authenticated in integrity and impartiality. A judge would take the testimony of such a witness to be valid and treated as vital to the case. In a similar way, an *al-'illa* sourced from the text is not invalid, but of the highest calibre. The second type, where an *al-'illa* is sourced from al-ijmā', is like a witness whose impartiality is yet to be established and a judge bases a verdict upon the witness's testimony. It is only after this that over time, the witness builds in integrity. The inclusion of such a testimony is considered necessary to the case. In a similar way, an *al-'illa* sourced from al-ijmā' is necessary to act upon. The third type, where *al-'illa* is sourced from insight and experience, is like a witness with an unknown background. The judge admitting such a testimony and basing a judgement upon it, will have to be enforced. In a similar way, the third type of al-qiyās will be enacted. If later, it is discovered that the wrong quality was identified as *al-'illa* it will invalidate the previous ruling.

Text And Translation

ونظيره إذا رأينا شخصا أعطى فقيرا درهما غلب على الظن أن الإعطاء لدفع حاجة الفقير وتحصيل مصالح الثواب، إذا عرف هذا فنقول: إذا رأينا وصفا مناسبا للحكم وقد اقترن به الحكم في موضع الإجماع يغلب الظن بإضافة الحكم إلى ذلك الوصف وغلبة الظن في الشرع توجب العمل عند انعدام ما فوقها من الدليل بمنزلة المسافر إذا غلب على ظنه أن بقربه ماء لم يجز له التيمم، وعلى هذا مسائل التحري، وحكم هذا القياس أن يبطل بالفرق المناسب؛ لأن عنده يوجد مناسب سواه في صورة الحكم فلا يبقى الظن بإضافة الحكم إليه فلا يثبت الحكم به؛ لأنه كان بناء على غلبة الظن وقد بطل ذلك بالفرق، وعلى هذا كان العمل بالنوع الأول بمنزلة الحكم بالشهادة بعد تزكية الشاهد وتعديله والنوع الثاني بمنزلة الشهادة عند ظهور العدالة قبل التزكية والنوع الثالث بمنزلة شهادة المستور.

An example of it is if we see a person giving a poor man a dirham, most likely the giving is to fulfil a need of the poor man and to achieve the prospect of reward. When this is known, we will say if we see an appropriate quality of a ruling, and the ruling applies to it in places of common agreement, the most probable outcome is attaching that ruling to that quality. A most probable opinion in the Shariah necessitates enacting it when there is no superior

QUICK TERMS

القياس: *al-qiyās*

Analogy. The reasoning of the learned.

QUICK ARABIC

التيمم: *at-tayammum*

Dry ablution. The ritual ablution performed without water.

evidence. It is like a traveller when he reasonably thinks that there is water nearby, he can not perform *at-tayammum*. Based on this are all cases of choice. The ruling of this al-qiyās is that it is invalidated with an appropriate difference because he has an appropriate thing other than it in the case of the ruling. So the thought is not connected to the ruling, so the ruling will not be established with it. This is because it was based on reasonable thought and that was invalidated by this difference. Based on this, enacting the first type is like a ruling with a testimony after cross-examination and having credibility. The second type is like a testimony when the credibility becomes clear before cross-examination, and the third type is like an anonymous testimony.

❖ ❖ ❖

Summary Of Authentic al-Qiyās and Its Types

The cause of both source and target cases must be the same. The cause itself can be realised from various sources:

1. al-Kitāb: Allah Almighty says ليس عليكم ولا عليهم جناح بعدهن طوافون عليكم بعضكم على بعض
   Frequenting is the cause of annulling the need for seeking permission. So, the cause to annul is understood from al-kitāb, and applied to different cases, such as frequenting of a cat and the annulling of impurity of water.
2. as-Sunna: The Prophet ﷺ said whomsoever sleeps whilst sitting, standing, in prostration or bowing does not invalidate the ablution, as it is invalidated when certain muscles relax. So, the Hadith is the origin and source of the cause for the breaking of the ablution being loose joints and muscles. We can extend this to when sleeping whilst leaning or propped up.
3. al-Ijmā': The guardianship of a father over a minor boy is due to him being a minor. This is known by way of al-ijmā'. This is also true of a minor daughter. So, as the father is a legal administrator for the minor son, he is for the minor daughter too.

In terms of where the common cause is being matched and the ruling applied, al-qiyās is of two types:

a) Homogeneous (النوع): The transfer of the ruling is to a similar kind of case. For example, matching the case of a minor boy's guardianship to the guardianship of a minor girl. Its ruling is: لا يبطل بالفرق
   "It is not invalid with discrepancies".
   This is because the source and target have the same cause, so they must have the same ruling; even if they are different in other ways.
b) Heterogeneous (الجنس): The transfer of the ruling is intended for a case similar in genus. For example, servants entering the home without permission, the cause of which is nuisance due to frequent entering and leaving, being transferred to cats. Transferring this cause to cats' nuisance in licking and drinking water, in annulling its impurity. The cases are different and heterogeneous, except with the common cause of nuisance. Its ruling is:
   فساده بممانعة التجنيس والفرق الخاص
   "It is invalid when no commonality is established or with a major difference".

4. Reasoning and derivation: This is the linking of a particular attribute or circumstance to a ruling. For example, observing a person drop a coin in the hat of a beggar would suggest he wants to eliminate suffering and wants to gain reward for himself. This is known through reasoning and commonly understood scenarios.

4.4 Countering al-Qiyās

Following a discussion on the conditions and components of al-qiyās, we now move on to those checks and queries that al-qiyās needs to satisfy. The queries can be used to counter al-qiyās, as well as to see if a constructed al-qiyās is correct. There are eight types of queries that can be asked of al-qiyās: 1) al-Mumāna'a; 2) al-Qawl bi-mūjib il-'illa; 3) al-Qalb; 4) al-'Aks; 5) Fasād ul-waḍ'; 6) al-Farq; 7) an-Naqḍ; and 8) al-Mu'āraḍa.

Text And Translation

فصل: الأسولة المتوجهة على القياس ثمانية: الممانعة والقول بموجب العلة والقلب والعكس وفساد الوضع والفرق والنقض والمعارضة

Chapter: There are eight queries al-qiyās is subjected to: al-mumāna'a, al-qawl bi mūjib il-'illa, al-qalb, al-'aks, fasād ul-waḍ', al-farq, an-naqḍ and al-mu'āraḍa.

❖❖❖

The first query is al-mumāna'a, refusal. This is when the enquirer refuses to accept all or some parts of the proposed al-qiyās. It has two types: to refuse a quality, and secondly to refuse the ruling. The first is for the enquirer to object that the quality that is proposed as *al-'illa* is not accepted as *al-'illa*, rather the true *al-'illa* is another quality. The latter is for the enquirer to accept the validity of the proposed quality but to object to the proposed ruling. The true ruling in the enquirer's opinion is different.

An example of a refusal of the quality is that the ash-Shawāfi' maintain that the *al-'illa* and cause of ṣadaqat ul-fiṭr is al-Fiṭr, the idea that the one who has witnessed sunset of the last day of the month of Ramadan. This would imply that if one witnessed the night of Eid ul-Fiṭr for the briefest of moments and then passed away, ṣadaqat ul-fiṭr would need to be paid posthumously. This is because *al-'illa* of al-Fiṭr was present and thus the duty to pay became necessary. After a duty becomes necessary, it is not fulfilled, except by undertaking it. The Aḥnāf disagree with this. The disagreement stems from refusal of the quality. The ascribed *al-'illa* for ṣadaqat ul-fiṭr is not what is mentioned but it is responsibility, the idea that the one who is the figurehead and responsible for other individuals needs to pay ṣadaqat ul-fiṭr for all those

QUICK TERMS

القياس: *al-qiyās*

Analogy. The reasoning of the learned.

العلة: *al-'illa*

The means. The method or instrument used to attain an end.

QUICK ARABIC

صدقة الفطر: *ṣadaqat ul-fiṭr*

Alms of fast breaking. Alms given on the conclusion of the month of Ramadan.

الفطر: *al-fiṭr*

Fast breaking. The conclusion of the continuous fasting of the month of Ramadan.

under their responsibility. This would imply that should someone pass away before the passing of that night and the rising of the Sun of Eid day, there would be no due payment on their behalf. Furthermore, if a child was to be born or a non-believer to become a Muslim, on that night, a payment would be due.

A second example of refusal of the quality is that after the passing of a whole year with excess wealth, zakah will be due. However, the Aḥnāf maintain that if the wealth was to be destroyed, the duty of giving zakah will be muted. ash-Shawāfi' disagree with this, saying the duty remains because its cause and *al-'illa* is established once an amount of zakah became payable. It is just like any other debt, because the cause in a debt is that it is necessary to be repaid and its ruling is that it remains obligatory until it is fulfilled. Whether the wealth itself perishes or not, the payment needs to be made once it is due. The Aḥnāf respond saying that the quality mentioned as the *al-'illa* is not accepted as the *al-'illa*. The duty to pay the zakah, *adā uz-zakah*, is the cause that keeps it necessary to be paid. So, if the wealth was to perish, there is no way to pay zakah as *al-adā* from it. As there is no necessity to fulfil the obligation after the wealth has perished, the cause is no longer present and consequently the ruling is annulled too.

Text And Translation

أما الممانعة فنوعان: أحدهما منع الوصف والثاني منع الحكم، ومثاله في قولهم: صدقة الفطر وجبت بالفطر فلا تسقط بموته ليلة الفطر، قلنا: لا نسلم وجوبها بالفطر بل عندنا تجب برأس يمونه ويلي عليه، وكذلك إذا قيل: قدر الزكاة واجب في الذمة فلا يسقط بهلاك النصاب كالدين، قلنا: لا نسلم أن قدر الزكاة واجب في الذمة بل أداؤه واجب

As for al-mumāna'a it is of two types: the first is refusal of a quality, and the second is refusal of the ruling. An example of it is in their saying: the offering of al-fiṭr is necessary due to al-fiṭr, and so will not be annulled by his death on the night of al-Fitr. We replied: we do not accept that it is necessary due to al-fiṭr, rather according to us it is necessary due to responsibility over an individual and guardianship. Similarly, when it is said: the amount of zakah necessary from one's account will not be nullified by losing the minimum threshold, just like debt. We said: we do not accept that the amount of zakah is necessary from one's account, rather handing it over is necessary.

QUICK TERMS

الأدآء: *al-adā*

Delivery. To observe a duty as per the requirement.

QUICK ARABIC

أدآء الزكاة: *adā uz-zakāh*

Delivery of zakah. To give a portion of wealth as necessary alms to the needy.

❖ ❖ ❖

An example of the second type of al-mumāna'a, refusal to accept the ruling, is found in the claim that an amount of zakah is payable even after the minimum threshold has been destroyed, just as a debt must be paid back when the creditor demands for it to be returned. This obligation cannot be fulfilled except by paying up. In response, the Aḥnāf refuse to accept that the repayment of the debt is necessary. This means that upon a demand from the creditor, it is not considered necessary for the debtor to pay anything; rather we say that *at-takhliya* is necessary. This means that the debtor should not be an obstacle between the creditor and his wealth. In this example 'paying the debt' was touted as the ruling, but we refused this and said that *at-takhliya* is the ruling. This makes this case an example of al-mumāna'a of the ruling.

A second example of al-mumāna'a from accepting the ruling is that according to ash-Shawāfi' it is sunna to wipe the head thrice in ablution. They support this by saying wiping the head is a major component of the ablution just like washing of the face, arms and feet. So, just as it is sunna to wash these three parts thrice, it is sunna to wipe the head thrice too. Querying this al-qiyās with al-mumāna'a in the ruling, the Aḥnāf say that we do not accept that it is sunna to wash the three parts thrice or for any number of times, rather the sunna is to prolong and complete the obligation, and that is the true purpose of all *as-sunan*. The completion of the obligation is achieved by prolonging the act of the obligation in the same location, as the completion of *al-qiyām* is achieved by lengthening the duration of recitation. Lengthening the recitation will prolong the obligatory *al-qiyām* and thus the required amount of recitation will be achieved by lengthening the time spent on recitation. However, when washing in ablution, it is not possible to prolong and lengthen the obligation except through repetition. This is because it is sunna to prolong the obligatory act in the rightful place of the obligation. The obligation to wash the face is accomplished by washing the entire face. Now, to conduct the sunna one has to prolong the act in the same place, but the place has already been covered. Now the only way to prolong it is to repeat washing the same area a second and third time. If one proposes to wash beyond the face to fulfil the sunna it will not be a sunna because by definition the sunna is to prolong the obligatory act in the very same place the obligatory act took place. Thus, the only way in which prolonging the act can occur is to repeat the act. It is for this reason that

QUICK ARABIC

التخلية: *at-takhliya*

To release. To free something from restraint, and to let it go.

السنن: *as-sunan*

Practices. The sayings, doings and approvals of the blessed Prophet ﷺ.

القيام: *al-qiyām*

Standing. The position of standing upright in prayer with the hands held right over left below the navel.

washing the parts in ablution thrice is considered the sunna and not because washing three times in itself is a sunna.

There is a similar narrative for the wiping of the head, in that the sunna is to prolong the obligatory wiping in the place of the wiping, the head. Now, as only a quarter of the head is obligatory to wipe, the sunna is complete by prolonging this wiping act over all the whole of the head. The obligation is thus fulfilled by wiping a quarter and the sunna is to extend the wiping to cover the whole of the head. There is no need to repeat any separate act to fulfil the sunna, as was the case on the parts that were washed during the ablution.

A third example of al-mumāna'a from accepting the ruling is that if one traded foodstuff for foodstuff, for instance wheat for wheat, the ash-Shawāfi' hold that both items must exchange hands and possession secured before the transaction can be deemed complete. The Aḥnāf maintain that this condition of taking possession is not necessary. al-Qiyās presented as evidence by the ash-Shawāfi' is that even according to the Aḥnāf when a transaction involves the exchange of money with money, possession is vital, so in a similar manner the foodstuff for foodstuff transaction will also require an exchange in possession. The Aḥnāf refuse this al-qiyās by saying that a transaction involving money on both sides does not require 'possession' as *al-'illa*, rather to avoid a transaction of *an-nasīa* both the merchandise and price must be specified; that is the condition. As money is not specified except after possession has occurred, we have as a consequence stated possession as the condition for the transaction. As for the foodstuff, it can be determined by simply pointing at it and as the item will be thus specified, taking possession of it is not required.

Text And Translation

ولئن قال: الواجب أداؤه فلا يسقط بالهلاك كالدين بعد المطالبة، قلنا: لا نسلم أنّ الأداء واجب في صورة الدين بل حرم المنع حتى يخرج عن العهدة بالتخلية وهذا من قبيل منع الحكم، وكذلك إذا قال: المسح ركن في باب الوضوء فليسن تثليثه كالغسل، قلنا: لا نسلم أن التثليث مسنون في الغسل بل إطالة الفعل في محل الفرض زيادة على المفروض كإطالة القيام والقراءة في باب الصلاة غير أن الإطالة في باب الغسل لا يتصور إلا بالتكرار لاستيعاب الفعل للمحل، وبمثله نقول في باب المسح: بأن الإطالة مسنون بطريق الاستيعاب، وكذلك يقال: التقابض في بيع الطعام بالطعام شرط كالنقود قلنا:

QUICK TERMS

القياس: *al-qiyās*

Analogy. The reasoning of the learned.

العلة: *al-'illa*

The means. The method or instrument used to attain an end.

QUICK ARABIC

النسيئة: *an-nasīa*

Postponement. An increase on growth due to postponement in repaying a loan.

لا نسلم أن التقابض شرط في باب النقود بل الشرط تعيينها كيلا يكون بيع النسئة بالنسئة غير أن النقود لا تتعين إلا بالقبض عندنا

If it is said: handing it over is necessary so it will not be nullified due to loss, just like a loan once recalled; we will reply, we do not accept that handing over is necessary in the case of debt, rather withholding it is forbidden, such that obligations will be fulfilled by handing it over. This is from the cases of refusal of the ruling. Similarly, if one said: wiping is fundamental in the chapter of ablution so it is sunna to repeat it thrice like washing; we will reply, we do not accept that repeating it thrice is sunna in washing. Rather it is prolonging the act in the necessary place, longer than the minimum requirement, just like prolonging the standing or recitation in the chapter of salah. Except, prolonging in the case of washing is not possible without repetition as the act entirely covers the place. Just like it we say in the chapter of wiping that prolonging is sunna by entirely encompassing. Similarly, it is said: possessional exchange is a condition in the trade of foodstuff with foodstuff, just like money. We said: we do not accept that possessional exchange is a condition in the chapter of money. Rather the condition is specifying it so that it is not a credit with credit trade, except that money is not specified without taking possession according to us.

❖❖❖

The second query is al-qawl bi-mūjib il-'illa. This is that the enquirer accepts the *al-'illa* but does not accept its outcome nor the consequent ruling. al-Qiyās in the enquirer's opinion contains the correct *al-'illa* but he or she believes the *al-ma'lūl*, outcome, and *al-ḥukm*, ruling, to be different to the one stated. An example of this is that the elbows are to be washed in the ablution just as the rest of the forearms and hands are to be washed. Imam Zufar رحمه الله disagrees. He says that this is because the elbow is a boundary and the boundary is not considered a part of the enclosure. The enclosure in this case is the washed part of the arm and the boundary, the elbow, is thus not a part of it. It therefore falls outside the area to be washed. The response to this is that we accept that the elbow forms the boundary, but it is a boundary for the unwashed part of the arm and not for the washed area. This is because the elbow forms a *ghāyat ul-isqāṭ*, a limiting boundary, and limiting boundaries are included within the enclosure. As it is within the enclosure it must also be washed with the rest of the area of the arm that is washed. In this example both

QUICK TERMS

العلة: *al-'illa*

The means. The method or instrument used to attain an end.

المعلول: *al-ma'lūl*

The effect. The outcome and end with respect to the method and instrument used.

الحكم: *al-ḥukm*

The ruling. An authentic decision of the Shariah regarding the level of importance of an act, whether an instruction or a prohibition.

QUICK ARABIC

غاية الإسقاط: *ghāyat ul-isqāṭ*

Limiting boundary. The limit at which the ruling is to cease. The limit is included in the ruling.

parties accept *al-'illa* to be the elbow as a boundary of the washing. They disagree whether it is a boundary of the washed area or the area that the washing is limited to. As an inevitable consequence they disagree on the ruling too, whether the boundary is to be washed or not.

Another example is whether a fast of Ramadan will be valid with an unqualified intention to fast or by a specific intention to fast for Ramadan. The Aḥnāf say just an intention to fast is sufficient and a specific intention is not required for the one fasting. The ash-Shawāfi' say that a specific intention is required because the fast of Ramadan is compulsory and it is just as the make up fast of a previous Ramadan is compulsory. When all agree that the make up fast for a missed fast of Ramadan requires a specific intention, then al-qiyās dictates that so does the fast of the current Ramadan. We respond by saying that we accept the stated *al-'illa* that the fast of the current Ramadan requires specification in its intention, however, we do not accept that a person needs to specify it. This is because the Shariah has already specified the current Ramadan for fasting and so does not require the person's intention of specifying it. The Shariah has specified the fast for Ramadan because the blessed Messenger of Allah ﷺ said: "When the month of Sha'bān has passed there is no fast except that of Ramadan." When the Shariah has specified it, there is no need for the worshipper to specify it.

If the ash-Shawāfi' were to counter this by saying that we formed al-qiyās of the fast of Ramadan upon the case of the missed fast of Ramadan. The missed fast of Ramadan requires a worshipper to intend the fast, and it follows that the fast of Ramadan will require the same. So just as the missed fast of Ramadan is invalid without a specific intention, the fast of Ramadan is also invalid without a specific intention. We would respond by saying that the worshipper is required to make an intention for the missed fast of Ramadan because there is no specified time to fast for it by the Shariah. As for the fast of Ramadan, the Shariah has specified a time and so the worshipper is not required to make an intention.

Text And Translation

وأما القول بموجب العلة فهو تسليم كون الوصف علة وبيانه أن معلولها غير ما ادعاه المعلل، ومثاله المرفق حد في باب الوضوء فلا يدخل تحت الغسل؛ لأن الحد لا يدخل في المحدود، قلنا: المرفق حد

حديث

لقوله ﷺ قال: إذا انسلخ شعبان فلا صوم إلا رمضان.

عليه الصلاة والسلام

(البناية في شرح الهداية: ج 3: كتاب الصوم: ص 608)

QUICK TERMS

القياس: *al-qiyās*

Analogy. The reasoning of the learned.

القضاء: *al-qaḍā*

To settle. To settle and make up a missed obligatory observance.

الساقط فلا يدخل تحت حكم الساقط؛ لأن الحد لا يدخل في المحدود، وكذلك يقال: صوم رمضان صوم فرض فلا يجوز بدون التعيين كالقضاء، قلنا: صوم الفرض لا يجوز بدون التعيين إلا أنه وجد التعيين هاهنا من جهة الشرع، ولئن قال: صوم رمضان لا يجوز بدون التعيين من العبد كالقضاء، قلنا: لا يجوز القضاء بدون التعيين إلا أن التعيين لم يثبت من جهة الشرع في القضاء فلذلك يشترط تعيين العبد وهنا وجد التعيين من جهة الشرع فلا يشترط تعيين العبد

As for qawl bi-mūjib il-illa, it is accepting an attribute as an effective cause. Its explanation is that the effect of it is other than what is claimed by the proposer. An example of it is that the elbow is a boundary in the chapter of ablution so it is not included in the washing, as a boundary is not included in the enclosed. We say: the elbow is the boundary for the exclusion so it will not be included in the ruling of the excluded, as the boundary is not part of the enclosed. Similarly, it is said: the fasting of Ramadan is compulsory so it is not permitted without specifying, just like al-qaḍā. We say: the compulsory fast is not permitted without specifying except that specification is present here from the Shariah. If it is countered: fasting for Ramadan is not permitted without specification from the subject like al-qaḍā. We reply: al-qaḍā is not permitted without specification except that specification is not found from the Shariah in al-qaḍā, therefore specification is a condition for the subject; here, there is a specification from the Shariah so the subject's specification is not a condition.

❖❖❖

The third query is al-qalb, reversal. It has two types: the first is to claim that the *al-'illa* stated in the al-qiyās is actually the ruling, and that which is stated as the ruling, *al-ḥukm*, is in actual fact the *al-'illa*. The second type is to claim that the *al-'illa* stated in al-qiyās for a particular ruling is actually the *al-'illa* for the exact opposite of that ruling. More details on this type will follow.

An example of the first type is that the ash-Shawāfi' say that *ar-ribā* in large quantities of foodstuff is forbidden, and it should follow by al-qiyās that it is unlawful in small quantities too, because gold and silver, in large and small amounts, are subject to the laws of *ar-ribā*. The *al-'illa* in foodstuff is being edible, *aṭ-ṭa'm*, and the *al-'illa* in gold and silver is value, *ath-thamanīya.* Both items have the common factor of being items of growth. When small quantities of foodstuff are subject to *ar-ribā*, it follows that a handful of grain cannot be

QUICK TERMS

القياس: *al-qiyās*

Analogy. The reasoning of the learned.

العلة: *al-'illa*

The means. The method or instrument used to attain an end.

الحكم: *al-ḥukm*

The ruling. An authentic decision of the Shariah regarding the level of importance of an act, whether an instruction or a prohibition.

QUICK ARABIC

الربا: *ar-ribā*

Usury. Excess to the legal standard permitted in a contract of exchange.

الطعم: *aṭ-ṭa'm*

Edibility/taste. To be fit to be eaten as food.

الثمنية: *ath-thamanīya*

Value. Monetary and material worth relative to demand.

sold for two handfuls. The Aḥnāf disagree that the *al-'illa* is unlawfulness of a large quantity and the *al-ma'lūl* and outcome is unlawfulness of the smaller quantity. The matter is the opposite, in that unlawfulness due to *ar-ribā* in a small quantity is the cause for unlawfulness in a large quantity. A small quantity in foodstuff is half of one *aṣ-ṣā'*, 1.1 kg, as this was the least denomination for measurement available. Any foodstuff less in weight than half of one *aṣ-ṣā'* that is sold for a similar genus of foodstuff is not subject to *ar-ribā* laws and is not required to be of equal weight. When equality is not a requirement in low quantities, then exchanging one handful of a grain for two handfuls will be permitted.

The second example concerns a murderer who takes sanctuary in the sacred lands of al-Ḥaram. The ash-Shawāfi' say that taking al-qiṣāṣ in al-Ḥaram is permitted and the Aḥnāf say it is not and such a person will be coerced into leaving the area and then the laws will be applied. If one was to severe the hand of another and then seek refuge in al-Ḥaram, then both parties agree that al-qiṣāṣ will be carried out in al-Ḥaram. The ash-Shawāfi' evidence their position by saying that sanctity of life dictates that each individual limb is sanctified. This means the impermissibility of taking the life of an individual in al-Ḥaram is the *al-'illa* and the impermissibility of severing the hand of an individual in al-Ḥaram is *al-ma'lūl* and the outcome. This is exactly as it is impermissible to hunt down an animal in al-Ḥaram just as it is unlawful to break any limb of an animal therein. When it is accepted that the hand of a criminal can be severed in al-Ḥaram, it follows that the criminal's life can be taken there too. Our response to this is that the reverse is true. The sanctity of each limb dictates that there is sanctity in the life of the individual. This means that the impermissibility of severing a limb is *al-'illa* and the taking of life is *al-ma'lūl*, just as it is unlawful to damage the limb of an animal in al-Ḥaram, it is unlawful to kill the animal therein.

al-Qiyās is to identify a particular *al-'illa* and in this al-qiyās the *al-'illa* provided by the claimant is rejected by reversal. In fact, the reversal means that the *al-'illa* is shown to be *al-ma'lūl*, so it means that the same thing is now *al-'illa* and *al-ma'lūl*. This is an impossible, so it follows that the al-qiyās is rejected.

The second type of al-qalb is that the claimant connects an *al-'illa* to a ruling but the enquirer associates the same *al-'illa* to the opposite of that ruling. At first the al-qiyās was a piece of evidence for the claimant but after the

QUICK TERMS

المعلول: *al-ma'lūl*

The effect. The outcome and end with respect to the method and instrument used.

QUICK ARABIC

الصاع: *aṣ-ṣā'*

A cubic measure. An ancient measure which equates to approximately 2.035kg.

الحرم: *al-ḥaram*

The sacred land. A sacred area around the blessed Ka'ba, where certain acts are unlawful.

القصاص: *al-qiṣāṣ*

Retaliation. The route afforded to the next of kin in the case of murder and to the afflicted in loss short of murder.

enquirer's query it now stands as evidence in favour of the opposition. An example of this is ash-Shawāfi' say that both the fast of the current Ramadan and the missed fast of a previous Ramadan are compulsory. As a specific intention is required for a missed fast, it is also required for the current fast of Ramadan. In this version the compulsory nature of both fasts is *al-'illa* for being specific in naming the fast in the intention as that is the agreed upon ruling in the missed fasts. The Aḥnāf retort that the *al-'illa* for specifying the intention in the fast of Ramadan is not because the fast is compulsory, rather it is because the fast is compulsory that you do not need to specify it. We elaborate by saying that because the fast of Ramadan is compulsory it does not need to be specified as the Shariah has already specified it. The al-qiyās started by saying the compulsory nature of the fast means it needs to be specified, but it was reversed, al-qalb, to say that the compulsory nature of the fast means it does not need to be specified.

Text And Translation

وأما القلب فنوعان: أحدهما أن يجعل ما جعله المعلل علة للحكم معلولا لذلك الحكم، ومثاله كقول الشافعية جريان الربا في الكثير يوجب جريانه في القليل كالأثمان فيحرم بيع الحفنة من الطعام بالحفنتين منه، قلنا: لا بل جريان الربا في القليل يوجب جريانه في الكثير كالأثمان، وكذلك في مسألة الملتجئ بالحرم حرمة إتلاف النفس يوجب حرمة إتلاف الطرف كالصيد، قلنا: بل حرمة إتلاف الطرف يوجب حرمة إتلاف النفس كالصيد فإذا جعلت علته معلولة لذلك الحكم لا تبقى علة له لاستحالة أن يكون الشيء الواحد علة للشيء ومعلولا له. والنوع الثاني من القلب أن يجعل السائل ما جعله المعلل علةً لما ادعاه من الحكم علة لضد ذلك الحكم فيصير حجة للسائل بعد إن كان حجة للمعلل، مثاله صوم رمضان صوم فرض فيشترط التعيين له كالقضاء، قلنا: لما كان الصوم فرضا لا يشترط التعيين له بعد ما تعين اليوم له كالقضاء

As for al-qalb, it is of two types: the first is to make what the proposer made the cause into the effect in the same case. An example of it is like the statement of ash-Shāfa'īya that usury applicable in large quantities necessitates it in small quantities, like in commodities. So it is forbidden to purchase a handful of foodstuff for two handfuls of it. We say: rather, that usury applicable in small quantities is applicable to large quantities like in commodities. Similar is the case of the one seeking refuge in al-Ḥaram; as it is prohibited to kill a person, it is forbidden to amputate, like hunting. We say: prohibition of amputation necessitates the prohibition of killing, like hunting. So when the cause has been made into the effect for the same case, it will no longer be the cause as it is impossible for the same thing to be the cause and effect. The second type of al-qalb is that the inquirer makes that which the proposer made the cause of the claimed ruling, into the cause for the opposite of that ruling. So it becomes a piece of evidence for the inquirer after it was evidence for the proposer. An example of it is that the fast of Ramadan is compulsory so it is necessary to specify it like al-qaḍā. We say: as the fast was compulsory it is not a condition to specify it after a day is already specified for it, like al-qaḍā.

❖ ❖ ❖

The fourth query is al-'aks. It is a query that involves the enquirer presenting the same source in the al-qiyās in a manner that compels the proposer to admit there is a crucial difference between the source and the target cases. If there is a vital difference between the source and the target the al-qiyās no longer remains valid. For example, the ash-Shawāfi' say that jewellery that is made for personal use is not subject to the payment of zakah because it is similar to personal items of clothing. Thus, they formulate a ruling of non-inclusion of personal jewellery in calculations of zakah based on personal items of clothing, which are unanimously exempt from zakah. The Aḥnāf respond by saying if jewellery is likened to personal clothing then there should be no zakah payable on men's personal jewellery too, as men's personal clothing is not subject to zakah either. However, the ash-Shawāfi' do not exclude men's jewellery from zakah. This response compels them to state that there is a difference between men's jewellery and women's jewellery. This is despite all jewellery being jewellery, which rises as well as decreases in value. Nevertheless, ash-Shawāfi' say the use of jewellery for men is forbidden and so their claim to jewellery for 'personal use' is not established. As jewellery for women is lawful, in their case there is such a thing as jewellery for personal use. They are compelled to alter their al-qiyās so it follows that women's personal clothes are exempt from zakah because they are for personal use and so women's jewellery that is for personal use is also not subject to zakah. The initial al-qiyās will not hold true for men's jewellery, so the enquirer has subjected it to al-'aks.

QUICK TERMS

القضاء: *al-qaḍā*

To settle. To settle and make up a missed obligatory observance.

القياس: *al-qiyās*

Analogy. The reasoning of the learned.

QUICK ARABIC

الحرم: *al-ḥaram*

The sacred land. A sacred area around the blessed Ka'ba, where certain acts are unlawful.

وأما العكس فنعني به: أن يتمسك السائل بأصل المعلل على وجه يكون المعلل مضطرا إلى وجه المفارقة بين الأصل والفرع، ومثاله الحلي أعدت للابتذال فلا يجب فيها الزكاة كثياب البذلة، قلنا: لو كان الحلي بمنزلة الثياب فلا تجب الزكاة في حلي الرجال كثياب البذلة

As for al-'aks, we mean by it that the inquirer adheres to the principle of the proposer in a manner that the proposer is compelled to the difference between the source and target case. An example of it is that jewellery is made to be worn so zakah is not necessary on it, like clothes for use. We say: if jewellery was in place of clothes, zakah would not be necessary for men's jewellery, like the clothes for use.

❖ ❖ ❖

The fifth query is fasād ul-waḍ'. It occurs when the proposer makes an attribute into an *al-'illa* that is inappropriate for the ruling. The enquirer highlights the inappropriate placing of the proposed al-qiyās and thus subjects it to fasād ul-waḍ'. For example, a couple are at first non-believers and then one of them embraces Islam. The al-qiyās concerns the status and validity of their marriage. The ash-Shawāfi' say that the acceptance of Islam of one of the couple will invalidate their marriage and separation needs to occur immediately. This is because when one of them has embraced Islam, there is a difference of religion in the marriage. Had the marriage been conducted before the change of religion the matter would be different, but as the marriage has now been subjected to this major difference between the spouses, it has annulled the marriage. It is just as when one spouse leaves the fold of Islam, may Allah ﷻ protect us; the marriage is annulled immediately. This al-qiyās means acceptance of Islam results in the breakup of marriage. The Aḥnāf maintain that only when the partner is given time to consider embracing too, that a ruling will be made; if the partner embraces Islam the marriage continues, and if the partner refuses, the marriage is annulled. This is because Islam protects rights and institutions such as marriage. The extent of this is that once someone embraces Islam, even in non-Muslim lands, their honour and wealth is protected. It is not appropriate to consider Islam as the cause of the destruction of one's marriage. Rather, a more sound and appropriate reason for the breaking of the marriage is the

QUICK TERMS

القياس: *al-qiyās*

Analogy. The reasoning of the learned.

العلة: *al-'illa*

The means. The method or instrument used to attain an end.

'refusal to embrace Islam'. This is a factor found in the spouse and will be established after the spouse is presented with the opportunity to accept.

Similarly, if one is able to wed a free-woman, it is not lawful for him to marry a slave according to the ash-Shawāfi', the Aḥnāf maintain that it is permitted. The ash-Shawāfi' liken the matter of the financially-able freeman marrying a free-woman to one who was previously married to a free-woman, as such a person is not permitted to marry a slave. The Aḥnāf respond by saying that for a man to be described as 'financially-able' and 'freeman' is inappropriate as an *al-'illa* to 'not be permitted to marry'. It is contradicting and not an appropriate connection. If one is able and free, it is reason enough to marry freely. This highlights the inappropriateness of the place, fasād ul-waḍ'.

Text And Translation

وأما فساد الوضع فالمراد به أن يجعل العلة وصفا لا يليق بذلك الحكم، مثاله في قولهم في إسلام أحد الزوجين: اختلاف الدين طرأ على النكاح فيفسده كارتداد أحد الزوجين فإنه جعل الإسلام علة لزوال الملك، قلنا: الإسلام عهد عاصما للملك فلا يكون مؤثرا في زوال الملك، وكذلك في مسئلة طول الحرة إنه حر قادر على النكاح فلا يجوز له الأمة كما لو كانت تحته حرة، قلنا: وصف كونه حرا قادرا يقتضي جواز النكاح فلا يكون مؤثرا في عدم الجواز

As for fasād ul-waḍ', what is meant by it is to make the cause an attribute that is not suited to that ruling. An example of it is what they say of the embracing of Islam of a spouse: the marriage is subject to difference of religion so it is nullified, like the apostasy of a spouse. That is making Islam the cause for the removal of ownership. We say: Islam is a state that protects ownership so it can not be effective in removing ownership. Similarly, in the case of having the capacity to marry a free-woman, he is a free and able man to marry. So a salve-girl is not permitted for him, just like if he had a free-woman. We say: the attributes of being free and able necessitate the permissibility of marriage, so they can not be effective in prohibiting.

❖ ❖ ❖

The sixth query is al-farq. It is when a significant difference can be found between the elements of the al-qiyās. It was discussed in detail in the discussion about the two different types of al-qiyās, *tajnīs ul-'illa*. [4.3.1 Types of Authentic al-Qiyās, page 397]

❖ ❖ ❖

The seventh query is an-naqḍ. It is when despite the presence of *al-'illa* of the presented case in another case, the ruling is still not realised. An example of this is that both *ablution* and *at-tayammum* are forms of purification, and *at-tayammum* requires an intention for it to be valid. This would imply that *ablution* also requires an intention. The Aḥnāf query this using an-naqḍ whereby washing impure clothes and dishes is also purification, but there is agreement that no intention is required in this purification. This means that despite the presence of the cause of purification, impurity, the ruling that an intention is required was not required to achieve the outcome.

Text And Translation

وأما النقض فمثل ما يقال: الوضوء طهارة فيشترط له النية كالتيمم، قلنا: ينقض بغسل الثوب والإناء

As for an-naqḍ, it is like what is said: ablution is purity so making an intention is a condition for it, like *at-tayammum*. We say: it is inapplicable to washing clothes or utensils.

❖ ❖ ❖

The eighth and final query is al-mu'āraḍa. It is reframing the presented quality that a claimant claims is the *al-'illa* in a manner that rather than supporting the claimant's position, it works as evidence against that position. An example of this is the claim of ash-Shawāfi' that wiping the head in ablution is a vital component, *ar-rukn*. All other vital components are washed thrice, so the wiping of the head should be undertaken thrice too. The query of al-mu'āraḍa by the Aḥnāf upon this is that wiping the head is a vital component just like wiping over the leather socks and wiping in *at-tayammum*. Just as there is no repeated wiping over the leather socks or in *at-tayammum,* there is also no repetition in wiping the head in ablution. The element, being a vital component, presented as the cause for repeating something thrice, is the very element presented as the reason not to repeat something at all. This is al-mu'āraḍa.

QUICK TERMS

العلة: *al-'illa*

The means. The method or instrument used to attain an end.

QUICK ARABIC

الركن: *ar-rukn*

Chief element. An essential and vital part, the absence of which would undermine the item.

التيمم: *at-tayammum*

Dry ablution. The ritual ablution performed without water.

وأما المعارضة فمثل ما يقال: المسح ركن في الوضوء فليسن تثليثه كالغسل، قلنا: المسح ركن فلا يسن تثليثه كمسح الخف والتيمم.

As for al-mu'ārada, it is like what is said: wiping is a an essential part of ablution so it is sunna to perform it thrice, like washing. We say: wiping is an essential part so it is not a sunna to perform it thrice like the wiping of the leather sock or *at-tayammum*.

❖ ❖ ❖

Summary Of Countering al-Qiyās

There are eight types of queries and checks that can be asked of al-qiyās:

1) al-Mumāna'a, Refusal; when the enquirer refuses to accept all or some parts of the proposed al-qiyās. It can be a refusal of a quality or of the ruling.

Example (Refusal of quality): The offering of al-fiṭr is necessary due to al-Fiṭr, and so will not be annulled by his death on the night of al-Fiṭr. Reply: It is not necessarily due to al-Fiṭr, rather it is due to responsibility over an individual and guardianship.

Example (Refusal of ruling): Handing zakah over is necessary so it will be nullified due to loss, just like a loan once it is recalled by the lender. Reply: handing it over is not necessary in the case of debt, rather withholding it is forbidden.

2) al-Qawl bi-mūjib il-'illa, Objection to the outcome of the cause; the enquirer accepts *al-'illa* but does not accept its effect nor the consequent ruling.

Example: The elbow is a boundary in the chapter of ablution so it is not included in the washing, as a boundary is not included in the enclosed. Reply: The elbow is the boundary for the exclusion so it will not be included in the ruling of the excluded.

3) al-Qalb, Reversal; to claim that *al-'illa* is actually the ruling, and *al-ḥukm* is actually *al-'illa.* Or the *al-'illa* is actually the *al-'illa* for the opposite of the stated ruling.

Example (*al-'illa* is *al-ḥukm*): The usury applicable in large quantities necessitates it in small quantities, like in commodities. Reply: Usury applicable in small quantities is applicable to large quantities, like in commodities.

Example (*al-'illa* cause of the opposite): The fast of Ramadan is compulsory so it is necessary to specify it like al-qaḍā. Reply: Not a condition to specify it after a day is already specified for it, like al-qaḍā.

4) al-'Aks, Counter; presenting the source such that the proposer is compelled to admit there is a crucial difference between the source and the target cases.

(...continued)

Summary Of Countering al-Qiyās (continued)

Example: Jewellery is made to be worn so zakah is not necessary on it, like clothes for personal use. Reply: If jewellery is like clothes, zakah would not be necessary for men's jewellery.

5) Fasād ul-waḍ', Misplacement; when the proposer makes an attribute into *al-'illa* that is inappropriate for the stated ruling.

Example: Embracing Islam of a spouse nullifies marriage, like the apostasy of a spouse. Reply: Islam protects ownership so will not remove ownership. Refusal of the other spouse is actual cause.

6) al-Farq, Difference; when a significant difference can be found between the elements of the al-qiyās. Example: Authority to administer financial affairs of a minor allows authority to administer personal matters of the minor. Reply: Authority to administer wealth is superior and more pressing than authority to administer personal affairs.

7) an-Naqḍ; when despite the presence of *al-'illa* the ruling is still not realised in another case.

Example: Ablution is purity so making an intention is a condition for it, like in *at-tayammum*. Reply: it is inapplicable to washing clothes or utensils, when purity is sought.

8) al-Mu'āraḍa, Reframing. It is reframing the presented quality that a claimant claims is the *al-'illa* in a manner that rather than supporting the claimant's position, it works as evidence against that position.

Example: Wiping is an essential part of ablution so it is sunna to perform it thrice, like washing. Reply: Wiping is an essential part so it is not a sunna to perform it thrice like the wiping of the leather sock or in *at-tayammum*.

al-Aḥkām

PART 5

5.0 Rulings

After concluding the four sources of rulings, from Parts 1 to 4, there are a few discussions regarding rulings, *al-aḥkām*, that need to be considered. This part on *al-aḥkām* first looks at three factors connected to a ruling, 1) *as-sabab*; 2) *al-'illa*; and 3) *a<u>sh</u>-<u>sh</u>arṭ*. The factor that is not an integral part of the ruling's existence but is effective in bringing about the ruling is called *al-'illa*. If a factor is ineffective in the ruling's existence but enables it, it is called *as-sabab*. If it is not vital to the ruling's existence or an enabler but the ruling is still dependent upon it is called *a<u>sh</u>-<u>sh</u>arṭ*. After introducing these elements with some revealing examples, the relationships between these elements are discussed. A discussion on the enablers of some legal rulings then follow the introductory discussions, with a particular focus on time as an enabler of salah. This chapter is followed by those elements that prevent and impede the establishment of a ruling. A chapter is included on the categories of rulings in worship, which is followed by highlighting rulings that may carry a degree of leniency in some circumstances. The part is concluded with a chapter on some methods adopted in producing rulings that have no real grounding in the Shariah, and are thus void and rejected.

❖ ❖ ❖

QUICK TERMS

الأحكام: *al-aḥkām*

Rulings. Decisions of the Shariah based on valid evidence.

السبب: *as-sabab*

The channel. The route and way in which the means attains an end.

العلة: *al-'illa*

The means. The method or instrument used to attain an end.

الشرط: *a<u>sh</u>-<u>sh</u>arṭ*

Condition. A required circumstance to enable performance of a duty.

5.1 *as-sabab, al-'illa* and *a<u>sh</u>-<u>Sh</u>arṭ*

A ruling of the Shariah is connected to its *as-sabab*, established with its *al-'illa* and present with its *a<u>sh</u>-<u>sh</u>arṭ*. *as-sabab* is a pathway that requires a means to lead to a particular point. For example, a path is like *as-sabab* that allows a person to reach a destination by the means of walking. This makes the pathway *as-sabab*, as it is the way that led to the destination. Similarly, a rope is the way that a bucket is lowered to collect water from a well, and so the rope is *as-sabab*. Everything that is the way and uses a means to arrive at a ruling will be called *as-sabab*. *al-'illa* is the means. So, continuing with the previous analogies, the walking and the bucket will be the means that were used to reach the destination and fetch the water respectively.

Another clear example showing *as-sabab* is the open gate to a stable, or the open door of a cage or the open chains of a slave. These are all *as-sabab* that lead to the escape of the beast, bird and prisoner. The escape of the animal was due to the bolting of the animal, this is *al-'illa* of the escape and the open gate is *as-sabab*. All rulings are directly associated with their *al-'illa* and not *as-sabab*, therefore the loss of an animal will not be compensated for by the one who left the gate open. The underlying reason the animal bolted was found within the animal, and not the open gate, the open gate was merely *as-sabab*.

Text And Translation

فصل: الحكم يتعلق بسببه ويثبت بعلته ويوجد عند شرطه فالسبب ما يكون طريقا إلى الشيء بواسطة كالطريق فإنه سبب للوصول إلى المقصد بواسطة المشي، والحبل سبب للوصول إلى الماء بالإدلاء، فعلى هذا كل ما كان طريقا إلى الحكم بواسطة يسمى سببا له شرعا ويسمى الواسطة علة، مثاله فتح باب الإصطبل والقفص وحل قيد العبد فإنه سبب للتلف بواسطة توجد من الدابة والطير والعبد.

Chapter: a ruling is connected to its *as-sabab*, established by its *al-'illa* and present with its condition. So *as-sabab* is the way to a thing by a means, like a pathway. It is *as-sabab* for arrival at a destination by means of walking, and a rope is *as-sabab* of fetching water by suspension. So based on this, every way to a ruling through a means is named *as-sabab* for it in the Shariah, and the means is called *al-'illa*. An example of it is opening the gates of a stable or cage, and untying the slave's shackles. It will be *as-sabab* for the loss by the means found in the animal, bird and slave.

QUICK TERMS

السبب: *as-sabab*

The channel. The route and way in which the means attains an end.

العلة: *al-'illa*

The means. The method or instrument used to attain an end.

❖ ❖ ❖

When both *al-'illa* and *as-sabab* are together and easily distinguishable, the ruling is connected to *al-'illa* and not to *as-sabab*. This is because *al-'illa* is directly effective in the ruling and will take precedence when it is noticeably distinct. When there is difficulty or confusion in distinguishing between *al-'illa* and *as-sabab*, then the ruling can be associated with *as-sabab*. It follows that if someone hands a child a knife, for example, and the child used the knife to kill himself, the one who hands the knife will not be a liable for *ad-diyya*. This is because giving the knife is *as-sabab*, and *al-'illa* is the child's own act. As both acts are distinct and separable, the ruling will be connected to *al-'illa*, which is the act of the child and not the *as-sabab*, the giving of the knife. However, if the knife was to accidentally fall from the child's hand as it was given, and to injure the child, the giver of the knife will be responsible and will have to compensate. This is because the falling of the knife was the cause and *al-'illa* of the injury sustained by the child, but the child had no control over this and it was not a voluntary act. As the knife was handed over, it fell and so the ruling is attached to the voluntary act of giving the knife. When the ruling is attached to the giving of the knife, the giver of the knife is the one responsible and will have to compensate for the resulting injury.

Similarly, another example is if one was to help mount a child onto a horse and the child was to ride the horse manoeuvring it left and right. If the child was to fall and die, the one who helped mount the child onto the horse will not be liable for the death itself because the mounting was *as-sabab* and the manoeuvring of the horse, an act that has the direct voluntary involvement of the child, is *al-'illa*. When both *as-sabab* and *al-'illa* are associated with a ruling, the ruling will be connected to *al-'illa* and thus the fatal connection will be to the manoeuvring of the child and thus the one who helped mount will not be liable.

Furthermore, if one was to point out the location of the wealth of another and a thief was to steal it, the one who notified of the location, will not be liable for the crime of stealing. This is because the locating is the way and *as-sabab* for the theft, whilst the theft itself is the means and *al-'illa* for the wealth being taken. When both *as-sabab* and *al-'illa* are together and distinguishable like this, the matter is connected to *al-'illa*. Moreover, if one located the victim of a murder for the murderer and the crime was committed, the locator will not

QUICK ARABIC

الدية: *ad-dīya*

Fine. A sum exacted for any offence upon the person or for retaliation.

be liable for that charge. Again, the ruling is connected to *al-'illa*, the act of murder, whilst *as-sabab*, the act of locating, is not connected, whilst both are distinct. This can be extended to bandits who are guided to a caravan. The one who directs is *as-sabab* and the bandits will be *al-'illa* for the crime. The charge of the crime will be connected to the bandits, *al-'illa*.

Text And Translation

والسبب مع العلة إذا اجتمعا يضاف الحكم إلى العلة دون السبب إلاّ إذا تعذرت الإضافة إلى العلة فيضاف إلى السبب حينئذٍ، وعلى هذا قال أصحابنا: إذا دفع السكين إلى صبي فقتل به نفسه لا يضمن ولو سقط من يد الصبي فجرحه يضمن، ولو حمل الصبي على دابة فسيرها فحالت يمنة ويسرة فسقط ومات لا يضمن، ولو دل إنسانا على مال الغير فسرقه أو على نفسه فقتله أو على قافلة فقطع عليهم الطريق لا يجب الضمان على الدال

When *as-sabab* and *al-'illa* are both together, the ruling is connected to *al-'illa* rather than *as-sabab*, except when the connection to *al-'illa* is difficult, at which point it will be connected to *as-sabab*. Based on this our scholars have said: when one hands a knife to a child, and he kills himself with it, he is not liable. If it falls from the hand of the child and injures him, he will be liable. If one mounted a child on a ride and he manoeuvred it, turning it right and left, and then fell off and died, he will not be responsible. If one guided a person to another's wealth and he stole it, to a person and he killed him, or a caravan and he ambushed it, there is no liability on the guide.

❖❖❖

There is an objection to the aforementioned rule that when there is a distinct *as-sabab* and *al-'illa*, the ruling is connected to *al-'illa* and not *as-sabab*. The objection is regarding a person who has been entrusted with valuables, who then goes on to inform a thief of their whereabouts, after which the thief steals the valuables. Under the mentioned rule, the entrusted individual is informing of the whereabouts of the valuables and is thus just *as-sabab*. The *as-sabab* is not charged for the crime when *al-'illa* is distinct, which in this case is the thief who stole the valuables. However, we find that the Aḥnāf do charge the thief and the one who was entrusted. Secondly, if an *al-muḥrim* informs a non-*muḥrim* of the whereabouts of a prey in al-Ḥaram, the pilgrim will be liable if the

QUICK TERMS

السبب: *as-sabab*

The channel. The route and way in which the means attains an end.

العلة: *al-'illa*

The means. The method or instrument used to attain an end.

QUICK ARABIC

المحرم: *al-muḥrim*

The pilgrim. The one who dons the dress of a pilgrim and makes the intention to perform the sacred rights of Hajj or 'Umrah.

الحرم: *al-ḥaram*

The sacred land. A sacred area around the blessed Ka'ba, where certain acts are unlawful.

animal is then killed by the non-*muḥrim*. This should not be so, because the *al-muḥrim* is merely *as-sabab* whilst the ruling is not associated with *as-sabab*.

The response to the first case is that the one entrusted with the valuables is not punished because of disclosing the whereabouts of the valuables to a thief but the punishment is for dishonouring the agreement of trust. The one entrusted had agreed to protect the valuables and then went on to breach that agreement. Similarly, the *al-muḥrim* is punished because the guiding to the location of an animal is a violation of the terms of donning *al-iḥrām.* It is similar to the violations of applying perfume or a sewn garment, which are also prohibited for *al-muḥrim*. The punishment is for this violation and not for guiding the non-*muḥrim* to the animal.

With respect to the answer given for the punishment of *al-muḥrim*, there is a further question. If the punishment is truly for a violation of *al-iḥrām*, then the punishment should be in place irrespective of whether the animal is killed or not. This is because he has violated the terms of *al-iḥrām* by guiding another to a kill. The Aḥnāf, however, do not hold him responsible if the animal is not killed. This query is answered by making it clear that the guidance given by *al-muḥrim* is only punishable after the kill because before the kill is actually realised, it is possible for the animal to escape. If the animal has escaped, then the act of the *al-muḥrim* is not realised as ‘guidance to a kill’. The true nature of this guiding is only realised once the act has come to completion. It is at that point that the *al-muḥrim* is culpable. It is helpful to liken this to an injury inflicted on another individual. If the injury heals entirely, the charge of 'infliction of an injury' becomes ineffective as though the injury never was. If the injury never was, there is no reprimand.

Text And Translation

وهذا بخلاف المودع إذا دل السارق على الوديعة فسرقها أو دل المحرم غيره على صيد الحرم فقتله؛ لأن وجوب الضمان على المودع باعتبار ترك الحفظ الواجب عليه لا بالدلالة، وعلى المحرم باعتبار أن الدلالة محظور إحرامه بمنزلة مس الطيب ولبس المخيط فيضمن بارتكاب المحظور لا بالدلالة إلا أن الجناية إنما تتقرر بحقيقة القتل، فأما قبله فلا حكم له لجواز ارتفاع أثر الجناية بمنزلة الاندمال في باب الجراحة

This is different to the entrusted when he guided a thief to the deposit and he stole it, or *al-muḥrim* guided another to the hunt of al-Ḥaram and he killed it.

QUICK ARABIC

الإحرام: *al-iḥrām*

Pilgrims garb and state. The dress of the pilgrim and the state in which he or she is held to be.

This is because liability is due on the entrusted for neglecting the security necessary upon him, not for guidance, and upon *al-muḥrim* because guidance is forbidden for his *al-Iḥrām* like touching a scent or wearing sewn clothes. So he is liable for committing a forbidden act and not guidance. However, the offence is established by the actual killing; as for before it, it is not ruled on as removal of the effect of the offence is feasible, like the case of healing in the chapter of injuries.

❖ ❖ ❖

Sometimes *as-sabab* is by all intents and purposes in the place of an *al-'illa*, and when this happens the ruling is associated with *as-sabab* directly. This occurs when *al-'illa* comes as a result of *as-sabab*. In this regard, it is as though *as-sabab* is the cause of the cause, *'illat ul-'illa*. As the ruling is to be connected to the *al-'illa*, in this case it will be connected to thing that causes *al-'illa*, which happens to be *as-sabab*. For this reason, we say that if one was leading an animal and the animal trampled and damaged someone's property, the one leading the animal will be responsible. This is because when the animal is being led, it is forced in that direction. So, the direction of destruction the animal has taken is because it is led that way. The destruction is the result and ruling, the *al-'illa* is the trampling of the animal, the *as-sabab* is actually the one leading the animal, but the animal would not have taken that course had it not been led there. The *al-'illa* has come about due to *as-sabab*, thus making *as-sabab* into the *'illat ul-'illa*. In such an intricate case, the ruling is connected to *as-sabab*. *as-sabab* is 'leading the animal' and so the one leading the animal will be liable for making up the damage caused.

Similarly, a claimant presented witnesses to his claim in a case. The judge gave the verdict in favour of the claimant. This resulted in the defendant having to pay the claimant for the amount that was disputed between them. It transpired that the witnesses withdrew the testimony and thus the evidence in the case was weak and there was a miscarriage in the judgment. As the judgement was wrong, the disputed payment paid by the defendant was consequently wrongly placed. The loss suffered by the defendant was a direct result of the judge's decision to rule in favour of the claimant and hence was *al-'illa* for the wrongful payment. The false testimony was *as-sabab* and way by which the judge made the judgement, which happened to be wrong in reflecting the truth. Associating the ruling to *al-'illa* would mean the responsibility lies

QUICK TERMS

السبب: *as-sabab*

The channel. The route and way in which the means attains an end.

العلة: *al-'illa*

The means. The method or instrument used to attain an end.

with the judge, but the judge only gave the judgement based upon the testimony provided by credible witnesses. The judge was compelled to give this verdict acting upon the apparent situation. In this regard, the judge has acted just like the animal that was led. In that case, the one leading the animal was liable and, in this case, the ruling is connected to the production of the false testimony, the *as-sabab*. It is not the judge's judgement to which the ruling will be connected.

Text And Translation

وقد يكون السبب بمعنى العلة فيضاف الحكم إليه ومثاله فيما يثبت العلة بالسبب فيكون السبب في معنى العلة؛ لأنه لما ثبت العلة بالسبب فيكون السبب في معنى علة العلة، فيضاف الحكم إليه، ولهذا قلنا: إذا ساق دابة فأتلف شيئا ضمن السائق، والشاهد إذا أتلف بشهادته مالا فظهر بطلانها بالرجوع ضمن؛ لأن سير الدابة يضاف إلى السوق وقضاء القاضي يضاف إلى الشهادة لما أنه لا يسعه ترك القضاء بعد ظهور الحق بشهادة العدل عنده فصار كالمجبور في ذلك بمنزلة البهيمة بفعل السائق

Sometimes *as-sabab* takes the meaning of *al-'illa*, so the ruling is connected to it. An example of it is when *al-'illa* is established by the *as-sabab*. So *as-sabab* will be in the meaning of the *al-'illa* because as the *al-'illa* is established by the *as-sabab*, *as-sabab* is in the meaning of being the *al-'illa* for the *al-'illa*, so the ruling is connected to it. For this reason we said: when one lead an animal and damaged something, the one leading is liable. A witness when he financially damages with his testimony and its falsehood comes to light by a retraction, he will be liable. This is because the moving of the animal is connected to his manoeuvring and the decision of the judge is connected to the testimony, as it was not in his power to abandon the judgement after the truth had surfaced with a sound testimony before him. So he was like the one forced in that, just as the animal under the act of the one leading it.

❖ ❖ ❖

When it is not possible to or there is an obstacle in determining the *al-'illa*, the ruling is connected directly to *as-sabab* in order to make matters easier to obey. The ruling will revolve around the *as-sabab* and it will be as though the *al-'illa* is non-existent. For example, if someone falls into a deep sleep and has no control over his muscles and joints, it is considered an invalidator of ablution.

The actual cause and *al-'illa*, emission of wind, is ignored. The invalidation of the ablution centres around deep sleep, which in fact is the *as*-sabab. So, if one sleeps in such a manner the ruling is that they must re-perform their ablution.

Another example is actual privacy of newly-weds, as it is considered to be intercourse and so the payment of the whole bridal gift, and a complete period of *al-'idda* will be spent if a divorce is given. There will be no consideration given to actual intercourse. Simply, if the newlywed couple were afforded actual privacy, it will be deemed that the whole amount of bridal gift is owed to the wife by the husband. If the husband were to divorce the wife after a period of actual privacy for both of them, then the wife would have to wait the length of the whole *al-'idda*.

Furthermore, travel is considered difficult; it is as though if one travels the minimum distance to be termed a traveller, they have endured hardship, and thus *al-qaṣr* is to be prayed and there is an option to forgo fasts. This would be true even if a sultan were to travel his territory with an intention to travel a distance in excess of the minimum threshold. Though every comfort and luxury is available it is still deemed a hardship, and prayers can be shortened and fasts forgone.

QUICK TERMS

السبب: *as-sabab*

The channel. The route and way in which the means attains an end.

العلة: *al-'illa*

The means. The method or instrument used to attain an end.

QUICK ARABIC

العدة: *al-'idda*

The term. The three-month period after a divorce.

القصر: *al-qaṣr*

Reduction. The reduction of 4-unit prayers to 2 units for the traveller.

Text And Translation

ثم السبب قد يقام مقام العلة عند تعذر الاطلاع على حقيقة العلة تيسيرا للأمر على المكلّف ويسقط به اعتبار العلة ويدار الحكم على السبب، ومثاله في الشرعيات النوم الكامل فإنه لما أقيم مقام الحدث سقط اعتبار حقيقة الحدث ويدار الانتقاض على كمال النوم، وكذلك الخلوة الصحيحة لما أقيمت مقام الوطيء سقط اعتبار حقيقة الوطيء فيدار الحكم على صحة الخلوة في حق كمال المهر ولزوم العدة، وكذلك السفرَ لما أقيم مقام المشقة في حق الرخصة سقط اعتبار حقيقة المشقة ويدار الحكم على نفس السفر حتى أن السلطان لو طاف في أطراف مملكته يقصد به مقدار السفر كان له الرخصة

Then, sometimes *as-sabab* takes the place of *al-'illa* when it is difficult to know the reality of al- 'illa, to make the task easier on the subject. Consideration of *al-'illa* is abandoned and the ruling revolves around *as-sabab*. An example of it in the Shariah is deep sleep, for it takes the place of invalidating the ablution. The consideration for actual invalidation is abandoned and the invalidation is based on deep sleep. Similarly, complete privacy takes the place of intercourse, so consideration for actual intercourse is abandoned and the ruling revolves around established isolation in respect to the whole bridal gift and necessity of the waiting period. Similarly, as travel takes the place of hardship with respect to concession, the consideration for actual hardship is abandoned and the ruling revolves around travel itself such that if a sultan was to circulate the borders of his sultanate, intending the distance of travel, he will have the concession.

❖ ❖ ❖

Sometimes a non-sabab is metaphorically called *as-sabab*. For example, a vow is deemed *as-sabab* for a penalty, *al-kaffāra*. The vow, *al-yamīn*, is not *as-sabab* for the penalty because by definition *as-sabab* is that which leads to the outcome. There should not be a contradiction between the two terms; one should exist immediately after the other. However, the penalty is payable when the vow is not intact and has been violated, known as *al-ḥinth*. Whilst the vow is still intact, there is no penalty, so a vow does not lead to a penalty, and as it does not lead to a penalty, it cannot be called *as-sabab* for it in reality. The real *as-sabab* is *al-ḥinth*. Only metaphorically is a vow called *as-sabab* for the penalty.

Similarly, the words that defer a matter of divorce or emancipation are only metaphorically *as-sabab*. This is because the actual occurrence of the divorce or emancipation occurs when the condition is met. The deferral itself no longer exists when the condition has been met. In other words, the utterance of the words is a deferral, but when the condition in the deferral is met, the matter is not of a deferral anymore but a matter that has been realised. This means that the words of the deferral do not lead to the divorce or the emancipation, and as they do not lead to either of them, they are not *as-sabab*. The true *as-sabab* for the divorce and emancipation is the actualisation of the condition the matter was deferred to. The words of the deferral are only metaphorically referred to as *as-sabab* of the divorce or emancipation.

Text And Translation

وقد يسمى غير السبب سببا مجازا كاليمين يسمى سببا للكفارة وإنها ليست بسبب في الحقيقة فإن السبب لا ينافي وجود المسبب واليمين ينافي وجوب الكفارة فإن الكفارة إنما تجب بالحنث وبه ينتهي

QUICK ARABIC

الكفارة: *al-kaffāra*

Expiation. The prescribed atonement for neglected duties.

اليمين: *al-yamīn*

The oath. A statement strengthened by a solemn appeal using the name of Allah ﷻ.

الحنث: *al-ḥinth*

Perjury of oath. To not fulfil one's oath by violating it.

اليمين وكذلك تعليق الحكم بالشرط كالطلاق والعتاق يسمى سببا مجازا وأنه ليس بسبب في الحقيقة؛ لأنّ الحكم إنما يثبت عند الشرط والتعليق ينتهي بوجود الشرط فلا يكون سببا مع وجود التنافي بينهما.

Sometimes other than *as-sabab* is metaphorically called *as-sabab*, like vows are said to be *as-sabab* of expiation, whereas they are not *as-sabab* in reality. The *as-sabab* cannot negate the existence of its own outcome. A vow denies the necessity of the expiation because expiation is necessary by dishonouring a vow and with it the vow ends. Similarly, deferring a ruling with a condition like in divorce or emancipation, is called *as-sabab* metaphorically. In reality it is not *as-sabab* because the ruling is established when the condition is met and the deferral ends with the met condition, so it cannot be *as-sabab* whilst there is a contradiction between the two.

❖ ❖ ❖

5.2 Causes of Legal Rulings

All the rulings derived from the four sources of Shariah are connected to their relative *as-sabab*. There is a need to have a recognisable thing that signals the ruling. The actual ruling that obligates anything upon us is the Command of the Almighty ﷻ, which is hidden. For example, the obligation to pray salah is from Allah ﷻ but we do not hear this command directly. There is a need for something that signals that a Divine Command obligates us to fulfil a particular task. To make this matter easier for us and to be able to fulfil the Command of Allah ﷻ all tasks are connected to such indicators that tell us a particular command needs to be fulfilled. For salah, the *as-sabab* is time. This means that *as-sabab* and way in which the actual obligation, *nafs ul-wujūb*, comes about is the Command of Allah ﷻ and the *as-sabab* and way in which the obligation to perform, *wujūb ul-adā*, is realised is the advent of time. The Command of the Almighty ﷻ does not demand a task before its due time, rather once the time for the duty has arrived the Divine Command demands it is performed. If the Divine Command demanded an action before its time, we as subjects would be unable to fulfil the duty until we arrived at that time. It would be as though we have been commanded to fulfil something, we are unable to and we simply do not have the means to. This would be particularly true if one was to die whilst the Divine Command had instructed a matter and the subject had not yet arrived at the time of delivery. This will be burdening the subject with that

QUICK TERMS

السبب: *as-sabab*

The channel. The route and way in which the means attains an end.

الأحكام: *al-aḥkām*

Rulings. Decisions of the Shariah based on valid evidence.

نفس الوجوب: *nafs ul-wujūb*

Actual obligation. The actual realisation of what causes an act to become necessary.

وجوب الأداء: *wujūb ul-adā*

Obligation to deliver. The point at which it becomes necessary to deliver and perform an obligation.

which he is incapable of fulfilling. Therefore, the Divine Command directs the subject to perform once the time for the task begins.

We can further understand the relationship of both *nafs ul-wujūb* and *wujūb ul-adā* in that Divine Address, *al-Khitāb*, is there to notify us that the time to perform has arrived, *wujūb ul-adā*, as well as informing us that the Divine Command is also present prior to the requirement to perform. The obligation itself is established when the time, *as-sabab*, arrives and the Command is established through the word-form of al-amr, which is the manner *al-Khitāb* is delivered. As both al-amr and *as-sabab* are two distinctly different things, it follows that the two obligations that are a result of them both must also be different. Hence, one is *nafs ul-wujūb* and the other *wujūb ul-adā,* the actual obligation and the obligation to perform.

We can understand the mechanism of the *al-Khitāb* in what normally transpires in our daily routines. A buyer is commanded, "Pay the dues for the merchandise", or a husband is commanded, "Give the bride her dues". The actual obligation to pay occurred when the contract was agreed in both cases. This was true whether the aforementioned reminders are issued or not. By entering the contracts, the buyer and the husband have agreed to the obligation of their respective payments. The purpose of the statements above is then understood to be a reminder to pay what is already previously due. In that regard they are a demand to pay what is obligatory and they are not the obligation itself. In a similar way the Devine Word and *al-Khitāb* is to establish the necessity to perform and there is no other method to know of the obligation itself other than the arrival of the time for the obligation. This will mean that the arrival of the time is establishing the obligation itself.

Another piece of evidence to show that time is *as-sabab* for salah, and not words, is that the obligation to pray is established for those people who are asleep too, and for those who are temporarily unconscious. The arrival of the time of prayer is enough for the performance of the prayer to be obligatory upon them. It is agreed that the obligation is not established before the time, so it is confirmed that it be established upon the arrival of the time.

The obligation of salah is established with the arrival of the time for it. This means the very first moment of a prayer-time is *as-sabab* for its obligation. If the whole time of a particular salah is deemed *as-sabab*, one will require the whole of the time to pass before the prayer can be performed, as *al-musabbab*,

QUICK TERMS

المسبب: *al-musabbab*

The effect. The outcome and end with respect to the route and way it is achieved.

QUICK ARABIC

الخطاب: *al-khiṭāb*

To address. A spoken or written statement directed to a particular group.

الأمر: *al-amr*

The imperative. A word form that informs of a demanded act.

outcome, only follows the completion of *as-sabab*. However, that would mean waiting for the whole time of the prayer to pass before the prayer becomes necessary; this would mean the performance of the prayer is out of its own time! It is necessary to understand that the first moment of the time is *as-sabab* and the obligatory *al-musabbab* is the particular salah of that time.

Text And Translation

فصل: الأحكام الشرعية تتعلق بأسبابها؛ وذلك لأن الوجوب غيب عنا فلا بد من علامة يعرف العبد بها وجوب الحكم، وبهذا الاعتبار أضيف الأحكام إلى الأسباب فسبب وجوب الصلاة الوقت بدليل أنّ الخطاب بأداء الصلاة لا يتوجه قبل دخول الوقت وإنما يتوجه بعد دخول الوقت والخطاب مثبت لوجوب الأداء ومعرف للعبد سبب الوجوب قبله، وهذا كقولنا: أد ثمن المبيع وأد نفقة المنكوحة ولا موجود يعرفه العبد ههنا إلاّ دخول الوقت فتبين أنّ الوجوب يثبت بدخول الوقت؛ ولأنّ الوجوب ثابت على من لا يتناوله الخطاب كالنائم والمغمى عليه ولا وجوب قبل الوقت فكان ثابتا بدخول الوقت، وبهذا ظهر أنّ الجزء الأول سبب للوجوب

Chapter: Rulings of the Shariah are connected to their enablers. This is because necessity is hidden to us, so a sign is required for a subject to recognise the necessity of a ruling by it. Considering this, rulings are connected to enablers. So the *as-sabab* for the necessity of salah is time, taken that the directive to perform the salah does not engage before the time has begun. It engages after the time has begun. The directive establishes the necessity to perform and the notifier for the subject is the *as-sabab* for necessity, before it. This is like us saying: "Pay the price of the merchandise" and "Pay the due of the bride". There is nothing here to notify the subject except the arrival of the time; so it is clear that necessity is established with the arrival of the time, as the necessity is established for the one who does not encounter the directive like the sleeper or the unconscious. There can not be necessity before the time so it is established by the arrival of the time. With this it becomes clear that the first moment is the reason for necessity.

❖❖❖

There are then two methods to proceed after establishing that the first moment is *as-sabab* for salah. The first is to allow the transfer of the quality of

QUICK TERMS

السبب: *as-sabab*

The channel. The route and way in which the means attains an end.

being *as-sabab* to the second moment, and then to the third moment, and so on, until we come to the last moment of that particular prayer's time. In this last moment of time, along with the nature of this moment even the status of the duty-bound individual will be taken into account.

Text And Translation

ثم بعد ذلك طريقان: أحدهما نقل السببية من الجزء الأول إلى الثاني إذا لم يؤد في الجزء الأول ثم إلى الثالث والرابع إلى أن ينتهي إلى آخر الوقت فيتقرر الوجوب حينئذٍ ويعتبر حال العبد في ذلك الجزء ويعتبر صفة ذلك الجزء

Then after that there are two models: the first is that *as-sabab* transfers from the first moment to the next if there is no performance in the first moment, then to the third and fourth, till it arrives at the end time, whereat the necessity is fixed. The subject's state at that moment is considered and the quality of that moment is taken into account.

❖ ❖ ❖

What is meant by the status of the individual is that for example in the first moment if one was still a juvenile, a non-believer, a woman was in her period or with post-natal bleeding, and then became an adult at the end time of the prayer, accepted Islam or the woman passed her bleeding phase, the prayer of that time will be necessary. This is because the status of the individual at the last moment is of one who is eligible and required to pray. All other situations of becoming eligible can be extrapolated from this. The reverse of this is also true. If a woman was not in her period at the first moment and at the end time entered her period or gave birth, or someone was conscious at the start time and became unconscious at the end moment of time, the prayer for that time will not be necessary. This is because their status at the end of the time is taken into consideration, and their status is such that they are not required or eligible to perform salah. It follows that if one was a traveller in the first time and became a resident in the last time, prayers must be completed in full. However, if he was resident at the start time and became a traveller at the last time, the shortened *al-qaṣr* is to be performed. The status of the individual at the end moment of time of the salah will be taken into account.

QUICK ARABIC

القصر: *al-qaṣr*

Reduction. The reduction of 4-unit prayers to 2 units for the traveller.

Text And Translation

وبيان اعتبار حال العبد فيه أنه لو كان صبياً في أول الوقت بالغاً في ذلك الجزء أو كان كافرا في أول الوقت مسلما في ذلك الجزء أو كانت حائضا أو نفساء في أول الوقت طاهرة في ذلك الجزء وجبت الصلاة، وعلى هذا جميع صور حدوث الأهلية في آخر الوقت، وعلى العكس بأن يحدث حيض أو نفاس أو جنون مستوعب أو إغماء ممتد في ذلك الجزء سقطت عنه الصلاة ولو كان مسافرا في أول الوقت مقيما في آخره يصلي أربعا، ولو كان مقيما في أول الوقت مسافرا في آخره يصلي ركعتين

The explanation of consideration for the state of the subject in it is that if one is a child in the start time and adult in that moment, or a non-believer at the start time and Muslim at that moment, or in menstruation or in post-natal bleeding at the start time and in purity at that moment, the salah is necessary. Based on this, are all cases of eligibility at the end time, and the reverse; such that menstruation, post-natal bleeding, complete insanity or sustained unconsciousness, begins in that moment, the salah will be annulled for them. If one was a traveller in the start time and resident in the last, he will perform four units. If one was resident in the start time and a traveller by the end time, he will perform two units.

❖❖❖

The consideration for the quality of the last moment of time means that if the last moment is complete, *al-kāmil*, the delivered responsibility also needs to be complete and *al-kāmil*. It will not be correct to perform that prayer in a disliked *al-makrūh* time. If one were to perform it in a disliked *al-makrūh* time, the prayer would need to be repeated. For example, the last moment of the al-Fajr prayer is complete; therefore, the prayer must be performed in a time that is complete. When the Sun rises the time becomes disliked and *al-makrūh*. This means that if one began his al-Fajr prayer and the Sun rose during the performance, the prayer will be invalid. This is because the requirement is to complete the prayer in time, which is *al-kāmil*, but the performance has run over into a time that is not of the same quality. This will result in the invalidity of the prayer; it must be made up later.

Contrast this to when the last moment of a prayer is incomplete, *an-nāqiṣ*. This occurs in the al-'Aṣr prayer. The prayer time lasts beyond the *al-kāmil*

QUICK TERMS

الكامل: *al-kāmil*

Complete. Executed as required and without deficiency.

المكروه: *al-makrūh*

Disliked. An act disliked due to a discrepancy.

الناقص: *an-nāqiṣ*

Deficient. Executed in an improper manner.

QUICK ARABIC

احمرار الشمس: *iḥmirār ush-shams*

Reddening of the Sun. The time before sunset when the disc of the Sun appears reddish in colour.

time to when the Sun's effect has weakened and until it sets. This time of the reddening of the Sun, *iḥmirār u<u>sh</u>-<u>sh</u>ams*, is incomplete. This means that as the last moment of al-'Aṣr prayer has an incomplete quality; the performance of the prayer can also be performed with an incomplete quality. The al-'Aṣr prayer at this time will thus be deemed valid.

Text And Translation

وبيان اعتبار صفة ذلك الجزء أن ذلك الجزء إن كان كاملا تقررت الوظيفة كاملة فلا يخرج عن العهدة بأدائها في الأوقات المكروهة، ومثاله فيما يقال: إن آخر الوقت في الفجر كامل وإنما يصير الوقت فاسدا بطلوع الشمس وذلك بعد خروج الوقت فيتقرر الواجب بوصف الكمال، فإذا طلعت الشمس في أثناء الصلاة بطل الفرض؛ لأنه لا يمكنه إتمام الصلاة إلاّ بوصف النقصان باعتبار الوقت، ولو كان ذلك الجزء ناقصا كما في صلاة العصر فإن آخر الوقت وقت احمرار الشمس والوقت عنده فاسد فتقررت الوظيفة بصفة النقصان، ولهذا وجب القول بالجواز عنده مع فساد الوقت

The explanation of consideration for the quality of that moment is that if that moment is complete the task will be required as complete. So one will not fulfil their obligation by performing it in disliked times. An example of it is in what is said: the last moment of al-Fajr is complete and the time becomes deficient with the rising of the Sun. That will be after the time has lapsed so the obligation will be established as complete. If the Sun rose during the salah the prayer will be invalid, because he is unable to complete the prayer except with deficient quality in terms of time. Had that moment been deficient like in the al-'Aṣr prayer, as the last moment of it is the reddening of the Sun where the time is impaired, the task would be required with a deficient quality. For this reason it is necessary to rule it permissible at the moment despite the deficient time.

❖ ❖ ❖

The second method of understanding how time is *as-sabab* is to consider each moment an independent *as-sabab*, separate and distinct from others. Unlike the first method, there is no transfer of *as-sabab* from the first moment to the second, and so forth. The added benefit of this independent *as-sabab* method is that when *as-sabab* is viewed as transferring it means that the previous moment that was *as-sabab* before, is no longer the *as-sabab*. However, the Shariah had proclaimed it to be *as-sabab*. By transferring the idea

QUICK TERMS

السبب: *as-sabab*

The channel. The route and way in which the means attains an end.

العلة: *al-'illa*

The means. The method or instrument used to attain an end.

of being *as-sabab*, one is rendering an *as-sabab* appointed by the Shariah into a non-sabab. This is not permitted. So, the current method allows each moment to be an independent *as-sabab* and thus the Shariah's appointment is adhered to. The objection to the independent method is that if each moment is *as-sabab*, it will mean that many obligations are necessary at one time. So, if one finds oneself in the middle of a prayer time, every moment that passed would independently ask for a performance. This query is dismissed because every independent moment is asking for the same performance, it is not asking for something independent and different. Though each moment is *as-sabab*, they all demand one prayer. It is exactly like having many *al-'illa* for one ruling or having many witnesses in one case, where each *al-'illa* does not result in multiple rulings nor do many witnesses indicate different incidents. In a similar way many *as-sabab* will not demand different obligations.

Text And Translation

والطريق الثاني أن يجعل كلّ جزء من أجزاء الوقت سبباً لا على طريق الانتقال فإنّ القول به قول بإبطال السببية الثابتة بالشرع ولا يلزم على هذا تضاعف الواجب، فإنّ الجزء الثاني إنما أثبت عين ما أثبته الجزء الأول فكان هذا من باب ترادف العلل وكثرة الشهود في باب الخصومات

The second model is to make every moment of time *as-sabab*; not by way of transfer as this will be admission of voiding *as-sabab* set by the Shariah. This does not necessitate multiple tasks as the second moment only confirms what the first moment confirmed. This would be like causes in tandem or multiple testimonies in the chapter of disputes.

❖ ❖ ❖

Along with the obligation of salah, various other practices of the Shariah also have their relative *as-sabab*. The *as-sabab* of sawm is witnessing the presence of the month of Ramadan. The evidence of this is that on the arrival of the month of Ramadan the Divine Word, *al-khiṭāb* of the Almighty ﷻ instructs it. Verse 158 of Sūrat ul-Baqara says:

﴿فَمَن شَهِدَ مِنكُمُ الشَّهْرَ فَلْيَصُمْهُ﴾ [البقرة: 185]

"...and whosoever of you finds the month, let him fast the month..."

حديث

عن عبد الله بن عمر رضي الله عنهما أن رسول الله صلى الله عليه وسلم ذكر رمضان فقال: لا تصوموا حتى تروا الهلال ولا تفطروا حتى تروه فإن غم عليكم قدروا له.

عليه الصلوة والسلام

(البخاري: 1906 ومسلم: 1080)

QUICK TERMS

السبب: *as-sabab*

The channel. The route and way in which the means attains an end.

العلة: *al-'illa*

The means. The method or instrument used to attain an end.

QUICK ARABIC

الخطاب: *al-khiṭāb*

To address. A spoken or written statement directed to a particular group.

النصاب: *an-niṣāb*

The minimum threshold. The minimum property upon which zakah must be paid.

Additionally, the Messenger of Allah ﷺ instructed, "Fast when you observe it", in other words when you see the moon of the first of Ramadan.

The *as-sabab* for the obligation of zakah is the ownership of a growing amount of eligible wealth above the minimum threshold, *an-niṣāb*. The growth can be an actual growth, like in trading stock, or a potential growth, as in the money that is in excess over the minimum threshold for a whole year, *ḥawlān ul-ḥawl*. It is because the potential growth, *as-sabab*, is present with the wealth all along that one is permitted to pay zakah before the term is up. This means that if one was to pay zakah as soon as they receive the wealth, even before the year has passed, the payment of zakah will be valid.

The *as-sabab* for the obligation of Hajj is the *Baytullāh*, the House of Allah ﷻ. This is because the Hajj is always connected to the *Baytullāh* and as the *Baytullāh* is only one, there is no repeated obligation of performing the Hajj. It means that Hajj must be performed just once in a lifetime as an obligation. It follows that as the *Baytullāh* is the *as-sabab*, if one was to perform the Hajj without having the adequate means to go on the journey, the obligatory Hajj will still be valid. This is because *as-sabab* of the Hajj, *Baytullāh*, is present. Compare this to one who does not have the minimum quota for zakah. Such an individual does not have the *as-sabab*, a minimum amount of wealth with potential growth, and so by paying zakah before having this amount, the donation will not be valid as zakah. In short, after the *as-sabab* is present, any delivery of the obligation is valid, and if the *as-sabab* is not present, the delivery will not be of the obligation.

Text And Translation

وسبب وجوب الصوم شهود الشهر لتوجه الخطاب عند شهود الشهر وإضافة الصوم إليه، وسبب وجوب الزكاة ملك النصاب النامي حقيقة أو حكما، وباعتبار وجوب السبب جاز التعجيل في باب الأداء، وسبب وجوب الحج البيت لإضافته إلى البيت وعدم تكرار الوظيفة في العمر، وعلى هذا لو حج قبل وجود الاستطاعة ينوب ذلك عن حجة الإسلام لوجود السبب وبه فارق أداء الزكاة قبل وجود النصاب لعدم السبب

As-sabab for the necessity of sawm is experiencing the month, as the directive engages when the month arrives and the sawm is associated with it. The *as-*

QUICK ARABIC

حولان الحول: *ḥawlān ul-ḥawl*

Yearly. The passing of a whole Islamic year for the necessity to pay zakah.

بيت الله: *baytullah*

House of Allah ﷻ. The building in the courtyard of masjid al-Ḥarām.

sabab of the obligation of zakah is ownership of the actively or potentially growing *an-nisāb*. Considering the necessity of *as-sabab*, it is permitted to be premature in terms of performance. The reason for the Hajj is the House, as it is associated with the House and the task doesn't repeat in a lifetime. Based on this, if one performed the Hajj before having the means, it will suffice for the Hajj of Islam as the *as-sabab* exists. With this, paying zakah before owning *an-nisāb*, differs as there is no *as-sabab*.

❖❖❖

The *as-sabab* for the obligation of *ṣadaqat ul-fiṭr* is the dependant, which a person is responsible for. Responsibility means that the head of household takes it upon their self to pay all the expenditures of an individual, and to act as a guardian for a person. As the *as-sabab* for *ṣadaqat ul-fiṭr* is the number of dependants, the paying is permitted before the day of Eid. This is because the *as-sabab*, dependants, is present before that day.

The *as-sabab* for the obligation of *al-'ushr* is land that has actual growing produce, and the *as-sabab* for the obligation of *al-kharāj* is the land that has the potential to be farmed. The land is by all intents and purposes of yielding quality, and so will have an obligation associated with it.

According to some, the *as-sabab* of the obligation of *al-wuḍū* is salah. For this reason, ablution is necessary upon the one whom prayer is obligatory. Those that are not eligible to pray, such as a woman on her period, are not required to perform ablution. Others have said that the *as-sabab* for the obligation of ablution is *al-ḥadath*, ritual impurity and the lack of a previous ablution. These jurists consider 'necessity to pray' as a condition for ablution. This is an opinion, which is clearly found in the works of Imam Muḥammad ﷫ This opinion works against the agreed concept of *as-sabab*, in that *as-sabab* is something that leads to the ruling. In this case, the *as-sabab*, absence of purity, does not lead to the ruling, which is the ablution, an act of obtaining purity. As one does not directly connect and lead to the other, it cannot be *as-sabab* for it.

The *as-sabab* for the obligation of bathing is bleeding during the period, post-natal bleeding and ejaculation.

QUICK ARABIC

صدقة الفطر: *ṣadaqat ul-fiṭr*

Alms of fast breaking. Alms given on the conclusion of the month of Ramadan.

العشر: *al-'ushr*

A tenth. A tithe given to the treasury of the Muslim state, for fruits and produce of the ground.

الخراج: *al-kharāj*

Land tax. A tax levied on the owners of land conquered and returned.

الحدث: *al-ḥadath*

Ritual impurity. An act or occurrence that necessitates either ablution or bathing

الغسل: *al-ghusl*

Ritual bathing. Washing the whole body after a major legal impurity.

وسبب وجوب صدقة الفطر رأس يمونه ويلي عليه وباعتبار السبب يجوز التعجيل حتى جاز أداؤها قبل يوم الفطر وسبب وجوب العشر الأراضي النامية بحقيقة الريع وسبب وجوب الخراج الأراضي الصالحة للزراعة فكانت نامية حكما وسبب وجوب الوضوء الصلاة عند البعض ولهذا وجب الوضوء على من وجبت عليه الصلاة ولا وضوء على من لا صلاة عليه وقال البعض: سبب وجوبه الحدث ووجوب الصلاة شرط، وقد روي عن محمد عليه الرحمة: ذلك نصا، وسبب وجوب الغسل الحيض والنفاس والجنابة.

The *as-sabab* for the obligation of *ṣadaqat ul-fiṭr* is responsibility and guardianship of an individual. Considering *as-sabab*, premature performance is permitted, such that it is permitted before the day of al-Fiṭr. The *as-sabab* for the necessity of *al-'ushr* is fertile land with actual produce. The *as-sabab* for the necessity of *al-khirāj* is arable land, as it has potential to produce. The *as-sabab* for the necessity of ablution is salah according to some. That is why ablution is necessary for the one who salah is necessary for, and there is no ablution for the one who need not pray. Some said: *as-sabab* for its necessity is *al-ḥadath* and the necessity of salah is a condition. This has been reported by Imam Muḥammad, mercy be upon him, in word. The reason for necessity of bathing is menstruation, post-natal bleeding and major ritual impurity.

❖ ❖ ❖

Summary Of Factors in a Ruling

There are three factors to a ruling under discussion: *as-sabab* (reason); *al-'illa* (cause); and *ash-sharṭ* (condition).

1. Details of as-sabab:
   i) Linguistic definition: لغة: ما يكون طريقا الى الشيء بواسطة
   "The path to something using a means".
   ii) Shariah definition: شرعا: كل ما كان طريقا إلى الحكم بواسطة
   "Anything that leads to the ruling by a means".
2. Details of al-'illa:
   i) Linguistic definition: لغة: ما يتغير به حال الشيء
   "That which alters the circumstance of a thing".
   ii) Shariah definition: شرعا: ما يكون واسطة بين السبب والحكم
   "The means between a as-sabab and a ruling".
3. Details of ash-sharṭ:
   i) Linguistic definition: لغة: إلزام الشيء أو التزامه
   "Coercion of something or commitment to it".
   ii) Shariah definition: شرعا: ما يتوقف عليه وجود الحكم ويستلزم من عدمه عدم الحكم
   "That upon which the ruling depends and at the lack of which there is no ruling".
4. Ruling: والسبب مع العلة إذا اجتمعا يضاف الحكم إلى العلة دون السبب إلا إذا تعذرت الإضافة الى العلة فيضاف الى السبب
   "When there is a clear as-sabab and al-'illa the ruling is connected to al-'illa and not as-sabab, except when there is obscurity in al-'illa whence it is connected to as-sabab".
   Example: If one untied another's animal and the animal bolted and fell fatally, the one who untied it will not be liable for the death of the animal. The as-sabab and reason for the death is his untying the animal, whereas the cause is the animal bolting.

5.3 al-Mawānī'

The jurist Qaḍī Imam Abū Zayd ﷺ says that the impediments and preventives, *al-mawānī'*, that prevent the effect of an *al-'illa* and thus do not allow a ruling to occur, are four: An impediment that prevents the:

1) *al-'illa* from establishing itself;
2) *al-'illa* from completion;
3) al-ḥukm from establishing; and
4) al-ḥukm from lasting.

Examples of the first impediment are the sale of a freeman, corpse or of blood. The sale is an *al-'illa* and its al-ḥukm is ownership. After the buyer enters an agreement to purchase and the sale is agreed, it results in the transfer of ownership from the seller to the buyer. However, the aforementioned items, a freeman, a corpse, and blood, are not sellable as they are not considered to be wealth. If they are not wealth, they cannot be bought or sold. The nature of the merchandise in this case is *al-mānī'*, an impediment, that prevents the ownership transferring because it stops *al-'illa*, sale, establishing itself.

In a similar way, any deferral also prevents *al-'illa* from being established. When a condition is used to defer a matter, it is as though nothing has been declared before the condition is realised. So, for example, if one said to his wife, "If you enter the house, you are divorced", before the wife enters the house, it is as though this statement does not exist. The statement "you are divorced" is the *al-'illa* and the al-ḥukm would be the realisation of divorce. The moment the condition is met and she enters the house, the statement becomes active. It is as though the deferral is preventing *al-'illa* from establishing itself. It is for this reason if one vowed never to divorce his wife, but then proceeded to give her a deferred divorce, the issuance of the divorce will not result in him violating his vow. The deferred divorce will only come into effect when the condition is met, and before this, the deferral is an impediment for it.

The second impediment is when *al-'illa* is prevented from completion. It is like the destruction of *an-niṣāb* and minimum threshold of zakah, during the running year. The *an-niṣāb* is the *al-'illa* for the compulsion of zakah, however it only becomes a complete *al-'illa* when the minimum amount of wealth has been in the ownership of the individual for a whole year. This is the very reason zakah is not obligatory before the year is up, though the *an-niṣāb* is present. The *an-*

QUICK TERMS

العلة: *al-'illa*

The means. The method or instrument used to attain an end.

الحكم: *al-ḥukm*

The ruling. An authoritative decision of the Shariah regarding the level of importance of an act, whether an instruction or a prohibition.

المانع: *al-mānī'*

Preventive. Something that serves to keep a matter from occurring .

QUICK ARABIC

النصاب: *an-niṣāb*

The minimum threshold. The minimum property upon which zakah must be paid.

niṣāb needs to become a complete *al-'illa* before the obligation is final. If *an-*niṣāb is destroyed during the year, it is an impediment to the completion of *al-'illa* and therefore zakah will not be payable.

Another example is the testimony of two individuals, which is *al-'illa*. If one witness testifies and the other refuses to, the *al-'illa* will be incomplete. The refusal of the second witness is an impediment to the completion of *al-'illa*. Furthermore, in a trade or marriage contract, both a proposal and acceptance are *al-'illa* for the validity of the contract. However, if a proposal is there and there is no acceptance, the *al-'illa* is incomplete, the lack of an acceptance is an impediment to the completion of the *al-'illa* and thus no agreement is reached.

Text And Translation

فصل: قال القاضي الإمام أبو زيد: الموانع أربعة أقسام: مانع يمنع انعقاد العلة ومانع يمنع تمامها ومانع يمنع ابتداء الحكم ومانع يمنع دوامه، نظير الأول: بيع الحر والميتة والدم فإن عدم المحلية يمنع انعقاد التصرف علة لإفادة الحكم، وعلى هذا سائر التعليقات عندنا فإن التعليق يمنع انعقاد التصرف علة قبل وجود الشرط على ما ذكرناه، ولهذا لو حلف لا يطلق امرأته فعلق طلاق امرأته بدخول الدار لا يحنث، ومثال الثاني: هلاك النصاب في أثناء الحول وامتناع أحد الشاهدين عن الشهادة ورد شطر العقد

Chapter: al-Qāḍī Imam Abū Zayd said: al-mawāni' are four types – an al-māni’ that prevents the cause, an al-māni’ that prevents its completion, an al-māni’ that prevents the ruling and an al-māni’ that prevents its continuity. An example of the first is the selling of a freeman, carcass or blood. The lack of eligibility prevents establishing usage as the cause, which yields a ruling. Based on this are all deferrals according to us. A deferral prevents establishing usage as a cause before the condition is met, according to what we have mentioned. For this reason if one vowed he would not divorce his wife, and then conditioned divorcing his wife with entering a house, he would not have broken the vow. The example of the second is: the loss of *an-niṣāb* during the cycle, the refusal of one of two witnesses testifying, and rejecting part of a contract.

❖ ❖ ❖

The third impediment is the prevention of establishing al-ḥukm. An example is agreeing a sale with the condition of a right to return. The *al-'illa* in a trade agreement, proposal and acceptance, is present but because there is an option to return the merchandise there is no immediate transfer of ownership, which is al-ḥukm. The option to return is an impediment that has prevented the al-ḥukm from establishing itself.

Another example of this impediment is an expanse in time for an excused individual. An individual with an excuse, such as uncontrolled urination, performs ablution for a set amount of time. The ablution remains for the duration of that period. Even though the urine drops were present, which would normally require a new ablution, the remaining time is *al-'illa* that prevents the al-ḥukm of a renewed ablution.

The fourth impediment is the one that prevents the al-ḥukm lasting. An example is the choice granted due to adulthood, emancipation, seeing, non-compatibility or healing. If a juvenile was entered into a contract by a guardian when they were younger the contract is permitted, however upon adulthood that individual will have the right to continue in the contract or annul it. The impediment of adulthood prevents the continuation of al-ḥukm of the valid contract. Similarly, if a slave-girl was married off by her master, the marriage will be valid. However, once the slave-girl has achieved her freedom she has a choice to continue the marriage or annul it. The choice granted after emancipation is the impediment to the lasting of the al-ḥukm of the valid marriage. Furthermore, a purchaser makes a purchase without seeing the merchandise. The transaction means that the trade is complete and the ownership has transferred to the buyer. After seeing the merchandise, the buyer can execute his right to refuse the sale if, for example, the merchandise is not to his liking. The choice of seeing for the buyer is an impediment that prevents the al-ḥukm of the valid sale lasting or remaining permanently. Moreover, a mature girl married to a non-compatible individual will be granted the right to divorce on the grounds of non-compatibility. Though the marriage contract was valid, non-compatibility is the impediment that prevents the al-ḥukm of the marriage lasting. Additionally, if someone injured another and the injury healed completely, there will be no compensation. The healing of the injury is the impediment that prevents the al-ḥukm of compensation from remaining.

These four types of impediments are according to those who agree to *takhṣīṣ ul-'illa*. *Takhṣīṣ ul-'illa* is the understanding that an *al-'illa* is not

QUICK TERMS

الحكم: *al-ḥukm*

The ruling. An authoritative decision of the Shariah regarding the level of importance of an act, whether an instruction or a prohibition.

تخصيص العلة: *takhṣīṣ ul-'illa*

Cause restriction. The understanding that a cause is restricted and does not by default lead to a ruling.

العلة: *al-'illa*

The means. The method or instrument used to attain an end.

automatically and inevitably followed by the ruling, al-ḥukm. There can be separation between *al-'illa* and al-ḥukm. However, those that insist that once *al-'illa* is established there is necessarily an al-ḥukm that follows, will reduce the number of impediments to three. The impediment that prevents:

1) the establishment of *al-'illa*;
2) the completion of the *al-'illa*; and
3) the al-ḥukm from lasting.

These jurists insist that the impediment that suggests that there is an *al-'illa* but al-ḥukm is prevented from establishing is not possible. An *al-'illa* of the Shariah will always result in an al-ḥukm. It is another matter whether that al-ḥukm lasts or not. All the examples cited by the first group of jurists as examples of the al-ḥukm not being established are cited by the second group of jurists as examples of when the al-ḥukm does not last. The disagreements between the two groups revolve around this principle.

Text And Translation

ومثال الثالث: البيع بشرط الخيار وبقاء الوقت في حق صاحب العذر، ومثال الرابع: خيار البلوغ والعتق والرؤية وعدم الكفاءة والاندمال في باب الجراحات على هذا الأصل، وهذا على اعتبار جواز تخصيص العلة الشرعية، فأما على قول من لا يقول بجواز تخصيص العلة فالمانع عنده ثلاثة أقسام: مانع يمنع ابتداء العلة ومانع يمنع تمامها ومانع يمنع دوام الحكم، وأما عند تمام العلة فيثبت الحكم لا محالة وعلى هذا كل ما جعله الفريق الأول مانعا لثبوت الحكم جعله الفريق الثاني مانعا لتمام العلة، وعلى هذا الأصل يدور الكلام بين الفريقين.

The example of the third is: trading with a right to return, and time remaining with respect to the excused person. The example of the fourth is: choice of maturity, emancipation, seeing, insufficiency and healing in the chapter of injuries, being on this principle. This is dependent upon the permissibility to isolate a cause in the Shariah. As for those who do not allow the isolation of a cause, the al-mawānī' are three types – al-mānī' that prevents the cause, al-mānī' that prevents its completion, and al-mānī' that prevents continuity of the ruling. As for when the cause is completed, there is necessarily a ruling established. Based on this, whatever the first group have counted as a

QUICK TERMS

المانع: *al-mānī'*

Preventive. Something that serves to keep a matter from occurring .

preventive for establishing a ruling, the second group have made them a preventive for the completion of the cause. Based on this principle, the discussion will alternate between the two groups.

❖ ❖ ❖

Summary Of Preventives

1. Definition of al-māni': وجود العلة وتخلف الحكم عنها
"A preventive is: Lack of a ruling despite the presence of the cause".

Occasionally there are preventives that obstruct the application of a ruling. There are four preventives:

a) Prevention of al-'illa: this is a preventive that doesn't allow al-'illa to be present from the onset. For example, to sell something, a right of ownership must exist. The ownership permits its disposal. However, blood and carcasses cannot be owned, so the cause is prevented in them. Therefore, they cannot be sold.

b) Effectiveness of al-'illa is prevented: This does not stop al-'illa being present, but stops it from functioning. For example, the passing of a whole term for zakah to become compulsory. If the term starts but is not complete, and the wealth is depleted or lost, the zakah is no longer due. So, al-'illa of the term was present but couldn't materialise as the loss of wealth prevented it from completion.

c) Prevention from application of the ruling: despite al-'illa being present and functioning, the ruling is still not applied. For example, when a sale contract concludes, ownership is transferred. But if a grace period exists ownership does not transfer. So, despite al-'illa functioning the ruling of ownership is still not applied.

d) Prevention of a continued ruling: this is a prevention that does not stop the ruling from the start but stops its continuation. For example, if without seeing the product a sale takes place, ownership will transfer immediately. However, upon seeing the purchase the contract is reversed, so ownership is halted. This means the ruling was initiated but not continued.

5.4 Types of Rulings in Worship

There are four categories of worship in the Shariah:

1) al-Farḍ (Mandatory);
2) al-Wājib (Necessary);
3) as-Sunna (Traditional); and
4) an-Nafl (Voluntary).

Lexically the word al-farḍ means evaluation. The evaluations of the Shariah mean those things that the Shariah has evaluated and determined, thus they cannot be increased nor decreased. In the terminology of the Shariah, al-farḍ is that ruling of the Shariah, which is proven from a definitive piece of evidence and contains no margin of error. An example of such worship is the obligatory five times a day salah. The ruling of al-farḍ is that it must be enacted and believed. The one who does not enact it is a sinner and the one who does not believe in it is out of the fold of Islam.

There are two lexical meanings of al-wājib. One is, to fall, and the other is, confusion. Considering the first meaning the relevance to the Shariah is that an act of worship described as al-wājib falls upon the subject without choice. It falls into the list of duties and requires the subject to complete them. The relevance of the second meaning is that al-wājib takes a confused and complicated position between al-farḍ and an-nafl. As for enacting it, it is like al-farḍ in that it must be fulfilled and ignoring it is not permitted, whilst one becomes a sinner by missing it. However, in terms of belief in it, it is like an-nafl, in that it is not definitively believed. This means that the one who rejects it entirely is not condemned as a non-believer, much like a disbeliever of an-nafl. al-Wājib in the Shariah terminology is that which is proven from a piece of evidence that has a remote chance of error. Examples of such things include interpreted verses and the sound khabar ul-wāḥid. Its ruling is that which is implicitly mentioned above, enacting is like al-farḍ and believing it is like an-nafl.

QUICK TERMS

الخبر الواحد: *al-khabar ul-wāḥid*

Singular tradition. Traditions related by single narrator chains.

Text And Translation

فصل: الفرض لغة هو التقدير، ومفروضات الشرع مقدراته بحيث لا يحتمل الزيادة والنقصان، وفي الشرع ما ثبت بدليل قطعي لا شبهة فيه، وحكمه لزوم العمل به والاعتقاد به، والوجوب هو السقوط

يعني: ما يسقط على العبد بلا اختيار منه، وقيل هو من الوجبة وهو الاضطراب سمي الواجب بذلك لكونه مضطربا بين الفرض والنفل فصار فرضا في حق العمل حتى لا يجوز تركه ونفلا في حق الاعتقاد فلا يلزمنا الاعتقاد به جزما، وفي الشرع وهو ما ثبت بدليل فيه شبهة كالآية المؤولة والصحيح من الآحاد، وحكمه ما ذكرنا

Chapter: al-Farḍ lexically is to evaluate. The obligations of the Shariah are its measures such that they can not be increased or decreased. In Shariah, it is what is established with definite doubtless evidence. Its ruling is that it must be enacted and believed. al-Wujūb is to fall, in other words, what falls upon the subject without his choice. It is said that it is from *al-wajaba* which means confusion. al-Wājib is called that because it is confused between the obligatory and the voluntary. So it is obligatory in terms of enacting, such that abandoning it is not permitted, and voluntary in terms of belief, as we are not obliged to believe it staunchly. In the Shariah it is that which is established with an evidence with a shade of doubt, like interpreted verses and sound *al-aḥād* narrations. Its ruling is as we mentioned.

❖❖❖

حديث

عن العرباض بن ساريه رضي الله عنه عن النبي صلى الله عليه وسلم قال: عليكم بسنتي وسنة الخلفاء الراشدين المهديين بعدي عضوا عليها بالنواجذ.

عليه الصلاة والسلام

(جامع الترمذي: 2619)

The lexical meaning of as-sunna is way or method. In the Shariah, it refers to that blessed course that is preferred in Islam. It is the way and method that is often observed and adhered to, but it is neither al-farḍ nor al-wājib. The way can be that of the blessed Messenger of Allah ﷺ or that of the Companions رضي الله عنهم. The blessed Prophet ﷺ has said, "My way is necessary for you and the way of the rightly guided caliphs after me. Hold on to it firmly." The ruling on as-sunna is that every individual is asked to uphold it and one will be scorned if it is not followed. The one with a legitimate excuse to leave it will be granted an excuse and there will be no repercussions.

Lexically the word an-nafl means extra. The spoils after a battle are called *an-nawāfil* because they are extra to the real purpose of honouring the religion of Allah جل جلاله. In the Shariah, it is the worship that is extra to al-farḍ and al-wājib. The ruling on an-nafl is that one is rewarded for performing them and there is no reprimand for leaving them. Another name for an-nafl is *at-taṭawwu'*.

QUICK TERMS

الأحاد: *al-aḥād*

Singular traditions. Traditions related by single narrator chains.

والسنة عبارة عن الطريقة المسلوكة المرضية في باب الدين سواء كانت من رسول الله صلى الله عليه وسلم أو من الصحابة، قال عليه السلام: عليكم بسنتي وسنة الخلفاء من بعدي عضوا عليها بالنواجذ، وحكمها أن يطالب المرء بإحيائها ويستحق اللائمة بتركها إلا أن يتركها بعذر، والنفل عبارة عن الزيادة، والغنيمة تسمى نفلاً ؛ لأنها زيادة على ما هو المقصود من الجهاد، وفي الشرع عبارة عما هو زيادة على الفرائض والواجبات، وحكمه أن يثاب المرء على فعله ولا يعاقب بتركه، والنفل والتطوع نظيران

as-Sunna is the accepted orthodox way in the religion, whether it comes from the Messenger of Allah, peace and blessings be upon him, or from his companions رضي الله عنهم. He, peace and blesings be upon him, said: "My practice is incumbent upon you, as is the practice of my caliphs after me; hold on to it firmly". Its ruling is that it will be demanded of a person to live by it and he will be ridiculed for abandoning it, except when left with an excuse. an-Nafl means extra. The spoils are called an-nafl because it is extra to the purpose of Jihad. In the Shariah it is what is extra to *al-farāiḍ* and *al-wājibāt*. Its ruling is that a man will be rewarded for enacting it and not admonished for abandoning it. an-Nafl and at-taṭawwu' are synonymous.

❖ ❖ ❖

QUICK TERMS

الفرائض: *al-farāiḍ*

The obligations. The observance of which is necessary and denial leads to disbelief.

الواجبات: *al-wājibāt*

The necessities. The non-observance of which is sinful, but denial does not lead to disbelief.

Summary Of Types of Rulings of Worship

There are four tasks asked for by the Shariah: al-farḍ; al-wājib; as-sunna; and an-nafl.

1. Details of al-farḍ:
   i) Linguistic definition : لغة: التقدير
   "To measure".
   Shariah definition: شرعا: ما ثبت بدليل قطعي لا شبهة فيه
   "That which is proven by definitive evidence without doubt".
   ii) Ruling: لزوم العمل به والاعتقاد به
   "Must be enacted and must be believed".

2. Details of al-wājib:
   i) Linguistic definition : لغة: سقوط واضطراب
   "To fall or be indecisive".
   Shariah definition: شرعا: ما ثبت بدليل فيه شبهة
   "That which is proven by evidence that has an element of doubt".
   ii) Ruling: لزوم العمل به والاعتقاد به نفلا
   "Must be enacted and belief in it is in addition".

3. Details of as-sunna:
   i) Linguistic definition : لغة: الطريق
   "The path".
   Shariah definition: شرعا: الطريقة المسلوكة المرضية في باب الدين سواء كانت من رسول الله ﷺ أو من أصحابه
   "The orthodox path in religion, whether from the Messenger ﷺ or his Companions رضي الله عنهم".
   ii) Ruling: يطالب المرء بإحيائها ويستحق اللائمة بتركها إلا بعذر
   "A person is encouraged to follow it and will be ridiculed for leaving it except with an excuse".

4. Details of an-nafl:
   i) Linguistic definition : لغة: الزيادة
   "Increase".
   Shariah definition: شرعا: ما هو زيادة على الفرائض والواجبات
   "That which is an increase and extra to the al-farḍ and al-wājib".
   ii) Ruling: يثاب المرء على فعله ولا يعاقب بتركه
   "A person is rewarded for doing it and not penalised for leaving it".

5.5 al-‘Azīma and ar-Rukhṣa

In terms of continuity of performance there are two types of rulings prescribed by the Shariah, al-'azīma and ar-rukhṣa. In the lexicon al-'azīma means a resolute and firm intention. It is due to this reason that should a person who committed *aẓ-ẓihār* make a resolute intention to have intercourse, it will be understood as a cancelling and going back on *aẓ-ẓihār*, just as it would if he actually had intercourse. A person who made such a firm intention in a case of *aẓ-ẓihār* will need to follow the procedure of the expiation because a firm intention is as though it occurred. If one said, "a*'zimu*", I firmly intend, using this word to make a promise, it will be a vow. Going against what one vowed will be invalidating a vow and will require expiation.

In the Shariah al-'azīma is the name given to those rulings that are necessary and obligatory from the onset. They are called this because the demand to fulfil them is from a very firm origin. The One Who has instructed and commanded them is the One Whom we worship, and we are His slaves. The types of rulings that come under al-'azīma are those that we have covered in the discussion of al-farḍ and al-wājib. [5.4 Types of Rulings of Worship, page 443]

In the lexicon ar-rukhṣa means ease and without strenuous effort. In the Shariah it is the leniency shown to a subject in a matter due to a mitigation and excuse. Many causes and mitigating circumstances are found in the Shariah, so there are just as many types of ar-rukhṣa.

Text And Translation

فصل: العزيمة هي القصد إذا كان في نهاية الوكادة، ولهذا قلنا: إن العزم على الوطيء عود في باب الظهار؛ لأنه كالموجود، فجاز أن يعتبر موجودا عند قيام الدلالة، ولهذا لو قال: أعزم يكون حالفا، وفي الشرع عبارة عما لزمنا من الأحكام ابتداء سميت عزيمة لأنها في غاية الوكادة لوكادة سببها وهو كون الآمر مفترض الطاعة بحكم أنه إلهنا ونحن عبيده، وأقسام العزيمة ما ذكرنا من الفرض والواجب. وأما الرخصة فعبارة عن اليسر والسهولة، وفي الشرع صرف الأمر من عسر الى يسر بواسطة عذر في المكلف، وأنواعها مختلفة لاختلاف أسبابها وهي أعذار العباد

Chapter: al-'Azīma is intention with an emphasised commitment. For this reason we said that determination to have intercourse is returning in the chapter of *aẓ-*

QUICK TERMS

العزيمة: *al-‘azīma*

Determination. This is the firm intention to carry out a duty and is the default position regarding duties.

الرخصة: *ar-rukhṣa*

Concession. Permission to resort to an easier alternative for a duty when faced with a mitigation or under duress.

QUICK ARABIC

الظهار: *aẓ-ẓihār*

Likening to a mother. A practice in which separation between husband and wife occurs until expiation is made.

ẓihār, because it is as though it exists. It is permitted to consider it as present when an indication is found. For this reason if one said: "*a'zimu*" (I firmly intend), he will have vowed. In the Shariah it is the rulings we are bound by from the beginning. They are called al-'azīma because they have an emphasised commitment due to the emphasised cause, which is that the Commander must be obeyed due to being our Lord ﷻ and we His slaves. The types of al-'azīma are what we've mentioned from al-farḍ and al-wājib. As for ar-rukhṣa it means ease and convenience. In the Shariah it is diverting the matter from hardship to ease due to an excuse from the subject. Its types are varied due to its different causes, which are the excuses of people.

❖ ❖ ❖

It is possible, however, to group rulings of ar-rukhṣa into two broad categories depending on their significance in the Hereafter. The first group is that which contains all acts that are temporarily permitted whilst the acts themselves remain forbidden. This means that the act is treated as an unrewarded and unpunished, *al-mubāḥ*, act whilst the excuse is there, even though the act is in itself forbidden. It is hoped in the court of Allah ﷻ the forbidden nature of the act is not taken into consideration and is mitigated by the excuse. An example of such an act is one being forced to utter words of disbelief under duress. So long as the disbelief is not actually held by the individual, the utterance is excused. This means that if a Muslim's health, wealth or life is threatened, or untoward words are aimed at the most Honoured Master and Beloved Ḥabīb, may the choicest peace, blessings and salutations of Allah Almighty be upon him, and the Muslim commits disobedience, it will not be reproachable. 'Under duress' and hardship implies that these acts are excused but it does not imply that the acts are permitted. They remain forbidden but no action will be taken against the perpetrator. The ruling of this type of ar-rukhṣa is that if the one compelled shows resilience and patience before committing such acts and is consequently injured or martyred, in the court of the Almighty ﷻ, the individual will be rewarded because the divine prohibition was upheld by the individual.

In the second type of ar-rukhṣa the instructed act is categorised differently. This means that the once prohibited becomes permitted. An example of this is if one was compelled to consume wine, swine or carrion, in the state of extreme thirst or hunger, where not consuming it permanently

QUICK TERMS

العزيمة: *al-'azīma*

Determination. This is the firm intention to carry out a duty and is the default position regarding duties.

الرخصة: *ar-rukhṣa*

Concession. Permission to resort to an easier alternative for a duty when faced with a mitigation or under duress.

المباح: *al-mubāḥ*

Indifferent. Permitted acts that are neither rewarded nor punished.

QUICK ARABIC

الظهار: *aẓ-ẓihār*

Likening to a mother. A practice in which separation between husband and wife occurs until expiation is made.

damages health or results in loss of life. The individual will be instructed to carry out the act because the amount of these prohibited items that will save a life has become permitted and halal for the person. The ruling of this type is that if a person desists from the acts, the individual will be a sinner. This is because he or she has desisted from a permitted act and has committed a crime akin to suicide.

Text And Translation

وفي العاقبة تؤول إلى نوعين: أحدهما رخصة الفعل مع بقاء الحرمة بمنزلة العفو في باب الجناية وذلك نحو إجراء كلمة الكفر على اللسان مع اطمئنان القلب عند الإكراه وسب النبي عليه السلام و إتلاف مال المسلم وقتل النفس ظلما، وحكمه أنه لو صبر حتى قتل يكون مأجورا لامتناعه عن الحرام تعظيما لنهي الشارع عليه السلام، والنوع الثاني: تغيير صفة الفعل بان يصير مباحا في حقه، قال الله تعالى: ﴿فمنِ اضطر فِي مخمصةٍ﴾ [المائدة: ٣] وذلك نحو الإكراه على أكل الميتة وشرب الخمر، وحكمه أنه لو امتنع عن تناوله حتى قتل يكون آثما بامتناعه عن المباح وصار كقاتل نفسه

In terms of outcome it divides into two types: the first is a permission to act whilst the prohibition remains. It is like pardoning in the chapter of crimes. This is like communicating words of disbelief from the tongue whilst the heart is content but is being coerced, or vilifying the Prophet, peace and blessings be upon him, or destroying the wealth of a Muslim, or wrongfully murdering someone. Its ruling is that if one was to be patient until he is killed, he would be rewarded for refraining from a prohibited act, showing respect for the prohibition of the legislator, peace and blessings be upon him. The second type is: changing the status of the act so it becomes permitted for him. Allah Almighty said: "...But if anyone is forced by hunger...". This is like being forced to eat a carcass or to drink wine. Its ruling is that if one refrains from engaging with it and is killed, he would be in sin for refraining from a permitted act. He will be like one committing suicide.

❖ ❖ ❖

Summary Of al-'Azīma and ar-Rukhṣa

1. Details of al-'azīma:
   Linguistic definition: لغة: القصد إذا كان في نهاية الوكادة
   "Intention with a strong sense of determination".
   Shariah definition: شرعا: ما لزمنا من الأحكام ابتداء
   "The rulings we are bound by, fundamentally".
   ii) Examples: salah, sawm etc
   iii) Types: al-farḍ and al-wājib.

2. Details of ar-rukhṣa:
   i) Linguistic definition: لغة: اليسر والسهولة
   "Comfort and ease".
   Shariah definition: شرعا: صرف الأمر من العسر الى اليسر بواسطة عذر في المكلف
   "Relaxing the difficulty of a matter due to an excuse of the subject".
   ii) Example: Not fasting in Ramadan when journeying.
   iii) Types: there are two types in terms of outcome:

3. First type of ar-rukhṣa:
   i) al-Ḥarām yet excused: the act is forbidden but is excused.
   ii) For example, if one was forced to profess disbelief. Disbelief remains al-ḥarām but is excused.
   iii) Ruling: لو صبر حتى قتل يكون مأجورا لامتناعه عن الحرام تعظيما لنهي الشارع
   "If one is patient and consequently murdered, they are rewarded for refraining from forbidden due to the honour of the Legislator ﷻ".

4. Second type:
   i) Change from al-ḥaram to permitted: this is when the status of the matter is changed from forbidden to permitted.
   ii) For example, if extreme hunger led to one consuming al-ḥaram.
   iii) Ruling: لو امتنع حتى قتل يكون آثما بامتناعه عن المباح
   "Had one resisted till they are killed they will be sinful, for resisting a permitted thing".

5.6 Rulings Without Evidence

There are a few techniques behind rulings that are not considered valid as sources of evidence. It is called, *istidlālun bilā dalīl.* There are a number of types of this non-evidencing.

One type of non-evidence is to suggest that the absence of an *al-'illa* shows that the al-ḥukm is also absent. For example, if one concluded that vomiting does not invalidate the ablution, and evidenced it by saying it is because vomiting does not exit the two passages and that which does not exit the two passages is not an invalidator of ablution. This evidencing is incorrect because the invalidation of ablution is not because something exits the two passages, but the cause is the exiting of impurity wherever it is from. This means flowing blood and pus etc are all invalidators of ablution too. This view is supported by tradition as well. Vomiting also draws up impurities from the stomach and would fit the cause and *al-'illa* stated. If the invalidation was based solely on something exiting the two passages, the conclusion drawn earlier may have been correct, but as that is not the case, the conclusion is also wrong.

Another example is if one said a brother buying a brother as a slave, will not result in emancipation of the slave because the two relatives are not connected through parenthood. They are both neither from each other's offspring nor each other's forefather. This is also incorrect. It is incorrect because the *al-'illa* for this kind of emancipation is not parenthood. The actual *al-'illa* is being *al-maḥram*. The blessed Messenger of Allah ﷺ said, "Whomsoever comes to own their *al-maḥram* will initiate their freedom." As brothers fall into this category of close relative, the slave brother will become free. Moreover, Imam Muḥammad رحمه الله was asked about a juvenile and adult who together commit murder and whether *al-qiṣāṣ* is carried out on both of them. He replied that it would not because the juvenile is excused and not duty bound. Anyone not duty bound is immune from *al-qiṣāṣ*. In the joint murder case, there cannot be *al-qiṣāṣ* because one accomplice cannot have a different punishment to the other for the same crime. The questioner then countered, that if a father took another accomplice and murdered his own child, *al-qiṣāṣ* should be necessary because the father is not immune from punishment. This is the use of the absence of an *al-'illa* to go against the ruling, which is to say that the previous ruling does not apply. This is not correct because the non-application of *al-qiṣāṣ* is not due to immunity from punishment but can be due

حديث

عن جابر بن جندب فيما يحسب حماد قال قال رسول الله ﷺ: من ملك ذا رحم محرم فهو حر.

عليه الصلاة والسلام

(سنن أبي داوود: 3949)

QUICK TERMS

استدلال بلا دليل: *istidlālun bilā dalīl*

Unproved evidencing. When a ruling is given using inadmissible techniques.

الحكم: *al-ḥukm*

The ruling. An authoritative decision of the Shariah regarding the level of importance of an act, whether an instruction or a prohibition.

العلة: *al-'illa*

The means. The method or instrument used to attain an end.

QUICK ARABIC

المحرم: *al-maḥram*

Unlawful. A near relative with whom it is unlawful to marry.

القصاص: *al-qiṣāṣ*

Retaliation. The route afforded to the next of kin in the case of murder and to the afflicted in loss short of murder.

to various other reasons. Ownership can, for example, be a reason for the non-application of *al-qiṣāṣ*, if a master kills a slave. Though a child is not owned by the father, he is still the legal guardian and has partial control over the affairs of the child. This partial guardianship is the reason why *al-qiṣāṣ* cannot be administered on the father, even though the act is a major and grave sin. If the father is immune from the punishment, then the accomplice is also not given the punishment of *al-qiṣāṣ*. The proposal for evidencing using the rule that the lack of an *al-'illa* means the lack of a ruling is just like proposing that so-and-so is still alive because he or she didn't fall off a roof. It is clear that death is not dependent upon falling from a roof; rather there are many other possible causes of death.

The only time that the lack of an *al-'illa* leads to the lack of its ruling is when the *al-'illa* is exclusive to a particular meaning, and that meaning is in turn bound to the ruling. It is actually a case of absence of the inseparably necessary, *al-lāzim*, resulting in the absence of its inseparable outcome, *al-malzūm*. There is no objection to this rule and such evidencing is valid. In this regard Imam Muḥammad رحمه الله has said that an usurped slave's child is not a part of the liability. His evidence is that the child was not usurped whilst the liability is only for usurping. As the child was not usurped, there is no liability. Similarly, if witnesses to a murder were to retract their statements after *al-qiṣāṣ* was carried out, they will not be punished with *al-qiṣāṣ* in return. The evidence presented for this is that the witnesses are not guilty of being murderers, and for *al-qiṣāṣ* to be sanctioned on them, they must have murdered.

QUICK TERMS

العلة: *al-'illa*

The means. The method or instrument used to attain an end.

QUICK ARABIC

القصاص: *al-qiṣāṣ*

Retaliation. The route afforded to the next of kin in the case of murder and to the afflicted in loss short of murder.

اللازم: *al-lāzim*

Inseparable. An item that is inevitably with another and cannot be disjointed.

الملزوم: *al-malzūm*

Attached inseparably. An item to which another is inevitably joined and the two do not separate.

Text And Translation

فصل: الاحتجاج بلا دليل أنواع منها: الاستدلال بعدم العلة على عدم الحكم، مثاله القيء غير ناقض؛ لأنه لم يخرج من السبيلين، والأخ لا يعتق على الأخ؛ لأنه لا ولاد بينهما، وسئل مُحَمَّد رحمه الله أيجب القصاص على شريك الصبي، قال: لا؛ لأن الصبي رفع عنه القلم، قال السائل: فوجب أن يجب على شريك الأب؛ لأنّ الأب لم يرفع عنه القلم، فصار التمسك بعدم العلة على عدم الحكم، هذا بمنزلة ما يقال: لم يمت فلان؛ لأنه لم يسقط من السطح إلا إذا كانت علة الحكم منحصرة في معنى فيكون ذلك المعنى لازما للحكم فيستدل بانتفائه على عدم الحكم، مثاله ما روي عن مُحَمَّد رحمه الله أنه قال: ولد المغصوبة ليس بمضمون؛ لأنه ليس بمغصوب ولا قصاص على الشاهد في مسئلة شهود

القصاص إذا رجعوا؛ لأنه ليس بقاتل؛ وذلك لأن الغصب لازم لضمان الغصب والقتل لازم لوجود القصاص

Chapter: Substantiation without evidence is of various types. Amongst them is evidencing using the absence of a cause, on the unsuitability of the ruling. An example of it is that vomiting does not invalidate, as it does not exit the two passages, and a brother is not emancipated for a brother, as there is no progenitor-ship between them. Imam Muḥammad, Allah have mercy on him, was asked if *al-qiṣāṣ* was necessary on an accomplice to a child. He replied: No, because the child is excused. The questioner countered: it is necessary to be established on the accomplice of a father, as the father is not excused. So the evidencing is of the lack of ruling due to the lack of cause. This is just like saying so-and-so has not died, as he did not fall from the roof. The exception is when the cause for a ruling is exclusive to an understanding. So that understanding is necessary for that ruling, so the lack of it is evidence for the lack of the ruling. An example of it is what is reported by Muḥammad, Allah have mercy on him, that he said: the child of the usurped is not in the liability, as he is not usurped; and there is no *al-qiṣāṣ* upon the witnesses in the case of witnesses in *al-qiṣāṣ* proceedings, when they retract; as he is not the murderer. This is because usurping necessitates the liability of usurping, and murder is necessary for the existence of *al-qiṣāṣ*.

❖ ❖ ❖

Another unacceptable method of evidencing is *al-istiṣḥāb*. *al-Istiṣḥāb* is to place a ruling on the present state based on a ruling that was previously true. This is because the existence of something is not a proof that the thing lasts. This means that if something was present and true in the past, it does not mean that it has continued to remain in the same state to the present; it is possible that it may have ceased to be. In this sense *al-Istiṣḥāb* may be an evidence to protect and reduce the negative impact, *ad-daf'*, on an individual but not to blame and increase negative impact, *al-ilzām*. This means that if a person is of unknown lineage and someone has claimed that he is of a slave background, and then the individual commits a punishable act against someone. The compensation due will be that of a slave and not of a freeman. The compensation of a freeman is greater than that of a slave, so if the compensation of a freeman were imposed it would be increasing the negative

QUICK TERMS

الاستصحاب: *al-istiṣḥāb*

To take along. The concept of carrying and taking along a state. That is to accept a current situation based on it being present in the past.

QUICK ARABIC

الدفع: *ad-daf'*

Rebuttal. To oppose and argue against by contradicting proof.

الإلزام: *al-ilzām*

Coercion. To compel and bring about by force and intimidation.

impact, whereas this is not an acceptable method of evidencing. This would mean that if the compensation is set at a freeman's, it is evidencing without valid evidence.

Based on the rule that a ruling without valid evidence is not established, it is said that if a woman's normal menstrual cycle is known and on one occasion the norm is broken, the matter will be resolved by referring back to her normal cycle. If her norm was five days of bleeding for example, anything in excess of this will be treated as the blood of *al-istiḥāḍa*. This is because the bleeding that is in excess of the woman's personal norm could be of either *al-ḥayḍ* or of *al-istiḥāḍa*. If we were to say that her norm has changed due to this one occurrence, it will be a ruling without any evidence. As the bleeding is undistinguished between *al-ḥayḍ* and *al-istiḥāḍa*, guessing both will be dismissed and the matter will be referred to her normal cycle.

Similarly, if a woman was to become an adult whilst already suffering from a continuous bleeding, ten days will be of *al-ḥayḍ* and the remaining days will be of *al-istiḥāḍa*. This is because what is more than three days of bleeding and less than ten days, has a possibility of being *al-ḥayḍ* or *al-istiḥāḍa*. If we decide the bleeding is of *al-ḥayḍ* up to any point before ten days, we will be extending the ruling of *al-ḥayḍ* to a limit without any evidence. This is not permitted. So, by extending the ruling of *al-ḥayḍ* to ten days and anything in excess of this being *al-istiḥāḍa*, we will be ruling in accordance with evidence. This is because the *al-ḥayḍ* of less than three days continues up to ten days due to the presence of blood as the evidence of this, and what is in excess of ten days is *al-istiḥāḍa* due to the norm of women that *al-istiḥāḍa* does not last more than ten days. In this manner evidence is being followed at all times.

QUICK ARABIC

الاستحاضة: *al-istiḥāḍa*

Non-menstrual bleeding. Blood flow seen by a woman that is not originating in the womb.

الحيض: *al-ḥayḍ*

The menses. A woman's periodic blood flow during a complete menstrual cycle.

Text And Translation

وكذلك التمسك باستصحاب الحال تمسك بعدم الدليل؛ إذ وجود الشيء لا يوجب بقاءه فيصلح للدفع دون الإلزام، وعلى هذا قلنا: مجهول النسب لو ادعى عليه أحد رقا ثم جنى عليه جناية لا يجب عليه أرش الحر؛ لأن إيجاب أرش الحر إلزام فلا يثبت بلا دليل، وعلى هذا قلنا: إذا زاد الدم على العشرة في الحيض وللمرأة عادة معروفة ردت إلى أيام عادتها والزائد استحاضة؛ لأن الزائد على العادة اتصل بدم الحيض وبدم الاستحاضة فاحتمل الأمرين جميعا فلو حكمنا بنقض العادة لزمنا العمل بلا دليل

وكذلك إذا ابتدأت مع البلوغ مستحاضة فحيضها عشرة أيام؛ لأن ما دون العشرة تحتمل الحيض والاستحاضة فلو حكمنا بارتفاع الحيض لزمنا العمل بلا دليل بخلاف ما بعد العشرة لقيام الدليل على أن الحيض لا تزيد على العشرة

Similarly, evidencing using continuity of a state, is evidencing with lack of evidence, because the existence of something does not necessitate its continuity. So it is appropriate for removal and not to enforce. Based on this we said: if one with an unknown lineage was claimed to be a slave by another and an offence was committed by him, compensation of a freeman will not be necessary upon him; because compelling the compensation of a freeman is enforcement, so cannot be established without proof. Based on this we said: when bleeding exceeds ten days in menstruation and the woman has a set cycle, it will default to her cycle days and the extra will be *al-istiḥāḍa*, because the extra to the norm is connected to the blood of *al-ḥayḍ* and to the blood of *al-istiḥāḍa*. So it has the possibility of both equally. If we ruled it to be against the norm, we would be acting without proof. Similarly, if one matured with *al-istiḥāḍa*, her *al-ḥayḍ* would be ten days, because less than ten days could possibly be *al-ḥayḍ* or *al-istiḥāḍa*. If we ruled the end of *al-ḥayḍ* we would be enacting without proof; as opposed to after ten days, due to the existence of proof that *al-ḥayḍ* does not exceed ten days.

❖ ❖ ❖

al-Istiṣḥāb as evidence to protect and not to damage can be seen in the case of the person lost without a trace. Such a lost individual is considered to be alive with respect to his own wealth. This is because before becoming lost, the person was alive, and so this status must continue based on the evidence at hand. The evidence is that the individual is alive and nothing has contradicted that, and that is why none of his relatives can become inheritors of the individual's wealth. However, if one of the lost individual's relatives was to pass on during the period of the person's disappearance, the lost individual is not set to inherit anything. This is because if the lost person is considered alive, using the evidence that the last bit of evidence is that the person was alive, it will diminish the amount allocated to others and will be damaging. Evidencing in this manner is not acceptable in such cases. The right of others is removed from the

QUICK TERMS

الاستصحاب: *al-istiṣḥāb*

To take along. The concept of carrying and taking along a state. That is to accept a current situation based on it being present in the past.

lost individual's wealth and the wealth is protected, whilst the lost individual has no right on others' wealth without any evidence.

Text And Translation

ومن الدليل على أن لا دليل فيه إلا حجة للدفع دون الإلزام مسئلة المفقود فإنه لا يستحق غيره ميراثه ولو مات من أقاربه حال فقده لا يرث هو منه فاندفع استحقاق الغير بلا دليل ولم يثبت له الاستحقاق بلا دليل

From the evidence that it is only evidence for removal and not for enforcement, is the case of the missing person. No one is permitted his inheritance and if one of his relatives were to die whilst he is missing, he would not inherit from him. Others' eligibility is removed without proof and his eligibility is not established without proof.

❖❖❖

The rule that one is not permitted to issue a ruling without evidence is challenged. Imam Abū Ḥanīfa ﷺ has stated without any evidence that ambergris has no *al-khums* due on it. If issuing a ruling without any evidence were permitted, then the Imam would not be permitted to do this. In response, the statement of the grand Imam ﷺ is not a ruling without evidence but a reason why all jurists have not issued any *al-khums* upon ambergris. The full explanation is that al-qiyās dictates that there should be no *al-khums* in ambergris. Furthermore, there is no tradition that has made a claim contradicting this al-qiyās. If such a tradition were to be found then it would be enacted rather than al-qiyās. As there is no tradition to state there is *al-khums*, the al-qiyās stands and a ruling of no *al-khums* is given by all. The al-Qiyās for ambergris not being subject to *al-khums* is that *al-khums* is taken from spoils of war, which is taken from the enemy by force. As ambergris is taken from the sea and not by force from an enemy, it is not spoils of war and thus not subject to *al-khums*. This al-qiyās is clearly highlighted when Imam Muḥammad ﷺ asked Imam Abū Ḥanīfa ﷺ, whether there was *al-khums* in ambergris or not. The grand Imam ﷺ replied how could there be? In other words, there is not. Imam Muḥammad ﷺ responded by asking what is the evidence for this? The grand Imam ﷺ informed that ambergris is just like the fish in the sea, and there is no *al-khums* on fish. Imam Muḥammad ﷺ probed further that why is there no *al-*

QUICK TERMS

القياس: *al-qiyās*

Analogy. The reasoning of the learned.

QUICK ARABIC

الخمس: *al-khums*

A fifth. The fifth of property from mines and buried treasure which is given to the Islamic treasury.

QUICK DICTIONARY

Ambergris: *am-ber-gris*

Whale secretion. A clear intestinal secretion of the sperm whale found floating on the ocean and used in perfumery.

khums due on fish. He replied that the fish are just like water, and there is no *al-khums* on water either!

Text And Translation

فإن قيل: قد روي عن أبي حنيفة رحمه الله أنه قال: لا خمس في العنبر؛ لأن الأثر لم يرد به وهو التمسك بعدم الدليل، قلنا: إنما ذكر ذلك في بيان عذره في أنه لم يقل بالخمس في العنبر، ولهذا روي أن مُحَمَّدًا سأله عن الخمس في العنبر، فقال: ما بال العنبر لا خمس فيه، قال: لأنه كالسمك فقال: فما بال السمك لا خمس فيه، قال: لأنه كالماء ولا خمس فيه.

If it is countered that it is reported from Imam Abū Ḥanīfa, Allah have mercy on him, that he said: there is no fifth due on ambergris as no report is transmitted about it and that is derivation without proof! We reply: this was stated as an explanation of his reason for not stating there is a fifth due for ambergris. For this reason it is reported that Imam Muhammad رحمه الله asked him رحمه الله about a fifth upon ambergris. He replied: why does a whale not have a fifth? He countered: as it is like fish. He queried: why is there not a fifth for fish? He answered: because it is like water, and there's no fifth in that!

❖ ❖ ❖

Text And Translation

والله تعالى اعلم بالصواب

And Allah Almighty knows best.

Summary Of Rulings Without Evidence

There are a few techniques behind rulings that are not considered valid as sources of evidence. It is called, *istidlāl bilā dalīl.*

Two types of this non-evidencing are:

1. Absence of a cause renders the ruling unsuitable.
   Example: Vomiting does not invalidate, as it does not exit the two passages
2. *al-Istiṣḥāb*: it is to place a ruling on the present state based on a ruling that was previously true. Only valid for removal and not to enforce.
   Example of removal: one with an unknown lineage was claimed to be a slave and he committed an offence; compensation of a freeman will not be necessary upon him.
   Example of enforcing: person lost without a trace is considered alive with respect to his own wealth. Lost individual does not inherit from the death of relatives.

About The Author

Mohammad Asrar ul-Haq is a British-born seminarian who has taught the renowned *Darse Niẓāmi* syllabus for over ten years. He is a full time lecturer, Imam and *Khaṭīb* based in Bradford, England. Shāshī's Principles of Ḥanafī Fiqh is his first book, compiled and presented after a decade of regularly teaching *Uṣūl ush-Shāshī*, the stalwart primer in elementary Ḥanafī principles of fiqh.

He is from a family of scholars and practitioners who have served the blessed *dīn* for generations. He currently lectures at al-Jamia Suffa-tul-Islam in Bradford and offers Islamic guidance at Jamia Masjid Bilal in Leeds. His educational background in Traditional Islamic Sciences (Darse Niẓāmi), Medical Engineering (BA Hons), Post-Compulsory Education and Training (PCET), and Arabic-English Translation (AUC - UN certified) has given him a broad base from which to approach many topics. He has an array of published articles and public lectures on matters concerning Muslim communities and traditional Islamic discourse.

He especially enjoys serving students of the *Dīn* through facilitating, training and offering general guidance in the lifelong quest to gain the closeness of Allah Almighty ﷻ, achieved through adherance to the way of the Beloved Prophet ﷺ. You may learn more about his services from Bradford Grand Mosque and Jamia Masjid Bilal, Leeds.